MW00604275

CONTEMPORARY CHINESE PHILOSOPHY

Dedicated to my mother Mrs Cheng Hsu Wen-shu and the memory of my father Professor Cheng Ti-hsien

Chung-ying Cheng

Dedicated to my granddaughter Amber Bunnin

Nicholas Bunnin

CONTEMPORARY CHINESE PHILOSOPHY

Edited by

CHUNG-YING CHENG AND NICHOLAS BUNNIN

Copyright © Blackwell Publishers Ltd 2002

First published 2002

2 4 6 8 10 9 7 5 3 1

Blackwell Publishers Inc.
350 Main Street
Malden, Massachusetts 02148
USA

Blackwell Publishers Ltd
108 Cowley Road
Oxford OX4 1JF
UK

All rights reserved. Except for the quotation of short passages for the purposes of criticism and review, no part of this publication may be reproduced, stored in a retrieval system, or transmitted, in any form or by any means, electronic, mechanical, photocopying, recording, or otherwise, without the prior permission of the publisher.

Except in the United States of America, this book is sold subject to the condition that it shall not, by way of trade or otherwise, be lent, resold, hired out, or otherwise circulated without the publisher's prior consent in any form of binding or cover other than that in which it is published and without a similar condition including this condition being imposed on the subsequent purchaser.

Library of Congress Cataloging-in-Publication Data

Contemporary chinese philosophy / edited by Chung-ying Cheng and Nicholas Bunnin
p. cm.
Includes bibliographical references and index.
ISBN 0-631-21724-X (alk. paper) — ISBN 0-631-21725-8
(pbk. : alk. paper)
1. Philosophy, Chinese—20th century. I. Cheng, Zhongying, 1935–
II. Bunnin, Nicholas.
B5231 C523 2002
181′.11—dc21
2001043245

British Library Cataloguing in Publication Data
A CIP catalogue record for this book is available from the British Library.

Typeset in 10.5/13pt Galliard
by Graphicraft Limited, Hong Kong
Printed in Great Britain by T.J. International, Padstow, Cornwall

This book is printed on acid-free paper.

CONTENTS

Notes on Contributors   vii

Preface   xii

Chung-ying Cheng

Introduction   1

Nicholas Bunnin

Part I   Pioneering New Thought from the West   15

1   Liang Qichao's Political and Social Philosophy   17
   Yang Xiao

2   Wang Guowei: Philosophy of Aesthetic Criticism   37
   Keping Wang

3   Zhang Dongsun: Pluralist Epistemology and Chinese
   Philosophy   57
   Xinyan Jiang

4   Hu Shi's Enlightenment Philosophy   82
   Hu Xinhe

5   Jin Yuelin's Theory of *Dao*   102
   Hu Jun

Part II   Philosophizing in the Neo-Confucian Spirit   125

6   Xiong Shili's Metaphysics of Virtue   127
   Jiyuan Yu

7   Liang Shuming: Eastern and Western Cultures and
   Confucianism   147
   Yanming An

8   Feng Youlan's New Principle Learning and
   His Histories of Chinese Philosophy   165
   Lauren Pfister

9   He Lin's Sinification of Idealism   188
   Jiwei Ci

Part III   Ideological Exposure to Dialectical Materialism   211

    10 Feng Qi's Ameliorism: Between Relativism and
        Absolutism   213
        Huang Yong

    11 Zhang Dainian: Creative Synthesis and Chinese
        Philosophy   235
        Cheng Lian

    12 Li Zehou: Chinese Aesthetics from a Post-Marxist
        and Confucian Perspective   246
        John Zijiang Ding

Part IV   Later Developments of New Neo-Confucianism   261

    13 Fang Dongmei: Philosophy of Life, Creativity, and
        Inclusiveness   263
        Chenyang Li

    14 Practical Humanism of Xu Fuguan   281
        Peimin Ni

    15 Tang Junyi: Moral Idealism and Chinese Culture   305
        Sin Yee Chan

    16 Mou Zongsan on Intellectual Intuition   327
        Refeng Tang

Afterwords   347

Recent Trends in Chinese Philosophy in China and
the West   349
Chung-ying Cheng

An Onto-Hermeneutic Interpretation of Twentieth-Century
Chinese Philosophy: Identity and Vision   365
Chung-ying Cheng

Glossary   405
Index   411

Notes on Contributors

Yanming AN is an Assistant Professor of Chinese at Clemson University. He previously taught at the University of Michigan and Princeton University. He was awarded a B.A. in 1982 and an M.A. in 1985 at Fudan University and a Ph.D. in 1997 from University of Michigan. He has written more than 20 articles on German and Chinese philosophy and has translated four academic books. His recent publications include *The Historical Hermeneutics of Wilhelm Dilthey* (*Di Er Tai de lishe jieshi lilun*) Yuanliu Chabanshe, 1999.

Nicholas BUNNIN is Director of the Philosophy Project at the Institute for Chinese Studies, University of Oxford and Chairman of the British Committee of the Philosophy Summer School in China: China Britain Australia. He received a A.B. from Harvard College and a D.Phil. from University of Oxford, where he was a Rhodes Scholar at Corpus Christi College. He previously taught at the Universities of Glasgow and Essex. He is coeditor (with E. P. Tsui-James) of *The Blackwell Companion to Philosophy* (Blackwell, 1996) and co-compiler (with Jiyuan Yu) of *Dictionary of Western Philosophy: English–Chinese* (People's Press, 2001). He was an Honorary Visiting Professor at the Institute of Philosophy, Shandong Academy of Social Sciences and at the Centre for Studies of Social Development, Chinese Academy of Social Sciences.

Sin Yee CHAN is an Assistant Professor in Philosophy at University of Vermont. She gained a B.A. from University of Hong Kong and an M.A. in Chinese Studies and a Ph.D. in Philosophy from University of Michigan. Her main interests are in ancient Confucianism and feminist ethics. She is interested in how Confucianism, especially the works of Confucius and Mencius, can help to develop a feminist ethics of care. Her publications include papers on the emotions, paternalism, the idea of *shu* (reciprocity) and the ethics of care, and the concept of *chung-shu* (doing-one's-best-for-others and likening-to-oneself) in ancient Confucianism.

Chung-ying CHENG was born in Nanjing and moved to Taiwan in 1949. He received a B.A. from National Taiwan University, an M.A. from University of Washington and a Ph.D. from Harvard University, where he held a Santayana Fellowship. He has taught at the University of Hawaii at Manoa since 1963. He has held visiting professorships at Yale, Queens College CUNY, National Taiwan University, International Christian University in Tokyo, Peking University, Berlin Technical University, and Hong Kong Baptist University and received a Doctoris Honoris from the Far Eastern Institute of the Russian Academy of Sciences, Moscow. Professor Cheng founded the International Society for Chinese Philosophy in 1973 and has been its Honorary President since 1983. He founded the *Journal of Chinese Philosophy* in 1972 and has since served as its Editor-in-Chief. He also founded the International Society for the Study of the *Yijing* in 1985. He has published 12 books in Chinese, four books in English and numerous articles on Chinese philosophy in Chinese and English. His main English work is *New Dimensions of Confucian/Neo-Confucian Philosophy* (SUNY Press, 1991).

CHENG Lian is an Assistant Professor in the Department of Philosophy, Peking University. He received a B.Sc. from Wuhan University in 1986, an M.A. from New York University in 1994 and a Ph.D. from Rice University in 1998. In 2001–2, he is a Visiting Fellow at the Institute for Advanced Study, Princeton. His main interests are in ethics and political philosophy.

Jiwei CI is an Associate Professor of Philosophy at the University of Hong Kong. His main philosophical interests include justice, the philosophical analysis of capitalism, and the ethics and politics of communist and post-communist China. He holds a Ph.D. degree from the University of Edinburgh. He has held post-doctoral fellowships at Brown University, Stanford University, University of Virginia, and North Carolina Research Triangle and has been a visiting fellow at the Institute for Advanced Studies, Princeton. He is the author, in English, of *Dialectic of the Chinese Revolution: From Utopianism to Hedonism* (Stanford University Press, 1994) and, in Chinese, of *Zhengyi de liangmian*, a book on justice in the Harvard-Yenching series (Sanlian Press, forthcoming).

John Zijiang DING is an Associate Professor at California State Polytechnic University at Pomona. He gained an M.A. from Peking University and a Ph.D. from Purdue University and previously taught at Peking University and Indiana University at Indianapolis. Dr Ding has been a visiting scholar at University of Chicago and Northwestern University and a research fellow at the Hong Kong International Center for Asian Studies, Center for Modern China, and East–West Center of Chinese Southeastern University. He was Vice President of the Association of Chinese Philosophers in America in 1997–9. Dr Ding's main interests are in comparative philosophy and sociopolitical philosophy. He is co-author of *Chinese Renaissance: The Reemergence of a Private*

Economy in China (M. E. Sharpe, 1998) and author of *Sino-American Inter-marriage*. He has also published numerous papers and two novels.

HU Jun is a Professor in the Department of Philosophy at Peking University, where he was awarded a Ph.D. in 1991. He lectures on Chinese philosophy and epistemology. Among his publications in Chinese are *Jin Yuelin* (Dongdutu Shugongsi, 1993), *An Introduction to Theory of Knowledge* and *Chinese Philosophy in the Twentieth Century* (Shandong Renmin).

HU Xinhe is a Professor at the Institute of Philosophy, Chubanshe, 1999 Chinese Academy of Social Sciences. He gained a B.Sc. in Physics from Nanjing Normal University and an M.Phil. in Philosophy from the Graduate School of the Chinese Academy of Social Sciences. His main interests are in the philosophy of science, especially in philosophy of physics, topics in realism and bioethics. He has paid an academic visit to the London School of Economics. His publications include *Exploring the Quantum Realm: A Biography of Erwin Schroedinger* (Fujian Education Publishing, 1993); "The picture of the world based on the theory of relativity and quantum mechanics," in *Frontiers of Science and Philosophy* (Qiushi Press); "From reform of the view of physical realism to relational realism," *Dialectics of Nature*, 3, 1993; "Discrimination of the conception of reality and relational realism," *Philosophical Research*, 8, 1996; "From separating to blending: on the relation between man and nature," in *New Conceptions of Nature* (Qiushi Press, 1998); and "On the relational paradigm in bioethics" (forthcoming).

HUANG Yong is an Assistant Professor of Philosophy at Kutztown University, Pennsylvania. He gained a Ph.D. in philosophy from Fudan University and a Th.D. in theology from Harvard University. He is currently the president of the Association of Chinese Philosophers in America. His main research interests are in philosophy of religion, social and political philosophy, and comparative philosophy and religion. In addition to a dozen articles in English and more in Chinese, he has recently published *Religious Goodness and Political Rightness: Beyond the Liberal and Communitarian Debate*, the Harvard Theological Studies series (Trinity Press International, (1998). He is currently writing *Confucian Philosophy of Religion: A Study of the Cheng Brothers*.

Xinyan JIANG is an Assistant Professor of Philosophy at the University of Redlands. She received a B.A. and an M.A. from Peking University and a Ph.D. from the University of Cincinnati. She previously taught at Peking University, Gonzaga University, the University of Memphis, and Grand Valley State University. Her main philosophical interests include Chinese philosophy and ethics.

Chenyang LI is an Associate Professor and Chair of the Department of Philosophy at Central Washington University. He earned a B.A. and an M.A. at Peking University and a Ph.D. at the University of Connecticut. His publications include *The Tao Encounters the West: Explorations in Comparative Philosophy* (Open Court, 2000) and *The Sage and the Second Sex: Confucianism, Ethics, and Gender* (ed.) (Suny Press, 1999). He has published articles in journals such as *Hypatia: A Journal of Feminist Philosophy, International Philosophical Quarterly, Philosophia, Journal of Chinese Philosophy, Philosophy East & West, Journal of Value Inquiry*, and *Review of Metaphysics*. In 1995–7, he was the first President of the Association of Chinese Philosophers in America.

Peimin NI is an Associate Professor at Grand Valley State University in Michigan and previously taught at Trinity College in Hartford, Connecticut and Montana State University. He received a B.A. and an M.A. from Fudan University and a Ph.D. from the University of Connecticut. He has published *On Reid* (Wadsworth, 2001) and *On Confucius* (Wadsworth, 2002) in the Wadsworth Philosophers' Series and is co-author of *Action of Non-action, East–West in Calligraphy and Philosophical Verses* (forthcoming). He has written over thirty journal articles and chapters of books. Ni's main philosophical interests include Chinese and comparative philosophy, the metaphysics of causation, and the history of modern Western philosophy. Dr Ni is a founding member of the Association of Chinese Philosophers in America and has served as the Association's Vice President (1995–7) and President (1997–9).

Lauren PFISTER is an Associate Professor in the Department of Religion and Philosophy at Hong Kong Baptist University. He received a Ph.D. in comparative philosophy at the University of Hawaii at Manoa. His main research interests include nineteenth- and twentieth-century Ruism (Confucianism), Ruist–Christian dialogue, and the history of European sinology. He is Associate Editor of the *Journal of Chinese Philosophy* and is currently collaborating on an annotated English translation of Feng Youlan's *New History of Chinese Philosophy* and on a critical edition of James Legge's *Chinese Classics*. He has been a Visiting Research Fellow at the University of New South Wales and a Guest Professor at the Sinology Institute of Bonn University.

Refeng TANG is an Associate Professor at the Institute of Philosophy, Chinese Academy of Social Sciences. She obtained a B.Sc. in psychology from Peking University and an M.Phil. in philosophy from the Graduate School of the Chinese Academy of Social Sciences. She has paid academic visits to the Universities of Hull, Oxford, and London.

Keping WANG is a Professor and Deputy Dean of the English Department, Beijing Second Foreign Languages University. He holds an M.A. from University of Canberra. His main academic interests are in aesthetics and intercultural studies. His works include *The Classic of the Dao: A New Investigation* (Foreign Languages Press, 1998); *Essays on Sino-Occidental Aesthetic Cultures* (Lüyou Jiaoyu Chubanshe, 1999); *Aesthetic in Tourism* (Lüyou Jiaoyu Chubanshe, 2000); *Sightseeing as an Aesthetic Activity* (Lüyou Jiaoyu

Chubanshe, 1991). He has paid academic visits to University of Toronto and University of Oxford.

YANG Xiao is an Assistant Professor in the Department of Philosophy at Middlebury College. His main philosophical interests include ethics, political philosophy, philosophy of history, and Chinese philosophy. He studies physics at Wuhan University and philosophy at the Graduate School of the Chinese Academy of Social Sciences, University of Oxford, and the New School for Social Research, where he gained a Ph.D. in 1999. He was an assistant fellow at the Chinese Academy of Social Sciences for five years and a post-doctoral fellow at the Centre for Chinese Studies, University of California, Berkeley in 1999–2000. His book *Human Rights and History* is forthcoming.

Jiyuan YU is an Assistant Professor of Philosophy at the State University of New York at Buffalo. He specializes in Ancient Greek Philosophy and in Greek–Chinese comparative philosophy. He has published a number of papers in these areas. He is cocompiler (with Nicholas Bunnin) of *Dictionary of Western Philosophy: English and Chinese* (People's Press, 2001) and coeditor (with Jorge J. E. Gracia) of *Rationality and Happiness from the Ancients to the Early Medievals* (forthcoming). He is currently working on a comparison of Aristotelian and Confucian virtue ethics.

PREFACE

Chung-ying Cheng

Although Western academics have come to know many things about Chinese philosophy in the last thirty years, what they know most is basically confined to classical Chinese philosophy. Through the efforts of many recent scholars a few Neo-Confucian and Neo-Daoist works and philosophers have found their places in sinological and comparative studies. As to contemporary Chinese philosophy one can readily see that students and scholars in the West have least knowledge and least access to such knowledge because of the complexity of source and resource materials and lack of expertise in explanation, translation, and evaluation.

For many years, I have wanted to write an analytical reflection on contemporary Chinese philosophy as a way of opening a new path to revitalize Chinese philosophy in the context of East–West dialogue. Although it is not an easy job, it is a challenging one because there are many different positions to analyze and evaluate. In my analytical notes, I find it possible to integrate these different positions under a common theme and then to characterize them in terms of some deep patterns and main directions. Needless to say, I also have a personal interest in this exploration because I can relate some of my own philosophical views to many of these philosophical works. I also came to know some of these philosophers personally as well as professionally.

I had brief personal contact with Professors Liang Shuming and He Lin when I was invited to give lectures at Peking University and the Chinese Academy of Social Sciences in 1985, marking my first return to China after 1949. I came to know Professor Feng Youlan in 1982 at our International Zhu Xi Conference at University of Hawaii at Manoa. I knew Professors Tang Junyi and Mou Zongsan in Hong Kong, but I first met them in 1965 at the 5th International East–West Philosophers' Conference in Honolulu. In Taipei, of course, I knew Professor Fang Dongmei (Thomé Fang) because he was my philosophy teacher at National Taiwan University for many years and Professor Xu Fuguan because he was my father's good friend in literature and poetry. In Shanghai I discussed philosophy with Professor Feng Qi when he invited me to give a series of lectures on Chinese–Western philosophy at East China Normal University in 1987. In the same period in Beijing, I visited Professor Zhang Dainian and came to know Li Zehou as a colleague and a friend.

I see each distinguished contemporary Chinese philosopher as engaged in a struggle to articulate some essence or aspect of Chinese philosophy through efforts to develop a method of thinking and a form of expression that met a high personal standard of articulation. All of them made efforts to link their thought with Western philosophical ideas, but they also tended to evaluate the Western tradition critically from the standpoint of the being of the human person and the well-being of humankind. Many lacked an opportunity to have dialogue, debate, or conversation with Western philosophers, but they succeeded in constituting a diversity of discourses with a central theme: understanding the Chinese mind in understanding the West and vice versa. Some of them used Western philosophy as a method and even adopted some fundamental theses from Western philosophers such as Bergson, Dewey, Russell, and Kant, but they always tried to argue and articulate some profound ontological, epistemological, and ethical insights from the Chinese tradition, whether manifest or hidden. They did not always wish to criticize the models and standards that they adopted from the West. Even though they were awakened to rational modernity, they carefully used aspects of the Chinese tradition to gain deeper understanding of the issues at hand. Their visions were always global in scope and suggested an optimistic prospect as their cultivation opened new roads of philosophical development. To say the least, they remind us that the task of philosophical thinking has unlimited potentiality and need not be limited to one or two paradigms. Humanity and culture never will end with one tradition and must not be dominated by one school. Our question is how we can effectively create and enjoy philosophical creativity through persuasion and equality rather than by coercion and dominance.

In 1997, I visited Nick Bunnin in Oxford when I was a visiting professor of philosophy at Berlin Technical University. I was much impressed by Nick's intensive work with young Chinese scholars on contemporary Chinese philosophers at the Institute for Chinese Studies at University of Oxford. Consequently, I proposed collaboration with him on a volume on contemporary Chinese philosophy to be published by Blackwell Publishers. I thought that a presentation of contemporary Chinese philosophers together with selected translations of their work would be useful and necessary before any analytical work could be done. He agreed and we worked hard together over a distance of half the earth for two years on this pioneering project, which involved collaboration with 16 young scholars in Chinese philosophy whom we invited to join the project. Each wrote a chapter on a philosopher from the list of names we had chosen and in a framework that we had developed.

We started with a rough division of contemporary Chinese philosophy into four stages that covers all the major philosophical developments and philosophical positions of Chinese philosophy in the twentieth century. The four stages, *pioneering new thought from the West; philosophizing in the Neo-Confucian spirit; ideological exposure to dialectical materialism;* and *later development of New Neo-Confucianism,* also constitute four orientations of contemporary Chinese philosophy: *Western orientation, Earlier Neo-Confucian orientation, Chinese Marxist orientation, and Later Neo-Confucian orientation.* On this basis, we set up four parts of the book in order to include the leading philosophies of each stage and to construct common measures and guidelines for the authors to follow in their chapters. We both looked at the contributed chapters and offered comments for revision. For myself, I commented on the organization, content, and ideas of the chapters from both logical–critical and historical points of view. All of the authors used our comments positively to improve the quality of their contributions.

Nick will provide a general introduction to describe the content and intent of each chapter. I shall write about very recent Chinese philosophers to bring the study up-to-date and shall also conclude with an overview and appraisal of contemporary Chinese philosophy and its nature based on my analysis of its origin and differentiation. I shall also explore the most recent concerns and directions of Chinese philosophy and its prospects for future development. With utmost modesty, I suggest that this book will initiate both a new era and a new area of contemporary Chinese philosophy and culture studies.

I wish to thank Nick warmly for our excellent collaboration and also to thank our contributors for their enthusiasm in joining hands with us.

Chung-ying Cheng
Honolulu, Hawaii
February 28, 2001

INTRODUCTION

Nicholas Bunnin

Contemporary Chinese Philosophy introduces the thought of sixteen of the most inventive and influential Chinese philosophers over the last century. This has been a turbulent period in which philosophical concepts, theories, and systems played a crucial role in China's continuing adjustment to modernity. Our primary aim is to expound and critically examine the work of figures whose creativity and sensitive interpretation of features of Chinese and Western thought are most worthy of philosophical attention. As a whole, the book depicts a complex philosophical culture and provides a platform for further investigation and innovative philosophical work. In addition, the editors take pride in offering a showcase for extremely talented Chinese contributors working in China, Hong Kong, and the United States. Our one non-Chinese contributor has long worked as a specialist on Chinese philosophy in Hong Kong. We are indebted to all the authors for their diverse perspectives, scholarly knowledge, and critical insights.

Because our purposes are philosophical, we have excluded lesser philosophers who have had greater public impact. Mao Zedong (1893–1976) is the most prominent of these. We have also omitted excellent Chinese philosophers whose work can be understood entirely as contributions to Western philosophy. For example, much sophisticated Chinese philosophy of science (dialectics of nature) can be understood without reference to the background of Chinese philosophy. The response of our readers is the test of our judgment in shaping this book. We hope that even those seeking a more comprehensive work of intellectual and cultural history will be attracted by the excitement of studying the deep, complex, original, and provocative thought of the philosophers who are included. This is especially important because the Chinese philosophical culture that was fragmented by bitter political conflict and exile in the middle of the twentieth century is currently being reunited. Contacts among Chinese philosophers in China, Hong Kong, Taiwan, and the United States are increasingly rich and productive. New approaches to comparative philosophy and world philosophy have also encouraged Western philosophers to cultivate interests in

Chinese philosophy. In his two concluding chapters, Chung-ying Cheng explores these developments and their implications for the future development of Chinese philosophy and presents an interpretation of contemporary Chinese philosophy. For now, we hope that readers will use *Contemporary Chinese Philosophy* to help determine an agenda of problems for their own further study and creative philosophical work

Readers are also encouraged to distinguish between what is valuable and what should be disregarded in the works considered. Several of the philosophers, for example, sought to determine the essence of Western philosophy and the essence of Chinese philosophy, initially to learn the secret of Western success and later to defend the value of Chinese culture and institutions. Others employed single developmental models of culture and philosophical thought. These approaches can be understood in the context of China's response to Western power and much can be retrieved to be deployed in more sophisticated analyses, but these essentialist or developmental models do not offer a suitable framework for understanding and assessing the complexity and variety of either Chinese or Western thought.

An important feature of the volume is the diversity of Chinese and Western influences on the authors discussed, and this variety in itself helps to undermine a monolithic or overly simplified vision of either tradition. Chinese influences include the *Yijing* (Book of Changes); Confucius, Mencius, and Xunzi; the Daoists, Laozi and Zhuangzi; the legalist Han Feizi; Mozi and the later Mohists; Mere Consciousness and Chan Buddhism; Zhu Xi, Lu Jiuyuan, Wang Yangming and other Neo-Confucians; and the Qing school of textual criticism. Western influences include Plato, Aristotle, Leibniz, Hume, Kant, Schiller, Mill, Hegel, Marx, Schopenhauer, Nietzsche, Heidegger, Green, Bergson, Woodbridge, Dewey, Russell, Moore, Wittgenstein, and Foucault. Many of the philosophers were deeply influenced by their studies abroad in Japan, the United States, Britain, France, Germany, or Austria.

Although there were personal rivalries and factional divisions among the philosophers discussed in *Contemporary Chinese Philosophy*, friendships and influences between teachers and students and among colleagues have also been important. In addition, the intellectual perspectives of many of the figures were shaped by their early education in the Chinese classics, in Buddhist or Daoist thought, or in Western scientific, political, and philosophical ideas. Institutional factors were also important. Different cities, institutions, philosophical and intellectual journals and publishers helped to shape the thought of philosophers who worked in them. Peking University throughout the period, Tsinghua University in the first half of the twentieth century, and the Institute of Philosophy of the Chinese Academy of Social Sciences since its foundation in the 1950s have been influential centers of Chinese philosophical thought in Beijing. Fudan University has played a similar role in Shanghai. During the Japanese occupation in the 1930s and 1940s, the Southwest Associated

University in Chungqing and later Kunming provided a focus of intellectual life in exile from Beijing and Tianjin. Several important figures migrated to New Asia College (later integrated into Chinese University of Hong Kong) and Taiwan National University and Academia Sinica in Taipei after the establishment of the People's Republic in 1949. Harvard University and University of Hawaii at Manoa have provided centers for Chinese philosophical thought in the United States.

New Youth, edited 1915–21 by Chen Duxiu (1879–1942), was remarkable as a focus of new and exciting ideas, but many other journals provided forums for popularizing thought in early-twentieth-century China. *Philosophical Review* maintained high intellectual standards in the publication of professional philosophical articles in the 1930s and 1940s. English-speaking readers have had access to the journals *Philosophy East and West* and the *Journal of Chinese Philosophy* for discussion of contemporary Chinese philosophy over the last several decades. Among publishers, Commercial Press had the most distinguished record of promoting philosophical discussion in China, but other presses have also been important.

Although the figures in the volume vary in the degree and orientation of their public involvement, the overwhelming presence of China in crisis overshadowed much of their philosophical work. An exploration of the causes, symptoms, and transformations of crisis in modern China would be out of place here, but a brief historical sketch will hint at the context of instability and the changing patterns of aspiration and despair in which philosophers have worked. In these circumstances, the depth and creativity of their philosophical work is remarkable.

Contemporary philosophy began in China as part of the response to the weakness, ossification, and corruption of the Qing dynasty near the end of the nineteenth century. Intellectuals feared that foreign powers would destroy China as a unified state and overwhelm Chinese culture. Japan, which had rapidly modernized after the Meiji restoration, was regarded as a special threat because it was so close to many aspects of Chinese thought and culture. The failure of early Republican institutions after the Revolution of 1911 and the slide into warlord rule, supplemented by disillusion over the carnage of the Great War in Europe, undermined the appeal of Western liberal models for Chinese modernization. A demand for reform and rejection of traditional Confucian culture culminated in the New Culture Movement and the May Fourth Movement, but this liberal moment was soon succeeded by the formation of the Guomindang and the Chinese Communist Party. The rivalry between these Leninist revolutionary parties with military wings produced civil war and further instability. Political and military conflict and the corrupt ineffectiveness of Guomindang governance formed a prelude to the Japanese seizure of Manchuria in 1931 and more extensive invasion of 1937.

After the Communist victory in renewed civil war, the People's Republic was founded in 1949 under the leadership of Mao Zedong (1893–1976), and Nationalist rule under Chiang Kai-shek (Jiang Jieshi) (1887–1975) was restricted to Taiwan. In China, the imperfectly effective Nationalist censorship gave way to more systematic intellectual control. The government and party reshaped universities on terms expressed in Mao's statements of cultural and intellectual policy in Yanan. Campaigns were organized to denounce ancient and contemporary intellectual rivals. The brief relaxation of the Hundred Flowers period led to the renewed control of the Anti-Rightist Campaign. The failure of the Great Leap Forward was followed by the decade of the Cultural Revolution in 1966–76, in which education was disrupted and intellectuals were sent to the countryside. Two decades of relative stability, economic success, and growing intellectual freedom under a policy of Openness and Reform were interrupted by the events of June Fourth 1989. In recent years, the despair and nihilism among intellectuals in the aftermath of the Beijing Massacre have given way to cautious anticipations of consolidating and extending reform, with Marxist, liberal, and Confucian thinking contributing to the debate. For most of the period since 1949, political dictatorship on the mainland was mirrored by political dictatorship in Taiwan, but an extended period of economic success has been followed by greater intellectual freedom and democratic reform.

Although there are liaisons, affinities, puzzles, and disputes that interweave among all the chapters of the volume, we hope that readers will be assisted by a division into four sections: Pioneering New Thought from the West; Philosophizing in the Neo-Confucian Spirit; Ideological Exposure to Dialectical Materialism; Later Development of New Neo-Confucianism. Each of the main chapters is accompanied by a bibliography and a set of discussion questions. Chung-ying Cheng supplements these chapters with an account of Recent Trends in Chinese Philosophy in China and the West and offers an Onto-Hermeneutic Interpretation of Twentieth-Century Chinese Philosophy: Identity and Vision. A Glossary of important Chinese philosophical terms used in the text concludes the work.

Pioneering New Thought from the West

Two writers can be seen to have been initiators of the Chinese intellectual response to modernity: Kang Youwei (1858–1927) and Yan Fu (1854–1921). Kang presented a vision of change that motivated the Hundred Days Reform in 1898. This movement offered hope of modernizing Qing dynasty rule, but was crushed by the empress dowager Cixi's palace coup. Although Kang had an appreciation of Western civilization, his thought was grounded in Confucian, Daoist, and Buddhist thought. He placed his criticism of late-Qing-dynasty China and his hope of reform in the context of ancient Han-dynasty controversies between new text and old text Confucianism. He claimed that the old text (*guwen*) versions of the classics, allegedly saved from the book-burning of China's first Emperor, were forgeries and that the true versions were those of the new text (*jinwen*) school of the Former Han dynasty. From this perspective, Kang argued that Confucius was a reformer and a utopian, with an ultimate vision of a society of great unity under the virtue of humanity (*ren*) and the rule of the people. His policy failed, but the strategy of marshaling available intellectual resources for reform and the recourse to utopian ideals recurred.

Yan Fu published translations and extensive philosophical commentaries on works by Thomas Huxley, Adam Smith, John Stuart Mill, and others as a means to understanding Western strength and Chinese weakness. His elegant commentaries related these works to a framework of Chinese thought, and the popularity of his writings extended the range of those seeking to assess and alter Chinese intellectual life and public institutions.

Other philosophers contributed to the revival of late-Qing intellectual life. Zhang Taiyan's (1868–1936) early collaboration with Kang Youwei ended because of conflict between Zhang's commitment to overthrowing Qing rule and Kang's more limited reformist aims. Zhang's training in philology and textual criticism supported his sophisticated assessment of Confucian, Daoist, and Buddhist texts and his rejection of Kang's new text Confucianism. His linguistic knowledge and understanding of logic informed his mature philosophical system, in which his account of perception was influenced by Kantian idealism.

At the beginning of the twentieth century, Zhang took part in radical educational experiments with Cai Yuanpei (1868–1940), a brilliant classical scholar who later became China's leading educator. Cai's works on aesthetics, religion, and moral philosophy were grounded in his mastery of the Confucian classics and his study of Western philosophy in Germany. He argued that the emotions, which were focused on irrational religious beliefs, would be better directed to aesthetic objects and that aesthetics could replace religion as a source of cultural unity and vitality.

As Chancellor of Peking University 1916–26, Cai attracted imaginative scholars with independent minds. The New Culture and May Fourth Movements arose from this milieu to embrace modernization and to condemn Confucian culture as a source of Chinese weakness. The various strands and figures of the May Fourth Movement have been subject to continuing investigation due to their emblematic status in marking China's commitment to modernity. Chen Duxiu (1879–1942), who argued for a transformation of Chinese culture through science and democracy, and Li Dazhao (1879–1927), who founded the first society in China to study Marxist theory, were leading figures in this radical setting.

We can note the work of three further philosophers who extended the range of Western ideas available to Chinese philosophical thought. Zhu Guangqian

(1897–1986) introduced themes from Croce in his aesthetic and psychological writings. The poet Zong Baihua (1897–1986) developed an aesthetic theory drawn from Kant, Goethe, Daoist thought, and the *Yijing* to explore the relationship between aesthetics and space in terms of fulfillment and emptiness. Hong Qian (1909–92) took part in the Vienna Circle as a student of Moritz Schlick. His lucid and rigorous search for a consistent and coherent logical empiricism influenced generations of Chinese philosophers.

In the first section of *Contemporary Chinese Philosophy*, we have selected five philosophers for detailed attention: Liang Qichao (1873–1929), Wang Guowei (1877–1927), Zhang Dongsun (1886–1973), Hu Shi (1891–1958), and Jin Yuelin (1895–1984). Each captures an aspect of the intense search for new ideas and new values.

After collaborating with Kang Youwei in developing a program of Confucian reform, Liang Qichao, who is discussed by Yang Xiao in chapter 1, developed a philosophically sophisticated and influential understanding of history, politics, culture, and law. He constructed a methodology for comparing Chinese and Western ideas and institutions and set out the first plan for a modern history of Chinese philosophy. His rejection of essentialism allowed him to shift attention from preserving Chinese Confucian culture to preserving China as an independent state. His assessment of democracy, citizenship, nationalism, liberty, rights, human relationships, and civil law founded the modern Chinese understanding of civic society. Of particular interest are his arguments for distinguishing between political and legal liberty and social and ethical liberty, and his understanding of the relationship between national rights and people's rights.

Wang Guowei, who is discussed by Keping Wang in chapter 2, responded to the thought of Kant, Schiller, Schopenhauer, and Nietzsche to establish an aesthetic theory of remarkable scope and sensitivity. His theory integrated German aesthetic thought into traditional Chinese theory of art and provided grounding for bold critical studies. His philosophy of criticism centered on six concerns: aesthetic education, spiritual detachment, art as play, the artist as genius, the refined, and the poetic state. Of these, his accounts of the poetic state and the refined show the greatest originality. Tension between Wang's attachment to idealist metaphysical, aesthetic, and ethical systems and his intellectual respect for positivism, hedonism, and empiricism persuaded him to give up philosophy early in his intellectual life. His romantic commitment to a royalist restoration led to his death by suicide in 1927.

Zhang Dongsun, who is discussed by Xinyan Jiang in chapter 3, was also influenced by Kant, but focused his philosophy on the theory of knowledge. A pluralist epistemology, which distinguished independent and mutually irreducible elements in cognition, led to an examination of cultural and linguistic factors shaping knowledge. He grounded his epistemology in a panstructuralist cosmology that was deeply influenced by Buddhist thought. Zhang rejected the concept of substance and proposed a sophisticated structuralism, according to which all that existed in reality were structures or orders. His identification of morphological differences between Chinese and Western languages as a source of different philosophical orientations, although still controversial, provided a framework for later explorations by Chinese and Western philosophers.

Hu Shi, who is discussed by Hu Xinhe in chapter 4, succeeded Zhang Dongsun as China's most influential liberal thinker. An article in *New Youth* initiated the vernacular revolution in Chinese literature. His doctoral dissertation at Columbia University asserted the claims of Chinese thought to be capable of supporting scientific practice. He followed Zhang's lead to create the paradigm of modern historical studies of Chinese philosophy and employed his historical theories and insights in an attempt to systematize the Chinese national heritage. His demand for clarity, bold hypotheses, and testability, drawn from Dewey's experimentalist pragmatism, extended to his accounts of culture, education, and politics. His politics were gradualist and democratic. In a famous exchange with Li Dazhou in 1919, Hu supported beneficial piecemeal reform in opposition to total revolutionary change.

Jin Yuelin, who is discussed by Hu Jun in chapter 5, replaced an early enthusiasm for Neo-Hegelian idealism with a passion for modern logic. He did much to introduce modern logic and its underlying philosophical thought in China. He was attracted to Russell's version of analytic philosophy, but rejected the claim that the method of analysis precluded the development of a metaphysical system. For his own metaphysics, he focused on the Chinese concept of *Dao*, but this exploration is also remarkable for his deployment of modality, centering on the notion of logical possibility. The clarity and sophistication of his argument has had wide influence in China.

Philosophizing in the Neo-Confucian Spirit

Reassessment of the complex traditions of Chinese philosophical thought played an increasingly important role as the century progressed. The diversity of commitment among philosophers concerning modernization and traditional values was shown in the 1923 debate on Science versus Metaphysics as some intellectuals, led by Zhang Junmai (1887–1969), powerfully contested the May Fourth Movement's optimistic endorsement of Western models of modernity.

A scholarly revival involving fresh interpretations of ancient Confucian, Daoist, Mohist, legalist, and Buddhist texts was crucially important, but the main inspiration from traditional Chinese thought derived from the great Neo-Confucian syntheses of the Song and Ming dynasties, especially in the writings of Zhu Xi (1130–1200) and Wang Yangming (1472–1529). The subtlety and scope of their philosophical intelligence and the tension between Zhu Xi's realism and Wang Yangming's focus on mind provided room for modern reflective interpretations of their work.

In the second section of the volume, we focus on four philosophers: Xiong Shili (1885–1968), Liang Shuming (1893–1988), Feng Youlan (1895–1900), and He Lin (1902–92).

Dissatisfaction with his early studies of "Mere Consciousness" Buddhism led Xiong Shili, who is discussed by Jiyuan Yu in chapter 6, to Confucianism and the project of recovering the true *Dao* of Confucius as a basis for Chinese revival. In this work he drew inspiration from Wang Yangming, but also wished to integrate Western learning in a system of modern Confucian thought. Using the *Yijing*, he sought to determine a metaphysical basis for Confucian ethics and an active Confucian conception of the self, linking original reality and function, which he held to be in some sense the same, with the processes of change and the grounding of human virtue. Xiong's system found legitimate roles for both philosophy and science, but sharply distinguished their two domains. His densely argued thought raised deep questions about the relationship between metaphysics and morality.

Liang Shuming, who is discussed by Yanming An in chapter 7, developed an account of Confucian spontaneity that was based on the thought of the Neo-Confucian Wang Xinzhai (1483–1541) and was also influenced by the writings of Henri Bergson. He argued that intuition as well as intellect was a source of knowledge and later incorporated his insights about intuition within a practically oriented conception of reason. He argued that Confucian concerns with intuition, harmony, and our capacity to live in accord with nature provided a basis for culture that was superior to a Western demand to conquer nature or an Indian rejection of the self and nature as illusory. He recognized a sequence in the appropriate temporal order of these three cultural inclinations and traced the weakness of China to the premature realization of the Confucian ideal. His comparative theory of human cultures was accompanied by a parallel theory of types of human personality and issued in the conviction that after the fulfillment of economic needs, the time for Confucian culture and the Confucian self would come.

Feng Youlan, who is discussed by Lauren Pfister in chapter 8, used the techniques of modern logical analysis to develop a philosophical system that aimed to correct and develop Zhu Xi's realist conception of principle (*li*) in a New Principle Learning. Like Xiong Shili, Feng sharply distinguished between philosophy and science, but grounded this distinction on a radical difference between the dimension of actuality and the dimension of truth-and-reality. His thought provided room for a philosophical mysticism based on the intellectual contemplation of the unity of reality. His ethics and politics retained a core of traditional values in the context of modernity. The sophistication and breadth of Feng's system were informed by a detailed historical understanding of the complexity and variety of Chinese philosophical thought. This understanding was manifested in three major histories of Chinese philosophy, in which Feng sought to reconstruct the arguments underlying the aphoristic and unsystematic surface of Chinese philosophical texts. The changing ambitions and emphases of these histories reflect Feng's intellectual development and his turn to materialism. His commitment to China's modernization and his conception of the true and faithful subject of a legitimate ruler provide an intellectual basis for his ambiguous relations to Maoist authority.

He Lin, who is discussed by Jiwei Ci in chapter 9, sought to reinterpret the doctrines of the School of Mind of Lu Jiuyuan (1139–93), and Wang Yangming (1472–1529) in order to provide a Chinese contribution to a universally true Hegelian idealist system of philosophical thought. In doing so, he aimed to resolve China's modern cultural crisis by returning to true philosophy. He construed mind objectively in terms of logic rather than subjectively in terms of psychology and considered mind to be the total of Kantian *a priori* principles or Neo-Confucian *li*. Like Hegel, he understood mind to be dynamic and developing rather than static. By using the identity of substance and application to erode distinctions between mind and principle and mind and matter, he sought to reconcile the traditions of the Neo-Confucian Schools of Mind and Principle. Within his idealist framework, He attempted to bring culture, nature, spirit, and the *Dao* into a single intelligible order. His philosophical universalism sanctioned the strengthening of Confucian philosophy of principle with truths that are explicit in Western philosophy, but only implicit in Chinese philosophy.

Ideological Exposure to Dialectical Materialism

After the victory of Bolshevism in Russia, Marxist thought came to dominate Chinese radical thinking. Chen Duxiu and Li Dazhao become China's first significant Marxist theorists and founded the Chinese Communist Party with Mao Zedong (1893–1976) and others. As the first party leader, Chen led many intellectuals away from earlier Chinese radical movements, such as anarchism, and Li's arguments for interdependent moral and economic revolutions founded Marxist ethical thinking in China. The political and social commentaries of Lu Xun (1881–1936), China's greatest modern writer and a sympathizer of the Communist Party's radical aims, called for popular reform and the recognition of democratic rights. Zhang Shenfu (1893–1986), whose 1927 translation of *Tractatus Logico-Philosophicus* introduced Wittgenstein's philosophy to China, attempted to integrate the philosophy of Confucius, Bertrand Russell, and dialectical materialism. The revival of the Communist Party under Mao after its near destruction under its urban-based leadership led to years of struggle and eventual triumph. Mao's populist and voluntarist Marxism established the parameters of public discussion over a wide range of subjects, including philosophy. The utopian aims and ideological rigidities of Mao's thought were used repeatedly to restrict the range of debate, even though Mao's theory of contradictions could distinguish between tolerable and dangerous disagreements. The imposition of orthodoxy curtailed much of the potential creativity of Marxist theory. Nevertheless, some philosophers contributed to serious Marxist thought and historical reassessments of Chinese philosophy. We can note the influence of Guo Moruo (1892–1978), whose periodization of Chinese philosophy on the basis of changing modes of production and his judgment of the philo-sophers who were therefore progressive or reactionary did much to shape the study of the history of philosophy in China. In the open exchanges earlier in the century, Guo's rejection of a static essence of Chinese society and thought contributed to the development of historical understanding, but, imposed as an orthodoxy, these views distorted and constricted philosophical study.

In the third section of the volume, we focus on three philosophers: Feng Qi (1915–95), Zhang Dainian (1909–present), and Li Zehou (1931–present). All are creatively heterodox in their interpretations of Marxism and in their use of other intellectual sources.

Feng Qi, who is discussed by Huang Yong in chapter 10, constructed an original philosophy of value on the basis of Daoist, Confucian, Buddhist, Kantian, Hegelian, and Marxist insights. His main study concerned the theory of wisdom, which he understood as knowledge of *Dao* as the fundamental prin-ciple of the universe and of human life. Wisdom found its application in our cognitive and practical activities and in our moral cultivation. Philosophers had the task of transforming knowledge, which requires an attachment to objects and the self, into wisdom, which sees reality as a whole without such attachments. This transformation came through the sudden enlightenment of intellectual intuition and moved from the realm of the nameable to the realm of the unname-able. Feng sought to transform the theory of *Dao* into method and into virtue. These transformations involved dialectic: the dialectic between analytic and synthetic methods, the dialectic between knowledge and practice, the dialectic between logical and historical methods, and the dialectic between agreements and disagreements. This last dialectical movement realized a notion of non-perspectival, yet nonfoundational, objectivity. Feng's account of virtue required an understanding of freedom as self-conscious, voluntary, and natural action, and this conception of freedom was to be realized in individuality.

Zhang Dainian, who is discussed by Cheng Lian in chapter 11, was inspired by his brother, Zhang Shenfu, to integrate analytic method, dialectic material-ism, and traditional Chinese philosophy in investigations of central philosophical problems and historical studies and in consideration of cultural questions facing China. According to Zhang, philosophy is the study of the principles of nature and the rules of human life, with humans seen naturalistically as a natural species. Matter is fundamental to life and mind, but Zhang held that it is a mistake to reduce ideals to the category of matter. He used the distinction between root and perfection to synthesize materialism and idealism. In his historical studies, Zhang sought to bring out the systematic nature of Chinese thought and approached his task through an analysis of fundamental categories and doctrines, rather than chronologically. *A Handbook of Concepts and Categories in Classical Chinese Philosophy* is a masterly expression of his mature understanding of Chinese thought. Zhang explored the materialist tradition of Chinese philosophy and interpreted its dialectical thought and humanitarian ideas. His cultural studies argued for a synthesis of Chinese and Western approaches to man and nature, the individual and society, and analytic and dialectical thinking.

Li Zehou, who is discussed by John Zijiang Ding in chapter 12, is best known for his aesthetic thought and for his interpretation of Kantian philosophy. Li has stressed the guiding role of practical rationality and the complementarity of Confucian and Daoist thought throughout the history of Chinese aesthetics. In his general philosophy, Li developed an "anthropological ontology" on the basis of his account of human subjectivity. In this post-Marxist practical philosophy of human subjectivity, Li sought to preserve Marx's fundamental ideas while relinquishing other aspects of Marxist theory. He held that Marxist philosophy must turn from the tasks of criticism to those of humane philosophical construction. He argued that through the humanization of nature, the rational and the social in human nature transforms the perceptual and the natural. Li used the thought of Kant, Heidegger, Wittgenstein, and Foucault to explain the role of human subjectivity in transforming Marxism and to present his vision of a post-Marxist philosophy.

Later Developments of New Neo-Confucianism

After 1949, philosophers in Taiwan and Hong Kong were eager to provide a more systematic reinterpretation of traditional Chinese culture and philosophy in light of a deeper and more informed understanding of Western philosophy, specifically the works of Plato, Kant, and Hegel. A mark of this commitment was the 1957 Declaration on Chinese Culture, promulgated by Tang Junyi, Zhang Dongsun, Mou Zongsan, and Xu Fuguan and giving rise to the Movement of Contemporary New Confucianism.

In the fourth section of the volume, we focus on four philosophers: Fang Dongmei (1899–1977), Xu Fuguan (1903–82), Tang Junyi (1909–78), and Mou Zongsan (1909–95).

Fang Dongmei, who is discussed by Chenyang Li in chapter 13, sought to synthesize Confucian, Daoist, Mohist, Buddhist, and Western thought in a comprehensive system of comparative culture and philosophy. He based the possibility of individual wisdom, integrating reason and emotion, on distinctive types of cultural wisdom. His system was animated by a universal urge to life and gave fundamental roles to the concepts of *Dao*, harmony, the unity of nature and value, and creativity. He stressed the importance of the *Yijing* as a metaphysics of change in constructing an account of reality. He was critical of classical Neo-Confucian thought for its narrow exclusion of rival views. His feeling for cultural detail and his integrative scope gave his philosophical exposition a rhapsodic power. He saw the facets of the world, from the natural world of physics and biology to the human world of psychology, aesthetics, morality, and religion, as organized in a hierarchy of layers, but gave each layer nonreductive autonomy as part of a harmonious whole.

Xu Fuguan, who is discussed by Peimin Ni in chapter 14, presented New Confucian views in a less systematic and metaphysical way than others considered in this section. He placed anxiety at the core of Chinese philosophical reflection in contrast to curiosity as the source of Western philosophy and sought to trace the consequences of this claim for understanding human life and the Chinese concern for the heart–mind. Because of human embodiment and the unity of the heart–mind, he saw bodily recognition, as a concrete and emotionally grounded method of knowing, as a crucial aspect of human knowledge. His scholarly appreciation of past philosophers was founded on a method of bodily recognition and tracing back, but he also saw bodily recognition as a method to discover and transform one's true subjectivity. In his political thought, Xu argued that although the Confucian tradition lacked a democratic dimension, the Confucian conceptions of the embodied self and the practice of virtue were both compatible with democracy and necessary for full realization of democracy. He argued that Zhuangzi's metaphysical notion of the *Dao*, when embodied in life, became the best representative of the Chinese aesthetic spirit as the realization of freedom in the unity between life and art.

Tang Junyi, who is discussed by Sin Yee Chan in chapter 15, interpreted the Neo-Confucian thought of Lu Jiuyuan (1139–93) and Wang Yangming (1472–1529) and the role that they assigned to the mind in intellectual and moral cultivation. He sought to ground these ethical concerns in a doctrine of universal metaphysical and moral substance. Moral life requires us to be self-governing and to transcend our actual selves by realizing ourselves as a universal rational moral substance: the ethical self. Through self-reflective and self-conscious thought at a moment, a thought that can create a moral world, we must resist indulgence. We can transcend our actual selves by taking part in moral activities. At the center of his ethical account are the heart–mind and our capacity for feeling–penetration, involving cognition, emotions and will. We use our feeling–penetration in relation to nine horizons dealing with the objective world, self-consciousness and the transcendence of the subjective and the objective. The transcendence of the self is a theme that united his ethical and metaphysical views. Tang understood cultures as different manifestations of the heart–mind as the ethical self and argued for the superiority of Confucian over Western culture. His notion of Confucianism, involving *ren* and unity, allowed room for democracy and reform by being abstracted from any pattern of institutions.

Mou Zongsan, who is discussed by Refeng Tang in chapter 16, used his deep understanding of Chinese and Western philosophy to criticize those who concentrated on chance parallels between Chinese and Western doctrines or who construed Chinese thought within a structure formed by a single Western school. He sought to revive Chinese philosophy while avoiding these interpretive dangers. After work on modern logic, he turned to Kantian theory of the self and the assessment of Daoist, Confucian, and Buddhist philosophy. Although he was fascinated by Kant, Mou developed his thought through criticism of Kantian claims. His mature system of moral metaphysics focused on human beings as moral subjects who, unlike Kantian selves, took part in infinite mind with a world-creating capacity for intellectual intuition.

With a renewal of officially sanctioned Confucian philosophy in China and greater contact among philosophers in China, Hong Kong and Taiwan, New Confucianism can contribute to the reintegration of Chinese philosophical life after the politically enforced divisions of half a century. Other Chinese and Western influences can also contribute to this reintegration. In addition, the schools of Chinese philosophy, from their origin to their modern interpretation, provide grounds for fusion with Western philosophy and a standpoint from which Western philosophy can be constructively criticized. In these circumstances, Chinese philosophers, holding diverse views but sharing a complex intellectual culture, can display subtlety, dynamism and openness to dialogue as Chinese philosophy takes its place in world philosophy.

I became interested in contemporary Chinese philosophy through work with the Philosophy Summer School in China: China Britain Australia. Since 1988, the Summer School has held intensive sessions in Beijing, Tianjin, Shanghai, Panyu, and Suzhou with British staff members and members drawn from an outstanding younger generation of Chinese philosophers. In recent years, Australian staff members and members from Hong Kong and Taiwan have also taken part. Chung-ying Cheng and I first met at a conference cosponsored by the Summer School. Several of our contributors were Summer School members or took part in projects that grew from Summer School roots. I am especially grateful to Professor Qiu Renzong and his colleagues at the Institute of Philosophy, Chinese Academy of Social Sciences and the Summer School staff members over the years for maintaining an institution that has produced so much friendship and good philosophy. I hope that they will see *Contemporary Chinese Philosophy* as further fruit of our work together.

Finally, I thank Chung-ying for his erudition and friendship and our contributors for their enthusiasm and hard work. I hope that readers will gain as much as I have from their efforts.

I

PIONEERING NEW THOUGHT FROM THE WEST

1

LIANG QICHAO'S POLITICAL AND SOCIAL PHILOSOPHY

Yang Xiao

Liang Qichao (1873–1929) was one of the foremost intellectual leaders of contemporary China and one of its major political figures. He was arguably the most widely read public intellectual during the transitional period from the late Qing dynasty to the early Republican era. Like Diderot in France and Herzen in Russia, Liang was a thinker whose opinions and activities changed the direction of political and social thought in his country. Liang and his teacher, Kang Youwei (1858–1927), often referred to as "Kang-Liang," transformed traditional Chinese philosophy into the kind of philosophy that we know today in China. Almost all the fundamental assumptions and ideas that we find in the work of contemporary Chinese philosophers can be traced back to Kang and Liang. This chapter will focus on Liang Qichao's political and social philosophy.

Liang was more than a political philosopher or theorist. His career as a public intellectual, journalist, and political activist began when he was still a young man. Liang was twenty-two years old when in 1895 he and Kang organized the scholars' protest in Beijing, an event that marked the beginning of the era of democratic mass movement in China.

The writings of Kang and Liang came to the attention of the young Emperor Guangxu and helped usher in the well-known "One-Hundred-Day Reform" in 1898. During this period the emperor acted on the advice of these scholars in an attempt to reform the imperial system. The suggested changes included setting up modern schools, remaking the 2,000-year-old civil service examination system, and publishing more translations of Western books on politics and history. Liang was recommended to the emperor and was granted an audience. The emperor placed him in charge of a newly authorized government translation bureau. Liang could have had greater influence, had he been able to speak proper Mandarin – the Emperor could not understand his Guangdong dialect.

The reform movement was suppressed by the Empress Dowager Cixi; on 21 September, 1898, she ordered the kidnap of the emperor, placed him under house arrest, and seized control of the government. Orders were also issued for the arrest of Kang, Liang, and other reformers. Six of the intellectual leaders of the movement were arrested and put to death. Liang escaped to Japan, where he was to remain in exile for 14 years until the fall of imperial China. Liang returned to China in 1912 after the establishment of the Republic of China. When the autocratic president Yuan Shikai attempted to overturn the republic and have himself declared emperor, Liang, with his former student, General Cai Er, organized successful military resistance (Liang, 1916). Liang held cabinet positions twice, each for a very short period of time: the minister of the Department of Justice (September 1913–February 1914), and the minister of the Department of Finance (July–November 1917). Although he wrote on theoretical and scholarly issues all his life, only in his last decade did he become a university professor. In the 1920s, Liang was considered, together with Wang Guowei, Chen Yinke, and Zhao Yuanren, one of the "Four Great Masters" of Qinghua University. He died when he was only fifty-six years old.

Liang was an extremely prolific writer. He started publishing when he was twenty-three, and *The Collected Works of Liang Qichao* contains about ten million words. Liang wrote on an extremely wide range of issues: political philosophy (especially nationalism, constitutionalism, anarchism, human rights, and women's rights), legal philosophy (including the first brief history of Chinese legal philosophy), international relations, philosophy of history, philosophy of science, metaphysics (especially the issue of free will and the law of causality), methodology of historiography, education, communication, journalism, economics, finance, and current political, social, economic, and financial policies, to give just a few examples.

Among his contemporaries, Liang was the most cosmopolitan. He invited Bertrand Russell to give a series of lectures in China. Liang spent 16 years in Japan and traveled extensively to the U.S., England, France, Sweden, Holland, Germany, Canada, Australia, and New Zealand. He met President Theodore Roosevelt and the financier J. P. Morgan and talked to the philosopher Henri Bergson. Liang had an imaginative and critical mind and was a marvelously gifted social observer. His books on his trips to America and Europe are full of insights about politics, customs, characters, and intellectual trends. Scholars in the future would do well to compare his book on his journey to the New World with de Tocqueville's *Democracy in America* (1954; first published in two volumes 1835, 1840). He wrote one short treatise on each of the following Western philosophers: Aristotle, Spinoza, Hobbes, Rousseau, Kant, Fichte, Montesquieu, Bacon, Bentham, Spencer, and Darwin. Many people in China were introduced to these figures through Liang's writings. Liang introduced a Chinese readership to the basic ideas of liberalism, anarchism, civic nationalism, constitutionalism, historicism, and the concept of a universal world history. Li Zehou, one of the most important philosophers writing in Chinese in 1980s,

assessed Liang as "the most influential propagandist of bourgeois enlightenment" (Li, 1979, p. 438). Indeed, a list of people who spoke passionately of
how Liang's writings transformed their life and thought would be a Who's Who
of modern Chinese history, regardless of their political positions.

Liang's Civic Nationalism and His Critique of Cultural Monism

One of Liang's central concerns was the problem of how to justify historical
changes that included "changing China from an empire to a nation" and
"*bianfa*" (reform; literally: changing institutions and laws). For Liang, reform
meant creating new institutions, such as railroads, newspapers, modern schools
(including schools for women), a parliamentary system, and the protection of
people's rights. And these institutions, according to Liang, were the essential
components of a modern nation or state (*guojia*). For most of the Chinese
in the late nineteenth century, these institutions were new and non-Chinese
and hence creating them was illegitimate and unjustifiable.

How to justify historical change to his contemporaries was already a
central problem in the first essay that Liang published, "*Bianfa tonglun*" (On
Changing Institutions) (1896). Liang's innovative solution to the problem can
already be found in this essay. Before Kang and Liang, there had been several
solutions to the problem of how to justify historical change. Liang's innovation consisted in his extremely keen reflective awareness of the deep-seated
assumptions or presuppositions that were taken for granted by his turn-of-the-
century contemporaries. These assumptions defined a general framework that
might be called the "framework of cultural monism." Liang called all deep-
seated assumptions *lixiang* (imagined principles):

> What was *lixiang*? The things that everybody imagines and are commonly taken
> as the most reasonable principles. In the mind of people of any nation, there
> are inherited social customs of thousands of years, and their great philosophers'
> teachings are eventually internalized in everyone's brain and cannot be erased
> or washed away. This was *lixiang*. It was the most powerful thing in the world.
> Its power can produce various customs and all kinds of events. Whenever there
> was an old *lixiang* that has ruled the world for a long time, if we suddenly
> want to replace it by an opposite *lixiang*, a giant force was needed. (Liang, 1999,
> vol. 1 p. 413)

Here we shall focus on a specific set of *lixiang* that define the framework
of cultural monism. Liang was the first to describe such a framework, and
his account obviously inspired Levenson's idea of "culturalism" (Levenson,
1959, 1968). The many assumptions in this framework focused on the views

that China is civilization or the world (*tianxia*); that the Confucian way (*dao*) or Confucian rituals and morals (*li-yi*) are universally true; and that the sovereignty of the empire (*tianxia*) lies in the emperor (*tianzi*), who is the Son of Heaven (*tian*).

In Liang's writings, cultural monism remained a major target throughout his life. For example, his civic nationalism, which holds that China is a nation and the sovereignty of the nation lies in the people or citizens, is the result of a direct negation of the assumption. Liang believed that the following three deep-seated assumptions were the main causes of China's weakness and its endless defeats in the modern world of nation-states:

> First, there has been no awareness of the distinction between *guojia* (nation) and *tianxia* (the world, empire). The Chinese have not been aware that its *guo* was one nation or state [among many]. For China has remained united since ancient time; it has been surrounded by "little barbarians," who do not have civilization or government and thus could not be called a nation or state. We Chinese people do not see them as equals. Therefore, for thousands of years, China has been isolated. We call China the world, not a nation. . . . Secondly, there has been no awareness of the distinction between a nation (or state) and a dynasty (or court). The biggest problem of the Chinese people is that we do not know what kind of thing a nation is and thus confuse the nation and the court, mistakenly believing that the nation is the property of the court. . . . Thirdly, there is no awareness of the relationships between the nation or state (*guo*) and the citizens (*guomin*). A nation consists in the people. Who is the master of the nation? The people of the nation. . . . The Western people regard the nation as being shared by the king and the people . . . This is not the case in China. One family owns the nation and all the rest of the people are slaves of the family. This is why, although there are forty million people in China, there are actually only dozens of human beings (*ren*). When such a nation of dozens of human beings encounters the [Western] nations of millions of human beings, how can it not be defeated? (Liang, 1999, vol. 1, pp. 413–14; also see Liang, 1999, vol. 2, p. 657, p. 736)

In his early essays, instead of distinguishing between *Chinese* learning and *Western* learning, Liang deliberately chose to speak of *political* learning (*zheng-xue*), which included, as he emphasized, both Chinese learning *and* Western learning. This enabled Liang to say that in order to change China into a modern nation and to make it strong, we should study both Western and Chinese political learning. Liang changed the subject by changing the question. Before Liang, the question was "Why should we study *Western* learning?" Liang started asking a very different question: "Why and how should we study *political* learning?" Liang's answer was, "If we really want to think about self-strengthening in China today, we must start with promoting political learning" (Liang, 1999, vol. 1, p. 43). "Regarding politics (*zheng*), there is no difference between China and the West. . . . These [rules and laws] are the same in both the ancient and present time, in both the West and China. They are common principles for all nations" (Liang, 1999, vol. 1, p. 137).

Liang shifted the focus from "civilization" to "nation" and from "Western versus Chinese learning" to "the universal laws of all nations." He wrote in 1899:

> The Westerners, such as Grotius and Hobbes, who were all ordinary people, have written the universal laws of all nations (*wanguo gongfa*), and the whole world obeys them. The *Chunqiu* written by Confucius was also the universal laws of all ages. How ridiculous for anyone to say that Confucius must not be as intelligent as Grotius and Hobbes! (Liang, 1999, vol. 1, p. 154)

Notice that in 1899 Liang still held the assumption that the source of all truth is Confucius; this is why in the above passage he had to claim that Confucius had already known the universal laws of all nations. Around the 1900s, Liang no longer held this assumption. He now thought that one came to know the universal causal laws of history by studying history. He stopped appealing to Confucius. For Liang, the most important law was the causal relationship between nationalism and the rise of Western nations. Here was what he wrote in 1902:

> That Europe has arisen, and the world has progressed since the sixteenth century was all because of the rising power of "nationalism" [Liang used the English term]. What is nationalism? Those people from different places, who are of the same race, language, religion and custom, see each other as fellows, seek independent self-rule and organize a government in order to seek the common good and to conquer other races. And by the end of nineteenth century (the last twenty or thirty years), this "ism" has developed to its extreme and has further become "national imperialism." [Liang used the English term] (Liang, 1999, vol. 2, p. 656)

The early Liang's justification for historical change and the creation of new institutions was based on such universal laws. For example, his justification for creating civil associations and parties in China was: "Among the strong nations in the West and East, there is no nation that has no parties and no one person who does not join an association" (Liang, 1999, vol. 1, p. 148). His justification for creating a national religion at the time was not different from his teacher Kang's justification; he said, "There are no ruling people who do not have a religion, and there are no nations that do not have a religion" (Liang, 1999, vol. 1, p. 150). His justification for creating local self-government was: "Cultivating the fashion of local self-government is the starting point of strengthening the nation. Today if we want to build a nation on this planet, the only art of doing it is through the citizen's self-government" (Liang, 1999, vol. 2, p. 758).

In the last decade of his life in the 1920s, Liang's role changed from a political activist to a historian; what Liang called the "historian's virtue of truthfulness" led him to reject his earlier belief in the *existence* of universal causal laws in history. However, in the 1900s, even though he still believed in the existence of universal historical laws, Liang had already changed his view regarding the *contents* of some of the universal causal laws. For example, he argued against his teacher Kang's claim that there was a causal relationship between religion (Christianity) and the rise of Western nations. He argued, rather, that it was freedom of thought that was partly responsible for the rise of the Western nations. For the same reason, he also opposed Kang's plan to establish Confucianism as a national religion modeled on Christianity. However, at this stage, Liang still took the freedom of thought as an instrumental value, as a means to the end of strengthening the nation. In his later life, Liang eventually came to see truth (and truthfulness) as an intrinsic value and never changed this position. He is one of very few Chinese intellectuals to have consistently taken freedom of thought as a value in itself (for detailed discussion, see Xiao, forthcoming).

Liang was the most original among the first generation of Chinese nationalists who articulated and introduced the fundamental idea of civic nationalism. His originality lay in two of his major ideas: his civic nationalism and his historicist concept of nationalism and nation. He believed that there was an intimate relationship between national rights (sovereignty) and the people's rights. He always reasoned on both levels: "The reason a nation has independent sovereignty (*zizhu zhi quan*) is because the people have independent sovereignty" (Liang, 1999, vol. 1, p. 344). The two rights were based on the same principle of self-mastery and independence:

> Nationalism is the most just and grandest doctrine in the world: no nations should violate my nation's liberty, and my nation should not violate other nations' liberty. When this doctrine is applied to my nation, it means the independence of human beings (*ren*); when the doctrine was applied to the world, it means the independence of nations. (Liang, 1999, vol. 1, p. 459)

For Liang, the location of sovereignty within the people and the recognition of the fundamental equality among its members constituted the essence of civic nationalism and this was at the same time the basic tenet of democracy. In his essay "On the Progress China Has Made in the Last Fifty Years" (1922), Liang argued that China's progress was due to the citizens' awareness of two principles. The first one is "Anyone who is not Chinese has no right to govern Chinese affairs." The second is "Anyone who is Chinese has the right to govern Chinese affairs." He called the first principle "the spirit of nation-building" and the second "the spirit of democracy" (Liang, 1999, vol. 7,

p. 4031). As we have seen, unlike cultural nationalists and other nationalists, Liang believed that nationalism is a product of history and it has a beginning and it also has an end in the future; thus he did not believe that there has always existed a Chinese nation. Rather, we had to create China as a nation. He tried to historicize nationalism and to show that nationalism was the product of a certain historical epoch, that is, the modern age. "The eighteenth and nineteenth centuries are the age of nationalism. The French Revolution [by giving rise to nationalism] has accomplished the greatest achievement by far in history" (Liang, 1999, vol. 1, p. 459). He argued that, as a matter of universal law, China should and would become a nation: "Any *guo* (country) that has not gone through the stage of nationalism cannot be called a *guo* (nation)" (Liang, 1999, vol. 1, p. 460).

In introducing the concept of civic nationalism in China, Liang introduced the concept of the people (*min*) at the same time. Before its link with nationalism, *min* meant no more than the population of a region. Liang played a crucial role in the process of the "nationalization" of *min* (the people), and he used a new term *guomin* (people of the nation, citizens). He held that the life and death of a nation depends on the life and death of its citizens (Liang, 1999, vol. 1, p. 259):

> What is a nation? It consists of the people (*min*). What is national politics? It is simply the people's self-government. What is love of country? It is the people loving themselves. Therefore, when the rights of the people arise, national rights are established. When people's rights or powers (*quan*) vanish, national rights or powers vanish. (Liang, 1999, vol. 1, p. 273)

From the last sentence of the above passage, we can see clearly that Liang's concept of "*quan*" means more than a normative and formal concept such as "rights." It also means "power." One might want to say it includes both "liberty" and what Rawls (1971) calls the "worth of liberty." But it might be more adequate to compare it with Hannah Arendt's concept of power. For both Arendt and Liang, power will be generated when people act together and, through power, people can found a new republic and make history. As Arendt puts it, "power springs up between men when they act together and vanishes the moment they disperse" (1958, p. 200). Liang would also agree with Arendt when she says that "power and freedom belonged together, . . . conceptually speaking, political freedom did not reside in the I-will but in the I-can" (1965, p. 148). Unlike Arendt, Liang also emphasizes that people's intelligence is essential for the generation of power. (For a discussion about the similarities and differences between Liang's and Arendt's concept of power, see Xiao, forthcoming.) It seems obvious that the word "*quan*" in the following passage should be translated as "power":

Those who speak of China must speak of "promoting the people's power (*quan*)."
It is necessary to promote the people's power, but the people's power cannot
be achieved overnight. This power grows from the intellect. When there is one
degree of intelligence, there is one degree of power. When there are six or seven
degrees of intelligence, there will be six or seven degrees of power. When there
are ten degrees of intelligence, there will be ten degrees of power. (Liang, 1999,
vol. 1, p. 177)

For this reason, Liang considered his agenda of cultivating the Chinese people
into new citizens (*xin-min*) as the crucial part of his political philosophy of
rights. His justification for a standardized public education is that it is the
passport to citizenship. For Liang, to increase the people's rights or powers is
to increase their will to self-mastery: "The reason the people have *quan* (rights
or powers) is because they have the will to self-mastery" (Liang, 1999, vol. 1,
p. 334). To achieve this aim of self-mastery, the ideas and techniques of Neo-
Confucian self-cultivation could be a very useful source, as Liang argued in
what might be his best-known essay *Xinmin Shuo* ("On the New People" or
"On Renewing the People"). This provides another example of his capacity
to transform traditional Chinese philosophy – in this case, moral psychology
and spiritual exercises – into contemporary discourse (for a more detailed discussion, see Chang, 1971). However, because of limited historical experience,
Liang was not aware of the possible conflict of the two meanings of *quan*,
and the possibility that the agenda of renewing people could dangerously
become an agenda of forcing people to become free. Also, he was not aware
of the possible conflict between national rights and people's rights, not to
mention the possible conflict between national rights and human rights.

Liang's Two Concepts of Liberty

Isaiah Berlin and Elie Kedourie have independently argued that the Kantian
idea of individual self-determination was one of the sources of nationalism
(the idea of national self-determination) in Europe (see Kedourie's 1960 book,
Nationalism, and Berlin's 1972 essay, "Kant as an Unfamiliar Source of
Nationalism" in Berlin, 1996). As we have seen, in Liang Qichao, the ideas
of individual and national self-determination went hand in hand.

The modern Chinese term *zhu-quan* (sovereignty) is an abbreviation of *zizhu
zhi quan* (literally: the right of self-determination or self-mastery or autonomy).
This phrase appeared as a translation of "[national] rights" or "[national]
sovereignty" in a Chinese version of the American legal scholar Henry
Wheaton's international law textbook, *Elements of International Law*. The book
was first published in 1836 in the U.S. There were several revised editions.
The American missionary W. A. P. Martin started the translation in 1862 when

he returned to China from the U.S. (Martin, 1966, pp. 221–2, 233–5). Martin used the 1846 edition of the book. With the aid of four Chinese scholars, he finished his rendering around 1864. His version, entitled *Wanguo gongfa* (Universal Laws of All Nations), could hardly be called a translation, not only because much of the original contents were omitted, but also because the translators mainly provided summaries of passages rather than word-by-word translations. In his preface, Martin used the idea that every human being has rights as an example to illustrate the idea of (national) rights.

Shortly afterwards, we also find Kang Youwei, Liang Qichao, Tan Sitong, and others applying the term *zizhu zhi quan* to *ren* (human beings) or *ren ren* (all human beings, every human being). The sentence "*ren ren you zizhu zhi quan*" (all human beings have the right to self-mastery or autonomy) thus became an extremely popular slogan at the time. We can also find this popular slogan in the books and magazines written, edited, and published by Christian missionaries, where the slogan was read not necessarily as a political one. Kang's and Liang's innovation is that they did not take it merely as a *metaphysical* claim about human nature. They took it as a *political* principle and went further to apply this principle to political, legal, and social issues. One result of these applications is their doctrine of *minquan* (the people's rights, popular sovereignty). The other is Kang's utopian idea that the family would be abolished in the future. No wonder some conservatives picked up this slogan as a major object of attack. We can find such an attack in Zhang Zhidong's essay on rectifying rights from his book *Quanxue pian* (Exhortation to Learn) (Zhang, 1995) which was published in 1898 and was given official distribution by the emperor. Zhang's essay was also included in *Yijiao Congbian* [Selected Writings on Protecting the [Confucian] Doctrine], a collection of essays attacking Kant–Liang's agenda of radical reform (Su, 1898). Zhang refused to take the idea of *zizhu zhi quan* as a political idea:

> Recently some people who chased after Western doctrines have even claimed that every human being has *zizhu zhi quan*. This is ridiculous. *This phrase came from the books of Christianity and its meaning was just that God gave human beings spirit and soul, and that every human being had intelligence, wisdom, and thus could achieve certain things* (emphasis added). Therefore, it is a big mistake for the translators to render it as "every human being has *zizhu zhi quan*." (Zhang Zhidong's essay on rectifying rights, in Su, 1898, p. 127)

This passage reflects the important fact that Kang and Liang had already transformed the slogan into a *political* one. Thus, not surprisingly, Zhang's strategy had to be to reinterpret the slogan as a *nonpolitical*, harmless, metaphysical/ religious claim about human nature.

Not long after W. A. P. Martin's translation *Wanguo gongfa* was published, Kang Youwei finished the manuscript of a book *Shili gongfa* (Substantial Axioms

and Public or Universal Theorems) around 1888. Its style was modeled on
the Euclidean axiomatic system of geometry and Wheaton's system of international law. The manuscript remained unpublished in Kang's lifetime, but
its basic ideas found their way into some of his published works, especially
his influential book on utopia, *Datong shu* (The Book of Great Unity). More
importantly, Kang showed the manuscript to his students, including Liang
(Liang, 1999, vol. 2, p. 958).

The proposition, "Human beings have the right to self-mastery" (*ren you
zizhu zhi quan*), was the first universal theorem (*gongfa*) of Kang's axiomatic
system. Kang applied this universal theorem to the five basic Confucian human
relationships (*wulun*): husband–wife, parent–child, teacher–disciple, emperor–
subject, and elder brother–younger brother. He appealed to this universal
theorem when he criticized the central aspects of Confucian moral teaching.
For example, he wanted to abolish the family; in his future utopia, children
would grow up in government-run units. "[When they grow up], they may see
their parents. But according to the *gongfa*, parents should not require children
to have filial piety, and children should not require parents to be benevolent,
because human beings have rights of autonomy" (Kang, 1987, p. 285).

Kang's approach was both revolutionary and utopian. He looked at parents
and children as if they were strangers armed with rights to self-mastery. He
wanted to impose on intimate human relations a moral principle that was more
properly applied to the relations of strangers. The New Culture Movement
in the 1910s and 1920s and the Cultural Revolution in the 1960s and 1970s
would seek to carry out radical utopian agendas that are not very different
from Kang's. In these periods, radical individualists, anarchists, and utopian
socialists promoted the abolition, among other things, of filial piety and the
institutions of family and marriage.

However, Liang never went as far as that. He did not believe that the
concept of rights should apply in the realm of intimate human relations.
This was one of the major reasons that Liang ceased to be read when radical
individualists, anarchists, and abolitionists of marriage in the New Culture
Movement dominated the national cultural life. Liang criticized misapplica-
tions of Kang's teaching:

> When some hear [Kang's] principles of Utopia, they learn nothing except
> that they should take their family members as strangers. . . . When they hear
> Locke's and Kant's theory of liberty, they immediately indulge in excessive
> and uncontrolled activities in the name of natural rights. (Liang, 1999, vol. 2,
> p. 763)

Liang distinguished political and legal liberty from social and ethical liberty
in a way that roughly corresponds to Isaiah Berlin's distinction between negative and positive liberty. Liang used the distinction to respond to a popular

communitarian critique of the principles of liberty and equality. He defended
these principles by recognizing that they are political and legal principles that
are only applicable to the domain of the political:

> I hope those older generations in our country understand that the function of
> liberty and equality is to be applied to politics. Outside politics, one should not
> appeal to these [two principles] as one's reasons for action. When they are applied
> to politics, they mean no more than that everyone has liberty protected by the
> law and that everyone is equal before the law. They should not be interpreted
> as going beyond this domain. (Liang, 1999, vol. 5, p. 2,845)

He argued that the older generation's objection to the principles of liberty
and equality was based on confusing the negative legal concepts of liberty and
equality with the positive ethical concepts of liberty and equality. He also held
that the legal concepts of liberty and equality are the necessary conditions for
any meaningful life:

> Liberty and equality are two principles from which many political principles are
> derived. How could we then take them lightly? Everyone has liberty protected
> by the law; everyone is equal before the law – are not these two principles
> those on which people's lives rely? In the last two years, the government has
> arbitrarily invented all kinds of taxes to exploit people, which has deprived
> people of the liberty of property; the government has put people under surveil-
> lance and spied on people's speeches in the streets, which has deprived people
> of the freedom of speech and association; the government has fabricated evid-
> ence to trap people and put people to death without trial, which has deprived
> people of the liberty of life; the government has used coercive force to manip-
> ulate people's will, which has deprived people of the freedom of conscience. How
> can anyone have a meaningful life under such a political system? (Liang, 1999,
> vol. 5, p. 2,845)

Liang, however, argued that, beyond the legal realm, the concept of liberty
means something very different:

> There are also cases where the principle of liberty and the principle of equality
> are applied to character and action. Ethical theorists respect freedom the most.
> What they mean by "freedom" is what makes the conscience absolutely free
> [from the bodily desires], not controlled by the bodily desires. If you indulge
> in excessive sexual activities and base behavior and try to return to your original
> conscience, you will know clearly that you should not act like this. When
> your bodily desires arise and intervene, you cannot control them. On the con-
> trary, you are controlled by them; you become the slave of desires. This is the
> opposite of freedom. If you still dare to say, "I am free," isn't this sad? (Liang,
> 1999, vol. 5, p. 2,845)

He held that the ethical concept of equality also means something very different outside the legal realm:

> The ethical concept of so-called "equality" means that every human being has the same basic capacity; if anyone can extend this capacity, then one can become a sage [here Liang used the phrases from Mencius]. If some give it up and want to be [ethically] inferior, then they will lose the worth of their humanity and become a beast. How can they then be equal to others? (Liang, 1999, vol. 5, p. 2,845)

It is extremely interesting that Liang claimed that the ethical concept of equality was based on Mencius's metaphysics of human nature, but did *not* claim that the legal concept of equality was based on any metaphysics. The contemporary New Confucian program of – to use Mou Zongsan's term – working out (*kaichu*) democracy from Confucianism has recently gained much popularity, with several attempts to derive the political idea of human rights from Mencius's concept of equality (see, for example, William Theodore de Bary, *Asian Values and Human Rights: A Confucian Communitarian Perspective*, Cambridge: Harvard University Press, 1998; William Theodore de Bary and Tu Wei-ming, eds, *Confucianism and Human Rights*, New York: Columbia University Press, 1997). In contrast to Liang's account, the disadvantage of this approach is that if we lose confidence in Mencius's metaphysics, we will lose confidence in the concept of human rights. To put the point in the later John Rawls's terms in his *Political Liberalism* (1993), Liang's *political* concept of human rights is a stable one whereas the others' *metaphysical* concept is not.

Modernity as Differentiation: Liang's Invention of the Sixth and Seventh Human Relationships

Like the later Rawls of *Political Liberalism* (1993), Liang was able both to accommodate a communitarian emphasis on basic intimate human relations and to retain a liberal emphasis on the political and legal concepts of liberty and equality. Instead of trying to change the nature of the five Confucian basic human relationships, Liang proposed recognizing two new relationships: (a) the relationship among private persons in general (*yibang siren*), including strangers and private persons of different countries (Liang, 1999, vol. 3, p. 1,310), and (b) the relationship between the state and its citizens (*guoming*). He held that these new relationships are within the domain of rights and legal regulations. I shall call these two new relationships the "sixth" and "seventh" relationships.

Liang thought that the two most unfortunate features of the traditional Chinese legal system were its lack of private law (*sifa*) to govern the sixth relationship and its lack of a constitution as the basic part of public law (*gongfa*) to govern the seventh relationship (Liang, 1999, vol. 3, pp. 1,311–12). According to Liang, civil law determines the rights and duties of strangers in general (Liang, 1999, vol. 3, p. 1,310) and the constitution determines the rights and duties of citizens in relation to the state (Liang, 1999, vol. 3, p. 1,312). Liang further argued:

> The most valuable thing about Roman law was that its civil law was comprehens-ive. . . . Modern civilization started from the study of Roman law. Its influence was so great that the legal systems of all modern countries are not duty-based, but right-based. This was all because of the influence of Roman law. Since rights were the basis of law, the purpose of law was thus not to limit people's freedom, but to protect people's freedom. This will then make it natural for people to be pleased to have law and respect law. Is not this revolutionary change of [legal] principle crucially important? China has three thousand years of legal history; there have been countless legal texts. But there was almost nothing about civil law. (Liang, 1999, vol. 3, p. 1,311)

In 1906, these were important innovative ideas, but unfortunately not many people followed Liang's line of thought. From Zhang Dainian's autobio-graphy, however, we know that Zhang's father, Zhang Zhongchin, who was a member of the congress in 1918, took this new approach to human rela-tionships very seriously, believed that besides the traditional five relationships, there was one more relationship between person and person, that is, between persons who are not friends. He even gave himself a new name "*Liulun*" (meaning: the sixth relationship).

Quite recently, China has seen a "right-based law movement" that started in 1988 at the First Conference on Basic Legal Categories with a debate on the question "What was the basis of law: right or duty?" Since then, hundreds of articles on this issue have been published in magazines and newspapers. Most contributors have criticized China's duty-based conception of law and its one-sided tendency to emphasize duty over right. One prominent member of the movement wrote, "Only when a government takes citizens' rights seriously can the people have trust, respect and obedience for the law." This claim reiterates Liang's idea and argument of eighty years ago for a right-based legal system.

The seventh relationship in Liang's civic nationalism took a constitutionalist form:

> However, if we do not have a constitution, we will not be able to have the rule of law. Why? Because a constitution is the basic law, without which all laws are without foundation and without protection. The Englishman Preston once wrote an article entitled "The constitutional law of the Chinese empire," comment-ing on the book *The Comprehensive Laws of the Great Qing* (*Daqing huidian*),

saying that it was the eternally unchanging basic law and was like a constitution. . . . But this was nonsense. The constitutions of all nations, good ones and
bad ones alike, generally have three parts: 1) the method of state structure;
2) the rules of state administration; and 3) the citizen's rights and duties with
respect to the state. Lacking any one of the three, it cannot be called a constitution. *The Comprehensive Laws of the Great Qing* has only the second part
and lacks both the first and the third. . . . Therefore, the difference between
the *huidian* and a constitution is not a matter of degree, but a matter of kind.
(Liang, 1999, vol. 3, p. 1,312)

When Mao Zedong was young and not yet a Marxist–Leninist, Liang was his
hero. He even gave himself a new name containing a character from Liang's
name. Under the influence of Liang's writings, the young Mao became a civic
nationalist and constitutionalist, believing in democracy, reform, and local self-
government. As a sixteen-year-old student in 1910, Mao read Liang's essay
"On National Consciousness" and was especially impressed by the following
passage:

A nation or state is like a company; the court is the management, and the head
of the court is just the manager of the department. . . . This is why the King
of France's statement "I am *guojia*" (L'état c'est moi) is today regarded as
absolutely incorrect. The children of Europe would ridicule this when hearing
it. (Liang, 1999, vol. 2, p. 663)

On the margin of this passage, Mao wrote:

When the country is legitimately founded, it is a constitutional nation: the constitution is made by the people and the crown is appointed by the people. When
it is not legitimately founded, it is a totalitarian nation: the laws are made by
the emperor who is not respected by the people. Today, Britain and Japan fall
into the former category, while the dynasties in the long history of China fall
into the latter. (Mao, 1990, p. 5)

We now know that, unfortunately, in his later years in power, Mao would totally
forget what he had read and believed.

Liang's proposal to add two ethical relationships resulted from his critique
of the traditional Confucian ideal of political and legal order, but he did not
dismiss every element of this ideal. He accepted certain of its assumptions
that were powerfully formulated in the *Great Learning* (*Da Xue*), one of the
"Four Books" of the Confucian canon. The Confucian ideal was a dynamic
conception of the transformative power of self-cultivation, which leads from
self to family, state, and empire. The cultivation of the self and the regulation
of the family are seen to be the "roots," and the governance of the state and
the universal peace of the empire are seen as the "branches." Liang still took

self-cultivation and the family as the roots in his new formulation of civic relationships. This commitment was reflected in his massive writings on self-cultivation and its crucial importance for his new ideal of citizenship (see, for example, "On Renewing the People").

Liang's innovation of adding the elements "citizen" and "private person in general" to his account of basic relationships led to changes in the nature of the traditional elements and changes in the structure of the traditional relationships. The "state" and "empire" now had different meanings, and Liang also wanted to change the structure of the Confucian ideal. He argued that civil associations and other communities are the missing links between the state and the family:

> Governance in Europe and America takes the individual person as a unit; governance in China [takes] the family. This is why people in Europe and America belong directly to the state, whereas people in China belong indirectly to the state. Confucian sages say that the root of the state is the family, and that when the family is well-regulated, the state can be well-governed. In such societies, there are no associations outside the family. . . . [T]hus I once said that there are only members of the family (*zhumin*), but no citizens (*shimin*) in China. For China never had *shimin*, the so-call "citizen" in English. (Liang, 1999, vol. 2, p. 730)

This emphasis on civil associations and communities was one of Liang's most important innovations, and it has obvious relevance for us today. To appreciate this, one must look at the efforts of contemporary Confucian scholars to deal with – or to avoid – this issue. In the *Great Learning*, the continuum of human cultivation and political transformation proceeds from the self to the family, to the state and to the world. Notice that in the sequence from the family to the state "community" or "civil associations" is not mentioned. In his commentary on the *Great Learning*, Tu Wei-ming regularly inserts the word "community" in the sequence from the family to the state. Here is a typical statement by Tu: "Family was the root, and harmony attained in the *community* [emphasis added], the state, and the world was a natural outgrowth of the well-regulated families. In this sense, what we do in the privacy of our own homes profoundly shapes the quality of life in the state as a whole" (Tu, 1988, pp. 115–16). What is missing in the Confucian version and is inserted by Tu is exactly what Liang wanted to create: civil associations and communities as the missing link between the family and the state.

If we agree with Max Weber, Niklas Luhmann, and Jürgen Habermas that modernity can be characterized as the differentiation of spheres of life, we should conclude that Liang Qichao's political and social philosophy has provided a fully articulated project for the modernization of China. It is thus necessary to understand Liang Qichao if we want to understand modern China.

Acknowledgments

My thanks must go first to Nick Bunnin and Chung-ying Cheng for their extremely
helpful editorial advice and comments. I was greatly helped by Chung-ying Cheng's
insightful comments on a much longer early draft. Earlier versions of this chapter were
presented at a panel on contemporary Chinese philosophy at the Eastern Division
Meeting, American Philosophical Associations, Boston, December 30, 1999 and at
the Joint Regional Seminar, "History and Memory in East Asia," at the Institute
of East Asian Studies, University of California, Berkeley, April 28, 2000. I was greatly
helped by the discussions following my presentation. The chapter was part of a larger
project I undertook while I was a postdoctoral fellow at the Center for Chinese Studies
at University of California, Berkeley; I want to express my thanks especially to the
following friends and colleagues: Fred Wakeman, Yeh Wen-hsin, Xin Liu, John Pang,
Peter Carroll, and Lauren Pfister. I am also grateful to Stephen Angle and Richard
Author who commented on earlier drafts of this chapter. Thanks to Anna Xiao Dong
Sun for living with "Liang Qichao" for two years. Finally, my deepest thanks go to
Nick Bunnin for his encouragement and unfailing support.

Bibliography

Works by Liang Qichao

Liang Qichao's nianpu [Life and Letters of Liang Qichao]

For Liang's life as a person, politician, journalist, political commentator and political
activist, as well as for the historical and intellectual context of Liang's thought and
especially for the development of his thought, a very useful tool is Liang Qichao's
nianpu. A *nianpu* is a collection of biographical and intellectual materials chronologically arranged. These two *nianpu* are a biographer's dream. They contain thousands
of Liang's letters (drawn from a collection of nearly 10,000 letters), summaries, contexts and responses to his essays and monographs and the editors' comments.

Ding, Wenjiang and Zhao, Fengtian 1983: *Liang Qichao nianpu changbian* 梁啟超
    年譜長編 (a chronological biography of Liang Qichao), Shanghai: Shanghai Renmin
    Publishing House. A first edition appeared as a draft in 1958 in Taiwan
Wu, Tianren 1998: *Minguo liangrengong xiansheng Qichao nianpu* 民國梁任公先生
    啟超年譜 (a chronological biography of Liang Qichao of the Republic of China),
    4 vols, Taipei: Shangwu Publishing House

Liang Qichao's quanji [The Collected Works of Liang Qichao]

There are many editions of Liang's collected works, but there is still no critical edition.
The first collection of Liang Qichao's writings was edited by He Qiangyi: *Yinbingshi
wenji* 飲冰室文集 (collected essays from the ice-drinker's studio), published by
Shanghai Guanzhi Publishing House in 1902. The latest collection was published in

1999. Between these two editions there have been about forty different editions. Until 1999, the most comprehensive and better edited was *Yinbingshi heji*, edited by Ling Zhijung. It consists of two parts: *wenji* (collected essays) and *zhuanji* (collected monographs and books):

Liang, Qichao 1936a: *Yinbingshi heji: wenji* 飲冰室合集：文集 (collected works from the ice-drinker's studio: collected essays), 103 vols in 24 books, Shanghai: Zhonghua Book Company

Liang, Qichao 1936b: *Yinbingshi heji: zhuanji* 飲冰室合集：專集 (collected works from the ice-drinker's studio: collected monographs), 45 vols in 16 books. Shanghai: Zhonghua Book Company. The 1999 edition is based on this 1936 edition and has inherited all of its virtues and flaws. For example, neither can be trusted when it comes to the dates of the essays, but the new edition is by far the most comprehensive

Liang, Qichao 1999: *Liang Qichao quanji* 梁啟超全集 (the collected works of Liang Qichao), 10 vols, Beijing: Beijing Publishing House. All references to Liang in my chapter are to this continuously paginated edition

There are only two critical editions of Liang's selected works:

Liang, 1984: *Liang Qichao xuanji* 梁啟超選集 (selected works of Liang Qichao), Li Huaxing and Wu Jiaxun, eds, Shanghai: Renmin Publishing House. The future critical edition of Liang's collected works should be modeled on this meticulously edited volume. All the pieces that are included have been compared with the original published texts; all the typographical errors and other mistakes are corrected. Mistaken dates in the early editions are also corrected. It includes 25 important essays that do not appear in the 1936 and 1999 editions. It is unfortunate that the editors of the 1999 *Quanji* did not make use of this critical edition

Liang, 1985: *Liang Qichao lun qin sh er zhong* 梁啟超論清史二種 (Liang Qichao's two books on Qing intellectual history), Zhu Weizheng, ed., Shanghai: Fudan Daxue Press. This is also a critical edition. The editor has corrected a lot of errors in the other editions. This should also be a model for the future critical editions of Liang's works.

English translations of Liang's works

Liang, Qichao 1916: *The So-Called People's Will* (A Comment on the Secret Telegrams of the Yuan Government). English and Chinese texts. Shanghai, n.d.

Liang, Qichao 1930: *History of Chinese Political Thought During the Early Tsin Period*, trans. L. T. Chen, New York: Harcourt, Brace & Company

Liang, Qichao 1959: *Intellectual Trends in the Ch'ing Period*, trans. Immanuel C. Y. Hsu, Cambridge: Harvard University Press [original work: (1920): Qingdai Xueshu Gailun]

Liang, Qichao 1999: "On Rights Consciousness," trans. Steven Angle, in *Sources of Chinese Tradition*, William Theodore de Bary, Wing-tsit Chan, and Richard John Lufrano eds, New York: Columbia University Press

Secondary Sources

Few figures in contemporary Chinese philosophy have received as much scholarly attention as Liang Qichao. The selective bibliography that follows contains some of the
best works.

Works in English

Angle, Stephen C. 2000a: "Should We All Be More English? Liang Qichao, Rudolf
von Jhering and Rights," *Journal of the History of Ideas*, 61:2 (April, 2000)

Angle, Stephen C. 2000b: *Human Rights in Comparative Perspective: The Challenge
of China* (book manuscript)

Arendt, Hannah 1958: *The Human Condition*, Chicago: The University of Chicago Press

Arendt, Hannah 1965: *On Revolution*, New York: The Viking Press

Berlin, Isaiah 1996: *The Sense of Reality: Studies in Ideas and their History*, London:
Chatto and Windus

Chang, Hao 1971: *Liang Ch'i-ch'ao and Intellectual Transition in China, 1890–1907*,
Cambridge: Harvard University Press

Cohen, Paul A. 1974: *Between Tradition and Modernity: Wang Tao and Reform in
Late Ching China*, Cambridge: Harvard University Press

Cohen, Paul A. 1984: *Discovering History in China: American Historical Writings on
the Recent Chinese Past*, New York: Columbia University Press

Crossley, Pamela Kyle 1999: *A Translucent Mirror: History and Identity in Qing Imperial
Ideology*, Berkeley: University of California Press

de Bary, William Theodore 1991: *The Trouble with Confucianism*, Cambridge:
Harvard University Press

Dikötter, Frank 1992: *The Discourse of Race in Modern China*, Stanford: Stanford
University Press

Elliott, Mark C. 2001: *The Manchu Way: The Eight Banners and Ethnic Identity in
Late Imperial China*, Stanford: Stanford University Press

Elman, Benjamin 1984: *From Philosophy to Philology: Intellectual and Social Aspects of
Change in Late Imperial China*, Cambridge: Harvard University Press

Elman, Benjamin 1990: *Classicism, Politics, and Kinship: The Chang-chou School of New
Text Confucianism in Late Imperial China*, Berkeley: University of California Press

Hsiao, Kung-chuan 1975: *A Modern China and a New World: Kang Yu-wei, Reformer
and Utopian*, Seattle: University of Washington Press

Huang, Philip C. 1972: *Liang Ch'i-ch'ao and Modern Chinese Liberalism*, Seattle and
London: University of Washington Press

Karl, Rebecca 1993: "Global Connections: Liang Qichao and the 'Second World' and
the Turn of the Twentieth Century." Durham: Asian/Pacific Studies Institute, Duke
University

Kedourie, Elie 1960: *Nationalism*, London: Hutchinson

Levenson, Joseph R. 1959: *Liang Ch'i-ch'ao and the Mind of Modern China*, Second
revised edition, Cambridge: Harvard University Press

Levenson, Joseph R. 1968: *Confucian China and Its Modern Fate: A Trilogy*, Berkeley
and Los Angeles: University of California Press

Martin, W. A. P. 1966: *A Cycle of Cathay: China, South and North*, Third edition. Distributed by Paragon Book Gallery, Ltd. (Original edition published by Fleming H. Revell Company, 1900)

McAleavy, Henry 1953: *Wang Tao: The Life and Writings of a Displaced Person*, London: China Society

Pusey, James Reeve 1983: *China and Charles Darwin*, Cambridge: Council on East Asian Studies

Rawls, John 1971: *A Theory of Justice*, Cambridge: Harvard University Press

Rawls, John 1993: *Political Liberalism*, New York: Columbia University Press

Tang, Xiaobing 1996: *Global Space and the Nationalist Discourse of Modernity: The Historical Thinking of Liang Qichao*, Stanford: Stanford University Press

Tocqueville, Alexis de 1954: Democracy in America, 2 vols, New York: Vintage Books.

Tu, Wei-ming 1988: *Centrality and Commonality: An Essay on Confucain Religiousness*, Albany: Press of State University of New York

Wakeman, Frederic, Jr. 1973: *History and Will: Philosophical Perspectives of Mao Tse-tung's Thought*, Berkeley: University of California Press

Wakeman, Frederic, Jr. 1975: *The Fall of Imperial China*, New York: Free Press

Xiao, Yang, *Human Rights and History*, Forthcoming

Works in Chinese

Chang, Peng-yuan 1964: *Liang Qichao yu qingji geming* 梁啟超與清季革命 (Liang Qichao and the late Qing revolution), Taipei: Academia Sinica, Institute of Modern Chinese History

Chang, Peng-yuan 1969: *Liang Qichao yu guomin geming* 梁啟超與國民革命 (Liang Qichao and the republican revolution), Taipei: Academia Sinica, Institute of Modern Chinese History

Feng, Qi 1997: *Zhongguo xiandai zhexue de geming hua jincheng* 中國現代哲學的革命化進程 (the revolutionary process of contemporary Chinese philosophy), Shanghai: Huadong College

Hsiao, Kung-ch'uan 1982: *Zhongquo zhengzhi sixiang shi* 中國政治思想史 (history of Chinese political thought), vol. 4 of *Hsiao Kung-ch'uan xiansheng quanji* 蕭公權先生全集 (the collected works of Hsiao Kung-ch'uan), Taipei: Lianjing Publishing Company

Huang, Ko-wu 1994: *Yige beifangqi de xuanze: Liang Qichao tiaoshi sixiang zhi yianjou* 一個被放棄的選擇：梁啟超調試思想之研究 (a rejected path: a study of Liang Ch'i-ch'ao's accommodative thinking), Taipei: Institute of Modern History, Academia Sinica

Kang, Youwei 1987: *Kang Youwei quanji* 康有為全集 (the collected works of Kang Youwei), vol. 1, Shanghai: Shanghai Renmin Publishing House

Li, Zehou 1979: "*Liang Qichao Wang Guowei jianlun*" 梁啟超王國維兼論 (on Liang Qichao and Wang Guowei), *Zhongguo jingdai sixiang shilun* 中國近代思想史論 (essays on early modern Chinese intellectual history), Beijing: Renmin Publishing House

Mao, Zedong 1990: *Mao Zedong zaoqi wengao: 1912.6–1920.11* 毛澤東早期文稿 (Mao Zedong's early writings: 1912.6–1920.11), Zhangsha: Hunan Press

Su, Yu, ed., 1970: *Yijiao congbian* 翼教叢編 (selected writings on protecting the (Confucian) doctrine), Taipei: Tailin Quaofen Publishing House (1970 reprint). Original edition 1898

Sun, Huiwen 1966: *Liang Qichao de mingquan yu junxian sixiang* 梁啟超的民權與君憲思想 (Liang Qichao's ideas of people's rights and constitutional monarchy), Taipei: Taiwan University

Wang, Ermin 1969: *Wan Qing zhengzhi sixiang shilun* 晚清政治思想史論 (historical studies on late Qing political thought), Taibei: Xuesheng Shuju

Wang, Ermin 1977: *Zhongguo jindai sixiang shilun* 中國近代思想史論 (historical studies on modern Chinese thought), Taipei: Taiwan Shangwu Yinshuguan

Wanguo gongfa 萬 國 公 法 (universal laws for all nations), The Chinese translation of Henry Wheaton's *Elements of International Law* by Martin with his Chinese assistants

A journal founded in 1986 is devoted to the study of Liang Qichao: *Liang Qichao yanjiu* 梁啟超研究 (journal of Liang Qichao studies), Xinhui, Guangdong Province

Discussion Questions

1. How can we justify the reform of institutions?
2. Are Liang Qichao's criticisms of cultural monism well-founded?
3. Are truth, truthfulness, and freedom of thought instrumental values or intrinsic values?
4. Does the concept of self-mastery help us to understand the relationship between national rights and people's rights?
5. Must political and legal rights be grounded in metaphysics?
6. Should we distinguish political and legal liberty from social and ethical liberty?
7. What follows from supplementing the five traditional Confucian relationships with the relationship among private persons in general and the relationship between the state and its citizens?
8. Did traditional China have a constitution?
9. Are self-cultivation and the family important for the governance of the state?
10. How should civil associations and communities affect relationships between citizens and the state?

2

WANG GUOWEI: PHILOSOPHY OF AESTHETIC CRITICISM

Keping Wang

Around the turn of the twentieth century, China witnessed a new cultural movement that featured the rapid introduction of Western ideas. It was during this
ideologically hectic period that Wang Guowei (1877–1927) established himself
as a pioneering scholar in fields as diverse as philosophy, aesthetics, literary
criticism, Chinese history, etymology, epigraphy, and ancient geography. He
was also highly celebrated as a poet in the classical form of *ci* lyrics that had
earlier flourished in the Song Dynasty (960–1279).

Wang Guowei was born in 1877 in Haining, Zhejiang province with a
family background in the patriot–scholar–official tradition. He obtained the
degree of *xiucai* at the age of 16 and became known as one of "the four
budding talents" in his hometown in recognition of his literary gifts and wide
learning. In 1893 and 1897 he took part in the examination for the *juren*
degree, but failed because he lacked motivation and quit halfway through the
examination. He became a private tutor and married. In 1898, he moved to
Shanghai, where he worked as a clerk and proofreader for the newspaper *Shiwu
Bao* (Current Affairs). While attending classes in the Oriental Institute, he came
upon passages from Schopenhauer and Kant in essays by a Japanese teacher
Taoka Reiun (1870–1912) and developed an interest in Western philosophy
and a desire to learn English. In 1901 he went to the School of Physics in
Tokyo, learning English during the day and mathematics in the evening. No
more than half a year later he returned to China because of illness and began
to edit the journal of *Jiaoyu Shijie* (Educational World) sponsored by Luo
Zhenyu. He wrote and translated for it in areas such as education, sociology,
psychology, and literature, as well as ethics, aesthetics, and general philosophy.
From 1903 to 1907, he read Kant's *Critique of Pure Reason* (1968) four times,
eventually understanding it through Schopenhauer's *The World as Will and
Idea* (1964). Soon afterwards, he found himself torn between his interest in
philosophical speculation and his success in writing poetry (Wang, 1907 "*Zi
Xu*" [Autobiographic Note II] in Wang, 1997. Unless otherwise indicated,
quoted passages are translated by Keping Wang). With growing doubts about

his dedication to philosophy, ethics, and aesthetics, he drew a line between "what is convincing but not likable and what is likable but not convincing," that is between the cool rationality of positivism and empiricism and the metaphysical, ethical, and aesthetic systems that he loved. This tension was one reason for his shift from philosophy to literature in 1907 and then to Chinese history in 1912.

After the Chinese Revolution in 1911, Wang went to Japan and studied the Chinese Classics, oracle records, history, and etymology. His outstanding achievements in all of these fields led him to a positive reassessment of the Chinese cultural heritage and to skepticism regarding the values of Western civilization. He therefore kept himself aloof from the antitraditionalist radicalism of the New Cultural Movement and the May Fourth Movement in 1919.

From 1916 to 1922 Wang taught in a private university in Shanghai founded by Silas Hardoon while editing *Xueshu Zazhi* (Journal of Scholarship) financed by Hardoon. During this period of time, his fame grew among Chinese intellectuals because of his pioneering explorations and new findings in history, epigraphy, and etymology. In 1923 he left Shanghai for Beijing to become a tutor of the deposed Emperor Henry Pu Yi. Wang became professor at Tsinghua University in 1925, but committed suicide in Kunming Lake at the Summer Palace in 1927, in part because of the political chaos caused by the civil war in China and the frustration of his desire to see a royalist restoration and cultural revival (Chen Hongxiang, 1998, pp. 268–93).

Scholarship

The development of Wang Guowei's scholarship was characterized by changes in his focal interests and fields of achievement. The process can be roughly divided into three periods:

1. Philosophical and aesthetic pursuits from 1898 to 1907,
2. Literary criticism from 1907 to 1911, and
3. Historical, etymological, and epigraphical studies from 1911 to 1927.

This division is by no means clear-cut, with overlaps resulting from his simultaneous exploration in several areas and from his obsessive engagement in writing poetry throughout nearly all of his career.

Wang Guowei's achievement and influence as a serious thinker and prolific writer are chiefly represented by six works. The first is *Honglou Meng Pinglun* (1904), a literary critique of *The Dream of the Red Chamber* that revealed his pessimistic understanding of human existence and reflected the influence of Schopenhauer, early Daoism, and Buddhism. The second is *Renjian Cihua* (1908), a selected edition of his discourses embodying the essence of his poetics. The third is *Song-Yuan Xiqu Kao* (1912), a historical review of Chinese drama that disclosed his evolutionary observations on literary progress and change. The final major works comprise three of his essays written in 1917: *Yin Buci Zhong Suojian Xiangong Xianwang Kao*, *Xu Kao*, and *Yin-Zhou Zhidu Lun*. The first two are philological and epigraphical studies of ancient oracle inscriptions on tortoiseshell and bone concerning Yin Dynasty lords and kings. The last essay is an historical investigation of the institutional systems and bronze-age cultures of the Yin and Zhou Dynasties.

His fruitful research in these areas introduced a fresh breeze into the old-fashioned arena of cultural studies and established his eminent position in the academic world. His importance rested on his individual methodology and on the boldness of his revolt against the cultural philistinism of traditional studies. The scientific aspects of his methodology were mainly inspired by his substantial learning from two major sources: the heritage of Chinese philological studies manifested in the Qian-Jia School (1736–1820) and the truth-oriented approach of Western philosophy. His methodology was characterized by three interrelated features: (a) mutual interpretation and attestation through comparing unearthed relics with relevant historical records, (b) mutual supplementation and correction through comparing old books of other ethnic groups with existing classics in China, and (c) mutual consultation and justification through using both Western concepts and sources available from Chinese literature. (Chen Yinque, 1934). Wang Gouwei applied the first two strategies to historical, epigraphical, and etymological studies and used the last strategy for his aesthetic thought and literary criticism. He did not, however, mechanically combine Western concepts with those drawn from Chinese literature, but sought an organic fusion of the two through a kind of intercultural transformation.

In his early preoccupation with aesthetics and literary criticism, Wang Guowei was inspired in part by German idealism and in part by the traditions of Chinese art. In Western philosophy, he was especially influenced by Kant, Schiller, Schopenhauer, and Nietzsche, and his revaluation of Chinese literature was marked by a preference for *ci* lyrics. His philosophy of aesthetic criticism gave a central role to the value of art. He held that even though pure art is instrumentally useless, it is crucially worthy and significant in terms of enlightenment. This is precisely because artistic works express philosophical, aesthetic, spiritual, and ethical values. The philosophical dimension of art exposes the truth of human existence in both a universal and a particular sense through imagery and artistic form. Wang Guowei's account is thus connected with Schopenhauer's Idea as the object of knowledge or the origin of art. The aesthetic dimension of art lies in a disinterestedness that helps us to go beyond the will to live and secular desires by entering an aesthetic state of serene contemplation. From this contemplative state we obtain a form of infinite delight and pleasure. The spiritual aspect of art as play expresses and releases suppressed feelings and emotions that give rise to pain and depression. By providing consolation and exoneration, art reduces the suffering and meaninglessness experienced in human life. In its ethical aspect, art is like a boat sheltering us in the bitter sea and frees us from worldly anxieties. Art aims not simply to depict the misery of the human world, but also to indicate that alternatives are available through a self-enlightenment that can help victims to extricate themselves from the human predicament.

These aspects of artistic value thread their way through the whole of Wang's aesthetic ponderings. For Wang, they parallel six cardinal doctrines: *meiyu shuo* (aesthetic education), *jietuo shuo* (spiritual detachment), *youxi shuo* (art as play), *tiancai shuo* (the artist as genius), *guya shuo* (the refined), and *jingjie shuo* (the poetic state). In his theoretical speculations, Wang hovered over the vast territory of Chinese culture with conceptual wings borrowed from the West. His aesthetic scholarship was grounded in his Chinese heritage, but greatly benefited from his ability to stand astride both Eastern and Western cultures.

Beyond East and West: An Intercultural Transformation

Wang Guowei's positive attitude towards both Chinese and foreign culture, which is noticeable throughout his early writings, can be attributed to his insight into the universal nature of all forms of learning. He held that learning is oriented towards truth by virtue of both scientific analysis and factual justification. He sought an intercultural standpoint that would disentangle him from any one-sided views. His chief motive for this strategy derived partially from his intention to reconstruct the Chinese cultural legacy and partially from his conviction that flourishing academic studies in a global sense must rely on progress through honest and unbiased investigations within significant existing cultures. Thus he affirmed the necessity of "going beyond any prejudiced preference or distinction (*xue wu zhongxi*) in sincere multicultural explorations" that recognized the intellectual diversity in the history of thought (Wang, 1905, "*Lun Jinnian Zhi Xueshujie*" ["About Academic Society in Recent Years" in Wang, 1997]):

> The nature of learning has nothing to do with the so-called discrepancy between the modern and the classical, the Western and Chinese, or the useless and the useful. Why is this so? The investigation of things in the world leads to different conclusions if considered from the perspectives of science or history. However, it all aims to seek truth from facts. . . . Human knowledge the world over is basically contained in such disciplines as science, history and literary studies which categorically exist in both China and Western nations. They only vary in their degree of width, roughness, superficiality or elaboration. In plain words, any biased discrimination between the two cultures is definitely groundless. For it originated in senseless worries that the imagined aftermath of the flourishing of

Western culture in China would prevent and impede the evolution of Chinese culture or vice versa. China is, as it were, exempt from such worries, but lacks real and substantial scholarship. Thus in Beijing, the capital and cultural center of the country, there are no more than ten scholars of great learning in the field of Chinese classical studies. As for those who are engaged in the study of Western culture, most tend to scratch the surface and hardly master either its profound spirit or broad scope. We cannot name even one or two figures for their devotion to the target subject and compare them with those who devote their lifetime to the learning of the Chinese classics. I personally maintain that Chinese and Western studies par excellence can interact on and promote each other to the extent that they thrive and decline in a synchronous fashion. That is to say, one cannot do without the other in terms of their respective rise and fall. This is especially so in the case of the contemporary world and learning (Wang, 1911 "*Guoxue Congkan Xu*" [Foreword to *The Journal of Chinese Studies* in Wang, 1997])

Wang's cultural openness and tolerance were grounded on observation. For instance, he held that the Chinese language features ambiguity in meaning and that Chinese modes of thought therefore appear logically weaker than ways of thought fostered by Western languages. Western cultural identity places greater emphasis on scientific speculation and hence has greater capacity for abstraction and classification. As a result, generalization and specification are two strategies that are widely applied in the West to both visible and invisible nature. They are, according to Wang, well manifested in Kant's analyses of reason and Schopenhauer's formulation of sufficient reason. In contrast, the identity of the Chinese people lies in a pragmatic or instrumental dimension. In theoretical pursuits, they tend to be easily contented with common factual knowledge and are reluctant to get down to the bottom of things. Consequently, the theoretical specification of things is rarely practiced unless it is imposed by practical needs. (Wang, 1905 "*Lun Xinxueyu Zhi Shuru*" ["On the New Terminology Imported from the West"] in Wang, 1997).

To verify his observations, he employed a strategy of intercultural transformation to handle three basic issues in Chinese philosophy, namely the questions of *xing* (human nature), *li* (principle), and *ming* (fate). He used the Kantian epistemological distinction between *a priori* and *a posteriori* knowledge to escape a dualistic trap that results from characterizing human nature as innately good or evil. In "*Lun Xing*" ("On Human Nature"), he held that *a priori* knowledge is based on theoretical hypotheses while *a posteriori* knowledge is based on empirical observations and relevant cases. In Chinese accounts of human nature (*xing*), an *a priori* perspective gives rise to two opposite views: the first maintains that all humans are innately good, and that the environment and *a posteriori* learning lead some people to be evil; the second holds that all humans are innately evil, and that education and enculturation make some people become good. The former view is represented by Confucius and Mencius, and the latter view is represented by Xunzi. Similarly, an *a posteriori* perspective leads to opposite views regarding the good or evil of human nature. Because both *a priori* and *a posteriori* perspectives lead to contradictory views, there is also room for an agnostic characterization of *xing* as "beyond human knowledge."

> Having good nature and having evil nature are antithetical to each other as empirically revealed in human deeds. Both of them could be tenable only if they happen to coincide with their corresponding evidence. But it is not reliable to infer human nature in general from sheer experience (for experience does not reflect the origin of human nature). When human nature is discussed in terms of human nature alone, a kind of absolute monism is produced in terms of either good or evil. This could be tenable only if it is conceived to be something non-empirical because contradictions and paradoxes tend to arise once it is applied to justifying practical acts or personal cultivation pertaining to good and evil. Hence I have deliberately pointed out this fact in the hope that young scholars in China will save up their breath by not engaging themselves in such fruitless debates over human nature. (Wang, 1904 "*Lun Xing*" ["On Human Nature"] in Wang, 1997)

Wang examined *li* (principle) in relation to Schopenhauer's principle of sufficient reason and Kant's distinction between theoretical reason and practical reason. He assumed that *li* in its narrow sense means *liyou* (causal reason) and in its wider sense means *lixing* (intellectual reason). Of the two basic meanings of *li*, *liyou* concerns the universal form of human knowledge while *lixing* concerns an intellectual power to fabricate and define ideas. As an object of knowledge, *li* contains both metaphysical values (*zhen*, truth) and ethical values (*shan*, goodness). *Zhen* and *shan* remained undifferentiated in ancient Chinese thought. This lack of differentiation between the metaphysical and the ethical is evident in Zhu Xi's conception of *tianli* (heavenly principles) (Wang, 1904 "*Shi Li*" ["Interpreting the Notion of Li"] in Wang, 1997).

Wang compared the conventional Chinese interpretation of *ming* (fate) with the Western concepts of fatalism and causal laws, even though he rejected the assumptions underlying the problem of free will and determinism. On this point he accepted Zhu Xi's analysis of the interconnection among *ming*, *xing*, and *li*, and derived a sense of practical moral responsibility from it (Wang, 1906 "*Yuan Ming*" ["The Original Fate"] in Wang, 1997).

In using an intercultural perspective, Wang never failed to detect fundamental dissimilarities between Chinese and Western culture. Chinese culture places more stress on personal cultivation and moral virtues that can harmonize human relations and sustain social stability, whilst Western culture emphasizes power and right, which are suitable for the conquest of nature and the conquest of other human beings. From his intercultural standpoint, Wang held that all these features can be gathered together to establish a complementary relationship of great significance.

Although Wang insisted on the need to learn from the West, he was neither a social activist nor a revolutionary. He remained a single-minded academic and an earnest advocate of intercultural method throughout his life. He succeeded in avoiding the relatively superficial debates about cultural preference as a political instrument of his time and served as a cultural bridge between the first wave of westernization that was launched by the generation preceding him and the New Cultural Movement that was formed by a group of radical intellectuals around the time of the May Fourth Movement in 1919.

Wang's new approach to historical studies also embodied intercultural features and was termed "a methodology of double proof" (*erchong zhengju fa*). This approach benefited from his commitments to German idealism and to the Chinese philological tradition that flourished in the Qing dynasty. In practice, it was derived from the features that I have mentioned above of mutual interpretation and attestation, mutual supplementation and correction, and mutual consultation and justification (Chen Yinque, 1934). Take his etymological study of the Chinese character *xun* for example. He applied his double-proof approach by "searching through all the oracle records available" and meanwhile looking into such classics as *The Book of Change* and *The Dictionary of Ancient Chinese Characters*. In seeking reciprocal interpretation and attestation between the oracle records as newly unearthed historical documents and the texts as old historical literature, he examined the evidence of ancient sacrificial vessels and their inscriptions to identify the contexts in which the character was used and to assess its possible interpretations. He concluded that *xun*, as "a ten-day period" related to *tiangan* (the heavenly stems), could be traced back to the Yin or Shang dynasty (1766–1154 B.C.) when it was deployed to tell fortunes (Wang, 1918 "*Shi Xun*" ["Interpreting Xun as a Ten-day Period"] in Wang, 1997).

Finally, Wang's concern for Western culture as a whole was marked by a passionate desire to introduce and promote German idealism, emphasizing its account of life (ethics) and art (aesthetics). He did this selectively, and his Chinese sensibility and expression modified the doctrines he received. In aesthetic criticism of Chinese literary texts, for example, he adopted and extended idealist concepts such as disinterested contemplation, aesthetic play, the will to live, genius, the beautiful and the sublime, the pure subject, serene contemplation, and the contrast between realism and idealism.

As a result, Wang structured his philosophy of aesthetic criticism in terms of six cardinal doctrines. This aesthetic theory exemplified his capacity for intercultural transformation, if not creative misinterpretation. The first four doctrines concern aesthetic education, spiritual detachment, aesthetic play, and the artist as genius. Although they were all borrowed from German idealism with minor modifications, the enlightenment that they brought to China remains a significant feature of Chinese intellectual and aesthetic culture. In contrast is the vision that flowed from his consideration of *guya* (the refined) and *jingjie* (the poetic state). His originality is best demonstrated in his investigation of *jingjie*, which marked the end of classical Chinese literary criticism and the beginning of modern Chinese aesthetic thought. *Jingjie* can be also seen as a product of intercultural transformation that invites care and cultivation today.

The Theory of the Poetic State (*jingjie shuo*)

Compared with his other essays on art and literature, Wang Guowei's *Renjian Cihua* (Poetic Remarks in the Human World) has a special importance. The notion of *jingjie* (the poetic state) that it formulated was central to the path of his aesthetic thought.

Renjian Cihua comprises 64 small sections. Its structure can be divided into two major parts: theoretical reflections and practical criticism. Sections 1 to 9 are devoted to a theoretical discussion of *jingjie*, and the remaining sections give examples of creating and appreciating *jingjie* in literature through sample texts (Ye Jiaying, 1997, pp. 186–8). *Jingjie* is conventionally taken to be a Chinese rendering of the Sanskrit word *Visaya*, which was used in Buddhist sutras to mean the scope of sense perception or the characteristic of sense experience. This original meaning has become extended in complex ways, with implications such as *jiangjie* (boundary), *zaoyi* (academic or artistic attainment), *jingxiang* (scene or site) and *yijing* (the mood, state, or significance of an artwork).

Against this background, Wang Guowei used *jingjie* as a term in literary criticism for the essential quality of art. On some occasions he used *jingjie* interchangeably with *yijing* (artistic state), and they are taken as equivalents by many Chinese scholars. I shall follow this precedent and translate *jingjie* as the poetic state par excellence. For Wang Guowei, *jingjie* was "the most important element in a consideration of *ci* lyrics."

> If a *ci* lyric has *jingjie*, it will naturally achieve a lofty form and naturally possess eminent lines. The unique excellence of *ci* lyrics of the Five Dynasties and Northern Song periods rests precisely on this point. . . . The poetic state is not limited to scenery and objects alone. Pleasure and anger, sorrow and joy are also a sort of *jingjie* in men's hearts. Therefore, those poems that describe true scenes and objects (*zhen jingwu*), true emotions and feelings (*zhen ganqing*), can be said to possess *jingjie*. Otherwise, they may be said to lack *jingjie*. "Red apricot blossoms along the branch, spring feelings stir." With that one word "stir" (*nao*), the *jingjie* of the poem is completely expressed. "As the moon breaks through the clouds, flowers play with their shadows." With that one word "play" (*nong*), the *jingjie* of the poem is fully expressed. (Wang, 1908 "*Renjian Cihua*" ["Poetic Remarks in the Human World"] as translated in Rickett, 1977, p. 42)

Elsewhere in discussing Chinese drama, Wang Guowei used *yijing* instead of *jingjie*:

> The subtlety of literary works can be summed up in one phrase: having *yijing*. Then what is *yijing*? It is in the expression of *qing* (feelings) that is heart-stirring and mind-freshening, in the description of *jing* (scenes) that is vivid and engaging, and also in the narrative of *shi* (events) that is lucid and authentic as though coming straight from the mouth [of a good story teller]. It is unexceptionally true of all the best pieces among the ancient *shi* and *ci* poems. It is also the case with the *qu* songs of the Yuan Dynasty. (Wang, 1912 "*Song-Yuan Xiqu Kao*" ["A Historical Study of the Drama in the Song and Yuan Dynasties"], in Wang, 1997, p. 389)

According to the first quotation, *jingjie* or *yijing* must have two sorts of components: *zhen jingwu* (true or authentic scenes and objects) and *zhen ganqing* (true or sincere emotions and feelings). In the second quotation, we notice similar things: *qing* (feelings) – as the shortened form of *ganqing*, *jing* (scenes) – as the shortened form of *jingwu*, and *shi* (events). All of these elements, when woven together and expressed in an artwork, should be true and sincere, vivid and touching, natural and suggestive; their presence without these merits would not make sense in terms of *jingjie*. *Qing* or *ganqing* (emotions and feelings) are subjective, while *jing* or *jingwu* (scenes and objects) and *shi* (events) are objective. Hence *jingjie* can be seen as a fusion of the subjective and objective aspects of experience. According to some theorists, *jingjie*, like *yijing*, is "an artistic integration of *yi* and *jing*," where *yi* stands for *qingyi* (feelings and affections) and *jing* stands for *jingwu* (scenes and objects) (Li Zehou, 1983, pp. 161–74). According to Chen Yong, *jingjie* is "the distinctive imagery in art" that involves "the emotional substance" and "the specific atmosphere". It stems from an artistic expression of how an objective scene or event is reflected and contemplated in the mind or aesthetic sensibility of the poet (Chen Yong, 1983, pp. 210–14). For Ye Jiaying, *jingjie* is a special term in literary criticism that emphasizes "the characteristic of genuine feelings and lively expressions. Feelings of this kind incorporate both inner and outer affective dimensions." *Jingjie* of this kind may well indicate either a real scene of sensory perception or a poetic vision of imaginative association (Ye Jiaying, 1983, pp. 147–59). The most frequently discussed definition of *jingjie* was proposed by Li Zehou: "As shown in Wang Guowei's usage, *jingjie* can be called *yijing*. . . . It is a higher category than *xingxiang* (image) and *qinggan* (feelings) in aesthetics, for it conjoins both image and feelings." Serving as the basis for *yijing*, *xingxiang* (image) signifies not only *xingsi* (resemblance in form) but also *shensi* (likeness in spirit). *Qinggan* (feelings) not only refers to *qing* (as the emotional aspect), but also implies *li* as the intellectual aspect concerning truth, concepts, and intrinsic laws or norms. The emotional aspect would become extremely wild without the mediation of the intellectual aspect.

Yijing, as the poetic state par excellence, can therefore be defined as "the unity of *yi* and *jing*, where the former (*yi*) is the fusion of *qing* (the emotional aspect) with *li* (the intellectual aspect), and the latter (*jing*) is the fusion of *xing* (resemblance in form) and *shen* (likeness in spirit). In other words, *yijing* is the bearing of uniting artistically objective scenes or events with subjective feelings and interest" (Li Zehou, 1983).

In spite of all these efforts at interpretation, we cannot easily locate *yijing* or *jingjie* by means of a single definition. The mist of its subtlety and ambiguity can be lifted to some extent by examining Wang Guowei's use of *jingjie* as the poetic state.

The creative state versus the descriptive state

Poetry has both the creative state (*zaojing*) and the descriptive state (*xiejing*), but it is difficult to distinguish between the two because the state (*jing*) that the great poets create must accord with what is natural (*ziran*), and the state that they describe must approach the ideal (Wang, as translated in Rickett, 1977, p. 40). This distinction is made from the perspective of producing art-works. The creative state, which is usually embodied in the works of idealists or romantics, employs means such as imagination, invention, exaggeration, and the grotesque to express subjective feelings and to characterize ideal models of society or romantic fantasies. The descriptive state, which is often reflected in the works of realists, represents and exposes a picture of the reality or actuality of the human condition. Yet, both the creative state and the descriptive state naturally share the common pursuit of the poetic state (*jingjie*).

The state of self-involvement versus the state of self-detachment

Poetry has both the state of self-involvement (*you wo zhi jing*) and the state of self-detachment (*wu wo zhi jing*). Self-involvement is present in the lines: "With tear-filled eyes I ask the flowers, but they do not speak. Red petals swirl past and swing away." In contrast, self-detachment is implied in the lines: "I pluck chrysanthemums by the eastern fence, far distant appear the southern mountains." In a state of self-involvement, the poet views objects egoistically in terms of himself, and everything therefore takes on his own coloring. In a state of self-detachment, the poet views objects *per se*, and one cannot tell what should be ascribed to the poet himself and what to the object. The state of self-detachment can be attained only in complete quietude. The state of self-involvement is attained in the quiet that follows a conscious act. The former is beautiful, and the latter is sublime (Wang, as translated in Rickett, 1977, pp. 41–2).

Wang Guowei drew a parallel between these two seemingly distinct states largely in terms of aesthetic appreciation. The state of self-involvement employs a self-identification with the object that is subjective and emotional and appears to be highly personified. It bears some analogy to the condition of empathy that Lipps depicts in his *Spatial Aesthetics* (Lipps, 1897). In the state of self-detachment, the self is so deeply lost in the object that it seems to disappear. The state of self-detachment is therefore more poetically subtle, natural, harmonious, and suggestive than the state of self-involvement. However, the difference between the two states is quantitative rather than qualitative. The state of self-involvement tends more to be "a state with an explicit self" (*xian*) whereas the state of self-detachment is a more "a state with an implicit self" (*yin*) (Zhu Guangqian "*Shi De Yin Yu Xian*" ["Of the Implicit and Explicit State in Poetry"], in Yao Kefu, 1983, pp. 87–9).

The state of self-detachment can be further explored in terms of the chan (*zen*) Buddhist concept of being desire-free (*wu nian*) or Schopenhauer's concept of the pure subject of knowledge. A person in the state of self-detachment would detach himself from any differentiation between subject and object and contemplate things in a purely objective manner.

The large poetic state and the small poetic state

Jingjie as the poetic state may be either large or small, but one cannot use this distinction as a basis for determining the excellence or inferiority of a poem:

> Why cannot [the poetic state] in lines such as "Little fish jump in the fine rain; swallows dip their wings in the faint breeze" stand in comparison with that in the lines "The large banners glow in the setting sun; horses neigh in the rustling wind"? Why is not [the poetic state] in lines such as "The pearled curtain idly hangs on the little silver hook" as impressive as that in the lines "Mist enfolds the tower and pavilion; the moon shines dimly on the ferry"? (Wang, as translated in Rickett, 1977, pp. 42–3; cf. Wang 1970, p. 5)

In the first example, the fish and swallows are small in size, and the rain and breeze are pleasingly gentle. These images suggest not only smallness and gentleness, but also playfulness, delight, delicacy, and peace. According to Wang Guowei, the lines contain small *jingjie*. In contrast, the banners and horses are large in size, and the sun and wind are dynamically powerful. These images imply greatness, power, a grand battlefield, excitement, motivating drive, pressure, and even terror. According to Wang Guowei, the lines contain large *jingjie*. Both sets of lines are aesthetically appealing and equally expressive, no matter what kinds of objects or scenes are presented in the poems. With reference to Edmund Burke's *Philosophical Enquiry into the Origin of our Ideas of the Sublime and Beautiful* (1757) we can say that the small type of *jingjie* shares certain features with the category of the beautiful and that the large type of *jingjie* shares certain features with the category of the sublime.

The veiled and the nonveiled

We can also distinguish between the poetic state as veiled (*ge*) and as non-veiled (*buge*). According to Wang Guowei, the veiled poetic state is weak in scenic description and leads us to approach some poems as if we were viewing flowers through a mist. Rather, the artistic excellence of lines such as "Spring grasses come to life beside the pond" and "Swallows drop bits of mud from the desolate beams" lies in their not being obstructed by a veil. In *ci* lyrics, it is just the same. For example, the first stanza of Ouyang Xiu's *ci* poem to the tune of "*Shao Nien You*" ("A Youth's Wandering") contains the lines:

> Against the twelve zig-zag railings I lean along in spring,
> The clear azure stretches far to the clouds.
> A thousand miles, ten thousand miles,
> The second month, the third month,
> To think of travel distresses the heart.

According to Wang Guowei, "Each image is directly there and is not obstructed by a veil. When we come to other lines in the same poem, such as: 'Beside the pond of Xie Lingyun, on the river-bank of Jiang Yan', we find that we are looking through a veil" (Wang, as translated in Rickett, 1977, pp. 56–7; cf. Wang 1970, pp. 26–7).

The reason that the last two lines are veiled is the use of two allusions. One refers us to Xie Lingyun's description in the line: "Spring grasses come to life beside the pond." The other is related to Jiang Yan's description in On Parting (*Bie fu*):

> The spring grasses blue-green in hue,
> Spring water all waves of green.
> As I see you off on the southern shore,
> What hurt, ah, what pain!

The original lines are direct and vivid, while the lines alluding to them are indirect and bewildering, as if they were veiled. The first stanza cited demonstrates an intuitively natural style with elements from sensory experience and immediate perception. The other two lines, which Wang Guowei saw as veiled, reveal a contemplative style that uses allusions as a basis for rational and associative inference.

For Wang Guowei, veiled poetry mainly embodied a pedantic use of allusions, overdecorative phrases and a pretentious style that deprives the reader of sincere feelings and vicarious experience. Nonveiled poetry is available through the natural expression of real feelings and scenes that enables the reader to attain intuitive apprehension and profound appreciation (Ye Jiaying, 1997, p. 220). This capacity is in accord with the chief qualities of *jingjie* that rest on the representation of both sincere feelings and emotions (*zhen qinggan*) and true scenes and objects (*zhen jingwu*):

> Only when "sincere feelings and emotions," as the soul, are blown into the fine imagery of "true scenes and objects," as the body, can the unique charm of the poetic state (*jingjie*) be fully displayed. Hence "sincere feelings and emotions" can be conceived of as the life of the poetic state whilst "true scenes and objects" [can be conceived of] as the manifestation and symbolization of this life. (Zhang Bennan, 1992, pp. 231–2)

In recognizing the difficulty of achieving *jingjie* through painstaking efforts as well as creative power and heart-felt sincerity, Wang Guowei quoted: "If all that is written, I love only what a man has written with his blood. [Write with blood, and you will experience that blood is spirit.]" (*Thus Spake Zarathustra*, Part I (1883) in Nietzsche, 1976).

The final analysis of *jingjie* as a special aesthetic category can be viewed holistically through the complex distinctions that I have suggested. *Jingjie* is concerned with style, imagery, mechanism, aesthetic value, significant form, truth content, criteria of judgment, and the creative activity of poetry, but all for the sake of "the investigation of the nature of art in general" (Nie Zhenbin, 1997, p. 139).

Wang Guowei's doctrine of *jingjie* was deeply rooted in the rich soil of Chinese philosophy of criticism and blossomed in that context. His views can be traced back to Zhuangzi's speculation of *yan* (words) and *yi* (meanings) and then down to Wang Changling, Yan Yu, Wang Shizhen, Liu Xizai, and others who have thought about *shijing* (the poetic realm) or *yijing* (the significant state). Wang Guowei's debt to this tradition is evident, for instance, in his comment:

> In his *Canglang Shihua* (Canglang's Poetic Discourse), Yan Yu said: "The poets of the Golden Tang period were concerned only about inspiration and interest (*xingqu*). Like the antelope that hangs by its horns leaving no discernible traces on the ground, their excellence lay in their crystal-like transparency, no more to be grasped than a sound in empty space, the changing colour in a face, the moon in the water or an image in a mirror. The words had a limit, but the meaning went on forever." However, what Yan Yu called inspiration and interest and what Wang Shizhen called spirit and tone (*shenyun*) only seem to touch the surface, while the term of two characters, *jingjie*, that I have chosen really probes the fundamentals of poetry. (Wang (1970), as translated in Rickett, 1977, p. 43)

Wang's connection with Chinese aesthetic tradition is strong. He was mainly inspired by the insights of Yan Yu's theory of "inspiration and interest" (*xingqu*) and Wang Shizhen's theory of "spirit and tone" (*shenyun*). Yet, he played down these theories because he considered *jingjie* to provide the most essential insight into poetic creation and its aesthetic values. For Wang, *jingjie* accommodates within itself both *xingqu* as an aesthetically touching and enlightening effect of poetry and *shenyun* as a stylistic outcome or magical power of imagery. Moreover, *xingqu* implies a subtle enlightenment that is connected with mystical Chan Buddhism, whereas *shenyun* indicates an obscure contemplation of the poetic style in terms of *qingyuan* (exquisiteness and far-reachingness). Neither of these accounts could be specifically formulated owing to their vagueness and ambiguity, but, for Wang, *jingjie* could be described in relatively more tangible terms such as "authentic scenes" and "sincere feelings." Some commentators, therefore, treat *jingjie* as a unity of the subjective and the objective, the ideal and the real, the emotional and the natural.

Wang Guowei enlarged the scope of *jingjie* both through his writings and aesthetic judgments and through his capacity to absorb relevant elements from Western sources. Many Chinese scholars associate his account of *jingjie* with Schiller's concept of "the aesthetic state" as elaborated in his 27th letter. In the specific context of Schiller's thought, however, the concept was intended to idealize things such as aesthetic culture, aesthetic man, and cultivated taste and related primarily to Schiller's concern for the advantages of aesthetic education rather than to a determination of the principles of artistic creation and appreciation.

Schiller's influence is found more in Wang's other theories concerning aesthetic education (*meiyu shuo*), spiritual detachment (*jietuo shuo*), and art as play (*youxi shuo*) than in his doctrine of the poetic state (*jingjie shuo*). There is a more direct link between *jingjie* and *Geist* (spirit or mind) as presented in Kant's *Critique of Judgment* (1788):

> Of certain products which are expected, partly at least, to appear as beautiful art, we say that they are without spirit; and this, although we find nothing to censure in them as far as taste goes. A poem may be very pretty and elegant, but is without spirit. . . . Even of a woman, we well say, she is pretty, affable and refined, but without spirit. What then do we mean by spirit? "Spirit" (*Geist*) in an aesthetic sense, signifies the animating principle in the mind. But that whereby this principle animates the psychic substance (*Seele*) – the material which it employs for that purpose that which sets the mental powers into a purposively swing, i.e., into a play which is self-maintaining and which strengthens those powers for such activity. Now my proposition is that this principle is nothing else than the faculty of presenting aesthetic ideas. (Kant, 1951, pp. 156–7)

Whatever their differences, *jingjie* and *Geist* are chiefly concerned with the essence, vitality, and significance of art.

Wang Guowei developed his theory of *jingjie* not only as an ultimate measure of artistic value, but also as an ideal of artistic creation. However, his account fails to offer any easily intelligible definition or systematically coherent clarification. *Jingjie* is like an eel that the reader may assume to have caught, only to find that it has slipped through his fingers. Hence, a contextual reading is required to gain greater confidence in understanding and assessing *jingjie* as the poetic state.

The Theory of the Refined (*guya shuo*)

Although Wang Guowei took literary invention to be the enterprise of genius (for example in Wang, 1906, *Wenxue Xiaoyan* [Notes on Literature]), his wider experience as a critic and a poet led him to examine another aspect of creative work. Among people of letters, only a few were naturally gifted with genius, but he saw that other works could be appealing and aesthetically significant. The question of how this could be so led to his hypothesis of *guya* as the secondary form of artistic creation:

> There are certain objects in the world that are neither original artworks nor practically useful stuff. Their producer is by no means a genius. However, works of this kind seem to have little difference from what is created by a genius. It can be called *guya* since there is no ready name for it. (Wang, 1907 "*Guya Zhi Zai Meixue Shang Zhi Diwei*" ["On the Position of the Refined in Aesthetics"])

The term *guya* combines two Chinese characters: *gu* (ancient or age-old) and *ya* (grace or elegance). Wang Guowei used the term mainly for a kind of classical gracefulness or refined elegance in art. We may render *guya* as "the refined." Wang Guowei offered *guya* as a kind of creativity in contrast with genius and as an aesthetic category in contrast with the beautiful and the sublime. He characterized *guya* in terms of its basic traits: as a kind of artistic creation, *guya* is produced not by a genius, but by a learned person of high personality. Its production depends on personal effort rather than on natural talent. As a kind of artistic form, *guya* is available solely in art and is thus distinct from the beautiful and the sublime, which are also found in nature. As a kind of aesthetic value, *guya* is independent to the extent that it does not possess the properties of the beautiful and the sublime. As a kind of technique, *guya* brings refinement or elegance into what is not beautiful in nature, for example in landscape painting. As a kind of aesthetic object, *guya* is subject to *a posteriori* judgment that is based on experience, in contrast to the universal and *a priori* judgment of the transcendental aesthetic categories of the beautiful and the sublime (Wang, 1907 "*Guya Zhi Zai Meixue Shang Zhi Diwei*" ["On the Position of the Refined in Aesthetics"]).

To facilitate understanding of *guya* as a new category of art, further clarification is required. First, Wang Guowei understood form in a broad sense. He asserted that all beauty is by definition formal beauty that lies in the symmetry, variety, and harmony of form. For example, the hero and his situation provide the subject matter of a novel or drama, but this subject matter can arouse aesthetic feelings only through adequate form. Only this form, which is distinct from the subject matter, can become an aesthetic object. There are generally two types of form. What is expressed naturally and perfectly in the primary form will produce an aesthetic object of either *youmei* (the beautiful) or *zhuangmei* (the sublime), and what is skilfully represented in the secondary form will produce an aesthetic object of *guya* (the refined). In this regard, form transforms something into an aesthetic object by arousing or provoking aesthetic feelings, but employs the subject matter as its content.

Secondly, *guya* is proposed as the secondary form to complement the primary form, which comprises both *youmei* (the beautiful) and *zhuangmei* (the sublime). The subdivisions of the first form, as formulated by Burke and Kant, exclusively represent the creative production of genius and provide other artists with exemplary models for mimesis. In contrast, a work of *guya* is produced by an artist who is not a genius, but who has highly cultivated aesthetic taste. This taste emerges naturally from learning, imitating, and refining. An artist who produces *guya* can be identified with artists of the first caliber in respect of what he makes. Nevertheless, his works are generally fashioned and refined far more by his effort than by his innate talent.

Thirdly, *guya* can be held to have an independent value. It helps to increase the beauty of the beautiful even though it lacks the properties inherent in either *youmei* (the beautiful) or *zhuangmei* (the sublime). By being "a special mode of formal beauty," *guya* serves as an indispensable element in the first form of the beautiful and the sublime. In this context, *guya* is the necessary method, skill, or technique without which beautiful or sublime artworks cannot be produced.

Finally, we must approach the concept of *guya* with reference to the concept of *tiancai* (genius). In aesthetic creation, there is a complementary relation between the two. Artistic geniuses, who offer works of originality and exemplariness, are extremely rare. Artists producing *guya* as excellent works of paramount aesthetic value supplement the output of genius and fill the gaps between its appearances. As supplementary works of art, *guya* does not negate the worth of the original and exemplary products of genius, but rather confirms the need for learning, experience, taste, and endeavor in the process of artistic creation. It is in this connection that *guya* has its independent value.

In spite of such explanations, the concept of *guya* remains perplexing and, in some aspects, self-defeating. Take for example the distinction between the primary form and the secondary form. The former, comprising *youmei* (the beautiful) and *zhuangmei* (the sublime), has two varieties: the natural and the artistic. The primary form in its artistic variety is supplemented by the secondary form *guya*, which is available only in an artistic variety. On this account, the beauty of all things is formal and should be capable of being increased when expressed through the second form, but this contradicts the claim that *guya* is available solely in art and not in nature. Wang Guowei needs an explanation of why this restriction is not arbitrary. Further, Wang's westernized delineation of *guya* hindered its reception and popularity in China.

Some Chinese critics treated *guya* so literally that they separated the term into *gu* and *ya* for interpretation. They saw *gu* (ancient, age-old) as the antonym of *jin* (present-day, modern) and saw *ya* (elegant, cultivated) the antonym of *su* (vulgar, popular). Accordingly, works of *gu* and *ya* were assumed to belong exclusively to classical or high art, which is appreciated by a cultivated minority and has nothing to do with present-day reality. Works of *jin* and *su* were seen to be typical of mass or popular art, which was appreciated by the vulgar majority and reflected present-day circumstances. On this basis, Wang Guowei was considered to be a conservative or elitist, and his doctrine of *guya* was condemned for being estranged from reality and life and for being antagonistic to both the social aspect and the mass appreciation of the beautiful (cf. Chen Yuanhui, 1989, pp. 71–5). This critique ignored the contextual implications that I have mentioned and thus failed to respond to Wang Guowei's actual views, particularly those regarding popular art. His historical review of Chinese drama and opera provided a pioneering study of a genre of art that scholars previously considered unrefined and unworthy of serious consideration. In an opening remark for this study, he showed his appreciation of both high art and this popular genre:

> Each era has its own literature; just like the *shi* poetry in the Tang dynasty, the *ci* lyrics in the Song dynasty, and the *qu* songs or drama in the Yuan dynasty, literature of a specific kind only flourishes during its own phase and cannot be revived continuously in later ages. (Wang, 1912 "*Song-Yuan Xiqu Kao*" ["A Historical Study of the Drama in the Song and Yuan Dynasties"]).

Wang Guowei's evolutionary view of literary development was free from any restriction to the classical or any bias against the popular. Critiques of his allegedly elitist stance are thus out of place.

Conclusion

Wang Guowei's theories of *jingjie* and *guya* are the chief innovative features of his aesthetic criticism. They are the fruit of his creative response to the Chinese and Western aesthetic traditions, especially Chinese concepts such as *qing* (feelings) and *jing* (scenes), *cai* (talents) and *xue* (learning), *xiang* (image) and *yi* (significance), *xingqu* (inspiration and taste) and *shenyun* (spirit and tone), and Western concepts such as idealism and realism, the beautiful and the sublime, genius and *Geist*.

The theories of *jingjie* and *guya* are formulated to explicate the aesthetic qualities of poetic works and to reveal the cultivated taste and high creativity of the poets. They are also recommended as overarching criteria for the aesthetic judgment of the arts, particularly of poetry. Philosophically, they are orientated towards the boundless pursuit of cosmic, social, moral, psychical, and artistic truth regarding the state of human existence and the system of human values. Ethically, these theories suggest a process of personal development and spiritual nourishment, as Wang illustrated through lines from three well-known *ci* lyrics:

> From the ancient time to the present day all those who have been highly successful in great ventures and in the pursuit of learning must of necessity have experienced three modes of *jingjie*. "Last night the West wind shriveled the green-clad trees. Alone I climb the light tower to gaze my fill along the road to the horizon" (Yan Shu, *Dielianhua*). This expresses the first stage (*jing*). "My clothes grow daily more loose, yet care I not. For you am I thus wasting away in sorrow and pain" (Liu Yong, *Fengqiwu* [mistakenly attributed by Wang to Ouyang Xiu's *Dielianhua*]). This expresses the second stage. "I sought her in the crowd a hundred, a thousand times. Suddenly with a turn of the head [I saw her], that one there where the lamplight was fading" (Xin Qiji, *Qingyuan*). This expresses the third stage. Such words as these could not have been uttered by other than great writers of *ci* lyrics. However, if we happened to use this idea of *jingjie* to interpret the meaning of the poems themselves, I am afraid the three writers concerned would have demurred. (Wang (1970), as translated in Rickett, 1977, p. 50; cf. Yao Kefu, 1983, pp. 10–11)

For Wang Guowei, this process of personal development progresses in enlightenment and achievement from the realm of necessity to the realm of freedom, thus sublimating the human spirit and aestheticizing human life.

Bibliography

Works of Wang Guowei

Wang, Kuo-wei 1970: *Poetic Remarks in the Human World*, trans. Ching-I Tu, Taiwan: Chung Hwa Book Company

Wang, Guowei 1987a: *Wang Guowei meilun wenxuan* 王國維美論文選 (Wang Guowei's selected essays on beauty). Liu Gangqiang ed., Changsha: Hunan Renmin Chubanshe

Wang, Guowei 1987b: *Wang Guowei wenxue meixue lunzhu ji* 王國維文學美學論著集 (Wang Guowei's anthology on literature and aesthetics), Zhou Xishan, ed., Taiyuan: Beiyue Wenyi Chubanshe

Wang, Guowei 1996: *Wang Guowei xueshu wenhua suibi* 王國維學術文化隨筆 (selected essays of Wang Guowei), Fo Chu, ed., Beijing: Zhongguo Qing Nian Chubanshe

Wang, Guowei 1997: *Wang Guowei wenji* 王國維文集 (collected works of Wang Guowei), vols. 1–4, Yao Ganming and Wang Yan, eds, Beijing: Zhongguo Wen Shi Chubanshe

Other works in Chinese

Beijing University, Department of Philosophy, ed., 1985: *Zhongguo meixueshi ziliao xuanji* 中國美學史資料選輯 (a source book of the history of Chinese aesthetics), Beijing: Zhonghua Shuju

Cai, Yuanpei 1983: *Cai Yuanpei meixue wenxuan* 蔡元培美學文選 (Cai Yuanpei's selected essays on aesthetics), Beijing: Beijing University Press

Chen, Hongxiang 1998: *Wang Guowei zhuan* 王國維傳 (a biography of Wang Guowei), Beijing: Tuanjie Chubanshe

Chen, Yinque 1934: "*Wang Jingan yishu xu*" 王靜安遺書序 ("preface to Wang Guowei's posthumous works"), Beijing: Shangwu yinshuguan, reprinted 1940

Chen, Yong 1983: "*Luetan Jingjie shuo*" 略談 "境界" 説 ("a note on the theory of *jingjie*"), in Yao, Kefu, 1983, pp. 210–14

Chen, Yuanhui 1989: *Lun Wang Guowei* 王國維論 (a study of Wang Guowei), Changchun: Dongbei Normal University Press

Fo, Chu 1987: *Wang Guowei shixue yanjiu* 王國維詩學研究 (a study of Wang Guowei's poetics), Beijing: Beijing University Press

Li, Zehou 1980: *Meixue lunji* 美學論集 (essays on aesthetics), Shanghai: Shanghai Wenyi Chubanshe

Li, Zehou 1983: "*Yijing qiantan*" 意境淺談 ("an initial enquiry into the theory of yijing"), in Yao, Kefu, 1983, pp. 160–78

Liu, Kesu 1999: *Shihang guyan: Wang Guowei biezhuan* 失行孤雁：王國維別傳 (a solitary wild goose: a separate biography of Wang Guowei), Beijing: Huaxia Chubanshe

Liu, Xuan 1996: *Wang Guowei pingzhuan* 王國維評傳 (a critical biography of Wang Guowei), Nanchang: Baihuazhou Wenyi Chubanshe

Lu, Shanqing 1988: *Wang Guowei wenyi meixue guan* 王國維文藝美學觀 (Wang Guowei's artistic and aesthetic views), Guiyang: Guizhou Renmin Chubanshe

Nie, Zhenbin 1997: *Wang Guowei meixue sixiang pingshu* 王國維美學思想評述 (critique of Wang Guowei's aesthetic ideas), Shenyang: Liaonig University Press

Yao, Kefu, ed., 1983: *Renjian cihua ji pinglun huibian* 人間詞話及評論匯編 (selected essays on Wang Guowei's poetic remarks in the human world), Beijing: Shumu Wenxian Chubanshe

Ye, Jiaying 1983: "*Dui renjian cihua zhong jingjie yici zhi yijie de tantao*" 對《人間詞話》中境界一辭之義界的探討 ("about the definitions of *jingjie* as a term in Wang Guowei's poetic remarks in the human world"), in Yao, Kefu 1983, pp. 147–59

Ye, Jiaying 1997: *Wang Guowei jiqi wenxue piping* 王國維及其文學批評 (Wang Guowei and his literary criticism), Shijiazhuang: Hebei Jiaoyu Chubanshe

Zhang, Bennan 1992: *Wang Guowei meixue sixiang yanjiu* 王國維美學思想研究 (a study of Wang Guowei's aesthetics), Taiwan: Wenjin Press

Zhu, Guangqian 1982: *Zhu Guangqian meixue wenji* 朱光潛美學文集 (Zhu Guangqian's collected works on aesthetics), vol. II, Shanghai: Shanghai Wenyi Chubanshe

Other works in English and German

Burke, Edmund 1958: *A Philosophical Enquiry into the Origin of our Ideas of the Sublime and Beautiful*, London: Routledge & Kegan Paul, (original date 1757)

Kant, Immanuel 1951: *Critique of Judgment*, trans. J. B. Bernard, New York: Hafner Press (original date 1788)

Kant, Immanuel 1968: *Critique of Pure Reason*, trans. N. Kemp Smith, London: Macmillan, (original dates 1781, second edn 1787)

Lipps, Theodor 1897: Raumaesthetik und geometrisch-optische täuschungen, Leipzig: J. A. Barth

Nietzsche, Friedrich 1976: *The Portable Nietzsche*. trans. and ed. Walter Kaufmann, Harmondsworth: Penguin Books

Rickett, Adele Austin 1977: *Wang Kuo-wei's Jen-Chien Tzu-Hua: A Study in Chinese Literary Criticism*, Hong Kong: Hong Kong University Press

Schiller, Friedrich 1967: *On the Aesthetic Education of Man*, trans. E. M. Wilkinson and L. A. Willoughby, Oxford: Oxford University Press (original date 1794–5)

Schopenhauer, Arthur 1897: *The Art of Literature*, trans. T. Bailey Saunders, London and New York: Swan Sonnenschein & The Macmillan Press

Schopenhauer, Arthur 1964: *The World as Will and Idea*, trans. R. B. Haldane and J. Kemp, London: Routledge & Kegan Paul (original date 1883)

Discussion Questions

1. Does an intercultural perspective help us to understand any basic concepts of Chinese philosophy?
2. Is *xing* (human nature) beyond human knowledge?
3. Should the metaphysical and the ethical be differentiated?
4. Does Wang Guowei provide a coherent account of *jingjie* (the poetic state)?
5. Can we use the same concepts to understand poetic creation and to provide standards for critical assessment?
6. How are creativity and description integrated in the poetic state?
7. Does the distinction between self-involvement and self-detachment help us to understand poetic works?
8. Are there any general grounds for preferring poetry that is unveiled to poetry that is veiled?
9. Does Wang Guowei's connection with Chinese aesthetic tradition help to justify his philosophy of criticism?
10. If we reject the concept of genius in aesthetic criticism, must we also reject the concept of the refined?

3

ZHANG DONGSUN: PLURALIST EPISTEMOLOGY AND CHINESE PHILOSOPHY

Xinyan Jiang

From the 1920s to the 1940s, Zhang Dongsun (1886–1973) was one of the most important philosophers in China. In his youth he went to Japan and studied philosophy for more than five years at Tokyo University. After returning to China in 1911, he taught in various universities, including Peking University, and published many works in philosophy. Among his best-known works are *Science and philosophy* (1924), *Philosophy ABC* (1929b), *Outlook on Life ABC* (1929a), *Essays on New Philosophy* (1929c), *Moral Philosophy* (1931), *Contemporary Ethics* (1932), *Epistemology* (1934a), *Philosophy of Value* (1934c), *Knowledge and Culture* (1946a), *Ideal and Society* (1946b), and *Ideal and Democracy* (1946c).

Zhang was deeply influenced by both traditional Chinese philosophy and Western philosophy. A Confucian education contributed much to his strong sense of responsibility for his country and people. The Buddhist view of the universe greatly inspired his cosmology. Kant's epistemology and other Western theories of knowledge provided a foundation for his epistemological pluralism (*renshi de duoyuan lun*). Zhang was very influential partly because of his excellent work in introducing Western philosophy to China. However, Zhang's significance in contemporary Chinese philosophy is mainly due to his role as the first contemporary Chinese philosopher to establish his own philosophical theory, especially in epistemology.

Unlike other Chinese contemporary philosophers, Zhang based his philosophy more on assimilating and synthesizing work in Western philosophy than on reforming traditional Chinese philosophy. As Chan Wing-tsit has pointed out, Zhang, indisputably, is the one "who has assimilated the most of Western thought, established the most comprehensive and well coordinated system, and has exerted the greatest influence among the Western oriented Chinese philosophers" (Chan, 1963, p. 744). Epistemology is the central part of Zhang's philosophy, which began with a pluralistic epistemology and culminated in a cultural epistemology. His pluralism is derived from a revised version of Kantian philosophy. To justify such an epistemology, he proposed a cosmology: panstructuralism (*fan jiagou zhuyi*). His cultural epistemology, although based on his pluralistic epistemology, sought to explore the social and cultural nature of knowledge. This stage of his philosophy is of greatest interest today and will provide the focus of this chapter. To illustrate and demonstrate his cultural epistemology, Zhang also undertook comprehensive and profound comparative studies of Chinese and Western philosophy. Especially insightful are his investigations of how differences in language influence differences in philosophy and how cultural differences determine differences in logical thinking. Although Zhang's comparative studies of Chinese and Western philosophy were written a half-century ago, they remain of great value even today. They will continue to throw light on current debates on cultural issues and to inspire comparative philosophy in our times.

Pluralistic Epistemology

For Zhang, knowledge is social and cultural. To argue this, he first discussed the process of cognition in order to show that the content of knowledge does not objectively represent external reality. He established his pluralistic epistemology (*duoyuan renshi lun*) or epistemological pluralism (*renshi de duoyuan lun*) to serve this purpose.

Zhang called his account of knowledge "epistemological pluralism" because he held that the various elements that make our cognition possible are mutually independent and irreducible to each other. In his view, sensation, external order, transcendental forms, logical postulates, and concepts are all indispensable for knowledge. Each has its own source and cannot be reduced to others: "from sensations we cannot know external things; from forms we cannot know sensations; from postulates we cannot know forms; from concepts we cannot know postulates" (Zhang, 1934a, p. 106). He held that a pluralist position of this sort distinguishes his theory both from epistemological monism, which reduces the known to the knower, and from epistemological dualism, which admits only the dichotomy between the subject and object (Zhang, 1934a, p. 45).

In this section, I will briefly introduce Zhang's epistemological pluralism and explain how sensation, external order, transcendental forms, postulates, and concepts are meant to play different roles in our cognition.

First, sensations are not representations of external things. The content of a sensation is nonexistent in the sense that it has no exact correspondence with its object in the external world. For example, when we see that there is a piece of purple clothing in front of us, there is no purple color in the external world but only something which makes us see things that way. So, through our senses, we cannot know how the external world really is. However, Zhang held that sensation has an external ground and is not caused by the mind alone. "It is not an external existence, but it does not exist in the mind either. It is something in between which does not exist in the world" (Zhang, 1934a, p. 47). There is something in the external world that stimulates our sensations:

> Although we do not yet know the nature of the external things stimulating us, there must be some sort of a correlation between them, because under certain conditions our sensation must be affected by certain changes while its object already changed. . . . In this connection, then, the causal theory of perception of Bertrand Russell, if I do not misunderstand him, is in a certain sense similar to this. (Zhang, 1932b, pp. 10–11)

There is a correlation between changes in sensation and changes in the external world. After all, sensation has its cause in the external world and differs when what is external to us differs. When we perceive a piece of clothing as purple, there is something in it that makes us perceive the purple color. If there is no such thing in it, we will not perceive the clothing as purple. But, the external cause of our sensation is not a substance, but is rather an order or structure outside us. What is reflected in our sensation is this external order (Zhang, 1932b, p. 12; and Zhang 1934a, pp. 47–9).

Secondly, external order does exist independently of us, although we can have almost no knowledge of it. For Zhang, however, there are three kinds of the external order that we can know. The first is atomicity, which signifies the atomic structure of the physical world without any reference to substance (Zhang, 1932b, p. 16). Atomicity is the equivalent of divisibility. In contrast to physical atoms, which are the smallest physical particles that constitute the ultimate stuff of the universe, Zhang's notion of atomicity concerns structure rather than substance. Structurally, the physical world can be infinitely divided into smaller units. The second kind of external order is continuity. Anything that can be divided also has continuity. Atomicity and continuity are two aspects of one thing: "what is continuous must be infinitely divisible" (Zhang, 1932b, p. 19). The third kind of order is creativity or novelty. If nothing new occurs in the world, there will be no change in the world. But, undoubtedly, there are changes in the world. Therefore, there must be new things in the world. These new things are not created by our minds. We recognize them but do not cause them, and they have their causes in the external world. "Hence, we must say that the reason why there are new things emerging is that there is something corresponding to these new things. That is a kind of order" (Zhang, 1934a, p. 61). However, the correspondence between the novelty we perceive and what is in the external world concerns only structure and does not concern content (Zhang, 1934a). Therefore, change in the external world only involves change in structure:

> We can make contact with the external world, but we can know very little about it. It is as though there were a thick curtain before us through which a few light beams can reach our eyes. What can reach us are the three kinds of order: atomicity, continuity, and creativity. Besides them, nothing is positively known by us. (Zhang, 1934a, p. 63)

Zhang's belief in the existence of external order is very significant to his epistemology, although he did not provide a sound ground for it. Zhang considered that his admission of the existence of an external order is one difference between his view and Kant's. In Zhang's understanding, Kant believed that the order of the objects of experience exists only within our consciousness (Zhang, 1934a, p. 51; 1932b, p. 14). However, Zhang's critique of Kant in this aspect is very weak, since he did not show how we know that there is external order and even did not try to explain how we can be so sure that atomicity, continuity, and creativity are external to us.

Internal order is another element of cognition. No matter how many kinds of external order there could be, without internal order, our cognition would be impossible. Zhang divided internal order into two kinds: cognitively *a priori* forms (transcendental intuitive forms) and logically *a priori* forms (logical postulates). According to Zhang, cognitively *a priori* forms or transcendental intuitive forms are the third element of cognition. They are the prior conditions of our cognition, such that only under such conditions is our cognition possible (Zhang, 1932b, p. 28). There are three kinds of transcendental intuitive forms: space, time, and the subject–object relation. His view of time and space is similar to Kant's. Like Kant, Zhang argued that space and time are subjective forms and not derived from experience. They are *a priori* conditions for the possibility of experience and necessary representations that underlie all intuitions. Space is nothing but the form of all appearance of our outer sense, and time is nothing but the form of all appearance of our inner sense (Zhang, 1932b, pp. 26–7; 1934a, pp. 69, 72). With regard to the subject–object relation, Zhang held that all cognition, even consciousness of the lowest kind, presupposes a subject and an object. He insists that in cognition the relation between known and knower is internal and that the two are inseparable (Zhang, 1934a, p. 80). Whenever there is a cognitive experience or an apprehension, there must be an object experienced and a subject experiencing it (Zhang, 1932b, p. 32).

According to Zhang, logically *a priori* forms or logical postulates are the fourth element of cognition. Such forms are the fundamental principles that make logic possible. They include postulates or categories in the Kantian sense and relations of logical implication (Zhang, 1934a, pp. 84–5). Postulates, which are static and immovable, are divided into many sets. Each postulate has an opposite, for example right and wrong or simplicity and complexity (Zhang, 1934a, p. 89). All postulates are useful, but some are more convenient than others (Zhang, 1934a). According to Zhang, postulates are cultural or social. Unlike cognitively *a priori* forms that are common to all knowers, postulates are different in different cultures. Their change depends upon culture (Zhang, 1934a, p. 128). In contrast to postulates, implicative relations or logical implications are dynamic and movable in the sense that different logical implications can be changed into each other and they are all manifestations of the same logical principle (Zhang, 1934a, p. 93). They are the foundation of all judgments and inferences. Without them, no proposition is possible because every proposition is an expression of logical implication. Zhang's implicative relations are logical rules or laws. For him, the three basic laws of logic, that is the Law of Identity, the Law of Non-Contradiction, and the Law of Excluded Middle, are all implicative relations (Zhang, 1934a, p. 90). Without implicative relations, there would be no logic. Logic is deduced from such relations but these relations cannot be deduced from logic. Therefore, implicative relations are *a priori* foundations of logic that we cannot analyze further (Zhang, 1934a, p. 91).

Concepts are the fifth element of cognition. According to Zhang, there is a hierarchy of concepts. The highest concepts are metaphysical concepts, such as substance, reality, matter, mind, and force. The second highest concepts are physical, followed by psychological, biological, logical, and ethical concepts (Zhang, 1934a, p. 95–6). Unlike postulates, concepts are empirical, even including the highest concepts of metaphysics. Concepts are formed by generalizations from experience. Regarding the function of concepts in logic, Zhang held that concepts are not logical presumptions from which inferences start but logical consequences that result from inferences (Zhang, 1934a, p. 97). This is because we need to apply postulates to experience in order to form concepts but not the other way around. In this sense, to say that concepts are logical consequences is not incompatible with holding that concepts are empirical. The different functions in logic between postulates and concepts lead to another difference between the two: postulates cannot be entirely invalid, whereas concepts can be false or out of date (Zhang, 1932b, p. 43). Concepts are contents while postulates are conditions. What we can know directly we know through concepts. Concepts are made through interpretation, while postulates are made for interpretation. Concepts are symbolic in nature; a concept is a symbol or class-name. The particulars that are included under the same concept need not share common attributes, but are classified as the same kind because our responses to them are similar (Zhang, 1934a, pp. 99–100). For example, a pen and ink are very different things, but we classify both under the concept of stationery because of the way in which we use them (Zhang, 1934a, p. 116). Every concept, according to Zhang, is a collection of our experience–attitudes or operations (Zhang, 1932b, p. 46) that has become comparatively fixed due to custom (Zhang, 1934a, p. 118). In this sense, class-names do not correspond to natural kinds in the external world but to our subjective classifications. Therefore, what class-names or concepts represent are actually nonexistent (Zhang, 1934a, p. 100). A concept is not a symbol that represents the way an external thing really is, but is determined by the way in which we respond to the external thing. A concept is a kind of collection of responses. For example, the concept of orange represents a group of our ways of handling an orange, such as "to be taken," "edible," "to be smelt," "sweet," "to be given," "to be put on a table," "to represent a three dimensional round object," and "to be squeezed into juice" (Zhang, 1934a, pp. 111–12).

Our classification of things is subjective but is not totally arbitrary. There are some objective grounds for our classification and some limits on our freedom in classifying things. For example, we cannot classify a mule as a tiger that eats meat (Zhang, 1934a, p. 114). Although our classification of things is based on our responses to them, our responses are related to certain qualities of things. For example, one of our responses to an orange is to eat it because it is edible, but we do not have such a response to a stone. Although "being edible" is a relational property which is not intrinsic to an orange and depends on our relation to an orange, this relational property has something to do with certain unknown qualities of an orange (Zhang, 1934a, pp. 116–17). Consequently, although concepts as class-names are subjective, they are still correlated with the external world in some way.

According to Zhang's epistemological pluralism, knowledge is the joint product of these five elements of cognition. He also believed that each simple apprehension is a whole and that therefore Kant's transcendental unity of apperception, which makes all of one's representations one's own, is not necessary. It seemed to Zhang that a major difference between Kant's theory and his can be explained in this way: Kant thinks that we first perceive disorderly stuff and then unify and order it by the transcendental unity of apprehension; Zhang's idea is that we first have a whole and then differentiate it (Zhang, 1934a, pp. 119–20). Zhang regarded his epistemology as a kind of pluralism, because he considered that the five elements of cognition are mutually irreducible and equally important for knowledge. So, for him, the debate between rationalism and empiricism over the ultimate single source of knowledge is meaningless (Zhang, 1934a, p. 123). Because Zhang's pluralistic epistemology was so deeply influenced by Kant, he saw it as a kind of revised Kantian theory of knowledge (Zhang, 1937, p. 96). Nevertheless, he insisted that his theory is unique in many ways. For him, his innovation did not lie in any specific part of the theory, but in the way in which he united all of its parts. Since the synthesis is new, his pluralistic epistemology is novel (Zhang, 1937, p. 96).

Whether or not Zhang's pluralistic epistemology was as original as he thought, it did argue that knowledge does not correspond to the external world and that truth as commonly understood in terms of such correspondence does not exist. Even scientific knowledge is recreation but not representation (Zhang,

1924, pp. 101–2). The fact that scientific knowledge may be valid across cultures does not prove that it is objective and culture-free. As human beings, people in different cultures share many qualities and therefore they must have something in common in their way of thinking and knowing. The cross-culture validity of science is compatible with its human subjectivity. On the one hand, Zhang believed that scientific knowledge is valid over the world (Zhang, 1922), and on the other hand, he holds that it is not a true reflection of the external world. Therefore, all kinds of knowledge are subjective in nature. Why, then, do we need knowledge? As it will be discussed in the next two sections, Zhang held that we need knowledge for the sake of convenience and for the sake of a meaningful life (Zhang, 1946a, p. 40). Therefore, knowledge should be seen as socially valuable and as part of culture. In this way, Zhang's pluralistic epistemology is a preliminary step towards his cultural epistemology. However, to justify his pluralistic epistemology, Zhang needed a cosmology whose account of the universe dispensed with the notions of substance, matter or physical entity. He called this cosmology "panstructuralism" (*fan jiagou zhuyi*) (Zhang, 1934a, p. 127).

Panstructuralism

Zhang claimed that his philosophy provided a cosmology, but contained no metaphysics. In his view, this constituted another difference between Kantian philosophy and his own. In Kant, metaphysics is not given up, although the priority of epistemology radically alters its role.

Zhang's revised Kantianism is limited to his pluralistic epistemology and does not apply to his cosmology. What did principally influence his cosmology was Buddhism. In his early age, it was Buddhist scriptures such as *Leng Yan Jing* and *Dacheng Qi Xin Lun* that intrigued him with philosophy (Zuo, 1998, p. 8). Although he gave serious criticism to Buddhism later on, he seemed always to have accepted Buddhist cosmology, especially certain ideas from the Great Vehicle School (*Mahayana, dacheng*) to a great degree. The close relation between Zhang's cosmology and Buddhist cosmology will be revealed in the following discussion of Zhang's panstructuralism.

In his pluralistic epistemology, Zhang already stated that there is no substance (Zhang, 1934a, p. 127). The objects of sensation do not have an ontological status (Zhang, 1934a, p. 127). As we have seen, the external world for Zhang comprises various structures, only some of which, atomicity, continuity, and creativity, are known to us. Underlying such conclusions is a cosmology holding that these structures or orders are all that really exist in the universe. Roughly speaking, these structures are arranged at three levels: so-called "matter," "life," and "mind." All of these structures are empty, and none are substances with certain natures. Rather than material substance, there are only physical relations and physical laws (Zhang, 1934a, pp. 128–9). "Matter" is a general concept covering a total domain of many specific concepts about physical properties. There is nothing that is in itself matter corresponding to our concept of matter. In his discussion of matter, Zhang wrote:

> First, what is so-called matter? As is well known, it is not the color, fragrance, sound or size that we perceive by our senses, because they tend to be subjective. Therefore, by "matter" we refer to an object's volume, tenacity, speed. This is just to make matter become a set of formulas of physics. Therefore, we have only physical laws but not matter. (Zhang, 1934a, p. 128)

So-called "life" is a generalization covering the domain of biological phenomena. "Mind" is a generalization too, but it covers psychological phenomena that differ from biological function (Zhang, 1934a, p. 130). Therefore, in our language, it is better to replace "matter" with "physical laws"; to replace "life" with "biological principles"; and to replace "mind" with "psychology" (Zhang, 1934a, p. 131). In short, terms for substance as carrier of attributes should be replaced by terms for structures or orders. In general, the universe contains no substance or essence, but only structures or orders. However, the structures or orders of the universe are not purely natural or objective, but rather depend on our cognitive activity (Zhang, 1934a, p. 133):

> There are many structures. For instance, mass is a kind of structure, so are density, speed, gravity. . . . I believe that these are indeed structures, but they are not completely external and real. A structure reflects on our internal world, i.e., goes through the middle portion discussed earlier [the portion between knower and known]. In other words, we must take the role of various cognitive forms and patterns into account in the formation of structures. (Zhang, 1934a, p. 130)

In explaining his cosmology, Zhang compared it to Buddhist cosmology. He believed that the two are very similar in that both deny substance and emphasize relationship. He said that "structure" in his theory resembled what Buddhism calls "relatedness" (Chinese: *yinyuan*; Sanskrit: *paccaya*). According to Buddhism, especially in Great Vehicle Buddhism, all things are constituted by relatedness, and there are not substances. The universe, like a big net, comprises countless numbers of relations that are dependent on each other and combine in various ways and at various levels. This illustrates the universe's emptiness. In Buddhist thought, "emptiness" is not equivalent to "nothingness," but means no substance, no fixed nature, and no self-sufficient being. Since there is only relatedness in the universe, nothing is an independent being by itself. Hence, there is no substance, and the world is merely a set of functional relations. Zhang believed that his cosmology is in accordance with this Buddhist idea (Zhang, 1979, p. 39), since it holds that the universe consists of structures that are not substances but relations.

There is further similarity between Zhang's cosmology and Buddhist cosmology. Buddhism holds that the universe is governed by a universal and unchanging law, holding that every thing is determined by relatedness or *yinyuan* and that nothing has an intrinsic nature in itself. In this sense, there is something objective in the universe. Zhang argued that this objectivity is consistent with his claim that the structures of the universe have some objectivity (Zhang, 1979, p. 40).

However, for Zhang there was an important difference in cosmology between his thought and Buddhism, namely, he accepted evolution, while Buddhist cosmology denied it. It seems that he absorbed a lot of ideas from theories of evolution in the West. Probably, what benefited him most was the theory of emergent evolution represented by C. Lloyd Morgan (1852–1936) and Samuel Alexander (1859–1938) in his time. According to Zhang's interpretation, the theory of emergent evolution holds that evolution involves the emergence of new kinds, that there are different levels of evolution which form a hierarchy and each lower level is controlled by the higher levels, and that new things from evolution are results of changes in structure but not in substance, etc. (Zhang Yaonan, 1998, pp. 232–3). Combining the Buddhist idea of nonsubstance with such a theory of evolution, Zhang held that the structures of the universe, although empty, are in evolution, and new kinds of structures may emerge due to changes in the combination of various structures. However, evolution is not simply change:

> To understand evolution, we first must know why "evolution" differs from "change." There are some characteristics of our evolving from the structure of "matter" to the structure of "life" and then to the structure of "mind." . . . Therefore, evolution refers to this: structures have been changed from simple and dispersed ones to closely bound and united ones. Although they are still structures, they are different kinds from before. (Zhang, 1979, pp. 40–1)

Evolution is change that brings structures to a higher and more complex level than before. Although all that exist are just relatedness or structures, they are changed in a progressive pattern. For Zhang, there is no inconsistency between holding that there is no substance and believing that there is evolution.

Zhang's cosmology not only served his pluralistic epistemology, but was also conducive to the intellectually oriented outlook on life that Zhang advocated. He firmly believed that one's outlook on life must be based on one's cosmology. As he put it:

> Nowadays, people love to talk a lot about an outlook on life, but, as a matter of fact, one's outlook on life cannot be separated from one's cosmology. An outlook on life is mainly aimed at elaborating how one ought to live in the world, i.e., what one ought to do. But, to understand how one ought to

live, one must make clear what a human life is. . . . Generally speaking, we
cannot talk about human life without talking about Nature; we cannot talk
about the essence of Nature without talking about the system of Nature. Since
the meaning of life is dependent on the position of human life in the universe, an outlook on life cannot be made without a cosmology. (Zhang, 1979,
pp. 42–3)

According to Zhang's cosmology, "mind" is at the top level among all the
structures of the universe, while "culture" is the top layer of the level of the
mind. There are many sub-layers of culture. Like all other structures, culture
is in evolution. The evolution of culture is not spontaneous, but depends
on the creativity of individual spirits. Culture aims to transcend living, which
is here and now and finite. Living in itself is a fact which bears no intrinsic
meaning and value, since the meaning and value of one's life do not come
with one's birth. First we come to live in the world and then create meaning
and value for our lives (Zhang, 1972, pp. 562–3, 567). The ideal of life is
to transcend the here and now of life (Zhang, 1972, p. 570). One's life here
and now is at a spatiotemporally coordinated point. The value of life lies in
transcending such a point and therefore in amplifying living in itself. Living
in itself is like a lamp-wick, with the enlarged life like the area lit up by the
lamp-wick. Different people enlarge their lives to different degrees, just as
different lamp-wicks light up areas of different size (Zhang, 1972, p. 562).
The larger we amplify living in itself, the greater are the meaning and value
of our life (Zhang, 1972, p. 568). Culture is created to make our life meaningful and valuable. It is the product of our effort to transcend living in itself
(Zhang, 1972, pp. 570, 574). To transcend and enlarge living in itself, one
first needs to have knowledge: "to know is to live" and "to live is to know"
(Zhang, 1972, p. 565):

> I need to discuss "enlightenment". "To be enlightened" is "to know." To know
> is the first step to transcend living here and now. . . . To know is to enlarge
> this life. Our life in itself is limited here and now, but we desire to amplify it.
> To know makes such amplification possible. It is appropriate to say that to
> know is to live. In this sense, one cannot live without knowledge. (Zhang, 1972,
> pp. 564–5)

> One's life in itself is like a lamp, and one's knowledge is like the light of the
> lamp. Just as the light gives value to the lamp, knowledge gives value to one's
> life. Knowledge enlarges one's life and makes one transcend living in itself. The
> more knowledge, the more one's life is amplified and the more one's life has
> value (Zhang, 1972, pp. 565–7)

Zhang did not explain much about what kind of knowledge one needs to
pursue in order to enlarge one's life. What he said about it is this:

To know is to turn "the thatness" (ci) to "the whatness" (he), to turn "change" to "eternal," to turn "disorder" to "stability," to turn "chaos" to "division." Therefore, only "knowing" can enable one to go beyond the spatiotemporally coordinated point where one's life in itself is; . . . only "knowing" is the characteristic of the mind; only "knowing" can enable one to lead one's life to an ideal . . . (Zhang, 1972, p. 570)

It seems that he was saying that it is the cognitive activity of human beings that transcends momentary experience, creates the meaning of human life, gives value to human life, and makes the existence of the individual life go beyond a particular time and space and become immortal in a cultural sense. Therefore, "to know" is what makes human life distinctive. In this sense, for human beings, to live is to know. By asserting "to live is to know," Zhang meant to say that one should live an intellectual life.

Furthermore, "to know" is a precondition for living a progressive and creative life that requires appropriate ways to deal with desires. For Zhang, in order to live a progressive and creative life, one should not simply control or eliminate desires, but also transform them and lead them in the right direction. According to Zhang, Buddhist elimination of desires is a kind of abnormal psychology, while Confucian control of desires can no longer work once confronted with Western culture (Zhang, 1922; Zuo, 1998, p. 172). What we ought to do is not to eliminate or control desires, but to transform them and elevate lower desires to higher desires. Instead of depressing selfish desires, one should enlarge our benevolent feeling (Zhang, 1922; Zuo, 1998, p. 172).

Zhang's account of desires also has a social and political aspect. He held that what is wonderful is to reconcile the various desires of individuals and to make them great desires. Then, rather than conflicting with one another, the well-being of individuals will become the great well-being of mankind. In other words, both self-interest and the interests of others will be satisfied and developed to a high degree. Such a way of life is vigorous and progressive. It is not a way of life in which one must hold the mean between extremes in regard to thought and desires (chi zhong yi yu) (Zhang, 1922). To live this way of life presupposes knowledge and a high level of intellectual development. At the beginning of one's intellectual enlightenment, one might intend to be selfish and follow desires wherever they lead (Zhang, 1979, pp. 43–4; Zuo, 1998, pp. 181–2). Selfishness is a symptom of the early stage of enlightenment:

Taking a small self [selfish self] as the temporary standard [for morality] is an inevitable phenomenon that accompanies the overthrow of custom-based morality. To overturn customs is the beginning of the awakening of intellectuality (lizhi). There is a process from no self-awareness, to half self-awareness, to full self-awareness. Egoism is a symptom of sickness which occurs at the stage of half self-awareness. In other words, it is an inevitable abnormality during the transition period. (Zhang, 1979, pp. 432–3)

To overcome egoism, the further enlightenment of intellectuality is needed. Zhang did not blame the new ideas brought to China by the May Fourth and New Culture movements for the prevalence of egoism after the May Fourth period, but believed that to go beyond this egoism the Chinese needed more knowledge:

> We should understand this: all negative effects caused by the acquisition of knowledge can be overcome only by the further acquisition of knowledge. We should not give up knowledge and go back to ignorance, just as we should not give up eating for fear of choking. . . . We can see that egoism is a negative thing that occurs at the beginning of the awakening of rationality and accompanies the overturning of traditional morals and customs. It can be corrected only when intellectuality is developed further and the great self is thus discovered. (Zhang, 1979, p. 433)

Once a person's intellectual level is raised and rationality can lead his emotions, he will be able to transform his desires and enlarge his self so that his desires will serve the common good and society at large. To live a creative and progressive life, one needs knowledge and fine intellect. As far as the function of knowledge in leading to a good life is concerned, Zhang's view seems similar to those of ancient Greek philosophers. "No one is intentionally doing wrong" is a well-known idea from Socrates. For Socrates, ignorance is the source of wrongdoing. To be morally good is the best for the individual. To further common good is also to further interests of the individual. Once one has understood this, one will desire to be morally good and to contribute to society. Such knowledge will transform one's lower desires, which will lead to immoral behavior and harm to society, into higher desires, which will lead to morality and common good. In general, it is clear that, for Zhang, the key to the ideal life is knowledge. In view of this philosophy of life, we can see why the theory of knowledge has been the most significant part of Zhang's philosophy.

Cultural Epistemology

Pluralistic epistemology reveals that knowledge is not an objective reflection of external things; and panstructuralism argues that there is no substance for us to know. To know is not to represent what is there outside us, but to construct or recreate the contents of knowledge in relation to the structures of the universe. On this account, the need for subjective elements in knowledge is obvious. How, then, are the subjective contents of knowledge decided? Zhang believed that, besides the common structure of human knowledge that is discussed in his pluralistic epistemology, culture plays a significant role in forming our knowledge, and that knowledge is culturally and socially determined. Therefore, to talk about knowledge, we must talk about culture. In this sense, the knowing mind is a collective mind. According to Zhang, epistemology in the past spoke only about the solitary mind, but with regard to knowledge, there is no solitary mind. We can have a new philosophy only when we have greatly reformed epistemology (Zhang, 1946a, p. 140).

To reform traditional epistemology, Zhang put forward a theory of knowledge that seeks to explain how cultural elements influence and shape our knowledge. It might be appropriate to call such a theory "Cultural Epistemology."

On the basis of examining how cultural products such as language affect the development of philosophy and science, Zhang held that to a certain degree different cultures have different ways of knowing. He used the differences between Chinese and Western philosophy as proofs of his cultural epistemology. To illustrate Zhang's theory about the cultural determination of knowledge, I shall examine Zhang's views on how philosophy, as a kind of human knowledge, is shaped by culture and discuss his comparative studies of Chinese and Western philosophy.

In his discussion of the nature of philosophy, Zhang held that philosophy is concerned with our highest concepts, that is the concepts that possess the greatest function of control and regulation (Zhang, 1946a, p. 68). Like all concepts, however, these highest concepts neither correspond to any objective reality nor refer to anything in the external world. Philosophy is not about truths that correspond to reality but is about ideals which express human wishes and satisfy human emotions. "All philosophers are those who passionately seek for ideals but are not scholars of truth" (Zhang, 1946a, p. 74). Philosophical knowledge is valuable and meaningful without the need or the possibility of being verified (Zhang, 1946a, p. 74). Philosophy is not meaningless, because it has the cultural function of expressing human wishes and satisfying human emotions. For instance, the reality of inequality leads us to desire equality. Our knowledge of social equality and justice expresses our wish for equality. In the same way, each philosophical issue is in the end a cultural issue (Zhang, 1946a, p. 77). Because philosophy is a matter of culture and culture is historical, therefore, philosophy is historical. Because of this understanding of philosophy, Zhang agreed neither with those who held that metaphysics can find final truth nor with logical positivists who held that metaphysics is meaningless:

> Those who oppose metaphysics and think that it is nonsense are in error, but those who think that metaphysics may find the ultimate truth independent of human emotions are also in error. Rather, what metaphysics expresses is ideal, and the ideal is the expression of human wishes. Because human beings feel empty, they have the desire to "unite with the universe." Since we have wishes or desires, we will make efforts. Culture is formed because of our desires and wishes. It originates from our dissatisfaction, not from the faithful representation of the world. All philosophical theories have their cultural functions and positions, but are not meaningless. (Zhang, 1946a, p. 74)

On the basis of this understanding of philosophy, Zhang argued that all existing philosophies actually conclude with moral issues and outlooks on life. In Western philosophy, epistemology, cosmology, and ontology are preludes to a philosophy of life. From Plato, Aristotle, and Epicurus to Hume, Kant, and Hegel, Western philosophers all constructed their philosophies in this way (Zhang, 1946a, pp. 74–5). This is inevitable because philosophy is about human ideals. For this reason, Zhang claimed that all Western metaphysics is essentially sociopolitical in nature and that "the pure theoretical aspect of Western philosophy is nothing but a disguised form of sociopolitical thought" (Zhang, 1959, p. 321). In Chinese philosophy, the philosophy of life is directly placed first, with other philosophical discussion clearly used to serve the philosophy of life. Regardless of this difference in structure, both Western and Chinese philosophy are expressions of human ideals and ultimately concern issues of human life. In spite of this similarity of function, philosophy in different cultures is constructed and developed differently, and the differences between Chinese and Western philosophy demonstrate how knowledge is culturally determined.

According to Zhang, there are several important differences between Chinese and Western philosophy. First, unlike Western philosophy, Chinese philosophy gives primacy to issues of human life. In this sense, Zhang says that Chinese philosophy is direct (Zhang, 1946a, p. 75).

> Strictly speaking, in China there is not "pure philosophy," but "practical philosophy." . . . It seems to the Chinese that we do not need metaphysics if it is irrelevant to human life. It is not necessary to study Nature either if it has nothing to do with our life. Therefore, Chinese philosophy obviously puts issues of human life first and makes people know that other issues originate from issues of human life. (Zhang, 1946a, p. 75)

Zhang argued that Western philosophy could not do the same because Western culture is centered on intellect or reason. To propose an ideal as desirable in a culture that regards intellect as the core of the good life, one must justify one's proposal in terms of theoretical knowledge about the universe. But Chinese culture is centered on morality. Since Chinese people are used to talking about human life, character, and behavior directly, they do not feel it necessary to justify their beliefs about human life by appealing to cosmology (Zhang, 1946a, p. 75). Therefore, there is no need in Chinese philosophy to justify views of how to live in the way that is required in Western philosophy. However, it might not be accurate to say that the Chinese do not feel that it is necessary to justify their beliefs about human life by cosmology. In Confucianism, especially in Neo-Confucianism, there is a cosmology that serves as a justification for the Confucian way of life. Actually, in Zhang's own writing, he also mentioned that cosmology is an inseparable part of Chinese thought and it is used to justify a certain kind of social order and way of life (Zhang, 1946a, p. 101). Perhaps, when he talked about the directness of Chinese philosophy, what he really tried to say was that the way Chinese philosophy appeals to cosmology to justify moral, social, and political beliefs is more direct than Western philosophy.

Secondly, Chinese philosophy, unlike Western philosophy, is not a philosophy of substance. Zhang believed that Chinese philosophy has no concept of substance and therefore no ontology. Chinese philosophy is concerned with possible changes and relations rather than with ultimate essences or substances. Although Chinese cosmology does contain the concept of the integral whole, this concept is not the same as substance in the sense of substratum or ultimate stuff. Rather, Chinese philosophy is concerned with how parts fit in the integral whole, and for this reason Chinese philosophy focuses discussion on the unity of humans and Heaven. Zhang regarded philosophy of this type as "function philosophy" which is focused on relations of different parts and functions of different parts in the whole:

> We need to know that the original ancestor of Chinese philosophy is the *Yijing* [the *Book of Changes*]. But the *Yijing* was merely used for divination. . . . Later on people gave it rational interpretations and made it philosophical. The reason why the *Yijing* could be rationally interpreted is that divination needs to use symbols. Each symbol represents one kind of possible way of change. When all changes in the universe are reduced to several possible kinds of change, many possible changes will be deduced from one kind of change. Then, a cosmology that concerns order and patterns of the universe is formed. . . . No matter whether Confucianism or Taoism, their views on the structure of cosmos do not go beyond those principles provided by the *Yijing*. . . . Because such philosophy concerns only possible changes and their relations and not the essence or ultimate being underlying them, and because the relations of various changes are determined by certain orders but are not connected by a cause–effect chain, it is not a so-called philosophy of substance and philosophy of causality in the Western philosophical sense. Roughly speaking, this kind of philosophy is similar to "function philosophy" in the West. But function philosophy occurred very late in the West. (Zhang, 1946a, p. 99)

Zhang did not make clear whose philosophy in the West is "function philosophy." He did mention that Plato's philosophy is similar to Chinese philosophy to a certain degree in the sense that Plato talked about society as a "functional whole" and held that different classes have different functions in society (Zhang, 1946a, p. 100). However, it is clear that Zhang did not think that there is much function philosophy in the West.

Zhang's denying Chinese philosophy a concept of substance and an ontology has been very controversial. His contemporaries such as Xiong Shili obviously objected to Zhang's conclusion. Even if we take Zhang's understanding of substance as the ultimate stuff or substratum, it is still hard to deny that there are some conceptions of substance in Chinese philosophical traditions. For example, in Daoism, the *dao* might refer to the ultimate source from which all things come to be. If the understanding of the *dao* is too disputable to be an evidence, the concept of *qi* (vital energy) that is widely accepted in Chinese philosophical traditions might be a better example. *Qi* as the ultimate stuff in the universe seems to fit the concept of substance well. Furthermore, to emphasize relations and functions of different parts in the universe does not have to exclude the concept of substance. Logically, it is compatible to believe that there is an ultimate substance and to investigate how various things that are produced by the ultimate substance are related at the same time. Perhaps, it is a great merit of Chinese philosophy to understand substance in such a dynamic way. As has been pointed out, there is holistic and process understanding of reality in Chinese philosophy. However, Zhang's comparison between Western and Chinese attitudes to substance and ontology is very insightful. Even if it is not totally correct to deny that there is the concept of substance and that there is ontology in Chinese philosophy, it might be worthy of notice that the concept of substance and the ontology based on it in Chinese philosophy are not exactly the same as those in Western philosophy and that Chinese philosophy concerns relations and changes much more than Western philosophy.

Zhang's claim that in Chinese philosophy there is no concept of substance and no ontology is based on his beliefs that there are certain differences between Chinese and Western languages and such differences have great impact on the formation of metaphysics. According to Zhang, although in the first place the way of thinking of a nation greatly affected the form of its language, once its language was developed it had great influence on its way of thinking. On the one hand, the structure of a language expresses the character and psychology of a nation, and on the other hand, it also determines the nation's way of thinking (Zhang, 1946a, p. 50). Since language is social, it must have some power to determine the direction of thought of individuals in society (Zhang, 1946a, p. 50). For example, Chinese grammar has had a certain impact on the way of Chinese philosophizing. Because the Chinese language does not mark differences between subject and predicate expressions through changes in suffix or in other ways, it lacks a clear distinction between subjects and predicates. Zhang argued that this grammatical feature has greatly influenced Chinese thought. Since the subject is not distinguished in the Chinese language, the Chinese do not have the concept of a subject; because the subject is not distinguished, the predicate is not distinguished either (Zhang, 1946a, p. 160). Also, the Chinese language often omits the subject of a sentence, unlike Western languages in which the omission of the subject of a sentence is an exception. This feature of Chinese gives the impression that the subject is dispensable (Zhang, 1946a, p. 180). Another difference is that Chinese lacks the equivalent of the expression "it." "*Zhe*" and "*ci*" in Chinese are equivalent to "this," but not of "it." "It" is an indefinite pronoun, but "this" is not. Chinese lacks sentences of the form "It is." "It is" expresses only the existence of something and not its attributes, and this separation of existence from attributes is a basic condition for forming the concept of substance (Zhang, 1946a, p. 180). Most important is the lack in Chinese of an equivalent of the expression "to be" in Western languages. "To be" implies "to exist" and being is existence. "*Shi*" ("is") in spoken Chinese does not imply "to exist." Ancient Chinese had the expressions "*you*" ("to have") and "*cheng*" ("to become") but not the equivalent of "to be" (Zhang, 1946a, p. 180). Since Chinese lacks an expression for "to be," it has difficulty in forming the subject–predicate propositions of standard logic.

For all of these reasons, Chinese thought did not develop the concepts of subject and substance. The philosophical concept of substance is derived from the logical subject (Zhang, 1946a, p. 161). The subject–predicate form implies that there is a substance that has attributes (Zhang, 1946a, p. 179). Western philosophy seeks substance because there must be a subject in Western logic, and the importance of the subject in Western logic is derived from the structure of Western languages (Zhang, 1946a, p. 162). Because the structure of the Chinese language does not emphasize the subject and does not have sentences of the subject–predicate form, Chinese thought cannot derive substance from the subject and lacks the fundamental metaphysical concept of being as being.

Also because of differences between Chinese and Western languages, the concept of category in the Aristotelian sense is not well developed in Chinese philosophy. Aristotle's ten categories are drawn completely from Greek grammatical forms. Basically, Western philosophy is founded on the concept of categories as the forms that are attached to an object. This relation between form and object can easily be expressed by changes in suffix. Since the Chinese language lacks change in suffix, the concept of category (as predicate) is hard to form (Zhang, 1946a, pp. 166–7).

Undoubtedly, Zhang's analyses on the differences between Chinese and Greek language and their impact on Chinese and Greek philosophical thinking are very insightful and valuable. However, to what degree the way of philosophical thinking is affected by the way of language might be subject to controversy. Will such differences make Chinese philosophy cancel ontology altogether? Or will they just make Chinese philosophy propose a different understanding of ultimate reality from Western philosophy? Given the differences between Chinese and Western language, Chinese and Westerners might not necessarily differ from each other dramatically in metaphysical speculation. Even if there are not exact equivalents of "being" and "substance" in Chinese language, that does not entail that Chinese philosophy is not concerned with underlying reality and ultimate stuff. Chinese philosophers might have their own way to express their metaphysical thinking. If the issue of "being" could be understood as one of substance, and substance understood as the ultimate stuff or underlying reality, it seems that at least some Chinese philosophers have been concerned with "being." For example, *qi*, *dao*, and *li* might be regarded as their expressions of the ultimate stuff or underlying reality. Nevertheless, whether there is a philosophy of "being" in the Chinese tradition is beyond the scope of this chapter. What needs to be pointed out here is just that this issue might not be answered simply by examining the structure of Chinese language. But, this does not deny that there are interactions between philosophy and language, as Zhang observed.

The third difference between Chinese philosophy and Western philosophy, according to Zhang, is that Chinese philosophy is not much concerned with the problem of knowledge. Because it lacks a concept of substance, Chinese philosophy tends toward phenomenalism: there is no need to investigate whether substance underlies all changes in the universe because we will know the truth about the universe by knowing how parts in the universe are related to each other. Because it assumes phenomenalism, Chinese philosophy lacks epistemological thought. Because it is not compelled to pursue ultimate substance, Chinese philosophy lacks a distinction between appearance and reality, and, hence, the problem of knowledge does not arise. Epistemology presupposes that there is a difference between what the subject perceives and what the object really is. The problem of knowledge starts with doubt. If one supposes that what the subject sees is what the object really is, one will not have a problem of knowledge (Zhang, 1946a, p. 101).

Fourthly, Zhang held that Chinese and Western philosophy have different types of logical thinking and explained this difference as well by differences in Chinese and Western languages. He argued that Aristotelian logic is derived from the structure of Western languages rather than from universal rules of human reasoning. The object of logic is the rules of reasoning in language. Because reasoning must be expressed in language, there can be no rule of reasoning without language, and the expression of reasoning must be implicitly affected by the form of language. Therefore, different languages will influence the formation of logics of different forms. This will become very obvious if we compare the Chinese language and Chinese ways of thinking with Western languages and Aristotelian logic (Zhang, 1946a, p. 178). Chinese thought lacks Aristotelian logic, but that does not mean that Chinese thought lacks logic. Rather Chinese thought has a different type of logic.

What, then, according to Zhang, are the main differences between Aristotelian and Chinese logic?

The first difference is that Aristotelian logic is based on the subject–predicate form and the law of identity while Chinese logic is based on the correlation between opposites. Zhang who called the former "identity logic" (*tongyi lü mingxue*) and called the latter "correlation logic" (*xiangguan lü mingxue*) or the

"logic of correlative duality" (*liangyuan xiangguan lü mingxue*). He was probably the first scholar to attribute correlative thinking to Chinese philosophy.

According to Zhang, the subject–predicate form of propositions and the
law of identity (A = A or something cannot be what it is and fail to be what it
is at the same time) determined Western logical division, definition, syllogism,
and other logical forms. The law of identity is the foundation of Western logic,
and the law of noncontradiction (not both p and not-p) and the law of excluded
middle (for every proposition, either p or not-p) are simply corollaries of
the law of identity (Zhang, 1946a, p. 181). Because of the law of identity,
Aristotelian logic is structured by dichotomous logical division in terms of
contradiction: A and not A. This division is exclusive in principle, that is, it
leaves nothing outside its terms. An object x must be either A or not-A. In
contrast, a division of the form "A and B" allows something to be neither A
nor B, and this nonexclusive division is often found in Chinese logic. Logical
definition in Aristotelian logic is an equation in which a sign of identity is
placed between the definiendum and the definiens. For example, a triangle is
a plane figure bounded by three straight lines (Zhang, 1946a, p. 181). But
such a method of definition cannot often be found in Chinese logic.

Relational propositions are the basic propositions of Chinese logic, just
as subject–predicate propositions are the basic propositions of Western logic.
In Chinese logic, correlations between opposites, such as above and below or
front and back, are emphasized and taken as the starting point. In Chinese
thought, opposites represented by *yin* (negative principle or force) and *yang*
(positive principle or force) are not mutually exclusive; rather they are dependent on each other and complete each other. Therefore, in Chinese logic, meaning is often expressed in terms of opposition, such as "great form has no shape"
or "blessing produces misfortune." According to this logic, the meaning of
a word can be understood or clarified by looking at its opposite. For this
reason, definitions found in Western logic do not exist in Chinese logic. The
meaning of a word is not made clear by a definition but by contrasting it
with its opposite. For example, a "wife" is a "woman who has a husband,"
and a "husband" is a "man who has a wife" (Zhang, 1946a, pp. 182–3). This
is not a strict definition but an explanation in terms of a relation.

In Chinese philosophy, the rectification of names has been an important
issue, but the rectification of names is not to give definitions, but to name.
Naming establishes and regulates a correspondence between names and things,
but the purpose of doing so is political and social. The rectification of names
aims to help establish and enforce the status of people in society. To give a
definition is to describe a thing in terms of its attributes and presupposes the
concept of substance and the separation between a substance and its properties.
For Zhang, since there is no concept of substance in Chinese philosophy, there
is correspondingly no strict definition in Chinese logic. A further consequence
is that Chinese philosophy lacks the Aristotelian concept of *genus*. To classify

things into *genera*, one needs a clear distinction between substance and attribute and a capacity to make a definition for each kind.

In addition to giving linguistic reasons to explain differences between Chinese and Western logic, Zhang investigated the connection between the political and social orientation of Chinese philosophy and the emergence of a Chinese logic of correlation. He believed that social phenomena, such as relations between men and women or relations between rulers and subjects, are always relative (Zhang, 1946a, p. 191). Through observation, one will naturally form the idea that all social phenomena are relative and that opposites are dependent upon each other. On this basis, he concluded that correlative thinking is a characteristic of politically and socially oriented thought (Zhang, 1946a, p. 191).

Another difference between Western and Chinese logic concerns their modes of inference. In contrast to syllogistic inference and its modern successors used in the Western logic of identity, Chinese logic uses analogy (Zhang, 1946a, p. 190). Analogical thinking is the characteristic form of inference in Chinese logic. In this sense, we may call Chinese logic the "logic of analogy" and call inference in Chinese logic "analogical argument." In Chinese philosophical writings such as the *Mencius*, there are numerous analogical claims. For example, "The goodness of human nature is like the downward tendency of water." This sort of inference is again related to the political and social orientation of Chinese philosophy. Analogical arguments are often inappropriate in scientific thought, but they are commonly of value in sociopolitical arguments. Analogical argument is one of the characteristics of political thought (Zhang, 1946a, p. 190).

Zhang clearly realized that underlying all these differences between Chinese philosophy and Western philosophy are differences in their larger cultural backgrounds. He believed that Western metaphysics and logic are based on religious culture, while Chinese cosmology and logic are founded on political culture (Zhang, 1946a, p. 189). It is because of their different cultural backgrounds that Western and Chinese philosophy do not raise the same questions.

> I think that Western philosophy is evolved from religion and therefore its questions are derived from religion. Chinese philosophy is the extension of political theories, therefore its questions originate from considerations about society and human life. (Zhang, 1946a, p. 101)

According to Zhang, in the West, the influence of religion has been very strong, and religion and politics have been sharply distinguished after the ancient Greek period. The pursuit of the supreme and ultimate substance in Western philosophy is clearly a reflection of Western religion. In China, as early as in the Spring and Autumn Period (770–476 B.C.), religious power started to weaken, and over time religion became less and less important in Chinese life. Eventually, religious influence almost vanished completely (Zhang, 1946a,

p. 189). Therefore, politics and not religion dominated ways of thinking. For this reason, Chinese philosophy is not occupied by the issue of the ultimate being but by the issues of relations and patterns of changes.

Chinese thought consists of four parts: cosmology, moral theory, social theory, and political theory. These four are united as a whole and serve social and political purposes in one way or another. Cosmology is used to analogize social organizations, social organizations determine individuals' positions in society, individuals' positions in society define their moral cultivation (Zhang, 1946a, p. 101). It seems that Chinese philosophy is derived from the need for the justification for a certain kind of social order. It is because of such a practical attitude that Chinese philosophy concerns itself much less with the nature of a thing than with how to deal with the thing. For example, the Chinese do not ask much about what Heaven really is in itself but very much want to know about the will of Heaven and its impact on their actions (Zhang, 1946a, p. 188). Zhang called this attitude the "how priority attitude." On the contrary, Western thought has a "what priority attitude" with which one asks "what a thing is" first before investigating "how to deal with it" (Zhang, 1946a, p. 189). Correlative logic and nonexclusive definition are related to the political background of Chinese philosophy, as identity logic, subject–predicate sentences, and the concepts of substance and category, are based on the religious background of the West (Zhang, 1946a, p. 189). As with some of Zhang's other ideas, this one is also very debatable. But it is certainly intriguing and thought provoking.

Zhang's comparative studies were focused on differences between Chinese and Western philosophy. According to him, it is more important in comparative studies to find the differences between the objects of comparison than to find the similarities between them. He did not regard finding similarities as the correct methodology of comparative studies. He argued that Chinese scholars did too much to find the similarities in comparative studies and wanted to open new directions which would distinguish his work from most comparative studies of his time (Zhang, 1946a, p. 157). He believed that one must respect one's own culture when doing comparative studies. "If a nation looks down on her own culture, she will lose self-confidence. . . . Actually, we certainly should know our shortcomings, but we should also see our merits" (Zhang, 1935. See Zhang Yaonan, 1995a, p. 409). By comparing Chinese and Western philosophy, Zhang concluded that their differences were indeed cultural differences but that they were not differences between the thought of ancient and modern times (Zhang, 1935. See Zhang Yaonan, 1995a, p. 408). Both have their own merits. Chinese and Western philosophy are compatible and potentially complementary. Western culture focuses on external beings but Chinese philosophy emphasizes inner cultivation. What Confucius taught has unique value for mankind (Zhang, 1935. See Zhang Yaonan, 1995a, p. 409). As a philosopher, Confucius is at least as great as Plato and Aristotle. For the Chinese, individuals' moral cultivation, as a workable political system, is indispensable for national rejuvenation. The problem in contemporary China is not that Confucian philosophy is wrong in itself but that it has not been really practiced much. If more Chinese practiced Confucianism, China would have a great hope of being a strong country again (Zhang, 1935. See Zhang Yaonan, 1995a, p. 413).

Zhang's comparative studies of Chinese and Western philosophy helped to establish his cultural epistemology and to show how our cognition is influenced by culture. His studies also contributed much to comparative philosophy itself and provided many valuable insights into the differences between Chinese and Western philosophy. His investigations of the influence of Chinese language on the development of Chinese philosophy is highly influential pioneering work. His proposal that correlative thinking is a characteristic of Chinese philosophy and analogical argument is a Chinese mode of inference has been widely adopted by scholars in comparative philosophy (see Hall, 1992, pp. xi–xii; Graham, 1985, 1992). Although his name and contributions are relatively unknown in the West, Zhang does deserve recognition in Chinese and comparative philosophy.

Acknowledgment

I would like to thank the editors of the volume and other readers for their valuable comments and suggestions on earlier versions of this chapter. I am also grateful to Grand Valley State University for awarding me a faculty research grant in 2000 for revising the chapter.

Bibliography

There is no literature in English on Zhang Dongsun except a few translations of his works. However, the literature on him in Chinese grew significantly in the 1990s. The most complete biography of Zhang is Zuo Yuhe 1998: *Zhang Dongsun zhuan* 張東蓀傳 (a biography of Zhang Dongsun), Jinan: Shandong People's Press). The most recent and detailed studies on Zhang's philosophy are Zhang Yaonan 1995a, *Zhang Dongsun zhishi lun yanju* 張東蓀知識論研究 (a study of Zhang Dongsun's theory of knowledge), Taipei: Hongye Wenhua, and Zhang Yaonan 1998: *Zhang Dongsun*, Taipei: Dongda Tushu Gongsi Zuo.

Works by Zhang Dongsun

Zhang, Dongsun 1922: "*Du dongxi wenhua jiqi zhexue*" 讀東西文化及其哲學 ("read east–west culture and [philosophy"], *Xue Deng*, March 19, 1922
Zhang, Dongsun 1924: *Kexue yu zhexue* 科學與哲學 (science and philosophy), Shanghai: Commercial Press

Zhang, Dongsun 1926: "*You zili de wo dao zizhi de wo*" 由自利的我到自製的我 ("from the selfish self to the self-controlled self"), *Dongfang Zazhi* 東方雜誌, **23:3**

Zhang, Dongsun 1929a: *Rensheng guan ABC* 人生觀 ABC (outlook on life ABC), Shanghai: World's Books

Zhang, Dongsun 1929b: *Zhexue ABC* 哲學 ABC (philosophy ABC), Shanghai: World's Books

Zhang, Dongsun 1929c: *Xin zhexue luncong* 新哲學論叢 (essays on new philosophy), Shanghai: Commercial Press, reprinted Taipei: Tianhua Press, 1979

Zhang, Dongsun 1931: *Daode zhexue* 道德哲學 (moral philosophy), Shanghai: Zhonghua Shuju, reprinted Taipei: Lushan Press, 1972

Zhang, Dongsun 1932a: *Xiandai lunli xue* 現代倫理學 (contemporary ethics) Shanghai: Xinyuo Shudian

Zhang, Dongsun 1934a: *Renshi lun* 認識論 (epistemology), Shanghai: World's Books

Zhang, Dongsun 1934b: *Weiwu bianzheng fa lunzhan* 唯物辨證法論戰 (debates on materialistic dialectics), 2 vols, Beijing: Beiping Minyou Shudian

Zhang, Dongsun 1934c: *Jiazhi zhexue* 價值哲學 (philosophy of value), Shanghai: World's Books

Zhang, Dongsun 1935: "*Xiandai de zhongguo zenyang yao kongzi*" 現代的中國怎樣要孔子 (how contemporary China needs Confucius), *Zhengfeng Banyue Kan* 正風半月刊, **1:2** (Reprinted in Zhang, Yaonan 1995b)

Zhang, Dongsun 1937: "*Duoyuan renshi lun chongshu*" 多元認識論重述 ("the restatement of pluralistic epistemology") in *Zhang Jusheng Xiansheng Qishi Shengri Jinian Lunwen Ji* 張菊生先生七十生日紀念論文集 (essays in memory of the 70th birthday of Mr Zhang Jusheng), Shanghai: Commercial Press (An earlier version of the essay was published in *Dongfan Zazhi* 東方雜誌), **33:19**

Zhang, Dongsun 1946a: *Zhishi yu wenhua* 知識與文化 (knowledge and culture), Shanghai: Commercial Press

Zhang, Dongsun 1946b: *Lixiang yu shehui* 理想與社會 (ideal and society), Shanghai: Commercial Press

Zhang, Dongsun 1946c: *Lixiang yu minzhu* 理想與民主 (ideal and democracy), Shanghai: Commercial Press

Zhang, Dongsun 1948: *Minzhu zhuyi yu shehui zhuyi* 民主主義與社會主義 (democraticism and socialism), Shanghai, Guan chushi

Zhang, Dongsun 1972: *Daode zhexue* 道德哲學 (moral philosophy), Taipei: Lushan Press (first published in 1931. See Zhang 1931)

Zhang, Dongsun 1979: *Xin zhexue luncong* 新哲學論叢 (essays on new philosophy). Taipei: Tianhua Press (first published in 1929. See Zhang 1929c)

Zhang, Dongsun 1995: *Zhishi yu wenhua – Zhang Dongsun wenhua lunzhu jiyao* 知識與文化 — 張東蓀文化論著輯要 (selections of Zhang Dongsun's works on culture), Zhang, Yaonan, ed., Beijing: Chinese Broadcast and Television Press

Translations of Zhang Dongsun's works

Zhang, Dongsun 1932b: *Epistemological Pluralism* (duoyuan reshi lun), trans. C. Y. Chang, with the collaboration of Zhang Dongsun. Unpublished

Zhang, Dongsun 1959: "A Chinese philosopher's theory of knowledge," in S. I. Hayakawa, ed. *Our Language and Our World*, New York: Harper

Secondary sources

Chan, Wing-tsit 1963: "Chang Tung-sun's theory of knowledge" in Chan, ed., *A Source Book in Chinese Philosophy*, Princeton: Princeton University Press, pp. 743–50

Chen, Shaofeng 1997: *Zhongguo lunli xue shi* 中國倫理學史 (a history of Chinese ethics), Beijing: Peking University Press

Fang, Keli and Wang Qibing 1997: *Ershi shiji zhongguo zhexue* 二十世紀中國哲學 (Chinese philosophy in the twentieth century), vols 2a and 3a, Beijing: Huaxia Press

Fang, Songhua 1997: *Ershi shiji zhongguo zhexue yu wenhua* 二十世紀中國哲學與文化 (Chinese philosophy and culture in the twentieth century), Shanghai, Xuelin cubanshe

Graham, A. C. 1985: *Reason and Spontaneity*, London: Curzon Press

Graham, A. C. 1992: "Conceptual schemes and linguistic relativism in relation to Chinese", in *Unreason within Reason*, LaSalle: Open Court

Guo, Zhanbo 1935: *Jin wushi nian zhongguo sixiang shi* 近五十年中國思想史 (a history of the past fifty years of Chinese thought), Beijing: Beiping Renwen Shudian

Hall, David Lynn 1992: "Foreword," in Graham 1992

He, Lin 1947: *Dangdai zhongguo zhexue* 當代中國哲學 (contemporary Chinese philosophy), Chongqing: Shengli Chuban Gongsi

Jiang, Guozhu 1989: *Zhongguo renshi lunshi* 中國認識論論史 (the history of Chinese epistemology), Zhengzhou: Henan People's Press

Li, Zhenxia and Fu, Yunlong, eds, 1991: *Zhongguo xiandai zhexue renwu pingzhuan* 中國現代哲學人物評傳 (critical biography of contemporary Chinese philosophers), Beijing: Zhongyang Dangxiao Press

Pan, Fu'en, ed., 1992: *Zhongguo xueshu mingzhu tiyao: zhexue juan* 中國學術名著提要：哲學卷 (outlines of Chinese academic classics: philosophy volume), Shanghai: Fudan University Press

Tang, Yijie 1995: Preface to *Zhang Dongsun de duoyuan renshi lun* 張東蓀的多元認識論輯要. See Zhang, Yaonan 1995a

Xie, Fuya 1976: "*Huainan Zhang Dongsun xiansheng*" 懷念張東蓀先生 ("cherish the memory of Mr Zhang Dongsun"), *Zhuan ji wenxue* 傳記文學, **29:6**

Xiong, Shili 1936: "*Yu Zhang Dongsun lun xueshu*" 與張東蓀論學術 (discuss scholarship with Zhang Dongsun), *Zhongxin pinglun* 中西評論, **9**

Xu, Quanxing, Chen, Zhannan, and Song, Yixiu, eds, 1998: *Zhongguo xiandai zhexue shi* 中國現代哲學史 (a history of contemporary Chinese philosophy), Beijing: Peking University Press

Ye, Qing 1931: *Zhang Dongsun zhexue pipan* 張東蓀哲學批判 (a critique of Zhang Dongsun's philosophy), Shanghai: Xinken Shudian

Ye, Qing 1934: "*Zhang Dongsun daode zhexue pipan*" 張東蓀道德哲學批判 ("a critique of Zhang Dongsun's moral philosophy"), *Ershi Shiji* 二十世紀, **2:8**

Yu, Songhua 1947: "*Lun Zhang Dongsun*" 論張東蓀 ("on Zhang Dongsun"), *Renwu Zazhi* 人物雜誌, **2:6**

Zhan, Wenhu, ed., 1936: *Zhang Dongsun de duoyuan renshi lun jiqi pipan* 張東蓀的多元認識論及其批判 (Zhang Dongsun's pluralistic epistemology and its criticisms), Shanghai: World's Books

Zhang, Heng 1931–3, "*Ping Zhang Dongsun shi de zhexue guan*" 評張東蓀式的哲學觀 ("on Zhang Dongsun's type of philosophical outlook"), *Jiaoyu Shehui* 教育社會, 1:4–6

Zhang, Yaonan 1995a: *Zhang Dongsun zhishi lun yanju* 張東蓀知識論研究 (a study of Zhang Dongsun's theory of knowledge), Taipei: Hongye Wenhua

Zhang, Yaonan 1995b: Preface to Zhang, Dongsun 1995

Zhang, Yaonan 1998: *Zhang Dongsun* 張東蓀, Taipei: Dongda Tushu Gongsi

Zuo, Yuhe 1998: *Zhang Dongsun zhuan* 張東蓀傳 (a biography of Zhang Dongsun), Jinan: Shandong People's Press

Discussion Questions

1. Can there be truth if our concepts do not correspond to external reality?
2. Are the elements of epistemology mutually independent?
3. Do we need a cosmology to justify our theory of knowledge?
4. If we accept that knowledge is social, cultural, and historical, must we be relativists?
5. How should we assess the claim that differences in language influence differences in philosophy?
6. Is there a specifically Chinese logic?
7. Is our world a world of structures rather than a world of substances?
8. Is there a harmony of structures?
9. What justifies placing different particulars under the same concept?
10. Is the cross-cultural validity of science compatible with Zhang Dongsun's account of human subjectivity?

4

Hu Shi's Enlightenment Philosophy

Hu Xinhe

Hu Shi had immense influence among his contemporaries and has growing importance in current intellectual discussions. Although his academic work has attracted conflicting evaluations, commentators agree that Hu Shi was a "central figure in the history of Chinese academic thought in the twentieth century" (Yu, 1984). His influence in literature, history, philosophy, and political thought was a product of his times as well as a creation of his innovative intellect.

Hu was born in 1891 as the youngest son of a low-ranking official. His father died four years later, and his mother "staked all her hope" on his education. Hu became intensely aware of the differences between the "long dead classical language" and the "living spoken language." In addition to his classical studies, he devoured every *peihua* (spoken language) novel in his village. In 1904, Hu went to Shanghai, where he studied the Western-style "new education" and read introductions to Western thinkers and translations of their works. In Peking, he passed the examination for the American Boxer Indemnity Scholarship and studied abroad 1910–17.

In America, Hu learned about the experimentalist pragmatism of John Dewey that shaped his own philosophy throughout his life. Hu also established the foundations of his political ideas and practice through studying Western political doctrines and institutions and by participating in student political activities. His doctoral dissertation, later published as *The Development of Logical Method in Ancient China*, initiated modern research on the history of Chinese philosophy and provided the framework for his own later academic works. His paper "Tentative proposals for the improvement of literature" led to the vernacular literary revolution in China.

In America, after three semesters as an agricultural student at Cornell University, Hu transferred to philosophy at Cornell University, in part because the 1911 Revolution in China greatly enhanced his interest in the history of politics. After completing his BA and a year of graduate studies at Cornell, Hu moved to Columbia University to study Dewey's philosophy.

After completing his doctorate in 1917 under Dewey's guidance, Hu returned to China to become Professor of Chinese and Western Philosophy at Peking National University. The period from 1917 to 1937 was the most creative time in Hu Shi's academic life. Together with Chen Duxiu and Cai Yuanpei, Hu promoted the literary revolution that he initiated. This soon grew into the New Culture Movement, a profoundly significant moderniz-ing movement that aimed to propagate new knowledge and new thought to promote social progress. It advocated the formation of a new literature against decayed classical literature, the development of a new morality against traditional morality, and the creation of a new pattern of culture to overcome the national cultural crisis in the face of foreign aggression. Hu practiced the new vernacular literature himself by writing poems, plays, and translations. He also advocated basic human rights, Ibsenism, and sound individualism, by which he meant that each person should liberate himself from the suffocating traditional ethical codes of China in order to promote political innovation and New Culture. All of this work won him fame as an Enlightenment thinker and teacher.

Hu also introduced pragmatism, experimentalism, and scientific research methodology in China, propounding the "attitude of the scientific laboratory," the "attitude of history," and the skeptical spirit of "the transvaluation of all values." Interest in experimentalism was stimulated by John Dewey's successful lecture tour in China. Hu's version of this philosophy was fundamental to the May Fourth Movement's program of liberating thought in China.

A third aspect of Hu's academic achievements in history, literature, and philosophy is represented by *An Outline of the History of Chinese Philosophy*, which used critical methods and modern ideas of history to establish a new paradigm of the history of Chinese philosophy. His writings also included much textual research and evidential investigation regarding Chinese classical novels, the history of Chinese literature, and the history of Chinese Buddhism. Through these works, Hu became one of the most influential leaders of Chinese thought and culture in the 1920s and 1930s.

Hu's intellectual pre-eminence reached a peak in the mid-1930s, after which violent changes at home and abroad interrupted his academic career. Although he was not a member of the Nationalist Party, he was appointed to important posts in foreign affairs in Europe and America, including the Chinese ambassadorship to the United States (1938–42). He later became President of Peking University (1946–8) and President of the Central Academy of Science in Taiwan (1958–62), but he neither recovered his leading role in Chinese intellectual life nor added significantly to his corpus of path-breaking academic work. In this period, his academic work centered on textual study of *Shui Jing Zhu* (Commentary on Water Cannon).

Literary Revolution and its Meaning

Literary revolution was the first step in China of the New Culture Movement, and Hu took the first step in literary revolution. His 1916 paper "Tentative proposals for the improvement of literature" in the journal *New Youth* stimulated an upsurge of debate on language and literature. Chen Duxiu collaborated with Hu in promoting the New Culture Movement. Hu's doctrine of literary revolution can be summed-up in four points:

1. Speak only if you have something to say,
2. Say what you have to say, and say it as it is said (in *peihua*),
3. Speak your own language, not the language of others, and
4. Speak the language of your own time. ("On a constructive literary revolution," Hu, 1921, p. 79)

Hu's justification for promoting the vernacular mainly lay in its historical timeliness. He held that each age has its own living literature, with a vitality in expressing human sentiments and thoughts that a rigid dead language cannot produce.

The theory of evolution and the Social-Darwinist doctrine of survival of the fittest played an important role in Hu's theory of literary revolution. Hu sought literary revolution to provide a national language that would make China fit for survival by breaching the wall of immobility in China and providing a tool for further social reform. Hu published papers on each major literary genre and wrote novels, plays, and poetry according to his principles.

The vernacular literary revolution took only four years to achieve a central aim. In 1920, the government in Peking ordered replacing classical language textbooks with vernacular ones in primary school. Prior to this reform, the literature of China was mainly restricted to the privileged literati, but now the paradigm of literature shifted to popular vernacular works. By developing a new mode of literary creation and a new manner of thinking, the literary revolution undermined institutions that maintained old and obstructive traditions and encouraged a critical attitude to the whole range of traditional values.

The real significance of the new thought lies simply in a new attitude. This attitude could be called "the critical attitude." In simple language, the critical attitude can be summarized as the application to all things of a fresh judgment as to whether or not they are good. In more detailed terms, the critical attitude comprises several specific demands:

1. Concerning institutions and customs handed down to us by habit we must ask: "Do these institutions retain at present any value to justify their existence?"

2. Concerning the sage precepts handed down to us by the ancients we must ask: "In the present day, does this phrase still hold true?"
3. Concerning [standards of] conduct and beliefs commonly acknowledged, in a muddled way, by society we must ask: "Must something be right because it is generally held to be so by all? If others do this, must I also do this? Can it be that there is no other way of acting that is better than this, more reasonable, more beneficial?"

Nietzsche said the current time is a time of "transvaluation of all values." These words: "Transvaluation of all values" are the best interpretation of the critical attitude." ("The meaning of the new thought," Hu, 1919, in 1921, p. 1023)

Hu praised Nietzsche's "fearless criticism" of traditional morals and the "destructive merit" inherent in his philosophy, but he did not restrict the critical attitude to its use against traditional prejudices. It would "guard against the uncritical acceptance of any idea, regardless of its origin" (Hu, 1921, p. 1031).

The critical attitude for Hu established the rational court in which each person should judge and accept or reject any idea. It set an intellectual standard that opposed the traditions of intellectual dogmatism and servility. According to Hu, the new thought, like the Copernican revolution in the West, constituted a fundamental change of the general pattern of Chinese thinking (Hu, 1998, I, p. 415).

As the spirit of the new thought, "the critical attitude really expresses two trends. One is to discuss a variety of social, political, religious and literary problems. The other is to introduce new thought, new doctrines, new literature and new beliefs from the West" ("The meaning of the new thought," Hu, 1998). Hu urged the Chinese people to "study problems" because in the course of radical changes in Chinese society, many customs and institutions that never caused trouble in the past grew unsuited to the requirements of the time. They had become the source of difficulties derived from Confucian tradition and the classical literary language. It was necessary to search for the crux of these problems and for the methods of resolving them in order to establish institutions that would be suitable for current requirements. Chinese society should "import theories" because Chinese modernization lacked not only advanced industry and technology, but also new ideas and new doctrines. China should draw lessons from modern thought in the West to resolve its difficulties. It should use the critical attitude to test the inheritance of traditional Chinese doctrines, rather than pursuing a policy of "blind following" and "conformity" to them. This critical evaluation could "systematize the national heritage" and reconstruct the civilization of China ("The meaning of the new thought," Hu, 1998, I, pp. 551–8). For Hu, studying problems, importing theories, systematizing the national heritage, and reconstructing civilization constituted the very meaning of the New Culture Movement and provided the program that he followed throughout his career.

The Naturalistic Conception of the Universe and the Experimentalist Method

The critical attitude at the core of Hu's philosophy was based on both his own skepticism and imported theories. The contribution of imported theories to the critical attitude began with his reading of Huxley and others in Shanghai, but mainly developed during his studies in America. For Chinese intellectuals at that time, science was the most convincing and acceptable achievement of Western civilization. On the basis of this common respect for science and the naturalistic inclination that he drew from his early education, Hu formulated his naturalistic conception of life and the universe. He summarized this "new credo" in his preface to *Kexue yu renshengguan* Shanghai, 1923, a volume of papers from the famous 1923 debate on science and metaphysics:

1. On the basis of our knowledge of astronomy and physics, we should recognize that the world of space is infinitely large.
2. On the basis of our geological and paleontological knowledge, we should recognize that the universe extends over infinite time.
3. On the basis of all our verifiable scientific knowledge, we should recognize that the universe and everything in it follow natural laws of movement and change. So that is "natural" in the Chinese sense of "being so of itself" and there is no need for the concept of a supernatural Ruler or Creator.
4. On the basis of the biological sciences, we should recognize the terrific wastefulness and brutality in the struggle for existence in the biological world, and consequently the untenability of the hypothesis of a benevolent Ruler.
5. On the basis of the biological, physiological, and psychological sciences, we should recognize that man is only one species in the animal kingdom and differs from the other species only in degree, but not in kind.
6. On the basis of the knowledge derived from anthropology, sociology, and the biological sciences, we should understand the history and causes of the evolution of living organisms and of human society.
7. On the basis of the biological and psychological sciences, we should recognize that all psychological phenomena could be explained through the law of causality.
8. On the basis of biological and historical knowledge, we should recognize that morality and religion are subject to change, and that the causes of such change can be scientifically studied.
9. On the basis of our newer knowledge of physics and chemistry, we should recognize that matter is full of motion and is not static.
10. On the basis of biological, sociological and historical knowledge, we should recognize that the individual self is subject to death and decay. But the sum total of individual achievement, for better or for worse, lives on in the immortality of the Larger Self. That to live for the sake of the species and posterity is religion of the highest kind; and that those religions that seek a future life either in Heaven or in the Pure Land, are selfish religions.

This new credo is a hypothesis founded on the generally accepted scientific knowledge of the last two or three hundred years. To avoid unnecessary controversy, I propose to call it, not "a scientific credo," but merely "the Naturalistic Conception of Life and the Universe."

In this naturalistic universe, in this universe of infinite space and time, man, the two-handed animal whose average height is about five and a half feet and whose age rarely exceeds a hundred years, is indeed a mere infinitesimal microbe. In this naturalistic universe, where every motion in the heavens has its regular course and every change follows laws of nature, where causality governs man's life and the struggle for existence spurs his activities – in such a universe man has very little freedom indeed. Yet this tiny animal with two hands has his proper place and worth in that world of infinite magnitude. Making good use of his hands and a large brain, he has actually succeeded in making a number of tools, thinking out ways and means, and creating his own civilization. He has not only domesticated the wild animals, but also studied and discovered a considerable number of the secrets and laws of nature. By means of which he has become a master of the natural forces and is now ordering electricity to drive his carriage and ether to deliver his messages.

The increase in his knowledge has extended his power, but it has also widened his vision and elevated his imagination. . . . Even the absolute universality of the law of causality does not necessarily limit his freedom because the law of causality not only enables him to explain the past and predict the future, but also encourages him to use his intelligence to create new causes and attain new results. Even the apparent cruelty in the struggle for existence does not necessarily make him a hardened brute. On the contrary, it may intensify his sympathy for his fellow man, make him believe more firmly in the necessity of cooperation, and convince him of the importance of conscious human endeavor as the only means of reducing the brutality and wastefulness of the natural struggle. In short, this naturalistic conception of the universe and life is not necessarily devoid of beauty, of poetry, of moral responsibility, and of the fullest opportunity for the exercise of the creative intelligence of man. (Hu, *Science and Our Philosophy of Life*, preface; see also Hu, 1931, pp. 260–3)

This long passage is the best description of Hu's "New Conception of Life" and his tendency towards scientism. These features reflected the view of modern Chinese intellectuals of the time that science was the most significant achievement of Western civilization and their belief that science could serve as the most rationally acceptable substitute for the discredited traditional feudal ethical codes and beliefs of China. This context can also partially explain why Hu was fascinated by Dewey's experimentalist doctrine and became its powerful advocate. According to Hu, the essence of science lies in its method: "science itself is nothing but a method, an attitude, a spirit" ("Manuscript," see Yu, 1984, p. 41). He held that "experimentalism" was a better name for this doctrine than "pragmatism" since:

though it paid attention to practical effects too, it could better point out that this philosophy paid most attention to experimental method. Experimental method is the very method that scientists employ in the laboratory. Peirce, the founder of this philosophical school, often said that his new philosophy is nothing but "the laboratory attitude of mind."

Experimentalism never admits that what we call the "truth" is the eternal truth; it admits only that all "truth" is an application of an hypothesis; the truth or not of the hypothesis depends on whether it could cause the effects that it should do. That is "the laboratory attitude of mind." The other scientific theory having an essential relation to experimentalism was Darwin's theory of evolution, which told us that species are not invariant. Not only are species changeable, but the truth is as well. A change of species is the result of adaptation to the environment; the truth is no more than one sort of tool to deal with the environment; when the environment changes, a change of truth would follow. Therefore, the feudal ethical codes that were once recognized as eternal truths, such as the Three Bonds and the Five Relationships, had now ceased to be true. Applying the concept of evolution to philosophy resulted in "the genetic method" by which it asks: how does a matter originate? Where did it come from? How did it evolve to its present state? That is a brief discussion of the two essential concepts of experimentalism: the first is the laboratory attitude of mind, the second is the genetic method. These two basic concepts are both the result of nineteenth-century science. So we could say that experimentalism is no more than the application of scientific method in philosophy. ("Experimentalism," Hu, 1998, II, pp. 208–13)

Hu's experimentalism was an important expression of his tendency of scientism, through which he took scientific method to be all-powerful in every field, including the study of society and history. His scientism led him to explore Dewey's philosophy and to accept it. What, however, was Hu's understanding of Dewey's philosophy? How, according to Hu, could this powerful scientific method be used to solve concrete problems? Hu answered in terms of Dewey's "five-step method," a formal procedure to guide thought:

The basic conception of Dewey's philosophy is: "the intellectual idea is the tool of man's response to his environment." The intellectual idea is the essential tool of human life, but not the luxurious toy of the philosopher. In one word, the fundamental purpose of Dewey's philosophy is how to make man cultivate "Creative Intelligence" and make him respond to his environment in a satisfying way. Here, ideas have the function of inferring other things or truths on the basis of known things, leading to a method that can be divided into five steps: (1) Finding a puzzling situation. (2) Defining and locating the puzzle. (3) Providing a variety of plans for resolving [the puzzle]. (4) Deciding which plan is capable of resolving the puzzle. (5) Verifying or falsifying this resolution. ("Experimentalism," Hu, 1998, II, pp. 232–3)

Hu summarized this approach in three principles:

1. Proceeding from concrete facts or situations,
2. Treating all doctrines, ideals, or knowledge as hypotheses to be proved and not as unalterable principles, and
3. Testing all doctrines and ideals by practice, with experiment as the only touchstone of truth. ("Mr. Dewey and China," Hu, 1998, II, pp. 533–7)

In a further simplification, Hu called for "bold assumption, careful verification" as a scientific method as well as a universal method to resolve practical social problems. Finding a method to cope with the problems of China was of central importance to Hu. This was his original motive for "importing theories" and a powerful ground for his fascination with Dewey's philosophy.

Hu was clearly conscious of the needs of his country and his responsibility to respond to them. In his diary, he wrote that his study should be "a preparation for being the teacher of the national population" (Hu, 1947). He held that "the urgent need of our country nowadays is not novel theories or advanced philosophies, but the methods of using inquiry, learning, discussing problems, surveying situations and managing the country" (Hu, 1947). Even before his conversion to Dewey's doctrine, he had written: "from my point of view, there are three methods which are the elixir of life for bringing the dying back to life: (1) Inductive method; (2) Historical perspective; (3) Evolutionary conception" (see Yu, 1984, pp. 18, 37). Hu's concern for methodology and practical application provided another motive for favoring experimentalism. Marx once said: "What philosophers have done is only to explain the world in different ways. But the problem is to change the world" (Marx and Engels, 1976, p. 8). Other philosophers have also taken practical relevance as a criterion of those theories that could be accepted universally. It was the practical quality of Dewey's philosophy, expressed in his claims that ideas are plans of action and tools of response to the environment and that philosophy should focus on devising social projects, that greatly influenced Chinese intellectuals. Their response partly reflected the needs of China as it entered the modern world but was also linked to the traditional Chinese doctrine that there is a unity of knowing and doing.

History of Chinese Philosophy and Systematizing the National Heritage

Hu's application of experimentalist method to the history of Chinese philosophy embodied his program of systematizing the national heritage. From the beginning of his career, Hu held that the reconstruction of civilization must be based on systematizing the national heritage. Confucianism was still dominant in academic thought and politics and its method of research remained dogmatic. Hu asked how to displace this dominance, how to use the critical attitude in research regarding Chinese philosophy to achieve a transvaluation of all values, and how to use other intellectual resources in the history of philosophy to lay a foundation for the New Culture:

> The real problem, therefore, may be restated thus: How can we best assimilate modern civilization in such a manner as to make it congenial and congruous and continuous with the civilization of our own making? This larger problem presents itself in every phase of the great conflict between the old civilization and the new. In fact, in literature, in politics, and in social life in general, the underlying problem is fundamentally the same. The solution of this great problem, as far as I can see, will depend solely on the foresight and the sense of historical continuity of the intellectual leaders of New China and on the tact and skill with which they can successfully connect the best in modern civilization with the best in our own civilization. For our present purpose the more specific problem is: Where can we find a congenial stock with which we may organically link the thought-systems of modern Europe and America, so that we may further build up our own science and philosophy on the new foundation of an internal assimilation of the old and the new? ("Introduction," Hu, 1922b, p. 7)

Hu began with the problem of philosophical method, because he held that "Philosophy is conditioned by its method and that the development of philosophy is dependent upon the development of logical method" ("Introduction," 1922b, p. 1). What Chinese philosophy lacked and needed to assimilate from Western learning was a proper method. As Yu Yingshi argued:

> There is a very obvious tendency of reductionism in Hu's ideas. He reduced all academic thought, even the whole of culture, to method. . . . What he attached importance to was always the method, the attitude and the spirit that underlay a school of learning, but not its specific content. Under the great influence of evolutionary theory and of experimentalist method, he held that the specific contents of all doctrines embraced the background, the historical situation and the personality of the author and were incapable of having permanent and universal validity. But methods – especially scientific methods that are verified by long-term use – have their own objective independence that is not open to the variety of subjective, specific factors of the author himself. . . . It is evident that he took all doctrines as "hypotheses," as "corroborated materials," as "tools" of ideas, meaning that doctrines could show their value only after being reduced to methods. (Yu Yingshi, 1984, pp. 40–1)

Thus, "the applications of specific propositions are finite, while the applications of methods are infinite" ("Mr Dewey and China," Hu, 1998, II, p. 280). The history of philosophy is the history of changes in philosophical method and we could retrospectively analyze the historical development of Chinese philosophy by an objective evaluation of the methods of each doctrine.

Another experimentalist influence on Hu's account of Chinese philosophy concerned the fundamental question of the selection of materials. In his preface to Hu's *Outline of the History of Chinese Philosophy*, Cai Yuanpei (Hu, 1919) pointed out that the choice of materials was of immense difficulty in writing a history of ancient Chinese philosophy. From ancient times, authentic and inauthentic materials were confused and even authentic materials contained many mistakes. In dealing with such materials, Hu's approach had the advantages of brevity and relevance. It would be difficult to extricate a purely philosophical system from the mass of half-mythic and half-political historical materials before Laozi and Confucius, especially if one enforced the experimentalist demand for careful verification. Therefore, Hu rejected consideration of early materials that he could not assess and began his account with the definite and well-authenticated texts of Laozi and Confucius. This procedure shocked students who expected to hear lectures starting from the very beginning of the legendary period (Gu Ji-gang, 1926, p. 36). Hu had sound training both in the textual and evidential researches of Han Learning and in the methods of research used in the history of Western philosophy. He paid detailed attention to materials that were available and could be checked. In the introduction to his *Outline*, Hu (1919) considered the research methods that could be used in writing the history of Western philosophy and gave detailed attention to the methods of dealing with historical materials. He considered what comprised historical material for the history of philosophy and what constituted its proper examination. He investigated how to use methods, such as textual criticism, the explanation of terms, and the threading together of the text, to place materials in order and claimed that such scholarly work provided the basis for writing the history of philosophy. This sophisticated account of methodology convinced his students that his selection of materials was coherent and that his ideas and methods could provide a sound new perspective from which to examine and systematize their knowledge. They were also convinced that Hu was an able philosopher.

The most fundamental feature of Hu's approach to research in the history of Chinese philosophy is what Cai called his "equal perspective," which broke down the traditional dominance of the Confucian classics by employing modern methods and perspectives to examine basic problems in the history of Chinese philosophy. At least since the Han dynasty, the Confucian school was thought of as superior to the Daoist, Mohist, and other schools. The dogmatic preference for the Confucian classics prevented scholars from giving just and objective appreciation to the doctrines of other schools. In contrast, Hu outlined a new model for the history of philosophy. He first defined philosophy: "Every learning that studies the crucial problems of life and searches for a radical resolution of them is philosophy" (Hu, 1919). To support his view, he gave examples of such problems, which separately belong to cosmology, theory of knowledge, ethics, philosophy of education, political philosophy, and philosophy of religion. He claimed that the history of philosophy comprised a chronological and systematic record of all the methods offered by different philosophers for studying and resolving these and similar problems. The history of philosophy should aim to:

> (1) realize the evolutionary clue to understanding ancient and modern thought; (2) search for the cause of these evolutions; and (3) judge the value of each doctrine. These judgments should be objective, that means they should clarify three aspects of the effects of each doctrine: its influences on thought at the same time and at later times; its influences on customs and politics; and its influences on shaping personalities. ("Introduction," Hu, 1919, also to be found in Hu, 1998, pp. 164–5)

By establishing these goals and setting up these criteria, Hu placed Confucian and non-Confucian doctrines in equal positions that allowed him to evaluate doctrines objectively and to derive conclusions that would enable modern Western ideas to enter Chinese thought:

> My own surmise of the problem is somewhat like this. Confucianism has long outlived its vitality. The new schools of Sung and Ming rejuvenated the long-dead Confucianism by reading into it two logical methods that never belonged to it. These two methods are: the theory of investigating into the reason in everything for the purpose of extending one's knowledge to the utmost, which is the method of the Sung school; and the theory of intuitive knowledge, which is the method of the school of Wang Yang-ming. While fully recognizing the merits of the philosophy of Wang Yang-ming, I cannot but think that his logical theory is wholly incompatible with the spirit and procedure of science. The Sung philosophers were right in their interpretation of the doctrine of "investigating into things." But their logical method was rendered fruitless (1) by the lack of an experimental procedure, (2) by its failure to recognize the active and directing role played by the mind in the investigating of things, and (3) most unfortunate of all, by its construction of "things" to mean "affairs." Aside from these two schools, Confucianism is long dead. I am firmly of the opinion that the future of Chinese philosophy depends upon its emancipation from the moralistic and rationalistic fetters of Confucianism. This emancipation cannot be accomplished by any wholesale importation of occidental philosophies alone. It can be achieved only by putting Confucianism back into its proper place; that is, by restoring it to its historical background. Confucianism was once only one of the many rival systems flourishing in Ancient China. The dethronement of Confucianism, therefore, will be assured when it is regarded not as the solitary source of spiritual, moral, and philosophical authority, but merely as one star in a great galaxy of philosophical luminaries. In other words, the future of Chinese philosophy would seem to depend much on the revival of those great philosophical schools that once flourished side by side with the school of Confucius in Ancient China. . . . For my own part, I believe that the revival of the non-Confucian schools is absolutely necessary because it is in these schools that

we may hope to find the congenial soil in which to transplant the best products of occidental philosophy and science. This is especially true with regard to the problem of methodology. The emphasis on experience as against dogmatism and rationalism, the highly developed scientific method in all its phases of operation, and the historical or evolutionary view of truth and morality, – these, which I consider as the most important contributions of modern philosophy in the Western world, can all find their remote but highly developed precursors in those great non-Confucian schools of the fifth, fourth, and the third centuries B.C. It therefore seems to be the duty of New China to study these long-neglected native systems in the light and with the aid of modern Western philosophy. When the philosophies of Ancient China are reinterpreted in terms of modern philosophy, and when modern philosophy is interpreted in terms of the native systems of China, then, and only then, can Chinese philosophers and students of philosophy truly feel at ease with the new methods and instrumentalities of speculation and research. (Hu, 1922b, pp. 7–9)

That is Hu's considered response to his problem of systematizing the national heritage. In addition to *The Development of the Logical Method in Ancient China* and *An Outline of the History of Chinese Philosophy*, Hu wrote many works on the history of Chinese philosophy. Most of these emphasized the need to pay attention to methodology, but some of them also stressed the scientific spirits and methods in Chinese philosophy such as doubting, searching for knowledge, the natural conception of the universe, evidential investigation, and textual research (Hu, 1962). He searched for points of juncture with modern thought and repeatedly urged the use of domestic resources to cultivate the soil for the new growth of Chinese thought.

Political Philosophy and Liberalism

In Hu Shi's opinion, the purpose of his efforts to study problems, import theories, and systematize the national heritage was to reconstruct a new Chinese civilization. But what is the ideal model for a new Chinese civilization? How should we choose such a model? These problems lead on to Hu's political thought.

Hu's political ideas and opinions were miscellaneous, evolutionary, and open to change, but the basic features of his political philosophy remained the same throughout his life by virtue of his commitment to idealism, gradualism, and liberalism. Hu paid close attention to American politics. He was fascinated by President Wilson's idealistic and humanitarian approach to politics and was moved by the ideals of internationalism, pacifism, and cosmopolitanism that were advocated by the student movements and associations in which he took part. He took American political institutions to be the ideal model of democracy and the goal of his later program of reform in China.

In contrast to Hu's ideals, the political realities of early Republican China were filled with menace and devastation. Yuan Shi-kai's monarchical farce, Chang Xun's attempt to restore the Qing Dynasty, and prolonged periods of brutal war among warlords dissuaded some elite Chinese from seeking political careers. This rejection of politics contrasted sharply with the traditional Chinese attitude that government service was the most desirable and honored route to success and personal satisfaction:

> When I arrived in Shanghai and saw the poverty and paucity of the publishing world and the inertia in educational circles, I realized that Chang Xun's restoration coup was quite a natural phenomenon. . . . I resolved to refrain from taking part in politics for twenty years and hoped to lay the foundations for the reform of Chinese politics based on thought and literature. ("My crossroads," Hu, 1924, II, iii, pp. 96, 108)

Hu's decision showed a naive idealism that was unsuitable for real politics and expressed an elitist view that was prevalent among his colleagues. By choosing to concentrate on cultural and intellectual work, their influence was limited to intellectuals and the educated. Their hope that their efforts would lay the foundations for political reform can be equated with the belief that recruiting the intellectuals of China would constitute a sufficient condition for reform. In addition, Hu and his colleagues were unrealistically optimistic in believing that their activities would convince the whole body of intellectuals. In fact, the pressure of political events and national crisis soon drew Hu into active political life. He sought "the objective of 'good government' as the minimum demand for the reform of Chinese politics" and raised constitutional government, public government, and government with a plan as the three fundamental principles of political reform. He demanded that "all the superior elements of the society ought to come out to do battle with the forces of evil [as] the only way to initiate the work of political reform" ("Our political proposals," Hu, 1924, II, iii, pp. 27–31). Hu's colleagues in the New Culture Movement responded to the national crisis in various ways. Chen Duxiu and Li Dazhao became founders of the Chinese Communist Party, while others entered government. Much later, even Hu accepted official posts.

Hu's gradualism regarding politics provided another reason for him to speak out. He combined idealism concerning the aims of political reform with a gradualist approach to its methods. His pacifist inclinations led him to dislike drastic revolution, and his admiration for Dewey led him to embrace the gradualism of Dewey's social and political philosophy that was manifested in his famous exchange on "Problems and Isms" with Li Dazhao. According to his understanding, "Experimentalism is, of course, also a kind of ism, but experimentalism emphasizes concrete facts and problems, and consequently it does not acknowledge any fundamental solutions. It recognizes only that kind of progress which is achieved bit-by-bit – each step guided by intelligence, each step making provision for automatic testing – only this is true progress" ("My crossroads," Hu, 1924, II, iii, p. 99).

Hu warned against the "empty talk of 'isms' imported from abroad" because theories, "isms," were nothing more than generalized statements of ideas that originated in a particular time and place as concrete proposals addressed to the solution of specific problems. Without study of their original contexts and of their applicability to new situations, they were abstract proposals that would neither help to resolve concrete social problems nor lead to social progress. "The great danger of 'isms' is that they render men satisfied and complacent, believing that they have found the panacea of a 'fundamental solution' and that they need not waste their energies by studying the way to solve this or that concrete problem." The study of specific problems, according to Hu, is the first essential step towards social reform. Each intellectual should "devote more study to the solution of this or that problem, and indulge less in high-flown talk of the novelty of this theory or the cleverness of that one" ("Study more problems, talk less of 'isms,'" Hu, 1921, ii, pp. 484–7). The task of "reconstructing civilization" will be achieved through the solution of problems, the "critical attitude" and the promotion of independence of personality rather than through the empty talk of "isms."

> Civilization is not created in a vague and general fashion; it is created bit by bit and drop by drop. Progress is not achieved in an evening, in a vague and general fashion; it is achieved bit by bit and drop by drop. . . . The work that must serve as the first step in the reconstruction of civilization is the study of this or that problem. The progress of such a reconstruction of civilization means simply the solution of this or that problem. (Hu, 1921, iv. pp. 1029–30)

In spite of his gradualist approach, Hu did not reject revolutions completely:

> I do not condemn revolutions, because I believe that they are necessary stages in the process of evolution. But I do not favor premature revolutions, because they are usually wasteful and therefore unfruitful . . . It is for this reason that I do not entertain much hope for the revolution now going on in China, although I have deep sympathy for the revolutionaries. Personally, I prefer to build from the bottom up. I have come to believe that there is no short-cut to political decency and efficiency. . . . My personal attitude is: "Come what may, let us edu-cate the people. Let us lay a foundation for our future generations to build upon." This is necessarily a very slow process, and mankind is impatient. But, so far as I can see, this slow process is the only process: it is a prerequisite of revolutions as well as evolutions. (Hu, 1947, pp. 842–3)

Here we come to the core of Hu's program for the smooth and steady reform of China: education. Even before he was attracted to Dewey's gradualism,

Hu suggested that the "fundamental plan to save China from destruction" was to "make our education flourish . . ." (Hu, 1947, p. 584):

> I believe that the proper way of creating causes at the present time lies in the cultivation of men. This properly depends upon education. Therefore I have of late entertained no extravagant hopes, and after returning home I will seek only to devote myself to the task of social education . . . believing this to be the only [possible] plan for the cultivation of men over a period of one hundred years. I am well aware that the cultivation of men is a long-range scheme, but recently I have come to understand that there is no short-cut that can be effective in national or world affairs. (Hu, 1947, pp. 832–3)

Hu's advocacy of reform through education expressed his democratic ideals and his commitment to liberalism. Hu is widely acknowledged as the most important representative of the first generation of Chinese Liberalism:

> Liberal movements in the East have never gone along the road of constructing democratic politics because they never grasped the special importance of political liberty. The great contribution of Western liberalism lies in the recognition that only democratic politics can ensure the basic freedom of the people, so the political implication of liberalism is to stress upholding democracy. ("Liberalism," Hu, 1998, XII, pp. 807–9)

Hu called his early individualistic liberalism "Ibsenism." Faced with suffocating traditional ethics that destroyed human lives, he agreed with Ibsen that "[n]o social evil is greater than the destruction of the individual's individuality and the prohibition of his free development." As the main goal of the Enlightenment, he urged each person to liberate himself from the bonds of traditional ethical codes and self-deceit, to recognize his own rights and independence and to "develop to the fullest his own natural ability . . . his own individuality." "What I most desire for you is a true and pure egoism. . . . Sometimes I feel that the whole world is like a ship sinking at sea, and that the most important thing is to save oneself." Because "Society is constituted of individuals, . . . one more person saved is one more prepared for the reconstruction of society. . . . Such egoism is in fact the most valuable kind of altruism" ("Ibsenism," Hu, 1953, IV, pp. 902–3).

Such egoism provided an individualistic basis for harmonizing the relation between individual and society. How could an individual save oneself, and how could Hu's individualist ideal be achieved? Hu was aware that one could not save oneself in isolation and that an "independent personality" could not be cultivated independent of society. "The individual is created by numerous forces in society. The reform of society must begin from the reform of these numerous forces that create society and the individual. The reform of society is the very reform of the individual" ("Non-individual new life," Hu, 1921,

IV, pp. 1053). He criticized attempts to separate "the reform of individuals" and "the reform of society":

> The fundamental error of this concept lies in . . . regarding the individual as something that can be set outside of society and reformed. It is important to understand that the individual is the result of numerous and varied forces . . . that together create society – institutions, customs, thought, education, etc. When these forces have been improved, so also will men have been improved. ("Non-individual new life," Hu, 1953, IV, pp. 1052–3)

Hu used his liberal principles to explore the social and political environment in which individuals live and act:

> The plainest meaning of liberalism is to stress respecting freedom. . . . In my humble opinion, liberalism is that great movement in the human history that advocates liberty, adores liberty, strives for liberty, enriches and spreads liberty. . . . The "liberty" we talk about now is the right not to be restrained and repressed by external forces, the right not to be restricted in certain aspect of life, such as the liberty of religious belief, the liberty of thought, the liberty of speech and publication. These rights are all not innate, not bestowed by god, but won by some advanced nations through long-term struggles. (Radio Broadcast, Radio Peking , 1948)

The second meaning of liberty is political liberty, which holds that only democratic politics can ensure these basic freedoms, and the third:

> is a special and unprecedented political meaning of liberalism in its two-hundred years of historical evolution, that is to tolerate the opposition and ensure the liberal rights of the minority. Modern democratic politics of the West has gradually cultivated a sort of magnanimity and atmosphere of tolerating dissident. . . . This is the most lovable and most basic aspect of modern liberalism. "Tolerance is more important than liberty" because tolerance is the source of liberty and without it, there is no liberty at all. . . .
>   Lastly I want to point that current liberalism also implies "peaceful reform." . . . Tolerating the opposition and respecting the right of the minority is the sole foundation of peaceful political and social reform. First, the toleration of the opposition sets up the most critical mechanism of supervision; secondly, it gives the opportunity of choice to people and allows the transformation of power in the nation in a legitimate and peaceful manner. (Radio Broadcast, Radio Peking, 1948)

To impatient young people who wanted "thorough reform," Hu said:

> I sincerely want to indicate that the history of the past 160–170 years has shown us that whoever conducts a thorough reform will go on to a politically absolute autocracy. That is natural because only absolute autocracy could uproot the

opposition and destroy all resistance; only absolutely autocratic politics can approach its goal of fundamental reform at any cost, by any sort of means. They admit neither that their views may be wrong, nor that there is any considerable reason in the opposition's idea, so they absolutely cannot tolerate dissent, cannot respect free thought and speech. Therefore, I frankly say that because it respects freedom and tolerance, liberalism of course opposes violent revolution and the violently autocratic politics necessarily led into by violent revolution. In sum, the first implication of liberalism is liberty, the second is democracy, the third is tolerance – tolerating the opposition – and the fourth is peaceful and gradual reform. (Hu, 1998, XII, pp. 806–10)

As the decisive battle between the Nationalist Party and the Communist Party reached a climax, Hu could not say how to establish the intellectual environment and political institutions that he sought. Nevertheless, the conception of liberty and liberal ideals that he outlined survives as a lasting theme in the process of Chinese modernization.

Hu Shi as an Enlightenment Philosopher

We can best understand Hu Shi as an enlightenment philosopher, both because of the content of his thought and because of his role in the intellectual and cultural reconstruction of modern China. Through the New Culture Movement, he sought to overcome the ossified and decaying traditional culture and to establish the authority of rationality and science against ignorance and superstition. His work for cultural renewal won him fame as an enlightenment thinker. He imported the philosophical doctrine of experimentalism that stressed the universality and invariability of methodology, and his *Outline of the History of Chinese Philosophy* applied experimentalism to open new possibilities for academic study in China. He advocated democracy, human rights, and liberalism and championed the critical attitude and independence of thought. He appealed for a liberal and tolerant social environment and saw the formation of the new individual as the main goal of enlightenment.

These great merits of Hu's philosophy also manifested its weakness. Although China needed an enlightenment philosophy and Hu's thought gained popularity among students and intellectuals, his work lacked profundity. Indeed, this deficiency was one reason for its popular support. Hu embraced experimentalism because it could help enlighten China, but his rejection of metaphysics relinquished one way of achieving greater intellectual depth. As a promoter of enlightenment, he was content to "initiate the trend but not to be the master." He anticipated that others would become masters on the basis of the universal problem-solving method that he imported. He opened broad academic territory as an initiator and pioneer, but recognized, "the aspects of my work were truly many, but they were all initial ones and had no further research" (Hu, 1984, p. 117). Because of his hostility to metaphysics and speculative philosophy, he evaded metaphysical problems concerning human beings and the world. When he did mention fundamental concepts, such as the concept of reality, he treated them solely in a pragmatic way. For example, he claimed that "reality is only the reality that we remake" ("Experimentalism," Hu, 1921, ii, p. 440). Hu restricted his philosophical interests mainly to dealing with practical social and political problems and reduced philosophical doctrines to methods for solving problems and justifying theories. His philosophy expressed, but did not examine, relatively crude utilitarian assumptions. By concentrating on solving discrete and limited concrete problems, Hu's philosophy emphasized method but lacked system. Because Hu made little effort to construct a coherent philosophical system, his philosophy lacks a deeper structure to support his arguments and inferences. He appealed to science rather than to philosophy for the grounding of his naturalistic conception of the universe. Further, his strict demand for evidence allowed little room for generalizations about philosophy or its history. He failed to establish a perspective from which to grasp the subject. For this reason, he spent most of his later years seeking evidence for a minor study rather than completing his *Outline of the History of Chinese Philosophy.*

A final criticism of Hu Shi's philosophy concerns his lack of originality. His philosophy contains few categories and principles that he created by himself. Although he recognized the importance of systematizing the national culture, he rarely sought to achieve a modern creative transformation of Chinese philosophy by using the plentiful resource of Chinese philosophical history. Aside from his popular slogan "bold assumption and careful verification," he simplified and applied experimentalism rather than developing it. Hu systematically expounded experimentalism in only one paper and much preferred to apply experimentalist conclusions uncritically as premises in problem solving. He held experimentalism to be universal and invariant and seemed to hold it exempt from the critical attitude and the evolutionary conception of truth. For these reasons, Hu may be considered to be an applied philosopher or as an historian of philosophy, but not a philosopher who established his own philosophical system with its own categories and arguments. His philosophy is significant more for its intellectual and cultural impact than for the details of its doctrines.

Both the limitations and the value of Hu Shi's philosophy can be approached by way of its historical context as well as through its intellectual content. Its merits and shortcomings result from both the situation of China in his unsettled times and his impressive abilities. Hu had much more immediate impact than his contemporaries whose philosophical understanding was deeper, more systematic, and more original. As a pioneer, however, he initiated powerful currents of intellectual and cultural innovation that will be recalled long after his program of enlightenment has been accomplished.

Bibliography

Works by Hu Shi (Hu Shih)

Hu, Shi 1919: *Zhongguo zhexue shi dagang, shang zhuan* 中國哲學史大綱上卷 (an outline of the history of Chinese philosophy, I), Shanghai: Commercial Press

Hu, Shi 1921: *Hu Shih wen-ts'un* 胡適文存 (HSWT) (collected essays of Hu Shi) Shanghai: Oriental Book

Hu, Shi 1924: *Hu Shih wen-ts'un* 胡適文存 (HSWT, II) (collected essays of Hu Shi), second collection, Shanghai

Hu, Shi 1930: *Hu Shih wen-ts'un* 胡適文存 (HSWT, III) (collected essays of Hu Shi), third collection, Shanghai: Yadong Tushuguan

Hu, Shi 1953: *Hu Shih wen-ts'un* 胡適文存 (HSWT, IV) (collected essays of Hu Shi), fourth collection, Taipei: Yuandong Tushu Gongsi

Hu, Shi 1998: *Hu Shi wen-ji* 胡適文集 (HSWJ) (collected writings of Hu Shi), vols I–XII, Beijing: Peking University Press

Hu, Shi 1922a: "Literary Revolution in China," *The Chinese Social and Political Science Review*, **6:2** 91–100

Hu, Shi 1922b: *The Development of Logical Method in Ancient China*. Shanghai: Oriental Book (reprinted, with intro. by Hyman Kublin; New York: Paragon Book Company, 1963)

Hu, Shi 1931: "My credo and its evolution," in *Living Philosophies*, New York: Simon & Schuster, pp. 235–63

Hu, Shi 1947: *Hu Shi liuxue riji* (Hu Shi's diary of studying abroad), Shanghai: Commercial Press

Hu, Shi 1962: "The Scientific Spirit and Method in Chinese Philosophy," in Charles A. Moore, ed., *Philosophy and Culture: East and West*, Honolulu: University of Hawaii Press, pp. 199–222

Hu, Shi 1981: *Autobiography by Hu Shi's Oral Account*, Tang De-gang trans. & notes (in HSWJ, I, 1998)

Hu, Shi 1984: Hu Shi Zhi Xiansheng Wannien Tanhualu 胡適之先生晚年談話錄 *Record of Hu's Talks in Later Years* ed. Hu Song-ping, Taiwan Lianjing Publishing House

Other works

Chou, Min-chih 1984: *Hu Shih and Intellectual Choice in Modern China*, Ann Arbor: University of Michigan Press

Grieder, Jerome B. 1970: *Hu Shih and the Chinese Renaissance: Liberalism in the Chinese Revolution, 1917–37*. Cambridge, MA: Harvard University Press

Gu, Ji-gang 1926: "Self-Preface," in Qushihpian Zishuh 古史辨・自序 *Discrimination of ancient history* Beijing: Pu Press, p. 36

Li, Zehou 1987: *Zhongguo xiandai sixiang shilun* 中國現代思想史論 (on modern Chinese thought), Beijing: Oriental Press

Marx, K. and Engels, F. 1976: *Collected Works*, vol. 5, Moscow: Progress Publishers

Yin, Hai-guang 1982: "The trend of liberalism', in Schwartz, Benjamin I. et al., eds, *Modern Chinese Scholars on Liberalism*, Taipei: Shibaowenhua

Yu, Yingshi 1984: Zhongguo jindai sixiangshi shan de Hu Shi 《中國近代思想史上的胡適 —《胡適之先生年譜長編初稿》序》 "Hu Shi in the history of Chinese modern thought," Preface to first draft of an extended chronology of the life of Hu Shi, Taiwan: Lianjing Publishing House

Discussion Questions

1. Does Hu Shi's critical attitude provide an acceptable basis for assessing new ideas?
2. Should we accept Hu Shi's naturalistic conception of the universe?
3. Does experimentalism provide an adequate theory of truth?
4. Does the concept of evolution help us to deal with any philosophical problems?
5. To what extent can Hu Shi's experimentalism be understood in terms of Popper's method of conjectures and refutations?
6. Can the same method be used to deal with theoretical academic problems and practical social problems?
7. Does Hu Shi succeed in providing a standpoint from which to systematize the Chinese national heritage?
8. Was Hu Shi justified in the idealism, gradualism, and liberalism of his political philosophy?
9. What is the relationship between the reform of the individual and the reform of society?
10. In what respects was Hu Shi a philosopher of the Enlightenment?

5

JIN YUELIN'S THEORY OF *DAO*

Hu Jun

Jin Yuelin (1895–1984) was born in Changsha, Hunan Province, China. After graduating from Qinghua College in 1914, he studied for a BA degree in political science at the University of Pennsylvania. In 1917, he enrolled at Columbia University to continue his study of political science for an MA degree and then obtained his doctorate at Columbia with a dissertation on "The Political Theory of T. H. Green." Under the influence of Green, Jin developed a strong interest in philosophy and, more specifically, in Neo-Hegelian thought. After completing his doctorate, Jin spent the next five years on a scholarly tour of Europe, spending time especially in Britain, France, Germany, and Italy. The most important effect of this journey was to bring Jin Yuelin into further contact with British philosophy, and his close examination of the works of Hume and Russell greatly influenced his further philosophical development. Hume's problem of induction remained a central concern of Jin's throughout his life, and from Russell's *Principia Mathematica* Jin was exposed to the claim that "analysis is philosophy." Under these influences, Jin abandoned his early commitment to Neo-Hegelianism.

Jin was attracted by the claim that philosophy is the profound and meticulous analysis of the concepts that we use in logic and mathematics, science, or our ordinary life rather than a system of peculiarly philosophical concepts. Like Russell, he was committed to analysis as a philosophical method, but Jin was never a loyal follower of Russell's philosophy, because he did not consider the method of analysis to be a proper part of philosophy. For Jin, analysis was only a very useful tool of philosophical thought, to be used in constructing his own philosophy system. In terms of method, we can see similarity between Jin and Russell, but it would be mistaken to claim that Jin was an analytic philosopher. In terms of philosophical thought, Jin differed greatly from Russell.

Jin was also deeply influenced by Chinese philosophy. *Dao* was the most important concept of his metaphysics, and he admitted that *dao* was his ultimate concern and the ultimate commitment giving impetus to his action and emotion.

Although he was not formally a student of Chinese philosophy, he began to read the "Four Books" and other Chinese philosophical works when he was a child and accepted the way of Chinese thought and Chinese life.

After returning to China, Jin Yuelin taught philosophy in Qinghua University and Peking University. In 1926, he founded the Philosophy Department at Qinghua University, where he was both Professor of Philosophy and Dean of the Philosophy Department. He held similar posts at Peking University from 1952 to 1955, and then became Vice-Director of the Institute of Philosophy, Chinese Academy of Social Sciences.

In the decade of the 1930s, Jin developed a system of philosophy in two parts, namely, the theory of knowledge and metaphysics. Among his numerous philosophical writings in Chinese were three principal publications: *Logic* (1935), *On Dao* (1940), and *Theory of Knowledge* (1983), which he completed in about 1948. These three publications are included in the four volumes of *Collected Works of Jin Yuelin* (1995). Jin's English publication *Tao, Nature and Man* (1995b) is drawn from *On Dao*.

Although Jin Yuelin's philosophical system contained both theories of knowledge and metaphysics, Jin considered his metaphysics to be the core of his philosophy, with his epistemology following from his metaphysical insights. Accordingly, this chapter will deal primarily with his metaphysics. Jin's metaphysics can also be called a theory of *dao*, since *dao* is his basic metaphysical concept, and his account of *dao* is the most important feature of his philosophy. According to Jin, *dao* can be analyzed into elements, namely, matter (or stuff) and form.

Matter and Form

By matter, Jin meant raw material. He held that "there is something in every particular thing or object, a 'thisness' or 'thatness' or an x that cannot be expressed" (Jin 1995b, p. 575). The inexpressible x is not a particular or a set of particulars, nor is it a universal or a set of universals. He argued that the inexpressible x cannot be known. Although Jin concluded on intellectual grounds that every thing has matter, this matter is incapable of being the object of conceptual knowledge or sensual experience. What is required in order to grasp matter is a sort of intellectual projection, in which recognition of the limits of one's intellect is accompanied by a leap out of the intellectual process with a proposition that extends into the great beyond instead of returning to the essence of intellectuality.

Jin identified matter with pure potentiality. Potentiality is the capacity of a thing at any given moment to be something that it is not at that moment.

Although matter cannot change by itself, its potentiality is responsible for all change. By being distinguished from any actuality, matter is pure potentiality. Jin also held that matter is pure activity, because the activity of matter is absolutely unhampered. It is entirely for its own sake that matter is active and can be actualized in things. Matter is pure substantiality as well. Matter is not any substance, just as it is not any expressible potentiality or activity of things or events or states and process. Because matter is pure potentiality, it cannot be limited to any specific category. Because matter is pure activity, it does not belong to the chain of changes comprising fleeting events, unstable objects, and contingent facts. But while matter is not itself a substance, it underlies all substances and is hence pure substantiality. Without matter, universals would be empty possibilities that lacked instantiation, and particulars would cease to be because there would be neither things nor events. According to Jin, matter is devoid of quality and constant in quantity.

In virtue of its activity and potentiality, matter enters into possibilities or withdraws from possibilities. For Jin, a possibility is something like a mold or scaffold that can be used to contain *neng* (matter). A possibility is realized when matter enters into it; a possibility ceases to be realized when matter departs from it. By possibility, Jin meant logical possibility. Anything that is contradictory is impossible, but everything else is a possibility. Jin used the term possibility to define form: "Form is a possibility formed by the exhaustive disjunction of all possibilities" (Jin, 1940, p. 22). The term "all possibilities" covers the totality of possibilities, but also covers the different hierarchies, orders, or types of possibility. Because disjunction is the familiar logical disjunction, form is without content and is itself absolutely formless. Since form exhausts all possibilities, there is no boundary dividing what is inside form from what is outside form, for the simple reason that there is nothing outside form. Everything must be within the scope of form. By exhausting all possibilities, form determines necessity. Logic, as the study of necessity, is essentially the exhibition of form. We could say that form is logic.

Matter and form are the basic analytical elements of *dao*. Rather than being isolated from each other, they are closely related. Matter must always remain inside of form, and form is unbounded. According to Jin, form without matter or matter without form is contradictory. Matter is active: by matter entering into a certain possibility, the possibility is realized. When it withdraws from the possibility, the possibility ceases to be realized. Whether or not matter enters into or withdraws from possibilities, it must stay within form. With ordinary raw material and molds, we can always raise the question of whether the mold fits the raw material. The absolute fluidity of form makes it a remarkable mold indeed: from one perspective it has every shape, and from another perspective it has no shape. With matter and form, there is no possibility that the raw material will fail to fit the mold.

Possibility

We can distinguish four kinds of possibility in terms of their realization:

1. A possibility is *necessary* if it cannot but be realized,
2. A possibility is *contradictory* if it cannot be realized,
3. A possibility is *eternally realized* if it must be realized, and
4. A possibility is *contingent* if it may be realized or unrealized or if once realized it may cease to be realized.

A possibility is eternally realized if it can be realized only when the sum total of contingent possibilities has been realized. An eternally unrealized possibility, that is the failure of an eternally realized possibility to be realized, is not contradictory, but is simply never contingent.

The first two kinds of possibilities are important because necessary possibility guarantees the absolute minimum of reality, while contradictory possibility furnishes the ultimate basis of factual givenness. The other two kinds of possibilities are also important, but for different reasons. The realization of contingent possibilities gives us the richness, variety, and completeness of *dao*, whereas the eternally unrealized possibilities supply us with implements in the realm of thinking and thought.

The realization of possibility is merely the entrance of matter into a certain possibility. When a possibility is realized, it becomes a universal. Through the notion of possibility, we can define a universal as a realized possibility. Jin used the term universal in a positive sense, so that existence is a universal, but nonexistence is not one possibility but is rather an infinity of universals or possibilities. As a consequence, a universal always indicates a class of objects, and a null class is not covered by any one universal. Also, the very notion of any one universal involves a logical conjunction of that universal with the universal "real." Reality is concrete if a plurality of possibilities are realized by one and identical matter.

Jin's theory of matter and form is similar to Western theories starting with Aristotle. However, the difference between Jin's account and Aristotelian theory can easily be seen. For example, in Aristotle's *Metaphysics*, form is the decisive aspect: it is active and is the aim of matter. Matter is seen as dead and passive. In Jin's metaphysics, matter is the decisive aspect: it is active and can enter into or withdraw from possibilities. For Jin, form is static and dead and is merely an empty and necessary mold for active matter. From this point of view, the relationship between Aristotle's form and matter is not necessary, that is to say, the realization of form or matter is not necessary and matter need not exist within form. Yet, according to Jin, the relationship between form and matter is necessary, and it is impossible for matter to be outside form. It is necessary that matter realizes possibilities, realized possibilities are universals, and universals cover all relevant particulars. We can easily see the differences between Jin's theory of metaphysics and Greek and European theories of metaphysics. Moreover, in Jin's theory, matter and form are subsumed as the most basic elements of *dao*.

Dao

With this background, it is time to introduce *dao*. *Dao* is simply mattered form or formed matter and is therefore neither pure form nor pure matter. *Dao* would be empty if it were pure form and would be fluid if it were pure matter:

> *Tao* as it is used here however is not confined to the expression and content of thought, it applies also to its object. In saying that there is *Tao*, we are not merely talking about there being thought or thinking, but also about there being the universe. (Jin, 1995b, p. 624)

We can speak of *dao* in at least two different ways, namely, the *dao* as one and the *dao* as infinite. *Dao* as one is the *dao* with the barest minimum of connotation, and *dao* as infinite is the *dao* with a connotation of the essence of that minimum. By *dao* as infinite, Jin meant the infinite possibilities of specific kinds of world. By affirming the *dao* as one, we affirm incidentally the reality of our present kind of world just as by affirming *logos*, we affirm the reality of a kind of world in which physics or chemistry or history describes and explains natural phenomena. We may have the *dao* as one, and yet our present kind of world need not exist. That is to say, in affirming *dao* we affirm nothing, and in affirming anything whatever, we also affirm the *dao* as one. Therefore, nothing can escape the all-pervasiveness of *dao*. Regarding the relation between the *dao* as one and the *dao* as infinite, Jin said:

> The relation between these two can be analyzed into two different aspects, both of which are important to our understanding of *Tao*. One of these is the relation of organic parts to organic wholes and the other is the relation of the inclusion of one class in another class. (Jin, 1995b, p. 31)

The relation of class inclusion enables us to say that what is true of a class is also true of any class that it includes. The relation of organic parts and wholes involves a system of external and internal relations. While parts in this system may be dependent on other parts, interdependent upon one another, or independent of other parts, the whole is always dependent upon its parts. While both the relation of class inclusion and the relation of organic wholes and parts have advantages and disadvantages, a combination of both relations enables us to talk of the *dao* as one in terms of the *dao* as infinite because the *dao* as infinite is not only included in the *dao* as one, but is also organically related to the *dao* as one. Given the relation of the *dao* as infinite to the *dao* as one, we can see not only that the sum total of the *dao* as infinite constitutes the entirety of the *dao* as one, but also that through its organic relation to the *dao* as one the *dao* as infinite constitutes the unity of the *dao* as one. Therefore, from the point of view of *dao*, a particular object or event reflects the whole universe. "From the point of view of epistemology, I hold that particular objects and events are both internally and externally related to each other" (Jin, 1995b, p. 631).

In Jin's metaphysics, *dao* not only is the most basic concept, but is also the highest ideal realm. Jin held that *dao* is the basic concept and the highest ideal realm of Chinese philosophy as well. However, he was clearly aware that Chinese philosophy was characteristically underdeveloped in terms of logico-epistemological consciousness. If the development of this consciousness was partly responsible for the presence of science in the West, its lack must be partly responsible for the absence of science in China. In order to modernize Chinese society, Chinese philosophy must introduce logic from Western philosophy. Jin was the first Chinese scholar who could fully understand modern mathematical logic and introduce it into China. Through his introduction of modern logic, Jin made a great contribution to contemporary Chinese philosophy. Through Chinese logicians, many of whom were Jin's students, logic continues to give the Chinese new ways of thinking and to transform their mentality. But for Jin, logic was not only the instrument of thought, but also had metaphysical meaning or ontological status. In his metaphysics, logic is both the expression and content of thought and the object independent of thought. Through logic thought can be about the world. Logic is the expression of form, or form is logic. As an analytic element of *dao*, form exhausts all possibilities. And everything has form or possibility as a basic element. From this point of view, Jin can be called a logical constructivist.

However important logic is for Jin, it is not itself his basic concept. As an analytic element of *dao*, it is subsumed under *dao*, the basic concept of Chinese philosophy for which Jin showed his deepest reverence. Jin considered logic to be too straightforward, too narrow, too cool, and too clear. On its own, it makes people uneasy and unhappy. However, *dao* reinforced by a consciousness of logic differs in all these respects from logic itself. *Dao* need not be too straightforward, too narrow, too cool, or too clear. Within *dao*, one can feel great ease and great happiness.

Chinese philosophy is so succinct and inarticulate regarding the interconnectedness of ideas that its suggestiveness is almost unbounded. Jin was emotionally attuned to the feeling or flavor of Chinese philosophy and used *On Dao* as the title of his work on metaphysics. His metaphysics can be properly called a theory of *dao*. Although he stressed the importance of logic as an instrument of thought, he cannot be called a logician, but was rather a Neo-Daoist.

Universal Sympathy

The importance of Jin's theory of *dao* is that it offers a very broad perspective that is not a special account for human beings, but is rather for all possible beings. This perspective differs from the complex Greek and Jewish tradition of the West. Western thought has made human beings anthropocentric in relation to the rest of nature and egocentric in relation to the rest of mankind. Hellenic light and Hebraic sweetness have produced a strain of human assertiveness, of pride in being what we are and of deeply seated belief in ourselves as the salt of the earth. According to this tradition, a person normally regards object nature either as an enemy to be conquered or as plastic material to be shaped according to one's desires and normally regards other human beings as enemies to be conquered according to one's will. In combating nature and other humans, a person may succumb to nature in himself and may be vanquished by others. Jin considered this attitude toward object nature and other human beings to be improper:

> Civilizations in the past may have been wiped out by glaciers, by floods, by earthquakes, or by desiccation and decay, but they are not likely to be wiped out through such agency in the near future; if their destruction ever takes place, it is likely to be effected through human beings themselves. (Jin, 1995b, p. 744)

In contrast, Jin's metaphysics maintains a universal sympathy, based on the claim that the universal is in us, not merely that we are in the universe. "Heaven and earth and I myself are contemporaneous, and I am at one with myriad other things." It is only by realizing that one is floating in an ocean of mattered form or formed matter that one gains universal sympathy and with it one's own all pervasiveness and one's own eternity. In terms of Jin's universal sympathy, we must not forget that a person is also an animal and an object. It is perfectly true that one differs from some objects in being an animal, and from some animals in being a person. From being a person with other persons as well as with other animals and other objects, we can hardly be excited about being a particular self. This realization enables us to feel at one with the world and everything in it: to acquire universal sympathy. We do not despise other objects for each of us is one of them. In a democracy of existents, a person gives as much as he takes. We do not frown upon other animals that like ourselves function in accord with their respective essences. We do not condemn certain animal proclivities in ourselves since being a human being does not release us from the function of realizing our essence as animals. For human beings, happiness comprises both harmony within and the ability to get along without. We realize that we cannot set ourselves apart and lord over nature, for in doing so we merely give comfort to the nature within us rather than transcending mere nature in order to save ourselves.

Possible Worlds

Here we should turn to Jin's theory of possible worlds. Form is the world of possibilities that exhausts all possibilities. Jin used possibility to define the concept of a universal. Among universals, there are necessary relationships, which Jin called "universal relationships." Because they are necessary, universal relationships are also possible relationships, but not all possible relationships are universal relationships. The concept of a possible world was first advanced by Leibniz, but was not accorded much importance in the history of philosophy until Kripke and Hintikka developed a semantics of modal logic in the 1950s based on Leibniz's theory of possible worlds. However, in the early 1930s, Jin used a theory of possible worlds to develop his systematic metaphysics. He put forward a theory of necessity and explained the relationship between necessity and contingency in terms of possible worlds.

Reality and Process

Jin held that reality is concrete if a plurality of possibilities are realized by one and identical matter. *Dao* is necessarily concrete because the realization of form involves the realization of a plurality of possibilities and the stuff that is in form must be one and identical. Here Jin introduced three principles concerning reality. The first is the *principle of congruence*: reality unfolds with congruence. If we regard different realized possibilities as the road and the same or different realities arrived at as the destination, the principle of congruence furnished us with a minimal character of reality, namely concreteness. The principle is a principle of concreteness only in the sense that congruence provides this minimal character of reality. The congruence with which possibilities are realized results in concreteness because the matter by which a plurality of forms are realized is bound to be one and identical.

The notion of concreteness used for this concrete table or that concrete apple is borrowed from the notion of concreteness applied to *dao*. The concreteness of *dao* is not open to doubt because a plurality of possibilities are realized by one and identical matter. The entirety or sum total of anything whatever must be identical with itself, and because the matter in form is all the matter there is, it must be identical with itself. The case is different for this concrete table or that concrete apple. A plurality of possibilities are realized in each case, but the matter involved can be called one and identical only roughly and indeterminately.

Concreteness is the minimal content of the principle of congruence. At a maximum, the principle is also the basis of the principle of consistency. We are all familiar with the claim that propositions must be consistent. Whatever consistency might mean, the dictum does not prevent the psychological occurrence of inconsistent thoughts in our mental processes. Rather, it logically invalidates inconsistent propositions in our structures of thought. If inconsistent propositions were not invalidated, the structures would not reflect the pattern of possible reality.

The ultimate basis of consistency is that concrete reality is congruent. In the broadest sense, consistency merely means the absence of contradictions. A body of propositions can all be false while also being consistent, but a proposition and its negation (or any proposition that implies its negation) are contradictory and cannot be consistent. We are liable to confine ourselves to a narrower sense of consistency: given the truth of certain propositions, the body of propositions that may be true with them are consistent with the given propositions. If we are guided by the extralogical consideration of the truth of certain given propositions, the criterion of consistency is often very fruitful. But this fruitfulness is obtained only on the condition that the truth of certain nonnecessary and yet true propositions is given. At the level of the necessary and eternal realities, the principle of congruence merely results in the concreteness of reality. But given the realization of certain contingent possibilities, the principle also provides us with contingent trends or tendencies. Were no contingent possibilities to be realized, this would not be so and the principle of congruence would be no more than a principle of concreteness.

Are we sure that any contingent possibilities will ever be realized? Jin argued that since time and change must be realized as a result of the metaphysical principle, contingent possibilities as a class must be realized because otherwise there would be no time and change. To say that contingent possibilities are bound to be realized is to say that reality unfolds itself with contingency. If reality unfolded itself merely with congruence, we would have a static concrete world. Because reality also unfolds itself with contingency, we have a world that is dynamic as well as concrete. Jin argued that to understand the world as dynamic we need a second principle, the *principle of contingency*. The principles of congruence and contingency together assure us of a world that is static in some respects and dynamic in others.

Although the principle of contingency enables us to have variety, it does not afford us an economy of interacting elements. Without economy, we could have temporal variation or variety in succession, but no spatial richness or richness that is contemporaneous. We could have a lumpy block-world that changes, but is devoid of any richness of shape or color. In order to supply us with such richness, we need a third principle, the *principle of economy*, stating that reality unfolds itself with multiple individuality. This principle assures us that the series of realizations is not in single file, but in multiple file, so that what might otherwise be a block-world is integrated into individuals that are capable of realizing almost all the possibilities that can be consistently realized at the same place and at the same time. If the world were one individual, only a few possibilities could be realized at any time, but since the world is integrated into a multiplicity of individuals, an enormous number of possibilities are realized.

Jin thinks that we cannot deny the concrete world given to us by the principle of congruence, no matter how skeptical we are or we try to be. The principles of contingency and economy supply us with a reality in process, a changing temporal and spatial world that is diversified into individual objects and events. These individuals realize universals through the birth and death of particulars that are catalogued by means of the scaffolding of space–time.

With the principle of contingency, we have change. The world is an eternal one in some respects, that is to say the possibility "change" is eternally realized. This feature of reality is implied not merely by the principle of contingency but also by the metaphysical principle. If matter enters into and departs from possibilities, there is obviously a change of realizations. Change is eternally realized because there is no time in which it will cease to be realized. The world did not start by being static and then proceed to become dynamic; rather change is the eternally realized possibility. Jin thinks that no philosopher will deny the fact of change since as sentient beings they experience change in their everyday life. However, there seem to be philosophical difficulties in the notion of change or in reasoning about change. The notion of change involves identity and difference, such that there must be identity in some things and difference in others. Both identity and difference are essential for obviously neither alone constitutes change on its own. If A is said to have changed into B, there must be something identical as well as something different. If there is not something different, there is not any change. A and B would simply be different names for the same thing. If, however, A and B are different without anything that is identical, they are simply two discrete entities. One may succeed the other in time, but the first cannot be said to have changed into the second.

The notion of change is an abstraction from experience in which most if not all changes are partial, but with partial changes the problem of identity and difference remains. Where there is a partial change, experience reveals to us certain identical aspects of a concrete object together with certain different aspects. But experience is often rough and ready and contains inferential elements that are often not well founded. Experienced differences may be final, but experienced identities are not. Identity as experienced is one of aspects, and identity of aspects is merely an indication of identity, not a conclusion based on a more radical identity of something else. The inference of an underlying identity from an experienced identity of aspects may not lead us to practical difficulties, but theoretical difficulties remain.

However unlikely, it is by no means impossible for there to be two different objects with identical aspects. Here experienced identity of aspects is not a conclusive indication of basic or radical identity. For this reason no change need take place even in cases where there is partial identity and partial difference. Even when A is experientially said to have changed into B on the grounds of partial identity and partial difference between them, one is theoretically never certain that a change has taken place because A and B might be two different entities from the beginning.

In order to solve this difficulty, Jin argued that the criterion of the identity of objects is not identity in aspects and that it can allow for difference in aspects. Identity and difference of objects and aspects are not on the same level or applied to the same kind of entities. When we say that it is possible to have two things with identical aspects we cannot understand "two things" as being identical combinations of identical aspects. On this understanding, no two things could have identical aspects, since there would be no sense in saying that they were two things rather than one.

What, then, can we mean by distinguishing between different things and the same identical thing? Aspects can be divided into universals and particulars. A thing cannot be equivalent to a set of universals, because at any time a thing may change while a set of universals cannot change, although in changing something emerges from one set of universals and enters into another set. Nor is a thing a nexus of particulars because a thing can endure while a nexus of particulars cannot endure, although in change a thing emerges from one nexus of particulars and enters into another nexus. There must be something in addition to the nexus of particulars that distinguishes a thing from other things. That something we have already found to be the inexpressible matter.

The identity of a thing or object is not the identity of a set of particulars or universals, but is the identity of its matter. The identity of its matter is what gives a thing its "thisness" or "thatness" that can be pointed to through its nexus of particulars and allows it to endure from one nexus of particulars to another. What constitutes change in a thing is identical matter having different aspects. According to Jin, any change is like the change of a man discarding his business suit and donning his evening dress or forsaking his brown shoes and putting on his black ones. Nothing has changed regarding the wearer except his clothes or shoes. In the final analysis, it is matter that is the wearer.

Change requires time and space. For Jin, time is the flow of objects and events, and space is their container or scaffolding. There are thus two aspects to the world: contents and their spatiotemporal scaffolding. Temporality and spatiality are eternally realized possibilities. This is simply another way of saying that there is always time and space.

Time cannot be said to begin or to end, nor can space be said to have boundaries, whether from the point of view of the scaffolding or from that of the contents. Since temporality is an eternally realized possibility and the world neither begins to change nor stops changing, one can see that time neither begins nor ends. The lack of spatial boundaries is somewhat different. One can easily see that as scaffolding space has no boundaries; given any starting point in space three lines in three different directions can be prolonged without returning to the original point. More significantly, to deny boundaries from the point of view of contents is to speak operationally: the contents of the world are not repeated.

In order to provide a purely theoretical account of the absolute scaffolding of time and space, Jin introduced terms that stand for limits of abstraction in order to give a more precise theoretical meaning to the structure of the scaffolding. A slice of time is indeterminate from the point of view of duration and may mean a second or an age. We need something that is determinate and invariant like the familiar notion of an instant, but differing somewhat from this notion. Jin used the term "instant" to mean the whole of space without any temporal dimension whatever. An instant is three-dimensional spatially but does not endure. It is a temporal surface without temporal thickness. Any finite slice of time has two instants as its boundaries and an infinity of instants in between. No slice of time is the totality of time. Of the two boundary instants to a slice of time, one is the beginning of the slice and the other is the end. Time neither begins nor ends, only slices of time begin or end. We can apply finite units to any slice of time and measure its length. An instant is an eternally unrealized possibility. While we cannot say that it is impossible, we are convinced that it is unreal. Unlike the possibility of being a dragon, the unreality of an instant does not lie in its present nonactuality or nonexistence. Rather, an instant is unreal because it is eternally unrealized. Its realization would depend upon the possibility of completing the infinite division of any slice of time. But no matter how short the slice, it can be further divided, so that there is no stage reached at which its infinite division is completed.

Although the possibility of an instant is eternally unrealized, the concept corresponding to it is not useless. Thus, the instant "12 o'clock" is never realized, but the concept is eminently useful since operations can be performed to approach it. Because a rough meaning can be given to the concept, it can be used for the practical purposes of life. Neither does the unreality of instants render the scaffolding organized or ordered by them unreal. The scaffolding is real because the slices of time bordered by instants are real and the order in which instants succeed one another is real.

Just as an instant is the whole of space without temporal dimension, so a space–time line is the whole length of time without spatial dimension. Just as an instant is not the usual instant, so a space–time line is not a Euclidean point. Euclidean space is an abstraction of space without time and consequently without events and objects. Its space is the space of a time surface or what we usually call space at a single instant. Like an instant or time surface, a space–time line is unreal. Although it is unreal, the concept corresponding to it is useful. By taking time and Euclidean space together, we can form scaffolding in which a time surface and a space–time line intersect in a point-instant. A point-instant is the Euclidean point, while a space–time line is not. Just as time can be ordered by time-surfaces, so space can be ordered by space–time lines.

Jin held that the scaffolding is not something apart from process and reality. The scaffolding is so inextricably conjoined with particulars that they are identified by it. Every particular is definitely and uniquely fixed in the scaffolding in terms of its position in time and location in space–time. No particular can change its position in time or its location in space–time. It cannot move. Motion is only possible when we absolutely separate the temporal from the spatial aspect of things.

Jin said: "When we say that the process of reality flows in accordance with pattern, we mean that objects and events obey natural laws" (Jin, 1995b, p. 669). By pattern, Jin meant the interrelatedness of universals. Corresponding to the interrelatedness of universals is the more familiar interrelatedness of concepts. He held that concrete reality unfolds itself in accordance with the pattern of natural laws with the consequence that reality is thoroughly intelligible. Its intelligibility does not mean that it is either rational or predictable. Rationality involves adopting adequate means towards an end as well as avoiding anything that does not contribute towards the end. If a person is rational, he does certain things and avoids others. Reality in its unfolding does not adopt certain things and avoid others even though an end can be attributed to it. Predictability involves a connection between the past and the future so that given the past, the future, although unactualized, is in some sense given. While we do not say the process of reality is rational, neither do we say that it is irrational. Reality is predictable in some ways and unpredictable in others. The emergence of particulars is unpredictable, while the realization of possibilities may sometimes be predicted with very high degrees of probability. Intelligibility is different from rationality and predictability. It involves the explanation of the present in terms of the past and the explanation of the actual in terms of the universal and the possible. A person who at least partly understands the intelligibility of reality has the ability to answer the questions of what, how, why, or when concerning the actual.

Jin argued that the pattern in which reality unfolds itself is the pattern of the interrelatedness of possibilities and universals and that this pattern in turn is the object of all of logic taken as the content of scientific knowledge. These claims raise a number of questions that we cannot pursue here concerning logic, the different sciences and their interrelation.

Now we turn to Jin's theory of particulars and individual objects or events. Particulars are distinguished from individual objects or events in that the former are an aspect and the latter are concrete wholes. Particulars can be pointed to, named or referred to, while strictly speaking individual objects and events cannot be expressed since they are identified in terms of their inexpressible matter. Let us take up the particulars first. A particular is different from a universal only because it is a particular. It remains an aspect and by itself it is as "bodiless" as a universal. An aspect is particular when it uniquely occupies a certain position in time and location in space. A set, nexus, or series of particulars is itself a particular, because taken as a whole these also uniquely occupy a position in time and location in space. The composition of a set, nexus, or series of particulars lies therefore in the scaffolding of space–time, not in a pattern of universals. A particular does not endure in time, since it does not persist beyond the period of time in which it is a particular into another period in which it is not a particular. A particular is finite, that is to say, there is no particular that occupies a point-instant nor any that occupies the whole of space–time. A particular cannot change since there is no difference in one particular nor is there any identity of two particulars. Because it cannot change, it cannot move. Each particular is both a particular and a set, nexus, or series of particulars. No particular is so simple that it ceases to be a set, nexus, or series of particulars or so complex that it ceases to be a single particular. There is no ultimate simplicity or complexity to a particular.

Next let us consider individual objects and events. These are distinguished from particulars in that they are concrete wholes not aspects and they house or contain inexpressible matter. Jin held that in practice we identify an individual object or event with a set of particulars at a particular place and time. This identification, however, is theoretically unsound, although in practice it does not lead to much difficulty. If we ignore the theoretical problems for the moment and follow the practice, we can easily see that through identifying particulars in terms of the scaffolding of space–time, we can also catalogue individual objects and events in these terms. Individual objects and events are the actualities that form the content of concrete reality in process. They are the things that sift through the pattern of universals. Concrete reality not only proceeds in accordance with the pattern of universals but also fills the scaffolding of space–time with individual objects and events. These latter not only realize possibilities, but also take place at certain times and in certain spaces. They can be understood in terms of the universals that they realize and can be ascertained in terms of their position in time and their location in space.

We have shown that the principle of congruence gives us a concrete world that cannot be denied, no matter how skeptical we are or try to be. The principles of contingency and economy supply us with a reality in process, a changing temporal and spatial world diversified into individual objects and events which realize universals through the birth and death of particulars and which are catalogued in terms of the scaffolding of space–time. In Jin's view, this is the world we experience.

Man and Nature

We can see that in the unfolding of *dao* or in reality and process an infinity of things have happened and an infinity of things will yet happen, although something that is impossible or, if possible, eternally unrealizable will never happen. Speaking from the point of view of the present as a slice of time, anything will be realized in infinite time. We cannot say when certain things will happen, but that they will happen sometime or other does not seem to be open to doubt. This claim needs clarification from another point of view. We do not attribute the existence of things or the emergence of actualities to the activity of any transcendent reason, to the will of a transcendent God or to the fulfillment of a transcendent purpose. Since *dao* is coextensive with the universe, there cannot be anything transcendent to *dao* or to its unfolding. If there were, it would be something that is a part of *dao* or that functions in the unfolding of *dao* and it would be transcendent only to some of things in reality or process rather than to all things.

Because all sorts of things happen in the unfolding of *dao*, all sorts of values will emerge in it. Jin thought that the emergence of purpose and mind can be accounted for in this way. *Dao* is neither purposive nor nonpurposive, neither knowing and conceiving nor not knowing and not conceiving. But because purpose may emerge in the unfolding of *dao*, the unfolding in which it emerges becomes partly purposive. The same is true of the emergence of the mind. *Dao* unfolds itself through the vehicle of actualities. Nothing can be predicated of *dao*-one, while all that can be predicated of the actualities separately are but a functioning of *dao*-infinite. Although *dao* cannot be said to be purposeful itself, it has purposefulness in its unfolding. "Purpose" is most generally used to mean desires or needs together with the adoption of means toward to their satisfaction. By "purpose" Jin meant ends to be achieved by means, whether or not the means are consciously adopted. In this sense, the ends are purposes and the means are purposive actions or activities to achieve the ends. The emergence of purpose brings with it the emergence of individuals capable of purposive acts. Because the concept of "purposiveness" is neither contradictory nor eternally unrealizable, purposiveness is a contingent possibility. Its realization is contingent with regard to any particular time or place; it is not contingent in the sense that it may never be realized. Because there is no contingent possibility that will not be realized, we can say that the sum total of contingent possibilities will be realized as time flows into infinity. The emergence of purpose is certain, but to determine when it emerged, which is quite a different matter, is a question of history. That there is purpose now is a question of fact.

With the emergence of purpose something most significant happened. There was a minimal bifurcation of reality, a faint separation of the self from others, or a slight demarcation of the inside from the outside. The whole field of reality actualized at any particular time and place was no longer quite lumpy with the emergence of purpose. Some items among the actualities set themselves apart, not by taking themselves out of time and space, but by introducing subjectivity.

The adoption of means toward ends, whether conscious or not, meant that ends would not be accomplished if means were not adopted. The adoption of means toward ends meant a modification of that part of reality that is the other, but not the self; that is outside, but not inside; that is the object but not the subject. The capacity to adopt means to ends is often accompanied by the capacity to avoid what is harmful. The objectified reality is modified in the direction of what the subjectified reality wants or needs. No matter how many or how few modifications there may be, it is only objectified reality that is modified. Reality as the nonbifurcated totality remains unmodified: it is what it is. Whatever innovations occur are what occasions and preordinations have actualized them to be. If one has a capacity to adopt means toward ends, one has a mind. A mind is something that may or may not function, but when it does, its function is entirely intellectual, although its intellectuality is a matter of degree.

The emergence of mind like the emergence of purpose is certain, although the timing of its appearance is again a different question. If the world is capable of waiting, it might have waited for ages for the appearance of mind. That we now have mind is essentially a point of historical interest quite devoid of philosophical significance. Mind might disappear altogether or disappear only to reappear under quite different conditions, that is, in a context of actualities that differ from those that are actual here and now.

Mind is active. Its activity is not itself directed toward the modification of objectified reality. It is aimed rather at understanding the objectified world. A thorough knowledge of that world leaves the world as it was or is or is going to be: it leaves the world unmodified. The emergence of mind bifurcates reality, but while the emergence of purpose bifurcates reality into the agent and patient, the emergence of mind bifurcates reality into the known object and the knowing subject.

Jin held that the emergence of purpose and the emergence of mind are both significant, each in its own way. But when they are combined so that individuals emerge endowed with purpose as well as with mind, the interrelation of what is congenial and what is uncongenial among actualities is enormously changed. Purpose without mind is sometimes effective and is sometimes ineffective, but is necessarily limited to purposive activities of limited scope. Mind without purpose distinguishes the knowing from known; by itself it cannot result in modification of the known. But when purpose and mind are combined, the adequacy and the scope of the means adopted toward the ends are increased by the help of the mind, and purpose becomes comprehensive, complex, and effective. With mind and knowledge, it is possible to have a series of ends and means such that an end may be a means to other ends and a means may be an end of other means. The longer the series of means, the more far-removed and complex the end and the easier it is to mistake the intermediate means for the ultimate end.

The link of the means to each other may be based on knowledge, on what is believed to be knowledge, or on what is falsely imagined to be knowledge. Hence, the adequacy of means towards ends may fail to be uniformly increased, although the scope of activities is bound to be enlarged when purpose is combined with mind. Values may come in to complicate the issue. Upon some criterion of valuation, the end may be eminently valuable while the means might be condemned. Moral problems or issues would never arise if mind were not joined with purpose. If there ever was any original sin, it was the alliance of mind with purpose. Through their alliance, both virtue and vice were realized.

An enormous number of other things emerged with the combined emergence of mind and purpose. Culture was born; artifacts were created; politics, ethics, and various sciences make reality more complicated than ever before. We shall not dwell on any of these, important as they are for the growth of civilization. From the point of view of time as an infinite evolutionary process, there is no reason why civilization should endure. Quite a different kind of world or a different kind of civilization may be actualized through future occasions and preordinations.

Reality is more dichotomized with the combined emergence of purpose and mind than by the emergence of either of them alone. We can call the bifurcated realities the objective and subjective realities. It is easy to have the agent and patient relation with these two realities. Mind and knowledge enable the subjective reality to be much more of an agent than purpose alone allows, hence objective reality becomes much more of a patient.

An agent can easily come to feel that almost anything can be done to transform a patient to suit the desires or needs of the agent. In so acting, the agent or subject is lifted out of the world of actualities and becomes their despotic ruler. Enormous modifications of objective reality may be accomplished, and an enormous number of artifacts may be created. Values relative to the purpose of the subject may be assigned to their modification. Creative progress may be maintained, and the agent may feel satisfaction in various lines of endeavor. But the demarcation between objective and subjective realities becomes more pronounced, and the separation of these realities becomes greater and greater, easily resulting in a sort of bloated self-importance on the part of the agent. It is also easy mistakenly to feel that in modifying objective reality, the subject is also modifying the whole process of reality or the unfolding of *dao*.

In Jin's view, human beings, up to the present, are the most effective combination of purpose and mind. He thinks that the emergence of humanity is neither accidental nor final. It is accidental only in taking place in this particular slice of time, that is, in being occasioned and ordained as it has been. Humanity, as a contingent possibility, was bound to emerge in time. Humanity is not necessary, and it is neither eternally realized nor eternally unrealizable. Because humanity is a contingent possibility, its realization comes in time. Its emergence should not be heralded with exaggerated glory, nor should its tenure of existence be falsely credited with finality. Compared to other contemporary actualities, or compared to other periods of actualization in the known span of natural history, human beings and the period in which they function may indeed be glorious. But no matter how glorious human beings may be in comparison with other contemporary species, they are also dependent upon the cooperation of other species. No matter how glorious the period in which they function may be, it is one station in the unfolding of *dao* and requires other periods to bring it to a focus. There is a sort of mutual dependence or mutual infiltration among species and among periods.

Human beings are, of course, immensely important to themselves. To us as human beings, our desires, hopes, needs, and whims are all important. Their importance differs only in degrees, because some are unimportant compared with others. The same is true of their satisfaction. Our minds alone are capable of filling us with pride. With the help of the force of our purpose, our minds give us our power. No species has ruled the world with greater power or more efficiency than the human species. Whether or not this rule has been benevolent, there is no prospect of revolution in sight. No species is currently powerful enough to overturn human power.

Nevertheless, the human species faces difficulties from within. There is greed and internal strife. Desires seem to run rampant, and luxuries become needs. Society becomes so integrated and so differentiated, that individuals may cease to be, and different social or economic strata become almost like different species. These difficulties may be overcome, and a long period of benevolent despotic rule may take place.

There is, however, a question of value that arises with the emergence of the human species. For Jin, value is a matter of a choice of criteria. A number of criteria may be adopted that fill human beings with pride. Others may be selected that fill human beings with trepidation. Like individuals, the human species is burdened with its strength; like individual strength, its strength is also its weakness. Mind is probably the strongest human asset, and yet it is through having a remarkable mind that human beings are sometimes made more calculatingly immoral, more disgustingly depraved, more painfully and falsely miserable, and more unnecessarily and cruelly at war with themselves than any other species. On the basis of value, there is no conclusive reason why the human species should survive. Fortunately or unfortunately, survival does depend not upon prescriptive values.

According to Jin, with the emergence of purpose and knowledge, reality is dichotomized into subjective and objective realities. Because human beings are endowed with both purpose and knowledge, they not only depend on modifications of object reality, but also increasingly know how these modifications are to be brought about. Objective reality is often resistant to these modifications, and its success or failure is in accordance with the power that the subject wields. This power is proportionate to the subject's knowledge. Once reality is dichotomized, struggle and resistance are inevitable. So far as objective reality is concerned, the issue seems decided, and the victory so far belongs to man. From some later point of view, this result need not be so conclusive, and the victor may also turn out to be the vanquished.

There is a good deal to be said about the plight of man. Human beings acquire purpose and knowledge after they are conceived and born. None of them become human beings with their own consent. Being assigned a human role, they have to function as human beings. They have to exist, to eat, to propagate, and to be clothed. The satisfaction of their basic desires and needs is not always easy, for there are often obstacles that cannot be overcome. Humans have to struggle for their existence, to gain power over their adversaries. They have to gain knowledge and its power in order to exist and have to exist in order to fulfill the function required of them. Whether conscious of it or not, their own nature, the nature of being human, drives them towards the acquisition of power. They are bound to modify objective reality to suit their needs and desires and to adopt means towards achieving their ends.

The combination of purpose and knowledge affords human beings power, and while power need not be dangerous, it often is. It breeds the desire for greater power and instead of being merely a means to an end, it tends itself to become an end. The struggle for existence turns into a struggle for power. As a means, power is limited. It ceases to function when an end is achieved. With the accumulation of power, there is an undreamed of expansion of desires that exceeds the requirements of existence. According to Jin:

> Knowledge by itself is harmonious, but purposes often conflict with one another, not merely between states or races or different men but also in a single individual himself. An individual with conflicting purposes is the enclosed battleground for spiritual struggle, and although stone walls do not make a prison, nor mere objective nature any obstacle to his yearnings, he is yet his own prisoner. The more power one acquires, the more one may be enslaved. We already pointed out that with the aid of knowledge purposes may become extremely complicated. There may be a chain of means to ends such that some ends are means to other ends and some means are ends to other means. If one tarries in this chain, one is liable to take means for ends. And value may enter to complicate the issue. The question of the justification of means by ends may be raised, and if one tarries with certain means so that the ends are lost sight of, the means which were formerly justified by the ends are no longer so when the ends are no longer in view. If the ends are not supposed to justify the means, then no matter how far removed the ends may be, whether or not they are lost sight of, they do not affect the means, since the latter will have to be justified on their own ground. But then the power to achieve ends is greatly diminished. Secondly, the longer the chain of means to ends, the more conflict of ends there

is likely to be. Conflict with mere objective nature is a straightforward issue, and one can march into it with a stout heart. Conflict with other human beings is liable to be accompanied by misgivings, and conflict with oneself may result in tragedies, since it is here that one's strength is also one's weakness, where one's victory is also one's defeat, and where a person is himself a house divided, and nothing can possibly console him. In the third place, with the aid of knowledge, purposes multiply and desires increase. Some desires are transformed into needs, while whims are changed into desires. The transformation may be highly satisfying, though it need not be so. But whether it is so or not, something is lost in the process. What was once only a whim or a wish or a hope with the softness, the lightness and the poetic quality that accompany it, is transformed into desires and needs with all the grossness and coarseness that accompany the will to achieve. But perhaps the important result of increased desires is that we are more enslaved by them. With the increased facility to satisfy, desires tend to increase in a geometrical ratio. In simple and native desires, we may not feel enslaved for the end is in view and the means are direct. . . . Where the end is not a sensed or felt need of the present, even a simple desire may give rise to the feeling of enslavement. (Jin, 1995b, pp. 727–9)

The chance of self-enslavement greatly increased by increased human power over objective nature and over fellow human beings. Civilization in the past may have been wiped out by glaciers, by floods, by earthquakes, by landslides, or by desiccation and decay, but it is not likely to be wiped out through such agencies in the near future. If the destruction of civilization takes place now, it is likely to be effected through human beings themselves.

The only way to liberate human beings from enslavement is to free them from egocentricity and anthropocentricity. Jin held that what we call an individual is an abstraction. An individual is a mobile area of accentuation where an enormous number of events take place in action and reaction. A mind that is aware of the universal interpenetration of individuals is bound to see things from a point of view that transcends individual difference. Jin pointed out that this mutual interpenetration is not limited to human beings. Each particular object reflects the whole particular world to which it belongs: each object is because the other objects of the particular world are. Each particular object is related to every other particular object in different ways. While some of these relations are internal and others are external, the qualities and relational properties of any single object depend upon the qualities and relational properties of every other particular object. This situation will enable human beings to know that one is permeated with the qualities and relations of one's coexistents and to be capable of universal sympathy in all its sincerity and purity.

In ceasing to be anthropocentric one may also cease to be egocentric. Once free of egocentricity, one is no longer plagued by the problem of self-enslavement. In so freeing oneself, one knows one's destiny, to be at peace with one's station in life much more comprehensively than in a merely social or political sense. What we must not forget is that a human being is also an animal and an object. It is perfectly true that we are different from some objects in being animals, from some animals in being humans, and from other humans in being oneself, but if we realize that what is known as oneself is permeated with other humans as well as other animals and objects, we will cease to be excited about being a particular self.

Bibliography

Major works by Jin Yuelin

Jin, Yuelin 1935: *Luoji* 邏輯 (logic), Beijing: Qinghua University Press

Jin, Yuelin 1940: *Lun dao* 論道 (on dao), Shanghai: Shangwu Press

Jin, Yuelin 1983: *Zhishi lun* 知識論 (theory of knowledge), Beijing: Shangwu Press

Jin, Yuelin 1988: *Luosu zhexue* 羅素哲學 (Bertrand Russell's philosophy), Shanghai: Shanghai Renmin Press

Jin, Yuelin 1995a: *Jin Yuelin wenji* 金岳霖文集 (collected works of Jin Yuelin) Lanzhou, Gansu Renmin Press

Jin, Yuelin 1995b: *Tao, Nature and Man* in Jin, Yuelin (1995a), vol. 2, pp. 568–749

Major books on Jin Yuelin

Chen, Xiaolong 1997: *Zhishi yu zhihui: Jin Yuelin zhexue yanjui* 知識與智慧：金嶽霖哲學研究 (knowledge and wisdom: on Jin Yuelin's philosophy), Beijing: Beijing Higher Education Press

Hu, Jun 1993: *Jin Yuelin*, Taipei, Dongda Publishing House

Hu, Weixi 1988: *Jin Yuelin yu Zhongguo shi zheng zhuyi renshi lun* 金嶽霖與中國實證主義認識論 (Jin Yuelin and positivist epistemology in China), Shanghai: Shanghai People's Press

Wang, Zhongjiang 1993: *Lixing yu langman* 理性與浪漫 (reason and romance), Zhengzhou, Henan People's Press

Wang, Zhongjiang and An, Jimin1 1998: *Jin Yuelin zhexue sixiang yanjiu* 金岳霖哲學思想研究 (on Jin Yuelin's philosophical thought), Beijing: Beijing Library Press

Discussion Questions

1. Is possibility more important than actuality for philosophical understanding?
2. Should we prefer Jin Yuelin's account of matter and form to those developed by Aristotle and his successors in the West?
3. Is Jin Yuelin justified in holding that *dao* is necessarily concrete?
4. How is it possible for there to be time and change?

5. Should we agree that there is no ultimate simplicity or complexity to a particular?
6. What are individual objects and events?
7. Will everything that is realizable happen?
8. Can there be anything that is transcendent to the *dao* and its unfolding?
9. What is the importance of purpose and mind?
10. Can human beings be liberated from enslavement?

II

PHILOSOPHIZING IN THE NEO-CONFUCIAN SPIRIT

6

XIONG SHILI'S METAPHYSICS OF VIRTUE

Jiyuan Yu

Since the May Fourth Movement in 1919, Confucianism has been blamed for China's weakness and decline in the face of Western aggression. The mainstream of Chinese intellectuals believed that the salvation of China as an integrated nation urgently required the introduction of Western science and democracy. Against this dominant intellectual trend, however, another voice disputed the claim that Confucianism was the reason for China's crisis and argued that, on the contrary, the underlying problem was the loss of the authentic Confucian *dao*. Accordingly, the way out was not to abandon Confucianism, but to rediscover and revive its real spirit. The main representative of this voice in contemporary Chinese philosophy was Xiong Shili (1885–1968). He declares his mission in this way:

> I try to illuminate the fundamentals of benevolence and righteousness. This was accused by many of being impractical and empty. However, if there is no way to stop the prevailing of the heresy and stop its flowing, our country and our nationality will be extinct. How could there be another way to save [China]. (Xiong, 1985, p. 29)

Xiong Shili, born in Hubei province, was never formally educated. He started to support himself and his family at the age of ten when his father, who was a village teacher, died. As a youth, Xiong was a devoted revolutionary who sought to overthrow the Qing dynasty. In 1920, he began to study Buddhism in Nanjing at the Institute for Inner Learning, which was organized by Ouyang Chingwu (1871–1943), the modern lay figure who revived the Buddhist School of Mere Consciousness ("mere consciousness," which is in Chinese *wei-shi* and in Sanskirt *Vijnanavada*, is also translated as "mere ideation," "consciousness-only," or "representation-only"). In 1922, Xiong became a lecturer on Buddhism in Peking University, where he soon became dissatisfied with Buddhism and turned to Confucianism. In particular, he was influenced by his study of the *Yijing* (*The Book of Changes*), which he regarded as the fundamental classic of Confucianism. In 1932 he published the first edition of his main work, *The New Doctrine of Mere Consciousness* (hereafter *New Doctrine*), in which he criticized Buddhism, but also appropriated many of its insights to reconstruct Confucianism. When the book first appeared, he was vehemently attacked by Buddhist scholars, including his teacher Ouyang Chingwu, who held that his treatment of Buddhism was not faithful. But Xiong's philosophical goal was not "to comment on the six classics," but for "the six classics to comment for me"; that is to say, he did not aim to be a faithful commentator, but saw himself as an original thinker who based his work on the ancient classics. It is now almost universally held that in the *New Doctrine* Xiong built the most creative philosophical system in contemporary Chinese philosophy.

Since Xiong's mission to reconstruct Confucianism was intended to assist in overcoming China's social and cultural crisis, one might wonder whether his committed philosophy could pursue the truth itself. In the Greek tradition, philosophy starts with a natural human sense of wonder and the desire to know the truth concerning things that puzzle us. (In Greek the word *aletheia* [truth] simply means "uncovering.") However, Xiong did not see his intended political mission and the pursuit of truth as conflicting with each other in his philosophy. He believed that only through explanation of its original meaning and spirit could Confucianism have real moral and political impact. Hence, his political and social concern motivated him to find the truth and was not an expression of narrow nationalist sentiment. Indeed, at the outset of Confucianism, Confucius himself put forward his vision in order to save the culture of the declining Zhou dynasty; but that does not entail that Confucius has no universal insights to offer about human nature.

In a sense, a history of Confucianism has been a process of discovering and rediscovering the true *dao* of Confucius. For Confucius, the real *dao* was the *dao* of the ancient sages and Zhou culture. Mencius claimed that his mission was to defend Confucianism against the attack of Mohism and Yangzhu's egoism (Mencius, 1970, 3B:9; see also Chan, 1963).

In the Tang Dynasty, Han Yu (768–824) asserted that after Mencius the "correct transmission" of Confucius' *dao* was broken and that he was the person to continue it. The Neo-Confucians of the Song and Ming Dynasties believed that they were the real successors of Mencius and the defenders of the Confucian *dao* in the face of the aggression of Buddhism. Xiong acknowledged the contributions made by Neo-Confucianism, particularly by the philosophy of Wang Yangming, but still saw many problems to overcome in explaining the Confucian *dao*. He criticized the Cheng-Zhu School: "Their *dao* is not broad. It is right for them to focus on human ethics and commonality, but they are too restricted. Their main trend is to follow the footsteps of the former masters and to safeguard the old, but with little new development." He also criticizes Wang Yangming: "His doctrine emphasized inwardness and is deficient in its external extension." Xiong regarded his own mission to be finding and developing the real *dao* of Confucius to meet the challenge of Western culture. "Now again we are in a weak and dangerous situation. With the strong aggression of European culture, our authentic spirit has been extinct. People are accustomed to self-disregard, self-violence, self-abandonment. Everything is copied from the outside, with little self-establishment. Hence the *New Doctrine* must be written" ("An outline of the main point of the *New Doctrine* – Reply to Mu Zhongshan," in Xiong, 1949).

Xiong's understanding of his own position in the long tradition of transmitting Confucianism has won general approval. The history of Confucianism is usually divided into three stages: Classical Confucianism, Neo-Confucianism, and Contemporary or New Confucianism. Xiong is widely regarded as the thinker who laid down the basis for the revival of Confucianism as Contemporary Confucianism in the twentieth century.

However, just as Neo-Confucianism sought to debate with imported Buddhism, Contemporary Confucianism has aimed to engage with Western culture. Xiong clearly had that task in mind, but he never studied abroad and could not read any Western language. His knowledge of Western philosophy was obtained from the very limited translations available in his time. As a result, Xiong's discussion of Western Philosophy is abstract, sketchy, and partial, in sharp contrast with his sophisticated and professional discussion of Buddhism. He argued that future learning must be based on the reconciliation of Western, Chinese, and Indian philosophies, but his central emphasis was that "there is indeed something solid in the inherited classics of Eastern philosophy, and I hope scholars could study this seriously and carefully" (Xiong, 1994, p. 156). His major philosophical contribution has been, through appropriating some aspects of Buddhism and combining them with his sophisticated understanding of the *Yijing*, to provide Confucianism – which has traditionally been regarded as being only an ethics – with a more solid metaphysical basis and a more dynamic character.

The 1932 first edition of the *New Doctrine* was written in Classical Chinese. In 1944, Xiong published a Colloquial Chinese version, which was not a mere translation, but was rather a complete rewriting of the original work. The Colloquial Chinese version is three times the length of the Classical Chinese version. In 1958–9, Xiong published *On Original Reality and Function* and *Illuminating the Mind*. These two books together formed a revised account of the *New Doctrine*. According to Xiong, once we have the later version, the earlier versions could be discarded (Xiong, 1994, p. 44). Nevertheless, some arguments are more detailed and more clearly expressed in his Colloquial version than in these later revisions. In the following synoptic account of Xiong's thought, I will use the texts in which his views are best expressed. Xiong wrote numerous other works, and a list of his major writings can be found at the end of this chapter. I have translated most of my quotations from the *Collected Works of Xiong Shili* (Chinese Book Bureau): the first volume (1985) contains the Classical and Colloquial versions of the *New Doctrine*; the second volume (1994) contains *On Original Reality and Function* and *Illuminating the Mind*; and the third volume (1996) contains *Important Remarks of Xiong Shili* (a series of short articles, essays, lecture notes, and letters). In addition, Xiong's *Original Confucianism* (1956), which is a develop-ment of his *Important Guide for Studying the Classics* (1945), presents his political philosophy.

After the founding of the People's Republic of China, Xiong stayed on the mainland and continued to be a professor at Peking University. In 1954, he moved to Shanghai and dedicated himself exclusively to writing. Exception-ally, the Communist Government did not require him, like most other intel-lectuals, to criticize his own earlier thinking in terms of Marxism. Not only could Xiong continue to revise and develop his own philosophy, but he also had government sponsorship in publishing many of his writings after 1949. Nevertheless, he suffered some physical abuse at the beginning of the Cultural Revolution. Seeing that Confucianism had suffered another disaster, he died in anger and despair in 1968 at the age of 84.

Daily Decrease and Daily Renovation

A major reason for Xiong's conversion from Buddhism to Confucianism was his recognition that Buddhism gives too much emphasis to negative or passive aspects of human nature and that it consequently fails to provide a positive and active guide to human life. The tenets of Buddhism hold that this world is unreal, immutable, and empty and that life in this world is a sea of suffering. Hence, it advocates the escape from this world through salvation. Borrowing a term from Laozi ["In the pursuit of learning one increases daily; in the pursuit of the *dao*, one decreases daily." (Laozi, 1970, chapter 48; see also Chan, 1963), Xiong Shili characterized Buddhism as "the learning of daily decrease [*ri shen*]," meaning that it is a philosophy which reveals the dark side of human nature and then directs us to eliminate it: "The learning of daily decrease . . . is devoted to the self-illumination of the inner consciousness and the overcoming of disorder and contamination" (Xiong, 1994, p. 180).

Buddhism, in Xiong's judgment, achieves an unparalleled depth in ana-lyzing the dark aspects of human life. Since Buddhism, in both Hinayana and Mahayana schools, concentrates exclusively on these aspects, it denies posit-ive features of human life and concludes that we should renounce this world. However, human nature also has a brighter side. The meaning of human life is not confined to eliminating bad desires, but also involves broadening and developing these brighter aspects of human nature. Buddhism as a learning of "daily decrease" completely ignores the good elements of human nature and its development. It is, Xiong asserts, learning against humanity (Xiong, 1994, pp. 182–202, 259–60).

Confucianism, according to Xiong, also pays attention to the negative aspect of human nature. One major aspect of the central Confucian virtue of *ren* (translated variously as "humanity," "virtue," or "benevolence") is "to restrain oneself and return to propriety" (Confucius, 1970, 12:1; see also Chan, 1963). Mencius distinguished between the small body (the bodily desires) and the major self (the heart/mind; *Mencius*, 6A:15). But in contrast to Buddhism, Confucian thought did not seek to reveal the details of human selfishness and appetites: "Confucius does not deny current human life, and so did not want to develop these views" (Xiong, 1985, p. 674). Instead, Confucianism upholds original human goodness, that is, the shining aspect of human nature. Orthodox Confucianism, from Mencius to Wang Yangming, insists that there is original benevolence in human nature (with the exception of Xunzi. Xiong judges that Xunzi fails to reach the essence of Confucianism. See Xiong, 1994, p. 194). Furthermore, Confucianism not only holds that human nature is originally good, but argues that the role of human *dao* is to develop this fundamental goodness. Mencius described human nature as consisting of four good seeds. These seeds must grow for an individual to become a really good person. A dynamic approach to human nature is indeed characteristic of Confucianism.

Accordingly, whereas Xiong labeled Buddhism as a learning of daily decrease, he borrowed a term from *Yijing* ("Daily renovation means the flourished virtue," see *Yijing*, "The Appended Remarks," part 1, chapter 5; see also Chan, 1963), to label Confucianism as a "learning of daily renovation [*ri xing*]":

> So Confucius' inquiry into *dao* characteristically seeks after benevolence, and by expanding daily intuitive and illuminating knowledge to penetrate into all things; it extends daily the seed of the unbearable mind, without excluding any human relation. Hence, the learning of *dao* focuses on daily renovation, rather than on daily decrease. (Xiong, 1994, p. 185)

In line with orthodox Confucian views, Xiong maintained that the human *dao* lies in expanding the good root of the original mind and making it grow daily. It is this learning of daily renovation that Xiong embraced and was determined to develop.

The contrast between the learning of daily decrease and the learning of daily renovation is significant. It reveals not only how Confucianism is distinguished from Buddhism, but also how Confucianism is an alternative to the main tradition of Western ethics. As is well known, the defining question of Western ethics is "why should I be moral?" This question is raised because the general assumption is that human beings are by nature selfish, and hence to be moral, which means to do good for others, needs justification. This is the fundamental challenge Thrasymachus poses in Plato's *Republic*, Book I. Various systems have been established to show why and how human selfish desires should be constrained. This sort of approach to ethics could also be regarded as a "learning of daily decrease" and is thus in contrast to Confucianism. Since Confucianism concentrates on the benevolence of human nature and attempts to develop this goodness, its central question is not "why should I be moral?" but "how should I cultivate my humanity?"

Original Reality and Function

Underlying the Buddhist learning of daily decrease, in Xiong's understanding, is its metaphysical belief that there is an unbridgeable split between an absolute unchanging reality (Dharma-nature or *fa-xing*), and a constantly changing and conditional phenomenal world (Dharma-characters or *fa-xiang*) (Xiong, 1994, pp. 69–77, 84–5, 111–12). These two realms are thought to be mutually exclusive, for Dharma-characters are things that lack any real nature of their own and are mere aggregates conditioned by many causes. Buddhism calls on us to transcend their conditionality and relativity to attain absolute knowledge. Hence, the only worthwhile life requires us to escape from this human world. For the convenience of argument, I call this theory the Separation Thesis.

Accordingly, to correct the Buddhist learning of daily decrease and to expand the Confucian learning of daily renovation, it is necessary to reject the Separation Thesis. Xiong repeatedly claimed that the central theory of his *New Doctrine* seeks to show that original reality, which he calls *ti*, and the phenomenal world, which he calls *yong*, function, are one and cannot be split into two separate realms. For convenience, I call it the Sameness Thesis. The word *ti* is generally translated as "substance." But this will lead one to read an Aristotelian conceptual framework into Xiong. To avoid unnecessary confusion, I choose to translate *ti* as "original reality."

Xiong admits that original reality and function should be described in different terms. Original reality does not have physical forms, while function does; original reality is the cause of all transformations, while function constitutes these transformations; original reality is hidden, while function is manifest; original reality is one, while function is many. Nevertheless, all these distinctions hold only at a level of description. More fundamentally, original reality and function are not two things with different natures, but one thing: the world of reality and function is a unity. Xiong's reasoning is as follows:

If they are separable, function will differ from original reality and exist independently, and in that way function will have its own original reality. We should not seek for some entity outside function and name it original reality. Furthermore, if original reality exists independent of function, it is a useless reality. In that case, if it is not a dead thing, it must be a dispensable thing. Thinking back and forth, I believe that original reality and function are not separable. This should be beyond doubt. (Xiong, 1985, p. 434)

If one talks about function, function is not something other than original reality. Otherwise, we might have to find another foundation for function. Xiong here assumes any function must presuppose a foundation and hence to separate function from original reality will result in a regress *ad infinitum*. Correspondingly, when one talks about original reality, it is not something other than function. Otherwise, original reality would not involve any change and transformation and therefore would be empty or void. "How can you still say that it is real?" (Xiong, 1985, p. 433).

Original reality is one, but is manifested in ten thousand things. Original reality becomes function when it reveals itself as many manifestations. Function is the manifestation of original reality. Ten thousand things manifest what original reality is, although this does not mean that original reality is the aggregation of the many functions:

> Original reality is one, but is manifested as function; hence it has to be differentiated. If we say that there are different parts, we are talking with respect to the appearances of function. Although the appearances of function are differentiated into various parts, these parts are not different with respect to original reality. Hence, insofar as there are different parts, these parts are mutually assimilable and integrable into an organic whole. Why is that? It is because function is original reality, and because it is not the case that function is something separate and different from original reality. The appearances of function are various. If they were not mutually assimilable, they would not form a whole. But if function were assimilable and reduced to original reality, then all the appearances of function would be the same. (Xiong, 1985, p. 446)

For Xiong, the sameness of original reality and function is best illustrated in terms of the metaphor of the ocean and the many waves:

> This meaning is subtle and profound. It is best illustrated in terms of the relation between the ocean and all the waves: 1. The ocean is analogous to original reality; 2. All the water in the ocean is manifested as waves. This is analogous to original reality's manifestation as function of ten thousand things, that is, one function and another; 3. All the waves are analogous to the innumerable functions; 4. All the waves are mutually assimilable to a whole; this is analogous to the mutual assimilation of all the functions into a whole. From the above, we can see that the metaphor of the ocean and the waves best illuminates the relation between original reality and function. (Xiong, 1985, p. 446)

The Sameness Thesis, according to Xiong, is implied although not explained in the Confucian classics. When Confucius says: "What does Heaven ever say? Yet there are the four seasons going round and there are the hundred things coming into being. What does Heaven ever say?" (Confucius, 1970, 17:19), he is indicating that Heaven as original reality is manifested in its actions. The Sameness Thesis is also in the spirit of the *Yijing*, which contains the remarks: "The successive movement of *yin* and *yang* constitutes the *dao* . . . It is manifested in *ren* (humanity) but is hidden in functioning" (*Yijing*, 1968, "The Appended Remarks," part I, chapter 5). In Xiong's interpretation, this word "hidden" (*cang*) means that ultimate reality "does not exist separately from its function" (Xiong, 1994, p. 119).

Xiong held that it is almost universal for the philosophies to separate reality from the phenomenal world. Hence, his Sameness Thesis can repair not only the Separation Thesis of Buddhism, but also the separation of principle (*li*) and material force (*qi*) in Neo-Confucianism and the separation between *phenomenon* and *noumenon* in Western philosophy. However, Xiong's argument supporting the claim that original reality and function are one and not two and are, therefore, the same, is quite thin. The metaphysics that separates the two worlds is built on a set of arguments. The Buddhist separation between Dharma-nature and Dharma-characters is predicated on a theory of change and a theory of causation. In Western philosophy, especially in the Platonic tradition, the arguments for the separation between *noumenon* and *phenomenon* include linguistic considerations (the difference between subject and predicate in predication), psychological considerations (the difference between soul and body and the difference between rationality and emotion), epistemological considerations (the distinction between opinion and knowledge and the distinction between sensation and reason), and metaphysical considerations (the distinctions between perfection and imperfection, between an original and its copies, and between the eternal and what changes). Xiong would have to deal with all or at least the most important of these arguments to have a convincing theory that the two allegedly separated worlds are actually one. But Xiong, while suggesting that the Sameness Thesis is "subtle and profound," frequently employs the metaphor of the ocean and its waves to substitute for the expected arguments.

The Sameness Thesis, however, has a great bearing on the Confucian learning of daily renovation. As we mentioned before, the metaphysical basis for the Buddhist learning of daily decrease is the thesis that reality is separate from the changing world. Accordingly, whatever we do in this world is meaningless at the level of reality. When Xiong proposed that original reality and function are one, he was indicating that the phenomenal flux of change is not illusory, but is intrinsically meaningful. Our world manifests in a tangible form what ultimate reality is. If original reality is in daily life, there is no point in human beings giving up this world. Instead, their lives should be devoted to daily cultivation in order to attain the vision of original reality.

Change and Transformation

Not only is the world a unity, but it also is a continuous process of becoming and transformation. Buddhism understands this change, but restricts it to the realm of Dharma-characters or the phenomenal world. It argues that precisely because phenomena are temporary and changing, they are illusory. In contrast, reality or Dharma-nature is held to be in absolute tranquillity. Following his metaphor of the ocean and waves, Xiong criticized the Buddhist view as being like "a child who goes to the coast, and recognizes only all the waves as reality, without knowing that all the waves are the manifestations of the sea water" (Xiong, 1985, p. 313).

Because Xiong believed that the world is in change, he used the dynamic term "function" to refer to what others call *phenomenon* or *fan-xiang*. "The word 'function,' also means 'effect,' 'usage,' 'tendency,' 'change,' 'work,' and 'arising anew again and again and flowing unceasingly'" (Xiong, 1985, p. 432). Based on his Sameness Thesis, Xiong maintained that if function changes, original reality transforms as well. In Xiong's view, the ability of changing into all things is precisely what characterizes original reality, and hence he also called original reality "eternal transformation" or "the ability to change" (Xiong, 1985, pp. 314, 352). It transforms at every instant and is permanently in such a state. In its perpetual transition, various manifestations or functions result.

In developing his metaphysics of change, Xiong inherited much from the *Yijing*. A. N. Whitehead famously claimed that the whole of Western philosophy is a series of footnotes to Plato. Xiong, who held a similar attitude towards the *Yijing*, said: "All Chinese scholarship and thinking have their source in the *Yijing*" (Xiong, 1994, p. 12). The basic themes of the *Yijing* are: "daily renovation means the flourishing of virtue," and "production and reproduction mean change" (*Yijing*, 1968, "The Appended Remarks," part 1, chapter 5).

In the *Yijing*, we read: "There is *qian* (heaven), the stillness of which is absorbed, and the motion of which is straightforward; thus it produces greatly; there is *kun* (earth), the stillness of which is *closing* (*xi*) the motion of which is *opening* (*pi*), so it produces extensively" (*Yijing*, 1968, "The Appended Remarks," part 1, chapter 6; my emphasis). Inspired by this passage and ascribing the two aspects of *kun* to original reality, Xiong suggested that the perpetual transformation of original reality consists of "closing" and "opening." These aspects are two tendencies of change, not two realities.

"The tendency of transformation which integrates to form things is called 'closing'" (Xiong, 1985, p. 317). The closing tendency is a tendency to integrate and to consolidate; in other words, to materialize. Because of it, various physical things are formed. However, as the closing tendency arises, there is an opposite tendency of opening that arises simultaneously. "The tendency of being strong, vigorous and not materialized is called 'opening'"

(Xiong, 1985, p. 318). In the tendency to opening, transformation is its own master and maintains its own nature by refusing to be materialized. This is how Xiong summarizes his ideas:

> Transformation manifests itself as the tendency to move, and is closing and opening, and it is not simple. The tendency to close is to consolidate. Because of this tendency of closing, there form things in shapes, which we, by way of hypothesis, call matter or the operation of matter. The tendency to open is strong and vigorous, and operates in the midst of closing and makes closing follow opening itself. Because of this tendency, we, by way of hypothesis, say that there is mind or the operation of mind. (Xiong, 1985, p. 319)

The two tendencies work simultaneously but in opposite directions. Both are indispensable. If there is no closing, there is only flowing but without matter. In that case, the tendency to opening would not have any instrument to use, and consequently there would be no real opening. If there were no opening, reality would be completely materialized, and the universe would be a solid and dead world.

Since closing and opening are not two separate things, but are two aspects or tendencies of the same reality, and since they are responsible for the apparent distinction between matter and mind, Xiong inferred that the dichotomy of matter and mind is not real. On this basis, Xiong criticized both materialism and idealism. Idealism, according to him, admits only the tendency to opening and reduces the tendency to closing to the tendency to opening. In contrast, materialism admits only the tendency to closing and reduces the tendency to opening to the tendency to closing.

In the final analysis, however, Xiong turns out to be an idealist. He claimed that in the opening tendency original reality manifests its true nature. Of the two tendencies, opening is the determining factor and the directing force in the whole process of transformation. It is the true nature of original reality that it is manifested in the myriad things, but in the constant transformation of reality it itself is not materialized. Xiong called the opening tendency "mind," but also called original reality "mind" or "consciousness." Both are mind in the following sense: "The meaning of mind is to master, in the sense that although it is the foundational reality of ten thousands things, it is not matter itself" (Xiong, 1985, p. 592). Sometimes he even directly called the tendency to open the mind of the universe: the closing can also be named as the mind of the universe, and we could call it "the spirit of the universe" (Xiong, 1985, p. 328). Like the Buddhist theory of Mere Consciousness, consciousness in Xiong's philosophy remains the ultimate reality. Probably this is the reason why Xiong calls his theory the "New Doctrine of Mere Consciousness," although in Xiong's view consciousness is actually a process rather than a static being.

Xiong further claimed that change follows a great rule that can be comprehended in terms of opposites: "We believe that it is the great principle of resulting from opposites. When we talk about change, it is oppositional, lively, and has inner contradiction; and the reason for change is in contradiction" (Xiong, 1985, p. 315). Change must be from opposites. This idea is inherited from the *Yijing* and the *Laozi*. The *Yijing* illuminates the principle of change in terms of trigrams. Each trigram contains three lines. Why three? According to Xiong, it should be interpreted by appeal to the remark of the *Laozi* that "one gives birth to two, and two gives birth to three." Three lines symbolize the principle of resulting from contraries, and they mean that one gives birth to two, and that two gives birth to three. If there is one, there is two, and they form a pair of opposites. Then the three is a combination. What this means is that the transformation (one) manifests itself as the tendency to close. In closing, it tends to be materialized and almost loses its own nature. Thus, the closing is two. This is what it means to say that one gives birth to two. But the transformation retains its own nature. Whenever there is a tendency to close, there simultaneously arises a tendency to open. This opening is called three, and this is what it means to say that two gives birth to three.

Here, the numbers one, two, and three do not represent a successive order and do not constitute three actual stages of change. Influenced by the Buddhist idea of instant generation and destruction (*shana shengmie*), Xiong held that change is not a process of development but is instantaneous. As soon as closing takes place, it disappears; and the same is true for opening. Both are instantaneous and disappear the very moment they arise: "All things are generated at this moment and are destroyed at this moment. So we say the time of birth is the time of death. None of the things will endure for a short while. It seems that there are enduring things in the world, but that is a distorted perception" (Xiong, 1985, pp. 334–5). Since change is instantaneous, nothing in this world has a history, for nothing stays. For Xiong, this instantaneous transformation is what the *Yijing* means by "the daily renovation of the universe." However, Xiong never satisfactorily explains why his theory of instantaneous transformation is better than a continuum view of change.

Furthermore, since original reality, although transforming instantly, keeps its own nature of transformation unaltered, it is also in a sense unchanging:

> Original reality is manifested into innumerable and boundless functions, that is, all the transformations; hence it is changing. However, although original reality is manifested as function of all the particulars or all the transformations, it does not change its own nature. Its own nature is pure, dynamic, obstructionless. In these senses it is said to be unchanging. (Xiong, 1985, p. 314)

Xiong's theory of transformation is often said to be similar to the philosophy of life of Henri Bergson or to the process metaphysics of A. N. Whitehead. Because Xiong could not read Western books, it is difficult to tell how much he was influenced by them. When he himself was asked to explain the similarity, Xiong said that he was not sure how similar his views were to Whitehead's, but he agreed that based on the account of Bergson's thought in the work of other scholars, there appeared to be some close similarities between Bergson and himself. Nevertheless, Xiong suspected that the similarities could be superficial. His doubt was based on the belief that he and Bergson had different ways of comprehending reality: "the original reality that the Western scholars talk about is constructed through inferential reasoning and is regarded as something external. The *New Doctrine* directly points to the original mind, connects the inner self and outer things and combines them as one. This is achieved through what Mencius says 'to be sincere through reflection,' not through inferential reasoning. So I doubt that Bergson is really similar to me" (Xiong, 1985, p. 679). Given that all three philosophers regarded reality as a process rather than as a static being, they do share a common outlook of dynamism. However, the dynamic picture each drew was from a different ground. Xiong drew upon the Buddhist theory of constant transformation and especially the *Yijing*; Bergson's vitalism was related to the development of the biology of his time, and Whitehead's process philosophy was based on field theory in modern physics. It would certainly be interesting to have a detailed comparison of these three theories of change, although the work cannot be done here.

Original Reality and Humanity

In presenting a process metaphysics, Xiong aimed to draw an ethical implication that a worthwhile human life should be a process of daily renovation. As he himself makes clear: "Everything is in the vigorous, lively and unceasing process of change. We call this kind of change the transformation of the great function. This cannot be disputed. When we guide our life attitude according to cosmology, the only conclusion is that human life should make effort to advance and move up" (Xiong, 1985, p. 307). The bridge for continuity between metaphysics and ethics is the view that heaven and human beings are one and that the mind of the entire universe is also the mind of human beings. "According to the tenet of the *New Doctrine*, heaven is in man; and man is heaven" (Xiong, 1996, p. 14). "Original reality is not separate from my mind" (Xiong, 1985, p. 251). Original reality is manifested in ten thousand things and is in all of them. Human minds are the manifestation of the original mind in human beings. Thus, the life of human beings and the great life of the universe are not two.

The first sentence of the *New Doctrine*, in both its Classical Chinese version and its Colloquial Chinese version, is:

> Today I invent this theory to show to those who intend to understand and inquire about metaphysics, that the original reality of all things is neither the objective world separate from the mind, nor that it is comprehensible through knowledge; it must be comprehended through reflective seeking and confirming. (Xiong, 1985, pp. 43, 247)

This sentence implies two theses: first, the human mind and original reality are not separate; and secondly, original reality must be grasped through reflection on what is in the human mind. Both theses are basic Confucian doctrines. In Chinese, the term for virtue (*de*) derives from "to get," that is, to get from the *dao* of heaven. For the Confucian tradition, *de* is the manifestation of the *dao* of heaven in human beings. This is why Confucius said: "Heaven produced the virtue that is in me" (Confucius, 1970, 7:22). Since the human mind and reality are the same, it follows that to know reality one should know one's own mind and that it is through this knowledge that we cultivate our virtue. The first sentences of *The Doctrine of the Mean* say: "What Heaven imparts to man is called human nature. To follow our nature is called the *dao*. Cultivating the *dao* is called education" (Legge, 1893). One central thesis of the philosophy of Mencius is: "to exhaust one's mind is to know one's nature, and a man who knows his own nature will know heaven" (Mencius, 1970, 7A:1). Both doctrines were much developed in the Lu–Wang School of Neo-Confucianism.

To meet the challenge raised by his times, Xiong further defended and developed these two basic Confucian doctrines. His Sameness Thesis provides a metaphysical basis to explain how the human mind and original reality are the same. Xiong also distinguished the human mind into the "original mind" and the "habituated mind." The habituated mind is the complex of thought, will, and the emotions. Habituated mind is inclined to know things through presupposing the external world and is conditioned by self-prejudice and self-desire. The original mind is our real nature (*xing*) and "the original self." It is the original mind that is one with original reality, and it is by exhausting the nature of the original mind that one who knows his own nature also knows the nature of heaven (Xiong, 1985, pp. 251–2). The assumption that there is a mind other than our psychological mind might seem to be unscientific. Here, however, we should be reminded of Plato's notion of pure soul in the *Phaedo* that is the subjective counterpart of the Ideas and of Aristotle's thinking of thinking in the *Metaphysics* and active intellect in the *De Anima*. Furthermore, to reinforce the idea that the human mind and the original mind are one, Xiong directly names the original mind *ren* (generally translated as "humanity" or "benevolence"), the fundamental virtue of Confucianism: "*Ren* is the original mind, and is the original reality which we human beings commonly share with heaven, earth and the myriad things" (Xiong, 1985, p. 567). Then, what is the content of *ren* that is identified with original reality? "*Ren* means generation and without end" (Xiong, 1985, pp. 391, 517; Xiong, 1994, pp. 118–19). In other words, *ren* is precisely the virtue of production and reproduction of original reality.

When the *New Doctrine* was first published, Xiong announced that this was only the part of his philosophy dealing with "objects" (*jin, Visaya*) and there would be another part on "calculation" (*liang, Pramana*). This part was supposed to answer the question of how we can know the original mind.

Unfortunately, although the *New Doctrine* was revised several times, the intended part on calculation was never completed. However, the preface to *The Original Confucianism* contains an outline of this part. The basic idea is related to the chapter "illuminating the Mind" of the *New Doctrine*, which was developed into a separate book *Illuminating the Mind*. By grouping these writings together, we are able to examine Xiong's contribution to the Confucian doctrine that to know reality is to know one's mind.

The most important point that Xiong makes in this aspect of his work is to distinguish between "calculative understanding" (*liang zhi*) and "nature understanding" (*xing zhi*). This distinction is the epistemological version of the distinction between the habituated mind and the original mind. From the point of view of the theory of calculation, the habituated mind is calculative understanding and the original mind is nature understanding. Xiong then associated scientific knowledge with calculative understanding and philosophy with nature understanding. In this way, he dealt with the relation between Confucianism and modern science.

Calculative understanding is "deliberating and inferring, or the logic of discriminating things" (Xiong, 1985, p. 249). It is scientific rationality and is bound to sense experience. Nature understanding is an inward process of intuitive experiencing that points back to the mind itself to discover the original reality within it. This understanding is the self-awareness or self-intuition of original reality. "Nature understanding is the illumination of the real self. What is meant here by 'the real self' is original reality" (Xiong, 1985, p. 249).

Calculative understanding is the function or the manifestation in the faculties of nature understanding. This understanding has its role and place, but cannot illuminate what original reality is. According to Xiong, calculative understanding "is an instrument to seek reason in the external world. This instrument, if used in the universe of daily life, i.e., the physical world, cannot be said to be inappropriate. But if we do not use it carefully and try to use it as an instrument to solve the problem of metaphysics, and in that way we take original reality as an external object to infer and inquire into, then it is fundamentally wrong" (Xiong, 1985, p. 254). Xiong suggests that ontology becomes a controversial matter mainly because both its practitioners and its critics deal with it in terms of calculative understanding. This limit that Xiong sets for science strongly echoes Kant's *Critique of Pure Reason* (1929) and also has parallels to Heidegger's treatment of technology (Heidegger, 1977).

Differing from Kant, however, Xiong maintained that original reality can be comprehended. He held that we cannot regard truth as something outside of our mind, waiting for us to explore, but that we must study ontology through understanding human nature. We must realize that original reality is in each of us, and that we cannot seek to know it in external things through reasoning. We should turn inward and let original reality present itself.

Furthermore, such an intuitive grasp of original reality accompanies our moral cultivation. Truth must be practiced before it becomes manifest.

Xiong did not reject science itself. He believed that science is significant in human progress and even called science the "learning of daily increase" (Xiong, 1994, pp. 178–9). His purpose in limiting the role of science was to show that science cannot contribute to the learning of daily renovation, that is, to the cultivation of virtue. In his understanding, science fails in this aspect for two reasons. First, scientific understanding is fragmented. If the original mind is concerned with fragmentary details, it will be broken into pieces and lose definite direction in life. Secondly, science directs people to be attached to the material world and could easily promote selfish desire. Xiong saw the introduction of Western science as a factor leading people to ignore the original mind that they share with heaven and earth, and he therefore regarded it as being responsible for the decline of Confucianism in his time.

There is a point in Xiong's distinction between science and philosophy. It is true that science cannot solve the problem of the meaning of human life, and hence it cannot replace philosophy. However, precisely because they have different areas of concern, we cannot blame scientific rationality simply because it cannot do what a metaphysics seeks to accomplish. It does not follow that by engaging in scientific activities one's mind will be fragmented and lose the general purpose of human life. Besides, science employs synthesis as well as analysis; and even intuition plays a great role. It is mistaken to believe that science must lead human beings to indulge in material passions and to be calculative and selfish. It is the attitude towards the results of science that affects human life, rather than the scientific activity itself. Scientific activity and the cultivation of virtue are not one and same process. It is a common problem for Confucians to confuse them and not to assess the merits of science from an appropriate standpoint. Moreover, Xiong had a special problem. The main trend in contemporary Chinese philosophy has been to develop logic and scientific methodology and to replace the mysterious intuitive thinking of traditional Chinese philosophy. Not surprisingly, Xiong's emphasis on intuition and direct experience was not echoed as widely as he wished.

Moreover, the sharp division between philosophy and science, or between calculative understanding and nature understanding, creates an inner tension in Xiong's philosophy. On the one hand, his Sameness Thesis proposed that original reality is not something separate from function and that they are one and cannot be split apart. On the other hand, calculative understanding, which is about functions and is itself a function of the original mind, cannot grasp original reality.

Xiong's theory of nature understanding is much influenced by the Buddhist method of "sitting in meditation" and by Wang Yangming's method of extending one's innate knowledge. However, in contrast to the presuppositions of these methods, Xiong insisted that the manifestation of the original mind is not an act once and for all. Rather it is a process of constant transformation. Furthermore, the transformation has a definite direction, and in this sense the mind is also called the will:

> What does it mean to say that it has a definite direction? It means that it forever unfolds itself in accordance with its original nature, which is generation and regeneration without stop, and resists being materialized. Hence this definite direction is also what life consists in, and is the unique reality. The self is established on this basis. (Xiong, 1985, p. 594)

The whole philosophy of Xiong Shili was intended to show that each of us has in us the creative spirit that is our real humanity. We will obstruct this spirit if we indulge in material desires and are conditioned by our prejudice, but we can and should manifest and extend our humanity in constant invention and creation.

Virtue and Metaphysics

Xiong's main work was to reconstruct a metaphysical basis for Confucian virtue ethics. That is, he synthesized several main doctrines of Confucianism and integrated them into a coherent system in order to show that the cultivation of virtue has an ontological and cosmological foundation. The significance of his work is evident for the development of Confucianism, but what is the place of such a philosophical orientation, assessed from the viewpoint of contemporary Western philosophy?

To answer this question, we can appeal to the framework provided by the reception of Aristotle's metaphysics in today's revival of virtue ethics. Like Xiong, Aristotle believed that human virtue has its metaphysical ground, although for Aristotle this ground was teleology and not the identity of the human mind and the universal mind presented by Xiong. According to Aristotle's teleology, each thing has its own nature, that is, its internal principle of moving and resting. Nature has two principles: matter and form, and it is form that is the decisive aspect and the primary substance of each thing. The formal nature, as a moving principle, directs a thing to develop from potentiality to actuality. It is the form or substance itself that develops or actualizes itself in the final end. The final actualization is nothing else but the actualization of the formal nature itself. To apply this theory to human beings, Aristotle held that each human being has its formal nature, which is its *ergon* (function), and that this formal nature is rationality. *Ergon* is etymologically related to actuality (*energeia*) (Aristotle, *Metaphysics*, 1050a21). Accordingly, rationality as human *ergon* must be active. It is exercising rationality well that is defined as human virtue. Despite all their differences, Xiong's metaphysics and Aristotle's metaphysics are comparable in several respects. In particular, both present a dynamic outlook. Xiong believed that we have an original mind, which is the shining light of humanity; Aristotle claimed that we have rationality, which is the essence of human beings. Xiong suggested that virtue is the unceasing manifestation, that is the production and reproduction, of the original mind; Aristotle held that virtue is the exercise rather than the possession of rationality (Aristotle, *Nicomachean Ethics*, 1098b33–4, 1175b34–5). Xiong claimed that the highest good is to be united with heaven and earth; Aristotle asserted that the highest *eudaimonia* is the full manifestation or the most free exercise of rationality, which is in the life of contemplation and that in such a life one is identical with God. It is clear that Aristotle's ethics, in Xiong's term, is also a "learning of daily renovation."

There has been a positive revaluation of Aristotle's virtue ethics in contemporary philosophy, but what is revived is Aristotle's theory of moral virtues. It is Aristotle's emphasis on moral character and its cultivation that some contemporary philosophers regard as being superior to Kantian principles or Mill's utilitarian consequentialism in providing insight into our ethical life. In contrast, Aristotle's teleological metaphysics is not welcomed at all. His function argument is highly controversial, and his emphasis on contemplation as the supreme good draws much criticism. In general, scholars doubt that the cultivation of virtue, which is thought to be a matter of moral education and habituation, is metaphysically determined.

Since Xiong's effort to revive Confucianism is through a reconstruction of a metaphysical basis of virtue, it is very natural to regard him as pursuing something which recent theorists of virtue ethics prefer to ignore. One might say that it is valuable for Confucianism to emphasize benevolence, family value, community engagement, moral education and cultivation, and in these areas Confucianism has much to offer. The mysterious Confucian theories that the human mind and heaven are one or that the highest human good is to be unified with heaven might on this view be discarded along with Aristotle's teleology. Xiong embraced Confucianism at a time when most Chinese intellectuals were trying to introduce Western science and democracy to replace Confucian tradition. Today, the revival of Aristotle's virtue ethics might be seen as a credit to Xiong as well, given that the Confucianism that Xiong revived is also a type of virtue ethics. But contrary to this expectation, Xiong's work seems once again to run contrary to the mainstream of philosophy.

In spite of the plausibility of such an assessment, a question emerges. Xiong is not providing a sort of metaphysics that is external to Confucianism and can be discarded by it. If Confucian virtue (*de*) is a matter of "getting," of embodying in oneself the *dao* of heaven, Confucian virtue ethics inherently requires a metaphysics. It has been the Confucian orthodoxy that moral ideas, cosmological insights, and ontological claims cannot be separated. It is a typical Confucian belief that how a person should be is inherently related to how the world really is, and that only a person living according to what the world really is can be a good person. Accordingly, when Xiong developed a metaphysical foundation of virtue, he was contributing to the authentic tradition of Confucianism. As he himself says: "the real philosopher must know that the theory of human life and cosmology cannot be viewed as two things. If one does not understand the true character of human life, one cannot comprehend the true nature of the universe. To exhaust one's own nature is to exhaust the nature of things. This is the spirit of the learning of the sage, and this is what is inherited by my theory" (Xiong, 1994, p. 4). It would be a great violence to Confucianism if one revived its account of moral virtue but abandoned its metaphysics.

We are therefore led to question how contemporary virtue ethics could take the account of moral virtue from Aristotle while discarding his metaphysics. Are they originally separable in Aristotle? Because the Western notion of ethics or morality is grounded in social custom (Greek *ethos*, Latin *mores*), we could easily think that ethics is related to society rather than to some metaphysical ground. However, whatever the merits of such a view, it is not faithful to Aristotle. Aristotle believed that to determine human life as a whole, we have to know what it is to be human. This leads to psychology and metaphysics. He divides virtue into moral virtue and intellectual virtue. Moral virtues are obtained through social habituation, but intellectual virtue is not. Aristotle concluded that the highest *eudaimonia* is the life of intellectual virtue, while the life of moral virtue is only second best. This is because contemplation, the highest intellectual virtue, shows the fullest actualization of human rational nature, whereas one's moral virtue is relative to the social environment in which one grows up and hence the exercise of practical wisdom is relative. Thus, by abandoning Aristotle's metaphysics, the Aristotelian revival in contemporary ethics is only partial. This indeed has created many problems, such as the difficulty that a nonmetaphysically based virtue ethics has in overcoming the charge of relativism. A full discussion of these problems is out of place here. What one can conclude from the above brief discussion is that Xiong's work cannot be dismissed because it is out of the mainstream of contemporary ethics. Rather, we should take Xiong seriously, because doing so might inspire us to reexamine the contemporary discussion of virtue. If we find difficulties in Xiong's own account of the metaphysical basis of virtue, we might be moved to seek a better metaphysics rather than to abandon a metaphysics of virtue entirely.

Acknowledgment

I wish to thank Nick Bunnin, Chung-ying Cheng, Xinyan Jiang, and Huang Yong for their helpful comments to earlier versions of this chapter and also Ouyang Kang for his assistance in obtaining texts.

Bibliography

The major works of Xiong Shili

Xiong, Shili 1926: *Yinming dashu shanzhu* 因明大疏删注 (commentary on the great treatise on Buddhist logic), Shanghai: Commercial Press

Xiong, Shili 1932: *Xin weishilun* 新唯識論 (new doctrine of mere consciousness), Classical Chinese version, Hangzhou: Zhejiang Provincial Library

Xiong, Shili 1933: *Po po xin weishilun* 破 "破新唯識論" (refuting the refutation of the new doctrine of mere consciousness), Peking: Pingxin Book Bureau

Xiong, Shili 1937: *Fojia mingxiang tongshi* 佛家名相通釋 (Buddhist concepts explained), Peking: Peking University

Xiong, Shili 1944: *Xin weishilun* 新唯識論 (new doctrine of mere consciousness), Colloquial Chinese version, 3 vols, Zhongqing: Commercial Press

Xiong, Shili 1945: *Dujing shiyao* 讀經示要 (important guides for the study of classics), Zhongqing: Commercial Press

Xiong, Shili 1935–46: *Shili yuyao* 十力語要 (important remarks of Xiong Shili), 4 vols, Printed by Hubei Provincial Government

Xiong, Shili 1949: *Shili yuyao chuxiu* 十力語要初續 (the first sequence to important remarks of Xiong Shili), Hong Kong: Dongsheng Book Bureau

Xiong, Shili 1955–6: *Yuan ru* 原儒 (an inquiry on Confucianism), Shanghai: Lungmen Book Bureau

Xiong, Shili 1956: *Yuan ru* 原儒 (original Confucianism), 2 vols, Shanghai: Lungmen Lienho Shuchu

Xiong, Shili 1958: *Tiyong lun* 體用論 (on original reality and function), Shanghai: Lungmen Book Bureau

Xiong, Shili 1959: *Mingxin pian* 明心篇 (illuminating the mind), Shanghai: Lungmen Book Bureau

Xiong, Shili 1961: *Qiankun yan* 乾坤衍 (an exposition of qun and kun hexagrams), Shanghai, Lungmen Book Bureau

Xiong, Shili, 熊十力論著集 (the collected works of Xiong Shili lunzuoji), Beijing: Chinese Book Bureau

Volume I (1985) contains the Classical and Colloquial versions of the *New Doctrine*; Volume II (1994) contains *On Original Reality and Function* and *Illuminating the Mind*; Volume III (1996) contains *Important Remarks of Xiong Shili* (a series of short articles, essays, lecture notes, and letters).

Further reading

A selected English translation of Xiong's works can be found in:

Chan, Wing-tsit 1963: "The New Idealistic Confucianism: Hsiung Shih-li," in *A Source Book in Chinese Philosophy*, Princeton: Princeton University Press, pp. 763–72

The following is the most comprehensive study of Xiong in Chinese:

Guo, Qiyong 1993: *Xiong Shili sixiang yanjiu* 熊十力思想研究 (a study of the thought of Xiong Shili), Tianjin: Tianjin People's Press

There is no single book dedicated to Xiong in English. The following papers are helpful:

Cheng, Chung-ying 1987: "*Xiong Shili zhexue ji dangdai xinrujia zhexue de jieding yu pinghia* 熊十力哲學及當代新儒家哲學的界定與評價 – Xiong Shili's philosophy and the definition and evaluation of contemporary Neo-Confucian philosophy", in *Wenhua: zhongguo yu shijie – Culture: China and the World*, Beijing: Sanlian Shudian, pp. 48–66

Tu, Wei-Ming 1979: "Hsiung Shih-Li's Quest for Authentic Existence," in *Humanity and Self-Cultivation: Essay in Confucian Thought*, Berkeley: Asian Humanities Press, pp. 219–56

See also

Aristotle, 1984: *Metaphysics*, in *The Complete Works of Aristotle*, J. Barnes, ed., 2 vols, Princeton, Princeton University Press

Aristotle, 1984: *Nicomachean Ethics*, in *The Complete Works of Aristotle*, J. Barnes, ed., 2 vols, Princeton, Princeton University Press

Confucius 1970: *The Analects*, trans. D. C. Lau, Harmondsworth: Penguin Books

Heidegger, Martin 1977: *The Question Concerning Technology, and Other Essays*, New York: Harper & Row

Kant, Immanuel 1929: *The Critique of Pure Reason* (first edn [A], 1781, second edn [B], 1787), trans. Norman Kemp Smith, London: Macmillan

Lao, Tzu (Laozi) 1970: *Tao te ching*, trans. D. C. Lau, London: Penguin Books

Legge, James 1893: "The Doctrine of the Mean," trans. James Legge in *The Chinese Classics*, vol. 1, Oxford: Clarendon Press

Mencius 1970: *Mencius*, trans. D. C. Lau, Harmondsworth: Penguin Books

Whitehead, A. N. 1957: *Process and Reality*, London: Macmillan

Yijing 1968: *The I Ching, or, Book of Changes*, 1968: third edn, trans. Cary F. Baynes, from the German translation by Richard Wilhelm, London: Routledge & Kegan Paul

Discussion Questions

1. Was Confucianism or the loss of Confucianism the source of crisis in China?
2. Should philosophers aim to be faithful commentators on philosophical classics or to use the classics for their own creative philosophical work?
3. How can we discover the real *dao* of Confucius?
4. Does Confucianism need a metaphysical basis? Does the *Yijing* (Book of Changes) provide this basis?
5. What is the role of cultivating benevolence in the human *dao*?
6. Does Xiong Shili give adequate grounds for accepting that *ti* (original reality) and the phenomenal world of *yong* (function) are the same?
7. Should we accept a metaphysics of change? Is change instantaneous or a process?
8. Do the concepts of opening and closing help us to understand the relationship between mind and body?
9. Can we accept the distinction between original mind and habituated mind?
10. What is the relationship between ethics and metaphysics?

7

LIANG SHUMING:
EASTERN AND WESTERN
CULTURES AND CONFUCIANISM

Yanming An

The prominent philosopher and social reformer Liang Shuming was born into a scholar–official family on October 18, 1893. His family had considered themselves to be natives of the remote southwestern city of Guilin, although the three generations preceding him lived in Beijing. His father was a cultural iconoclast, who actively supported the reform of society, institutions, and education. Because of his encouragement, Liang enjoyed a thorough but unconventional early education.

After a short study of basic Chinese characters, Liang read *The Earth in Rhyme*, a primer of world geography, instead of memorizing the Four Books. He then entered a "new style" elementary school and middle school, whose curriculum mainly comprised mathematics, science, and foreign languages rather than classical Chinese learning. As Liang later recalled, he neither "recited (a traditional way to memorize) the Four Books and the Five Classics," nor seriously studied them until he reached adulthood (*Wo de zixue xiaoshi* [a short history of my self-education] in Liang, 1989–93, II, p. 667). After graduating from middle school, rather than applying to a university as his father wished, Liang joined a revolutionary group and started a professional career in journalism. He neither went to college nor studied abroad. His broad knowledge came mainly from "self-education" (Liang 1989–93, II, p. 661).

Liang's intellectual development had three major stages. In adolescence, Liang was influenced by his father to hold views that were close to British utilitarianism, although the names of Jeremy Bentham or J. S. Mill were then unknown to him:

> At that time I devoted myself to saving our country and people, and wanted to do something praiseworthy to establish myself. My mind and spirit seemed to be extremely broad and high. But, in essence, my philosophy of life was pitifully shallow and simplistic. I simply ignored the more profound problems of human life. . . . I held a narrow utilitarian point of view, which valued concrete

achievement, but contemned scholarship and learning *per se*. I gave some attention to studies with practical value, but simply discarded the subjects, such as
literature and philosophy, as being that which misled and deceived people. (Liang,
1989–93, II, p. 683)

The years from 1913 to 1916 witnessed the second phase in Liang's development. In 1913, he suffered a serious psychological crisis. Unable to continue his social activities, he retired from society to engage completely in
the study and practice of Buddhism. This solitary self-therapy lasted until the
middle of 1916, when he recovered from the period of crisis and reentered
the world.

The most important stage of Liang's intellectual history was initiated by
his shift to Confucianism:

After a period engaged in the study of Buddhism, I turned to Confucianism
after 1920. At the beginning of this shift, it was the Confucian scholar of the
Ming dynasty, Mr. Wang Xinzhai (Wang Gen) (1483–1541) who gave me the
greatest stimulation and led me through the door [of the Confucian school].
What he praised the most was spontaneity (*ziran*). This was the very point from
which my comprehension of the Confucian school began. (*Zhong xi xueshu zhi
butong* [the difference between Chinese and Western learning] in Liang,
1989–93, IV, p. 252)

The concern for spontaneity decisively influenced Liang's understanding of
Confucianism as a philosophical tradition. It provided him with an intellectual criterion with which to weigh and measure the problems confronting his
country and himself. According to Liang, these problems could be grouped
under the interrelated headings of the problem of human life and the problem of Chinese society:

In order to resolve the problem of life, I have studied Western philosophies,
Indian religions and the Chinese schools in the Zhou, Qin, Song, and Ming
times. This won me the title of philosopher. Similarly, in order to resolve the
problem of society, I have participated in the Chinese revolution and played a
role in the social movement until today. (A Short History of My Self-education
in Liang, 1989–93, II, p. 679)

Liang's social activities mirrored the whole history of the political endeavors
of Chinese intellectuals in the twentieth century. As a child, Liang was attracted
to the Movement of Constitutional Monarchy around 1898. He then enthusiastically took part in the Revolution of 1911. From 1927, he actively promoted the movement of rural reconstruction. During the decade of 1937–47,
he was a leader of the Chinese liberals. He devoted the first eight years of this
decade to campaigning throughout the country against the Japanese aggression.
In the last three years, he led the "third political force," the Democratic League,

to seek to avoid renewed civil war between the Nationalist Party and the Communist Party.

After the Communist triumph in 1949, Liang suffered political persecution and theoretical attacks because he opposed the government's decision to adopt the Soviet model for the Chinese economy and maintained ideas that he has stated in his earlier works. The attacks on Liang included fierce criticism by Mao Zedong himself (1953). Despite the reclusive situation that the government enforced on him, Liang continued his research on Chinese thought and society. Remarkably, this research showed no sign of academic opportunism that plagued China at the time. People generally agree that, as his self-evaluation tells us, "he is a person who has his own idea, and acts in accordance with the idea" (*Zhongguo wenhua yaoyi* [the essence of Chinese culture] in Liang, 1989–93, III, p. 6). Liang passed away on June 23, 1988 after seeing the publication of two new books and the establishment of an Academy that he chaired.

Eastern and Western Culture

In 1921, Liang published a major philosophical book, *Eastern and Western Cultures and Their Philosophies* (*Dongxi wenhua jiqi zhexue*). This book is of importance in three ways. First, in China it pioneered the examination of Chinese, Indian, and Western philosophies from a comparative perspective. Secondly, it contained in embryonic form most of the key ideas that were developed in Liang's later works. Thirdly, and most important, it became one of the sources of the Contemporary Confucian movement. In this book, Liang provided a powerful and positive interpretation of the essence of Confucius' doctrine. It directly opposed the intellectual tide of antitraditionalism and anti-Confucianism of the New Culture Movement that began around 1919, and helped to weaken the movement's influence on Chinese society.

Cultures and directions

From Liang's point of view, there have been three kinds of problems facing humans. First are the basic human needs for food, clothing, shelter, and procreation. The second are the needs of human emotional life, including the maintenance of harmonious relationships in the family and society and the acquisition of inner contentment even in relatively poor situations. The third are the needs of the transcendent realm, in which people may find the ultimate meaning of their life.

In parallel to these three problems, Liang held that there have been three cultural approaches or directions regarding their solutions. Western culture represents the first direction. It straightforwardly seeks to conquer the environment, including nature and other people, in order to satisfy the basic needs. Chinese culture represents the second direction. Instead of struggling with the environment directly, it obliquely seeks to harmonize itself with the environment and looks for mental satisfaction within it. The third direction is represented by Indian culture. It stresses that ultimately the tension between humans and their environment is illusory and claims that human happiness lies in spiritual enlightenment through which this tension is overcome by being completely ignored.

Liang argued that all three directions are legitimate, because what they strive to satisfy are human needs at three levels. Humans could not enjoy thorough happiness unless all three kinds of problems are completely resolved. Nevertheless, Liang insisted that there existed a "proper order" and a "normal process" for resolving these problems. Humans should begin by taking the first direction to resolve the first problem. They should not shift their focus to the second or third problems before the first one is sufficiently resolved. Westerners have great accomplishments because of their unwavering persistence in following the normal process. The terms "science" and "democracy," which were promoted by the New Culture Movement's instigator Chen Duxiu (1880–1942), respectively identify a tremendous freedom from nature and an admirable social system. In contrast, Chinese and Indian cultures turned to the second or third direction before the time was ripe.

Liang further argued that the cultures taking three directions would never have met without stimulation by external force. For example, if China had completely shut itself off from the foreign world and had no contact with the West, it would never have produced things such as steamboats, railroads, airplanes, scientific methods, and democratic spirit. However, one should not conclude that the Chinese people are intelligently weak or that Chinese culture is essentially behind its Western counterpart. What is relevant here is the difference between the two paths:

> If China were just traveling more slowly on the same path, then there would be a day when it would catch up with the West. However, if they are going on separate roads, or in different directions, then no matter how long China travels, it will never reach the point that the Westerners do! (Eastern and Western Cultures and Their Philosophies in Liang, 1989–93, I, p. 392)

Intellect and intuition

Henri Bergson (1859–1941) and the Neo-Confucians, especially Wang Xinzhai, were two sources of Liang's insight concerning the antagonism between "intellect" (*lizhi*) and "intuition" (*zhijue*). According to Liang, these two concepts respectively characterize Western and Chinese cultures and account for the principal differences between them. The typical form of intellect is an attitude of "deliberation" and "calculation" toward nature and other people.

Liang claimed, "we always feel that the action of intellect is too flourishing and too strong in the modern Western people" (Liang, 1989–93, I, 485). This emphasis on intellect leads simultaneously to two consequences. Overflourishing and overstrong intellect brings about efficient methods of knowledge, the achievements of science and a praiseworthy democratic system. However, because of the same intellect, people in the West distance themselves from nature and other people. They artificially divide nature into many small pieces for the sake of easy manipulation. Also, they draw a clear line between oneself and others and even calculate and deliberate regarding relationships with their own family members. The same thing happens in the sphere of people's spiritual life. As a result, arts, religions, and metaphysics are gradually losing the eminent positions that they enjoyed until the modern age.

In contrast, Chinese culture has a tendency toward intuition, which Chinese philosophy, especially Confucius' doctrine, has thoroughly explored. In Liang's view, Chinese metaphysics fundamentally differs from both Western and Indian metaphysics in both problem and method. With regard to the problem of metaphysics, the ancient Chinese philosophers never bothered to discuss a "stagnant and static problem" such as monism versus dualism or materialism versus idealism:

> In Chinese metaphysics transmitted from very ancient times, there is a principal issue permeating all learning, no matter how great or trivial, profound or shallow. This is a set of ideas referring to what changes, not the static. What they [Chinese philosophers] talk about is simply abstract rules of change, not problems concerning concrete things. (Liang , 1989–93, I, p. 442)

The concepts of *yin* and *yang*, the creative (*qian*) and the receptive (*kun*) in Chinese philosophy, and the concepts of metal, wood, water, fire, and soil in Chinese medicine, do not refer to any visible, physical things in either the human body or the universe. Instead, they symbolize certain kinds of "significance" in them. Liang warned that people must be extremely careful when dealing with these concepts. For instance, they should not equate the Chinese concepts of the five elements with the Indian concepts of the four Greats: earth, water, fire, and wind. "The former refers to abstract significance, the latter to concrete substance" (Liang, 1989–93, I, p. 442). The particularity of the problem calls for a corresponding method to deal with it:

> What do we use to recognize that kind of significance or tendency? It is intuition. In order to know the significance or tendency, we have to use intuition to experience and ruminate. What are called "*yin*" and "*yang*" and "the creative" and "the receptive" cannot be grasped through sensation; also, they are not abstract concepts formed through the operation of intellect. Those are dynamic and harmonious concepts, whereas the concepts that are formed through intellect are all definitive and fixed ones. (Liang, 1989–93, I, p. 443)

Here intuition was described by Liang as a tool of knowledge distinct from the intellect. The significance or tendency is the object of intuition, and the dynamic or harmonious concepts are formed through its operation. This tool, as Liang said, is not used to make clear distinctions between things. Accordingly, it is not very useful for making observations and analyses of concrete matters in nature and society. It provides no support to the attitude of calculation and deliberation.

The concept of harmony, which occupies a central position in the *Yijing* (Book of Changes), is another major reason for the formation of Chinese attitudes against calculation and deliberation:

> In the universe, there exist no absolute, single, extreme, partial, and disharmonious things. Even if those things actually existed, they must be in concealment, rather than being revealed. All that appear are relative, pairing, impartial, balancing, and harmonious things. That is true for everything that exists. This idea comes from the observation of the universe. What it notices is not a universe in a static state, but that in change and flow. The so-called "change" simply means [a process] from harmony to disharmony or from disharmony to harmony. (Liang, 1989–93, I, pp. 444–5)

This idea helped the Chinese people to live a life with harmony, yielding, and compromise. They would like to regard themselves as being partners and friends of nature and as being compassionate members of their family and society.

Confucius' doctrine

According to Liang, Confucius was one of the inventors of this philosophy of intuition and harmony and was its untiring practitioner. Confucius regarded it as most desirable to be in correspondence with the rhythm of the universe. He believed that the universe is a great flow, a constant process of production and reproduction. Parallel to the universe, society is also constantly undergoing changes. It is simply a dream to seek out some fixed rules that will ensure our correct response to all challenges. The only valid course of action is to follow the guidance of intuition:

> [The way chosen through] intuition is always right. We do not need to seek correctness in the external world. The life of human being is a flowing and changeable integrity. One will naturally take for himself the most right, secure, and proper path. (Liang, 1989–93, I, p. 452)

A dialogue from the *Analects* perfectly exemplifies Confucius' opinion of intuition. In Confucius' time, the practice of "being in mourning three years over the death of one's parents" was respected by most people as an unchanging rule. However, when one of his disciples inquired if he could mourn his parents only for one year, instead of giving a definitive answer, Confucius raised another question. For the sake of the huge love you had received from your parents, "would you then (after a year) feel at ease in eating good rice and wearing silk brocades?" (*Analects*, 17:21). If not, you should mourn them in the traditional way. If so, you might mourn in the way in which you prefer, no matter how intense might be the pressure from society, relatives, and friends.

Here the "feeling at ease" (*an*) is simply another expression for intuition. Confucius certainly approved of the practice of "being in mourning three years." However, this approval is not based on any fixed rules or social customs, but rather on people's feeling or intuition. Intuition is constant and universal, because its existence and movement always comply with the rhythm of the universe. Rules, on the contrary, are partial and temporary, because they come into existence in special historical situations, and all rules will sooner or later be out-of-date. We should read in this light the famous saying in the *Analects*: "There are four things from which the Master was entirely free. He had no forgone conclusions, no arbitrary predeterminations, no obstinacy, and no egoism" (*Analects*, 9:5). Liang argued that this is a fundamental doctrine left by Confucius to his disciples and to the Chinese nation as a whole. It is directly opposed to the attitude of intellect, namely the attitude of calculation and deliberation.

In conclusion, Liang's analysis of Eastern and Western cultures revealed a social and intellectual tension that has tormented Chinese intellectuals since the mid-nineteenth century. Facing the powerful challenge of the West, they have had to ponder the question whether China could realize modernization like the Western countries while preserving its own culture. In general, Liang's answer to the question was affirmative and optimistic. China could reach both goals so long as its people acquired a clear knowledge of the essence of their culture and the position it occupies in the human world.

By means of a comparison of the Western, Indian, and Chinese cultures, he highlighted the characteristics of Chinese culture as represented by Confucius' doctrine. In terms of this understanding, it also became necessary and urgent to reinterpret and revivify Confucianism. Moreover, the method of comparison allowed Liang to draw a map of major human cultures in which Chinese culture occupied its own position. What an observer could find from the map was not only the weakness, but also the strength of Chinese culture. At a time when support for wholesale Westernization prevailed and national confidence was totally lost, his emphasis on the positive side of Chinese culture was particularly important and meaningful. Finally, Liang's comparison of cultures and its discovery exhibited his vision, hope, and effort to construct the best type of culture for the future: a universal culture for the Chinese people and for humanity as a whole.

Evolution of Terms

In more than half a century after the publication of *Eastern and Western Cultures*, Liang expanded his theory of culture through many further publications. The most important among them are: *The Final Awakening of the Chinese People's Self-salvation Movement* (*zhongguo minzu zijiu yundong de zuihou juwu*) (1930), *Theory of Rural Construction* (*xiangcun jianshe lilun*) (1937), *The Essence of Chinese Culture* (*zhongguo wenhua yaoyi*) (1949), *Human Mind and Human Life* (*renxin yu rensheng*) (1984), and *The General Introduction to the Learnings in the East* (*dongfang xueshu gaiguan*) (1986). The basic concerns of these works remained the same, but Liang introduced a new concept, "reason" (*lixing*). It replaced the role of intuition in the first book and provided the basis of Liang's final account of what characterized Chinese culture. In line with this important modification, Liang adjusted his ideas of instinct, intuition, and intellect and his account of their mutual relations.

Intuitive knowledge

Scrutiny of *Eastern and Western Cultures* reveals that Liang used the term "intuition" in three senses and did not always realize or identify its change of meaning. They are "intuition as a method of knowledge," "intuition as the equivalent of 'instinct' (*benneng*)," and intuition as the equivalent of 'intuitive knowledge' (*liangzhi*)."

It is useful to understand Liang's own opinion on the three uses. On intuition as a method of knowledge, he held a negative view in the first edition of *Eastern and Western Cultures*. "Since intuition is not something unselfish and unsubjective, but something subjective and emotional, how could it attain the real?" (Liang, 1989–93, I, p. 406). The use of intuition as a major method to acquire knowledge was directly responsible for the backwardness of the Chinese nation in many fields. With regard to intuition as the equivalent of instinct, Liang realized this confusion shortly after the publication of the book and severely criticized himself for this mistake. In contrast to the fate of the first two uses, the use of intuition as the equivalent of intuitive knowledge remained in Liang's later works, although he employed a new term "reason."

"Intuitive knowledge" is an important concept in the mainstream of Confucianism. Mencius introduced the term in a philosophical context. He wrote, "what makes a man know without having to deliberate is his intuitive knowledge" (*Mencius*, 7A:15). Intuitive knowledge spontaneously arises in a person's mind, whereas "deliberation" must involve a discursive operation of mind.

For Wang Yangming (1472–1529), "intuitive knowledge is a nature conferred on us by Heaven, a spontaneous, intelligent, and enlightening element in the substance of our mind. Any ideas that arise are, without fail, automatically comprehended by this intuitive knowledge of our mind" (Wang, 1986). Here, "intuitive knowledge" seems to be a function of the evaluative mind that underlies people's moral decisions. It always indicates the rightness or wrongness of the decision and encourages people to live a virtuous life.

This analysis explains why Liang abandoned the term "intuition" in his later works. First, the term masked a theoretical confusion by having three simultaneous uses. For Liang, this confusion nullified the validity of intuition as a major source of knowledge. More profoundly, the conflation of these three uses of the term suggests that Liang vacillated in choosing his position regarding the relation between Chinese and Western cultures. He later admitted that when writing *Eastern and Western Cultures*, he was still in the midst of a theoretical transition from Buddhism to Confucianism and "had not yet reached the final destination" (*renxin yu rensheng* [Human Mind and Human Life], in Liang, 1989–93, III, pp. 595–6). The fluctuation between theories was partly responsible for the various ways in which he used the term "intuition." When he eventually completed his conversion to Confucianism, he needed a new concept to retain the unique meaning of intuition as an equivalent of intuitive knowledge and to breathe fresh life into the traditional Confucian term. This double function was fulfilled by the term "reason."

Reason

In Western philosophy, practical reason is the counterpart of Liang's conception of reason. Practical reason, which people use to guide their action, is contrasted with theoretical reason, which people use to guide their thought. According to Aristotle, practical reason enables a man to decide on each particular occasion what would be fair, kind, or generous, and what would be the right thing to do (*Nicomachean Ethics*, VI). In the same vein, Kant stressed that practical reason should address "the world at large," that is, everyone conducting reasoning, regardless of their time, location, and social background. In these two cases, this term appears to be a principle to direct people to act morally, and to justify the rightness of their action.

In contrast, reason for Liang is not only a principle for directing and justifying action; it also initiates moral action. Reason brings people to do what is right and to live a virtuous life. Liang believed that reason in this sense constitutes the cornerstone of Chinese society. First, it bestows a precious inner discipline and moral consciousness on the people. This results primarily from the effort of Confucius:

> He always encouraged people to examine themselves, to ponder everything with their own minds, and to cultivate their own capabilities of differentiation. . . . Confucius offered people no doctrine except the idea of self-reflection. He taught

people to believe in nothing but their own reason. Since the establishment of
the Confucian school, the Chinese nation has been imbued with this teaching.
(*The Essence of Chinese Culture*, in Liang, 1989–93, III, p. 107)

Secondly, reason contains moral sentiment and ethical motivation. "Reason
in Chinese refers to a force, a direction of life. It demands you to do so and
so," unless you do not wish to see your society, including yourself, continue
to survive (*Xiangcun jianshe lilun* [theory of rural reconstruction] in Liang,
1989–93, II, pp. 267–8).

Liang further described reason as a "clear, bright, peaceful, and harmonious
mind." Reason manifests itself in two ways. The first manifestation is "a mind
that is inclined to go forward or upward"–a mind that refuses to surrender
to mistakes, differentiates right from wrong, appeals to fairness, and advocates
justice. It is a mind that dislikes calculations and deliberations in practical life.
The second manifestation is "honesty in interpersonal relations" (*The Essence
of Chinese Culture*, in Liang, 1989–93, III, p. 133). It follows the Confucian
tradition of expanding love, starting with love among family members. People
who have this emotional attachment may expand their love of family to include
other people, birds and animals, and even grass and stones. Through this
all-encompassing love, humans may fully enjoy their lives in a harmonious
community and a harmonious universe.

Liang argued that the exploration and wide application of reason should
be regarded as the most fundamental feature of Chinese culture:

> I often say that if the Chinese have not lived in vain for several thousand years,
> if the Chinese have contributed anything at all, then it is because they first under-
> stood why a human is human. That is to say, from very early the Chinese ancients
> have understood reason. . . . And the sum total of the spirit of the Chinese people
> is bringing this reason into play. (Liang, 1989–93, III, p. 130)

> How could reason constantly sustain its vitality in Chinese society? How could the
> Chinese people tend to follow the guidance of reason for several thousand years?
>   It is because there existed in Chinese society a [physical] representative of
> reason, namely the scholar–gentry. Traditionally, Chinese society was composed
> of four ranks: scholars, peasants, artisans, and merchants. The scholars were
> the leaders of all the other three ranks. They made an extremely important con-
> tribution to society, although they did not undertake any physical work. They
> represented reason in their sustaining of education and [personal] cultivation
> and in the maintenance of social order and stability. (*Xiancun jianshe lilun* [theory
> of rural construction], in Liang, 1989–93, II, p. 186)

In terms of this analysis, the triumph of reason ultimately meant that scholars
could maintain a universal control over society. Through their efforts, reason
prevailed throughout China, and the other social ranks acquired proper positions in the social structure.

Reason and intellect

Along with introducing the concept of reason, Liang developed a new model for the relations among instinct, intellect, and reason. It not only dissolved the antagonism between intellect and intuition, but also allowed a reconsideration of the relation between Chinese and Western cultures.

Liang defined instinct as an innate ability that is passed to an individual through biological inheritance. It can be neither eliminated from an individual's experience nor acquired by individuals during their lifetime. "Because the life of animals in particular depends on instinct, so an animal's instinct should be regarded as its typical form" (*Human Mind and Human Life*, in Liang, 1989–93, III, p. 562). In contrast to instinct, both intellect and reason characterize human life. They are the "two aspects of the operation of mind (*xinsi zuoyong*)" in humans:

> The aspect of knowing is called "intellect," while the aspect of feeling is called "reason." In actuality, they are connected closely and inseparably. For example, in mathematics, the mind that does the calculating is the intellect, while the mind that seeks accuracy is the reason. (*The Essence of Chinese Culture*, in Liang, 1989–93, III, p. 125)

In contrast to the relationship of intellect and intuition in *Eastern and Western Cultures*, this model contained something remarkably new. First, it began with an analysis of instinct and underscored its difference from both intellect and reason. Secondly, it employed a new term, the "operation of mind," to designate the integral unity of intellect and reason. Thirdly, these two concepts were no longer antagonistic, but supplemented each other in building the unity of the human mind.

However, we can still identify some similarities between the works of the two phases. Liang believed that there is a difference in degree in Chinese and Western cultures concerning the development of intellect and reason. "The Chinese are advanced in reason, but backward in intellect, whereas the Westerners are advanced in intellect, but backward in reason" (*Lixing yu lizhi de fenbie* [the distinction between reason and intellect], in Liang, 1989–93, VI, p. 406). In his final analysis, reason is superior to intellect, and, therefore, Chinese culture is higher than its Western counterpart.

Liang used two approaches in seeking to verify this superiority. First, he argued that reason represents the true essence of human beings:

> The intellect has numberless functions: analysis, calculation, assumption, reasoning, etc. Nevertheless, it could not make any decision. What could make decisions is reason. (*Lixing yu lizhi de fenbie* [the distinction between reason and intellect], in Liang, 1989–93, VI, p. 412)

Secondly, the relation between reason and intellect can be compared to that of substance (*ti*) and function (*yong*):

> What we call "intellect" is a wonderful function of the human mind; what we call "reason" is a good virtue of the human mind. The latter is substance, while the former is function. In order to know the human mind as such, we have to differentiate one from another, although they are inseparable in essence. (*Human Mind and Human Life*, in Liang, 1989–93, III, p. 603)

Here, substance and function are understood as an agent and its tools. Intellect is free from connotations of good or bad, because it can be applied by any people for any purpose. In contrast, reason is categorically good because it brings about only morally correct consequences. For instance, weapons were effective tools in the Sino-Japanese war. The Chinese army with reason could apply them for the cause of justice, whereas the Japanese army without reason or short of reason could apply them for the cause of injustice. In the hands of the Japanese army, the more advanced a weapon was, the more severe the evil it could cause.

Analysis of Chinese Society

The evolution of Liang's philosophical ideas influenced his historical, economic, and sociological studies of Chinese society. Now by means of the concept of reason, he further explored Chinese society and strove to reveal what features its structure contained.

The premature birth

Liang regarded the idea of the "premature birth of Chinese culture," which first appeared in *Eastern and Western Cultures*, as one of his most important findings. He later stated that it should be "more accurately phrased as the 'premature birth of human reason'" (*Theory of Rural Construction*, in Liang, 1989–93, II, p. 181). He elucidated this idea as follows:

> Humans are rational animals, but reason in humans must develop gradually. As for the life of an individual person, the development of his reason must go along with that of his age, body, and physiological and psychological maturity. Speaking in terms of the life of a society, it must slowly develop in accordance with economic progress and other cultural conditions. The "premature birth of reason" in Chinese society means that reason was fully developed [in China] when the proper time had not yet arrived, and the conditions were insufficient. (*Theory of Rural Construction*, in Liang, 1989–93, II, p. 182)

Here, the insufficient conditions mainly concerned ensuring the satisfaction of people's material needs. It is the task of intellect to strive for their sufficiency. The proper time for the birth of reason is the time at which people turn their attention to moral perfection because material needs do not particularly concern them any more. This signals the beginning of a period in which reason properly functions as a dominant principle. For Liang, reason improperly flourished in China before intellect had fully completed its task, and the Chinese people focused on moral perfection when they should have been primarily concerned with the satisfaction of material needs.

Why did China not develop like the West according to the normal process? Liang has two explanations. The first appeared in *Eastern and Western Cultures*. He assumed that the geniuses in ancient China might have been more intelligent than their counterparts in the West. An ordinary genius could discover truth bit by bit, and left his successors a large space for their further exploration. Accordingly, detailed knowledge of nature and society would be gradually accumulated. In contrast, if early geniuses were too profound to be restrained by the surrounding conditions, they might go beyond the immediate problem to ponder something deeper. Thus, they might leave their successors no alternative but following the path determined by them. Liang concluded that the first account fits the case of the West, while the second account fits the case of China (*Eastern and Western Cultures and Their Philosophies*, in Liang, 1989–93, I, p. 481).

The second explanation appeared in his later works. Liang claimed that the root of the "premature birth of reason" lay in the "absence of major religion" or the "failure to produce any major religion." Confucius was mainly responsible for this nonreligious aspect of Chinese culture and society:

> Confucius did not strive to establish an ultimate goal of belief, and did not offer people a dogmatic criterion [of good or evil]. He simply demanded people to conduct self-reflection. . . . He never applied the notions of sin and fortune as tools to manipulate and control people's mind. . . . Instead, he encouraged people to discard the notions of fortune and misfortune, gain and loss, and to bring the minds of right and wrong, good and evil, which they innately possessed, into full play. He believed that humans were endowed with reason. He expected to enlighten people's reason. (*Theory of Rural Construction*, in Liang, 1989–93, II, p. 182)

Confucius and his disciples did their utmost to channel people's religious feeling into the framework of social rituals. In addition, they insisted that everybody should play his own role in a social hierarchy that the rituals represented. By virtue of these endeavors, they created a moral philosophy that could fulfill two major functions of religion, namely "to unite people together" and "to maintain an order in a society." Liang argued that "after the wide propagation of Confucius' doctrine, no religion could be truly successful in China" (*Theory of Rural Construction*, in Liang, 1989–93, II, p. 182).

Liang held that for the Chinese nation, the "premature birth of reason" was at once the greatest achievement and the greatest fault. It helped to maintain a culture that lasted longer, spread further, assimilated more people, and shaped more neighboring cultures than any other. Nevertheless, it accounted for almost every social and cultural disease with which the Chinese have had to contend throughout their history and still encounter even today.

Two features

Liang claimed that China is an ethic-based (*lunli benwei*) society and a profession-differentiated (*zhiye fentu*) society. These characterizations identify two features of Chinese social structure.

The first feature can be understood through comparison with Western society. According to Liang, Westerners have lived a "corporate life," first in Christian organizations and later in nation-states. Because of the constant competition and struggle among different groups and because of religious asceticism, society left no room for the development of individuals. This eventually induced a violent reaction of individualism and liberalism, which brought out a new type of life, which Liang called an "individual-based" life. He held that in recent times more and more people in the West have realized the negative consequences of the excessive advocacy of individual interest and have begun to return to the idea of corporate life. From medieval times until today, Westerners perpetually oscillated between the two kinds of lives.

In contrast, the Chinese "had not a corporate life at all, and therefore, had no chance to think about the problem of individualism. They had neither of the two types of lives. What they had was simply a thing in between, namely an ethical relationship" (*Theory of Rural Construction*, in Liang, 1989–93, II, p. 167). This relationship started from family life. Because of blood-ties and common experience in a family, its members share an intimate feeling toward each other and regard it as a duty to serve the other members voluntarily. Entering the social world, people have to deal with a variety of qualitatively different relationships, such as teacher and student, employer and employee, superior and inferior. Nevertheless, this difference was blurred in premodern China. People tended to extend family relationships to all other relationships in society. It was the idea to make everyone participate in a relationship similar to what he enjoyed at home, and jointly to constitute a huge family-society.

Liang's study of profession-differentiation as a feature of Chinese society was inspired by the "Debate on the Social History of China" that occurred in 1930s. In that debate, many Marxist scholars argued that China had been a class society since remote antiquity. In opposition to their opinion, Liang contended that the Marx's class framework did not quite fit the reality of China:

In Western society, there is class antagonism between feudal nobles and serfs in the medieval age, and that of capitalists and workers in modern times. However, Chinese society resembled neither of them. If Western society can be named a "society of class antagonism," then China is simply a "profession-differentiated society." (*The Essence of Chinese Culture*, in Liang 1989–93, III, p. 139)

In contrast to Western society, China saw no class monopoly of the tools of production. Liang attributed this to three reasons. First, land could be freely bought or sold. Consequently, everyone had an opportunity to possess a piece of land. Secondly, inheritance was equally allotted to each son. This avoided a monopoly of land through primogeniture. Thirdly, there was no invention of the steam engine, electrical engine, or other powerful machines. Therefore, it was not easy for a small group of people to control a multitude by controlling these formidable means of production.

Other reasons also contributed to this profession-differentiation. For example, except the imperial household, China generally had no hereditary ruling class since the Qin–Han period (around the 3rd century B.C.). The country was run by a system of bureaucracy whose members were selected through the national civil service examination that was open to individuals from the four ranks (scholars, peasants, artisans, and merchants). In other words, there were no legal or hereditary barriers to an individual's social mobility through examination.

The ethic-based life and profession-differentiation interacted in China and collaborated in shaping the social structure. For example, due to the absence of a large-scale monopoly of land and tools, families were the basic unit in agriculture, handicraft, and commerce. Since there were no legal or hereditary barriers to social mobility, a family could combine their energy and resources to ensure that one or more members could be promoted in the social hierarchy. These relations, built on the processes of production, distribution, and political cooperation, solidified the ethical basis of the family.

Furthermore, due to the absence of class antagonism, Chinese politics operated through morality and ethics. In turn, because of the overwhelming influence of morality and ethics on politics, the society increasingly denied room for class antagonism. Liang concluded that "these eight characters [two phrases] – 'ethical basis' and 'professional difference' exhaust [the essence of] the Chinese social structure in the past" (*Theory of Rural Construction*, in Liang, 1989–93, II, p. 174).

A dilemma and its solutions

According to Liang, the premature birth of reason was the basic explanation for all the points of inferiority in China. At the same time, reason is the appropriate dominant principle for the second phase of cultural development after people satisfy their material needs.

This analysis presented a dilemma for Liang. The Chinese must abandon the present cultural direction in order to rid themselves of the negative consequences of their premature birth of reason. However, it would be neither realistic nor desirable for them to abandon this direction. Just as an adult cannot return to childhood, a culture in the second phase cannot return to the first phase, no matter how admirable it is. Moreover, Liang believed that by attempting to abandon the Chinese direction for the Western direction, the Chinese would suffer the dehumanization and spiritual distress that modern Westerners are undergoing.

Liang offered two solutions to the dilemma. First, the evolution of "objective realities" is forcing Westerners to change their direction, just as it is now compelling the Chinese to continue their imitation of the West. Therefore, we have grounds to anticipate the emergence of a universal culture that will replace both Chinese and Western cultures. In this analysis, the main agent in resolving the dilemma is history itself.

The second solution invokes the emergence of a new cultural entity that combines the advantages of Western and Chinese cultures:

> Should there appear in China a [new mode] of social organization, it must be something fused out of concrete facts from both China and the West. . . . This is an organization based on reason. It not only sufficiently ensures the development of the human spirit, but also contains the advantages of Western culture. (*Theory of Rural Construction*, in Liang, 1989–93, II, pp. 308–9)

This solution is a variation of the famous motto, "Chinese learning for substance, while Western learning for function," which was advocated by Zhang Zhidong, a leading nineteenth-century Confucian official. In contrast to the first solution, this one has as its main agent the Chinese people, especially their intellectuals.

Bibliography

Works by Liang Shuming

Liang Shuming 1989–93: *Liang Shuming quanji* 梁漱溟全集 (the complete works of Liang Shuming), vols 1–8, Jinan: Shandong Renmin Chubanshe

Other works

Alitto, Guy S. 1986: *The Last Confucian*, Berkeley: University of California Press
An, Yanming 1997: "Liang Shuming and Henri Bergson on intuition: cultural context and the evolution of terms," *Philosophy East and West*, **47:3**, Honolulu: University of Hawaii Press

Aristotle, 1984: *Nicomachean Ethics*, in *The Complete Works of Aristotle*, J. Barnes, ed., 2 vols, Princeton: Princeton University Press

Cao, Yueming 1995: *Liang Shuming sixiang yanjiu* 梁漱溟思想研究 (a study of the thought of Liang Shuming), Tianjin: Tianjin Renmin Chubanshe

Guo, Qiyong, and Gong, Jianping 1996: *Liang Shuming zhexue* 梁漱溟哲學 (the philosophy of Liang Shuming), Wuhan: Hubei Renmin Chubanshe

Liang, Peikuan, ed., 1993: *Liang Shuming xiansheng jinian wenji* 梁漱溟先生紀念文集 (selected works in memory of Mr. Liang Shuming), Beijing: Zhongguo Gongren Chubanshe

Ma, Yong 1994: *Liang Shuming jiaoyu sixiang yanjiu* 梁漱溟教育思想研究 (a study of Liang Shuming's thought on education), Shenyang: Liaoning Jiaoyu Chubanshe

Shan, Feng 1996: *Liang Shuming shehui gaizao gouxiang yanjiu* 梁漱溟社會改造構想研究 (a study of Liang Shuming's thought on social reform), Jinan: Shandong Daxue Chubanshe

Wang, Donglin 1989: *Liang Shuming yu Mao Zedong* 梁漱溟與毛澤東 (Liang Shuming and Mao Zedong), Changchun: Jilin Renmin Chubanshe

Wang, Yangming 1986: *Wang Yangming chuan xi xiandai xin ruxue* (questions on the great learning), Taipei: Liming Wenhua Siye Gongsi

Zheng, Dahua 1993: *Liang Shuming yu xiandai xin ruxue* 梁漱溟與現代新儒學 (Liang Shuming and contemporary Confucianism), Taipei: Wenjin Chubanshe

Zhu, Hanguo 1996: *Liang Shuming xiangcun jianshe yanjiu* 梁漱溟鄉村建設研究 (a study of Liang Shuming's theory of rural construction), Taiyuan: Shanxi Jiaoyu Chubanshe

Discussion Questions

1. Does Liang Shuming provide an adequate basis for the comparative study of cultures?
2. Can we determine when it is appropriate for a culture to seek to conquer its environment, harmonize itself with its environment, or reject its environment as illusory?
3. What special role has intuitive knowledge played in Chinese thought?
4. How should we understand Liang Shuming's concept of reason? Was he right to regard reason as the most fundamental feature of Chinese culture?
5. What is the relationship between intellect and reason?
6. Should we accept the claim that the "Chinese are advanced in reason, but backward in intellect, whereas Westerners are advanced in intellect, but backward in reason"?
7. Can we explain the backwardness of nineteenth and early twentieth-century Chinese society in terms of "the premature birth of Chinese culture"?

8. What are the philosophical implications of an analysis of Chinese social structure in terms of being ethic-based and profession-differentiated?
9. Can we accept Liang Shuming's account of the difference between Western and Chinese societies?
10. How persuasive are Liang Shuming's predictions about the future of culture?

8

FENG YOULAN'S NEW PRINCIPLE LEARNING AND HIS HISTORIES OF CHINESE PHILOSOPHY

Lauren Pfister

Feng Youlan (1895–1990) became famous through his publication in Chinese and English of the first critical and comparative study of the history of Chinese philosophy, but he also published between the years 1939 and 1946 a six-volume account of his own philosophical system. Although Feng's philosophy was significantly influenced by his earlier research in Chinese philosophical history, he presented his own thought as a modern reconstruction of metaphysical, moral, cultural, and political concepts that were drawn from the Song dynasty Ruist (Confucian) School of Principle Learning (*Lixue*). Feng developed a rationalist system of Confucian realism that was deeply influenced by the philosophy of Zhu Xi (1130–1200), but he also employed specific concepts from later Daoist and Chan Buddhist works. In addition, Feng's philosophy reflected his response to aspects of Platonic metaphysics, Aristotelian logic, and Hegelian philosophy of history. He initially absorbed these Greek and European philosophical influences during his doctoral studies in the early 1920s at Columbia University, where his dissertation chairman was the famous American pragmatist, John Dewey (1859–1952). The modernized metaphysical and epistemological Platonism promoted by the New Realism of W. P. Montague (1873–1953) had a particularly notable influence on his work.

Feng's system of New Principle Learning (*Xin Lixue*) was a creative synthesis of rationalist and mystical teachings self-consciously developed within a modern Chinese context. He sharply distinguished between philosophical discussion and scientific methods and interests, examining also aesthetic, political, and religious questions in the light of his conception of what is "most philosophical." He generally supported a traditional Confucian approach to morality, but sought to reconstruct this morality for a modernizing Chinese world. At the same time, he promoted a conservative political ethics that he linked to a modern nationalistic concern for Chinese political development.

Principles

Discerning principles

Central to the whole philosophical project of New Principle Learning is the understanding that "principle" itself is the basic category for understanding language, human life, and ultimate reality. Feng claimed that his logical account of the status of principle was a modern correction and extension of previous descriptions of the concept in medieval Neo-Confucian teachings. It corrected a confusion between cosmological and metaphysical realms which Feng's logical analysis of principle resolved and consequently provided new ways of answering a number of classical problems in that tradition. In this way Feng's logical understanding of principle served as a kind of philosophical chisel to dispose of unwanted philosophical confusions within earlier Confucian traditions. The starting point for grasping this new and critical understanding began for Feng in the proper philosophical discernment of principles within everyday language and life. In order to understand what words for "things and affairs" (*shiwu*) represent, Feng insisted that something "is present" (*you* or *zai*) which makes a particular thing be a certain kind of thing. Consequently, any "thing" must, at the very least, be constituted by some matter and by a principle that makes it the kind of thing it is. A principle is "something" that initially is an intellectually discernible "class" (*lei*) of things. A principle is not a thing at all, but "subsists" (*qiancun*) as ontologically prior and metaphysically connected to the dimension of actuality and any actual thing. Because Feng was not interested in investigating things or discovering the physical universe in its objective presence and was not convinced by any skepticism concerning the existence of objects and the external world, he left these tasks primarily for natural scientists to pursue. Rather, he sought to understand the principles underlying thought, life, and living things, taking this to be the task that is particularly appropriate for philosophers. A single "thing" or "event" is very complex in and of itself. Not only is it formed by one or more intelligible principles, but it is also materially "in-formed." Besides principles, there is "vital energy" (*qi*) which materializes each thing and affair. Like principles, vital energy is not a thing itself, but is an objective item in the dimension of truth-and-reality.

> Vital energy is definitely not an actual thing (*shiti*), because we cannot say what vital energy is. Because this is the case, we can discuss two points. First of all, if we say what vital energy is, then we must explain how this existent affair or thing is constructed from whatever made it to be this (affair or thing). Talking in this manner is to have something to confirm about the dimension of actuality. This is a summary or general proposition (*zonghe mingti*) which is, however, unverifiable. According to the standards of the Vienna School, this proposition is meaningless and is not a proposition. Secondly, if we say what

vital energy is, then this so-called vital energy is an affair or thing that is able to exist (*neng cunzai*) and is not that which enables all affairs and things to exist. We cannot confuse it with what science calls "capacity" (*neng*) or with the vital energy found in air or electricity. . . . all these are able to exist, and so are not that which enables them to exist. Therefore, they are not what New Principle Learning calls vital energy, for what New Principle Learning calls vital energy is not some-thing. . . .

What is called "matter" (*zhiliao*) in the philosophies of Plato and Aristotle is similar to vital energy discussed in New Principle Learning. What the Old Principle Learning called vital energy came out from Zhang Zai's philosophy . . . and is an affair or thing . . . and so confirms something about the dimension of actuality. (*Discussions about New Knowledge*, in Feng, 1986, vol. 4, pp. 63–4)

The unity of principles

Feng was drawn by this analysis towards an ever higher and more comprehensive awareness: to think of the sum of all principles as the supreme ultimate (*taiji*); to conceive of the sum of all the processes of things in their movement in and out of actual existence as the embodiment of the Way (*daoti*); and ultimately, to conceive and maintain in awareness the totality of the philosophical universe, the dimension of truth-and-reality together with the dimension of actuality, in a great whole (*daquan*).

Affairs and things exist. When we do a formal analysis of affairs and things as well as of existence, then we arrive at the concepts of principle and vital energy. When we do a formal summation (*zongkuo*) of affairs and things together with existence, then we come to the concepts of the Great Whole and the embodiment of the Way. These analyses and summations are formal explanations of actuality and experience.

The first major proposition about metaphysics in New Principle Learning is that affairs and things are all necessarily whatever affairs and things they are. Whatever affairs and things they are must all be some certain kind of affair and thing. A certain kind of affair and thing is a certain kind of affair and thing, and so there must be that which makes a certain kind of affair and thing to be that certain kind of affair and thing. (*Discussions about New Knowledge*, in Feng, 1986, vol. 4, p. 59)

All affairs and things (*shiwu*) are necessarily whatever affairs and things they are; whatever affairs and things they are must be certain kinds of affairs and things. . . . Affairs and things necessarily exist. Existing affairs and things necessarily are able to exist. Those affairs and things which are able to exist must have that which makes them able to exist. . . . Existence is a flowing whole (*yi liuxing*). All existence is the existence of affairs and things. The existence of affairs and things is the vital energy's (*qi*) realization of the flow of a certain principle or several principles. . . . In referring to the totality of everything that is present (*you*), we speak of the "great whole" (*daquan*). The great whole is everything that is present. (*New Treatise on the Nature of the Way*, in Feng, 1986, vol. 4, pp. 844–50)

[W]e recognize that "existence is a flow" (*liuxing*) and "the flow stores up or entails (*hanyun*) movement" are analytic propositions. However, what we consider to be analytic propositions do not, or not only, represent the definitions of words. It is not the case, according to our theory, that existence is a flow because "existence" is a verb; [the concept of] flow entails movement. Rather, because existence is a flow, and flow entails movement, then "existence" is a verb. . . .

The fourth major proposition about metaphysics in New Principle Learning is that everything that there is (*zong yiqie di you*) is called the Great Whole, so the Great Whole is all that there is.

The terms for "all," *fan* and *yiqie*, are precise, philosophical terms, because what they refer to transcends experience. . . . For example, this or that horse can be experienced, but "all horses" cannot be experienced. This point is the greatest difficulty encountered by empiricism. (Feng, 1946, p. 65)

Living philosophically in the actual world

At this highest point, Feng asserted, one passes beyond the understanding of principles to the philosophical boundary of thought, experiencing the presence of the All, the One, the Totality. In referring to this as a kind of mysticism, Feng did not intend to promote a feeling of ecstasy or a mystical union with the cosmos in any classical religious sense, but to indicate the highest awareness achieved by contemplation on the presence of principles. This mystical conception drew heavily on Daoist visions of the Way and the Whole, especially in Guo Xiang's (d. 312) commentary to the *Zhuangzi*. In addition, he was influenced by Chan enlightenment portrayed in Seng Zhao's (384–414) writings and the mystical experience of unity with all things taught by Mengzi (372 B.C.–289 B.C.) and Wang Yangming (1472–1529). Rather than taking these as religious experiences of cosmic unity, Feng insisted that they constitute the philosophical insights into reality that are the basic attainment of all Chinese sages. Though the awareness of the great whole may or may not be expressed in religious rhetoric, its essential character is contemplative noesis, a philosophical grasp of the totality of a multidimensional universe.

For Feng, this mystic contemplation is not a justification for retreating from the everyday world, but is a state of consciousness to be applied to normal life so that the inner transformation obtained in the realm of Heaven and Earth can reveal a form of life available to all thinking persons. A sage of this highest realm expresses supermoral values in the midst of a world influenced by people living within natural, utilitarian, and socially defined moral realms. Feng's philosophical sage, who is both other-worldly and this-worldly, is a modern version of what traditional Chinese philosophy described as "sageliness within and kingliness without" (*neisheng waiwang*), which might also be rendered "internal sageliness and external regalness":

> That is to say, in his inner sageliness, he accomplishes spiritual cultivation; in his kingliness without, he functions in society. . . . [This saying] means only that he who has the noblest spirit should, theoretically, be king. As to whether he actually has or has not the chance of being king, that is immaterial. . . .
>
> Since what is discussed in philosophy is the Way of sageliness within and kingliness without, it follows that philosophy must be inseparable from political thought. Regardless of the differences between the schools of Chinese philosophy, the philosophy of every school represents, at the same time, its political thought. . . . [T]he study of philosophy is not simply an attempt to acquire this kind of knowledge, but is also an attempt to develop this kind of character. Philosophy is not simply something to be *known*, but is also something to be *experienced*. It is not simply a sort of intellectual game, but something far more serious. (Fung, 1948, pp. 201–3)

Summary

This claimed "necessary connection" between philosophy and political thought provokes a number of important questions that we will deal with later, but at this stage a summary statement about the general nature of the philosophy of principle within Feng Youlan's New Principle Learning should be made. Feng's abiding claim is that he had a new insight into the nature of principle, and that this insight initially came from a logical awareness of the nature and status of class concepts within everyday language. Insisting that this new logical awareness is the proper account of all principles, consequently distinguishing it radically from any simple empirical or scientific assessments of the empirical attributes of things, Feng persistently employed this reconception of principle to establish three other basic logico-metaphysical concepts within the system of New Principle Learning. Once principles are properly understood, they are recognized to "exist" not as things in the world but as logical entities metaphysically discerned by the human heart–mind. In this sense, principles transcend time and space as logically discerned entities that need not be bound to the dimension of actuality. Individually distinguished principles can therefore also be combined together, forming a whole which Feng, following traditional Confucian terminology, called the "supreme ultimate." Principles are the metaphysical ground for the existence of actual things, and while things flow in and out of temporal and spatial existence, which Feng called the dimension of actuality, principles remain fixedly "present" as subsistent metaphysical patterns, the ontologically prior foundations for the existence of all these various things. In Feng's system, the total process of things moving in and out of actuality in connection with their principles is called the embodiment of the Way.

Ultimately, the whole of this transforming actual dimension and its metaphysical foundation of principles in the dimension of truth-and-reality, including the thinker who thinks this thought, is captured in the all-embracing conception of the great whole.

New Principle Learning

Feng's new system

New Principle Learning, both the title of Feng's first book (1939) in the exposition of his system and the title of his philosophical system as a whole, constituted the first systematic and comprehensive presentation of Feng's "new" Chinese philosophy. After examining what constitutes philosophy in general, Feng asserted that his modernized notion of principle (*li*), which he derived from a central Confucian metaphysical concept employed and developed in the Song and Ming dynasties, provided a criterion for discerning what is "most philosophical" in all systems of philosophy. Feng applied this test to a wide range of traditional Chinese problems concerning metaphysics, philosophical anthropology, self-cultivation, the history of the diverse schools of Chinese philosophy, aesthetics, religious teaching, and the sage ideal. In all of these explorations, Feng referred frequently to Song and Ming dynasty Neo-Confucian philosophical discussions. In using Neo-Confucian terminology, however, Feng regularly redefined crucial terms in the light of a formal analytic system that he based on a twentieth-century logical and metaphysical understanding of the nature of principle. Consequently, Feng sharply distinguished three levels of the way things are: various things in the empirical world, the dimension of actuality, and the dimension of truth-and-reality (*zhenji*) that is constituted by principles:

> That which makes a square thing be square is "square." . . . "Square" can be not "actual" (*shi*) and yet still be "true-and-real" (*zhen*). If in fact no square thing actually exists, then "square" is not actual. But if in fact a square thing actually exists, then it must have four corners. An actual and square thing must be dependent on that which makes something square, and cannot escape from it. On this basis we can see that "square" is true-and-real. If "square" is not actual but true-and-real, then "square" is purely true-and-real.
>
> Actual things are stored up (*hanyun*) in the dimension of actuality (*shiji*); the dimension of actuality is stored up in the dimension of truth-and-reality (*zhenji*). Being "stored up" is equivalent to the relationship expressed in "if . . . then" statements. If there is an actual thing, there must be the dimension of actuality; if there is the dimension of actuality, there must be the dimension of truth-and-reality. But the dimension of actuality is there without entailing that any actual thing is there; the dimension of truth-and-reality is there without entailing that there is the dimension of actuality. (Feng, 1939, pp. 22–3)

Because Feng assigned the highest ontological status to principles and placed similarly high epistemological value on knowing principles, he can be considered a philosophical realist. For Feng, the "most philosophical" philosophy is the system that can be constructed precisely and self-consciously upon these principles. To establish this system is the philosophical task of his subsequent five volumes.

The present and actual world

In applying New Principle Learning to problems of modernization and morality in his next two books (1940), Feng supported the modern transformation of Chinese life on the basis of a strongly deterministic economic understanding of industrialization. These volumes are replete with references to traditional Chinese philosophy and literature and touch upon other traditions of thought only when the discussion of modernity requires it.

In the first of these two volumes, Feng contrasted the general concept of society with a great variety of particular kinds of societies, employing the logical distinction between the general or universal (*gongxiang*) and the particular (*shuxiang*) that was generated from his methodological commitment to principle:

> When we talk about society based on family, the family is an economic unit and the foundation of social organization. The family is the foundation of the social organization because for a person in a society based on family, their first duty is to secure the family organization. Therefore, in this kind of society, "filial piety is the first among a hundred tasks" and is "the standard of Heaven and the righteousness of Earth." . . .
>
> In a society based on industry, the production methods of this kind of society break through the walls of the home. . . . In these societies, the family is no longer the foundation of social organization, and so persons also do not take the security of the family as their first duty. . . . In these societies, persons naturally do not count filial piety as the first of a hundred tasks. This is not to say that they "hit their grandfathers and curse the widows," but it is to say that in these societies "filial piety," even though it is a kind of morality, is only one kind of morality, and it is definitely not the center and root for all morality. (*New Treatise on Practical Affairs*, in Feng, 1986, vol. 4, p. 271)

Modern society is a general kind of society based on industrialization, but also constituted by values that earlier Chinese philosophers recognized as the five constants (*wuchang*): cultivated humaneness (*ren*), rightness (*yi*), ritual propriety (*li*), wisdom (*zhi*), and faithfulness (*xin*). Certain Chinese traditional values, Feng argued, are unsuitable for modern society – specifically filial piety (*xiao*) and loyalty (*zhong*) – and so must be discarded:

> According to Chinese traditional ways of speaking there are five constants:
> cultivated humanity, rightness, ritual propriety, wisdom, and faithfulness. . . .
> These five constants are needed in every kind of society. They are unchanging
> moral values, no matter (whether discussed in relation to societies) new or old,
> ancient or contemporary, Chinese or foreign. . . . Loyalty and filial piety are moral
> values found in societies based on family. . . . We can say that loyalty and filial
> piety are old moral values. Although today we still speak about loyalty and filial
> piety, so that even now we regularly hear people talk about how we ought to
> be completely loyal to the country and completely filial to the people of our
> nation, nevertheless the meanings of these words are no longer the same as their
> meaning in ancient times. (*New Treatise on Practical Affairs*, in Feng, 1986,
> vol. 4, pp. 359–60)

Ultimately, Feng's moral and political vision remained tied to a core of traditional values and concepts, but he reconsidered their general cultural significance in relation to the understanding of principle. He subsequently readdressed
questions relating to the role of these concepts and values in the process of
social modernization in general as well as specifically in China. In the 1950s,
he referred to this method of selective adoption and careful reconsideration of
traditional Chinese philosophical values and concepts as "abstractly inheriting"
these traditions:

> We feel that when people during the last years of the Qing dynasty spoke
> about "taking Chinese studies as the substance and Western studies for practical
> matters," what they said was unacceptable from one perspective and yet from
> another point of view one could agree. If what was understood by this phrase
> is "We can take the Five Scriptures and the Four Books as the substance of our
> studies, but use firearms (from the West)," this is truly not acceptable. To study
> the classical scriptures means that they would not be able to study and truly
> understand the use of firearms. . . . But if what was understood by the phrase
> is "The morality used to organize society is the one which Chinese persons
> originally had, and what we need to add to it is Western knowledge, technology
> and industry," then this can be supported. (*New Treatise on Practical Affairs*,
> in Feng, 1986, vol. 4, p. 364)

Intellectual-spiritual realms

A more rigorous philosophical discussion about a hierarchy of four
intellectual-spiritual realms (*jingshen jingjie*) of human experience and attainment appeared in *New Treatise on the Nature of Man* (1943), where Feng
argued, in ways that were only implicit in earlier volumes, that all human beings
are characterized by individuated consciousness (*juejie*) which orients them
in four possible realms: the natural (*ziran*), utilitarian (*gongli*), moral (*daode*),
and universal Heaven and Earth (*tiandi*) realms.

Through normal growth a person lives within the first two realms, but through types of moral and intellectual understanding that transcend the natural and self-centered stances of these realms one can attain the latter two realms. Furthermore, the highest and most philosophical realm involves a comprehensive grasp of the principles of Heaven and Earth, a form of knowledge that transforms one's way of life into a sagely presence on earth by embodying a philosophical mysticism attained and maintained by this awareness:

> The human within the realm of Heaven and Earth is "self"-less and yet also has a self. . . . This so-called "self" has two meanings: that which is "selfish" and that which is "sovereign" (*zhuzai*). The person within the realm of Heaven and Earth is naturally in unity with the Great Whole. . . . The difference between "self" and "no self" no longer exists for him. So in referring to a "self" involved with "selfishness," he has no "self." But because his person (*shen*) is united with the Great Whole, then he can say, "All things reside in 'me'." From the perspective of this natural unity with the Great Whole, it is not the case that the "self" has been completely extinguished, but rather that the "self" has been immeasurably expanded. The "self" within this immeasurable expansion is the sovereign of the Great Whole. (*New Treatise on the Nature of Man* in Feng, 1986, vol. 4, p. 636)

Feng understood the realm of Heaven and Earth to be the highest philosophical attainment of New Principle Learning, characterizing this supreme realm as the sublation and synthesis of all lesser realms:

> Someone may ask: Humans are a part of the universe. Though it is the case that human beings have individuated consciousness of the universe, these nevertheless are discernments by a part of the universe. . . . How can a part be able to gain unity (*tong*) with the whole?
>
> To this we respond: The physical body of humans is a six foot tall organism, and so truly is only a part of the universe. Nevertheless, the human heart–mind can think, and this thought extends, and so it is a part of the universe that is unlimited, even though it is only a part of the universe. The human heart–mind can have intelligent comprehension and so it is able to take all that there is and summarily conceptualize it. Because of this ability, thinking up concepts such as "the universe" and "the Great Whole" is possible. (*New Treatise on the Nature of Man*, in Feng, 1986, vol. 4, p. 633)

> The realm of unity with Heaven (*tongtian jingjie*) basically is mysticism. What Buddhist scholars call "Tathagata" (*zhenru*) and Daoist scholars call the Way is, according to their own theories, inconceivable and inexpressible (*bu ke siyi di*). Similarly, what we have called the Great Whole is also, according to our theory, inconceivable and inexpressible. . . . The Great Whole referred to in discussions is the object of the discussions and does not include the discussions themselves, and so it is relative to those discussions. Consequently, the Great Whole referred to in discussions is necessarily not equivalent to the Great Whole. (*New Treatise on the Nature of Man*, in Feng, 1986, vol. 4, p. 634)

On the basis of the above discussions Feng's understanding of the philo-sophical mysticism experienced in contemplation within the realm of Heaven and Earth can be further clarified. Although in contemplation humans may realize the "natural unity" they have with Heaven and Earth, this was not for Feng a strictly natural mysticism, as one experiences in a moment of aesthetic ecstasy before an inspiring natural panorama. Nor is it a form of cosmic mys-ticism involving a transcendent feeling attained passively in one's openness to the physical universe. The "self" in the realm of Heaven and Earth is not passively attentive, but is actively the "sovereign of the great whole," the philo-sophical mind that has attained full comprehension of the sum of the dimen-sions of actuality and of truth-and-reality in a vision that transcends the limits of the actuality of time and space. It is for this reason that he carefully placed his account of the contemplation of the great whole in parallel with religious conceptions in Daoism and Chinese Buddhism. Similarly to these religious attainments, the person in the realm of Heaven and Earth reaches a state of ineffability, but this is generated by logical discernment and not by other forms of meditative technique or by religious rituals. Consequently, Feng regularly asserts that his "most philosophical philosophy" should be a replacement for religious life, and not stand merely as another kind of religious attainment. In this light one can see how Feng's philosophical mysticism shares certain char-acteristics with religious mysticism: it presents a similar experience of totality, advocates stages of ascent to the highest achievement, claims that the highest attainment accompanies a refinement of human consciousness and recognizes the ineffability of this final vision. It is also similar to religious mysticism because comprehending the great whole transcends normal boundaries of time and space, leading to a stable illumination that maintains this philosophical attain-ment. Nevertheless, in contrast to religious mystical claims, Feng's sage lacks any expression of ecstatic feelings and asserts an active state of intellectual engagement and control throughout the two higher realms, resisting any claim that this vision participates with or embodies eternity. Feng's account is also distinguished by its strict employment of a formal analytical method unembellished by intuitive insights or transconscious awareness of an ultimate reality encountered in radical transcendence.

The history of philosophy

In the final two volumes, Feng presented two lengthy descriptive explanations of the role of New Principle Learning as the culmination and completion of major themes in the history of the interweaving patterns of the different schools of Chinese philosophy (*New Treatise on the Nature of the Way*, 1944) and of methodologies that were promoted in the complex variety of philo-sophies of the ancient Mediterranean and modern Europe (*Discussions about New Knowledge*, 1946). In the former work, he proudly described his own philosophy as the "new standard system" (*xintong*). He also explained how his logical method could be employed – starting with the sentence "Something exists" – to produce an analytically consistent set of propositions that proved his metaphysical claims. In the latter volume, Feng sought to explain how New Principle Learning could overcome philosophical problems evident in Platonic and Kantian systems and to show how his Spinozistic cosmology and his formal analytic method could overcome the metaphysical skepticism and reductionism of Vienna Circle logical empiricism.

While providing a new positive method for modern Chinese philosophy through formal analysis based on the logical implications of the nature of principle, Feng also promoted a negative method that is distinctively Chinese and particularly indebted to Neo-Daoist and Chan Buddhist philosophical visions of the universe. By this negative method, a philosopher could imitate logically what is accomplished aesthetically in Chinese poetry and painting by expressing and understanding how the boundaries of the inexpressible arise. The "unutterableness" and philosophical "inconceivability" of the ultimate led Feng to his special claims about philosophical mysticism experienced in the realm of Heaven and Earth:

> What New Principle Learning calls "one" is the Great Whole and is not an entity. Also, the "one" discussed by Buddhist scholars and some Western philosophers is taken to be the origin or the essence (*benti*) of affairs and things. They believe that there is an internal relation between affairs and things, so that all affairs and things are essentially "one." The diverse particularities of things and affairs are superficial; they are phenomena, this "one" is either mind or matter, or as some Western philosophers claim, there is an internal relation between affairs and things. . . . If this so-called "one" has this kind of meaning, . . . then it is a general proposition, and it is confirming something about the dimension of actuality. But the "one" spoken about by New Principle Learning is the general name for all. . . . What is commonly called idealism, materialism, monism, and dualism have generally nothing which is relevant to New Principle Learning.
>
> From the four propositions of New Principle Learning there arise four concepts. Of these, . . . three of its proposed representatives are inconceivable and inexpressible. That is to say, they cannot be represented by concepts. . . .
>
> From this viewpoint we can say that metaphysics cannot be discussed. Talking about the fact that metaphysics cannot be discussed is the negative method of discussing metaphysics. (*Discussions about New Knowledge*, in Feng, 1986, vol. 4, p. 66)

In what was possibly an allusion to the final sentence of Wittgenstein's *Tractatus Logico-Philosophicus* (1922), Feng claimed at the very end of his *Short History*, "One must speak very much before one keeps silent."

In his six-volume system, Feng pursued many varied questions about human life and thought in order to reveal what a logic and metaphysics informed by principle can show according to the "most philosophical" philosophy. Feng's own modern form of Chinese philosophy regularly privileged the general over the particular, the theoretical over the practical, the analytically formal over the sensuously spontaneous, and the rational over the emotional or intuitive.

Feng's Histories of Chinese Philosophy and New Principle Learning

In his historical studies of the different traditions of Chinese philosophy, Feng sought to demonstrate that Chinese thought was fully and seriously philosophical in spite of differences in style and rhetoric between Chinese and Western philosophical works. Bodde's English translation of Feng's first history added the following questions at the very beginning of the work, emphasizing the kind of questions Feng was considering in the late 1920s:

> First, what is the nature of Chinese philosophy, and what contribution has it to make to the world? Secondly, is it true, as is often said, that Chinese philosophy lacks system? And thirdly, is it true that there is no such thing as growth in Chinese philosophy? (Feng, 1952, p. 1)

Conscious that the term "philosophy" would raise certain expectations for non-Chinese readers, Feng offered the following explanation of where the philosophical content of Chinese philosophy would be found:

> When one begins to read Chinese philosophical works, the first impression one gets is perhaps the briefness and disconnectedness of the sayings and writings of their authors. . . . A student accustomed to elaborate reasoning and detailed argument would be at a loss to understand what these Chinese philosophers were saying. He would be inclined to think that there was disconnectedness in the thought itself. If this were so, there would be no Chinese philosophy[, f]or disconnected thought is hardly worthy of the name of philosophy. . . . In China, there were far more philosophers who produced no formal philosophical writings than those who did. If one wishes to study the philosophy of these men, one has to go to the records of their sayings or the letters they wrote to disciples and friends. . . . Disconnectedness or even inconsistency between them is, therefore, to be expected. . . . The fact is that Chinese philosophers were accustomed to express themselves in the form of aphorisms, apothegms, or allusions, and illustrations. . . . Aphorisms, allusions, and illustrations are thus not articulate enough. Their insufficiency in articulateness is compensated for, however, by their suggestiveness. Articulateness and suggestiveness are, of course, incompatible. . . . These sayings and writings of the Chinese philosophers are so inarticulate that their suggestiveness is almost boundless. . . . According to Taoism, the *Tao* (the Way) cannot be told, but only suggested. So when words are used, it is the suggestiveness of the words, and not their fixed denotations or connotations, that reveals the *Tao*. (Feng, 1948, pp. 194, 204–6)

In order to help his readers, Feng introduced a method of intellectual reconstruction that sought to display the underlying argumentative coherence
beneath the surface of Chinese philosophical texts. Whereas the first volume
of *A History of Chinese Philosophy* (published in 1931), which dealt with the
"period of studies by philosophers" (*zixue shidai*), is putatively descriptive and
does not promote any one school or position, the second volume (published
in 1934) covered the "period of Classical learning" or "scriptural studies"
(*jingxue shidai*) in a different way. Feng supplemented descriptions of schools
with his own evaluations along the orthodox lines of the Cheng–Zhu school
of Principle Learning (*Cheng Zhu Lixue*). Although this philosophical inclination continued to influence him when he began writing the New Principle
Learning three years later, Feng by that time had qualified this orthodox philosophical preference in several ways.

The "newness" of New Principle Learning

Feng's basic understanding of principle within New Principle Learning altered
the original concept of principle found in the Cheng–Zhu school in several
ways. First of all, he saw principle as a logical term that is metaphysically distinct from anything "actual." Because earlier Neo-Confucian philosophers,
including Zhu Xi, had not restricted their conception of principle in this way,
Feng considered their metaphysics to be confused at critical points:

> If there is a round thing, then there must be a round which makes it be round.
> When we speak like this, no matter if we repeat it everywhere, it can be of no
> service to either science or philosophy. This criticism was exactly the criticism
> Aristotle made against Plato. . . . These propositions are originally dealing with
> the dimension of actuality and (yet) they confirm nothing . . . , but they do have
> something to express about the dimension of truth-and-reality. This is precisely
> what metaphysics needs. (*Discussions about New Knowledge*, in Feng, 1986,
> vol. 4, p. 60)

In particular, Feng considered Neo-Confucian moral discussion to be unsatis-
factory in its account of the relationship of principle to the heart–mind (*xin*)
and (human) nature (*xing*). Their persistence in taking principle to be part
of the actual world of time and space was for Feng a category mistake confusing metaphysics with cosmology. As a result, Neo-Confucians continued to
assert too much about the nature and functions of principle. By chiseling away
these cosmological claims, Feng presented a more restricted logical account
of principle that refined and clarified the metaphysical status of human nature
and claimed to overcome the dualism inherent in Neo-Confucian discussions
about the relationship between principle and vital energy. It follows that
Feng's attention to formal analytic logic, the methodological fulcrum of his

philosophical system, constituted a major modern departure from traditional Principle Learning.

Another significant departure arose from Feng's advocacy of a form of historical materialism as early as 1936. Since principle was itself logically free from time and space, a historically limited materialism did not stand in complete contradiction to his historically unrestricted metaphysics. He apparently believed that changes within the dimension of actuality could be accounted for on the basis of materialism without threatening the metaphysical status of any principles. Consequently, his understanding of modernization was informed by a distinctive view of economics and modernity involving industrialization, something completely new and separate from the positions of his philosophical predecessors and from the views of many other contemporary scholars influenced by Confucian thought.

New Principle Learning and Feng's histories of Chinese philosophy

By the time Feng wrote his *Short History of Chinese Philosophy* (1948) for an English-speaking audience, his own New Principle Learning philosophy had been completely published. While seeking to draw out comparative likenesses between European and Chinese philosophical histories, Feng simultaneously revealed more of his own interpretive interests. This is evident in the section on "Mencius," which ended with a description of Mengzi's philosophical "mysticism" and names the two main Neo-Confucian schools of the Song and Ming dynasties as the school of "Platonic Ideas" and the school of "Universal Mind." Feng also explicitly mentioned the transformative influence of Western logic on modern Chinese philosophy, ending the volume with an account of his own New Principle Learning as an illustration of a contemporary Chinese philosophy that used logical methods. Significantly, Feng admitted that the Universal Mind school that opposed the Cheng–Zhu philosophical system was the dominant philosophical influence after the May Fourth Movement in 1919, thus suggesting how very new and different was his own philosophy.

This more reflective and contextualized description of New Principle Learning was extended and sharpened in the seventh and last volume of Feng's last major historical study, the *New Edition of the History of Chinese Philosophy* (*Zhongguo zhexueshi xinpian*). This posthumous volume constituted a long and detailed completion of his Marxist interpretation of the whole range of Chinese philosophical history. Much more could be indicated about the scholarly changes and Marxist categories employed in the whole seven volume work, but in relation to his own philosophical interests it is significant that there is a greater emphasis on Chinese logic and epistemology as well as occasional discussions of the "realms" attained by various philosophical schools. In the last volume, Feng reviewed his own system of New Principle Learning from a very different interpretive perspective from that informing its composition some forty years earlier. First of all, his philosophy was no longer presented as something unique. Instead, it was classed with the works of Jin Yuelin as a representative of the New Principle school. The alternative and more influential school was the New Heart–Mind philosophy (*Xin Xinxue*) of Liang Shuming and Xiong Shili. More significantly, Feng accepted a metaphysical criticism of his own philosophical system: rather than maintaining a distinct ontological difference between the subsistence of principles and the existence of actual things and the dimension of actuality as a whole, he had written at times of principles being there (*you*) as if they existed (*cunzai*) along with actual things:

> As a philosophical system the New Principle Learning made a fundamental error when it did not clearly distinguish between what "there is" (*you*) and what "exists" (*cunzai*). While Feng Youlan endorsed Jin Yuelin's way of speaking, saying that principle "is there but does not exist," he also followed the explanations of the contemporary New Realists in the West and acknowledged that what "there is" involves a kind of existence. . . . New Realism had created an explanation that seemed to be logical: the existence of the general [or universal] aspect is "subsistence" (*qiancun*), a kind of existence that is hidden and has not yet revealed itself. This was opposite to the meaning of Jin Yuelin's phrase, . . . [and] is a great contradiction in the New Principle Learning. (Feng, 1992, pp. 222–3)

While Jin Yuelin had more carefully examined the differences and connections between probability, potentiality, and actuality, Feng had at times eroded the distinction between the dimension of truth-and-reality and the dimension of actuality without a coherent explanation. Within his own system, Feng wanted to portray the processural "embodiment of the Way," but he had failed to do so adequately. Feng's assessment of his own philosophy is important, but it also suggests other critical questions about Feng's philosophical system.

Problems of a Modern Confucian Rationalist

Feng remained in mainland China after the Communist victory in 1949 because of the nationalist hopes that he had publicly expressed in his own philosophy. Although he quickly made a decisive turn toward Marxist–Maoist materialism, he was made to publish a series of self-criticisms about his own philosophy over the subsequent thirty years. While his early self-criticisms were clearly politically motivated, some later self-criticisms were willingly produced and included much that is insightful. During the last decade of his life, Feng reshaped his philosophical commitments into an unswerving materialism that was more or less Marxist and could also express his own philosophical point of view. Was this final intellectual transformation a complete and incoherent break with

Feng's previous philosophical writings? We can approach the issues raised by this question only by answering two further questions. If there was not a complete break, how can the direction of these developments be best described? In the end, was Feng's criticism of his earlier philosophical system a complete rejection of that position?

Non-Chinese philosophical influences within New Principle Learning

Much has been made of the influence of American New Realist philosophy on the Platonic inclinations of Feng's New Principle Learning, but this judgment needs qualification. Certainly, Feng's philosophy, with its distinction between the dimension of truth-and-reality and the dimension of actuality, resembles the ontology found in Plato's *Republic*, and Feng tended at times to describe the nature of a thing in terms very similar to Plato's participation theory of Forms. Nevertheless, Feng's logical account of principles reflected Aristotelian doctrines of universals and the meaning of propositions. In addition, his concern for the processural "embodiment of the Way" suggests an aspect of New Principle Learning that focuses more on the union of principles and vital energy than on their ontological separateness. Although Aristotle's conception of the entelechy within every individual thing is not reflected in Feng's account of actual things, his insistence on the relation between principle and vital energy reflects the harmony between form and matter that Aristotle advocated. This connection between principle and vital energy underscored the persistence of a metaphysical inconsistency pointed out in Feng's later self-criticism quoted above. Here the comprehensive vision of an undivided multidimensional reality, a Great Whole mirroring cosmological and intellectual visions found in Spinoza and Guo Xiang, revealed Feng's philosophical desire to harmonize and unify the metaphysical realms that include principle and vital energy. Consequently, the tension created between the analytical side of Feng's New Principle methodology and his mystical goal of attaining a philosophical awareness of the Great Whole and expressing it in the midst of daily life is not fully resolved.

Furthermore, the influence of Hegel on Feng's conception of philosophy of history and metaphysics should also be noted. In his *New Treatise on the Nature of the Way*, Feng manifestly adopted a dialectical account of the historical progression of the realization of the "spirit of Chinese philosophy" across more than two millennia. This dialectic was worked out from the time of Confucius to the twentieth century, when Feng's own system "realized" a modern philosophical synthesis that sublated past errors and employed new logical methods learned from Western philosophy. His previous work in the history of Chinese philosophical traditions had not been so clearly linked together, even though Feng had already been positively impressed by Hegel's philosophical system in the early 1920s. In this sense, Hegel's dialectical history of philosophy provided a new foundation for the understanding of the essential development of Chinese philosophical traditions in Feng's New Principle Learning.

Hegel's influence was also evident in Feng's later philosophical transitions after he had published the six books of New Principle Learning. Feng claimed that his metaphysical turn towards materialism in the early 1950s grew from a fuller awareness and final acceptance of the Hegelian conception of Absolute Spirit as a concrete universal. In Feng's own terms, this was realized through the unity of principle and vital energy. Having previously accepted the hermeneutic importance of Hegel's understanding of the dialectic, worked out in various historical periods among different philosophical schools, Feng moved toward a Marxist version of dialectical materialism because he accepted the final metaphysical claims concerning the role of Absolute Spirit in Hegel's philosophy of history. From this point of view, one might summarize Feng's life-long philosophical journey as a metaphysical transition from philosophical realism to philosophical materialism, but this assessment would not fully portray the shifts within the synthetically unified philosophical commitments that Feng aspired to maintain in the midst of this transition and afterwards. Although Feng ceased to be a metaphysical realist, he continued to value the logical recognition of principles as class terms and to promote his distinct hierarchy of intellectual–spiritual realms. The goal of his system, the philosophical mysticism experienced in the realm of Heaven and Earth, was reduced to a matter of psychological comprehension and personal transformation and could no longer hint at further metaphysical claims about sageliness. Precisely because there was not a complete break between the philosophical positions taken by the early and later Feng, we can see a gradual transformation that accommodated shifting commitments within a larger synthetic whole.

Feng's Marxist turn and New Principle Learning

The changes in Feng's philosophical views are not merely a terminological camouflage for Feng's Marxist turn. As a result of the adjustments in his synthesis, the later Feng was able to criticize the utopian and destructive development of Mao Zedong's philosophy during the Cultural Revolution for its ultimate incapacity to reconcile revolutionary means with the goals of political and social harmony. This philosophical critique arose from Feng's revised materialistic New Principle philosophy. From this standpoint, Feng criticized Mao's thought for lacking a sagely balance between practice and thought and for its failure to attain the level of the "most philosophical" philosophy.

What remains puzzling and controversial for many biographers and critics when they view Feng's philosophical transformation after 1949 was his willingness to work within the Maoist ideological regime as a philosophical advocate of various Marxist positions. At certain times, Feng openly supported Maoist revolutionary changes. At other times, he suffered much from the self-criticisms that he was forced to write and from public disgrace as the object of abusive ideological campaigns. Although the complex psychology of those suffering propagandistic attacks should not be discounted, there are at least two other issues relating to Feng's New Principle Learning that should be considered. In his own writings, Feng presents himself as a Chinese nationalist who advocated the modernization of Chinese philosophy as well as the modernization of China as a whole. He believed that Mao would accomplish much to promote China's modernization, and in many respects he later believed that these initial hopes were vindicated. Yet in another aspect of his philosophy, Feng held that sagely understanding of devotion to a "country" ought not to be bound solely to a particular country, but should extend to the principle of "a modern country" itself. In his discussion within New Principle Learning of political philosophy and sagely engagement in the world, Feng held that those beneath a ruler in a modern society should remain true and faithful to enable the ruler to become a truly regal and moral leader. This he presented as a modern principle of "devotion to a country," although it appears to be quite traditional and one-sided.

The leader is aloof from ordinary activities, but legitimately uses rewards and punishments, a doctrine inspired by the legalist thought of the Qin dynasty:

> [A ruler] does not personally get involved with managing [the country's] affairs, and yet everything gets done. This then is "getting everything done without doing anything" . . .
>   A ruler has authority, and this authority is expressed in giving out rewards and punishments. Legalists called these the "two powers." . . . Being a ruler is like driving a Western-style horse carriage. The driver sits high above on the top of the carriage, and lets the horses pull the carriage forward. If the horses go too slowly, he gives them a lash from his whip. When he sees that the horses go along quickly and well, then in the evening he gives them a little extra hay to eat. He does only this and nothing more. It is useless for him to crawl down from his perch and help the horses pull the carriage. If he does so, the amount of strength he adds is limited, and the horses begin to gallop wildly, pulling the carriage in the wrong direction, because there is no one guiding them. (*Teachings for the New Age*, in Feng, 1986, vol. 4, pp. 499, 501–2)

> The greatest function of employing rewards and punishments is not only in encouraging and warning people during an affair, but also in causing people in general to know what is encouraged and what will be punished. . . . Therefore besides "doing nothing," the method of leadership we are describing must also include three other points: unselfishness, maintaining sincerity, and dwelling in respect. . . . When the results (of a task) are good, (a leader) must reward the person, even if they are an enemy; if the results are bad, he must punish those responsible, even if they are his relatives. (*Teachings for the New Age*, in Feng, 1986, vol. 4, p. 503)

Although Feng justified a revolution of systems to accomplish change in a modern society, he was also willing to question the legitimacy of a tyrannical ruler in at least a few passages of his first volume, *New Principle Learning*. On what basis, then, could a true and faithful citizen justifiably choose political dissent as a means to promote political justice, social modernization, or to achieve sagely wisdom in the midst of daily life?

> Someone may ask: If there is a leader who is able to do completely what you have explained above, would he not have to be a sage king? We would answer: Certainly. Though there may not in fact be a sage king necessarily present, nevertheless, any ruler really must do more or less of these in order not to be a complete failure. A ruler who wants to be a perfect leader must take the sage king as his ideal standard. This we can say with certainty. (*Teachings for the New Age*, in Feng, 1986, vol. 4, p. 508)

Feng offered little concrete guidance in political realms, but was himself involved in precisely such choices while living under Mao's regime. In this sense, he may be seen as a Chinese Heidegger, a philosopher compromised by his questionable alliance with what many now consider to be evil political powers of his own day. For many years before the Cultural Revolution, Feng acted as an educational and philosophical consultant to high-ranking officials and accepted prominent positions in both educational and political institutions. Significantly, he did so without becoming a member of the Chinese Communist Party. Feng chose to engage modern Chinese revolutionary traditions while not fully identifying himself with them. Although he maintained a measure of philosophical independence at times from the current political line, Feng's own philosophy did not provide clear standards for dealing with the excesses of Mao's political ideology. Because Feng's "most philosophical philosophy" was dangerously susceptible to political and ideological misappropriation, we have grounds for criticizing the version of the sagely ideal that emerged from his philosophy.

The character and significance of Feng's new system

Feng's philosophical tendencies, as expressed in the New Principle Learning, can be characterized in the following way. It is decidedly Neo-Confucian in tone. In spite of the recognizable influences of Daoist metaphysics and Buddhist logic, its main task was the critical development of Zhu Xi's school of Principle Learning. Metaphysically Feng was a mystical realist, methodologically a logical universalist, epistemologically a modern Ruist or Confucian rationalist, cosmologically a nontheistic Daoist in the style of Guo Xiang, aesthetically a paradoxical Chan Buddhist, stylistically analytic, and politically an idealistic socialist. Feng attempted to reconstruct these diverse philosophical commitments into a modern synthesis of his own making, not allowing himself to be merely an imitator or transmitter. In this way, his work presented a formidable achievement of modern Chinese philosophy. Nevertheless, Feng's pursuit of an unusual philosophical synthesis and the shortcomings of an unresolved tension in his metaphysics ultimately attracted few contemporary philosophers to become followers of his school.

If we add the influence of Feng's massive corpus of three separate histories of the various traditions of Chinese philosophy to the creation of his own school of New Principle Learning, we must recognize that Feng's account of what constitutes "Chinese philosophy" remains both influential and problematic. By writing his first history about these traditions, Feng succeeded in presenting a new vision of Chinese philosophy for the twentieth century. In fact, the term for "philosophy" itself (*zhexue*) was a late-nineteenth-century coinage that was initially employed to describe "Western" philosophy. Feng decisively brought Chinese and Western thought under the same concept. The fact that Feng wrote two further histories of Chinese philosophy indicates that Feng was self-consciously engaged in the conception and reconception of the periods, schools, and prominent issues expressed over 2,500 years of Chinese intellectual discussion. Unquestionably, these historical studies influenced the Confucian terminology and content of his New Principle Learning. His later Marxist revision of that history retained important conceptual continuity with his own earlier philosophical writings. In spite of his ambitions for New Principle Learning, Feng's histories have become far more influential than his own philosophy, both inside and outside China. Although the range of his writing in the history of the various traditions of Chinese philosophy has been paralleled in extensive works by Fang Dongmei, Tang Junyi, and Mou Zongsan, Feng alone produced works while remaining within mainland China under the Maoist regime.

Bibliography

Major works by Feng Youlan (Fung Yu-lan)

Fung, Yu-lan 1924: *A Comparative Study of Life Ideals*, Ph.D. Dissertation, Columbia University. In Fung, Yu-Lan, *Selected Philosophical Writings of Fung Yu-Lan*, Beijing: Foreign Languages Press, 1991, pp. 1–189

Feng, Youlan 1939–46: *Zhen yuan liu shu* 貞元六書 (上下) (purity descends, primacy ascends: six books) Changsha, Shanghai, and Chongqing: Commercial Press, 1939–46: Also fourth volume in Feng 1986

Feng, Youlan 1939: *Xin Lixue* 新理學 (new principle learning), Changsha: Commercial Press

Feng, Youlan 1940a: *Xin shilun* 新事論 (new treatise on practical affairs), Shanghai: Commercial Press

Feng, Youlan 1940b: *Xinshi xun* 新世訓 (teachings for the new age) Shanghai: Kaiming Bookstore

Feng, Youlan 1943: *Xin yuanren* 新原人 (new treatise on the nature of man), Chongqing: Commercial Press

Feng, Youlan 1944: *Xin yuandao* 新原道 (new treatise on the nature of the way), Chongqing: Commercial Press, 1944. Also in English, *The Spirit of Chinese Philosophy*, trans. E. R. Hughes, London: Kegan Paul, Trench, Trubner & Co., 1947

Feng, Youlan 1946: *Xinzhi yan* 新知言 (discussions about new knowledge), Shanghai: Commercial Press. Also in English, *A New Treatise on the Methodology of Metaphysics*, trans. Chester C. I. Wang, Beijing: Foreign Languages Press, 1997, and in German, with annotations and introduction, *Die Philosophischste Philosophie: Feng Youlans Neue Metaphysik*, trans. Hans-Georg Möller, Wiesbaden: Harrassowitz, 2000

Fung, Yu-lan 1948: *A Short History of Chinese Philosophy*, ed. Derk Bodde, New York: The Macmillan Company

Fung, Yu-lan 1952: *A History of Chinese Philosophy: Volume I – The Period of the Philosophers (from the beginnings to circa 100 B.C.)*, trans. Derk Bodde, Princeton: Princeton University Press (Original work: *Zhongguo zhexueshi – shangce* 中國哲學史 (上冊) published 1931)

Fung, Yu-lan 1953: *A History of Chinese Philosophy: Volume II – The Period of Classical Learning (from the Second Century B.C. to the Twentieth Century A.D.)*. trans. Derk Bodde, Princeton: Princeton University Press. 1953 (Original work: *Zhongguo zhexueshi – xiace*, 中國哲學史 (下冊) published 1934)

Feng, Youlan 1964–89: *Zhongguo zhexueshi xinpian* 中國哲學史新編 (第一至六冊) (new edition of a history of Chinese philosophy), 6 vols, Beijing: The People's Grand Press

Feng, Youlan 1984: *Sansong tang xueshu wenji* 三宋堂學術文集 (collected scholarly essays from the hall of the three pines), Beijing: Beijing University Press

Feng, Youlan 1986: *Sansongtang quanji* 三宋堂全集 (the complete works from the hall of three pines), Beijing: Beijing University Press, Tu, Youguang, ed., Zhengzhou: People's Press

Feng, Youlan 1992: *Zhongguo xiandai zhexueshi* 中國現代哲學史 (a history of contemporary philosophy in China), Hongkong: Zhonghua Bookstore

Feng, Youlan 2000: *The Hall of Three Pines: An Account of My Life*, trans. Denis C. Mair, Honolulu: University of Hawaii Press

Studies of Feng Youlan's life and philosophy

Cai, Zhongde 1994: *Feng Youlan xiansheng nianpu chubian* 馮友蘭先生年譜初編 (first draft of a chronology of Feng Youlan's life), Zhengzhou: Henan People's Press

Cai, Zhongde 1995: "*Lun Feng Youlan de sixiang licheng*" 論馮友蘭的思想歷程 ("on the historical development of Feng Youlan's ideas"), *Qinghua xue bao* 清華學報, *Tsing Hua Journal of Chinese Studies*, **25:3** 237–72. Hsinchu, Taiwan, 1995

Cai, Zhongde, ed., 1997: *Feng Youlan yanjiu (di yi ji) – Jinian Feng Youlan xiansheng danchen yibai zhounian guoji xueshu taolunhui lunwen xuan*. 馮友蘭研究

（第一輯）— 紀念馮友蘭先生誕辰一百週年國際學術討論會論文選 (studies on Feng Youlan vol. 1), Beijing: Guoji wenhua chuban gongsi

Cheng, Weili 1994: *Xinnian de lucheng – Feng Youlan zhuan.* 信念的旅程 — 馮友蘭傳 (journey of convictions: a biography of Feng Youlan), Shanghai: Literary Arts Press

Yin, Ding 1991: *Feng Youlan*, Taipei: Great Eastern Library

Yin, Lujun 1992: "Against Destiny: Feng Yu-lan and a New Hermeneutics of Confucianism." Ph.D. dissertation, Stanford University

Major works on Feng Youlan's philosophy

Chen, Lai 1997: "*Lun Feng Youlan zhexue zhong de shenmizhuyi*" 論馮友蘭哲學中的 神密主義 ["on the mysticism within Feng Youlan's philosophy"), In Cai, Zhongde, ed., *Feng Youlan yanjiu* (studies on Feng Youlan), vol. 1, pp. 294–312, 1997

Fang, Keli, and Li, Jinquan, eds, 1991: *Xiandai xinruxue yanjiu* 現代新儒家研究 (collected essays of studies on contemporary new ruism) Beijing: Chinese Social Sciences Press

Fang, Keli, and Zheng, Jiadong, eds 1995: *Xiandai xinrujia renwu yu zhuzuo* 現代新 儒家人物與著作 (contemporary new ruists: persons and works), Tianjin: Nankai University Press

Gievers, Bie 1999: "New Wine Requires New Bottles: Feng Youlan and the Modernization of Chinese Philosophy." Ph.D. dissertation, The Catholic University of Leuven

Lomanov, A. 1998: "Religion and Rationalism in the Philosophy of Feng Youlan." In *Monumenta Serica*, **46** 323–41

Masson, Michel C. 1985: *Philosophy and Tradition: The Interpretation of China's Philosophic Past, Fung Yu-lan 1939–49*, Taipei: Ricci Institute

Obenchain, Diane B., ed. and trans. 1994: *Feng Youlan: Something Exists – Selected Papers of the International Research Seminar on the Thought of Feng Youlan.* In *Journal of Chinese Philosophy* **21:3/4** Honolulu

Standaert, Nicolas 1995: "The Discovery of the Center through the Periphery: A Preliminary Study of Feng Youlan's *History of Chinese Philosophy* (New Version)," *Philosophy East and West* **45:4** 569–89, Honolulu

Tian, Wenjun 1990: *Feng Youlan xinlixue yanjiu.* 馮友蘭新理學研究 (studies in Feng Youlan's new school of principle), Wuhan: Wuhan Press

Wang, Zhongjiang, and Gao, Xiuchang, eds 1995: *Feng Youlan xueji.* 馮友蘭學記 (recorded studies of Feng Youlan), Beijing: Sanlian Bookstore

Wu, Xiaoming 1998: "Philosophy, philosophia, and zhe-xue," *Philosophy East and West*, **48:3** 406–52, Honolulu

Yin, Ding 1991: *Feng Youlan.* 馮友蘭, Taipei: Big Eastern Library

Zheng, Jiadong 1995: *Dangdai xinruxue lunheng.* 當代新儒學論衡 (discussions and evaluations of contemporary new ruism), Taipei: Guiguan Library

Other works

Wittgenstein, Ludwig 1922: *Tractatus Logico-Philosophicus*, trans. C. K. Ogden, London: Routledge. Also trans. D. F. Pears and B. McGuinness, London: Routledge 1961

Discussion Questions

1. Is Feng Youlan's understanding of principle (*li*) an improvement on that of Zhu Xi?

2. Do the methods of modern logic help us to understand traditional Chinese philosophical concepts and doctrines? Do these methods justify Feng Youlan's metaphysical claims?

3. Is rationalism compatible with philosophical mysticism?

4. Can we accept a distinction between the dimension of actuality and the dimension of truth-and-reality?

5. What does traditional Chinese philosophy need in order to meet the requirements of modernity?

6. Can we "abstractly inherit" traditional philosophical concepts in detachment from the historical circumstances in which they originated and developed?

7. Should our account of the self alter according to the "realm" that we have attained?

8. Must Chinese philosophy be intellectually reconstructed for it to be assessed together with Western philosophy?

9. What are the philosophical consequences of Feng Youlan's turn to materialism?

10. What is the role of the "true and faithful citizen" in modern Chinese philosophy? How does it alter traditional Chinese political values?

9

HE LIN'S SINIFICATION
OF IDEALISM

Jiwei Ci

He Lin is probably the least known of the generation of Chinese philosophers, among them Feng Youlan and Xiong Shili, who collectively, and in some cases individually, reached the high point of Chinese philosophy in the twentieth century. In part, this reflected his apparent lack of ambition or ability to develop a philosophical system of his own. In spite of this, He was a strong believer in philosophical systems and left numerous clues to what his own system would look like had he built one. He Lin was a system-builder without a system or, put another way, he provided pieces of a system, which lacked either full development or explicit connection.

The reasons for He's absence of a system are intrinsically connected with his conception of the project of philosophy. He Lin believed in the existence of one true philosophical system for all humans regardless of differences in their cultural and historical backgrounds. Accordingly, he saw the task of philosophy as the attempt to discover this system, but believed that the essentials of such a system had already been found in idealism, in particular the idealism of Hegel. He Lin was sufficiently happy with Hegel's system to see no need for anyone, including himself, to build another one.

The fact that the author of this system was a Westerner and a German rather than a Chinese did not matter, but He Lin did see the Chinese philosophical tradition, especially in the Lu–Wang School (or School of Mind) of Lu Jiuyuan (1139–93) and Wang Yangming (1472–1528), as the Chinese counterpart of the Hegelian system, albeit in a less sophisticated and explicit form. In view of this, He Lin saw his task as a Chinese philosopher to be one of updating the philosophy of the Lu–Wang School in the light of modern idealism in general and Hegel in particular. This work would enable China to partake, in terms already familiar to itself, in an ultimate philosophical truth that is neither Western nor Chinese. In this light, when He Lin explained his lack of system-building ambitions in terms of the time-honored Chinese practice of "commenting [on great works produced by others] without inventing [one's own ideas]" (*shu er buzuo*), he did so for the time-honored reason that a uniquely correct system was already in place. Accordingly, the task left to him, just as to his predecessors in the tradition, was primarily exegetical.

He Lin's exegetical task took on an especially important cultural function in his own eyes because China was in the grip of a deep national crisis that had begun with defeat in the Opium War of 1839–42. True to his roots in the Confucian scholarly tradition, he regarded the crisis as more than anything else a cultural crisis. True to his philosophical idealism, he saw the cultural crisis, in turn, in terms of China having gone astray from the ultimate philosophical truth. In this way, He Lin's task was as philosophically modest as it was culturally ambitious: it was philosophically modest because the ultimate philosophical truth had already been uncovered; it was culturally ambitious because it sought to restore the vitality of Chinese culture and, given He's belief in the pivotal importance of culture, to restore the strength of Chinese society.

Performing his philosophical task was to be He Lin's whole life, and his life in turn was to mirror for close to a century the historical vicissitudes of the country he wanted to serve with his philosophy. Born to a well-to-do gentry family in Sichuan province in 1902, He Lin received a Confucian education from the age of eight and in the course of his study developed an interest in the Song–Ming School of Principles (*songming lixue*). In 1919, the year of the May Fourth Movement, he was admitted to what was to become Qinghua University, where he came under the influence of Liang Qichao (1873–1929) and Liang Shuming (1893–1988). Thanks especially to Liang Shuming, he became a devoted follower of the teachings of Wang Yangming, one of the leading representatives of the School of Mind. Neither his education nor his temperament prepared him for the pragmatism that he encountered when he went to the United States in 1926 to further his study of philosophy. After two years at Oberlin College, he enrolled at the University of Chicago but soon left because of deep dissatisfaction with the pragmatism that then dominated philosophy at the university. He found a more congenial environment at Harvard and pursued a deep interest in Spinoza and Hegel that he first acquired at Oberlin, immersing himself especially in the work of the Neo-Hegelians T. H. Green and Josiah Royce. After obtaining his Master's degree from Harvard in 1930, He Lin went to Germany in search of a deeper understanding of Hegel and German idealism at the University of Berlin. His studies were interrupted by news of the Japanese invasion of north-east China in 1931, and he returned home in this hour of crisis.

He Lin's first book, *The Attitude of Three German Philosophers at the Time of National Crisis* (1934), highlighted what was to become a long-standing feature of his intellectual life, namely, the unity of his philosophical interest in idealism and Hegel and his political interest in national salvation and betterment. In its more philosophical aspect, this combination led to the publication of *A Brief Exposition of Modern Idealism* (1943) and *Contemporary Chinese*

Philosophy (1945) while He's more immediate political and cultural concerns found expression in *Culture and Human Life* (1947/1988). These books established his reputation as a major representative of idealism in Chinese philosophy and as a specialist in Western idealism, especially Hegel.

After the founding of the People's Republic of China, He Lin continued to teach at Beijing University until 1955, when he was put in charge of the study of Western philosophy at the Chinese Academy of Social Sciences. Although he became an energetic organizer of philosophical activities, a major influence on later generations of philosophers, and an accomplished translator of works of Western philosophy, he produced little in the second half of his intellectual life that matched the energy and inventiveness of his earlier philosophical output. In 1950 he announced his conversion to Marxist materialism, a decision that showed some signs of sincerity but which also reflected the political pressure of the day. Nevertheless, He wrote little of enduring value in the field of dialectical and historical materialism, being content for the most part to offer perfunctory critiques of so-called idealist philosophers, both Chinese and Western, including his contemporaries such as Hu Shi and Zhu Guangqian. His critical expositions on Hegel, collected in his *Lectures on the Philosophy of Hegel* (1986), were wide-ranging but did not explain how and why Hegel's idealism arose and were not informed by twentieth-century criticisms of Hegel from the perspectives of realism and science. In the more open atmosphere of post-Mao China, He quietly softened his critique of idealism and of his former philosophical self but it was also during this period, in 1982, that he joined the Communist Party. He Lin died in 1992.

Idealism and the Reconciliation of the Cheng-Zhu and Lu-Wang Schools

The heart of He Lin's philosophy is his conception of idealism. What is distinctive about his idealism is his injection of Western idealism, especially certain ideas of Kant and Hegel, into Confucianism, especially Song-Ming Confucianism, and within the latter, his reconciliation of the Cheng–Zhu School (Cheng Yi, 1033–1108; Zhu Xi, 1130–1200) and the Lu–Wang School. Since his main philosophical allegiance in the Chinese tradition was to the Lu–Wang School or School of Mind (*xinxue*), He's own contribution was dubbed by others, though not by himself, the New School of Mind (*xin xinxue*). This was not an inaccurate label as far as He's philosophical sympathies in the Chinese tradition went. But at its most eloquent, He Lin's idealism was an almost seamless weaving of Chinese and Western elements, with little explicit reference to the Lu–Wang School except in the use of certain key terms taken over from that school but made to carry new and more sophisticated meanings.

One such term is *xin* (mind), with which He began his key essay on idealism "A brief exposition of modern idealism," first published in 1934 and later made the title essay of a major collection of his papers:

> Mind has two meanings, one psychological, the other logical and what is called "matter" by lay people is, according to those who subscribe to idealism, something whose attributes and appearance are brought into being with the help of consciousness, and whose meaning, organizing principle, and value all issue from the subject of cognition and valuation. This subject is what I call mind. If a thing possesses attributes and appearance, meaning, and value that are objective, this is because the subject of cognition and valuation is constituted by categories of cognition or principles of valuation that are objective, necessary, and universal. (He, 1990, p. 131)

What He Lin meant by "mind in the logical sense" is close to what Kant meant by *a priori* principles. He explicitly stated that "mind in the logical sense is a principle of the spirit that is ideal and *a priori* in character" (He, 1990, p. 131). Following Kant, He Lin insisted that such *a priori* principles are the conditions of the possibility of all knowledge and experience. "To express the same point in terms of an old Chinese saying, this is because 'mind is the same for every person, and principles are the same for every mind'" (He, 1990, p. 131). That He studiously followed Kant here is further evidenced by his division of mind into three aspects, namely, to use He's own terms, "the governor or organizer of knowledge," "the agent of conduct," and "the judge of values." This threefold division of mind corresponds quite neatly to Kant's division of the subject matter of philosophy into his three Critiques.

For He Lin, to construe mind in the Kantian way was just to say that mind is the totality of *a priori* principles. Inasmuch as the term *a priori* principles has its Chinese equivalent in the term *li*, it turns out that the idealism that He took over from Kant was already roughly encapsulated in the Chinese philosophical epigram "mind is principles" (*xin ji li*). As He puts it, "mind in the logical sense is the same as *li* (principles); thence the saying 'mind is principles'" (He, 1990, p. 131). It is in this Kantian sense that He Lin undertook to reinterpret this time-honored epigram, which originated with the School of Mind philosopher Lu Jiuyuan. In so doing, he clearly intended to place himself in the tradition of the School of Mind, but to bring its insights to a higher level of philosophical sophistication.

The need for reformulating the School of Mind arose, for He Lin, because the idea that mind is principles was traditionally construed in a narrow and insufficiently rigorous way. As expressed in the School of Mind and implied by its precursor Mencius, this idea sometimes appears to be essentially ethical in character, since the *li* or principles involved are by and large moral principles rather than general principles of making sense, of which moral principles make up only one category. What goes together with this narrowly ethical focus is the even more important fact that the mind is not yet fully or explicitly taken in the logical sense, as the condition of the possibility of all that is humanly meaningful. At least to some degree, mind is treated instead as the locus of principles, and the distinction between mind in the psychological sense and mind in the logical sense is consequently blurred.

On the basis of this understanding of the School of Mind, He Lin proceeded to draw a sharp line between mind in the psychological sense and mind in the logical sense and to understand "mind is principles" in terms of the latter, that is to construe mind as the totality of those *a priori* principles that make all human cognitive and ethical activities possible. In his view, "mind is principles" was no longer narrowly ethical or practical but encompassed the whole spectrum of human knowledge and experience. Such a reinterpretation of the School of Mind was very radical indeed and represented a major gain in epistemic insight comparable to that accomplished by Frege through his rejection of psychologism in logic.

It is arguable, however, that He Lin's distinction between the logical and the psychological (where "psychological" was more or less given a modern scientific meaning) did not adequately capture the Lu–Wang School's understanding of mind (*xin*) as the ontological, if also psychological, realization or embodiment of reality. For this reason, He's logical interpretation of the School of Mind cut itself off from all those ideas of the School that were predicated upon treating mind in the ontological sense. It might be said, for example, that Wang Yangming's whole philosophy was based on ideas of this kind, among them innate knowledge of the good (*liang zhi*), and the manifestation of clear character (*ming mingde*). This is also the case with Mencius (371–289 B.C.), the most important precursor of the School of Mind, whose central idea of the four beginnings (*siduan*) of human goodness is not only ontological but also psychological and resists logical reformulation. In making short shrift of the ontological aspect of the School of Mind and jettisoning its psychological aspect, He Lin left many of its insights largely unexplored, while his emphasis on the logical aspect of mind provided an epistemic sophistication and clarity of argument from which modern reformulations of the School stand to benefit.

In reformulating the School of Mind, He Lin drew on Kant and German idealism to such a degree that it seems appropriate to see the resulting hybrid product as an expression of Kantian ideas in School of Mind terms rather than the other way around. The idea at the center of He's idealist position, namely, that *a priori* principles underlie our experience and knowledge of the world and that these principles are a function not of the world as such but of the cognitive character of our very humanity, is Kantian through and through and, in its emphasis on the conditions of the possibility of knowledge, is a far cry from the ontological or psychological investigations of the School of Mind. What He Lin retains from the School of Mind are chiefly two things:

the emphasis on mind in making sense of the human relation to the natural and moral order, and the idea that mind and the natural and moral order are ultimately inseparable. These features bear some resemblance to the idealism of Kant but such resemblance should not be exaggerated, since neither the emphasis on mind nor the inseparability of mind and world is at all clearly conceived by the School of Mind in logical terms.

One major consequence of He Lin's Kantian transformation of the Lu–Wang School of Mind is that this School no longer seems so sharply divided from the Cheng–Zhu School of Principles (*lixue*). Indeed, this latter is arguably superior to the School of Mind as far as the explicit formulation of principles is concerned. From He Lin's perspective, all that has to be done to rectify the School of Principles is to realize that the principles do not pertain to things in themselves but are grounded in our subjective constitution. Thus, as He Lin saw it, the human mind and *a priori* principles, which are brought together in German idealism, were emphasized respectively in the School of Mind and the School of Principles. He Lin's achievement was to unify the insights of these two Chinese Schools from a single Kantian perspective, although in the process he had interpreted the two Schools in ways that are open to question.

How does mind, so understood, enter into relationship with matter? In working out his answer, He Lin drew heavily, on the side of Western philosophy, on Spinoza and, especially, Hegel. He Lin held that mind and matter are inseparable. "Strictly speaking, mind and matter make up an inseparable unity," and it is only "for the sake of convenience [that] we may speak of them separately" (He, 1990, p. 132). But what kind of inseparable unity? We may characterize He Lin's answer by saying that it is a hierarchical unity. This is not just a question of "giving the name mind to that which comprehends and thinks, and giving the name matter to that which has extension and shape" (He, 1990, p. 132). Much more important, mind and matter "constitute the two sides of reality, with mind as the controlling component and matter as the instrumental component" (He, 1990, p. 132). Here we need to distinguish two senses in which mind is "superior" or "prior" to matter. First, mind is superior to matter because mind is the logical condition of the possibility of matter. Secondly, mind is superior to matter because matter is mind's instrument. It is the second sense of mind's superiority to matter that He Lin is referring to in this passage, the first sense having already been covered in his logical interpretation of mind. If Kant is the decisive influence behind He Lin's insistence on the logical priority of mind, Hegel takes center stage when it comes to what we may call the dynamic priority of mind. This Hegelian sense of priority, more than the Kantian one, lends itself to being formulated in terms of Chinese philosophy, as the distinction between substance (*ti*) and application (*yong*). Thus, "mind is the substance of matter, while matter is the application of mind; mind is the essence of matter, while matter is the manifestation of mind" (He, 1990, p. 132).

One important consequence follows from the inseparability of mind and matter and their hierarchical unity. In a loose fashion typical of much of his philosophical writing, He Lin explained this consequence as follows:

> For this reason, an upholder of idealism must not talk about mind in the abstract without reference to culture or the science of culture. To talk about the priority of mind without the nourishing context of culture would be to empty idealism of content. To talk about the priority of mind without reference to creations of culture and the actual life of the spirit would be to deprive idealism of vitality. (He, 1990, pp. 132–3)

Vitality is a key term here, for it is a nontechnical way of conveying He Lin's fundamental philosophical conviction that idealism, or "the inseparable unity of mind and matter," must be so conceived that mind can act on matter. This is what the hierarchical unity of mind and matter is all about. For He Lin, mind and matter form a kind of unity in which one is "higher" than the other, and in which being higher amounts to being able to act on what is lower.

However, following from He Lin's treatment of mind as the totality of *a priori* principles rather than as the psychological locus of individual thought and will, the active character of mind has little to do with will, still less with willfulness. Thus, to say that mind acts on matter is the same as saying that matter moves and changes in accordance with *a priori* principles. Part of what is meant by the inseparability of mind and matter is that such principles do not exist "outside" of matter, with matter conforming to them; rather, principles inhere in matter, making a thing, as an instance of matter, what it is. In this sense, *a priori* principles make up the essence (*xing*) of matter or an individual thing:

> *Xing* means the essence of matter. A thing exists by virtue of its essence, without which it ceases to exist. Therefore, to understand a thing it is especially important to investigate its essence. When philosophers understand a thing, they mean to grasp its essence, which is then made manifest through definitions. For example, in the proposition "A human being is a rational animal," rationality is taken to be the essence of a human being. Rationality is that which gives value to a human being, the original principle by virtue of which a human being is a human being. Every human conduct, qua human conduct, is an exercise of rationality. When one loses one's rationality, one loses that by virtue of which one is human. The essence of a thing is that which makes it what it is and what it ought to be, the original principle or prototype which determines a thing in all its changes and developments. (Hu, 1990, p. 133)

Once mind is understood as *a priori* principles, and principles in turn are understood as the nature or essence of a thing, idealism begins to shed its subjective connotations. This emphasis on essence shows why He Lin found it necessary to combine the Cheng–Zhu School and the Lu–Wang School. Without the Cheng–Zhu School's appreciation of the importance of principles, He Lin believed, allegiance to the Lu–Wang School would lead in the direction of willfulness and, worse, in the direction of the psychological understanding of mind. However, firmly siding with the Lu–Wang School, He Lin was adamant that it does not make sense to speak of matter, or the principles inherent in it, except through the categories of the human mind. It is only in this sense that He Lin insisted, using a famous formulation of the School of Mind, that there is no matter outside of mind (*xin wai wu wu*). Thus, the equation of mind and essence is yet another place where He Lin brought about a supposed reconciliation of the two schools. *Xing* or essence, at its highest or most comprehensive, is something for which He Lin found an equivalent in Hegel's Absolute Idea. Following Hegel, he insisted that essence be understood in terms of concrete universals. He explained this point with reference to a nation's essence:

> In the realm of politics, idealism sets great store by the study, understanding, and development of a nation's essence. By a nation's essence is meant the lifeblood and spirit that determines the fate of the whole nation. It is only through a full understanding of a nation's essence that guidelines can be found for the further development of the nation. However, as life is understood through investigating the evolution of myriad living organisms, and as reason is understood through examining the totality of human cultural activities, so a nation's essence is something that can be grasped only by studying the cultural life and history of the entire nation. Thus, essence is the universals or key features derived from the totality of objective material in all its diversity. Essence, then, is universal and concrete, and such concrete universals are "*li.*" (He, 1990, p. 134)

Here He Lin followed Hegel for two reasons, both involving a sharp contrast between Hegel and Plato. First, for Plato there is a fundamental division between the world of essence (Ideas) and the world of appearance or phenomena, whereas for Hegel the two form a unity. Secondly, for Plato essence (Ideas) is static and abstract, whereas for Hegel essence (the Absolute Idea or Spirit) is active and concrete. According to He Lin, the conception of essence and phenomena as a unity and the conception of essence as dynamic permitted Hegel's idealism to make room for all the complexity of the world and to account for the movement of the world toward a positive end. Moreover, thanks to his understanding of essence as law-like principles rather than as the individual human will, Hegel's idealism could explain and foresee this movement because of the imperfections or contradictions in the world rather than in spite of them.

He Lin had a particularly keen appreciation of Hegel's idea of the "cunning of reason," according to which the objective rational development of history uses subjective and seemingly irrational human desires to achieve its ends. He claimed to find the same idea in the Ming dynasty scholar Wang Chuanshan (1619–92), who predated Hegel by about one hundred and fifty years. Largely on this account, He Lin considered Wang Chuanshan to be the most import-ant Chinese philosopher since Wang Yangming. It is not hard to see why He Lin was drawn to the idea of the cunning of reason. In the first place, the cunning of reason allows a reconciliation between *li* (principles) and *yu* (desire), a reconciliation He Lin found especially important in modern times. Through the cunning of reason, it would be unnecessary to follow an imperative of the Cheng–Zhu School, namely, "to preserve heavenly principles and eradicate human desire," in order to bring about the conformity of everything to *li*. Resolving this tension between principles and desire is very much in keeping with He Lin's advocacy of a politics that combines utilitarianism, moderation, and conformity to principles. In the second place, the cunning of reason helps to reconcile realism and optimism, that is to reconcile a sober appreciation of the dark side of things and a sense of confidence that gradually and eventually everything will turn out to be all right.

Although these claims for the cunning of reason may not seem entirely coher-ent upon reflection, one can nevertheless understand why Hegel's idealism profoundly appealed to He Lin, particularly given the political and cultural circumstances in which he became fascinated with Hegel's philosophy. In the epilogue to his 1936 translation of Josiah Royce's *The Spirit of Modern Philosophy*, He Lin wrote: "The time in which we live has in common with Hegel's time . . . the fact of the threat of invasion by a more powerful neighbor, internal division, and the collapse and disintegration of spirit. . . . Hegel's doctrine contains a lot that can help us find a solution to the problems of our time" (He, 1936, p. 200).

In spite of the un-Hegelian nature of his belief in the practical efficacy of philosophy, there is no mistaking why He Lin found Hegel so compelling. If philosophy were to contribute to improving and perfecting the world, He Lin found in Hegel all the necessary pieces: the inseparable unity of mind and matter; the power of mind to act on matter; an understanding of this power in terms of the operation of essence (the Absolute Idea) as an active and motive force in the teleological unfolding of events rather than as the exercise of individual will; and, following from these, the inevitable prospect of a final conformity of everything to principles that will be reached from a present situation that is full of imperfection and tragedy.

Substance and Application in the Philosophy of Culture

Given He Lin's understanding of idealism, it is only natural that he should extend his philosophical idealism to the realm of culture, for it is in this realm that mind as principles and matter as the material world meet. Thus He Lin developed a philosophy of culture to supplement his philosophical idealism and to make it more concrete. Central to the structure of this philosophy is the distinction between substance and application. As we have seen, this distinction is relatively straightforward when applied to mind and matter: it picks out one dimension of the priority of mind over matter, namely, the dimension involving control and instrumentality. When applied to culture, however, the substance–application distinction becomes more complicated, and it must be said that He Lin's understanding of substance–application is neither Confucian nor Daoist but very much his own. Here, instead of the two concepts of mind and matter, He Lin operates with four concepts:

1. The idea of *dao*, namely, the substance of culture,
2. The idea of Culture, namely, the manifestation of *dao* in the form of consciousness,
3. The idea of Nature, namely, the manifestation of *dao* in the form of non consciousness,
4. The idea of Spirit, namely, the enabling condition of the manifestation or realization of *dao* in the form of Culture, or the spiritual condition by virtue of which culture is culture, and hence the dividing line between Culture and Nature. (He, 1990, p. 347)

As in the case of mind and matter, these four basic concepts or categories make up a hierarchy in terms of substance and application, with the two intermediate categories being simultaneously substance in relation to a lower category and application in relation to a higher category: "Nature is the application of Culture while Culture is the substance of Nature. Culture is the application of Spirit while Spirit is the substance of Culture. Spirit is the application of *dao* while *dao* is the substance of Spirit" (He, 1990, p. 347). *Dao* alone is pure substance and, in this sense, the highest concept in the hierarchy. It is to Spirit, however, not to *dao*, that He Lin gave priority, treating it as "the most important but also the most difficult and strange" (He, 1990, p. 347). The reason for this is that, unlike in the case of mind and matter, the order of hierarchy in terms of substance and application does not quite correspond to the order of activity. He Lin singled out Spirit as the most important because it alone is active whereas *dao*, otherwise higher, is not. "Without the mediation of the activity of Spirit, *dao or li* will not be able to realize or manifest itself as Culture but will remain latent and obscure principles, mere substance without application" (He, 1990, p. 348). Recall that He Lin believed in the identity of mind and principles. Here, in his philosophy of culture, mind and principles seem to come apart, with principles corresponding to *dao* and mind reduced to a psychological locus. Once they come apart, that which is highest, namely, *dao* construed as principles divorced from mind, is no longer that which is active. It is only with this separation of *dao* and mind that it becomes necessary to introduce an intermediate category to link them together.

This intermediate category is Spirit. "Spirit is the coming together of mind and truth. In other words, Spirit refers to the activity of *dao* or *li* in the mind" (He, 1990, p. 347). Thus, Spirit alone is *dao* in active form or mind in principled form: Spirit is the medium through which "mind is principles":

> In terms of substance and application, Spirit is an activity of consciousness that takes *dao* as its substance and Nature and Culture as its application. It follows that Spirit occupies the dominant, active, and governing position in the philosophy of culture. Nature is but the material with which Spirit operates or realizes itself, while what is called Culture is Nature as molded by the human Spirit. What is called *li* or *dao* comprises nothing but laws and principles in the depths of the human mind. The activity of Spirit consists in enhancing and bringing to the forefront of consciousness such otherwise implicit and obscure laws and principles so as to turn them into conscious and concrete truths. Without the mediation of the activity of Spirit, *dao* or *li* will not be able to realize or manifest itself as Culture but will remain latent and obscure principles, mere substance without application. From this point of view, Nature is pure application or material without substance, while *dao* or *li* is pure substance or prototype without application and hence is just an abstract concept. It is Spirit alone that is a reality which combines substance and application and is both. (He, 1990, p. 348)

Was this mere confusion or inconsistency on the part of He Lin, who simply forgot what he had proposed elsewhere, namely, the identity of mind and principle or the identity of mind and *dao*? What inconsistency there is seems to be motivated by a desire to recover something which was lost when He Lin, in his general exposition of idealism, construed mind entirely in the logical sense and in so doing put mind in the psychological sense beyond his philosophical reach. Now, with mind no longer identified by definition with principles, mind could become psychological again and flesh-and-blood human actors could give a tangible, human form to the otherwise extremely abstract idea of mind as an active and motive force. Then, with the introduction of the further category of Spirit, it became possible to unite mind in the logical sense with mind in the psychological sense. Whereas in his general account of idealism, mind is either logical or psychological, in his philosophy of culture mind is both logical and psychological, although the detailed workings of his categories in the philosophy of culture are nowhere spelled out beyond saying that "It is Spirit alone that is a reality which combines substance and application and is both." Such unification, in turn, was designed to render the idea of mind as an active force on matter, or Spirit as an active force on Culture, more tangible, and to put *dao* or principles in concrete touch with Culture. "Spirit is Truth in concrete, effective, and social form" (He, 1990, p. 348). Clearly, for Spirit to perform this function, it has to be something like the Absolute Spirit in the Hegelian sense, and this sits ill with He's concept of *dao* as the highest substance.

Implicit in He Lin's discussion of the mediating function of Spirit is the idea that substance and application are inseparable, an idea that goes together with the belief, expounded in He's general account of idealism, in the inseparability of mind and matter. "Substance and application are necessarily united and inseparable. Any application must be of some substance, and any substance must contain some application. There is no substance without application, nor application without substance" (He, 1990, p. 349). This belief in the inseparability of substance and application informed He Lin's clear-headed and sometimes prescient remarks on the heated debate in the late nineteenth and early twentieth centuries over the wisdom of China maintaining its culture (substance) while trying to adopt Western technology (application) for the sake of national survival:

> Given the principle of the unity of substance and application, it is clear that the idea "Chinese culture as substance, Western culture as application"(*zhongxue weiti, xixue weiyong*) is completely wrong-headed. Since Chinese culture and Western culture each form a comprehensive system of its own, each with its own substance and application, it will not do to violate the integrity of each system and sever its component parts as if a part could be appropriated in isolation from the whole. . . . Even when the idea "Chinese culture as substance, Western culture as application" is interpreted in terms of taking spiritual civilization as substance and material civilization as application, or taking knowledge of *dao* (*daoxue*) as substance and knowledge of matter and practical know-how (*qixue*) as application, it still does not work. For Chinese culture is not pure knowledge of *dao* or pure spiritual civilization, and no more is Western culture pure practical knowledge of matter and know-how or pure material civilization. Western science, or Western knowledge of matter and practical know-how, has as its substance Western metaphysics or knowledge of *dao*. And Western material civilization has as its substance Western spiritual civilization. For this reason, the outdated Chinese morality, way of thinking, and philosophy is absolutely incapable of serving as the substance of modern Western science and material civilization. Nor can it appropriate the latter as its application. When China has developed its own new science, it will also have developed its own new philosophy as its substance. . . . The aim is to promote the unified development of substance and application. (He, 1990, pp. 352–3)

Within the unity of substance and application, Spirit and Culture, He Lin assigned a higher place to substance and hence to Spirit. This priority of Spirit entails a cultural universalism, for Spirit itself is not culture-specific but something of which all cultures, past and present, Chinese and foreign, are applications. As the substance of Culture, and hence the substance of all cultures, Spirit is universal. By the same token, all cultures, no matter how specific they are *qua* applications, are applications of this universal Spirit, the universal substance of culture. "The culture of the whole world is the process wherein

the Absolute Spirit gradually realizes or manifests itself" (He, 1990, p. 348).
We see here the philosophical rationale for He Lin's distinctive, highly ecumen-
ical and comprehensive approach to philosophy, his refusal to draw a sharp
line between Chinese philosophy and Western philosophy. But this tendency
existed side by side, not without tension, with a particularistic or even nationalistic tendency in He Lin's thought that set great store by Chinese culture.
He Lin sometimes came close to saying or implying that there is a Chinese
Spirit. Both sides of He Lin are at work, almost seamlessly, in the following
passage:

> On the basis of the principle that Spirit . . . is the substance of Culture, I want
> to put forward the proposal that Spirit or Reason be treated as substance and
> the cultures of past and present, Chinese and foreign, be treated as application.
> The idea is to proceed from the free and independent Spirit or Reason as sub-
> stance and thereby to absorb and assimilate, select from and move beyond,
> foreign cultures and past cultures. We should do our best to appropriate the
> strengths of those cultures and grasp their essence and, in so doing, we should
> take upon ourselves not only the legacy of Chinese culture but also the legacy
> of Western culture, until we have internalized them and turned them into our
> own resources. Especially with regard to Western culture, it is important not
> to look upon it as a culture imported from a foreign nation but to treat it as a
> set of resources for actualizing our own Spirit and perfecting our own Reason.
> (He, 1990, p. 353)

Our own Spirit? Our own Reason? Such incoherence, if it is that, expressed
a deep tension between He's universalistic aspirations and his deep sense of
rootedness in the Chinese cultural and philosophical tradition. It is this incoherence or tension that allowed He Lin to attach great importance to a revival
of Confucianism. But even as he tried to inject new life into Confucianism
as Chinese Spirit, he sought to reinterpret Confucianism in a universalistic spirit.
Behind this universalism lurked, in turn, his deep admiration for Western philosophy, which He Lin saw as the substance of the technological and military
might of the West.

Strengthening Confucianism with Western Philosophy

It was in keeping with He Lin's belief in the priority of Spirit that he should
regard China's plight since the Opium War as first and foremost a crisis of
Spirit, specifically of the Chinese Spirit. Since he regarded Confucianism as the
principal expression of the Chinese Spirit, it should come as no surprise that,
for him, "The greatest crisis of the Chinese nation is that Confucianism has
lost its sovereignty in Chinese cultural life and is without new vitality" (He,
1988, p. 5). By the same token, he held that the way out of China's crisis

was to give new life to Confucianism and thereby to revive the Chinese Spirit. On the strength of his 1941 article "The New Unfolding Confucianism," (in He, 1995) as well as other writings, it would be fitting to regard He Lin, after Liang Shuming and Xiong Shili, as one of the earliest proponents of what has come to be known as New Confucianism (*xinruxue*). Not surprisingly, He's brand of New Confucianism bears the distinctive stamp of his philosophical idealism and his idealist philosophy of culture.

He Lin proposed to bring about a Confucian revival with the help of the cultural and philosophical resources of the West. "The new unfolding of Confucianism is not predicated on the rejection of Western culture but on a thorough understanding of Western culture" (He, 1988, p. 7). He called such a proposal "enriching [Chinese] substance with [Western] substance" (*yi ti chong shi ti*), and it came in large part from He Lin's cultural universalism, the belief that Spirit, as distinct from its applications, is not culture-specific:

> For the saints of East and West are of one mind and one principle. To bring the philosophy of Confucius and Mencius, Laozi and Zhuangzi, Cheng Yi and Zhu Xi, Lu Jiuyuan and Wang Yangming into unity with the philosophy of Socrates, Plato, Aristotle, Kant, and Hegel so as to produce a new philosophy that strengthens the national spirit and thereby overcomes the new cultural crisis of the nation – this is the path of development which new Confucianism must follow. Once Confucianism is made richer in content, more cogent as a system, and more transparent in its arguments, it can serve not only as a theoretical foundation that makes morality possible but also as a theoretical foundation that makes science possible. (He, 1988, p. 8)

This is perhaps the best description of He Lin's own philosophical project or, at any rate, of his philosophical aspirations, although nowadays the idea of bringing Eastern and Western philosophers, old and new, into one room to find one best universal philosophy seems a very odd recipe for reconstructing a new Chinese culture. The underlying cultural universalism, however, does not explain He Lin's almost exclusive interest in Western culture among the cultures outside China, and, within Western culture, his almost exclusive interest in what he calls the mainstream philosophy of the West. By the mainstream he clearly has in mind the part of Western philosophy that constitutes the substance of the technological and military power of the West. "Western science, or Western knowledge of matter and practical know-how, has as its substance Western metaphysics or knowledge of *dao*" (He, 1990, p. 352). It is largely for this reason that He Lin was eager to draw upon mainstream Western philosophy in reviving Confucianism. Indeed, he seems to have deduced the excellence of Western substance from the power of Western application, so impressed was he with the latter, as have been most Chinese in his time and since then. This ambiguous mixture of cultural universalism and practical concern with power lay behind He Lin's open-mindedness towards

Western philosophy and does much to explain both his diagnosis of the crisis of Confucianism and his recipe for its revival:

> The introduction of Western culture confronts Confucianism with a test, a huge test or juncture with survival at stake. If Confucianism can enrich and develop itself by grasping, absorbing, assimilating, and transforming Western culture, it will be able to sustain and revive itself and develop in new ways. If it cannot stand this test or pass through this juncture, it will die off or go under without any prospect of a comeback. (He, 1988, p. 6)

Following from his understanding of the make-up of Confucianism, He Lin advanced a three-fold recipe for its revival:

> Confucianism itself contains three components, namely, the study of principles (*lixue*), which is aimed at the investigation of things and the understanding of principles; the cultivation of character through rituals (*lijiao*), which serves to exercise and strengthen the will and regulate conduct; and cultivation of character through poetry and music (*shijiao*), which is designed to mold temperament and sensibility and add color to life. Therefore, to promote the new unfolding of Confucianism, the first thing to do is to strengthen the *lixue* of Confucianism with the help of Western philosophy. . . . The second thing to do is to enrich the *lijiao* of Confucianism with the best part of Christianity. . . . The third thing to do is to strengthen the *shijiao* of Confucianism through an appreciation of Western art. (He, 1988, pp. 8–9)

He Lin attached equal importance to these three ways of reviving Confucianism. As a philosopher, however, he saw his own role as falling especially in the first domain. We could indeed view his whole philosophical output as an attempt to contribute to the Confucian revival through the study of principles, were He Lin, in other moods, not to see his philosophical endeavor as guided by his universalism. From the standpoint of this commitment to universalism, any attempt to revive a national philosophy *qua* national philosophy would be philosophical activity of an inferior order. Be that as it may, it is worth giving a concrete example of how He Lin went about strengthening Confucianism with Western philosophy, and nowhere did he go into greater detail than in the case of his controversial interpretation of the traditional doctrines of the Five Relations (*wulun*) involving rulers and ministers, fathers and sons, husbands and wives, elder and younger, and friends, and the Three Bonds (*sangang*) governing the conduct of ministers, sons, and wives.

He Lin was quite right to consider his examination of the concept of the Five Relations entirely new. His innovation lay in detecting a qualitative difference between the concept of the Five Relations and its subsequent incarnation as the concept of the Three Bonds. He Lin gave a "two-tier account of the logic that inevitably leads from the Five Relations to the Three Bonds" (He, 1988, p. 58). The central idea at the first tier is that the Five Relations are reciprocal and hence conditional whereas the Three Bonds impose moral duties that are unilateral and hence unconditional or absolute. This makes a world of difference both in theory and in practice, and He Lin explained the logic at work with admirable clarity:

> Let the ruler behave like a ruler, the minister a minister, the father a father, the son a son, the husband a husband, and the wife a wife. If the ruler does not behave like a ruler, the minister does not behave like a minister. If the father does not behave like a father, the son does not behave like a son. And if the husband does not behave like a husband, the wife does not behave like a wife. The "does not" in the case of the minister and the son contains two meanings, namely, "ought not" and "will not." If the ruler does not do what is expected of a ruler, it is only natural that the minister will not do what is expected of a minister and, moreover, he ought not so to act. . . . The same applies to the relations between father and son and between husband and wife. In this way, as long as there are often rulers who do not behave like rulers, fathers who do not behave like fathers, and husbands who do not behave like husbands, then it is both reasonable and to be expected that ministers will murder rulers, sons will behave unfilially, and wives will fail to discharge wifely duties. The reason for this is that all these human relations are reciprocal and inconstant. As a result, there is an element of instability in human relations and in the foundations of society, and revolts and chaos might happen at any moment. Thus, the Three Bonds are meant to remedy the instability of reciprocal relations, and it does so by requiring of one party within each relation that they absolutely perform their prescribed role, practice unilateral love, and carry out unilateral duties. The essence of the Three Bonds consists, then, in the requirement that the minister should not stop behaving like a minister when the ruler does not behave like a ruler, that the son should not stop behaving like a son when the father does not behave like a father, and that the wife should not stop behaving like a wife when the husband does not behave like a husband. In other words, the Three Bonds require the minister, the son, and the wife to discharge their respective duties of loyalty, filial piety, and chastity in a unilateral and absolute manner so as not to fall into a pattern of unstable reciprocal relations marked by mutual revenge and bargaining. (He, 1988, pp. 58–9)

As the reciprocity of the Five Relations thus evolves into the nonreciprocity and absoluteness of the Three Bonds, there also occurs a qualitative change in the status of the superior parties in the Five Relations. Whereas in the Five Relations, the ruler, father, and husband are concrete persons, in the Three Bonds they have turned into *li*, that is, Ideas. It is only to the ruler, father, and husband conceived as *li* that unilateral, absolute duties can be owed. This conception, then, is the second tier of He Lin's account, and it is a natural extension of the first.

The idea of Five Relations in the pre-Qin period focuses on relations between humans, whereas the idea of Three Bonds in the Western Han dynasty transforms relations between humans into a unilateral, absolute commitment on the part of humans to *li*, to prescribed roles, and to constant virtues. For this reason, the idea of Three Bonds is more profound and more effective than the idea of Five Relations. To take a concrete example, where the idea of Three Bonds regards the ruler as the standard (*gang*) of the minister, the ruler is understood as a universal, and accordingly it is the idea (*li*) of the ruler that serves as the standard and measure of the position of minister. When it is said that the minister must not be disloyal even if the ruler is malevolent, it is meant that the minister, that is, a person who occupies the position of minister, must respect the ruler qua idea and status, and this also means acting in strict accordance with the nature of one's position. What is involved here is loyalty to a status and to an idea rather than subservience to an individual tyrant. It is only when every person is prepared unilaterally to carry out their absolute duties in keeping with their position and status that the Three Bonds and Five Relations governing human relations in society can be maintained. (He, 1988, p. 60)

So interpreted, the concept of Three Bonds, otherwise distinctively Chinese and hopelessly reactionary and outmoded, began to show some affinity with certain modern and enlightened ideas in Western philosophy, or so He Lin claimed:

What is most extraordinary, and this has come as a surprise even to myself, is that in the idea of Three Bonds, this uniquely Chinese, this most moribund and most roundly criticized doctrine . . . , I have discovered affinities with certain profound ideas in mainstream Western moral thinking and with the forward-looking and ever expanding modern spirit of the West. In its emphasis on loyalty to eternal ideas or constant virtues rather than subservience to the inconstant commands of individuals, the doctrine of Three Bonds is akin to Plato's thinking. In its emphasis on individuals unilaterally carrying out pure moral duties without regard to contingent situations in the empirical realm, the doctrine of Three Bonds contains ideas similar to Kant's. . . . Likewise, the moral thinking of Jesus is characterized by treating love as an end in itself and unilaterally carrying out pure duties, thereby rising above the kind of worldly morality marked by mutual advantage and exchange. In this regard, it bears a strong resemblance to the doctrine of Three Bonds, in that the latter rises above the relativity and natural reciprocity in the way relations are governed by the idea of Five Relations and insists on the unilateral fulfillment of absolute duties. (He, 1988, pp. 60–1)

He Lin would be the last to deny that his reconstruction of Confucianism, specifically of the Three Bonds, brought to the fore something that is only latent in it. Indeed, the unconditional sense of duty and the pure freedom of will behind it not only were philosophically latent but had also been politically suppressed.

What makes the Three Bonds different [from unconditional morality based on reason] is that its true spirit has been hidden through imprisonment by *lijiao* (the cultivation of character through rituals) and suppression by authoritarianism. Without purification by the Enlightenment, the unilateral element in the Three Bonds does not yet amount to pure freedom of the will, pure compulsion by conviction. (He, 1988, pp. 61–2)

He Lin's approach to reviving Confucianism lay precisely in uncovering what was latent philosophically and what had been suppressed politically. Once a latent or suppressed value is retrieved from the past, it can point the way to the future. "To follow one's own will as the ultimate authority, to discharge fully one's love and one's duties unilaterally . . . is the path which must be followed by the Confucian conception of the person" (He, 1988, p. 62).

Recourse to Western philosophy went hand in hand with this approach because much of what is latent in Chinese philosophy is explicit in Western philosophy, just as much of what has been suppressed in Chinese society has been allowed to grow in Western society. This way of viewing the relationship between Chinese and Western philosophy can be illuminating, especially when He Lin first explained the difference between the Five Relations and the Three Bonds in terms of the absence of the idea of unconditional duty in the former and its presence in the latter, and then explained the difference between the latency of this idea in the Three Bonds and its explicit and well-articulated presence in Western culture. He Lin's account of these differences is highly astute, both as moral psychology and as cultural analysis. Possibly influenced by Max Weber, he put his finger on a crucial factor that sets the West apart from China: "The Western tendency to attend to pure morality and pure love, the perseverance in carrying out one's calling or one's position, all this contains the spirit of dedication involved in unilateral love and the unilateral performance of duties" (He, 1988, p. 61).

Although He Lin failed to notice the subtle kind of reciprocity or exchange which is often at work in the unconditional sense of duty fostered by Christianity, his diagnosis of Chinese culture in terms of the lack of an explicit ideal of unconditional duty is on target and remains relevant today.

This way of bringing to the fore something that is latent in Chinese philosophy but is explicit in Western philosophy is what He Lin meant by "enriching [Chinese] substance with [Western] substance." As a matter of general methodology, this approach assumes that "the saints of East and West are of one mind and one principle" (He, 1988, p. 8). Not surprisingly, instead of applying this assumption across the board, He Lin was highly selective and sought to find latent in Confucianism only those things which were not merely explicit in Western philosophy but which were normatively attractive to him. This selectiveness need not be a flaw, but his failure to see the intrinsically normative character of all philosophical interpretation or reconstruction does point to a serious weakness that pervaded He Lin's whole philosophy and went to the heart of his idealism. It is most clearly illustrated by his discussion of the Three Bonds.

As we have seen, He Lin found the latent philosophical core of the Three Bonds in the idea that the ruler, father, and husband are not concrete persons who deserve only reciprocal and conditional duties but ideas which enjoin nonreciprocal and unconditional duties. For He Lin, these ideas were simply given and hence beyond question. In this regard, he saw himself as following Kant, assigning to the ideas of ruler, father, and husband the status of Kant's synthetic *a priori* principles. But he failed to notice an important difference between his use of Kant's notion of *a priori* principles and Kant's own. However one may question Kant's notion of *a priori* principles, one can say in Kant's favor that he restricted his list of such principles to a minimum, in keeping with their character as the conditions of the possibility of knowledge and morality. In the case of morality, the *a priori* principles identified by Kant, such as the Categorical Imperative, are formal and, in the first instance, empty of empirical content.

What vitiates He Lin's use of Kant is that he was too quick to give empirical content to supposedly *a priori* principles. Instead of saying that there are things in principle which serve as the conditions of the possibility of knowledge or morality, he told us exactly what these things are, and as the example of the Three Bonds shows, they happen clearly to have empirical content. In this way, the notion of *a priori* principles can easily degenerate into a defence of contingent human institutions by elevating them to the status of eternal truths. This does not seem to be He Lin's intent, but such a practice was facilitated by an idealism that contained no principled grounds for resisting the injection of empirical content into supposedly *a priori* categories.

He Lin's empirical version of idealism, so to speak, closed off the Kantian possibility of understanding reason procedurally rather than substantively. Further, it obstructed the possibility, pursued by philosophers such as Nietzsche, Heidegger, the pragmatists, and the later Wittgenstein, of understanding the conditions of knowledge and morality as *a posteriori* rather than *a priori* and as contingent rather than necessary. Besides being more defensible in epistemic terms, either of these possibilities would be morally and politically more enlightened and would leave much greater room for autonomy on an individual level and democracy on a collective level. It is a pity that He Lin's idealism, in several respects an advance over earlier Chinese versions of idealism, did not move in these directions. In this regard, at least, his philosophical outlook was still traditional rather than modern, exhibiting a closer affinity with the substantive idealism of Song–Ming Confucianism than with the more logical or formal idealism of Kant and Hegel. This characterization of He Lin's philosophy does not imply a general equation in philosophy of the traditional and the Chinese and of the modern and the Western. He Lin can be seen as a precursor of developments in philosophy that are Chinese and modern.

Conversion to Materialism

It is customary to distinguish two main periods in He Lin's philosophy, with 1949 as the dividing line. Such a division, often applied to scholars of He's generation, seems especially clear-cut in his case, since his main contributions to philosophical writing fell almost exclusively within the first period. Nevertheless, his philosophical activity after 1949 deserves a brief discussion, both in its own right and as a way to shed light on his philosophy as a whole.

He Lin's "official" philosophical transformation took place in 1951, with the publication in the influential newspaper *Guangming Daily* of his article "Participation in the Land Reforms Changed My Outlook." In this article, He openly renounced his idealism in favor of dialectical materialism and historical materialism. Like most of He's accounts of his philosophical change, this article was philosophically insubstantial and was filled with the political jargon of the day. On the evidence of this and other articles, one might conclude that after 1949 He Lin underwent not so much a philosophical transformation as a political one and that his political conversion was a matter of enforced conformity rather than voluntary change. The problem with this interpretation, as applied to He Lin, is not that it is incorrect but that it is too general. The picture that emerges from He's publications after 1949, including his own proclamations of his philosophical transformation, is ambiguous. His conversion from idealism to materialism was not as deep as he claimed at the time, but it was not as superficial as the harsher critics of He's post-1949 output have argued.

At least to some degree, He Lin's switch from idealism to materialism can plausibly be seen in part as a philosophical transformation, in the sense that his move was facilitated by philosophical considerations. Despite the enormous gap between idealism and materialism, He clearly found a philosophical bridge between them. He Lin was not obliged to cross from one side to the other, but the bridge was there to facilitate such a move, whatever the causes might have been. The bridge comprised certain common features between He's understanding of idealism, including both its Hegelian and its Confucian elements, and his understanding of materialism. Prominent among such features was an understanding of reality that is holistic, teleological, and objective. In moving from idealism to materialism, He Lin had to change the order of priority between mind and matter, reverse the direction of causation between them, and shift to a different substantive teleology. All of this was made easier by the fact that he did not have to abandon the role of objectively given law-like principles in his nonconstructivist understanding of humans and their world. In these respects, He Lin's philosophical transformation was not a complete departure from his earlier idealist position. By the same token, his partial reconciliation with his idealism in the more open atmosphere of post-Mao China did not amount to a total abandonment of the materialist philosophy to which he verbally subscribed to the end of his life.

In terms of philosophical substance, however, He Lin's criticisms of his erstwhile idealist philosophy seldom went beyond the philosophical clichés of the time, which he indeed helped to create and consolidate, with significant borrowings from the philosophical orthodoxy in the Soviet Union. The same must be said of his criticisms of idealism in general. In both cases, he operated within an overarching framework comprising the distinction between materialism and idealism, itself subdivided into a subjective and an objective variety, and the further distinction between dialectics and metaphysics. Through the rigid use of this framework, he presented a master-narrative in which the philosophers of the past, both Chinese and Western, suffered from either idealism or metaphysics until Marxism united materialism and dialectics and thereby yielded the ultimate philosophical truth in the shape of dialectical materialism. Even He Lin's article "On Reflection," in some ways his most serious and substantial critique of idealism and defence of dialectical materialism, is largely a rehashing of such vague generalizations, a service neither to Marxism nor to He Lin himself.

In the last decade or so of his life, He Lin found it possible to soften his critique of idealism in general and of his own idealism in particular, but he stopped short of retracting such criticism or reverting to idealism, and he did not explain why. Nor did he give a more than anecdotal account of his philosophical life in which his diverse philosophical contributions and activities were brought together and given their proper place. In many ways his overall philosophical legacy is as ambiguous as the conduct of his entire life as a philosopher and as a human being.

Further Reading

He Lin published most of his work in the form of articles, which were subsequently published as collections, often with considerable overlap among them. Two such collections, He (1943) and He (1947/1988), contain most of his major writings before 1949. The first is no longer in print, but its more important pieces, such as the title essay "A brief exposition of modern idealism," are available in He (1990), the most comprehensive collection of He's entire philosophical output. Another general collection, He (1995), brings together his contributions to New Confucianism (in a very broad sense) but has considerable overlap with He (1947) and He (1990). He Lin's writings on Western philosophy, especially on Hegel, are conveniently found in He (1984) and He (1986).

He Lin has not attracted a large secondary literature, and much of what has been written about him is less than impressive. Zhang Xuezhi wrote some of the better commentaries, especially his book *He Lin* (1992a), which is easily the most comprehensive and reliable study available. Another worthwhile work, more narrowly focused on the currently fashionable topic of

New Confucianism, is Song Zhiming (1998). A more multifaceted picture emerges from Song and Fan (1993), which contains some thirty articles of uneven quality and interest by colleagues, friends, and students on various aspects of He Lin's life and scholarship.

Bibliography

Works by He Lin

He, Lin 1934: *The Attitude of Three German Philosophers at the Time of National Crisis*, Chongqing: Duli Chubanshe

He, Lin 1936: *Heige'er xueshu* 黑格爾學術 (translation of Josiah Royce, *The Spirit of Modern Philosophy*), Shanghai: Shangwu Yinshuguan

He, Lin 1943: *Jindai weixinlun jianshi* 近代唯心論簡釋 (a brief exposition of modern idealism), Chongching: Duli Chubanshe

He, Lin 1945: *Xiandai Zhongguo zhexue* 現代中國哲學 (contemporary Chinese philosophy), Sheng Li Publishers

He, Lin 1984: *Xiandai xifang zhexue jiangyanji* 現代西方哲學講演集 (lectures on modern European philosophy), Shanghai: Shanghai Renmin Chubanshe

He, Lin 1986: *Heige'er zhexue jiangyanji* 黑格爾哲學講演集 (lectures on the philosophy of Hegel), Shanghai: Shanghai Renmin Chubanshe

He, Lin 1988: *Wenhua yu rensheng* 文化與人生 (culture and human life), Beijing: Shangwu Yinshuguan, 1988 new edn. (1st edn 1947)

He, Lin 1990: *Zhexue yu zhexueshi lunwenji* 哲學與哲學史論文集 (collected papers on philosophy and history of philosophy), Beijing: Shangwu Yinshuguan

He, Lin 1995: *Rujia sixiang de xinkaizhan: Helin xinruxue lunzhu jiyao* 儒家思想的新開展：賀麟新儒學論箸輯要 (the new unfolding of confucian thought: He Lin's key writings on Neo-Confucianism), Song, Zhiming, ed., Beijing: Zhongguo Guangbo Dianshi Chubanshe

Works on He Lin

Han, Qiang 1993: "*Helin xin xinxue wenhua zhexue shuping*" 賀麟新心學的文化哲學理論述評 (commentary on He Lin's mind school philosophy of culture), *Journal of Nankai University: The Philosophy and Social Science Edition*, 2 8–13, Nankai Daxue Xuebao: Zhesheban

Song, Zhiming 1998: *Helin xinruxue yanjiu* 賀麟新儒學思想研究 (a study of He Lin's Neo-Confucianism), Tianjin: Tianjin Renmin Chubanshe

Song, Zuliang, and Fan, Jin, eds 1993: *Huitong ji: Helin shengping yu xueshu* 會通集：賀麟生平與學術 (building bridges: He Lin's life and scholarship), Beijing: Sanlian Shudian

Zhang, Maoze 1997: "*Helin yu husai'er xianxiangxue*" 賀麟與胡塞爾現象學 (He Lin and Husserl's phenomenology), *Journal of Northwestern University: The Philosophy and Social Science Edition*, 4 36–40, Xibei Daxue Xuebao: Zhesheban

Zhang, Xuezhi 1990: "*Lun helin dui sibin'nuosha sixiang de xishou yu gaizao*" 論賀麟對斯賓諾莎思想的吸收和改造 (on He Lin's absorption and transformation of the thought of Spinoza), *Wenshizhe (Literature, History, Philosophy)*, 1 34–9

Zhang, Xuezhi 1992a: *He Lin* 賀麟, Taipei: Dongda

Zhang, Xuezhi 1992b: *Helin de xin xinxue* 賀麟的新心學 (He Lin's new mind school) n. p.

Discussion Questions

1. For the purposes of philosophy, is the mind (*xin*) best understood in terms of logic or psychology?
2. Must we use the concept of mind to make sense of the relation between human beings and the natural and moral order?
3. Does He Lin succeed in reconciling the teachings of the School of Mind and the School of Principle?
4. In what sense, if any, can mind act on matter?
5. Can we accept He Lin's use of the "cunning of reason"?
6. Do the concepts of substance and application help us to formulate a philosophy of culture?
7. Should we accept He Lin's account of how Spirit and Culture are related?
8. What should be the project of a new Confucianism?
9. Does He Lin provide an acceptable account of the Five Relations and the Three Bonds?
10. What is preserved philosophically in He Lin's conversion to materialism?

III

IDEOLOGICAL EXPOSURE TO
DIALECTICAL MATERIALISM

10

FENG QI'S AMELIORISM: BETWEEN RELATIVISM AND ABSOLUTISM

Huang Yong

Feng Qi (1915–95) was a student of Jin Yuelin, Feng Youlan, and Tang Yongtong. Of the three, Jin undoubtedly had the greatest influence on him. Although Feng, a devoted communist revolutionary, did not graduate from the masters degree program at Qinghua University during these turbulent years (1935–44), he finished his thesis and published it in 1947 under the title "On Wisdom," and, indeed, the topic of wisdom was at the center of his life-long philosophical concerns. After 1949, Feng taught at Yunnan University, Tongji University, Fudan University, and, from 1951, at East China Normal University in Shanghai. By the mid-1960s, he had completed philosophical manuscripts of several million Chinese characters, but all of these disappeared during the Cultural Revolution (1966–76). Thus, he had to start again to record his philosophical thoughts in the last two decades of his life. In the 1980s, he published *The Logical Development of Ancient Chinese Philosophy* (3 volumes) and *The Revolutionary Process of Modern Chinese Philosophy*, which in both spirit and style can be compared to Hegel's *Lectures on the History of Philosophy*. In the 1990s, he prepared his major philosophical work, *Three Treatises on Wisdom*, which he finished shortly before his death in 1995. In this work, which was posthumously published as the first three volumes of the *Collected Works of Feng Qi*, Feng presented a tripartite philosophical system of wisdom. The first part is an epistemological and metaphysical theory of wisdom, focusing on our knowledge of *dao*; the second is a methodological treatment of dialectic logic, dealing with the application of the theory of *dao* as a method to our cognitive and practical activities; and the third is a moral theory of human freedom, centered on the application of the theory of *dao* to our moral cultivation.

Wisdom: Theory of *Dao*

In his 1947 article "On Wisdom," Feng distinguished wisdom from opinion and knowledge: "opinion is from my perspective, knowledge is from the perspective of the object, and wisdom is from the perspective of *dao*" (Feng, 1996–8, vol 9. p. 3). In other words, opinion is something subjective, reflecting different people's different views; knowledge is objective, representing the actual reality of some particular objects; and wisdom is universal, intuiting the *dao* as the ultimate reality of everything. Such an idea of wisdom is still important in his *Three Treatises on Wisdom*, but he now acknowledged:

> It was too simplistic of me to make such a distinction merely among different perspectives. Therefore, I feel a need to change the way of expression, so that our knowing process becomes a movement from ignorance to knowledge and from knowledge to wisdom. My task is to explain the dialectics of such a movement. (Feng, 1996–8, vol. 1, p. 10)

Both in his earlier distinction among opinion, knowledge, and wisdom and in his later distinction among ignorance, knowledge, and wisdom, Feng emphasized that a philosopher's task is to transform knowledge into wisdom.

Transforming knowledge into wisdom (zhuangshi chengzhi)

The term "transforming knowledge into wisdom" was borrowed from Buddhism. In the consciousness-only school, this term originally means "to transform the conscious activities that focus on the distinction between the attachment to myself and attachment to *dharma* into a wisdom that understands things as they are without any distinctions and attachments" (Feng, 1996–8, vol. 1, p. 409). To use this phrase in his own philosophical system, Feng first defined the terms knowledge and wisdom in relation to ignorance. In Feng's view, in the state of ignorance (as of a child), no distinctions are made either among different objects or between subject and object. Everything is in a primordial unity without distinctions. In contrast, knowledge (including both common sense and science):

> divides objects into different facts and different laws and tries to understand the relationships among these facts and among these laws. The realm of empirical knowledge is the world that can be divided by names and categories. (Feng, 1996–8, vol. 1, p. 412)

In this sense, knowledge is a progressive step out of ignorance. For without such distinctions and understandings, things can only exist as things-in-themselves. Only through knowledge can human beings become self-conscious beings and objects become things-for-us. However, Feng claimed that "knowledge cannot grasp the ultimate cause, the totality, or the whole of the universe, and therefore is not the highest realm," which belongs to wisdom (Feng, 1996–8, vol. 1, p. 412).

Feng used the term "wisdom" as it is used in "the wisdom of sages" (*shengzhi*) and in translations of the Buddhist term *prajna* and the Greek term *logos*. In all these senses, it is "the knowledge of the fundamental principle of the universe and human life, of the *dao* that penetrates all" (Feng, 1996–8, vol. 1, p. 413). Thus, the main distinction between knowledge and wisdom is that, while knowledge emphasizes the abstract, the analytic, and the parts, wisdom focuses on the concrete, the synthetic, and the whole. It might sound peculiar to say that our view of an individual thing (knowledge) is abstract, while our view of the whole (wisdom) is concrete. The point that Feng was making is that our knowledge of an individual thing takes place when we distinguish, separate, and, therefore, abstract this thing from other things. Our wisdom becomes concrete because it focuses precisely on the interconnections among individual things since they are all comprehended in terms of a single *dao*. Thus, in order to understand the *dao* that penetrates all, no distinctions are to be made between one thing and another and between nature and humans. In this sense, the result of the transformation from knowledge to wisdom is a return to ignorance:

> Humans originally belonged to nature and there were no distinctions between heaven and humans, between the subject and the object, between the knower and the known. Only after the step from ignorance to knowledge was taken do such distinctions occur. The transformation from knowledge to wisdom has as its goal the unity between heaven and the human, the realm in which "heaven and earth grow together with me and ten thousand things become one body with me." It is a kind of returning to the original. (Feng, 1996–8, vol. 1, p. 418–19)

Yet this is not a simple return to the original. It is a return on a higher level. The unity between heaven and humans is no longer a spontaneous unity. It is a unity that is not only clearly understood in consciousness but is also purposefully appropriated in practice.

Intellectual intuition (lixing zhijue)

In Feng's view the transformation from knowledge to wisdom is made possible not by the step by step logical analysis of knowledge but by a sudden enlightenment (*dunwu*):

> The parts put together is not the whole. Only through a leap can we suddenly obtain the overall and concrete knowledge of the whole. Of course, to have a separate knowledge of the different parts, aspects, and stages is a necessary preparatory step to know the totality, the whole, and the process. Yet there must be a leap, a feeling of sudden enlightenment in the transition between these two. (Feng, 1996–8, vol. 1, p. 419)

Feng called such a sudden enlightenment "intellectual intuition":

> [Wisdom] grasps the absolute from the relative, the infinite from the finite, the unconditional from the conditional. It is only through transforming our [scientific] knowledge into [metaphysical] wisdom, through intellectual intuition, that we can reach the nameless realm. (Feng, 1996–8, vol. 1, p. 42)

Here, Feng had in mind Kant's distinction between sense and intellect. Using our ability to sense, we can have intuitions of things, but such intuitions, being finite, relative, and particular, cannot be used to know *dao*, which is infinite, absolute, and universal; using our intellectual ability, we can have universal and necessary knowledge, but such knowledge, being the result of the projection of our *a priori* categories, cannot be used to know *dao*, which is a thing-in-itself. To know *dao*, therefore, there is a need for intellectual intuition, an intuition of the universal, infinite, and necessary. However, Kant categorically denied the possibility of such an intellectual intuition. It was Feng's task, therefore, to prove its existence.

Intellectual intuition has often been regarded as mysterious by both those who deny it and those who claim to have it. In Feng's view, it has not received the credit it deserves largely because people do not understand how it is to be obtained and communicated. According to Feng, intellectual intuition is a very common phenomenon: "Every field of our intellectual activity, whether artistic, scientific, moral, or religious, is full of intellectual intuitions" (Feng, 1996–8, vol. 1, p. 422). For example, Newton's discovery of the law of gravitation was an intellectual intuition that he obtained when he saw an apple falling from a tree; Mencius' discovery of the universal goodness of human nature was an intuition that he obtained when he saw a child fall into a well. Moreover, although intellectual intuition is not the result of logical analyses of sense data, it is inseparable from them:

> Intellectual intuition is nothing but a sense activity penetrated by reason. As a sense activity, of course, intellectual intuition is inseparable from distinguishing among different colors, judging among different sounds, and knowing different tastes. (Feng, 1996–8, vol. 1, p. 430)

Here, Feng was appropriating the view of Wang Fuzi (1619–92). Unlike ordinary people, who entirely rely upon sense perceptions, and Buddhists and Daoists, who entirely deny the function of sense perceptions, Wang argued, correctly in Feng's view, that we have to "rely upon them and then transcend them" (Feng, 1996–8, vol. 1, p. 431). For Wang, the common assumption of both common people and Buddhists and Daoists is that sense perception is all that we have. Common people deny our knowledge of *dao* since we cannot perceive *dao*, and Daoists and Buddhists define *dao* as nothingness since sense perception is not real. They all forget, in Wang's view, that "the five colors, five sounds, and five tastes are actually the manifestations of *dao*" (quoted in Feng, 1996–8, vol. 1, pp. 430–1). In this sense, *dao* is immanent, since it is in perceivable things, but it is also transcendent, since it is not immediately perceivable.

Of course, wisdom as the philosophical intellectual intuition of *dao* is unique in comparison to other forms of intellectual intuition. Intellectual intuitions in science and morality, while different from sensible intuitions that are entirely particular, can be applied only to their limited spheres. In contrast, intellectual intuition in philosophy is universally applicable:

> The core of philosophy is its doctrine of the natural and heavenly *dao*. It aims to be not only true but also thorough. Philosophy tries to grasp the *dao* that unifies, and is the source of, heaven and the human and the object and the self, and to cultivate the free virtue unified with the heavenly *dao*. Philosophy wants to investigate the first cause of ten thousand things in the universe and reveal the highest realm of human life. Thus what it explores is the unconditional, the absolute, and the infinite. (Feng, 1996–8, vol. 1, pp. 423–4)

Intellectual intuitions in religion and art, while also concerning the whole of the universe, are not speculative. In contrast, intellectual intuition in philosophy aims at "grasping the world in the form of theoretical thinking," which can be rationally argued about and practically tested (Feng, 1996–8, vol. 1, p. 424). People may have objections to Feng's view of religion and art, but his point here is that the intellectual intuition of *dao* is not merely relative and subjective.

In Feng's view, as soon as we obtain wisdom through such an intellectual intuition, we will be able to see things as they are without making any distinctions among them and without attachment to any one of them. Appropriating and yet reversing the order of the three realms is discussed in the "Equality of Things (*Qiwu*)" and "Autumn Water (*Qiushui*)" chapters of *Zhuangzi* (*Chuang-tzu*, 1968; see also Graham, 1986 and Chan, 1963). Feng claimed that such a realization comprises three stages of transcendence:

> First, we divide and equalize all things. This is to equalize the affirmation and its negation so that we can transcend mutual disagreements of various opinions and their respective limits. Secondly, we affirm the being of all things and unify them. This is to negate all distinctions among things such as big and small and similar and dissimilar so that one can see them all as one and grasp the totality. Yet at that stage, there is still a distinction between the knowing subject and the known object and so there is a need for the third stage to affirm the being of all things and then negate them. This is to transcend all distinctions such as those between heaven and the human, between the inner and the outer, between the subject and the object, and between the knower and the known. (Feng, 1996–8, vol. 1, p. 429)

In Feng's view, it is at this last stage that the intellectual intuition of *dao* is finally realized, where one is no longer burdened with any things. Because one hears and sees things without perceiving their differences and one's thinking corresponds to reality without making affirmative or negative judgments about things, "one becomes identical with *dao* and is in one body with *dao*" (Feng, 1996–8, vol. 1, p. 430).

The language of wisdom

One important way in which Feng made the distinction between knowledge and wisdom is that, while the former is related to the realm of the namable and speakable (*mingyan zhiyu*), the latter is related to the unnamable and unspeakable (*chao mingyan zhiyu*):

> In the realm of namable and speakable, saying must have something to be said about and knowledge must have something to know about. Thus, it is inseparable from the distinction between the thing and the self, the knower and the known. In the relationship between the name and the reality, the names and categories always try to grasp reality by dividing it into this and that, such and so, this kind and that kind. (Feng, 1996–8, vol. 1, p. 432)

However, as we have seen, wisdom denies all these distinctions in order to grasp the *dao* that unifies all. It is in this sense that Feng claimed that "what is grasped in [philosophical] intellectual intuition is beyond the realm of the namable and speakable. Because it is beyond the reach of empirical knowledge, it is of course inconceivable and unspeakable" (Feng, 1996–8, vol. 1, p. 432).

How to deal with the unconceivable and unspeakable is of course a problem not unique to Feng. Wittgenstein's solution is the easiest: just keep your mouth shut. This, however, cannot be a way out for Feng, who was confident that a metaphysics of *dao* is possible. So when Feng said that wisdom is about the realm of the inconceivable and unspeakable, he meant only that it is inconceivable and unspeakable in the common way; he did not mean that we cannot talk about *dao* at all. When you say that *dao* cannot be said, you have already said it. By this, Feng was not merely saying that *dao* can only be said in a negative way: "it is something that cannot be said." He believed that we could say something positive about *dao* as well. Nor was Feng merely saying that when we use "*dao*" to refer to what is grasped in our intellectual intuition, we have already said it. Following Wang Bi (226–49), Feng drew a distinction between names and ways of addressing: names (*ming*) originate from what is named, while ways of addressing (*chen*) originate from the one who addresses (see Feng, 1996–8, vol. 1, p. 434). For example, "John" is only a way of our addressing (*chen*) a person: it is not a name (*ming*) that tells us who and what this person is. Similarly, "*dao*" is only a way of our addressing what we intuit in philosophy and not a name that tells us what it is.

In Feng's view, to say that *dao* is unspeakable only means that it cannot be spoken about in our ordinary language in its ordinary way. Here again, Feng got his inspiration from *Zhuangzi*, where three different ways to express our intuition of *dao* are mentioned: quotations from ancient and old people (*zhongyan*), metaphors (*yuyan*), and words with infinite applications (*zhiyan*). Among the three, Feng believed that the last, which is "to use what others say to equalize yes and no and you and me to reach a natural balance" (Feng, 1996–8, vol. 1, p. 276), is most appropriate as a philosophical language of *dao*. He used an example in the "Autumn Water (*Qiushui*)" chapter of *Zhuangzi* to explain what he meant:

> With regard to the difference among various kinds of things, people generally think that heaven and earth are big, while grains of rice are small; the mountain is big, while the tip of a hair is small. Now "from the perspective of *dao*," I can still use the words "big" and "small" but will change the meaning, as suggested by the Daoist Guoxiang . . . so that "big" means "enough" and "small" means "without leftover." Then heaven and earth, mounds and mountains can be regarded as without leftover and therefore as small, while a grain of the smallest rice and the tip of a hair can be regarded as enough (in relation to their own nature) and therefore as big. There is thus no distinction between big and small. (Feng, 1996–8, vol. 1, pp. 276–7)

Thus, the language to express our intuition of *dao* is still our ordinary language. Our ordinary language cannot be used to talk about *dao* if it is used merely according to a formal logic that focuses on fixed distinctions among things, among concepts, and between things and concepts. However, it becomes an appropriate language if it is used according to a dialectical logic.

Dialectical Logic: Theory Transformed into Method

While his interest in an epistemological and metaphysical theory of *dao* was shown in his 1947 article "On Wisdom," Feng applied this theory in the 1950s according to two slogans: "transform theory into method" and "transform theory into virtue." We will see that these two slogans are sometimes misleading. They create an impression that one first knows what is *dao* and only then applies this knowledge in one's intellectual (method) and practical activities (virtue). Rather, Feng believed that there is a two-way movement between the theory of *dao* on the one hand, and method and virtue on the other. Thus, in the final systematic presentation of his philosophy, Feng saw his theory of *dao* as the main body and the ideas expressed in these two slogans as two wings. We shall discuss the first transformation in this section and the second transformation in the next section.

One of Feng's fundamental themes is the unity of theory and method: theory can be used as a method to gain new knowledge. For example, our biological theory can be used as a method to know biological phenomena. So our theory of *dao* (wisdom) can also be used as a method to know *dao* (see Feng, 1996–8, vol. 2, p. 406). From the formal logical point of view, there seems to be a vicious circle here: in order to have a theory of *dao*, we need to have a method to know it; yet in order to have a method to know *dao*, we need to have a theory of *dao*. Feng acknowledged that there is indeed a circle, but insisted that it is not a vicious one. In his view, neither our theory of *dao* nor our method to know *dao* is perfect at any given time, but both can be improved infinitely. When we have a theory of *dao*, we can use it as a method to know further about *dao* so that we can have a better theory of *dao*, which will in turn help us to have an even better method to know *dao*. Feng called such a view a dialectical logical point of view in the Hegelian–Marxist sense. Other familiar expressions of this insight in the discourse of contemporary Western philosophy are the antifoundationalist idea of reflective equilibrium (for example, between particular moral intuitions and general political principles in the work of John Rawls) and the idea of the hermeneutic circle (for example, between text and preunderstanding in the work of Hans-Georg Gadamer). The unique feature of such a view is that it denies the existence of one single foundation and yet avoids relativism by emphasizing the progressive movement resulting from the interplay of contrasting elements. As a Marxist philosopher, Feng clearly derived his interest in dialectical logic from Hegelian–Marxist philosophy, but his actual formulation of this logic is largely drawn from his study of Chinese philosophy. In the following, we will examine several important applications of dialectical logic in Feng's philosophy.

The dialectic between analytic and synthetic methods

The classical hermeneutic circle discussed by Schleiermacher is the between the part and the whole of a text. While Feng's discussion of analytic and synthetic methods is related to this circle, it has a wider scope and is concerned with the part and the whole of any object of knowledge:

> By analysis I mean dividing the concrete object of knowledge into different elements, parts, and features, and examining them separately. By synthesis I mean grasping the object of knowledge by combining its different elements, parts, and features into a unified whole. (Feng, 1996–8, vol. 2, p. 286)

The analytic method examines an object by looking at its different parts, while the synthetic method examines an object by looking at it as a whole. They are indeed two different methods, since knowing something as a whole (a house, for example) is different from knowing its different parts (its doors, windows, and roofs).

In both Chinese and Western traditions, there are philosophers who emphasize the importance of analytic method and those who emphasize the importance of synthetic method. However, in Feng's view, not only are these two methods both necessary, but there is also a dialectical movement between them. It is necessary to have an overall view of an object in order to understand its parts appropriately. One cannot have an appropriate understanding of any parts of an object without an appropriate understanding of the object as a whole (a door separated from a house will no longer be a door). However, "it is necessary to have a separate knowledge of different parts, aspects, and stages of a thing in order to obtain a comprehensive, overall, and thorough knowledge of it" (Feng, 1996–8, vol. 1, p. 419). One cannot have an appropriate understanding of an object as a whole without an appropriate understanding of its constituent parts (a house without its constituent parts will no longer be a house).

From a formal logical point of view, there is an obvious contradiction here: to know the whole (using the synthetic method) we need to know its parts (using the analytic method), and yet to know the parts we need to know the whole. However, from Feng's dialectical logical point of view, there is no contradiction at all: one's better understanding of the object as a whole (by using the synthetic method) will help one to have a better understanding of its constituent parts (by using the analytic method), which will further help one to have a better understanding of the object as a whole. Through this open-ended spiral movement, we can obtain an increasingly better (though never perfect) understanding of both the parts and the whole of an object.

The dialectic between knowledge and practice

In his second slogan, "transform theory into virtue," to be discussed in the next section, Feng was concerned with how to apply our knowledge of *dao* to our moral cultivation: "to exemplify the *dao* to form virtue" (*ningdao er chengde*). This, however, is only one side of the coin. The other side is to acquire our knowledge of *dao* from our moral cultivation: "manifesting one's nature (virtue) to expand *dao*" (*xianxing yi hongdao*) (see Feng, 1996–8, vol. 1, p. 441). Here Feng seems to present us with another dilemma: moral cultivation presupposes knowledge of *dao*, and yet knowledge of *dao* presupposes moral cultivation. To understand this, we need to examine Feng's more general view of the relationship between knowledge and practice.

According to Feng, through our knowledge and practice, we are establishing two different relationships between the subject (*neng*) and the object (*suo*), the internal relationship and the external relationship:

The internal relationship is the one in which the qualitative change of one item will lead to a corresponding change of the other related item. The relationship established by practice between the subject and object is an internal one, while that established by knowledge is an external one. The latter is external because the object is not changed simply because it is known by the subject. (Feng, 1996–8, vol. 1, p. 80)

The question is then how these two relationships that are established by theory and practice respectively are related to each other:

Practice and knowledge are inseparable. On the one hand, knowledge develops when practice develops, since it is in the process of transforming the object that we get to know the object; it is only when we establish an internal relationship with the object in our practice that we can establish an external relationship with the object in our knowledge. On the other hand, it is only when we establish an external relationship with the object that we can establish an internal relationship with the object in practice. (Feng, 1996–8, vol. 2, p. 39)

If we have not established some appropriate internal relationship with the object by dealing with the object (practice), we will never be able to establish an appropriate external relationship with the object (true knowledge), since knowledge always comes from practice. However, if we have not established some appropriate external relationship with the object (knowledge), we will be unable to establish an appropriate internal relationship with it (successful practice), since practice is always guided by knowledge. In this sense, knowledge and practice are inseparable. The better knowledge we acquire, the more appropriate practice we can perform; and the more appropriate practice we perform, the better knowledge we can have. It is in this dialectical movement between knowledge and practice that we can have increasingly better knowledge and more successful practice. It is not realistic to try to start from absolutely true knowledge or absolutely appropriate practice, or to try to avoid any practice until we have absolutely true knowledge or avoid believing anything until it is verified through absolutely appropriate practice. An ideal person for Feng is not one who has perfect knowledge or who never fails in practice, but is one who is never off the spiral of the dialectical movement between knowledge and practice.

The dialectic between logical and historical methods

Wisdom aims at knowledge of *dao*, and *dao* for Feng is essentially the *dao* of change and development. In this sense, one important way to know *dao* is to examine historical events to discern the *dao* displayed in them. This is what he called the historical method:

Historical method grasps the fundamental outline of historical phenomena and their causal relationships by following the sequence of history. . . . In order to do so, one has to see history as a process of necessary movement, as a logical process, caused by movements among contradictory forces. Therefore, the historical method is nothing but grasping the logic of history. (Feng, 1996–8, vol. 2, p. 444)

Here Feng emphasized the importance of the historical method to understanding *dao*. Obviously, if you do not spend time doing detailed historical examinations, analyses, and syntheses, you will have no way to understand the logic (*dao*) of historical development. However, Feng pointed out at the same time that if you know nothing about the logic (*dao*) of history, you may not be able to do your historical study properly:

[In history] there are many accidental elements. Thus, if our thinking follows every step of history, much of our energy will be wasted in dealing with insignificant materials and our thinking process will often be interrupted. Thus we have to use the logical method really to grasp the logic of historical development. (Feng, 1996–8, vol. 2, p. 445)

Therefore, there is a need for logical method, which applies our knowledge of *dao* to our historical study (see Feng, 1996–8, vol. 2, p. 413). Only then can the vast and complicated historical data become simple and relationships among some apparently unrelated historical events be easily established.

From a formal logic point of view, there is again a contradiction here: in order to use the logical method, one has first to use the historical method to find the actual logic of history and to avoid empty speculation; but in order to use the historical method, one must already know the logic of history in order to avoid being lost in a sea of historical data. In Feng's dialectical logic, however, we have to see the dialectical movement between the historical and logical methods. The better we conduct our historical study, the better we will be able to grasp the logic of history; and the better we are able to grasp the logic of history, the better we will be able to conduct our historical study. While we can never have a perfect understanding of either historical events or the *dao* displayed in them, we can always improve our understanding in this dialectical movement.

The dialectic between disagreement and agreement (bailü yizhi)

Feng used this term from the *Commentary on the Book of Change* to explain the relationship between individuals and the community in a theory of knowledge. Philosophy is a theory of wisdom. Wisdom differs from opinion because it tries to see things not from "my" perspective but from the perspective of *dao*. In this sense, philosophers should have consensus (*yizhi*) on what *dao* is, since there is only one *dao*. However, philosophers are notorious for their disagreements (*bailü*), each believing that his or her own view of the world and human life is the view from the perspective of *dao*. The result is that "everyone is talking about *dao* which is not the *dao* I am talking about" (Feng, 1996–8, vol. 1, p. 235). This is because "any perspective has its subjectivity and everyone has to see things from 'my' perspective" (Feng, 1996–8, vol. 1, p. 395). However, Feng argued against relativism. In his view, if we follow Xunzi's advice "to speak with a loving heart, to listen with a learning heart, and to argue with an impartial heart" (see Feng, 1996–8, vol. 1, p. 226), we can reach agreement on *dao* from disagreement about *dao*:

> On any particular issues, people will have different opinions from their different perspectives. Thus they seem to disagree with each other a lot at the beginning. After debate, their views may edify, supplement, correct each other and finally reach an agreement. (Feng, 1996–8, vol. 1, p. 227)

In this sense, Feng had the same concern as Jürgen Habermas in his communicative ethics: to reach universal agreements in an undistorted communication. Of course, people may have reasonable doubt about the possibility of such an agreement, and it is also true that Feng did not provide convincing reasons to show that it is possible. This, however, is perhaps because reaching agreement for Feng was only one aspect of this dialectic. The other aspect moves from agreement to disagreement. While trying to avoid relativism, Feng also cautioned against dogmatism. For "it is one thing to reach agreement and it is another to reach truth" (Feng, 1996–8, vol. 1, p. 239). Because truth is the perspective from *dao* (and not merely on *dao*), there can only be one truth. Relativism has to be avoided, and the agreement of opinions is desirable. However, even if agreements can be reached, agreement cannot be identified with the perspective from *dao*. Rather, *dao* itself should be understood as an open-ended process of development (see Feng, 1996–8, vol. 1, p. 261), and because any agreement can be superseded, we should avoid dogmatism even when we have reached agreements. When individuals have reasons to question or reject an established agreement, it is important to let their opinions and the previous agreement debate with, learn from, enrich, and criticize one another, so that a new agreement may be reached:

> In the knowing process, people can come to an agreed conclusion after debates among different opinions and reach the same goal from different ways. Yet this agreement may again lead to disagreement among different opinions and therefore new debates may occur again. . . . It is in this circular movement between agreement and disagreement that knowledge becomes an ever-ongoing process of the occurrence and solution of problems. (Feng, 1996–8, vol. 1, p. 227)

In other words, undistorted communication aims at neither agreement nor disagreement but at the increasingly comprehensive knowledge of *dao*, which is obtained in the infinite progressive movement between agreement and disagreement.

Although we have contrasted Feng's dialectical logic with formal logic, Feng did not seek to replace formal logic with dialectic logic. He argued against the dogmatic Marxist view that rejects formal logic or makes formal logic dialectical (see Feng, 1996–8, vol. 2, p. 231). In Feng's view, dialectical logic focuses on the movement of both objects of our thinking and our thinking process, while formal logic stresses their stability. "Formal logic has its objective ground. The whole world is indeed moving, but it also has its relative stability" (Feng, 1996–8, vol. 2, p. 246). In this sense, even dialectical logic cannot violate formal logic, although we do need to go beyond formal logic in order to apply dialectical logic fully.

Freedom: Theory Transformed into Virtue

Feng's second slogan enjoins us to transform theory into virtue. In Feng's view, wisdom is not merely a theoretical understanding of *dao*. We must apply this understanding to our moral cultivation, a step from "understanding *dao* (*zhidao*) to possessing virtues (*youde*)" (Feng, 1996–8, vol. 3, p. 318). For Feng, to transform theory into virtue means to construct and realize an ideal of being a human according to our wisdom. In Chinese (especially the Confucian) tradition, the ideal of being a human is to become a sage. Although the tradition emphasizes that we can earn to be a sage and that everybody can become a sage, in Feng's view, the fact that very few people have been recognized as sages indicates that such an ideal is beyond the reach of common people. Thus, Feng felt it necessary to develop a modern ideal of being a human that is within the reach of ordinary people:

> Unlike the ancient ideal of sages, worthies, and heroes, the modern ideal is that of an ordinary free person. This is not an ideal too high to reach: everyone can reach this goal if they try. The new personality that we want to cultivate is the personality of a free ordinary person and not that of an omnipotent and omniscient sage. We do not think that there is consciousness and freedom in their absolute sense. We cannot deify humans, since all are ordinary human beings who have shortcomings and make mistakes. Yet the essence of human beings is to become free and to perform free labor. (Feng, 1996–8, vol. 3, p. 309)

Central to Feng's modern ideal of being a human is his conception of freedom. Feng repeatedly used *Zhuangzi*'s story of the cook Bao Ding cutting up an ox for his ruler Wen Hui to explain his idea of freedom:

Whenever Bao Ding applied his hands, leaned forward with his shoulder, planted his foot, and employed the pressure of his knee, in the audible ripping off of the skin, and slicing operation of the knife, the sounds were all in regular cadence. Movements and sounds proceeded as in the dance of the Mulberry Forest and the blended notes of the *Jing Shou.* . . .

And responding to the admiration of the King, the cook said: "What your servant loves is the method of *dao*, something in advance of any art. When I first began to cut up an ox, I saw nothing but the entire carcass. After three years I ceased to see it as a whole. Now I deal with it in a spirit-like manner, and do not look at it with my eyes. The use of my senses is discarded, and my spirit acts as it wills." (*Zhuangzi* I.3b, see Legge, 1891, pp. 198–9)

In Feng's view, the cook Bao Ding, as a common person, certainly fell short of the ancient ideal of a sage, but he was an almost perfect example of Feng's modern ideal of a free person: he becomes free in his labor of cutting up the ox. Labor for him was no longer forced work; nor is it merely physical work. It became a means of enjoyment or rather the process of enjoyment (see Feng, 1996–8, vol. 3, p. 11). What this story tells us is that to become free (*ziyou*) in one's activity, one has to act self-consciously (*zijue*), voluntarily (*ziyuan*), and naturally (*ziran*), all in one's own way (*ziwo*). In the following, we shall examine these central features of Feng's conception of freedom.

The principle of being self-conscious (zijue)

We often use a bird flying in the sky or a fish swimming in the ocean to exemplify freedom. By analogy, a free person is one who performs uninhibited instinctual or habitual actions. In this sense, being free is equivalent to being spontaneous (*zifa*). In Feng's view, however, this conception of freedom ignores two fundamental distinctions between human beings and animals. The first distinction is that only humans act with self-consciousness, and this capacity is constitutive of human freedom:

Human freedom is particularly displayed in the purposefulness of their actions. Humans become free in their activities by acquiring rational knowledge, choosing from the potentialities provided by nature to meet human needs, and making plans to realize the potentialities chosen; humans also become free by developing the essential powers inherent in them and using them in making up themselves. (Feng, 1996–8, vol. 3, p. 48)

A bird flying in the sky and a fish swimming in the water are not free in this sense, since they do not know what they are doing, why they do what they are doing, and how they do what they are doing. They just perform their actions spontaneously. Humans, of course, also perform spontaneous actions, and these may even produce morally good consequences. In Feng's view, however, "such spontaneous and instinctual good actions, while being legitimate moral actions, are not free moral actions" (Feng, 1996–8, vol. 3, p. 220). To be free is first of all to have intellectual knowledge about the nature, reasons, and ways of your actions. An action is free only if it is based on the agent's true knowledge that this action will realize the potentialities offered by nature (including human nature) and that it is beneficial to human beings.

The principle of being voluntary (ziyuan)

The second distinction between humans and animals is that only human actions can be based on their free choices, and this capacity is also constitutive of any genuinely free actions. To explain this, Feng drew a distinction between two senses of law: as a moral norm and as a natural law. Although law in the latter sense:

> provides various possibilities from which people can choose, the law itself does not change according to human will: human will has no way to determine what possibilities the law will provide. In this sense, humans have no alternative to obeying laws of nature. However, a norm or rule is different. Although reasonable norms or rules must have objective grounds, they are established by humans, and humans can choose to obey or not obey them. (Feng, 1996–8, vol. 3, pp. 26–7)

A bird flying in the sky and a fish swimming in the ocean are thus not free, since they have not chosen to fly or swim. Humans are different. Although they equally have no choice and cannot be said to be free in relation to natural laws (for example, they must grow older every year and eventually die), they have choices and are free to follow or violate moral norms and rules. A free action must be an action out of one's free will. To have free will:

> is the presupposition of moral responsibility. A person's moral or immoral actions are actions of one's voluntary choices, of one's autonomous decisions. Thus the person has moral responsibilities and should be responsible for the consequences of his or her action. (Feng, 1996–8, vol. 3, pp. 221–2)

Feng observed that, while Chinese tradition stresses intellectual knowledge, the first principle of freedom, Western tradition based on the Christian doctrine of original sin puts more emphasis on free will, the second principle of freedom. In Feng's view, each of these two traditions has its strength and weakness. The Confucian tradition, emphasizing self-consciousness, may help us avoid blind actions but can easily lead to determinism or even fatalism. The Christian tradition, emphasizing human free choice, may help us avoid determinism but can easily lead to blind actions. Thus, to be a truly free person, one has to learn how to synthesize these two principles of freedom:

On the one hand, one's conformity to moral standards in one's action originates from one's rational knowledge and therefore is self-conscious; on the other hand, it is out of the free choice of one's will and therefore is voluntary. (Feng, 1996–8, vol. 3, p. 220)

Genuinely free moral actions must be both self-conscious and voluntary. The former is the character of the intellect, while the latter is the character of the will. Moreover, in Feng's view, there is no reason to prefer either of these two principles over the other, since "in moral practice, intellect and will promote each other" (Feng, 1996–8, vol. 2, p. 225). In other words, our better understanding of our actions can help us perform these actions more willingly; and our more willing performance of these actions will help us to understand them more completely.

The principle of being natural (ziran)

Because self-conscious and voluntary actions distinguish human beings from nonhuman beings, Feng's two principles of freedom are humanistic principles that enable us to make an important and necessary step from nature (*tian-xing*) to virtue (*dexing*). In Feng's view, the Chinese schools of Confucianism and Mohism have rightly emphasized these humanistic principles. However, humanistic principles, taken in isolation and with their overemphasis on the distinction between the human and the natural, will lead to artificiality. Indeed, if a self-conscious and voluntary action has to be performed with extraordinary efforts, it cannot be considered as a free action. Bao Ding in Zhuangzi's story is a free person, not only because he knows what he does and does it out of his free will, but also because he does it effortlessly, happily, and without any artificiality. Feng argued that genuine freedom needs a third principle, the principle, emphasized by Daoism, of being natural, to bring virtue back to nature. By "bringing virtue back to nature," Feng intended to make two claims. First, virtue has to be from nature:

The creation of values must be consistent with the potentiality of reality and human need. Objective reality provides some real potentialities, and humans have some needs according to human nature. The combination of the two becomes the demands of nature. (Feng, 1996–8, vol. 3, p. 312)

Secondly, virtue has to be performed in a natural way:

Because of the "advancement of skill into *dao*," labor becomes an element of enjoyment. The laborer and nature, the subject and the object, have reached an entire unity and coherence so that the laborer can intuit himself or herself in the result of labor. Thus, labor becomes an aesthetic activity. (Feng, 1996–8, vol. 3, p. 27)

What we regard as virtues must be naturally grounded. A virtuous activity must be both naturally possible and beneficial to human beings. In this sense, neither an action intended to make human beings immortal nor an action intended to extinguish the whole of humanity is virtuous, since the former, while desirable, is naturally impossible and the latter, while possible, is undesirable. In addition, a free person must be able to perform virtuous actions effortlessly, naturally and with ease, just like a bird flying in the sky and a fish swimming in the ocean. In Hegelian fashion, Feng claimed that the virtue that returned to nature is at a higher stage than the nature from which the virtue developed. Thus, while the truly free person can perform virtuous actions as effortlessly as the flying bird and the swimming fish, only free persons are able to enjoy the actions they clearly understand and voluntarily choose to perform.

The three principles of freedom, namely the principles of being self-conscious, voluntary, and natural, in Feng's view, represent the three traditional philosophical ideals: epistemological truth, moral goodness, and aesthetic beauty. To act with self-consciousness is to have true knowledge of one's actions; to act voluntarily is to have free will as the precondition for moral responsibility; and to be natural and to lack artificiality in one's actions is to be harmonious with nature. Thus, Feng insisted, in order to have a full understanding of freedom, one must examine freedom from all three of these points of views:

> From the epistemological point of view, freedom means to transform the world according to one's true knowledge. It is the realization of scientific ideals based on both the predictions of possibilities offered by reality and on human needs. From the moral point of view, freedom means to make voluntary choice and voluntarily to follow moral principles in one's action so that the moral ideals that reflect the human demand for progress can be realized. From the aesthetic point of view, freedom means to intuit oneself in humanized nature so that aesthetic ideals can be realized in vivid images full of human passions. (Feng, 1996–8, vol. 3, pp. 27–8)

It is in this sense that Feng believed that a genuinely free person must also be a true, good, and beautiful person.

The principle of the individual self (ziwo)

Freedom as the modern ideal of being a human is not a uniform formula to be applied to everyone. In Feng's view, although it is the essence of all human beings to become free, the way of becoming free varies from one individual to another:

> A free individual is not merely a member of the species, a cell in social relations. The individual also has its unique identity, which distinguishes the person from all others and makes the person independent in complicated social relations. (Feng, 1996–8, vol. 3, p. 320)

Rather than setting up an abstract and universal standard to measure everybody, Feng urged us to encourage every individual to develop into an authentic personality, that is, a personality true to one's own nature and feeling (*xingqing*) in one's own way. In order to be free, there is a need for a fourth principle, the principle of the individual self (*ziwo*) as the subject of freedom (see Feng, 1996–8, vol. 1, p. 453). Here, it is important not to confuse what is universal to all human beings with what is essential to each individual human being:

> When we talk about human purposes we are talking about the purposes of individual human beings. The essence [of these individual human beings] lies right in those individual human beings, each with its individual characteristics. (Feng, 1996–8, vol. 3, p. 60)

In this relation, he criticized Confucianism and even Chinese communism for their tendency to:

> overemphasize the social while ignoring the individual in relation to human values and ideals; to pay too much attention to universal characteristics while being negligent about concrete existence in relation to the individual self; and to stress too much self-transformation while not daring or willing to talk about self-realization and self-development [in relation to human activities]. (Feng, 1996–8, vol. 3, p. 194)

However, Feng believed that his emphasis on individuality is not inconsistent with the ideal of solidarity. He always cited Li Dazhao's "individual freedom and universal solidarity" as an ideal of the relation of individuals to society. Crucial to such an ideal, in Feng's view, is free labor organization. Primitive labor organizations depend on an authoritarian personality, while modern labor organizations depend on the market. Thus, "only if both of these two types of dependence are sublated can the organization of labor become a united association of free individuals" (Feng, 1996–8, vol. 3, p. 331). Clearly, Feng's united association of free individuals is very close to the idea of the voluntary association in contemporary Western public discourse. The members of a voluntary association have the freedom to join and withdraw from the association. According to Western views, voluntary associations are both made possible and limited by a nonvoluntary association, the political state, but for Feng the political state and even the whole human community should become a voluntary association of all free individuals. As a life-long communist, Feng held this noncoercive ideal of communism, where, quoting from Marx and Engels, "the free development of every individual becomes the precondition for the free development of all individuals" (see Feng, 1996–8, vol. 3, p. 55). In Feng's ideal state, there is still a common good or a common will, but in contrast to orthodox Marxism and even contemporary Western communitarianism, this common good or common will is not an additional good or will of the state above and beyond the goods and wills of its individual members. It is rather the common good or will of the community to develop and promote the good and will of each of its individual members.

It might seem ironic for Feng to propose his ideal of a free person for the common people to replace the traditional ideal of a sage for a selected elite on the grounds that becoming a sage is too difficult for most people to achieve. Is it any less difficult to become a free person in Feng's sense? It is true that not many people have been recognized as sages, but how many people have become free? Even Bao Ding was only an almost free person, in Feng's view, since he worked for a king in a class society. One can become a sage individually, but one can become a free person only in a society that is a voluntary association. However, Feng argued that his ideal of a free person focuses more on the process than the result: one is free as long as one is on the way to freedom. In this sense, his ideal is indeed more accessible to common people than the traditional ideal of a sage.

Feng Qi was an unusual figure among contemporary Chinese philosophers. Most philosophers included in this volume developed their philosophical ideas either before 1949 or, if after 1949, outside the communist mainland. In the mainland after 1949, most philosophers became either exponents of Marxist philosophy or historians of philosophy. Feng Qi, however, was one among the very few in this period who not only developed their own philosophical ideas but also constructed their own philosophical system. Feng Qi was, of course, a Marxist, but to the same extent he was also a Confucian, a Daoist, a Kantian, and a Hegelian. When asked to which school he belonged, he answered that no important philosophical school should be bypassed and yet every one should be transcended (see Feng, 1996–8, vol. 9, p. 561). Thus, although he mentioned Zhuangzi when forced to name one philosopher who most influenced his own philosophy, his philosophical system is thoroughly "Fengian." The defining character of Fengian philosophy is its antifoundational ameliorism that finds a way between relativism and dogmatism. This feature is most directly reflected in his dialectical logic, but it is also essential to his theory of *dao* and his idea of freedom. In his view, we can never fully understand *dao*, but we can always improve our understanding of *dao*. We can never become perfectly free, but we can always become more authentically free. For Feng, *dao* is indeed absolute, but it is not some thing that is absolute. Rather, it is the absolute movement, process, and way of all finite things (see Feng, 1996–8, vol. 1, p. 427). After all, *dao* is nothing but the Way.

Acknowledgment

I would like to thank Professor Jiyuan Yu, who has read an early version of this chapter and provided helpful comments. I would also like to thank Professor Chung-ying Cheng, the co-editor of this volume, for his detailed constructive comments and suggestions for revision. I have benefited greatly from their comments in preparing this chapter.

Bibliography

Works by Feng Qi

All major works of Feng Qi have been published in the ten volumes of Feng Qi 1996–8: *Feng Qi wenji* 馮契文集 (the collected works of Feng Qi), Shanghai, East China Normal University. The first three volumes are the three treatises on wisdom, the main focus of this chapter. They are followed by the three volumes of the logical development of ancient Chinese philosophy and one volume of the revolutionary process of modern Chinese philosophy. Then there are two volumes of essays and short books on wisdom, entitled *On Wisdom* and *More On Wisdom*, respectively. The last volume is a collection of Feng's lectures and correspondence.

Works on Feng Qi

All major works on Feng Qi published before 1996 were collected in Philosophy Department, East China Normal University, ed., 1996: *Lilun fangfa he dexing* 理倫方法和道性 (theory, method, and virtue) Shanghai: Xuelin Chubanshe. Works on Feng Qi after 1996 have appeared in several important journals. For general discussion of Feng's philosophy, see Cheng, Chung-ying, 1997, He, Ping and Li, Weiwu, 1996

For discussion of Feng's theory of *dao*, see Cheng, Xiaolong, 1999, Min, Shijun, 1999; Chen, Weiping, 1996, Ding, Zhenyan and Jing, Rongdong, 1996; Yang, Guorong, 1996, Zhang, Tianfei, 1996a

For important discussions of Feng's dialectic logic, see Jing, Rongdong, 1999, Peng, Yilian, 1996, 1999, Liang, Qingyan, 1999, He, Shankai, 1999

For important discussion of Feng's conception of freedom, see Yang, Guorong & Jing, Rongdong, 1996, Ren, Jiantao, 1997, Wu, Genyou, 1996, 1997

For discussion of Feng as a historian of Chinese philosophy, see Fang, Xudong, 1999, Gao, Ruiquan, 1996a, Chai, Wenhua, 1997, Chen, Weiping, 1996

Chai, Wenhua 1997: "*Lun Feng Qi dui zhongguo zhexueshi yanjiu de gongxian* 論馮契對中國哲學史研究的貢獻" (Feng Qi's contribution to the study of history of Chinese philosophy), *Zhexue Yanjiu*, No. 2

Chen, Xiaolong 1999: "*Zhuanshi chenzhi*" 轉識成智 (transformation of knowledge into wisdom), *Zhexue yanjiu*, No. 2

Cheng, Chung-ying 1997: "*Feng Qi xianshen de zhihui zhexue yu benti sikao* 馮契先生的智慧哲學和本體思考" (Mr Feng Qi's philosophy of wisdom and the ontological reflection), *Xueshu yuekan*, No. 3

Cheng, Weiping 1996: "*Zhihui shuo he zhongguo chuantong zhexue de zhihui: Feng Qi de zhongguo zhexueshi yanjiu* 智慧説和中國傳統哲學的智慧：馮契的中國哲學史研究" (the theory of wisdom and the wisdom of traditional philosophy: Feng Qi's study of the history of Chinese philosophy), *Lilun fangfa he dexing*, pp. 242–57

Cheng, Weiping and Tong, Shijun 1996: "*Zhihui de tansuo zhe: Feng Qi xiaozhuan* 智慧的探索者：馮契小傳" (the seeker of wisdom: a biography of Feng Qi), *Lilun fangfa he dexing*, pp. 302–14

Ding, Zhengyan, 1998: *Lujia de lixiang renge he xiandai xinren de peiyang* 儒家的
理想人格和現代新人的培養 (the Confucian ideal of personality and the cultivation
of the modern new personality). In The Shanghai Society of Comparative
Philosophy and Culture between East and West, ed., *Zhongxi wenhua yu ershi shiji
zhongguo zhexue* 中西文化和二十世紀中國哲學 (East–West cultures and twentieth-
century Chinese philosophy), Shanghai: Xuelin Chubanshe, pp. 71–87

Ding, Zhenyan & Jin, Rongdong 1996: "*Luelun Feng Qi dui zhuanshi chengzhi wenti
de tantao* 略論馮契對轉識成智問題的探討" (on Feng Qi's appropriation of the
transformation of knowledge into wisdom), *Lilun fangfa he dexing*, pp. 144–57

Fang, Xudong 1999: "*Qian xiandai de zhongguo zhexue shi shuxie: yi Feng Qi wei li*
前現代的中國哲學史述解：以馮契為例" (writing of the pre-modern history of
Chinese philosophy: the example of Feng Qi), *Zhexue yanjiu*, No. 7

Gao, Ruiquan 1996a: "*Bawo minzhu jingshen de zhuliu: lun Feng Qi de zhongguo jindai
zhexueshi yanjiu* 把握民族精神的主流：論馮契的中國近代哲學史研究" (grasping
the main trend of the national spirit: Feng Qi's study of the modern history of Chinese
philosophy), *Lilun fangfa he dexing*, pp. 258–72

Gao, Ruiquan 1996b: "*Tianren heyi de xiandai quanshi* 天人合一的現代詮釋" (a modern
interpretation of the unity between heaven and humans), *Xueshu yuekan*, No. 3

He, Ping & Li, Weiwu 1996: "*Chonggou Makexi zhuyi zhexue tixi de kegui chanshi*
重構馬克思主義哲學體系的可貴闡釋" (the valuable exploration of the Marxist
philosophical system), *Lilun fangfa he dexing*, pp. 158–69

He, Shankai 1999: "*Lun bianzheng siwei tuili de jiben yuanze* 論辯證思維推理基本
原則" (on the fundamental principles of reasoning in dialectical thinking), *Huadong
shifa daxue xuebao*, No. 6

Jin, Rongdong 1999: "*Feng Qi kexue luoji sixiang tantao* 馮契科學邏輯思想探討" (an exploration of Feng Qi's scientific logic), *Shanghai shehui kexueyuan xueshu jikan*, No. 3

Liang, Qingyan 1999: "*Feng Qi dui bianzheng luoji zhong liangge yinan wenti de jiejue*
馮契對辨證邏輯中兩個疑難問題的解決" (Feng Qi's solution to two difficult prob-
lems in dialectical logic), *Huadong shida xuebao*, No. 2

Min, Shijun 1999: "*Shilun Feng Qi xiansheng de zhongji guanhuai* 試論馮契先生的
終極關懷" (on Feng Qi's ultimate concern), *Huadong shifa daxue xuebao*, No. 6

Peng, Yilian 1996: "*Feng Qi woguo bianzhen luoji yanjiu de xianquzhe he changdaozhe*
馮契：我國辨證邏輯研究的先驅者和倡導者" (Feng Qi, the pioneer and proponent
of the study of dialectical logic in our country), *Lilun fangfa he dexing*, pp. 184–205

Peng, Yilian 1999: "*Lun gainian de lishi xingtai* 論概念的歷史形態" (on the ideal
modes of concepts), *Huadong shifa daxue duebao*, No. 2

Ren, Jiantao 1997: "*Xiang dexing lunli huigui* 向德性倫理回歸" (a return to virtue
ethics), *Xueshu yuekan*, No. 3

Tong, Shijun 1996: "*Feng Qi he xifang zhexue* 馮契和西方哲學" (Feng Qi and western philosophy), *Lilun fangfa he dexing*, pp. 287–301

Wu, Genyou 1996: "*Pingminhua ziyou renge shuo qianshi* 平民化自由人格說前釋" (a
preliminary interpretation of the ideal of free personality for ordinary people), *Lilun
fangfa he dexing*, pp. 233–41

Wu, Genyou 1997: "*Feng Qi pingminhua de ziyou renge shuo shending* 馮契平民化的
自由人格說審定" (on Feng Qi's theory of free personality for ordinary people), *Zhexue
yanjiu*, No. 5

Yang, Guorong 1996: "*Zhishi yu zhihui* 知識與智慧" (knowledge and wisdom), *Lilun fangfa he dexing*, pp. 127–43

Yang, Guorong and Jing, Rongdong 1996: "*Hua lilun wei dexing* 化理論為德性" (to transform theory into wisdom), *Lilun fangfa he dexing*, pp. 217–32

Zhang, Tianfei 1996a: "*Feng Qi xiansheng de zhihui xueshuo* 馮契先生的智慧學說" (Mr Feng's theory of wisdom), *Lilun fangfa he dexing*, pp. 108–26

Zhang, Tianfei 1996b: "*Feng Qi xiansheng de guangyi renshilun* 馮契先生的廣義認識論" (Mr Feng Qi's wide epistemology), *Lilun fangfa he dexing*, pp. 170–83

Other works

Chan, Wing-tsit 1963: *A Source Book in Chinese Philosophy*, Princeton: Princeton University Press

Chuang-tzu (*Zhuangzi*) 1968: *The Complete Works of Chuang-tzu*, trans. Burton Watson, New York: Columbia University Press

Graham, A. C. 1986: *Chuang-tzu: The Inner Chapters*, London: Mandala Books, Unwin Paperbacks

Legge, James 1891: trans., *Chuang-tzu*, in *Sacred Books of the East*, vols. 39, 40, Oxford: Oxford University Press

Discussion Questions

1. What is the difference between knowledge and wisdom? Can we transform knowledge into wisdom?
2. Do we have intellectual intuition?
3. How does intellectual intuition of *dao* differ from other intellectual intuition?
4. Can we transcend distinctions between heaven and the human, between the inner and the outer, between the subject and the object, and between knower and the known? Should we seek to do so?
5. Is philosophy incomplete without a *dao* that unifies all?
6. Does language have the resources to deal with the unnamable and unspeakable?
7. Can we transform wisdom into method?
8. Can we apply our knowledge of *dao* to our moral cultivation?
9. Do we need a modern ideal of the citizen to replace the traditional ideal of the sage?
10. Can we accept Feng Qi's account of freedom?

11

ZHANG DAINIAN: CREATIVE SYNTHESIS AND CHINESE PHILOSOPHY

Cheng Lian

Both as a historian of Chinese philosophy and as a philosopher in his own right, Zhang Dainian has staked out an important position in contemporary Chinese philosophy. His works on the history of Chinese philosophy have established him as a pivotal scholar with a significance comparable to that of Hu Shi and Feng Youlan. Zhang also advanced his own systematic philosophy.

Born in 1909, Zhang began to publish philosophical papers in the 1930s under the guidance of his brother Zhang Shenfu, who was then a professor of philosophy at Tsinghua University. Zhang Shenfu was famous for introducing Bertrand Russell's philosophy into China, and he also translated Wittgenstein's *Tractatus Logico-Philosophicus* into Chinese. On the basis of Zhang Dainian's philosophical publications, Feng Youlan and Jin Yuelin recommended him for his first teaching job at Tsinghua University. Since 1952, Zhang has been teaching at Peking University. He is now Professor Emeritus of Philosophy at Peking University.

During his twenties, Zhang was enormously influenced by Zhang Shenfu, one of the earliest Marxists in China, who believed that a new Chinese philosophy would emerge from a synthesis of the thought of Confucius, Lenin, and Russell. For Zhang Shenfu, these figures represent three different sources of philosophical insight, namely Chinese tradition, dialectical materialism, and philosophical analysis. Although Zhang Shenfu never provided such a synthesis, a very similar project has dominated Zhang Dainian's philosophical career. In his preface to the *Academic Writings of Zhang Dainian Selected by Himself*, Zhang wrote that he tries in his philosophical research "to synthesize modern materialism, the method of logical analysis, and the excellent tradition in Chinese philosophy" (Zhang, 1993, p. 2). A passage from his early article "A Possible Synthesis in Philosophy" (1936) provides a good illustration of his lifetime project:

> We should make a further synthesis out of materialism and idealism, with the method of logical analysis. The reason why we need such a synthesis is that we demand a philosophy that is true, credible, powerful and life-guiding. By

analyses we promote clear-mindedness and remove confusions; by materialism
we approach reality and keep away from illusions; by idealism we overcome the
limits of nature and arrive at perfection. (Zhang, 1996, vol. 1, p. 263)

Over time, this ideal has become widely known as "the creative synthesis
doctrine." Its three major aspects have occupied Zhang's continuing academic
career in his explorations of the basic problems of philosophy, his studies in
the history of Chinese philosophy, and his contributions to debates concerning cultural problems. In the course of his productive writings, Zhang has
developed his own philosophical system, presented a unique interpretation of
classical Chinese philosophy, and participated in significant cultural debates.
In the following account of Zhang's philosophy, I will present and assess the
first two aspects of his thought and will sketch his cultural views.

The Study of Nature and Man

At the beginning of his philosophical activities, Zhang became interested in
problems at the center of Western philosophical discussion. "On the Existence
of External World" (1933) displayed his receptiveness to the philosophical
analysis of Moore and Russell that had only recently been introduced in China.
His argument for the existence of external objects has two steps. First, he tried
to demonstrate that whether there are external objects or not is independent of the perceiver's sense impression. Then, he claimed, "I know about
other objects just in the same way that I know about my body; therefore, if
I acknowledge that I exist, then I must acknowledge that external objects exist"
(Zhang, 1982, p. 7). The structure of the argument is clear and the strategy
is interesting, but one may find that there is a leap in the second step, in which
Zhang identified himself with his body.

Zhang's basic concern has been with Chinese philosophy, and he used the
method of analysis as a means of reconstructing Chinese philosophy. After the
1930s, he turned from discrete problems like the existence of the external world
to construct his own systematic thought. The completion in the 1940s of
what was later called *Five Essays concerning Heaven and Man* gave birth to his
philosophical system. Of these five monographs, the first four were devoted to
a different aspect of his thought: "On Philosophical Thinking" for methodology, "On Perception and Reality" for epistemology, "On Events and Laws"
for cosmology, and "On Character" for a theory of value. The fifth essay, "A
Short Theory of Heaven and Man," offered a brief general summary of the
main theses proposed in the other four works. In these essays, Zhang carefully delineated his view of philosophy. "Philosophy is a study of heaven and
man. Heaven is nature, whereas men are the most outstanding living species.
What philosophy studies are the fundamental principles of nature and the
ultimate rules for human life" (Zhang, 1996, vol. 3, p. 216).

According to Zhang, the following ten propositions characterize his substantial philosophical insights:

1. Nature is the ultimate root, and men are the highest achievement of nature's evolution (*tian ren ben zhi*).
2. Any thing is a process of many continuous events that obey some laws (*wu tong shi li*).
3. Matter is the headstream or source and mind is its branch (*wu yuan xin liu*).
4. Everything is in constant change, and any contradiction has its unification (*yong heng liang yi*).
5. The universe has meaning at three levels: matter, universal law, and the highest standard of value. This highest standard is not moderation, but compatibility and balance (*da hua san ji*).
6. Knowledge consists in the communication of human minds and the external world (*zhi tong nei wai*).
7. There are three criteria for true knowledge: consistency, correspondence to sense experience, and the prediction of results (*zhen zhi san biao*).
8. Individuals are inseparable from their community (*qun ji yi ti*).
9. The ideal conditions for human life depend on three kinds of activity: changing nature, establishing advantageous social institutions, and improving human nature (*ren qun san shi*).
10. Morality varies from time to time, and new social life needs new morality in so far as it aims toward the greatest interests of most people (*ni yi xin de*). (Zhang, 1996, vol. 3, pp. 216–28)

Roughly speaking, the first five propositions constitute the core of Zhang's metaphysics; propositions 6 and 7 express his epistemological claims; and propositions 8 through 10 sketch his moral and political thoughts. The whole system was a significant achievement of his time. None of the philosophical systems of his admired contemporaries, such as Xiong Shili, Jin Yuelin, and Feng Youlan, incorporated so many divergent sources into so comprehensive a philosophical theory. Although it appeared more than half a century ago, many of its elements continue to make good sense and raise controversy today. First, the materialistic tone distinguished Zhang from his great contemporaries in Chinese philosophy. He claimed that all that is could be understood as matter and that mind and life spring from matter. Zhang provided an evolutionary account of the relationship between mind and matter:

> The rough process of the universe's evolving is from matter (in general) through living beings (matter with life) to conscious beings (matter with mind). Matter has fundamentality, and life and mind are the advanced form of evolved matter. Mind is a function or property uniquely owned by advanced living beings. (Zhang, 1996, vol. 3, pp. 217–18)

This materialist perspective, although oversimplified in his texts, remains popular today. Zhang rejected the classical *ben-zhi* (root-perfection) identity doctrine, which he saw as prevailing in the history of Chinese philosophy. The traditional view is that the root and perfection are one and the same and that one ultimate thing governs every aspect of the universe, from the movement of material bodies to the way of human life. This one thing is identified as *dao* by Laozi, *taiji* by Zhu Xi, and *ben xin* by Lu Xiangshan and Wang Yangming. According to Zhang, all of these claims involve a confusion of the root and perfection:

> Things have a root and perfection. The root is the original upon which everything else relies or from which everything develops, and the perfection is the consummation to which everything aims.
>
> The ancients thought that the root and perfection are one and the same. The so-called *taiji, taihe,* and *dao* of ancient Chinese philosophers and the absolute of Western philosophers comprise both root and ideal. What is true is that the root is not necessarily perfection, and perfection is not necessarily the root. The root as the original of the universe and perfection as the acme of the accomplishment of the universe are not one but two. . . . The root is matter, while perfection is the ideal situation. (Zhang, 1996, vol. 1, p. 442)

Zhang's distinction led him to conclude that human ideals and the root of the universe fall under different categories. In a sense, this reminds us of the fact-value distinction, although Zhang held that the root and perfection are not utterly distinct, but stand in a dialectical relation to each other:

> It is not difficult to synthesize materialism and idealism if the distinction between the root and perfection is known. Matter is the root; mind is perfection; and life is between them. Mind is the achievement of the development of matter and is hence subject to matter. But mind can also react on matter. Therefore, men can reform their environment and ideals have the function of overcoming reality. The truth revealed by materialism is that matter is prior to mind and the environment is prior to man, while the truth revealed by idealism is that mind can change matter and man can change the environment. Actually, mind, while coming from matter, can overcome it; man, while being subject to the environment, can change it. The truth about the universe is that "matter is most fundamental" whereas human ideals consist in "overcoming matter." (Zhang, 1996, vol. 1, pp. 268–9)

Zhang sought to defend the idea that even though there is only matter in the universe, a suitable variety of idealism can preserve ultimate human standards and values and the claim that it is the business of mind to promote human perfection. This discussion of matter and mind is hard to assess because Zhang had more than one definition for each of these terms. An unambiguous conception of matter can hardly be found in Zhang's writings. In the texts, he sometimes defined matter as "the process of many continuous events that obey certain laws', and sometimes wrote of matter as being composed of low-level particles like atoms and molecules. The former is philosophical speculation with the imprint of Whitehead's thought, while the latter is derived from modern physics. There is little evidence in his texts that Zhang understood the need to accommodate these different conceptions of matter. Zhang also elaborated his conception of mind in ways that seem to conflict with his materialistic convictions. In his writings, the mind is sometimes treated as a property of advanced living matter (the product of matter's evolution), sometimes as an agent with the capacity to know and to change matter, and sometimes as the bearer of ultimate human values.

Zhang also has two notions of perfection as the ideal situation. First, the ideal situation is a particular configuration of the root (matter) that gives rise to perfection (mentality). Secondly, the ideal situation is a state in which ultimate human values are realized. These two notions of perfection cannot be the same. Perfection as the realization of ultimate human values through the mind requires that the mind can cause changes in the material world, but how can mental causation be explained in a materialistic framework? Although this question seems obvious, it is not clear that Zhang took it seriously. Rather, he claimed that there are no difficulties in his project of synthesizing modern materialism and the kind of idealism that he held to be inherent in the Chinese tradition.

Characteristics of Classical Chinese Philosophy

Investigating the fundamental character of classical Chinese philosophy has been of compelling interest to Zhang throughout his lifetime. He wrote his masterly *Outline of Chinese Philosophy* at the age of 27. This work not only is a milestone in the study of the history of Chinese philosophy, but also forms a part of Zhang's own philosophical system. As indicated by its subtitle *A History of Chinese Philosophical Problems*, the work explores Chinese philosophy from the perspective of the problems raised in its development. Unlike Feng Youlan, whose *History of Chinese Philosophy* presents major figures in chronological order, Zhang was concerned with the classical Chinese contribution to systematic philosophical thought about the universe and human life, even though their work, unlike Western philosophy, never constituted a general discipline. In his *Outline of Chinese Philosophy*, Zhang agreed with Feng Youlan's claim that "although Chinese philosophy did not have a formal system, it had a substantial one" (Zhang, 1982, p. 18). One of the main purposes of the *Outline* was to discover and elaborate a complete systemic account of Chinese philosophy.

Zhang considered three aspects of classical Chinese philosophy. The first section of the *Outline*, "Cosmology," discusses ontological or metaphysical problems. The second section, "The Theory of Human Life," discusses problems such as the place of human beings in the universe, the meaning of life, human nature, and human ideals. The third section, "The Theory of Approaching

Knowledge," discusses epistemological and methodological problems. The work makes taxonomic efforts to untangle the interweaving constituents of Chinese thought and to order various doctrines, ideas, and concepts so that a clear structure of ancient Chinese philosophy can be revealed. Unlike a general history of philosophy, the *Outline* paid extensive attention to the analysis and exposition of the development of the essential categories and doctrines of Chinese thought. It thus became the first work on the history of the categories of Chinese philosophy. Further, Zhang's comparative studies of Chinese and Western philosophy in the *Outline* are quite remarkable. To a considerable degree, they succeeded in giving an explicit and powerful account of the character of Chinese philosophy.

According to Zhang, Chinese philosophy has six general characteristics: combining knowing and acting; unifying heaven and man; identifying truth with goodness; valuing life over knowledge; valuing understanding over argument; and clinging to neither science nor religion (Zhang, 1982, pp. 5–9). Other particular features of Chinese philosophy are explained in later sections of the *Outline*. Zhang's exposition always contains observations about how Chinese philosophy differs from Western philosophy. An influential example taken from his discussion of Chinese ontology displays his approach. Ontology is an account of ultimate reality. On Zhang's interpretation, the ultimate reality for Chinese is *bengen* (the root), which can perhaps be understood as parallel to the Western notion of *noumenon*:

> Indian philosophy and Western philosophy speak of the *noumenon* as something more real [than the *phenomenon*] and think that the *phenomenon* is delusion while the *noumenon* is reality. What is *noumenon*? It is the uniquely ultimate reality. This conception really has never emerged in original Chinese philosophy. Chinese philosophers recognize the distinction between the root and things. It rests not with the distinction between reality and delusion, but with the distinction between root and branches, between headstream and offshoots. Ordinary things are all real, and it is not the case that only the root is real. Chinese philosophers really do not hold a theory that treats the *noumenon* as the only reality. (Zhang, 1982, p. 9)

It should be noted that *noumenon* was originally translated into Chinese as *benti*, but in later work Zhang used *benti* to translate substance. Substance and *phenomenon* do not form a proper contrast in Western philosophy, which instead distinguishes between substance and attribute and between *noumenon* and *phenomenon*.

The root, according to Zhang, has four characteristics: (a) it is independent: everything else is derivative, but the root comes from nowhere and depends on nothing; (b) it is invariable: everything else changes, but the root stays constant; (c) it is infinite and absolute; and (d) it is unembodied or intangible: tangible things could not be the root, and the root is beyond any configuration. The further question of what the root is can be answered by ontological investigation. Zhang carefully examined the major candidates for the root that have been proposed in Chinese philosophy, including *dao* (the way), *qi* (vital energy), and *xin* (mind). Although many commentators have praised Zhang's comparative expositions of Chinese and Western philosophy, we should note that Zhang's tendency to take Western philosophy as a homogeneous whole gives rise to inaccuracy when he examines specific problems. This is shown by considering the above example. It is plain that not all Western philosophers endorse the distinction between *noumenon* and *phenomenon* or think that *noumena* are real and *phenomena* are delusive. One can draw an epistemological distinction between seeming and being without accepting Kant's distinction between *phenomena* and *noumena*. Kant himself held that *phenomena* are real and in his *Critique of Pure Reason*, at least on one interpretation, took *noumenon* as a negative term that is correctly employed to restrict knowledge to *phenomena*. Even in ordinary thinking, it is unavoidable to separate perception from illusion. There is no reason to think that the Chinese and Western distinctions are incompatible, if the Western view is understood as claiming no more than that something hidden is responsible for all that appear to us. In sum, something seems to be overstated in Zhang's comparative discussion of the root and *noumenon*. His text contains many more comparisons that suffer from insufficient discrimination among distinct Western positions. In "Several Features of Classical Chinese Philosophy" published in the 1950s, Zhang restated the first characteristic of Chinese philosophy as "the unification of *noumenon* and *phenomenon*." This claim is difficult to accept insofar as his original view was that there had never been a distinction between *noumenon* and *phenomenon* in Chinese thought for ancient Chinese philosophers to unify. *The Outline of Chinese Philosophy*, although full of insights, exemplifies the fifth general feature of Chinese philosophy as listed by Zhang: it values understanding above argument.

Zhang's work on the history of Chinese philosophy also constituted a part of his project of creative synthesis. After 1949, these writings focused on commending the materialist tradition of Chinese philosophy, articulating its dialectical thought and revealing its humanitarian ideas. Works representing these aspects of his thought include *A Short History of Materialistic Thought in China* (1957a), *Zhang Zai: an Eleventh Century Materialist Philosopher in China* (1957b), *Studies in Chinese Ethical Thought* (1989c), and a series of articles. On Zhang's interpretation, Chinese thought has had an enduring materialist tradition. Moreover, materialism is the mainstream of the development of Chinese philosophy. In each period, there have been philosophers who advocated materialism in various ways, such as Wang Chong (Han dynasty), Fan Zhen (Southern dynasties), and Zhang Zai (Song dynasty). Zhang stressed the importance of dialectical thinking in China. In his interpretation of Chinese moral thought, Zhang made use of Marxist methodology, including class analysis and dialectics, and examined what he judged to be positive and negative elements in ancient Chinese moral thinking. Readers may be willing to make allowances for the excessive use of Marxist jargon in most of his writing after 1949.

Zhang's excellent work *A Handbook of Concepts and Categories in Classical Chinese Philosophy* (1989b), deserves special attention. It is a companion to his early *Outline*, but the exposition of classical Chinese philosophy is developed from another perspective. The *Handbook* carefully enumerates and examines the fundamental concepts and categories of classical Chinese natural philosophy, philosophy of life, and epistemology. It serves both as a systematic examination of classical Chinese thought and as a valuable reference book to guide reading of classical texts. For example, Zhang devoted nine pages to exploring what different figures or schools meant by the crucial classical philosophical concept of *li* (principle, law). In this mature work, Zhang is fully sensitive to the diversity of doctrines that can be attached to a fundamental philosophical term.

A Sophisticated View of Chinese Culture

From Zhang's early childhood, a succession of cultural crises have had impact on the minds of Chinese intellectuals. The May Fourth Movement provided a platform on which a variety of competing views on culture could be expressed. Zhang and most of his contemporaries did not pursue a general philosophy of culture as a means of determining what culture is, but raised the particular question of what kind of culture China should develop in order to regain its affluence and power. From the proposals that emerged, radical and conservative intellectuals developed two influential and competing views of the reconstruction of Chinese culture. Radicals called for wholesale Westernization, while conservatives responded by promoting a revival of the national essence. Zhang was satisfied with neither view. He participated in the cultural debate of the 1930s and formulated his view of Chinese culture in a paper of 1933:

> Sticking to our old culture and refusing to adjust it to world culture will necessarily lead to extinction. Meanwhile, totally throwing away our native culture and accepting exotic culture will eventually incur assimilation by other cultures and make our own culture disappear. So, both attempting wholesale acceptance of Western culture and attempting revival of the old culture are doomed to failure in today's China. (Zhang, 1996, vol. 1, p. 230)

The way out of this predicament, according to Zhang, would be to "synthesize the advantages of both the East and the West, promote the excellent heritage inherent in Chinese culture and adopt valuable Western profferings, and to form one single new culture, which is not a flat concoction, but a creative synthesis" (Zhang, 1996, vol. 1, p. 229). This view of culture has obtained popularity in China over the last two decades as the "synthesizing innovation theory of Chinese culture." This view of culture, which Zhang held all along, has a structure that is extremely similar to that of his view of philosophy. An enhanced version was developed and expounded during another period of cultural debates in the 1980s. For Zhang, the important question is not what to synthesize, but how to synthesize. In "The Way of Developing Chinese Culture: On the Synthesis and Innovation of Culture," Zhang discussed three aspects of synthesizing the advantages of Chinese and Western culture in some detail. First, he considered the relationship of man to nature. Zhang claimed that Chinese culture advocates harmony between man and nature, while Westerners proclaim opposition and struggle between man and nature. In his view, "it is necessary and unavoidable to combine the idea of 'unifying heaven and man' and the idea of 'conquering nature.'"

Zhang discussed the second aspect of synthesis with respect to the relationship of individuals to community. He observed that "thinkers either emphasize the promotion of spiritual life and national interest or emphasize individual rights and freedom." In fact, he claimed, "individuals are inseparable from society or the nation, and people's material interest and spiritual life are interdependent" (Zhang, 1993, pp. 599–600). According to his synthesis, collective goals and individual interests are all honored by a good society.

The third aspect of synthesizing Chinese and Western culture concerns ways of thinking. Zhang observed that the Chinese are good at dialectical thinking, but weak in scientific and analytical thinking. To remedy this, he proposed to combine dialectical and analytical thought. He concluded by arguing that synthesis is an ongoing process:

> The creation of the new Chinese culture must synthesize all relative truths ever discovered by human beings and achieve the union of all known truths. Truths are to be constantly discovered, and culture is to be constantly updated. (Zhang, 1993, p. 601)

Zhang's stance has much subtlety. Rather than proposing a balance between radical and conservative views, Zhang finds no truth in either of them and rejects them both. A cultural synthesis is not a simple aggregation of disconnected pieces that one finds valuable in either scientific or moral terms. Zhang sought the innovative development of a new integral culture. For him, a cultural project is a never-ending endeavor that constantly absorbs new truths.

Zhang Dainian Scholarship

Zhang's work has not attracted the scholarly attention that it deserves. Because of political and historical factors, his ideas received little notice until the last two decades. Although his major works were written before 1949, only a few were published. His older contemporaries Feng Youlan and Jin Yuelin established their academic reputation before 1949, but Zhang did not share this good fortune. After 1949, Zhang was deprived of his right to teach and publish for twenty years during the antirightist campaign and the Cultural Revolution. His major work *Outline of Chinese Philosophy* obtained public recognition only when it was republished in 1982. In spite of the delay in his recognition, Zhang Dainian is one of the most important thinkers in contemporary China. His system of thought displays a passion for truth and morality, a capacity to incorporate a wide range of human values, and an attachment to the needs and prospects of his countrymen. A picture of contemporary Chinese philosophy without him would be incomplete.

Bibliography

Works by Zhang Dainian

Zhang, Dainian 1957a: *Zhongguo weiwu zhuyi sixiang jianshi* 中國唯物主義思想簡史 (a short history of materialist thought in China), Beijing: China Youth Publishing House. This work also appears in Zhang, 1996, vol. 4

Zhang, Dainian 1957b: *Zhang Zai – shiyi shiji zhongguo weiwu zhuyi zhexue jia* 張載 — 十一世紀中國唯物主義哲學家 (Zhang Zai: an eleventh-century materialist philosopher in China), Wuhan: Hubei People's Publishing House. This work also appears in Zhang, 1996, vol. 3

Zhang, Dainian 1958: *Zhongguo zhexue dagang* 中國哲學大綱 (outline of Chinese philosophy), Beijing: Commercial Press, (published under the pen name Yu Tong); revised edition, 1982: Beijing: The Publishing House of the Chinese Academy of Social Sciences. This work also appears in Zhang, 1996, vol. 2. The first draft of this work was completed in 1936

Zhang, Dainian, 1982: *Qiu zhen ji* 求真集 (essays in pursuit of truth), Changsha: Hunan People's Publishing House. These essays also appear in Zhang, 1996, vol. 1. These are most of Zhang's early papers from the 1930s, which were originally scattered in several newspapers

Zhang, Dainian 1988: *Wenhua yu zhexue* 文化與哲學 (culture and philosophy), Beijing: Educational Science Press. This volume is a collection of essays on cultural problems

Zhang, Dainian 1989a: *Zhongguo lunli sixiang yanjiu* 中國倫理思想研究 (studies in Chinese ethical thought), Shanghai: Shanghai People's Publishing House. This work also appears in Zhang, 1996, vol. 3

Zhang, Dainian 1989b: *Zhongguo gudian zhexue gainian fanchou yaolun* 中國古典哲學概念範疇要論 (a handbook of concepts and categories in classical Chinese philosophy), Beijing: The Publishing House of the Chinese Academy of Social Sciences. This work appears in Zhang, 1996, vol. 4

Zhang, Dainian 1993: *Zhang Dainian xueshu lunzhu zixuan ji* 張岱年學術論著自選集 (academic writings of Zhang Dainian selected by himself) Beijing: Capital Normal University Press. This collection contains what Zhang took to be his most important writings

Zhang, Dainian 1996: *Zhang Dainian quan ji* 張岱年全集 (the complete works of Zhang Dainian), 8 vols, Shijiazhuang: Hebei People's Publishing House. Since the publication of Zhang, 1996, most of Zhang's works are conveniently accessible to both scholars and general readers

Zhang, Dainian: *Tian ren wu lun* 天人五論 (five essays concerning heaven and man) appears in Zhang, 1996, vol. 3. The first three essays were published as *Zhenyu shande tansuo* (in search of truth and goodness), Jinan: Qi Lu Publishing House, 1988

Secondary works

Philosophy Department of Peking University, ed. 1999: *Zhongguo zhexue de quanshi yu fazhan* 中國哲學的詮釋與發展 (interpretation and development of Chinese philosophy: essays in honor of Mr Zhang Dainian's ninetieth birthday), Beijing: Peking University Press

Wang, Zhongjiang 1991: "Zhang Dainian: an untiring explorer" in Li, Zhenxia, ed. *dangdai zhongguo shizhe* 當代中國十哲 (ten contemporary philosophers of China), Beijing: Hua Xia Publishing House

Discussion Questions

1. Can there be a philosophical synthesis of Chinese tradition, dialectical materialism, and philosophical analysis?
2. Can individual philosophical problems be dealt with more successfully on their own or within the context of systematic philosophical thought?
3. Is it a mistake to think that the root and the perfection are the same? What are the consequences of distinguishing them?
4. What are the consequences for philosophy if we think that everything is in constant change?
5. What follows from the claim that the highest standard of value is found in compatibility and balance, rather than in moderation?
6. Do consistency, correspondence to sense experience, and the capacity to predict results provide adequate criteria for a theory of knowledge?
7. Does holism, as opposed to individualism, follow from the claim that individuals are inseparable from their community?
8. Does materialism have room for Zhang Dainian's account of life and the mind?
9. Are there advantages in dealing with the history of Chinese philosophy from the perspective of problems, categories, and concepts rather than chronologically in terms of main figures?
10. Does Zhang Dainian's approach to Chinese philosophy provide a suitable basis for comparing Chinese and Western philosophy?

12

LI ZEHOU: CHINESE AESTHETICS FROM A POST-MARXIST AND CONFUCIAN PERSPECTIVE

John Zijiang Ding

Li Zehou (1930–) is widely considered to be the most creative living Chinese philosopher as well as the most controversial. Some colleagues have risen in academic status through praising Li, while others have achieved eminence by criticizing him. Since the late 1970s, Li has launched many views that have had great impact on Chinese intellectual life, and even his opponents recognize Li's scholarly influence and academic achievements.

Kantian Subjectivity and Post-Marxian Anthropological Ontology

Li's general philosophical framework is a post-Marxist anthropological ontology. He argues that the task of post-Marxism is to surpass and transcend traditional Marxist thought. Li has sought to preserve Marx's most fundamental ideas, but has been willing to abandon other parts of Marxist theory. Indeed, Li's work, including his aesthetics, his studies of traditional Chinese thought, and his accounts of Western philosophy, has developed within this framework. At the center of Li's work is the concept of *zhutixing* (subjectivity), and his entire philosophy is a practical philosophy of *zhutixing*. Originally, *zhutixing* had four meanings: (a) a principal body, part or role, in contrast to a subordinate body, part or role, (b) a subject, in contrast to an object, (c) a perceiver, in contrast to the perceived external world, and (d) human initiative, subjective activity or a conscious dynamic role, in contrast to nonhuman roles, forces or powers from the natural and physical world. As used by Li, *zhutixing* includes all of these meanings.

Zhutixing has two sets of implications. First, *zhutixing* has two ontological structures: *gongjubenti* (instrumental *noumenon*) within a technical–social structure and *xinlibenti* (psychological *noumenon*) within a cultural–psychological structure. Secondly, *zhutixing* involves human collectivities, such as societies, nations, classes, and organizations, as well as individuals. These four factors are interrelated and interact. Each provides a complex composite structure by which we may examine the development of mankind and individual persons. In particular, we can combine material and spiritual aspects in an account of complete human development. The structure of the instrumental *noumenon* provides a fundamental distinction between humans and animals: unlike animals, human beings consciously make and use instruments and change their design. In order to make instruments, humans evolved language as a symbolic system with semantics and grammar to serve a cognitive and practical function. The structure of the psychological *noumenon* provides the framework for more individual roles. There are two types of *zhutixing*: one is for humanity as a whole and another is for personal individuality. Marx examined the former, but individual *zhutixing* will be questioned by post-Marxism.

Recently, Li has attempted to distinguish *zhutixing* from conventional notions of subjectivity:

> Sometimes there is a kind of misunderstanding regarding my so-called *zhutixing*. It does not have the Western sense of "subjectivity" (*zhuguan*). I feel we should rather use a new term "subjectenity" – even though there is no such word in the English dictionary – that means that a human person is the capacity of an active entity. *Zhutixing* is not a concept of epistemology; instead it implies that a human being is considered as a form of material, biological, and object-ive existence and as an active capability in relationship to the environment. (Li Zehou, 1999f)

Li is greatly influenced by Marx and accepts the practical philosophy of Marx's historical materialism, according to which human beings must first attend to eating and drinking and finding shelter and clothes and then can engage in politics, science, art, religion, or other social activities. However, Li disagrees with the dialectical materialism that was developed by Engels and completed by Lenin and Stalin. Following Marx, Li emphasizes the humanization of phys-ical nature and argues that through its own initiative human practice transforms physical nature so that physical nature belongs to human beings and becomes part of their nature. He criticizes Mao Zedong's essay "On Practice" as well as some Frankfurt School studies of practice on the grounds that they con-sider practice in a manner that is too broad and all-embracing. Li tries in his philosophy to go "from Marx to Kant and also from Kant to Marx," but he does not simply copy these two great thinkers. Rather, he uses Marx as his starting point to reexamine issues initiated by Kant and then deals with unsolved problems arising from these considerations.

Marxism must transform itself from a critical philosophy to a constructive philosophy, because negation, criticism, and revolution are means, not ends, of human development. God is dead, but human beings are alive and as living beings constantly move forward, propelled by their own forces in their principal roles. It is unnecessary to pray to have supernatural powers or to build a revolutionary utopia for the human future. The ideal society must be constructed, but deconstructive activity alone cannot achieve it. Although there will be difficulty, suffering, and loss, human beings will attain a realm of spirituality in which they are unified with heaven in their actual lives. In attempting to answer the questions of how to live and why to live, human beings have produced philosophical theories or religious doctrines. In this sense, philosophy deals with the theme of human destiny. Anthropological ontology seeks to explain the existence and development of human beings in material and spiritual fields and to help people to choose their personal values and individual priorities and to determine their own destiny.

Human nature mixes and unifies the perceptual and the rational as well as the natural and the social. This unification is not a simple mechanical addition. The perceptual and the natural contain the rational and social. In a process of the humanization of nature, the rational and the social can bring about internal transformations of the perceptual and the natural. There is a distinction between human subjects and natural objects, between human being and natural being, but there is no similar distinction between animals and nature. Unlike animals, human beings throughout history have played subjective, conscious, and dynamic roles that are beyond nature, but are functionally related to it. Human subjectivity represents real human nature. Kant's most important contribution to philosophy was to present a systematic *a priori* framework for human subjectivity. This framework, however, lacks individuality and contingency. Kant's cognitive forms and categories are logical, *a priori*, and rational, but need to be psychological, historical, and perceptual. Although anthropological ontology and the practical philosophy of human subjectivity have the same meaning and content, they offer slightly different emphases. Anthropological ontology deals primarily with the forces and structures of human subjectivity, including their physical aspects, while practical philosophy stresses knowing, feeling, and consciousness as the psychological structures of human subjectivity and gives more prominence to individuality, sensibility, and contingency. To reconstruct the psychological *noumenon* after the deconstruction of language, we must rely on an account of individual subjectivity.

Li stresses that art is prior to science because it involves psychological and emotional *noumena* and real perceptual accumulation. The essence of beauty is the most complete representation of the human essence, and the philosophy of beauty is the highest human philosophy. Philosophically, beauty fundamentally concerns the problem of human subjectivity, although in scientific terms it is reduced to the problem of cultural–psychological structure. A study of human subjectivity in terms of beauty can provide the basis of the future development of historical materialism.

Relations to the Thought of Heidegger, Wittgenstein, and Foucault

Li compares Marx, Kant, Heidegger, Wittgenstein, and Foucault with his own framework. In order to transform Marxism from a critical style to a constructive one, he pays more attention to so-called ends of human development than to means of human development. In his view, besides Kant, Heidegger was also a significant philosopher for this transformation. In his "Fourth Outline of Human Subjectivity" (see the excerpt at the end of this chapter), Li discusses the relationship between "co-existence" and "personal existence," "being," and "individual beings" in a synthetic and comprehensive way.

According to Heidegger in *Being and Time* (1927), one's self as "being-there" (*Dasein*) or "being-in-the-world" is the one being – human being – with which we are intimately acquainted. Human being as *Dasein* must be distinguished from any other beings. Human existence with the awareness of *Dasein* can be understood differently from any other existences. There are two kinds of human existence: the existence of "I" and the existence of "they." During the process of "being-toward-death," human individuality will become human collectivity: one's self will lose one's "I" in "they." For this reason, one's self must have freedom to release *Dasein* from the unreality of collectivity and help it to get back the reality of individuality. Generally speaking, Li disagrees with Heidegger's "pessimism." He does not accept that "being-toward-death," which is filled with Angst (dread), is the final cause of the awareness of *Dasein*. "Being-toward-life" should be a real driving force of the human development. Li's *Dasein* emphasizes the material existence of human being as "a part of collectivity in the lower level," and entrusts the spiritual existence of individuality to the human being in a higher level.

Regarding language, Li prefers Wittgenstein's later account of "language games" in *Philosophical Investigations* to his earlier "picture theory" account in *Tractatus Logico-Philosophicus* (1922). Wittgenstein's earlier thought intended to posit an ideal language with a perfect logical form to explain the possibility of actual languages. It would be far distant from people's everyday life and their social, political, and economic activities, and even would exclude as senseless the propositions of ethics, metaphysics, and religion. By contrast, Wittgenstein's later thought provides a more open framework to overcome the narrowness of his earlier account. It is impossible to create a so-called ideal language, and it is also unnecessary to analyze propositions in terms of a perfect logical form. An understanding of a sentence can be reached through an examination of the "forms of life" out of which the sentence arises and meaning is understood in terms of use. Wittgenstein's later understanding of language has connections with Li's anthropological ontology. Language, like any consciousness, ideology, thought, and spiritual activities, ultimately arises from the social environment and communal interactions, cultural conditions, historical context, and political structures.

Li supports Foucault's "archeology of knowledge" for developing a method of intellectual history. Foucault's later "genealogy of language," however, could be more valuable for Li's purposes than this archaeology. With Foucault's genealogy, (a) new systems of thought can be considered contingent products of many small and unrelated causes, (b) there are essential connections between knowledge and power, (c) bodies of knowledge are tied to systems of social control, and (d) power can be a creative source of positive values. But in Li's "Outline," power is inadequately interpreted and explained. For example, in discussing power and knowledge, he does not determine whether "power" relates to "social control" or to "individual control." Li's critics have pointed out inconsistencies and even contradictions between his Marxian account of anthropological ontology and his Kantian account of individual subjectivity.

More recent critics have questioned Li's Westernization of Chinese spirituality. Some young critics have challenged what they allege to be his "conservative framework" by proposing a more liberal perspective.

The Future of Philosophy

What is the possible future of philosophy? Like most Chinese philosophers, Li's methodology is basically prescriptive and synthetic, rather than descriptive and analytical. Like many Western scholars of Marxism, Li follows earlier Marx in adopting Feuerbach's concept of alienation and applying it to social, political, and economic interactions. Human beings have been separated from animals through alienation. We can distinguish between rational alienation through the internal structure of human nature and perceptual alienation through psychological-final being. Alienation will be overcome through the development and perfection of human freedom and through the development and perfection of our instrumental *noumenon* and individual subjectivity. Individual subjectivity, as expressed in protest and resistance arising from alienation, is present in modern and contemporary humanism but lacks a solid grounding in an acceptable theory of subjectivity. Alienation inevitably arises in social development and resistance by individual subjectivity can be understood in terms of good and evil: two forces that constituted historical tragedy and ground the antithesis between historicism and morality. Evil, as the lever of historical progress, and good, as the value of human beings, can become compatible and identical when individual subjectivity is liberated from collective subjectivity. Individual subjectivity can be fully established only when morality, including humanism, becomes identical with historicism.

According to Hegel's Dialectic, a method of uniting or overcoming contradictions by moving to a higher level of truth, Being and Nothing are held in tension within the higher truth of Becoming. Hegel's perspective of dialectical progress was accepted by Marx, who rejected the idealism of Hegel's Absolute Spirit. Like most other Chinese Marxists, Li attacks the dialectical idealism of Hegel's Absolute Spirit, but he also rejects what he considers to be Hegel's devaluation of humanity. Unlike most other Chinese Marxists, he abandons dialectical materialism, especially in its Stalinist development, leaving many aspects of Li's thought closer to the Frankfurt School critical theory of Marcuse and Habermas than to orthodox Marxism. Li has attempted to create a new path for political reforms and revolution. Ideally, "reforms without blood" and "revolution without violence" could be realized through aesthetic education. As one of the central studies in the construction of material and spiritual civilization, this education would promote the full development of human beings and the full realization of individual potentiality.

Li sees the source of human rationality in *jidian* (accumulation or long standing practice) and uses this notion to construct the psychological forms that make up human nature. That nature, as psychological *noumenon*, has been constituted by culture. The explanation of psychology lies in culture, but culture exists through the accumulation of the psychological. Because cultural structure is closely related to psychological structure, we can combine these two structures to form a cultural–psychological whole that gives rules to individuals in their various roles. The ethical significance of human subjectivity is grounded in the practical philosophy of anthropological ontology. This ethical significance can be seen as a demand for a subjective will aiming at human good for all individual practices. We should ask all individuals to undertake duties and responsibilities for the existence and development of all human beings. Philosophy is the embodiment of the ideals, intentions, and responsibilities of human subjectivity, and ethics constitutes the subjectivity of the human free will. The structures of subjectivity comprise the internal transformations of rationality through the structure of intelligence, the coagulation or embodiment of rationality through the structure of will, and the accumulation of rationality through the structure of aesthetics. These structures, as general forms, reveal the importance of human collectivities. Through fulfillment in individual psychology, the creative psychological functions of these structures are constantly opened and enriched. The functions become free intuition by enlightening truth through beauty. They become free will by preserving goodness through beauty. They become free impression by feeling happiness through beauty. The subjectivity of human nature thus concerns the structural forms of general psychology and the creative functions of individual psychology.

Philosophers should emancipate themselves from the collectivity, rationality, and necessity of Hegelian and Stalinist doctrine by emphasizing individuality, sensibility, and contingency in the whole of human life. Because history has been created by human initiative, it does not conform to any objective laws. Historically, to give more importance to individual subjectivity is to expand the scope of contingency. By emphasizing individual subjectivity, one uses contingency to construct necessity. Every individual person actually or potentially participates in creating the whole of history. The destiny of individuals should be determined by themselves rather than by authorities, environments, conditions, powers, or any external consciousness.

Philosophy is science plus poetry or occupies an intermediate zone between science and the poem. Philosophy should combine the oneness, individuality, invention, ambiguity, vagueness, irrationality, and purposelessness of poetry with the truth, falsifiability, discovery, rationality, and purposefulness of science. In these regards, there is room for different philosophies to have different inclinations or emphases.

Accordingly, human subjectivity is compatible with traditional Chinese philosophy, and Daoism, Confucianism, and Chinese Buddhism can be understood as investigations of anthropological ontology, psychological and emotional structures, and subjectivity. In a sense, Li advocates a new movement of going back to Confucianism to transform people from "common men" to *junzi* (superior men), with higher moral virtues and aesthetical characters.

To sum up, Li proposes that philosophy of the future will:

1. Find a full cultivation and representation of individual potentiality through "accumulation," the unification of history and psychology and the examination of beauty in a full mixture of individuality and totality;
2. Practice the examination of beauty, rather than morality, in the system of *zhutixing* as its final goal;
3. Analyze the objective history of social development, but also initiate the creation of history;
4. Examine human destiny through understanding the structure of subjectivity;
5. Avoid absurdity and anxiety and obtain historicity through the search for transcendence by contingency and individuality;
6. Overcome tragic conflicts and dissensions between human beings and nature, society and individuals, emotion and reason, history and psychology, and ideal and reality.

Li's attempt to overcome the deficiencies of "cold philosophy" by proposing the goals of subjectivity and "hot philosophy" can be criticized for exaggerating the role of individual subjectivity. Although he has developed an ambitious strategy, he has never completed any of his programmatic aims.

Aesthetics

Li has made major scholarly contributions to aesthetics. In *The Path of Beauty*, which is the most influential recent Chinese study in this field, he argues that the main development of traditional Chinese aesthetics, like other branches of Chinese philosophy, was a rationalism that freed itself of primitive magic and religion and laid the foundations of cultural and psychological structure for the Han people. This rationalism was manifested primarily in Confucian thought but also in the Daoist doctrines represented by Zhuangzi. The mutual and complementary roles played by Confucianism and Daoism are an important thread that has run through all Chinese aesthetic thinking for more than 2,000 years. Traditional Chinese philosophy, including aesthetics, has been guided by the practical rationality of daily life, human relations, and political concepts, rather than by any abstract and abstruse rationalist theory. The basic characteristics of the Confucian outlook, as the cornerstone of Chinese spirituality, combined a skeptical or atheistic world outlook with a positive and energetic attitude towards life. Following Confucius, many traditional Chinese intellectuals tried to direct and incorporate human emotions, concepts, and rites into worldly relationships and human life, rather than orienting them towards an external object of worship or supernatural realm.

The leading aesthetic characteristics of traditional Chinese art have stressed a variety of concerns. Chinese art has celebrated a general sensory pleasure that is related to social ethics and politics. It has focused on function, relationship, and rhythm, rather than on substance and objects. It has dealt with the harmony of intercourse or interaction between various opposites, rather than with conflict. It has sought to express an intrinsic interest in human life, rather than providing exact imitation and faithful reproduction. It has tried to integrate emotion and reason and to employ the intuitive wisdom of the emotions to achieve harmony and satisfaction within human life, rather than to dwell on irrational fantasy or supernatural belief. It has appreciated both the soft and gentle emotional beauty of feminine grace and the bold and vigorous beauty of masculine strength, rather than fixing on a fatalistic concern for terror or tragedy.

For many Westerners, Confucianism, Daoism, and Chinese Buddhism appear to be mutually opposed, but they balance and supplement one other in many ways. For example, Zhuangzi preached that one should withdraw from the world, but he still considered the natural life of humans. His account of the omnipresence of gods and his aesthetic view of life are aspects of Daoism that scintillate with emotion and supplement and deepen Confucianism. Confucianism is also supplemented by the concern for significant social change within the exoteric sects of Chinese Buddhism. In Li's opinion, Confucianism, Daoism, and Buddhism took part in an important ideological process, through which the Chinese tradition of clear-headed rationalism and historicism triumphed over mysticism and fanaticism.

"The Fourth Outline of Human Subjectivity"

One of Li's papers, entitled "The Fourth Outline of Human Subjectivity," is a particularly representative exposition of what is frequently referred to as Li's Anthropological Ontology:

(1) "Human beings are living" is the first fact. "Living" is more fundamental than "why they are living," because it is the given fact.

(2) What does "Human beings are living" mean? (a) Human beings are thrown into this world, namely, they were born not by their own choices. Life is not the choice and decision of human beings; it is only a fact. The reason why human beings have never chosen nonliving is that their births seem to be mystical (scientifically, this is the racial continuation of living beings) and to represent a demand for continuous living after being born (scientifically, this is the instinct of animals in their consciousness and nonconsciousness). (b) Human beings live in a world of "co-existence with others," just as Heidegger says, "to be with others, within-the-world." But this situation is not chosen and decided by human beings themselves (individual persons). (c) "Co-existence with others" – to get together to live in this world is "everyday life" (Wittgenstein) or "everydayness" (Heidegger). It is also Marx's "social existence." As Marx says, human beings cannot choose the productive modes into which they are born.

(3) The first implication of "Human beings are living" is how they live, namely, how they eat, dress, are sheltered and transport themselves. (a) "How to live" is prior to "why live." "Living" is prior to the "implications of living," and also the existence of the "nonoriginal-real" is prior to that of the "original-real." We should suspend the latter and focus our attention on the former, on "human beings are living" and "how they are living." (b) Marx's historical materialism adopts just this way of examining how human beings live and correctly and significantly distinguishes human beings from other animals. This is the "social-final being" – human productive practices by using and producing instruments. The foundation of "human beings are living" and "how they live" is ultimately in those practices, rather than in language or internal mental activities. In fact, Heidegger also recognizes that using instruments is a basic fact (*Being and Time*), and really emphasizes "non-original-real" and "decadent" everyday life. Similarly, Wittgenstein believes that the basis of language games is our acting rather than the problem of truth and falsity. His book *On Certainty* points out that everyday life and life patterns are the roots of language.

(4) The endless, everlasting and common time seem to have the "first implication," and its universal necessity (Kant) actually is social objectivity (see the third chapter of my *Critique of Critical Philosophy*). Therefore, history and the nature of history can have an objective and "necessary" significance.

(5)   Grammar (language) and logic (thought) are also the needs, regulations and laws of human "co-existence with others" in this world. They are separated from nature. For this reason, morality is prior to cognition. Cognitive rules (grammar and logic) were separated or transformed from moral regulations. This is the most important point. Cognition is guaranteed to have the initiative to the future. Cognition, life and reality are "ready to hand" rather than "present at hand." Cognitive content (empirical knowledge) is transferred to power (M. Foucault). There is not any knowledge as "power" that is unrelated to human beings, just as there is not any nature that is unrelated to human being. This is involved in the "humanization of nature." "Humanization of nature" goes forward in two directions: instruments (the social world) and psychology (the cultural world). We may call them "objective-instrumental-final being" and "subjective-psychological-final being." "What is life for?" (The meaning of life) comes from the cultural world. Suspended and unsolved problems have appeared again to become a mark for a new era. "How to live?" (How human beings can continue to live) ceased to be a problem, but now it is strongly and significantly questioned. Although raising doubts, human beings still need to live. What should we do?

(6)   We propose to construct the psychological *noumenon*, especially the emotional *noumenon*. Human beings attach and submit to heavy pressure from the instrumental *noumenon* and objective sociality that are necessary for "human living." Therefore, they want to seek "selves" that are "forgotten" and "lost" and to examine the meaning of life. Human beings raise issues about "death," "care" and "dread," but they cannot find any real solutions. According to Heidegger, real existence is conscious of the possibility of nonexistence. If human beings are separated from the two "*noumena*" mentioned above, they will only have an animal-like existence and will also not have any problems about "being conscious of." The meaning of life and the consciousness of human life that are separated from life and human life would become a real paradox of language, but life and human life are, after all, different from the meaning of life and consciousness of human life. The objective sociality, psychological accumulation, and eating, dressing, housing and transport and so on are not equal to the finite existence of individuals that is unrepeatable and ceases at death. The "human beings are living," "how to live" and "why to live" of others cannot determine, dominate and identify my "why to live" or the meaning of my life. This is the main problem at the present.

(7)   The meaning of life and consciousness of human life have not jumped out of the void. It is not easy to survive realistically and historically without sharp paws, strong arms, dagger teeth and giant bodies. To struggle for "living" in difficult circumstances can be considered a meaning and consciousness by itself. The metaphysical roots of "human touch" (human relationships) and the "feeling of homeland" are "living," "coexistence with others" and "living together in one world." The key point here is that "who to live" and the meaning of life are born from the process of "how to live."

(8)   This is also the traditional spirit of Chinese philosophy. Traditional Chinese philosophy relies on Confucianism and makes Daoism subsidiary. It considers "happiness" and "living without stopping" as the leading importance of life

and the spirit of the universe. This can also be considered my anthropological ontology (namely, the practical philosophy of subjectivity). Here, "subjectivity" (*zhutixing*) is the anthropological *noumenon*, because there is not any objective being that is completely unrelated to or against human beings. Anthropological ontology needs two types of utopias. One is external: the world of the great harmony or "communism"; the other one is internal: the perfect psychological (emotional) structure. We may find a new way of internal sageliness and the external kingliness. "Living" without utopia is losing the way in contemporary times. To believe in "God" or to seek "Being" is to construct an internal utopia. Zhu Xi, a leading neo-Confucian scholar, points out that Buddhism can only know the big universal views rather than fine and detailed items. This comment also applies to Heidegger and other contemporary philosophers. Those "fine and detailed items" can be treated as the concrete examination of the psychological *noumenon* or emotional structure. This emotional structure has roots, sources and transformations and can be considered "human nature," or psychological accumulation. According to my aesthetic theory, art and the history of art are the concrete homologues that reveal the emotional structure of human nature. "Real and original" time that puts the past, present and future together are saved and preserved in this structure. It still has a common nature of accumulation, but its formation may have the pious feeling similar to the formation of God.

(9)　Human beings are, after all, always individual. The structure of human nature (the cultural–psychological structure and the psychological structure) from historical accumulation does not force and intervene in individuals. The contingencies of "living" (the experience and choices of human beings from "being born" to "being thrown in their life tours") and the impression they will make on the reception, resistance and attendance of individuals to final being are significantly different from the construction of instrumental-final being. So, the individuals may have mysticism, sacredness, uncertainty, multiplicity and challengeability. The meaning of life, the consciousness of human life and the motive force of life come from accumulated human nature and also from the attacks of resistant forces of the accumulated human nature. This can be considered eternal suffering and happiness.

(10)　All of the above involve destiny. Religions offer destiny. Art and literature express and philosophy ponders destiny. Human nature, contingency and destiny are the main subjects of my philosophy, which will be widely disseminated in the twenty-first century. (Translated by John Ding from Li, Zehou, 1994, pp. 499–503)

Conclusion

Li has attempted to combine the most important aspects of traditional Chinese philosophy with those of Western philosophy and to establish a methodology for the study of philosophy that embraces both Chinese and Western thought. Many students and intellectuals in the early 1980s were fascinated by his erudition, the variety of his academic insights and the poetic diction of his romantic style. There have also been significant and penetrating criticisms of Li from both the left and the right. Critics on the left reject what they consider to be his pseudo-Marxism. Critics on the right condemn him for degenerating into the dogmatism of outworn Marxism. Some critics consider his theoretical frameworks to be a "mixed stew" of Marx, Kant, and other philosophers or, at most, a "creative imitation" of those figures. Others classify him as a contemporary follower of the eclectic school of thought that flourished at the end of the Warring States Period and the beginning of the Han dynasty over two thousand years ago. Furthermore, there are critics who argue that he is always satisfied with a smattering of a subject when he says that philosophy is only an outline, rather than monumental work.

In spite of such criticism, Li's innovative and reforming thought continues to be influential among Chinese intellectuals. Li has touched on many areas of social progress, individual developments and human existence, and even those who criticize his viewpoints have been impressed with the breadth of his examination. Because they are written in Chinese and present a post-Marxist framework for human subjectivity that stands outside the mainstream of Western philosophical development, Li's works are unsurprisingly ignored outside Chinese intellectual circles. It is possible, however, that Western readers who rediscover the problems that Li has examined will be drawn to explore his inventive thought.

Bibliography

Li, Zehou 1957: *Men wai ji* 門外集 (the outdoors), Wuhan: Changjiang Literary & Art Press

Li, Zehou 1958: *Kang Youwei Tan Sitong sixiang shilun* 康有為譚嗣同思想研究 (on the thought of Kang Youwei and Tan Sitong), Shanghai: Shanghai People's Press

Li, Zehou 1979a: *Pipan zhexue di pipan: Kangde shuping* 批判哲學的批判：康德述評 (the critique of critical philosophy: a study of Kant), Beijing: People's Press

Li, Zehou 1979b: *Zhongguo jindai sixiang shilun* 中國近代思想史論 (on pre-modern Chinese thought), Beijing: Beijing People's Press

Li, Zehou 1980: *Meixue lun ji* 美學論集 (essays on aesthetics), Shanghai: Shanghai Literary & Art Press

Li, Zehou 1982: *Mei di li cheng* 美的歷程 (a path of beauty), Beijing: Wenwu Press

Li, Zehou 1983: *A Path of Beauty*, Oxford: Oxford University Press

Li, Zehou & Liu, Gangji 1984: *Zhongguo meixue shi* 中國美學史 (history of Chinese aesthetics), Beijing: Chinese Social Science Press

Li, Zehou 1985a: *Li Zehou zhexue meixue wenxuan* 李澤厚哲學美學文選 (selections from Li Zehou's philosophical and aesthetic works), Changsha: Hunan People's Press

Li, Zehou 1985b: *Wo di zhexue tigang* 我的哲學提綱 (my philosophical outline), Taipei: Taiwan: Sanmin Press

Li, Zehou 1985c: *Zhongguo gudai sixiang shilun* 中國古代思想史論 (on classical Chinese thought), Beijing: Beijing People's Press

Li, Zehou 1986: *Zuo wo ziji di lu* 走我自己的路 (take my own path: essays of Li Zehou), Beijing: Sanlian Press

Li, Zehou 1987a: *Liang han meixue shi* 兩漢美學史 (history of Han dynasty aesthetics), Taipei: Jinfeng Press

Li, Zehou 1987b: *Zhexue bai ti* 哲學百題 (a hundred topics on aesthetics), Taibei: Danqing Press

Li, Zehou 1987c: *Zhongguo xiandai sixiang shilun* 中國現代思想史論 (on modern Chinese thought), Beijing: Beijing Dongfang Press

Li, Zehou 1989a: *Dangdai sichao yu Zhongguo zhihui* 當代思潮與中國智慧 (contemporary thought and Chinese wisdom), Taipei: Fengyunshidai Press

Li, Zehou 1989b: *Huaxia meixue* 華夏美學 (Chinese aesthetics), Beijing: Zhongwai Cultural Press

Li, Zehou 1989c: *Meixue si jiang* 美學四講 (four aesthetic essays), Beijing: Sanlian Press

Li, Zehou 1989d: *Meixue, zhesi, ren* 美學，哲思，人 (aesthetics, philosophical thought, and human beings), Taipei: Fengyunshidai Press

Li, Zehou 1989e: *Wu si: duoyuan de fansi* 多元的反思 (the May Fourth movement: plural thinking), Taipei: Fengyunshidai Press

Li, Zehou & Ru, Xin, eds, 1990: *Meixue baike quanshu* 美學百科全書 (encyclopaedia of aesthetics), Beijing: Social Sciences Documentary Press

Li, Zehou 1991: 美學譯文 (translations on aesthetics), Beijing: Chinese Social Sciences Press

Li, Zehou 1993: *A Study on Marxism in China*, Hong Kong: Joint Publishing

Li, Zehou 1994: *Li Zehou shinian ji, 1979–89* 李澤厚十年集 (ten years of Li Zehou's selected works, 1979–89), 6 vols, Hefei: Anhui Literary and Art Press

Li, Zehou 1998a: *Li Zehou xueshu wenhua suibi* 李澤厚學術文化隨筆 (Li Zehou's academic and informal cultural essays), Beijing: Chinese Youth Press

Li, Zehou 1998b: *Lunyu jindu* 論語今讀 – *Reading the Analects Today*, Hefei: Anhui Literary and Art Press

Li, Zehou 1998c: *Shiji xinmeng* 世紀新夢 – *New Dream of the Century*, Hefei: Anhui Literary and Art Press

Li, Zehou & Liu Zaifu 1999a: *Gaobie geming: ershi shiji duitan lu* 告別革命：二十世紀對談錄 (a critical dialogue on twentieth-century China), Taipei: Maitian Press

Li, Zehou 1999b: *Li Zehou zhexue wencun* 李澤厚哲學文存 (philosophical works of Li Zehou), Hefei: Anhui Literary and Art Press

Li, Zehou 1999c: *Meixue san shu* 美學三書 (three treatises on aesthetics), Hefei: Anhui Literary and Art Press

Li, Zehou 1999d: *Yi mao wu shuo* 已卯五説 (five talks), Beijing: Chinese Dianying Press

Li, Zehou 1999e: *Zhongguo sixiang shilun* 中國思想史論 (on Chinese thought), Hefei: Anhui Literary and Art Press

Li, Zehou 1999f: "歷史眼界與理論的"度"：李澤厚先生訪談錄" ("interview with Mr Li Zehou", *Tianya* 天涯, vol. 2, 1999

Li, Zehou 2000: *Tan xun yu sui* 探尋語碎 (to seek), Shanghai: Shanghai Wenyi Press

Other works

Heidegger, Martin 1962: *Being and Time*, trans. J. MacQuarrie and E. Robinson, Oxford: Blackwell, original work published 1927

Wittgenstein, Ludwig 1922: *Tractatus Logico-Philosophicus*, trans. C. K. Ogden, London: Routledge. Also trans. D. F. Pears and B. McGuinness, London, Routledge 1961

Discussion Questions

1. If we need a post-Marxist philosophy, what should be its character?
2. Should ontology be an "anthropological ontology"?
3. Can we accept Li Zehou's account of subjectivity?
4. What follows from the claim that there is one type of subjectivity (*zhutixing*) for humanity as a whole and another type for personal individuality?
5. What are appropriate roles for construction and deconstruction in philosophy?
6. Should we accept Li Zehou's claim that art is prior to science?
7. How is Chinese aesthetics related to Confucian and Daoist thought?
8. Should we criticize Heidegger's account of *Dasein* for its focus on "being-toward-death" rather than "being-toward-life"?
9. Is Foucault's "genealogy of language" more helpful than his "archeology of knowledge" in furthering Li Zehou's philosophical purposes?
10. Does Wittgenstein's approach to language in his later work help to illuminate Li Zehou's anthropological ontology?

IV

LATER DEVELOPMENTS OF NEW NEO-CONFUCIANISM

13

Fang Dongmei:
Philosophy of Life,
Creativity, and Inclusiveness

Chenyang Li

Born in 1899 in Tong Cheng, Anhui province, China, Fang Dongmei (Thomé H. Fang) was the sixteenth generation descendant of Fang Bao (1668–1749), founder of the Tong Cheng Movement in Chinese literature. His family undoubtedly had a deep influence on his development. He was able to recite the entire *Book of Poetry* when he was only three years old. At sixteen, he attended the University of Nanking and later studied philosophy at University of Wisconsin at Madison, where he received his Ph.D. He also studied Hegel's philosophy at Ohio State University. During his studies in the United States he was greatly influenced by the philosophy of Hegel, Bergson, and Whitehead. This influence is evident in his interpretation of Chinese philosophy and the development of his own philosophical position.

After returning to China in 1924, Fang taught philosophy for fifty years at National Wuchang University, National Southeastern University, Central Institute of Political Sciences, University of Nanking, National Central University, National Taiwan University, and Fu Jen Catholic University. He also held visiting professorships at the State University of South Dakota, University of Missouri, Michigan State University, and Oberlin College. Among his students are such well-established scholars as Chung-ying Cheng and Shu-hsien Liu. He retired from National Taiwan University in 1973 and died in 1977.

Among his philosophy writings are three English publications: *Creativity in Man and Nature* (1980a), *The Chinese View of Life: The Philosophy of Comprehensive Harmony* (1980b), and *Chinese Philosophy: Its Spirit and Its Development* (1981a). His numerous publications in Chinese include *Philosophy of Science and Life* (1936), *Outlines of Chinese Ancient Philosophers' Philosophy of Life* (1937a), *Three Types of Philosophical Wisdom* (1937b), *Creative Virtue and Power* (1979), *The Philosophy of Huayan Buddhism* (1981b), *Eighteen Lectures on Neo-Confucianism* (1983a), *The Philosophy of Primordial Confucianism and Daoism* (1983b), and *Chinese Mahayana Buddhism* (1984). A recent collection of Fang's philosophical works is *Shengmin Lixiang yu Wenhua Liexin* (The Ideal of Life and Cultural Types: Selected Works of Fang Dongmei on Neo-Confucianism), by Chinese Broadcasting and TV Press, Beijing, 1992. It has an informative introduction. A useful interpretative volume of Fang's philosophy is *Philosophy of Thomé H. Fang*, including essays both in English and Chinese, edited by the Executive Committee of the International Symposium on Thomé H. Fang's Philosophy, Youth Cultural Enterprise Co., Ltd., Taipei, 1989.

Fang's General Philosophy

Answering a Westerner's query about his philosophy affiliation, Fang said "I am a Confucian by family tradition; a Daoist by temperament; a Buddhist by religious inspiration; moreover, I am a Westerner by training." Indeed, Fang's philosophy is a combination of all these philosophical traditions.

In an essay that made him famous, "Three Types of Philosophical Wisdom" (1937b), Fang defined philosophy through the study and synthesis of the emotive (*qing*) and the rational (*li*). Following the *Yijing* (*The Book of Change*), Fang maintained that *qing* and *li* emerged from the Ultimate Original, which is unnamable and undescribable. The existence of humankind is rooted in *qing* and *li*. Without *qing* and *li* there can be no philosophy. *Qing* and *li* are mutually determining and interdependent. Philosophy captures the source, truth, and mystery of both *qing* and *li* in their actualities and possibilities. Because there are different degrees of grasping *qing* and *li*, the greatness of philosophers also varies. Fang differentiated between intelligence (*zhi*) and wisdom (*hui*), even though he believed that the two are not entirely separate. Intelligence, according to Fang, is knowledge that is based on reality and accords with *li*. Wisdom, however, is human inspiration or desire (*yu*) that corresponds with *qing* and proceeds in accordance with *li*. He maintained that there are three types of wisdom. One type focuses on learning and knowledge, another on exploratory thinking, and the third on cultivation. Each of these three types of wisdom is an independent system, but Fang considered cultivation to be the highest type.

Fang held that ancient Greek philosophy represents a type of culture that emphasizes truth. Truth was symbolized by Apollo, who was the first of three symbols of the original spirit and ideals of the ancient Greeks. The other two were Dionysius, symbolizing great passion, and Olympian, symbolizing truth and passion in moderation. Fang took Socrates to be the representative of Greek philosophy and argued that Socrates' grave mistake was to make knowledge the only criterion for evaluating virtue, life, and the entire universe. Socrates pushed rationalism to an extreme and lost the Greek ideals symbolized by Dionysius and Olympian. Therefore, Greek philosophy was built solely on *li* (rationality), lacking *qing*. Fang argues that without *qing*, rationality is crippled and that such a philosophy can only wither.

For Fang, modern European philosophy represents the wisdom that searches for utility or usefulness, symbolized by Faust, who passionately endeavored to conquer the world. The weakness of European philosophy, according to Fang, is threefold. First, it puts everything into an unharmonious and uncompromising dualism. Being stuck in deep contradictions, it cannot reach truth. Secondly, European philosophy is obsessed with the quantitative pursuit of trivial details and ignores the interconnectedness of the world. Thirdly, Fang criticized European philosophy for confusing truth and falsity and ending up with nihilism. He held that European philosophy has too much *qing* and not enough *li* to be a balanced and healthy philosophy.

In contrast, Chinese philosophy maintains a balance between *qing* and *li*. Through cultivation, Chinese philosophy aims at a grand harmony in life; it is like a symphony, with all notes contributing to its harmonious unity. This idea of harmonious unity underscores his interpretation of Chinese philosophy as the interplay of various schools of thought, Confucianism being just one of them. Indian culture, Fang maintained, is based on religion, because the Indian tradition was influenced by Hebrew culture. He held that only Chinese culture is authentically eastern (Fang, 1992, pp. 85–106).

Fang's interpretation and evaluation of Greek, European, and Indian philosophies are open to dispute. In his attempt to locate Chinese philosophy at the pivot of world philosophy, he may have judged others in a too harsh and oversimplified fashion. But because Fang worked at a time when comparative philosophy was not as widely studied as it is today, it may have been inevitable for him to proceed as he did.

The concept of Life occupies a central place in Fang's philosophy. He maintained that all Chinese traditions converge on one essential point: they all hold that the universe represents an all-comprehensive Urge of Life, an all-pervading Vital Impetus, that never for a single instant ceases to create and procreate and never in a single place ceases to overflow and interpenetrate (Fang, 1980b, p. 33). He interprets the concept of *sheng sheng* in the *Book of Change* as "Creative Creativity," which symbolizes the vitality of life. The universe is a living entity that cannot be reduced to mere inertial physical stuff. This living universe is full of energy, and everything in it is somehow connected to the living process that penetrates the entire realm. This view may be called a "life-ontology." For Fang, it is more than a "Gaia hypothesis"; it is reality. In this regard, the influence on Fang of Western philosophers such as Hegel, Bergson, and Whitehead is evident:

Throughout the Universe there is an all-pervasive Flux of Life. Whence does it come and whither will it go are the sorts of mysteries that are forever hidden from the knowledge of men. Life in itself is infinite in extent. So from beyond the Infinite, infinite Life comes; and to the Infinite, finite life extends. All is in the process of change and of incessant change, getting and spending inexhaustible energy. It is a path; it is a way, good in its track to be followed by good steps. It is *Dao* in perpetual creative advance. (Fang, 1980b, pp. 12–13)

Another concept central to Fang's philosophy is harmony, or "Comprehensive Harmony." The Chinese, he claimed, hold that the universe is a kind of well-balanced and harmonious system that is materially vacuous but spiritually opulent and unobstructed (Fang, 1980b, p. 35). And the Chinese ideal of life is that of grand harmony: "We keep up with ourselves the supreme excellence of balance and harmony, never tending to be selfish and partial, and never tending to be narrow and stubborn" (Fang, 1980b, p. 39). In Fang's reading of the history of Chinese philosophy, he saw more the harmonious interplay of various schools of thought than conflict. It may be argued that Fang was too idealistic and romantic in his reading of the harmonious interplay of these philosophies, but for him, if harmony was not a reality, it was at least the ideal for the Chinese:

For several thousands of years, we Chinese have been thinking of these vital problems in terms of comprehensive harmony that permeates anything and everything. It sounds like an eternal symphony swaying and swinging all the sky, all the earth, all the air, all the water, merging all forms of existence in one supreme bliss of unity.

In what, by what, toward what, and for what shall man live?

Man lives in Nature where the passage from the Primordial to the Consequent stage is an overflow of Life, getting and spending with inexhaustible energy. Should anyone come in contact with this directional energy from without, he would feel that something has encompassed him with hardness. Like a raindrop falling into the river, it is being borne away and forever lost. Nature encountered by any one individual man in this way is felt to be an encumbrance and blind necessity. But when the drops of water have been deeply merged in the river, they become ingredients of its waves. Now they are one surf, rising and falling in the same rhythm as the lover and the beloved beat their hearts together in the same measure of music.

The force of propulsion in the on-going process of Nature passes into an ideal excess, swinging in concurrent motion, as it is displayed in an elegant dance, full of the sense of joy. The feeling of restraint and compulsion entirely expires in a new ecstasy of freedom. Therefore, Nature, confronting Man as necessity, is finally transformed into communal fellowship fostered through the magic of felicitous sympathy. Nature is a continuous process of creation, and Men are co-creators within the realm of Nature. Nature and human nature are two in one, giving form to what I have called comprehensive harmony, a harmony between ingrowing parts as well as a harmony with surroundings. In this form of primordial unity, all that seems various and antipathetic is so intrinsically related that it strikes together chords to the accompaniment of a song of love, which is an encomium of life. (Fang, 1980b, pp. 11–14)

The third most important concept in Fang's philosophy is the unity of nature and value. He holds that the universe is filled with the attribute of morality and the attribute of art, and it is fundamentally the realm of value. The universe is not a totality of material stuff, but is a living organism laden with value. There is no gap between fact and value. In the Chinese view, "a realm of precious value permeat(es) all forms of existence and await(s) to be enhanced through the creative efforts of men in various walks of life" (Fang, 1980b, p. 43). He subscribed to a kind of pantheism that puts the divine into the natural world. Thus, the world is not only natural, but also spiritual; it is not only fact, but also value:

> We have understood Nature not in the same way in which the Westerners have understood it. Nature, for us, is that infinite realm wherein the universal flux of life is revealing itself and fulfilling everything with its intrinsic worth. Nature is infinite in the sense that it is not limited by anything that is beyond and above it, which might be called Supernature. The fullness of reality in Nature does not prejudice against the potency of God, for the miraculous creation may be continually accomplished within it. Nor is there any gulf between Nature and human nature inasmuch as human life is interpenetrating with the cosmic life as a whole.
>
> Furthermore, man's mission of cultural creations in different realms of art, literature, science, religion, and social institutions is being carried on so as to bring any imperfections that there may be in Nature and Man into ideal perfection. Thus we see that the magnificence of Nature is linked up with the glory of Man through the development of culture. History, as the unfolding of the fine spirit of culture, is Man writ large and Nature writ beautiful.
>
> (. . . .)
>
> It gushes out and swells forth in the form of primordial Nature that is the essence of the Good. Being so good that it excels all in value, it must be the transcendental, nay, the transcendent. The *Dao* is the Infinite endlessly continuing itself into the infinite in the form of Consequent Nature that is the fulfillment of the Good. Being so good in its way that it brings all creative forces under its sway, it must be the immanent – the Creator revealing creativity in the created. Hence between Primordial Nature and Consequent Nature, there is a nexus, a chain of creations constituting the cosmic order.
>
> Such a theory of Nature as creative advance has been best expressed in the *Book of Change* in which you also find the following statement: "The fulfillment of Nature which is life in perpetual creativity is the gate of Wisdom bodying forth the value of *Dao* and the principle of righteousness." From this you can see that, according to the Chinese philosophical tradition, a system of ontology is also a theory of value. All forms of existence are charged with intrinsic worth. Nothing in the entire universe is void of meaning. Everything is valuable as it is, since it participates in that Universal life which is immortal in virtue of its infinite ideal of perfection and its eternal continuity of creation. (Fang, 1980b, pp. 11–13)

Therefore, in Fang's view, truth, goodness, and beauty are a unity; *qing* (the emotive) and *li* (the rational) are connected. Indeed, Fang's moral philosophy is established on his "life-ontology":

> Morality is the essence of life inasmuch as it is the concrete embodiment of the values of life. . . . We are not living merely for the sake of living. . . . What we really want in life is to elevate it into the plane of ideal perfection in which we can augment its value by doing what is good as a step to the attainment of what is better and best. We must live for the realization of supreme value. (Fang, 1980b, pp. 102–3)

This philosophy is also called "value-centered-ontology" (Fang, 1992, p. 494). His "life-ontology" and "value-centered-ontology" are directly connected because, for him, life is value and both life and value are rooted in the *dao*. The *dao*, as the all-encompassing and all-pervading unity, is the ultimate source of life, value, and harmony:

> The great *Dao* that is the primordial source of life is all-pervasive in the universe and is, therefore, not limited to any particular boundary. In the words of Zhuangzi, "Heaven, Earth, and I are living together, and all things and I form an inseparable unity." "Notwithstanding the greatness of heaven and earth, their transforming power proceeds from one lathe; notwithstanding the infinite varieties of things, their conduct of life is one and the same." "The Pivot of *Dao* lying in the very centre of the Cosmos can readily respond to the infinite variety of things." "The *Dao* is an all-pervading unity. . . . And all things in the process of change and transformation are comprehended in this unity. It is only the wise who is fully aware of this." "It is the *Dao* that overspreads and sustains all things. How great It is in its overflowing influences! . . . . The excellent men ought by all means to be free from narrow-mindedness. Action without attachment to the fruits thereof is what is called Spontaneity. Utterance without egocentricity is what is called Excellence. Loving men and benefiting things are what is called Benevolence. The reconciliation of differences is what is called Greatness. The conduct that is entirely free from perversity is what is called Generosity. The possession of infinite variety of attributes is what is called Plenitude. . . . The complete accordance with *Dao* is what is called Perfection." The fine spirit bodied forth by these statements is congruous with the Confucian attempt to conceive all things under the form of an all-pervading unity. (Fang, 1980b, pp. 50–1)

Fang's interpretation is grounded in his selective reading of Chinese classics. For him, *dao* as the source of life and value is a given rather than something to be argued for; the unity of life and value is to be evident in actual life experience, rather than the implication of logical argument. He thus left out any answer to the Nietzschean question of "why be good?"

Fang's Interpretation of Chinese Classic Philosophy

Like most Chinese philosophers of his time, Fang's philosophical work pro-
ceeded mostly through his interpretation of traditional Chinese philosophy.
Although he has been regarded as a contemporary New-Confucian along with
Mou Zongsan, Tang Junyi, and Liang Shuming, Fang's work stands beyond the
Confucian tradition. Unlike Mou Zongsan, Fang did not regard Confucianism
as the only legitimate philosophy and all others as heresies; he argued that
Laozi's Daoism was the leading and most legitimate philosophical school
during ancient times (Fang, 1992, pp. 476–7). Fang saw Confucianism, Daoism,
Mohism, and Buddhism as mutually interacting and integrating compon-
ents of a holistic cultural process, rather than as several distinct schools of
thought. Among the six Confucian classics, the *Book of Poetry*, the *Book of
History*, the *Book of Music*, *Li Ji*, the *Book of Change*, and the *Spring and Autumn
Annals*, Fang regarded the *Book of Change* as the foundation of all learning
(Fang, 1992, pp. 472–3). He correctly rendered the "*Yijing*" as the "*Book
of Change*" instead of the "*Book of Changes*," because "*yi*" as a philosophical
concept stands for the ontological status of change rather than ontic acts of
change. He did not hold that the *Book of Change* is solely a Confucian classic,
but claimed that it is also Daoist (Fang, 1992, p. 479). In addition to the
Book of Change, he regarded the *Book of History*, particularly the chapter of
"*Hongfan: Jiuchou* (Grand Matrix of the Ninefold Categories)," as a central
classic in the Confucian tradition.

Fang argued that primordial Confucianism, primordial Daoism, and Mahayana
Buddhism, diverse as they are, possess in common three important features. First,
they all subscribe to the doctrine of pervasive unity, believing that the universe
is one and that the ultimate truth is one. Accordingly, reality is not divided into
dualistic segments. This Oneness may be called the *bodhi-dao*. Secondly, they
all accept the doctrine of *dao*, even though their interpretations vary greatly.
The Confucians recognize the *dao* of Heaven, the *dao* of Earth, and the *dao*
of Man. The Daoist *dao* is "the mysteriously mysterious Mystery." Mahayana
Buddhism approaches the *dao* through the principle of nullity, which is a prelude to the principle of realization. Thirdly, all three schools purport to exalt
the individual. In *Chinese Philosophy: Its Spirit and Its Development*, he wrote:

> We think of the human individual in terms of observed actualities and idealized
> possibilities. From actuality to possibility, there is an elaborate process of self-
> development, an arduous task of self-(cultivation) as well as a full range of self-
> realization. (Fang, 1981a, p. 27)

Thus, between the two paths of self-abnegation and self-approbation, the Chinese
traditions emphasize a third way, that is, self-development and self-realization
(Fang, 1981a, pp. 23–8).

In his typically poetic language, Fang spoke highly of all three philosophies. Daoists turn everything that is relative and limited within the cogwheel of special conditions into Nothing, a spontaneously adorned Nothing that is absolutely infinite, a mystery that is inscrutably profound, a Nothing that is "really real Reality" in the form of a dynamo generative of everything. Confucians begin where Daoists end. In sharp contrast, Confucians confront Nothing at the wide open gate of the heavenly *dao*, whose magic touch of creation has the marvelous power of transmuting it into everything which is not once diminished but is always augmented. In Confucianism, a boundless horizon of creative advance is spread before humankind for its partaking of this infinitude, for its participation in the continual creativity of creation, and for its assumption of a pivotal position in the universe of dynamical transformation. The Confucian conception of the world is homocentric, which early Buddhism found unacceptable. Allied with Daoism, early Buddhism drew the human interest of life to the transcendent world for an assured satisfaction. Later Buddhism, however, came to see the strong points of Confucianism and found in it a spiritual affinity in affirming the perfection of human nature in the form of Buddha–nature. Buddhists set their eyes on the final destiny of humankind and the universal emancipation of all beings in the future. Fang called the Confucian the "Time-man," because the Confucian "cast(s) all conceivable realities into the mould of dynamical transformation." He called the Daoist the "Space-man," because the Daoist "soar(s) high up into the unobstructed acme of the Celestial where the realm of eternity is transfigured into the enjoyed space of lyrical art, and especially of romantic poetry, contemplated by the spirit all at once." "The Buddhist starts searching into the bottomless pit of incessant change which swallows up the world – all in blunder and suffering and thus regards eternity as nil while, after swinging through the loop of the defiled, he sweeps everything clean and rejoices at the fullness of the *Dharma* conceived, once again, under the form of eternity." Therefore the Buddhist is the Space-Time-man, with an alternative sense of forgetting (Fang, 1981a, p. 34).

Fang distinguished between two phases of primordial Confucianism. In the first phase, Confucianism accepted a primeval heritage and tried to bring it to bear on rational philosophy. In the second phase, it constructed a profound system of thought, which was followed by Han Confucianism as the third phase. The most important document in the second phase is the *Book of Change*. Fang maintained that the philosophy of change as found in the *Book of Change* includes four principles. The first is the Principle of Life; life embraces within itself all beings and creatures interwoven with, and connected to, the great path of *dao*. The second is the Principle of Extensive Connection; the world is an organic whole, in which everything is profoundly interconnected. The third is the Principle of Creative Creativity; he quotes the *Book of Change* that "of all values, the Good exhibited in the primordially creative-procreative is towering in its supremacy." The fourth is the Principle of Creative Life as a Process of Value-Realization; the universe is "an all-comprehensive urge of life and all-pervading vital energy, not for a single moment ceasing to create and procreate and not in a single spot ceasing to overflow and interpenetrate."

> (F)rom beyond the infinite primordial creative power, the infinite Life comes; and to the ultimate infinite consequence, the finite Life of every form extends. All is in the process of change and of incessant change, getting and spending inexhaustible energy. It is the heavenly *Dao* in perpetual creative advance, gushing out and swelling forth in the form of the primordial creativity that is the essence of the Good excelling all relative values in worth. (Fang, 1981a, p. 112)

Fang's Critique of Song-Ming Neo-Confucianism

Fang's interpretation of classic Chinese philosophy set criteria for his evaluation of philosophers and philosophical works in general. While he gave the *Book of Change* a very high score and often drew from it, he held that Confucius' *Analects*, which has been the "Bible" for later Confucians, is at best a "moralogy" and cannot represent the whole thought of Confucius (Fang, 1992, pp. 454–6). He praised Confucius for incorporating into his own philosophy the thought from various other schools, but criticized Mencius for being intolerant toward philosophers who held different views. For instance, Mencius attacked Mohism, which had important achievements in science, religion, and philosophy (Fang, 1992, p. 437). In Fang's view, Mencius' example of narrow-mindedness and initiation of the idea of an orthodox tradition had very negative influence on later Confucians. Fang denounced the Han Confucian philosopher Dong Zhongshu for his failure to understand the Confucian classics, the *Book of History* and the *Book of Change*, for his failure to understand the overall trend of ancient Chinese thought, and for his attempts to glorify Confucianism and to eliminate all other doctrines (Fang, 1992, p. 439).

In his later years, Fang developed a significant interest in Song–Ming Neo-Confucianism. He held that these Confucians had great achievements in reviving the ancient culture. He praised them for upholding the most fundamental Confucian idea of the unity of nature and humanity and for their dedication to their noble cause instead of materialistic gains. Nevertheless, he also criticized them for being narrow-minded, mainly because of their hostility towards Buddhism. Although Fang expressed great appreciation of Ming Neo-Confucianism, his view of Song Neo-Confucianism was generally critical. In his Fifth Lecture on Neo-Confucianism, he wrote:

> The weakness of Song Neo-Confucianism is that its life spirit is closing, retreating, not exploring and expanding. The best cure for this kind of cultural disease

is to borrow the spirit of Daoism. Some Song Neo-Confucians may not admit this problem. Then listen to the Qing Neo-Confucian Chinese classicist Dai Dongyuan, who said, "the Song Neo-Confucians kill people under the name of '*li*'. Killed this way, there is no hope for rescue." Dai may have overstated it, but his words are directed to the Song Neo-Confucian problem of over-adherence to *li*. It makes one think deeply on this matter.

The Song Neo-Confucians go overboard with their adherence to *li*. They try to eliminate all human desires, feelings, and sentiments, including the good ones. This is a one-sided philosophy. It cannot integrate with literature, poetry, art, and the open spirit of other general culture. This way, it easily becomes a withering philosophical system. It makes it even worse to uphold the idea of the orthodox heir of tradition. It is a vital injury to its philosophical thought. Therefore, I think the philosophical spirit of Daoism and that of Confucianism should deeply integrate together. If so, Confucianism must uphold the idea of "becoming one with Heaven and Earth and being open to myriad things." Advocating "the unity of Heaven and Earth," the Daoist Zhuangzi says "I live with Heaven and Earth, and I am one with myriad things." Both Confucianism and Daoism were prominent schools during the time of Warring States. There was no problem of "the orthodox heir of tradition," and they shared the same view without planning to do so. But later Han Confucians were influenced by the Yin-Yang school, the Five-Element School, and eclecticism. They devalued positive artistic values, moral values, and religious sacred values in the universe. After this devaluation, the world is but a materialistic system as viewed by the Yin-Yang scholars and the Five-Element scholars. Therefore, precious values were neglected. Song Neo-Confucians oppose Han Confucianism in name, while they accept the doctrines of the Yin-Yang school and the Five-Element school. They gradually turned the system of value of the universe into a realm without value. Afterwards, experiencing the collapse of society during the Wei-Jin times and the abundant evil in the society of the later Tang and Five Dynasties, the Song Neo-Confucians developed a narrow-minded and resentful mentality. Therefore, I think, if the Song Neo-Confucians want to mend this defect, they not only need to accept the Daoist spirit, but also need not to misunderstand the Buddhist spirit. (Fang, 1992, pp. 507–8)

Fang divides Song–Ming Neo-Confucianism into three types. Philosophers of the first type were realists, represented by Zhou Dunyi, Zhang Zai, Cheng Hao, Cheng Yi, and Zhu Xi. Fang considered Zhou to be an important philosopher and claimed that his *Insight into the Book of Change* brought together the *Book of Change*, the *Grand Matrix of Ninefold Categories*, and the *Doctrine of the Mean*. Fang held that in doing so Zhou established a system of dynamic ontology, an axiological unity, and a picture of the progressive course of life. Fang argued that another major work by Zhou Dunyi, the *Schema and Explanation of the Great Ultimate*, is actually a Daoist work, mistaken by Zhu Xi to be Confucian (Fang, 1992, p. 495). In contrast, Cheng Yi, according to Fang, was baffled by dualistic thinking. Philosophers of the second type were idealists, represented by Lu Xiangshan and Wang Yangming. These philosophers considered the mind to be the fulcrum of all existence. Philosophers of the third type were naturalists or materialists, represented by Wang Tingxiang and Wang Fuzhi.

In Fang's view, Song–Ming Neo-Confucianism was simply not authentic Confucianism. He criticized these philosophers for fighting among themselves over the orthodox tradition of Confucianism and their claims to the sole legitimacy in interpreting Confucianism. Fang dismissed Song Neo-Confucian claims concerning an orthodox tradition as "historically unfounded" and strongly opposed it. He also maintained that Song Neo-Confucians were heavily influenced by Daoism and Buddhism and that they unfairly attempted to undermine these two philosophies (Fang, 1992, pp. 480, 483).

There is one crucial difference between the thought of Fang and that of the Song–Ming Neo-Confucians: whereas Fang's central concept is life, the Song–Ming Neo-Confucians based their philosophy on *li* or the righteous principle of the cosmos. Fang was critical of the narrow Song–Ming Neo-Confucian adherence to *li*. In placing *li* in opposition to emotion, sentiment, and human desires, they formed a Chinese "Puritan" philosophy. Unlike Confucius, Song–Ming Neo-Confucians eliminated the elements of art and literature from philosophy. In Fang's view, the narrow focus on *li* and their exclusion of all other elements was a fatal defect in their thought. In order to remedy this flaw, Neo-Confucianism must learn from Daoism and Buddhism.

Now, was Fang a Neo-Confucian? His thought certainly differed from that of many contemporary Confucians. Mou Zongsan followed the Confucian tradition of Mencius, Lu Xiangshan, and Wang Yangming. Feng Youlan asked whether today one should speak according to Song–Ming Neo-Confucianism or further develop it. Feng's New Principle Philosophy developed on the basis of Song–Ming *li* philosophy, but also went beyond it. Although they differed in many ways, both Mou and Feng were within the Confucian tradition. They both argued for the legitimacy of Confucianism as the orthodox philosophy of Chinese culture. Fang asked a different question, namely whether to philosophize within or beyond the Confucian tradition, and he chose to form his thought beyond Confucianism. He openly accepted Laozi's Daoism as the leading school of thought – or the orthodox school of Chinese culture – in the ancient time (Fang, 1992, pp. 477–8). He openly embraced the value of Buddhism. While criticizing Song–Ming Neo-Confucianism for being narrow-minded, he maintained that the path of future Confucianism must "start with and follow the *Book of Change*, borrow from Laozi and Zhuangzi, and learn from Mozi" (Fang, 1992, p. 474). Perhaps his early statement about his philosophical affiliation should be taken at face value: Fang was a Confucian-Buddhist-Daoist who was influenced by Western thought.

Excerpts from Fang's Publications

Cosmology

The universe which is congenial to our philosophical nature has been properly characterized as (*a*) the confluence of universal life in the mode of perpetual creativity, (*b*) a system of finite substantial forms magically transmuted into ideally infinite spiritual functions, and (*c*) a realm of precious values permeating all forms of existence and waiting to be enhanced through the creative efforts of men in various walks of life. The universe thus characterized can only be adequately understood through a set of fundamental principles that I have tried to develop elsewhere. Here I enunciate them in summary as the following.

(1) Principle of Life. Life embraces within itself all beings and creatures interwoven with, and enlinked to, the great path of *Dao*. In its fulfillment through change and transmutation it roots itself in Primordial Nature, which is the spring of inexhaustible energy, and passes through the steps of creative advance into Consequent Nature, which is the achievement of the Supreme Good. As a universal active substance, Life manifests itself in Space and, withal, conquers its limitations by the great momentum of the infinite creative urge. It is energetic in nature but reposed in visage. As a never-ending function, life gushes out in Time, propelling and expanding it into infinity. It is dynamic in propulsion and progression, but static in subsistence and continuum.

Universal life is imbued with five excellent qualities: (*a*) fulfillment through generation of new species; (*b*) expansion through ever-new achievements; (*c*) perpetual creativity; (*d*) emergence of novelty from what is already accomplished in the continual process of change and transformation; (*e*) efficacious efforts to attain to actual immortality, the state of creative creativity which perpetually goes on and never comes to an end. (For the sake of space, not included here is Fang's elaboration of *a*, *b*, *c*, *d*, and *e*.)

(2) Principle of Love (Erotic Impulse). The spirit of life gives expression to the spirit of love. The sentiment of love bears the semblance of universal change whereby the motive of comely life is actuated and the relation of affective unity is established among all beings in the world through the rhythmic movements of Yin and Yang. What is here called love is just the intimate communion in intensified emotional contrasts, like the convection of opposite electric charges across a spark-gap. It is a universal process wherein Heaven and Earth lead all things to play important parts in the sport of bliss. The strong and the tender supervene upon each other concordantly; men and women are happily consorted; creatures of different nature are congruently concerted; and societies and institutions are beautifully interfused and interwoven. In a word, life of all forms is fulfilled and the value of all kinds is achieved through the spirit of love.

Thus the phenomena of love may be classified under six different forms: (*a*) the mutual embracement of Yin and Yang; (*b*) the union of male and female; (*c*) the matrimony of man and woman; (*d*) the congruous illumination of the sun and the moon; (*e*) the happy interaction of heaven and earth; and (*f*) the established order of Qian and Kun, representing the powers of origination and procreation.

There are four fundamental properties of love: (*a*) communion through adverse contrast; (*b*) alluring admiration; (*c*) fellowship in unity through intercommunication; (*d*) eternity of love. (For the sake of space, not included here is Fang's elaboration of *a*, *b*, *c*, and *d*.)

(3) Principle of Creative Advance. Life is the primordial active substance exhibiting itself in the mode of creative advance. The primordial substance is one, but is not limited to being one. Therefore it diversifies itself into Qian and Kun, which are the powers of origination and procreation pertaining to Heaven and earth. The former is always dynamic; the latter is static in a way. Through the combined operation of these two powers, universal life is to be fulfilled and all beings are to be completed. Moreover, the primordial substance of life performs its splendid function in the steps of creative advance. It flushes into the rhythmic movements of Yin and Yang, which concentrate their energies so as to expand them all the more fervidly. The stupendous expenditure of these energies in the midst of modulation gives rise to formations of concord and harmony in which all things live and move and have their being. The great function of life is the nexus of existence running through heaven, earth, men, and all things. The power of origination, being continued into that of procreation, penetrates into infinite varieties of life, brings them along and leads them to the final destination of immortality. This is the fundamental chord of creative advance.

(4) Principle of Primordial Unity. The substance of life is primarily one to be magically transmuted into origination, whose functioning takes various forms and issues in infinite varieties of entities. Laozi tells us: "The *Dao* produced One; One produced Two; Two produced Three; Three produced All things." *Dao* as the fundamental root of life is the original begetter, bringing into existence that which is begotten, which, in turn, is also a begetter of the further begotten. Thus the universal life comprised in the *Dao* is an iterative process of creativity, generative of the unlimited variety of things. The infinite variety of things is evidently a plurality. But if we get to the bottom of reality, all things embraced within Life stand in a universal context of essential relativity and form an inseparable unity. According to the Chinese Philosophy of Change, the universe is an array of activities subsumed under the form of One. This is also the reason why Laozi has told us to hold all things within the one embrace of *Dao*. The entire Universe is permeated with life every form of which, while partaking of the original One, comes to achieve the specific oneness of its own. Thus the manifolds of the specific ones, taken in summation, constitute a system of the many, namely, pluralities which, through the ingression of the original One and by the mutual implication of essential relativity among the many, must ultimately enter into the enriched form of a higher unity. Wang Pi's statement that "comprised in the form of unity and consolidated by the power of origination, all things are orderly and unmistakable despite their variance and multiplicity" is a good characterization of the mysterious *Dao* as revealed in the universal process of change.

(5)   Principle of Equilibrium and Harmony. This cardinal principle is the true embodiment of Chinese spirit and the nice measure of Chinese culture. It is vindicated by the Philosophy of Change. It is imbued in Chinese music and poetry. It regulates Chinese history and social customs. And, furthermore, it shapes the rules of conduct and the ideals of political life. Equilibrium expresses the spirit of impartiality; harmony exhibits the relation of essential relativity. They are to be conceived in terms of the following characteristics: (*a*) thorough-going equality; (*b*) equity and unselfishness; (*c*) permeation by empathy and sympathy; (*d*) ideal representation through ethereal vacuity or eidetic freedom; (*e*) comprehension of all things in the unity of *Dao*. (For the sake of space, not included here is Fang's elaboration of *a*, *b*, *c*, *d*, and *e*.)

(6)   Principle of Extensive Connection. The great function of universal change and the constant procedure of all-comprehensive *Dao* are intelligible only in the light of the principle of extensive connection. Taken all in all, the principle comprises the following set of characteristics: (*a*) the concatenated order of life in the mode of creative creativity; (*b*) the mutual relevance of all forms of existence in respect of the inherent possession of meaning and value; (*c*) the never-ending process of change and transformation issuing in the emergence of novelty; and (*d*) a thread of connection running through all forms of life, which, by reason of mutual relevance and interpenetration, constitute the integrative Universe. The universal process of change, exhibiting the creative advance of *Dao*, comprehends as in a mould the transformation of Heaven and Earth without failure and completes, by an ever-ready adaptation, the nature of all things without exception. As it embraces all, it is said to be great and extensive in the way of appropriate functioning.

Such a principle of extensive connection has been most elaborately elucidated in the *Book of Change*, the profound meaning of which is too technical to expound here. There are, however, three essential features to be noted. Logically, it is a system of deduction demonstrated by reason of a set of rigorous rules. Semantically, it is a syntax of language in which the rules of formation and transformation of significant statements are carefully worked out. Philosophically, it is a system of dynamic ontology based upon the principle of perpetual creativity as exhibited in the incessant change of Time as well as in a system of general axiology in which the origin and development of the idea of supreme Good is shown in the light of comprehensive harmony. All of these features bear out the fundamental principle of extensive connection. (Fang, 1980b, pp. 43–52)

Moral philosophy

In his appraisal of the values of life, Laozi always traces them back to the primordial root of life for the purpose of showing that *Dao* together with *De* is a living spring of moral excellence, ever running out with benevolence, justice, and propriety. Any attempt to reverse the order by laying the emphasis merely upon benevolence, justice, and propriety apart from their origin in the *Dao* would be a blunder.

Confucius, Mencius, and almost all Confucians of later periods try to elucidate the meanings of benevolence, justice, propriety, and wisdom on the basis of the nature which has been conferred by Heaven for the reason that, setting aside the fundamental root of life, there will be no possibility of any proper moral evaluation.

And Mozi, not being so metaphysical as the thinkers of the other two schools, also develops his theory of universal love on the assumption that Heaven likes to have the world live. Thus it is that Heaven's will to live is the foundation-stone of human morality.

Through the above discussions we come to see that the metaphysical foundation of morality is, in point of method, spirit, and fundamental principle, quite the same for the three predominant schools of Chinese philosophy, namely, Daoism, Confucianism, and the theory of Mozi. It is rather unfortunate, I think, for the philosophers themselves to have been unaware of such an important spiritual unity as is vindicated in the above.

We have already demonstrated that the foundation of morality is to be found in the universal life that is permeated with values. Now let us inquire into the nature of the common moral standard. Why should we have morality? And in what spirit shall we put this morality into practice? Morality is the essence of life inasmuch as it is the concrete embodiment of the values of life. As we Chinese have a vehement love for life, a reverence for life, we are quite unwilling to look upon it as a set of blind impulses. For the edification of life we must deliberately appeal to the supreme ideals that are to be perfectly realized through the utmost of our efforts. We are not living merely for the sake of living. Any creature can do that, however rude and ruthless the mode of life may be. What we really want in life is to elevate it into the plane of ideal perfection in which we can augment its value by doing what is good as a step to the attainment of what is better and best. We must live for the realization of supreme value. (Fang, 1980b, pp. 102–3)

Political philosophy

According to the Chinese Classics, the word "*cheng*" (politics) means many things, namely, correctness, straightness, straightening, being-in-right-direction, rectification, rectitude, edification, and lawfulness. Hence the original meaning of politics is the correction of what is wrong, the straightening-up of what is crooked through moral rectification, cultural edification, and conformity to law. What is called statute, order, command, ordinance, prohibition, or punishment only indicates its derivative meaning.

The political thought of Chinese philosophers about ideal politics is centered round three different types of government: (a) government by virtue; (b) government by cultural refinement; and (c) government by law. But government by fraudulent tricks and government by coercive force are too corrupt to be worthy of mention here. In general, the primordial Daoists and the primordial Confucians and the Mohists all approve of (a); Later Confucians are inclined to hold to a combined form of (a) and (b); the Legalists abide by (c); but some members of the later Legalist school are so degenerate as to fall into the trap of tactics by setting aside the validity of law. (Fang, 1980b, p. 152)

To proceed from the Spirit of Heaven and to extend it over to the spirit of men for the sake of practising affectionate universal love – this is the fundamental political thought in the system of primordial Confucianism. And later Confucians from the period of Han onwards have all regarded extensive love as the fundamental spirit underlying political life. This is clearly evidenced by the voluminous writings of any array of thinkers such as Jia Yi, Dong Zhongshu, Yang Xiong, Cheng Hao, Cheng Yi, Zhu Xi, Lu Xiangshan, Wang Yangming, Wang Fuzhi, Dai Zheng, Jiao Xun, and others.

The reasons that underlie the Confucian conception of political life may be enunciated as follows:

(a)   Confucius and the Confucians that follow in his footsteps are the pure type of the Chinese people. The Chinese look upon man and the universe as one inseparable confluence of universal life in which Man and Nature, men among themselves, and men and other things stand in a harmonious relation of essential relativity whereof any relatum cannot go without its converse. We live and move and have our complete being on the necessary condition that the universe, men, and other things are all at one in the creative steps of advance. And, therefore, we cannot fail to go deep into the experience of life, seeking after its fundamental root, in order to express our comprehensive and profound sympathy to the beings that are so intimately connected with us. All the noble motives for the love of men naturally find their adequate expression in political activities which, when elevated into the ideal plane, will be in keeping with the benevolent spirit that is in Heaven or with the supreme good that has been bestowed upon men by Nature.

(b)   The State is a perennial field of moral activities. The concrete values of human life, when borne away by imagination to the transcendent heavenly paradise, will be too high up in the air as to be unrealizable in this world, and, again, if kept within the confine of the actual human individual, will be too egocentric and narcissistic to be of any benefit to mankind. The only sure ground, on which human beings can exert themselves to accomplish their great tasks and have the good intention to overrun and conquer the narrow sphere of self-interests by striving after that form of enlarged existence in which the greatest happiness of the greatest number can be achieved, is the State.

To obtain this objective in view, inasmuch as we are actual beings in this actual world chained to its limitations and imperfections, we have to overcome many difficulties that stand in our way through effort, courage, perseverance, and sagacity; to set ourselves free from self-bondage, for one thing, and from social constraint and enslavement, for another; and, in short, to transcend any imperfection that weighs us down either from within or from without. When all this has been done, we can escape above from the fatality below and behold the light of day in perfect freedom and happiness.

Thus, political life in a State provides, as it were, a "ladder-way," through the instrumentality of which we can, in one direction, descend down to the bottom of the world of actuality and, in another, ascend and reach up to the heavenly height of ideal perfection. Ideal politics is the endeavour to frame a scheme of life in which the gap between actuality and ideality may be bridged over.

The useful function of government by virtue is to promote this fascinating scheme.

(c) The Chinese, again, conceive the universe and political society to be of the same pattern, namely, the ideal realm of balance and equilibrium or the beautiful prospect of great harmony. When we observe the universe, we are fascinated by its beauty; when we enter into the experience of life, we must rectify our moral nature. Hence the framework of political organization in which the nobleness of human nature is to be displayed must be patterned upon the beautiful melody of poetry and the congruous harmony of music. Only in this way can human beings enter into an intimate fellowship of sympathetic unity enjoying to the utmost the excellent virtues of love and benevolence. (Fang, 1980b, 156–8)

(Quotations from Fang, 1992, are in my own translation. Quotations and excerpts from Fang, 1980b and Fang, 1981a are taken from Fang's original English publications, although I have made some changes.)

Bibliography

Fang, Thomé 1936: *Kexue zhexue yu rensheng* 科學哲學與人生 (philosophy of science and life), Shanghai: Shangwu Publishing House

Fang, Thomé 1937a: *Zhongguo xianzhe rensheng zhexue gaiyao* 中國先哲人生哲學概要 (outlines of ancient Chinese philosophers' philosophy of life), Shanghai: Shangwu Publishing House

Fang, Thomé 1937b: *Zhexue sanhui* 哲學三慧 (three types of philosophical wisdom), Taipei: Sanmin Shuju

Fang, Thomé 1979: *Shengsheng zhide* 生生之德 (creative virtue and power), Taipei: Limin Wenhua Shiye Gongsi

Fang, Thomé 1980a: *Creativity in Man and Nature: A Collection of Philosophical Essays*, Taipei: Linking Publishing

Fang, Thomé 1980b: *The Chinese View of Life: The Philosophy of Comprehensive Harmony*, Taipei: Linking Publishing

Fang, Thomé 1981a: *Chinese Philosophy: Its Spirit and Its Development*, Taipei: Linking Publishing

Fang, Thomé 1981b: *Huayan zong zhexue* 華嚴宗哲學 (the philosophy of Huayan Buddhism), Taipei: Limin Wenhua Shiye Gongsi

Fang, Thomé 1983a: *Xin rujia zhexue shiba jiang* 新儒家哲學十八講 (eighteen lectures on Neo-Confucianism), Taipei: Limin Wenhua Shiye Gongsi

Fang, Thomé 1983b: *Yuanshi rujia daojia zhexue* 原始儒家道家哲學 (the philosophy of primordial Confucianism and Daoism), Taipei: Limin Wenhua Shiye Gongsi

Fang, Thomé 1984: *Zhongguo dacheng fojiao* 中國大乘佛學 (Chinese Mahayana Buddhism), Taipei: Limin Wenhua Shiye Gongsi

Fang, Thomé 1992: *Shengmin lixiang yu wenhua liexin* 生命理想與文化類型：方東美新儒學論著輯要 (the ideal of life and cultural types: selected works of Fang Dongmei on Neo-Confucianism), Beijing: Chinese Broadcasting and TV Press

Executive Committee of the International Symposium on Thomé H. Fang's Philosophy, ed. 1989: *Fang Dongmei de zhexue* (philosophy of Thomé H. Fang), Taipei: Youth Cultural Enterprise

Discussion Questions

1. Should philosophy seek to combine the emotional and the rational?
2. How should we assess Fang Dongmei's claim that different cultures have produced different types of wisdom?
3. Is comprehensive harmony a more important philosophical goal than truth or utility?
4. Is Fang Dongmei a Confucian?
5. What difference does it make to view Confucianism as only one of many schools of Chinese philosophy rather than as the main orthodoxy?
6. Can we accept Fang Dongmei's account of the *dao*?
7. How should we understand "Creative Creativity"?
8. Is there a gap between fact and value?
9. Should ontology be a "life-ontology"?
10. Should we accept the judgment that the Song Neo-Confucians killed people under the name of "*li*"?

14

Practical Humanism of Xu Fuguan

Peimin Ni

Together with Tang Junyi, Mou Zongsan, and Carsun Chang, Xu Fuguan signed the famous 1958 "Manifesto for a Re-appraisal of Sinology and Reconstruction of Chinese Culture" (Chang, 1962, pp. 455–83). Unlike his cosigners, who devoted themselves to scholarship, Xu placed himself between politics and scholarship. While the intellectual work of his cosigners was entirely devoted to constructing their own versions of New-Confucianism, Xu's scholarly activity was diversified, ranging over philosophy, history, literature, politics, and art criticism. His philosophical theory, compared to the others, was less systematic and metaphysical. All of these aspects are indications of Xu's own philosophical position. He held that one of the greatest features of the Chinese philosophical tradition is its deep concern for human reality and its active embodiment in real life. His method of scholarship was to "rake the sand" in order to "find the gold" that was scattered in different areas of study in history and to reveal and restore their original connections. His aim was to capture the spirit of Chinese cultural tradition that links all of its parts together so that its intrinsic values can be revealed, revitalized, and reappropriated, rather than to construct a theoretical system to force upon the tradition.

Xu was born in 1903 in a farmer's family in Hubei province, China. In response to a suggestion from Xiong Shili, he replaced his original given name of Binchang with Fuguan, taken from a line in Laozi's *Daodejing* "All things come into being, and I see [*guan*] thereby their return [*fu*]." His adopted name can serve as a concentrated autobiography because his life returned to examine the root of Chinese tradition after a great excursion. Xu joined the army in his youth to rescue his country from crises provoked by foreign invasions. He was promoted to the level of major general and came close to the center of political power. Yet he was deeply disappointed with politicians. Convinced by Xiong Shili that "those who lose their own nation and nationality usually first lose their culture," he voluntarily retired from his powerful political–military post and, from his late forties, devoted himself to the critical evaluation and revitalization of Chinese cultural tradition. This decision took place in an era when the political conflict between China and the foreign powers molded the conflict between Chinese and Western cultures, so much so that "those who were against Western culture did it more from nationalistic senti- ments than from critical evaluation of Western culture itself, and those who were against Chinese culture did it more from admiration of Western powers than from reflections of Chinese culture itself" (Xu, 1980, p. 423). In his youth, Xu was attracted to the position of Lu Xun, the "flag man" of the May Fourth Movement, who was extremely critical of the Chinese cultural tradition. For a time, Xu refused to read any traditional Chinese "thread-bound books." "To transcend resentfulness to moral courage in culture and scholarship was an existential decision made by master Xu, after his awakening through reflection on the root of Chinese wisdom," says Tu Wei-ming (1983). But instead of turning himself into a mere observer and commentator, he remained an active and passionate participant in social and political life through his posts as a journal editor, university professor, and writer until his death at the age of 80 in 1982.

The Sense of Anxiety and the Heart–Mind Culture

According to Xu, the basic characteristic of the Chinese tradition is its origin in anxiety, in contrast to the beginning of Western tradition in curiosity. The sense of anxiety leads the Chinese tradition toward the search for virtue and value rather than for science and understanding, and it leads to moral practice rather than to speculation:

> In order to identify the status of Chinese culture within the global cultures of today, it is better to look at the unique features that differentiate it from Western culture than to look at their similarities. I think that Chinese culture and Western culture, at the very beginning of their undertakings, were already different in their motivations, and therefore developed two aspects of human nature and formed two opposite characteristics. Of course in their long history, cultures will not always develop in a linear way. But before people realize their own shortcom- ings, their activities will always be limited by those basic characteristics. That is why those things in the West that carried the Eastern spirit, such as pantheism and Stoicism, were never able to develop fully, and why those things in Chinese history that carried the Western spirit, such as the School of Names in the Warring States period, were also usually short-lived. When basic cultural characteristics are different, the similarities in vocabulary or in some beliefs, if any, would be insignificant. (Xu, 1996, pp. 196–7)

Xu maintained that although Western culture has two main sources, the Greek and the Hebrew, the mainstream of modern Western culture is derived from its Greek origin. Greek culture was motivated by a sense of curiosity to know the natural world. The Greeks held rationality to be the defining feature of human being, and the love of wisdom or contemplation the source of happiness. They took knowing as a leisurely activity pursued for the sake of itself. These characteristics of Greek culture resulted in the pursuit of objective knowledge, especially the development of metaphysics and science. Modern Western thinkers inherited this tradition. However, while the Greeks took "knowing" as a way of education, modern Western thinkers shifted knowledge to be the persistent search for power through possessing and controlling the external material world, as expressed by Francis Bacon's famous motto "knowledge is power."

In contrast, the entire Chinese traditional culture "is based on *youhuan yishi* – a sense of anxiety," which leads to the discovery, understanding, and transformation of human beings themselves. The sense of anxiety is "the key linkage that runs all the way through Confucius, Mencius, Laozi, Zhuangzi, Song and Ming Neo-Confucianism and even the Sinicized Buddhism" (Xu, 1991, p. 176). By "sense of anxiety," Xu meant a psychological state in which one feels responsible to overcome difficulties by virtue of one's own efforts:

> The biggest difference between the sense of anxiety and the sense of dread and despair is that the sense of anxiety originates from a person's vision obtained through deep thinking and reflection about good fortune and bad fortune, success and failure. The vision entails the discovery of a close interdependence between the fortunes and the person's own conduct and the person's responsibility to his conduct. Anxiety is the psychological state of a person when his feeling of responsibility urges him to overcome certain difficulties, and he has not got through them yet. . . . In a religious atmosphere centered around faith, a person relies on faith for salvation. He hands all the responsibilities to God and will therefore have no anxiety. His confidence is his trust in God. Only when one takes over the responsibility oneself will he have a sense of anxiety. This sense of anxiety entails a strong will and a spirit of self-reliance. (Xu, 1984, pp. 20–2)

The idea of "*jing*" (reverence) in the early Zhou dynasty is an important attitude that resulted from anxiety. It differed from religious piety in that:

> Religious piety is a state of the mind when one dissolves one's own subjectivity and throws oneself entirely before God, and takes refuge thoroughly in God. The reverence of the early Zhou is a humanitarian spirit. The spirit collects itself from relaxation to concentration; it dissolves bodily desires in front of one's own [moral] responsibility, and manifests rationality and autonomy of the subject. (Xu, 1984, p. 22)

Xu shows, with citations from *Yizhuan*, the Appendix of the *Book of Changes*, that this characteristic of the Chinese tradition can be traced back to the time of King Wen of Zhou, as it is exemplified in *Yijing* (*The Book of Changes*). He further quotes *Shujing*, the *Book of History*, to show that it was developed by the Duke of Zhou and Zhao. Through Confucianism, it became eminent in the Chinese culture. As an outflow of this primary motivation, Confucianism centered around two inseparable aims – the cultivation of oneself and the manifestation of virtue to affect the world. Both aims are about real life and value, and show no pure theoretical interest in pursuing objective knowledge of the natural world (See Xu, 1984, pp. 20–2 and 1996, p. 199).

The importance of this point was explicated by Mou Zongsan: "The sense of anxiety is an idea brought up first by my friend Xu Fuguan. It is an excellent idea. It may quite well be used to contrast with the Christian idea of the sense of guilt in original sin and the Buddhist idea of suffering and impermanence." Christian "original sin is a deep abyss of fear, the shore of the abyss is salvation, and the refuge of salvation is Heaven, to be close to God. Heaven is the final refuge originated from the Christian idea of original sin." The Buddhist "idea of suffering can be seen from the Four Noble Truths. . . . Impermanence and frustrations caused by craving form an abyss of suffering. Its salvation . . . is to take refuge in the tranquil realm of Nirvana." The Chinese sense of anxiety is different. It was "not generated from original sin or the suffering of human life. It originated from a positive moral conscience, an anxiety over not having one's moral quality cultivated and not having learned. It is a sense of responsibility. What it leads to are ideas such as reverence, respect for morality, the manifestation of moral character and the Decree of Heaven" (Mou, 1963, p. 13).

The recognition that one should try to find the resources for overcoming difficulties within oneself led the early Chinese thinkers to study and cultivate "the governing part of the self," *xin* or the heart–mind. Xu believed that Chinese culture could be characterized as "the culture of the heart–mind." According to Xu, what represented *ren wen* (the humanities) in the Spring and Autumn period were *li* (rules of propriety). Confucius located the ground of *li* in what is in the heart–mind: *ren* (benevolence or human-heartedness). *Ren* is a conscious state of the mind that includes at least the following two aspects: the enduring quest for self-perfection and the awareness of unconditional duties toward others. When put into practice, the two aspects are identical – the perfection of the self is carried through one's perfection of others and vice versa. Confucius thereby turned an external world of human rules (ritual proprieties) inward, and opened up "an internal world of moral character" as the ground of morality, the source of value for a human life. That was Confucius' greatest contribution to Chinese civilization. Given this internal world, people no longer sought physical dominance of the external world in order to gain freedom. One cultivates oneself morally and is thereby able to find one's own autonomy and freedom. Plato's world of ideas and Hegel's world of absolute spirit are products of speculation, and the theologian's Heaven is a conjecture of faith. None of them have anything to do with this internal world of humanity. The access to this internal world requires deep reflection and cultivation, but it is an actual world that can be experienced (Xu, 1984, pp. 67–71, 90–100).

Scholars generally credit Mencius with establishing a Confucian theory of human nature. Xu argues, however, that the Mencian theory concerning the goodness of human nature was already implicit in Confucius' own teachings. Xu offered textual analysis of the *Analects* to point out that Confucius and his disciples took *ming* (fate) and *tianming* (Decree of Heaven) very differently – they simply accepted *ming* and advised not to fight against it, but they held *tianming* in awe and felt that they were bestowed with a mission to carry it and manifest it. What Confucius meant by "the Decree of Heaven," "the *dao* of Heaven," or simply "Heaven" is "the transcendental characteristic of morality," says Xu (Xu, 1984, pp. 77–80, 83–90). If the *dao* or the Decree of Heaven meant fate, a concept that was popular in primordial religions, why would it take Confucius so long to get to know it at the age of fifty? And once he came to know it, why would he still spend the next eighteen years of his life in political efforts only to feel defeated? (Xu, 1980, pp. 440–1). It must be his awareness of the moral responsibility – something that, through his constant practice, turned from external requirements to be internally grounded in his own heart–mind. Xu calls this Confucius' "Copernicus Turn" (Xu, 1980, pp. 446–7). But the turn was not a result of speculation; it was a result of Confucius' moral practice and cultivation. The heart–mind that has gone through this process is saturated with moral character, and is therefore both empirically accessible through introspection and yet also transcendental – it is so compelling that one will feel that it is irresistible and so *a priori*, i.e., it has nothing to do with external experience. This conception marked a fundamental transition from the early Zhou worship of the Decree of Heaven that issued from external deities. It also differed vastly from the Decree of Heaven as conceptually abstract moral principles in the Spring and Autumn period. It turned the Decree of Heaven into moral demands existentially identifiable in the human heart–mind. Although the specific wording "What Heaven imparts is called (human) Nature" appeared later in the *Doctrine of the Mean*, and clear statements about the goodness of human nature appeared still later in *Mencius*, the identification of human nature with the moral Decree of Heaven actually took place in the *Analects* (Xu, 1967, p. 77). Since the moral virtues were seen to be the Decree of Heaven, Confucius felt a strong sense of mission, of responsibility, and a sense of reverence and awe. This mixed feeling was as much a religious feeling as it was moral. Humans were no longer merely passive and inactive receivers of external imperatives. Heaven showed up in one's own nature, and the requirements of Heaven became the requirements of the nature of the subject himself (Xu, 1984, pp. 98–99). For this reason, Confucius could say, "I want *ren*; *ren* is there!" The confidence in the self and the power of self-determination in Confucianism all germinated from here.

The "Great Appendix" of the *Book of Changes*, allegedly written by Confucius, says "What is beyond *xing* is called *dao* (the Way). What is below *xing* is called a vessel." According to Xu's research, in the Warring States period (403–221 B.C.) the word "*xing*" meant the human body. Since the central point of Chinese culture, the heart–mind, is inside the human body and is a part of the body (Mencius called it *da ti*, the great part of the body), the culture should be called "the learning of what is within *xing* (*xin er zhong xue*)," rather than "the study of what is beyond *xing* (*xin er shang xue*)," a phrase usually employed to translate the term "metaphysics," The heart–mind is "a concrete being, entirely different from the metaphysical constructs of speculation or faith." It is totally misleading to interpret the heart–mind as the idealist concept of mind. The principles (*li*) of the heart–mind are moral principles, not ideas of natural phenomena (Xu, 1967, pp. 243–4).

Xu held that the dominance of "the learning of what is within *xing*" explains why the primordial religions of China were replaced by a humanitarian spirit at a very early time. It also explains why Buddhism, when introduced into China, was appealing (because it provided answers to questions that "the learning of what is within *xing*" could not provide, such as questions about an afterlife), and why it was soon sinicized as another form of learning about the heart–mind, as shown in the teachings of *Chan* (*Zen*) Buddhism. It also explains why Chinese culture is a popular culture. Xu quoted the story about Wang Yangming's lectures at Long Chang Yi. While people in the cities found Wang's lectures difficult, the farmers at Long Chang Yi, who never received any formal education, were able to understand them well, because they had no preconceptions and what Wang was talking about could be directly experienced from their own heart–mind (see Xu, 1967, pp. 246–9).

History shows that humans have been torn on the horns of a dilemma: If, like the Empiricists, one locates the ground of morality in external conditions, morality would not be based on self-determination and human behavior will neither be moral or immoral. There would be no necessary connection between humans and morality. If one locates the ground of morality inside oneself, from a biological perspective, morality would lack universality, and rights and wrongs would be isolated individual preference; from a transcendental perspective, morality might be a regulative force over one's behavior, but it would not take root in life and would not constitute a value that is the consummation of the self. Rather, the self would be sacrificed for the sake of universal principles, and the universal principles themselves would thus become abstract and empty terms. Xu believed that Confucianism had actually provided a solution to the dilemma long ago. By identifying the moral character of our heart–mind as human nature imparted from Heaven, the ground of morality is both inside and beyond, both biological and rational. The *Doctrine of the Mean* summarizes this view: "What is imparted from Heaven is (human) nature, and following (human) nature is the Way" and calls the Way "*zhong he*" (*The*

Doctrine of the Mean). *Zhong he* "refers to the 'nature' that unifies the internal and the beyond and to the harmonizing function of the nature that consummates both the self and the things around. The internal aspect is what consummates the self, and the beyond is what consummates the things around." The sages are those who are sincere (*cheng*) to this nature and can fully manifest this nature. They are therefore participating in Heaven and Earth in transforming the universe. Because the full manifestation of this nature is the full implementation of morality in ordinary daily life, the greatest height of brilliance and the "ordinary" are not separated. Most people are not sages, and need to make their will sincere to nature (*xing*), which means "to choose what is good and adhere to it" (*The Doctrine of the Mean*). This only requires practice and cultivation, nothing extraordinary (see Xu, 1967, pp. 78–86).

Xu's identification of the sense of anxiety as the origin of Chinese culture and of its subsequent emphasis on the human heart–mind is both insightful and inspiring. It makes good sense of the differing overall orientations of the Chinese and Western philosophical traditions. It provides an excellent starting point from which to see that the questions Asian philosophers try to answer are by and large different from the questions which concern Western, especially contemporary Western, philosophers (see Kupperman, 1999).

Bodily Recognition and Embodiment: A Methodology of Chinese Learning

One major ambiguity, however, remains to be clarified: On what ground did Confucius and Mencius identify human nature as the Decree of Heaven? Did they merely discover the identification through introspective experience or is more involved in the identification of the two? Xu frequently used the word "*chengxian*" (emerge) to describe the presence of *ren* in Confucius' mind, and he used "*faxian*" (discovery) for Confucius' realization of its presence as the Decree of Heaven (Xu, 1963). But at other times he suggests that this identification was also a decision and an act of affirmation, as the quotation from *The Doctrine of the Mean*, "select the good and adhere to it," indicates (Xu, 1967, p. 84). Hidden behind this ambiguity is the deep question regarding the relation between "is" and "ought." Through a process of retrospection, one may discover within oneself moral feelings, such as compassion for the sufferings of others and a sense of shame over accepting intimidating treatment, but one also finds other tendencies in the heart–mind, such as the craving for possession, for comfort, and for fame. Confucius said that "humans are born straightforward," but he also said that "I have yet to see people who are truly fond of *ren* [human-heartedness], and abhor the contrary" (*Analects*, 4:6), and "I have yet to meet a person who is fond of virtue more than of physical beauty" (*Analects*, 9:18). The tension between discovery and decision is

evident in the following passages from *Mencius*. First, Mencius clearly reveals
the pragmatic considerations behind his choice of the "goodness" in us as our
nature:

> It is due to our nature that our mouths desire sweet taste, that our eyes desire
> beautiful colors, that our ears desire pleasant sounds. But there is also fate (*ming*)
> [whether these desires are satisfied or not]. The superior man does not say they
> are man's nature [and insist on satisfying them]. The virtue of humanity in the
> relationship between father and son, the virtue of righteousness in the relationship
> between ruler and minister – these are [endowed in people in various degrees]
> according to fate. But there is also man's nature. The superior man does not
> [refrain from practicing them and] say they are matters of fate. (*Mencius*, 7B:24,
> Wing-tsit Chan trans.)

In another passage, Mencius says "men have the four beginnings (incipient
good tendencies), just as they have their four limbs." This makes goodness
seem to be a matter of empirical fact, but shortly after this he also says that
anyone devoid of the incipient good tendencies "is not a human." The two
sides of Mencius' account clearly show that his theory of human nature is also
stipulative, for in cases where a person is found not to have such tendencies,
Mencius would not modify his universal assertion of the goodness of human
nature, but would deny that the person is human.

Xu's own study of history reveals that historians did not simply record history in a "scientific" way. Xu held that by mixing "historical knowledge together
with their own wishes" the historians contributed greatly to the transition of
the Chinese world from a world of primordial religions to a humanitarian one.
They replaced religious immortality with historical immortality through the
so-called "three establishments": to be immortal is to establish virtue, to establish achievement, and to establish words. They replaced religious judgment
with historical judgment: the reward for good and the punishment for evil is
achieved through placing both good and evil deeds into the historical record
for people to praise or condemn. Consequently the mentality of the nobles
of the time was more afraid of the judgment of history than the judgment of
the gods. Xu recognized that Confucius himself played an important part in
this process. In editing the *Spring and Autumn Annals*, Confucius sought
"to differentiate right from wrong, to reward goodness and to punish evil
and to use the judgment of history to direct the main orientation of history"
(Xu, 1979a, p. 256). Xu also mentioned the famous Han dynasty historian
Sima Qian, saying that he was also motivated by the aim of establishing morality and orienting history, and that Sima Qian made a great contribution to
the establishment of Confucian moral authority (Xu, 1979a, pp. 321–37).

The answer to the question lies in Xu's analysis of the Confucian account of
bodily recognition and embodiment. Xu believed that Confucius would not claim
to know about something unless he really knew it, as shown by his attitude

toward the afterlife and toward gods and spirits. Therefore, his claim that "at fifty, I knew the Decree of Heaven" must be genuine. Yet the Decree of Heaven is not subject to sense experience like colors, sounds and other sensory objects; rather it is transcendent. How, then, did Confucius obtain his knowledge of the moral Decree? Xu held that it was obtained through *tizhi* (bodily knowing), or *tiyan* (bodily experiencing), or as he most often calls it, *tiren* (bodily recognition). The subject engaged in *tiren* neither passively receives impressions nor reasons intellectually about the logical relations between premises and conclusions. Rather, *tiren* is a retrospective and active process in which "the subject uncovers moral subjectivity from the pseudo-subjectivity of human desires and affirms it, develops it" (Xu, 1996, p. 214). Here the word *"ren"* (recognition) means both realization and acknowledgment. One reveals one's own moral nature through "overcoming the self" and "reducing sensual desires." By freeing oneself from these constraints, the subject lets the original mind emerge (Xu, 1967, p. 248). The way to determine what desires and inclinations need to be overcome is the same as the way to reveal moral subjectivity: Bringing whatever feelings and ideas that one experiences before the light of moral subjectivity in one's own heart–mind, and seeing whether one can still take the feelings and ideas at ease (Xu, 1996, p. 214). The fact that one can take certain feelings at ease is an indication of the Heavenly imparted human nature, and in getting rid of the feelings and ideas that the heart–mind cannot take at ease, one recognizes, affirms, and develops one's moral subjectivity.

Xu criticized the Han Confucians for mixing concepts of Yin-Yang and Five Elements into Confucianism, and for turning the Decree of Heaven into something external. He held that some Song and Ming Neo-Confucians were able to return to the original insight, especially the Cheng brothers, Lu Xiangshan, and Wang Yangming. The Cheng brothers seldom mentioned their teacher Zhou Dunyi's work on *Tai Ji* (the Supreme Ultimate). Instead they stressed the identity between the human heart and Heaven, and advocated direct bodily recognition of the heart–mind. Lu and Wang were more straightforward on the point, and thus, according to Xu, were even closer to the spirit of Confucius and Mencius (see Xu, 1980, pp. 450–4).

Xu calls our attention to the fact that the Neo-Confucians did not call bodily recognition a method of gaining knowledge; instead, they called it a *gongfu*, both a way of doing something with genuine bodily effort and a talent or ability that is gained through receiving training from masters and through one's own diligent practice. For Xu the main application of the bodily experience *gongfu* lies in *weiji zhi xue* (learning for the self), a phrase from Confucius that Xu believed to express the aim of Confucian learning. The learning is not merely for understanding others, but rather "for discovering, opening, transforming and completing oneself" (Xu, 1982, p. 570). Through this learning, one turns the biological self into the moral, rational and artistic self:

Whether in China or out of China, today or in the past, many people who succeeded in attaining achievements in scholarship can only be called "scholars,"
not *ren* "persons," This is not because their scholarship is opposed to *ren*, nor
because their scholarship cannot be entailed in *ren*. It is because they merely
have self-awareness at the level of the intellect, and are unable to raise themselves to the level of *ren*, a level in which the perfection of oneself and the perfection of things around oneself are one and the same. (Xu, 1984, p. 96)

In other words, these scholars are *zhong* (loyal, doing one's best, being
fair-minded) in their scholarship, but they lack the *gongfu* of *shu* (engaging
the heart in feeling easiness and uneasiness) (Xu, 1984, p. 9). The *gongfu* of
shu marks a great difference between ordinary scholarship and the way of
Confucius:

Decisions on the basis of knowledge are usually made by comparing gains and
losses. When they are reasonable, they may also consider the well being of the
public. But most of the time they will be limited within the parameter of the
personal interest and lack moral necessity. Yet through the turn made by learning for the self, my relationship with other people and things and my motiva-
tions and actions are no longer comparisons of gains and losses centered around
my interest; they will arise out of the requirements of moral duty, such as overcoming the self and avoiding egotism. (Xu, 1982, p. 571)

Confucian moral duty differs from Kantian moral duty in that Kantian duty
has nothing to do with one's dispositions, and yet Confucian learning aims
at the full embodiment of moral duty so that one will take pleasure in being
moral. However, since moral dispositions grow from within a person after
a process of learning, they are autonomous and necessary. According to Tu
Wei-ming, this process of embodying moral qualities is in fact to learn to be
a human (Tu, 1985, p. 96). Late in his life, Xu wrote that even though Laozi
and Zhuangzi differed from Confucians in their attitude toward knowledge
and life, their way of scholarship was similar to Confucian learning: both were
learning for the self. "That is what I finally was able to recognize; I regret
that it came to me too late" (Xu, 1982, p. ii).

Because Chinese cultural tradition has to be understood in light of moral
practice and cultivation and from bodily recognition, Xu held that it is entirely misleading to seek the real spirit of Confucianism through speculative
metaphysics. Many scholars take Confucianism to be something like Western
metaphysics and compare it with aspects of Western philosophy, such as
idealism or materialism. Of course, Confucians do consider problems such
as the ground of the heart–mind or the origin of the universe, and both
Confucius and Mencius thought about these issues using notions such as Heaven
and Decree of Heaven, but Confucians did not seek to elaborate on these
notions:

That is because from the Confucian point of view, morality is practice. Moral progress and moral understanding have to be obtained through each individual's own practice. So when the sages taught others, they merely guided the practice. If they were to use language alone to describe the ontological ground of morality, even if what they described was from their genuine practice, the readers would have gotten no more than a mere intellectual understanding. To approach the ground of morality from the intellect, even if one were able to get something, it would be, using Zhu Xi's words, "merely seeing a shadow from the outside." Furthermore, it would easily twist the true nature of morality. The *Analects* shows that when asked about *ren* by the disciples, Confucius never tried to describe what *ren* was like. He just gave instructions according to each disciple's particular condition and let them know on which level and in which aspect they could start their practice. (Xu, 1996, p. 218)

In this regard, Xu criticized Feng Youlan for interpreting Confucianism in terms of Western metaphysics, saying that this is no more than "scratching one's feet across the booth." To force Confucianism into the framework of Western metaphysics is to suffocate the vital spirit of Confucianism. Xu was also openly critical of his friends, such as Tang Junyi, and even of his teacher, Xiong Shili. He gave full credit to Xiong's work of constructing a profound, coherent, and all-encompassing metaphysical system. Yet this approach:

to reason from concrete life and activities up to metaphysics, to the Decree of Heaven, the *Dao*, to try to find a ground for the entire Chinese culture there, and to think that otherwise the ground is not solid, is going the opposite way from Chinese philosophical tradition. [Xiong and Tang] did not realize that metaphysical theories in the history of Chinese thought went by one after another like a carrousel, and none of them could ever stand solidly still. (Xu, 1982, pp. 432–3)

The whole notion of embodiment is a point with profound philosophical significance, and Xu has left much room for further elaboration and discussion. One might say that when Xu speaks of the human heart, human nature, and Heaven, he seems to be admitting himself into a realm of moral metaphysics and accepting some ontological entities. To this objection, I think Xu would reply that his "heart" or "nature" or "Heaven" are all identical, and it is something concrete that can be identified by bodily recognition; they are not abstract "metaphysical entities" constructed by the mind. In this regard, Xu seems closer to Wang Yangming than to Zhu Xi. But his admiration is not based on Wang's move from the concrete heart to a metaphysical "idealism"; it is rather based on Wang's unification of Heaven with the concrete heart. This heart cannot be understood metaphysically. It has to be brought up by a bodily approach (see Xu, 1980, pp. 452–3).

Xu's insights about the importance of embodiment in the Chinese way of learning contain two aspects. On the one hand, embodiment must be recognized as an essential aspect of the tradition. Without an awareness of the importance of embodiment, we can hardly understand the Confucian account of human nature, nor can we appreciate the significance of the Six Arts in the classical Confucian program of education. On the other hand, we cannot understand the tradition without using the method or *gongfu* ourselves, that is without embodiment and our own practice of the human mind. Xu's own application of the *gongfu* is a demonstration. In his study of past great masters, he used a special hermeneutic method. He would first approach the texts through a process of induction, starting from understanding the words, to the sentences, the chapters, and the books, until he grasped the basic thoughts of the author. He would then proceed in the opposite direction: reinterpreting the books, chapters, sentences, and words from the basic thoughts and principles:

> But if one merely reaches this level, one obtains something that is merely abstract. The thought processes of ancient people were concrete actualities with flesh and blood. There is still a distance between one's abstract grasp and the concrete reality. Therefore one should take a further step from abstract thought into the actual life of the person behind the thought, to see his spiritual development, to see the cultivation that his personality went through, to see vertically the kind of heritage in which he developed and to see horizontally what his environment was able to offer him. All thoughts are centered around questions: thoughts that do not respond to any question are not thoughts. How did the ancient author find or determine the questions that shaped his thought? How did he answer his questions? How did he engage his thought and personality to answer his questions? What kind of process did he endure in order to reach his destination? Was his method for solving problems feasible and effective? Did the problems that he tried to solve and the method he used have any significance for that time and the people? We need actually to experience all these. (Xu, 1967, p. 116)

He called this method "*zhui tiyan*" (tracing-back and bodily experiencing). The application of this method accounted for his solid scholarship and for his penetrating insights into many issues in the history of Chinese thought.

In this kind of epistemology, objectivity requires one to immerse oneself in what is to be known, and the act of knowing involves displaying what is known in action. Only when one has enough *gongfu*, when one has achieved enough ability and has made enough effort in applying the ability, can one have knowledge of the transcendent moral self behind the *gongfu*; and only when one fully embodies this knowledge, acknowledging it and making it one's own rational dispositions, is the knowledge fully attained. In this case there is no dichotomy between the knower and the known, and the embodiment of what is known becomes a condition of knowing it. This may account for the fact that Xu's articulation of the notion of embodiment appears to be somewhat less than satisfactory, because the notion of embodiment itself has to be embodied for it to be fully understood and appreciated.

While crediting Xu for identifying the crucial role of embodiment in Confucianism, we must ask if he was too radical in his criticism of metaphysics. Xu thought that "the special feature of Chinese culture is to descend step by step from the *dao* of Heaven and the Decree of Heaven to the concrete life and activities of human beings" (Xu, 1982, p. 432). But without sometimes ascending to this higher level, how could it descend from above? As Cai Renhou puts it, it is more plausible to say that "the way of Confucianism is both a unity of the inside and the outside and a unity of the beyond and the below" (Cai, 1992, p. 66). Song and Ming Confucians tried to reinterpret Confucianism metaphysically to meet the challenge of Buddhism. If this fact accounts for the subsequent revitalization of Confucianism, would it not be beneficial or even necessary for contemporary Confucian scholars to do the same in order to meet the challenge from Western philosophical traditions? A modern metaphysical reinterpretation could reappropriate the value of Confucianism and protect it from rejection as irrelevant or inadequate for dialogue with its Western rivals.

Xu did not tell us whether the *gongfu* applies solely to the recognition and transformation of human nature and the study of human thought, or more broadly, to the learning of other subjects as well. The Daoists used retrospection, calmness, and emptiness – "fasting the mind" – as a way of knowing the *dao*, and the knowledge they searched for was more than the human heart–mind and encompassed the natural world. According to Xu, however, Confucians never had a strong interest in knowing the objective natural world:

> Confucians feel close to nature. But they neither place their admiration of the infinite in their view of nature like the Western Romantics, nor do they perform dispassionate objective analysis of nature, like the scientists. Their view of nature is merely the objectification of their moral sentiments and virtues. The names of plants and animals in the three hundred Odes are sentiments and virtues of the poets, not botany or zoology. Western science interprets the human as part of nature; the Confucian spirit interprets nature in terms of the human. That is because the foundations of the two cultures are different and therefore the characteristics of nature [in their view] also became different. (Xu, 1996, pp. 214–15)

Xu claimed that even though the Confucian spirit lacked a scientific dimension, it does not mean that it was against science. Xu answered the accusation that Chinese culture lacks a methodology for scientific investigation, such as logic, by saying that this was not because Chinese intellectual tradition is naive. Rather, given that the aim of Chinese tradition was different, the methodology that the Chinese needed was different. Because Confucians aimed at cultivating their human nature and manifesting it, they needed *gongfu* rather than methodology. Confucians look for a world with objectified moral feelings and virtues. The selection of plum, orchid, bamboo, and chrysanthemum as representatives of the four seasons reflects more their moral ideals (endurance, modesty, integrity, and courage) than features of the natural world. "We should straightforwardly admit that the Confucian spirit lacks a scientific dimension, just as the Hebrew spirit lacks that dimension. But there is nothing in the Confucian tradition that is against science" (Xu, 1996, p. 215).

I am not sure that Xu has assessed Confucianism fairly in this respect. Xu did not seem to suspect that Western science may also be value-laden and is therefore also objectification of human values and assumptions. Secondly, he did not even mention the holistic and correlative way of thinking that characterizes the Chinese philosophical tradition, including Confucianism. One can dispute whether this mode of thinking offers an alternative way of scientific thinking. If one defines science in terms of the model developed in the modern West, one might argue that China never had scientific thought. Yet the Chinese, including the Confucians, used correlative thinking to understand nature and attained remarkable achievements and insights into how the universe functions, as best exemplified in Chinese medicine. In this regard, Joseph Needham's work on science and civilization in China and more recent discussions of Chinese correlative thinking by A. C. Graham and others deserve our serious attention.

Confucian Government by Virtue and Democracy

Like the other modern Chinese philosophers, Xu was confronted by a fundamental charge that Confucianism was an outdated basis for the Chinese political system and, even worse, that it has fundamental flaws which made it responsible over the preceding two hundred years for social and political crises and evils, such as the lack of political freedom, the lack of respect for human rights, and the absence of democracy. Xu's position was unequivocally that Confucianism is not to blame. He held not only that it is compatible with democracy, but also that democracy cannot be complete without being integrated with Confucianism.

Xu argued that Confucianism is compatible with democracy because it entails taking people as *ben* (the root or substance) of a society, an idea that appeared in *Shang Shu* (the *Book of History*) and other pre-Confucian texts. Statements such as "Heaven looks through the eyes of the people, Heaven listens through the ears of the people" (*Shang Shu*) indicate that "the people were not merely 'the ruled' who were below the rulers; they were the representatives of Heaven and the gods, above the rulers" (Xu, 1980, p. 51). This spirit was inherited by the Confucians, and was most clearly reflected in Mencius' statement that "the people are the most important; the spirits of the land and grain are the next; the ruler is the least important" (*Mencius*, 7B:14). Mencius also made it clear that the people have a right to rebel and to overthrow unqualified rulers. Xu found that even the idea of a government run by the people existed in *Mencius* in a rudimentary form (*Mencius*, 1B:7), though Mencius never knew a system that could put the principle into social practice (see Xu, 1967, p. 136).

Xu further held that a "democratic political system can be firmly established and fully utilized only when it takes a step forward to accept Confucian thought" (Xu, 1980, p. 53). In the ideal Confucian rulership:

> the ruler and the ruled are in morally reciprocal relation, not in a right-enforcement relation. Morality is the common ground that makes us all human. When everyone is able to exert moral virtue to his or her best ability, people will all encounter each other on the basis of the common ground of being human, without feeling otherness. That is exactly the purpose of politics and the uttermost ideal of politics. (Xu, 1980, p. 49)

> The relationships maintained by legal rights are at best external relations. External relations are not reliable, and they do not allow human nature to develop freely, unless they are grounded on internal relations. To govern by virtue is to establish internal relations between individuals through the moral virtues that everyone possesses, which from the Confucian point of view is the only natural and rational relation. (Xu, 1980, p. 50)

Xu was not uncritical of the Chinese tradition. He pointed out that since the Chinese grounded morality internally in human nature rather than on an external source, a person can take a moral stand without relying on anything external; yet because of its internal basis Confucian morality cannot be indisputable like the size and weight of an object. So the foundation stone of Chinese culture, the "heart–mind," cannot be defined objectively, and one has to rely on the criterion of seeing whether one's own heart–mind is at ease or not. Xu cited a story from the *Analects* in which Confucius' disciple Zai Yu argued with Confucius over whether a three-year period of mourning was necessary. Confucius asked Zai Yu whether he felt that his own heart–mind was at ease or not. When Zai Yu replied positively, Confucius could do nothing but say "if that is the case, so be it" (Xu, 1980, p. 180).

When the object of knowledge is external, it is publicly observable and open to justification. When the object of knowledge is the heart–mind, it can only be introspected subjectively. Those who were reckless and selfish took advantage of this difference.

> In the Chinese moral culture, human being is really the most sacred being among all the things between Heaven and Earth. Thus, "up to the emperor and down to the ordinary people, all should take the cultivation of the person as the basic obligation." Every individual is supposed to take the weight of the entire history and transform oneself into the great personality that responds to all aspects of the entire world. However, even though the "gifted" and the extremely well-cultivated are able to take their stand by their inner strength, the less gifted and

the ordinary people mostly would still have to rely on external forces to stand up. Religion is such an external force; the idea of law and the idea of state are also external forces. From the standpoint of Chinese culture, the focal point is naturally "to manifest one's heart–mind to its uttermost and to know [human] nature," and the lesser ideal is "to prevent [something bad] from happening before it actually takes shape by teaching people rules of propriety." The aim is the far remote indefinite ideal of "bringing peace to the world," or "forming a ternion with Heaven and Earth." Consequently in Chinese culture religion was not taken as necessary, nor were the ideas that regulate human behavior from the outside, such as law and state, taken seriously. (Xu, 1980, p. 179)

Furthermore, Confucianism lacked a democratic dimension. The Confucian tradition always looked from the standpoint of the rulers to see how they might provide a benevolent government, and seldom from the standpoint of the ruled to restrict the rulers. The virtue of the rulers is a virtue of giving, offering, and the people are always the passive receiver of the offers. Thus politics was always in the hands of the emperors and their ministers, and the political subject-ivity of the people was never established. Because there is no effective means for the common people to participate in politics, initiation of political change had to come from the imperial court, and not from the society. When intel-lectuals wanted to influence society, they had no way but trying to get into the imperial court themselves. Since the selection of officials was determined by those who were above, the upright candidates were constantly defeated by the flatterers (Xu, 1980, pp. 49–56). As Chinese intellectuals lacked a tradition of pursuing knowledge for its own sake, the only social and economic ground for their existence was in the political circle as consultants or advisors. The Chinese terms *"you shi"* (wandering gentry) and *"yang shi"* (fostered gentry) show clearly this feature of Chinese intellectuals. "Wandering" shows that they had no root in the society; "fostered" shows that they had no other means of life except for being fostered by someone. Yet the realm of their wander-ing was political, and the realm in which they were being fostered was also political. So Chinese intellectuals were from the very beginning parasites of politics, beggars of the ruling class (Xu, 1980, p. 182). However, when morally conscientious emperors and ministers wanted to bring some political change, they also lacked a solid social body that was capable of supporting them (Xu, 1980, pp. 54–5).

The solution, according to Xu, is to incorporate democracy into the Confucian moral tradition. More specifically, we need to rectify a misinterpretation of Confucian political thought according to which the Emperors are the State. The political subjectivity of the people must be restored, and a political system must be established to ensure that this subjectivity will no longer provide mere lip service to the ruler, but is a genuine power of the people by which the rulers will be constrained. "The polity should achieve rational harmony on the basis of reasonable competition, the coexistence beyond individuals on the basis of independence of the individuals, the ritualistic transformation beyond individual rights on the basis of stipulations of individual rights" (Xu, 1980, p. 59).

Xu argued passionately that the modern Chinese polity has combined the worst parts of the Chinese and Western traditions. It took the unlimited political responsibility of the rulers from the Confucian tradition but discarded its moral conscience, and it took the modern Western competition for power but discarded the recognition of basic individual rights. That was the worst kind of polity in the world. Once we implement the Confucian idea of the political subjectivity of the people with a democratic political system, "democracy can obtain a more supreme ground from the revival of the Confucian spirit, and Confucianism can complete its actual objective structure through the establishment of a democratic polity" (Xu, 1980, p. 60).

Recent discussions on the compatibility of Confucianism and democracy have enriched our thought on this issue. As this is no place to survey the whole field, I will just mention a few contrasting views to enhance our understanding of Xu's position. Some scholars argued against Xu, in one way or another, regarding the compatibility. In China, for instance, Qi Liang argues that the traditional Chinese idea of "the people as the substance" is fundamentally anti-democratic, since it is based on the premise that the people should be treated in a certain way by their rulers, and not that they should be placed in a position to determine their own fate. It advises the rulers what they should do (that is, that they should take the people's interest seriously) rather than saying what is required of them. By expecting the ruler to treat them as "the substance," the mentality of the advocates of the idea is no different from that of the beggar who expects alms (Qi, 1995, pp. 438–40).

In the United States, Henry Rosemont Jr. argues that Western democracy is based on the notion of human beings as rational, autonomous, rights-bearing individuals and that this notion is crucially flawed because, as an abstraction, it leads us away from actual concrete persons in social relations. He claims that this notion should be held accountable for the increasing moral conflicts in America today, where individuals' rights are protected at the cost of the loss of reciprocity, maldistribution of wealth, and so on. The Confucian notion of human being is the opposite. It shows how we make our actual decisions – we do not choose in the abstract without "real hopes, fears, joys, sorrows, ideas and attitudes of flesh-and-blood human beings," nor do we choose as autonomous individuals who are solely responsible for becoming who we ourselves are. Our choices affect and are affected by the people to whom we have specific relationships (Rosemont, 1997, p. 63). As a rival to the rights-talk, Confucianism allows us to express our moral sentiments fully without ever invoking the language of rights (Rosemont, 1997, p. 64).

In favoring Xu Fuguan's view about the compatibility between Confucianism and democracy, Chung-ying Cheng rejects both views mentioned above. According to Cheng, Qi Liang misconstrued Mencius' idea of *minweigui* ("the people

is the most important, . . . and the ruler is the least important," Mencius, 1970,
VIIB:14), and Rosemont, in establishing an opposition between the Confucian
moralist and the Western liberal, presupposed that Western democracy is the
only democratic model. Cheng believes that Xu Fuguan failed to bring out the
way in which democratic rights can be introduced into the Confucian morality
of virtues. He argues that a rational and relational rights-talk can be readily
generated from classic Confucianism. In Confucianism, the immediate concern of a person is virtue, and all the specific virtues take the form of duties
to both self and society. "When the duties attached to virtues are performed,
one naturally receives a place of dignity and respectability in society" (Cheng,
1997, p. 146). One will then become simultaneously the agent and recipient
of virtues. A "theory of explicit virtues could be turned into a theory of implicit
rights if it could be seen as a theory of correlative duties among members of
a community. The only thing lacking would be an explicit assertion of these
rights as a basis for their political recognition." In taking this last step, promotion of a rational way of thinking could be very useful (see Cheng, 1997,
pp. 142–53). According to Cheng, we have to see that Confucianism is an
open system and that compatibility between Confucianism and democracy is
not only possible, but desirable for both the further development of Confucian
morality and for the moral development of a rights-based society.

One dimension that deserves more attention concerns the timing and conditions of bringing Confucianism and democratic rights together. Democracy must
be based on certain minimum levels of maturity of its participants and on the
availability of certain minimum amounts of information. It is hard to imagine
that ancient farmers, who had virtually no education and had no means for
getting relevant information, could effectively participate in democratic politics.
At that stage, a sage ruler, although difficult to get, was far more realistic
to propose than an effective democracy. However, when the maturity of the
people and the other conditions are adequately present so that people who
enjoy political rights can live together harmoniously, the system of rights might
also become less important or even unnecessary. As Chenyang Li suggests,
between well-related family members, "it is meaningless or even destructive
to talk about their rights against each other" (Li, 1999, p. 175). Yet between
the stage that relies on sage rulers and the stage at which harmony prevails,
Confucianism must provide room for something less ideal. As Shu-hsien Liu
says, in the current historical state "we have to negate the tradition in order
to reconfirm the ideal of the tradition" (Liu, 1986, p. 350).

The Chinese Aesthetic Spirit

Xu held that "morality, art and science are three pillars of human civilization"
(Xu, 1983, p. 1). After painstaking examination of an enormous amount of

ancient literature, Xu identified Zhuangzi as the best representative of the "Chinese aesthetic spirit," exemplifying the synoptic unity between life and art. Xu recognized the metaphysical nature of the Daoist notion of *dao*, but held that when *dao* is looked at through its embodiment in life, it is actually an aesthetic ideal and that the lives pursued by Laozi and Zhuangzi constituted an artistic way of life. This can be seen everywhere in the *Zhuangzi*. Take, for example, the story of Cook Ding cutting up an ox. His great performance showed far more than mere perfection of a technique:

> Cook Ding said that what he pursues is the *dao*. *Dao* is more than mere technique. From the story we can see that *dao* and technique are closely related. Cook Ding sees the *dao* inside his technique, not external to it. As I said, the Western notion of art meant technique in its origin as well. Even today, artworks are still inseparable from techniques or skills. But we can still ask whether a technique is merely technical or artistic. [The two] actually differ in spirit and in function. Zhuangzi has a very deep and clear awareness of the difference. Speaking merely from a technical perspective, the performance of cutting up an ox should be evaluated by nothing more than its practical results. It would be completely superfluous to speak of its being "in perfect rhythm, as though he were performing the dance of the Mulberry Grove or keeping time to Chingshou music." The enjoyment that one obtains from pure technique is material enjoyment brought about by the technique and is not in technique itself. Yet what is special about Cook Ding's performance in Zhuangzi's imagination is exactly his "being in perfect rhythm." That function is not required by the technique; it is an artistic function brought by the technique. After the completion of his performance, Cook Ding's satisfaction is his "standing there holding the knife and looking all around, completely satisfied and reluctant to move on." This kind of artistic function and enjoyment is the very content of what Cook Ding means by his remark that "what I like is the *dao*." The long section in the story that begins with "When I first began cutting up oxen" concerns his journey from learning technique to [the embodiment of] the *dao*, and it is actually also about his journey from learning technique to the realm of artistic creativity. (Xu, 1983, pp. 52–3)

This journey involves two aspects: dissolving the opposition between the heart–mind and the objects (from seeing the ox to no longer seeing the whole ox) and dissolving the opposition between the heart–mind and the hands or technique (perception and understanding come to a stop and spirit moves where it wants). In this way, one eventually achieves one-ness, a state of being both free and satisfied, which is the aim of art. This is also the state in which one finds supreme happiness. Xu quoted Tolstoy, Lipps, Heidegger, and Hegel to show that artistic experience is often identified with a state of being free. Zhuangzi's *you* (often translated as wandering) is such a state. It has no external aim, but is a harmony or unity in one-ness with no constraints and no coercion. To reach such a state, one has to "fast the mind" and "sit in forgetfulness," to free the heart–mind from the constraints of one's cravings and from one's sense of "usefulness," and to free the heart–mind from the pursuit of knowledge. One must stop trying to grasp the world conceptually and analytically and directly experience the world itself. This direct experience is not a means for obtaining knowledge or a guide for action; it rather aims at its own satisfaction. When Zhuangzi enjoyed watching fish or dreamed that he was a butterfly, he was having such direct aesthetic experiences. In them, forgetfulness and directness transcended time and space and overcame the dichotomy between the subject and the object. Because of the completeness of the satisfaction, they even transcended life and death. They were able to form a consistent whole because they were all from his pursuit of the *dao* and its embodiment.

Xu contrasted the Chinese aesthetic spirit exemplified by Zhuangzi with Western aesthetics:

> The main difference between the aesthetic spirit displayed and understood by Zhuangzi and the one seen in Western aesthetic theorists is not that Zhuangzi obtained the complete and the ordinary aesthetic theorists obtained only the partial. It is rather that the difference between the complete and the partial derives from the fact that Zhuangzi obtained his understanding from his *cultivation in his life*, whereas ordinary theorists got theirs *from reasoning and generalizing* from their experiences in dealing with particular aesthetic objects and artworks. Because what they obtained are in both cases aesthetic spirits, they will coincide here and there unexpectedly. Yet since for Western aesthetic theorists, their aesthetic spirit did not sprout and generate from the root of humanity, as far as the entirety of life is concerned they would inevitably leave room uncovered in their understanding. It is therefore inevitable that what they obtain is partial. The situation is much better in Phenomenology. However, since the phenomenologists are unable to *grasp the calm and empty nature* of the heart–mind, they are only "riding the horse to look for the horse": trying to grasp [the spirit] from its function. To explain this from our traditional ideas, they are still unable to see the substance: the subjectivity of aesthetic spirit. (Xu, 1983, p. 132, italics mine)

Xu believes that in both Confucianism and Daoism the paths of *gongfu* aim at dissolving biological functions and letting subjectivity emerge. That is what "overcoming the self," "no ego," "no self," and "losing myself" mean. The emergence of subjectivity is both the completion of the person's humanity and the unification of the subject and the myriad objects. Therefore, one of the most striking differences between Chinese culture and Western culture is that there are no dichotomies between subject and object and individual and community at the fountainhead of Chinese culture (Xu, 1983, p. 132). In this regard, Confucianism and Daoism carry the same spirit. The reason that Zhuangzi, and Daoism in general, represent the Chinese aesthetic spirit better than Confucianism is that the Confucian aesthetic spirit is filtered through morality. In Daoism, especially in Zhuangzi, the unity between life and art is more direct. Confucian subjectivity appears more as a moral subjectivity, and Daoist subjectivity appears to be more an aesthetic one.

Xu claimed that Confucianism has the same aesthetic spirit as Daoism, only that Daoist subjectivity is more directly aesthetic, but he did not explain why Confucianism (an indirect aesthetic spirit) can nevertheless be taken as more typically Chinese. One barrier that prevented him from doing so was his failure to distinguish between the nonutilitarian functions of an aesthetic activity and the aesthetic activity's being nonutilitarian. It is true that there is a nonutilitarian aesthetic dimension in both Daoist and Confucian ways of life, yet this does not mean that the ways of life must eschew utilitarian functions in order to retain their aesthetic function. The unity between life and art entails a unity between utility and aesthetic appreciation, and in this sense the Confucian way of life is no less a complete unity of the two than Daoism and might even be a greater unity. Yet when Xu took uselessness as a necessary condition of the aesthetic *you*, he seemed to say that an activity can be aesthetic only if it is useless or disinterested. This is certainly not the case for Confucianism, but it is also quite uncharacteristic of Chinese thought in general.

Against this background, we can talk about Confucian aesthetics. Confucius also used the notion of *you* in his saying "*you yu yi*" (take excursions in art). That Confucius placed *you* at a very high level in the ideal life can be seen from the fact that in the *Analects* "*you yu yi*" follows immediately after a significant summary of Confucius' central principles: "Set your will on the way. Have a firm grasp on virtue. Rely on humanity" (*Analects*, 7:6). In this context, *you* is a state of freedom achieved by the understanding of the *dao*, the determination to follow the *dao*, and the exercise of the ability to participate effortlessly and creatively in the *dao*. The state is "following the will of the heart–mind without overstepping or transgressing the line (moral principles)" (*Analects*, 2:4). For Confucius, "knowing that it cannot be done and yet doing it" is at its best when one "takes pleasure" in doing it. When Duke of She asked Tzu Lu about Confucius, and Tzu Lu did not answer, Confucius said: "Why didn't you say that I am a person who forgets his food when engaged in vigorous pursuit of something, is so happy as to forget his worries, and is not aware that old age is coming on?" (*Analects*, 7:18). These passages indicate that there is a nonutilitarian aesthetic dimension in the Confucian way of life, and some of them endorse "forgetfulness" as crucial to that way of life. Mencius' choice of music as a metaphor to characterize the sageliness of Confucius also displays the aesthetic dimension of the Confucian ideal life (Tu, 1985, p. 108). The ideal life aims at satisfaction of the heart–mind, although it also has utilitarian purposes.

Bibliography

Works by Xu Fuguan

Xu, Fuguan 1967: *Zhongguo sixiangshi lunji* 中國思想史論集 (collected essays on the history of Chinese thought), Taiwan: Xuesheng Shuju

Xu, Fuguan 1971: *Xu Fuguan wenlu* 徐復觀文錄 (the collected essays of Xu Fuguan), vols 1–4, Taiwan: Huanyu Press

Xu, Fuguan 1974: *Liang han sixiang shi* 兩漢思想史 (the history of eastern and western Han thought), vol. 1, Taiwan: Xuesheng Press

Xu, Fuguan 1976: *Liang han sixiang shi* 兩漢思想史 (the history of eastern and western Han thought), vol. 2, Taiwan: Xuesheng Press

Xu, Fuguan 1979a: *Liang han sixiang shi* 兩漢思想史 (the history of eastern and western Han thought), vol. 3, Taiwan: Xuesheng Press

Xu, Fuguan 1979b: *Rujia zhengzhi sixiang yu minzhu ziyou renquan* 儒家政治思想與民主自由人權 (confucian political thought and democracy, freedom, and human rights), Taiwan: Bashi Niandai Press

Xu, Fuguan 1980: *Xueshu yu zhengzhi zhijian* 學術與政治之間 (between politics and scholarship), Taipei: Student Book Company

Xu, Fuguan 1982: *Zhongguo sixiangshi lunji xubian* 中國思想史論集續編 (continuation of collected essays on the history of Chinese thought), Taiwan: Shibao Wenhua Chuban Shiye Gongsi

Xu, Fuguan 1983: *Zhongguo yishu jingshen* 中國藝術精神 (the Chinese aesthetic spirit), 8th edition, Taiwan: Xuesheng Shuju

Xu, Fuguan 1984: *Zhongguo renxinglun shi – xianqin pian* 中國人性論史－先秦篇 (the history of Chinese theories of human nature: pre-Qin period), 7th edition, Taiwan: Commercial Press

Xu, Fuguan 1991: *Xu Fuguan wenchun* 徐復觀文存 (posthumous collection of essays by Xu Fuguan), Taiwan: Xuesheng Press

Xu, Fuguan 1996: "Rujia jingshen de jiben xingge jiqi xianding yu xinsheng" 儒家精神的基本性格及其限定與新生 (basic characteristics, limitations, and revival of the Confucian spirit), in *Zhongguo renwen jingshen zhi chanyang – Xu Fuguan xin ruxue lunzhu jiyao* 中國人文精神之闡揚－徐復觀新儒學論著輯要 (elaboration of the Chinese humanitarian spirit – selected works on new-Confucianism by Xu Fuguan), edited by Li Weiwu, Beijing: Zhongguo Guangbo Dianshi Chubanshe, 1996. The paper was originally published in *Minzhu pinglun* 民主評論 (democracy forum), vol. 3, supplement to no.10, April 1952

Commentaries and Related Material

Cai, Renhou 1992: "Xu Fuguan xiansheng dui song-ming lixue de jianjie" 徐復觀先生對宋明理學的見解 (on Xu Fuguan's interpretation of Song and Ming Confucianism), in *Donghai daxue Xu Fuguan xueshu sixiang guoji yantaohui lunwenji*, 1992

Chan, Wing-tsit 1963: *A Source Book in Chinese Philosophy*, Princeton, Princeton University Press

Chang, Carsun 1962, *Development of Neo-Confucian Thought*, vol. 2, New York: Bookman Associates

Cheng, Chung-ying 1997: "Transforming Confucian virtues into human rights: a study of human agency and potency in Confucian ethics," in de Bary and Tu, 1997

Confucius 1970: *The Analects*, trans. D. C. Lau, Harmondsworth: Penguin Books

de Bary, William Theodore and Tu, Wei-ming, eds, 1997: *Confucianism and Human Rights*, New York: Columbia University Press

Donghai daxue Xu Fuguan xueshu sixiang guoji yantaohui lunwenji 東海大學徐復觀學術思想國際研討會論文集 (essays presented at the Donghai University International Symposium on Xu Fuguan's scholarly thought) 1992: Tai Chung: Donghai University. The articles in these volumes provide good surveys of Xu's scholarly contributions, although most of them are not critical

Kupperman, Joel J. 1999: *Learning from Asian Philosophy*, Oxford: Oxford University Press. This book, although containing no mention of Xu, is useful for following Xu's ideas that are discussed in the first part of this chapter. It provides more concrete understanding of how the Chinese and Western philosophical traditions developed their own questions and their own approaches

Li, Chenyang 1999: *The Tao Encounters the West*, Albany N.Y.: SUNY Press. In this book, Li argues against Xu's claim that Confucianism and democracy are compatible

Liu, Shu-hsien 1986: "*Cong minben dao minzhu*" 從民本到民主 (from people-as-substance to democracy), in *Wenhua yu zhexue de tansuo* 文化與哲學的探索 (exploration of culture and philosophy), Taipei: Xuesheng Press

Mou, Zongsan 1963: *Zhongguo zhexue de tezhi* 中國哲學的特質 (the uniqueness of Chinese philosophy), Hong Kong: Rensheng Publishing Company. Mou credits Xu with the modern thematization of the concept of anxiety in which the moral nature of Chinese philosophy is rooted

Qi, Liang 1995: *Xinruxue pipan* 新儒學批判 (critique of Neo-Confucianism), Shanghai: Sanlian Shudian

Rosemont, Jr. Henry 1991: *A Chinese Mirror: Moral Reflections on Political Economy and Society*, La Salle, Illinois: Open Court

Rosemont, Jr., Henry 1997: "Human rights: a bill of worries," in de Bary and Tu, 1997

Tu Wei-ming 1983: "*Wei wangsheng ji juexue*" 為往聖繼絕學 (continuing the lost scholarship of the ancient sages), in 1984: *Xu Fuguan jiaoshou jinian wenji*. This is a speech made at the first anniversary memorial service of the death of Xu Fuguan in 1983

Tu, Wei-ming 1985: *Confucian Thought: Selfhood as Creative Transformation*, Albany: SUNY Press. Tu broadens the scope of Xu's study of the Chinese Aesthetic Spirit to include Confucianism, especially Mencius, in the same aesthetic interpretation with Daoism

Wu, Kuang-ming 1989: "Chinese Aesthetics," in *Understanding the Chinese Mind: The Philosophical Roots*, Robert E. Allinson, ed., Hong Kong: Oxford University Press, pp. 236–64. This article develops Xu's work in interpreting the Chinese philosophical tradition from the perspective of aesthetics.

Xu Fuguan jiaoshou jinian wenji 徐復觀教授紀念文集 (essays in memory of Professor
    Xu Fuguan) 1984: Taipei: Shibao Wenhua Chuban Shiye Youxian Gongsi
Xu Fuguan xiansheng jinian wenji 徐復觀先生紀念文集 (essays in memory of Mr. Xu
    Fuguan) 1986: Taipei: Xuesheng Press

Discussion Questions

1. Can features of Chinese culture and philosophy be traced to an under-
    ling sense of anxiety?
2. What is the heart–mind?
3. Can we accept Xu Fuguan's account of the relationship between *li* and
    ren in Confucius' thought?
4. Is the Decree of Heaven external or internal? How can we gain know-
    ledge of it?
5. Does the method of bodily recognition contribute to our knowledge?
6. Is it a mistake to consider Confucianism to be a doctrine of speculative
    metaphysics?
7. Is Xu Fuguan justified in claiming that democracy is incomplete with-
    out Confucianism?
8. Is it better to be governed by virtue or legality?
9. In what sense might *dao* be an aesthetic ideal?
10. How should we understand "overcoming the self"?

15

TANG JUNYI: MORAL IDEALISM AND CHINESE CULTURE

Sin Yee Chan

Tang Junyi was born in 1909 in Sichuan province, China. As an undergraduate, he studied at Beijing University and Nanjing Zhongyang University with Fang Dongmei and Tang Yungtung. He also befriended Xiong Shili and discussed philosophy with him in his youth. After moving to Hong Kong in 1949, he cofounded New Asia College with Qian Mu and Zhang Pijie. Tang visited Taiwan University, and took part in many overseas conferences on Chinese philosophy. In 1978 he died from cancer in Hong Kong.

Tang's works can be divided into three main areas:

1. Traditional Chinese philosophy,
2. ethics and metaphysics, and
3. writings on cultural questions, especially the comparison of Western and Chinese culture, and the modernization of Chinese culture.

Because a discussion of Tang's work on traditional Chinese philosophy will require extensive exegesis of Chinese philosophy itself, this chapter will focus solely on his contributions to the second and third areas, especially his writings on ethics and metaphysics.

Ethics and Metaphysics

Although Tang developed his philosophy in the context of dialogues with Western philosophy, his thought can more appropriately be seen as a modern reinterpretation of Neo-Confucianism, especially that of the Lu–Wang school. This school, which focused on the writing of Lu Xiangshan and Wang Yangming, is often described as the idealistic wing of Neo-Confucianism because of its emphasis on the role of the mind in moral and intellectual cultivation. Like these Neo-Confucians, he sought to use metaphysics to ground ethics. Like them, he believed in a metaphysical reality (*xin er shàng ti benti*) that is immanent in everything in the universe. Because of this immanence, cosmic unity is achieved. Moreover, Tang believed that the metaphysical reality possesses moral qualities, such as the Confucian virtue of *ren*. To fulfill our nature by embodying the metaphysical reality and achieve a full union with it, human beings should lead a moral life.

From the time of his earliest works, ethics was the focus of Tang's philosophy. According to him, the moral life requires us to be self-consciously self-governing. To do this, we must assume full responsibility for ourselves and believe that we are free. Free and self-governing moral activity is basically the activity of transcending one's actual self:

> One common nature shared by all moral conduct and moral psychology is the self's transcending the limits of the actual self. . . . Often people say that working diligently and spending thriftily are moral conduct. What is diligence? It is the continuous use of present strength. What is thriftiness? It is the suppression of present desires. Both express transcendence over the actual self. (*Daode jiwo zhi jianli*, in Tang, 1986, vol. 1, p. 54)

With whom can we identify if we are to transcend our actual selves? Tang asked us to distinguish between the actual self and the ethical self and to take the latter as one's genuine self. The ethical self is described in terms of reason:

> What we call Reason (*li xing*) is the nature that can manifest and follow what is rational. That is to say, what is rational is natural. Reason is what the Chinese Confucians call natural reason (*xing li*). It is the nature or essence that makes our ethical self, or spiritual self or transcendental self be what it is. (*Wenhua yishi yu daode lixing*, p. 19)

In contrast, the actual self is "the self that is trapped in present space and time" (*Daode jiwo zhi jianli*, p. 29). Because what exists in time is transitory and therefore illusory and what exists in space is restricted and therefore neither universal nor real, the actual Self is not real. The ethical self, which is not limited by space and time and is permanent and true, represents one's genuine self.

More importantly, the ethical self is a universal metaphysical reality that is shared by everybody:

> I strongly believe that this reality of the mind must be all-perfect. This is because it transcends and stands above infinite time and space. . . . I believe that the reality of mind in me is the same reality of mind that is in others. For the reality of mind in me is all goodness. It expresses itself as my moral psychology, commands my actual self to transcendence and to see others as myself. This shows that it originally is the reality of mind that is shared by the actual selves of myself

and others. . . . This reality of mind is the master of the world, i.e. God. (*Daode jiwo zhi jianli*, pp. 109–10)

Since the reality of mind is good, our nature, as Mencius claimed, must be good as well. But if this is so, what is the source of evil and vice? Tang answered this question in terms of our indulgence (*chen ni*). If, for example, we indulge in the delight that results from being praised by others, we will become greedy for fame and power. But why do we become indulgent? According to Tang, from one act of indulgent thinking we can develop an infinite greed because it is the nature of our spirit is to desire infinity. Originally infinity itself is the object of actuality-transcending activities. However, when an actual thing becomes the object of our indulgent thought, we seem to become arrested by it. Our desire for the infinity of the actual object is the origin of our infinite greed (*Daode jiwo zhi jianli*, p. 156).

To emerge from indulgence, Tang suggested a method of "self-reflective and self-conscious thought at the moment" (*dangxia zixing zijue zhi yinian*), "realize clearly your responsibility. Realize clearly the importance of a thought. Then you will know that a thought at the moment can create an ethical world" (*Daode jiwo zhi jianli*, p. 92). A thought of this sort initially stems from a feeling of discomfort concerning one's actions. Discomfort leads to reflections on these actions, which in turn give rise to a judgment of goodness and badness. One can then consciously act to eliminate badness and to pursue goodness.

By succeeding in emerging from indulgence, one can control oneself with the genuine or ethical self. On this account, the intrinsic nature of the ethical self is transcendence: by engaging in moral activity one transcends one's actual self or, more precisely, transcends limitations of all kinds.

Tang believed that moral activities will help us develop the four cardinal Confucian virtues of benevolence (*ren*), rightness (*yi*), propriety (*li*), and wisdom (*zhi*). The point of all these virtues is to transcend the limitation of oneself and to become united with others. This is most obvious in the case of *ren*, which Tang held to be the most fundamental virtue:

> *Ren-ai* (benevolence–love) in its primitive form is the first virtue that becomes manifest [when we] develop the concept of ourselves and others as independent and individual beings. According to Confucianism, one's *ren* towards others need not at first be manifested as love that actively involves oneself in actions. It can be manifested as an undifferentiating and non-separating gentleness and simplicity, or the commiserating mind which cannot bear to see the sufferings of others. (*Wenhua yishi yu daode lixing*, pp. 537–8)

Because moral activities involve transcendence, Tang held that ethics and religion cannot be entirely separated. To cultivate the moral virtues fully, we must also develop our religious spirit. Gratitude is a paradigmatic example of the ethical–religious spirit that we must cultivate because gratitude enables us to transcend ourselves and to connect with virtues and moral personalities that have accomplished good deeds. In this light, he saw ethical significance in the traditional Chinese religious practice of the three worships (*sanji*), that is the worship of parents, ancestors, and sages:

> In Chinese culture, the most fundamental expression of the spirit of gratitude lies in the gratitude one shows towards parents and all those who have done good deeds. From this, we derive the rituals for the veneration of ancestors, for those who have contributed to the world, for the sages, and for the "gods" of the nation and heaven and earth for creating and fulfilling things. (*Shuo zhongguo renwen zhong zhi bao'en jingshen*, *Legein Monthly* 16, 1975, p. 104)

Wang Yangming had an obvious influence on Tang's ethics. The idea of a genuine self, the claim that evil is a result of indulgence that can be overcome by thinking, and the doctrine of a universal moral metaphysical reality that accounts for cosmic unity all have affinities to Wang's own views. These ideas remained the core of Tang's ethics throughout his life.

A refined and elaborate system containing these themes was developed in Tang's most important work, *Shengming cunzai yu xinling jingjie* (Life, Existence, and the Horizons of the Heart–Mind) (1977), which he completed shortly before his death. We shall now turn to look at his philosophy as expounded in this book, which contains extensive discussions and critiques of a wide range of major philosophical ideas found in the Western, Buddhist, and Chinese philosophical traditions.

To Tang, the human heart–mind holds the key to understanding of the world. The heart–mind knows the world through a function that Tang described as feeling–penetration (*gantong*). Feeling–penetration includes cognition as well as emotions and willing. In its ideal operation, one responds to an object or a situation in correct ways (*dangran zhi li*), and achieves an integration of reason and emotion. When applied to knowing another human being, feeling–penetration is a kind of empathetic response. Exercising this feeling–penetration, we can achieve a vision or cognition which Tang called horizon (*jing*). *Jing* is a Buddhist concept for an object to which the mind is directed and implies a unification of the subjective understanding and the objective situation. It can therefore be compared to the Kantian account of perception, according to which perception is also a product of the mind's unification of sensory data by means of categories supplied by the mind.

Tang identified a total of nine horizons. The first three horizons deal with the objective world as perceived by the heart–mind. The next three horizons are the product of the heart–mind reflecting upon itself. The final three horizons are the most important because they constitute the different ways in which the heart–mind unifies the subjective and the objective. Tang called the last three horizons the trans-subjective–objective horizons. Tang described the nine horizons as follows:

> In the beginning, our cognition is about external, not internal observation, that is [our mind] is conscious of others and is not self-conscious. . . . Hence the first horizon of the nine horizons is the horizon of manifold separate individuals (*wanwu sanshu jing*). From this we observe the realm of individuals. . . . The second horizon is the horizon of transformation according to classes (*yilei chenghua jing*). From this we observe the realm of classes. The third horizon is the horizon of functioning in sequence (*gongneng xuyun jin*g). From this we observe the realm of cause and effect, and the realm of means and ends. (*Shengming cunzai yu xinling jingjie* I, pp. 47–8)

The middle three horizons are horizons about self-consciousness, not about consciousness of others. The first horizon [in this group] is the horizon of mutual perception (*ganjue hushe jing*). . . . In this horizon, a subjective substance first knows that the manifestations of the objects of its cognition are included in its perceptions. And the space and time in which we find the manifestations are internal to the heart–mind which has conscious reflections following perceptions. One then knows from inference that all existing substances are subjective substances that have the ability to perceive. These subjective substances can mutually perceive each other and also are independent of each other. . . . The second horizon in the group is the horizon of observation in suspension (*guanzhao lingxu jing*). From this we observe the realm of meaning. . . . This world of pure manifestations, pure meaning can be expressed in language, words and symbols . . . literature, logic, mathematics are collections of linguistic symbols. They indirectly express the various pure manifestations, pure meaning. Our music, painting and arts use collections of voice, sounds and shapes directly to express the various pure manifestations, pure meaning . . . The third horizon of this middle group is the horizon of practicing morality (*daode shijian jing*). From this we observe the realm of moral conduct. Its main point is to discuss our having self-conscious ideals and seeking to universalize them. (*Shengming cunzai yu xinling jingjie* I, pp. 49–50)

The last three horizons are the horizons in which the subjective incorporates the objective and transcends the distinction between the subjective and the objective. It is the horizon where we transit from self-consciousness to trans-consciousness. Yet this trans-subjective–objective [horizon] still follows the order of having the subjective incorporating the objective and develops further from there. Hence it still takes the subjective as the chief. . . . In these three horizons, knowledge must all be transformed to wisdom, or belongs to wisdom, and be used in our lives to help us to achieve real and valuable existence of our lives. . . . Of these last three horizons, the first horizon is named horizon of returning to one God (*guixiang yishen jing*). From this we observe the realm of God. Its main point is to discuss the horizon of the trans-subjective–objective, unifying–subjective–objective God as described in monotheism. This God is the substance that occupies the highest position. The second horizon is the horizon of the dual-emptiness of self and dharma (*wofa erkong jing*). From this we observe the realm of dharma. Its main point is to discuss the Buddhist views on the classification and meaning of all realms of dharma and manifestations. [Buddhism] sees that for both emptiness is their nature, their real manifestation. Both belong to the category of emptiness. This destroys our attachment to the [distinction between] the subjective and the objective, [between] self and others, thus transcending the distinction between subjective and objective. . . . The third horizon is the horizon of flowing of Heavenly Virtue (*tiande liuxing jing*), which is also named as the horizon of exhausting one's nature and establishing one's mandate. From this, we observe the realm of nature and mandate. Its main point is to discuss the Confucian idea of exhausting one's subjective nature and to establish the objective mandate from Heaven. [Following this Confucian idea has] the consequence of creating a connection between the subjective and the objective. . . . This [horizon] can be seen as connected to the horizon of practicing morality, and can be called the ultimate horizon of practicing morality or the horizon of establishing the Great Human Ultimate. (*Shengming cunzai yu xinling jingjie* I, pp. 51–2)

In brief, the nine horizons are about (a) individuals (things or persons), (b) classes to which individuals belong, (c) cause–effect relationships among individuals, (d) mutual perceptions by the subjective minds, (e) concepts and pure meaning, (f) practicing morality, (g) unifying with a single deity, (h) realizing the illusoriness of the world and the self, and (i) fulfilling human nature which is the embodiment of Heavenly Virtue.

The nine horizons are supposed to encompass all varieties of knowledge, but the last three horizons, the trans-subjective–objective horizons, were the most important for Tang. He saw them as having the highest concerns. The purpose of his philosophy, he claimed, is to help people achieve genuine existence. In the last three horizons our knowledge is transformed into wisdom. Tang sought to anchor his ethics in metaphysics, and it is within the last three horizons that different metaphysical theories are discussed and compared.

The three horizons can be seen as representing, respectively, Christianity, Buddhism, and Confucianism. Tang believed that all three religions point to the same absolute metaphysical reality, but that they give this reality different names. Their major difference, however, lies in the different directions that they recommend humans to follow in order to achieve unity with this metaphysical existence:

For this so called horizon of the flowing of heavenly virtue, we can see simultaneously the flowing of heavenly virtue in the accomplishment of human virtues. Hence it is simultaneously the trans-subjective–objective horizon. This differs from the horizon of returning to one God, where there is a vertical vision proceeding from below and extending to above, enabling us to see the existence of God or Spirit who unifies the subjective and the objective, making our faith extend upwards, and transcending the opposition between the subjective and the objective. This also differs from the Buddhist idea of destroying the subjective attachment to the self and the objective attachment to the dharma. [If we follow Buddhism] we look at the world in its ten directions and observe truly the nature of all subjective–objective, internal–external dharma that exists in the realm of dharma. This makes our wisdom flow downwards, and transcend the opposition between the subjective and the objective. Now when I talk about the flowing of the human and the heavenly virtues, the main point is to proceed in accordance with the order of the existence of our lives and the sequence in which the present world manifests itself, moving from what comes first to what comes later. (*Shengming cunzai yu xinling jingjie* II, pp. 155–6)

This order proceeds from what is immediate to reach what is far away. We should start with what concerns our human lives here and now. Since morality addresses that very question, we can achieve transcendence by practicing morality. Tang considered this to be the message of Confucianism. Confucianism affirms our human lives and this world, instead of seeing them as illusory (Buddhism), or requiring us to abandon them in search for a transcendent God (Christianity).

In brief, this philosophy of nine horizons seeks to establish two conclusions: the existence of a transcendent heart–mind and the supremacy of the horizon of the flowing of heavenly virtue (Confucianism). Let us examine each in detail.

Tang gave three reasons for saying that Confucianism is superior to Christianity and Buddhism. First, the other two religions require people to look beyond the present life and the world: Christianity focuses on a transcendent God, Buddhism believes that the world is an illusion. These different emphases, Tang held, will lead people to overlook the present for the sake of the future. People will then tend to employ the utilitarian mode of thinking, which severs them from the union with the infinite metaphysical reality.

Secondly, Buddhism is appropriate only for those who are so attached to the world that they require enlightenment about the illusoriness of the world, and Christianity is appropriate for those who are so dependent on others that they need help from an all-powerful God. These two religions are medicines only for those who are "sick."

Thirdly, Confucianism encompasses Buddhism and Christianity, but they do not encompass Confucianism. Confucianism can regard Jesus and Sakyamuni as sages, but Buddhism and Christianity will not see Confucius as enlightened or as divine.

Tang used two arguments to establish the existence of a transcendent, infinite metaphysical reality, the heart–mind: the ontological and the moral argument (see Ng, 1988). Tang considered all ontological arguments in Western philosophy to be wrong-headed because they attempt to go beyond the existence of empirical things and claim that empirical things could be nonexistent. Tang also applied this accusation to the cosmological and teleological arguments for God's existence.

His ontological argument starts from remedying this mistake:

> We can start from the existence of the things in the world, and the deficiencies and imperfections in their attributes. Then we can think about supplementing what they lack, so as to form an existence that is not imperfect, [but] perfect. (*Shengming cunzai yu xinling jingjie* II, p. 28)

Traditional ontological arguments claim that since a perfect being, that is God, must include all attributes, and since existence is an attribute, God must exist. Tang's argument, in contrast, claims that if we negate the imperfection of an existent being, we end up with an existent being with all attributes, that is a perfection being.

For Tang, however, the more suitable way to prove the existence of the infinite being is through ethical–religious experience. Like Kant, he thought that the postulate of an infinite being was required by rationality and moral sentiments:

> In the beginning, people only believe in the spiritual existence of those they respect and love. This original affirmation stems from the emotions of their moral minds. Since this affirmation stems from the emotions, they will not bear to think that these spiritual beings are left lonely, without companionship and unattached. As these spiritual beings do not have the obstacles of possessing material forms as people and things in the world do, their transcendent mind should be able mutually to shed light on each other and form one body, hence forming an absolute spiritual existence. . . . Doubting the reality of this absolute spiritual existence and that of the spiritual beings whom we respect and love is to counter the moral mind. (*Shengming cunzai yu xinling jingjie* II, p. 10)

Tang was well aware that the Kantian line of argument alone does not prove the objective reality of the infinite being. He went on to say that our moral experience actually reveals its objective existence:

> In our moral lives, so long as there are real common emotions and feelings between others and ourselves, and so long as we can genuinely reflect, we can see that our moral minds and those of others are united to form a spiritual existence. (*Shengming cunzai yu xinling jingjie* II, p. 62)

Tang believed that common emotions and feelings occur when people give help to one another and that they are especially apparent in situations such as natural disasters and wars:

> At those moments, each person subjectively has the feeling of sharing one mind with the multitudes. And objectively speaking, it can also be said that there is

one mind genuinely existing among the multitudes. Simultaneously people can be conscious of the actions of this one mind existing between heaven and earth. . . . Here we should not say that the one mind belongs separately to individual persons, or to us, or to heaven and earth. . . . For when we are facing heaven and earth, heaven and earth make us transcend our respective limitations, resulting in the manifestation and existence of this one mind. (*Shengming cunzai yu xinling jingjie* II, p. 64)

We should note that Tang was not talking about intersubjectivity here. He was not saying that there is a common mind in the sense that everybody shares the same goal. He is talking about a transcendent mind which is a union of minds of individual persons when they transcend themselves to unite with others. He held:

In our mutual moral conducts and moral lives, we have direct feeling (*zhigan*) of the existence of the moral minds and moral personalities of others. . . . From our mutual direct feelings of the existence of each other's moral minds and personalities, there comes the expansion and enhancement of our moral minds and personalities. From this we can see that a person's moral mind and personality do not just belong to that person, but also belong to others. Originally, this mind does "belong to oneself." Yet when it expresses itself before others, when it is directly felt by others, then it also belongs to others. . . . With regard to the reality of this unified spirit which results from mutual incorporation and mutual feelings, [we can] describe it as an Absolute Self, and Absolute Spiritual Reality. (*Shengming cunzai yu xinling jingjie* II, p. 61)

Why does our recognition of the moral minds of others through our direct feelings imply a union of our minds with theirs? Tang's answer was that when other minds exist in our direct feelings, those minds exist in us. Others and ourselves are united in our direct feelings.

To understand these claims, we need to understand Tang's idealism. Sometimes he seemed to equate conceptual reality with objective reality. That is, he took an idea to be an objective existence. His idealism was discernible even in his early argument for the existence of an infinite metaphysical reality:

Our discontent with the universe evidences our desire for a real universe, a good and perfect universe. This desire is absolute: [we] cannot merely take it as a psychological fact. If it were a psychological fact, how could it place itself forever above the present universe and [make us] feel discontented with it? This desire therefore must have a source which transcends the so-called present universe and which accounts for its transcendence. (*Daode jiwo zhi jianli*, p. 102)

Tang argued that when the mind takes the entire universe as its object of judgment, the mind must transcend the universe because the universe is in our mind.

Tang's idealism was rooted in the belief that the perceiving mind and what the mind perceives are inevitably connected together:

> Our ability to perceive and that which can be perceived cannot be separated. The basic reason is this: When we are conscious of our perceptions, on the one hand, we are conscious of our ability to perceive. On the other hand, we are conscious of the manifestations of what is perceived. In this consciousness, we clearly have a unified consciousness, thus we cannot say that the two can exist separately. (*Shengming cunzai yu xinling jingjie* II, p. 352)

Tang drew a phenomenalist conclusion that things which seem to be objective and independent of us can be understood in terms of actual and potential perception:

> Yet when people see that these manifestations can transcend our subjective, particular perceptions and have universal meaning, they say that these things exist by themselves, or exist in the bodies of the particular things. They even claim that their existence is independent of human perception. This is confusing the "universal" with the "external." . . . If we say that for this perceived manifestation, it itself still exists when it is not perceived, in relation to perception, it is only a possible existence or a potential existence. (*Shengming cunzai yu xinling jingjie* I, p. 351)

Hence, in criticizing Berkeley, Tang did not criticize Berkeley's idealism. In his view, Berkeley's mistake was to claim that all ideas must be perceived, thus requiring the existence of a perceiving God. Tang's idealism led him to confuse conceptual reality with objective reality and to take mere ideas to be existing objects. Hence, he inferred from our perception of the moral minds of others that those minds are in our own minds and that there is a union of minds. We can see how these beliefs led him to conclude that in perceiving all minds, in his terms, the mind of heaven and earth, we become united with an infinite mind.

Discussion of Tang's Account of Ethics and Metaphysics

Tang did not succeed in establishing his claims for the superiority of Confucianism. If pursuing an ideal in the future leads to a utilitarian mode of thinking, Confucianism faces the same problem as Buddhism and Christianity. The Confucianism affirmation of the value of the present life and the world by no means implies that Confucian ideals are not directed at the future. Even for Tang, one must engage in moral cultivation and exhaust one's nature before one can fully participate in the heavenly virtue of transcendence.

Furthermore, Christianity and Buddhism, by providing no more than a panacea for the "sick," are inferior to Confucianism only if the majority of humans are not sick in this way. The Confucian belief in the goodness of human nature can admit general human sickness by ascribing this sickness to external factors. Which religion best meets the needs of a society to overcome sickness does not admit an absolute answer that is universally true.

Finally, to claim that Confucianism alone encompasses the other two religions can also be challenged. If Confucianism recognizes Jesus and Sakyamuni as sages on a par with other Confucian sages, it does not recognize them as they are understood in their own religions. Jesus would not be identified as an omnipotent, omnibenevolent, and omniscient Creator. The religions encompassed by Confucianism would not be Christianity and Buddhism.

Nor was Tang successful in his ontological and moral arguments for the existence of an infinite reality. His ontological argument starts with an existent being, negates its imperfections by supplementing it with all the attributes it lacked for perfection, and arrives at a perfect being. His argument rests on the claim that we can supply all the attributes that an existent being lacks in order to make it perfect, thus absurdly suggesting that we can create God ourselves.

An alternative interpretation of Tang's argument is that we can think about the additional attributes needed to supplement the concept of an existing imperfect being to transform it into a concept of an all-perfect being. This interpretation, however, only proves that we can have a concept of God, not that God exists.

Tang's moral argument also encounters problems. Tang argued for a unity among individual minds, hence arriving at an infinite mind. Yet, uniting finite minds, no matter how numerous, will not lead to the formation of an infinite mind. More importantly, we have seen that his argument relies on his idealism. But his idealism is too crude to be plausible. Even idealists like Berkeley tried to maintain a distinction between a mere idea and a real existence. Berkeley would say that a mere idea is less vivid than a real existence and maintains less coherent causal relations with other ideas, but Tang's idealism seems to overlook such a distinction. Following his line of reasoning, we should say that our bodies are all in our perceptions and are, therefore, all united. But this claim is absurd.

Finally we should note that in the following respects, Tang's philosophy of the heart–mind was inherited from Neo-Confucianism. First, Tang described the relationship between individuals and the infinite heart–mind as one of various manifestations (*fenshu*):

> We know that this spiritual being is an absolute and infinite spiritual being, and that it penetrates through every subjective mind and the myriad things in heaven and earth. All the subjective minds and the myriad things in heaven and earth are places of its manifestation. When the manifestations of our subjective minds correspond to the existent virtues of this spiritual being, they can be seen as the manifestations of this spiritual being. We can say that our subjective minds

are the various manifestation (*fenshu biaoxian*) of the spiritual being itself. (*Shengming cunzai yu xinling jingjie* II, p. 65)

This relationship between the heart–mind and its various manifestations conforms to the Neo-Confucian claim "the principle is one, its manifestations are many" (*liyi fenshu*).

Secondly, Tang's idea of reaching the state where there is no distinction between the self and others through the exercise of feeling–penetration echoed the Neo-Confucian idea of "forming one body with the universe":

> This empirical horizon (*xianliang jing*) stems from the mind's feeling–penetration to the external things, that is, it is the horizon where there is no distinction between the self and the non-self. (*Shengming cunzai yu xinling jingjie* II, p. 178)

Thirdly, both the Neo-Confucians and Tang considered *ren* to be the primary virtue of the universe, by means of which universal unity is achieved. We should note that in Neo-Confucianism, *ren* was sometimes considered to be the metaphysical reality itself, rather than its virtue. Tang understood *ren* as feeling–penetration, with all other virtues being seen as its different manifestations. Because feeling–penetration leads to universal unity, Tang concluded:

> To know Heaven's *ren* in universalizing the myriad things without any partiality, we have to see it through our *ren* in universalizing the myriad things without any partiality. (*Shengming cunzai yu xinling jingjie* II, p. 243)

However Tang departed from Neo-Confucianism in one important respect. Neo-Confucianism described the metaphysical reality as the Principle (*li*) or the *dao* of "production and reproduction," a description connoting development, but not necessarily in the sense of progress. In contrast, Tang described the metaphysical reality as transcendent, which does connote progress. Along the same lines, Thomas Metzger notes that the Neo-Confucian emphasis on the pole of stillness (*jiran budong*) is not included in Tang's philosophy (Metzger, 1977, p. 92).

The Principle in Neo-Confucianism is a principle of "production and reproduction" because it is the source of existence or the origin of life and because it underlies and governs the activities of all things, and these activities evolve around production and reproduction. Because of the commonality between the intrinsic nature of the Principle and the nature of the activities of the myriad things, the Principle is embodied in the myriad things, and the myriad things are the various manifestations of the Principle.

Tang claimed that the same kind of relationship holds between the heart–mind and individuals in the universe. But there are problems if we conceive metaphysical existence as transcendence because it is difficult to establish the intrinsic nature of the heart–mind as transcendent. If the heart–mind is all-perfect, and encompasses all kinds of attributes, then it is difficult to see how the already perfect being of the heart–mind can transcend itself.

One might try to make sense of this transcendence by understanding the heart–mind as becoming a perfected being, rather than as an already perfect being (Ng, 1988, p. 305). Tang did claim that a being can be considered to be perfect even though its attributes take turns in becoming manifest rather than all being manifested together. He also claimed that the heart–mind does not reveal all its attributes at the same time because the heart–mind has "inclusive transcendence" (*chaoyue de baohan*):

> The so-called "inclusive transcendence" refers to the inclusion of these opposites and contradictions, at the same time allowing these opposites and contradictions mutually to cancel and eliminate one another in order to become a "being of nonbeing," a "being in nothingness" or an "empty being." (*Shengming cunzai yu xinling jingjie* II, p. 44)

The heart–mind can contain contradictory attributes only if it takes turns in manifesting the attributes that contradict each other. Thus Tang emphasized the flexibility and diverse nature of the heart-mind:

> Therefore, the more a being can respond to different situations and manifest different natures to the extent that it can transform without limit and act without obstacles, the greater is its ability to be, and the more perfect its being becomes. (*Shengming cunzai yu xinling jingjie* II, p. 44)

The description of the heart–mind as transcendent and including contradictions is like that of Hegel's *Geist*, but the resemblance is only apparent. Hegel's *Geist* undergoes a process of development to achieve its full freedom, but Tang's heart–mind is already perfection.

In any case, an interpretation of the heart–mind as becoming perfect does not really work. Tang never described the heart–mind as a potential being. Instead, he held that the degree of perfection of a being is a function of the number of attributes that the being can manifest. The process by which more and more attributes become manifest cannot be understood as a process of becoming perfect, and the heart–mind should not be understood as a being that becomes perfect.

The problem remains: how can a perfect being have the intrinsic nature of transcendence? Tang did address the issue of the transcendent nature of the heart–mind:

> That this Reality has the meaning of transcendence lies in the fact that it has one activity transcending another. Hence, the meaning of transcendence of this Reality is first revealed in the succession of its activities, that is in the eclipse, contraction,

and recession of the previous activity, and the manifestation, extension and advance-ment of the next activity. (*Shengming cunzai yu xinling jingjie* II, p. 329)

This passage, however, illustrates changes and not transcendence and does not justify the claim that the two are equivalent. Transcendence, unlike change, implies betterment. Because Tang failed to show that the heart–mind has the intrinsic nature of transcendence, he was unable to establish that the myriad things are the various manifestations of the heart–mind.

Tang also had difficulty in establishing transcendence as a cosmic principle governing the activities of the myriad things of the universe. He did not rely on the theory of evolution to establish cosmic transcendence. Instead, from the various adjustments that living things make to their environment, we can see that living things express mutual tolerance of each other's existence. According to Tang, this tolerance of one another's existence shows that living things transcend their nature, that is their survival instinct. This claim is unten-able because adjustment to one's environment is an expression of one's survival instinct, not its transcendence.

Despite this failure to establish transcendence as a cosmic principle under-lying everything in the universe, perhaps Tang's claim about the *human* heart–mind can still hold. He would just have to admit that the human heart–mind is finite, not infinite. This finite human heart–mind then could undergo the process of transcendence through moral perfection and would eventually achieve unity with the infinite heaven and earth.

Culture

Tang has been accused of being a pan-moralist because he reduced all human cultural activities to moral activities and claimed that the transcendent moral mind runs through them. Tang understood different cultural realms as par-ticular manifestations of the transcendent heart–mind and held that the func-tion of cultural activities is to facilitate human moral development. Because the heart–mind can proceed in different directions in its different manifesta-tions, Chinese culture and Western culture have different characteristics. Tang held that Chinese culture is superior to Western culture because it realizes the nature of the transcendent heart–mind to a greater degree. In his view, Chinese culture is humanistic and focuses on ethics, arts, and human relationships, while Western culture is materialistic and emphasizes science, religion, and indi-vidual freedom. Nevertheless, Tang held that Chinese culture must strengthen itself in science and democracy and that in order to achieve successful modern-ization, it needs to have confidence in its own traditions. Indeed, it should lead the search for a perfect culture through the integration of various cultures. Let us examine his cultural theory in more detail.

According to Tang, morality underlies all human cultural activities. "All human cultural activities belong to an ethical self, or spiritual self, or transcendent self. They are its particular manifestations (*fenshu biaoxien*)" (*Wenhua yishi yu daode lixi*, p. 5). All cultural activities aim at certain ideals, that is they have goals which the actors seek to implement in objective reality. Reflecting and having goals are the functions of one's reasoning mind. Because the ethical self is Reason, the ethical self is the source of our cultural activities, even including very primitive activities such as the creation of tools:

> For the primitive man who first discovered the simplest form of stone axe, if in his mind there were no goal of splitting an object, how could he think of making a stone into a sharp stone axe? If he could not reflect on his experience, and thereby know how to make a stone sharp, how could he make a stone become sharp and form a stone axe? (*Xinwu yu ren-sheng*, p. 184)

The ethical self or reason also underlies the more developed forms of cultural activities. Tang classified these activities in terms of social cultures (family, economics, and politics), pure cultures (philosophy, science, literature, arts, religion, and ethics), and maintenance cultures (education, physical education, military, and law). Without governing by the ethical self, none of these activities is possible. Take the example of economic activities:

> Why do animals not develop social and economic organizations? This proves that the ground for the establishment of a human economic society is not individuals' desires for of goods. . . . Our wish to privatize our property (including the consumption of goods and the means of production) stems from our selfish mind. Yet each has a regard for each other's selfish mind, and each recognizes each other's private property. These stem from the public mind and the principle of reciprocity (*shu*). . . . We must first recognize the rights of ourselves and others in controlling our respective property before we can have an exchange. (*Wenhua yishi yu daode lixi*, pp. 120–39)

Tang held that historical contingencies can also influence cultural development. Western culture is pluralistic because it developed from multiple sources and underwent many cultural conflicts. In contrast, the different tribes that ruled China's different dynasties shared one common culture. Until the nineteenth century, Chinese culture managed to respond to external influences, such as Buddhism and Islam, without changing its core ideas. Tang rejected the crudely deterministic version of Marxism that sees culture as being completely determined by the economic and technological conditions of a society. He insisted that environmental factors do no more than set parameters for a culture by ruling out some of the possible forms that cultures can take. It is the ethical self that determines the distinctive form of a culture because the ethical self judges whether we should conform to environmental constraints.

Because the ethical self or mind determines the particular configuration of a culture, the direction of the mind explains the expression of the culture. One major difference between Chinese and Western culture, according to Tang, is that Chinese culture emphasizes ethics and arts, while Western culture focuses on religion and science. This difference is explained by Chinese culture being guided by the mind of harmony and integration and Western culture being guided by the mind of distinctions. Chinese ethics is concerned about how to eliminate the distinction between the self and others through the smooth working of human relationships. In Chinese arts, the distinction between the subject and the object dissolves in the experience of artistic appreciation, when subjects are absorbed in the object of appreciation or express themselves through the object. In contrast, Western religion is based on distinctions: God, as transcendent, is distinct from human beings. Western science distinguishes between the inquirer and the object of inquiry. Tang explained the characteristics of Western culture:

> Concerning the special spirit of Western culture, I try to include it under four items. The first is the transcendent spirit which moves upwards and outwards, for example, the "transcendent God." . . . The second is the spirit that tries fully to objectify rational epistemic activities . . . From this spirit, we have in the West logic, mathematics, geometry, algebra . . . The third is the respect for individuals' freedom. This is mainly manifested in the Christian belief that God created man to be the only being that has freedom. . . . The fourth is the pluralistic development in the different divisions of scholarship and culture. The different cultural divisions in Western culture such as religion, literature, art, science, philosophy, politics, economics all are clearly categorized. (*Zhongguo wenhua zhi jingshen jiazhi*, pp. 4–5)

In contrast, the Chinese culture is characterized by integration rather than distinctions:

> In China, social class distinctions are not prominent. There is a high degree of job mobility. In scholarship and culture, the emphasis is on synthesis and not classification, on the harmonization of the spirits of different scholarship and culture. Scholarship and culture with different foci and principal themes can be mutually inclusive and coexist. (*Zhongguo wenhua zhi jingshen jiazhi*, pp. 494–6)

Tang believed that Chinese culture expresses the virtue of *ren*, which implies unity, and Western culture expresses the virtue of wisdom, which implies distinctions. Because of this emphasis, Western culture has significant problems. It has a history of cultural conflict and no particular Western culture endures. Because of the distinction between the object of inquiry and the inquirer, Western culture has developed an attitude of trying to control and manipulate nature to increase one's wealth and power. Although the aspiration towards transcendence leads to the creation of many excellent theories, the lack of attention to integration renders the culture incapable of transforming baser human impulses. As a result, these theories have been usurped by untamed impulses, as expressed in relentless capitalism, materialism, and communism.

In contrast, Chinese culture, because of its emphasis on integration, has strength in its enduring existence:

> The spirit of Chinese culture is unsurpassed in terms of its inclusive capacity and its moral capacity. . . . When something is adequate in its inclusive capacity and moral capacity, often we only see that its spirit is round and divine. . . . Hence, today we must include the square into what is round so as to support and expand the roundness. (*Zhongguo wenhua zhi jingshen jiazhi*, p. 497)

The square that Tang held should be brought into the round and divine Chinese culture is the objectifying and differentiating mind:

> That is, our spirit follows the ideal of differentiation and sheds its light upwards and outwards, so as to objectify and achieve scientific knowledge, industrial mechanical civilization, productive technology, various kinds of objectified and diversified social and cultural developments, organizations of civil society and state laws. . . . With regard to the spirit of democracy and freedom, it is an objective spirit that mediates between "the individual spirit" and the "objectified spirit" . . . (*Zhongguo wenhua zhi jingshen jiazhi*, p. 497)

Tang's recommendations for the path of China's modernization differ completely from the position "Chinese culture as the substance, Western culture as the functioning" (*zhongxueh weiti, xixueh weiyong*) that was advocated by Zhang Zhidong and others in the nineteenth century. Indeed, Tang severely criticized that position and argued that successful modernization required China to incorporate certain Western cultural spirits, and not merely its technologies and practical skill. In terms of introducing science and democracy into China, Tang agreed with people like Hu Shi and Chen Duxiu. Yet unlike those favoring complete Westernization, Tang believed that Westernization should be partial and should be built on the foundation of Chinese culture. This was possible, in his view, because Chinese culture contained seeds enabling it to develop science and democracy.

With regard to science, Tang held that Chinese culture traditionally developed technologies to improve the people's livelihood, but that this development had been limited by its scientific progress. Tang suggested that science progressed slowly in China because Chinese culture tends to reduce epistemic inquiry to moral activity. He noted that this problem was not totally ignored by traditional Chinese scholars. Some attempted to extend their epistemic activity to the external world, although this often resulted in nothing more than philological research and textual exegesis. In spite of these limitations, Confucians in the late Ming and early Qing periods emphasized the value of irrigation work, farming, medicine, and astronomy. This trend, which continued in the self-strengthening movement in the late Qing period, expressed a desire to know about nature in order to promote moral development and improve the livelihood of the people.

Similarly, Tang believed that there are seeds of democracy in Chinese culture. He pointed to the Confucian belief that the opinion of the people represents the Mandate of Heaven. From the Confucian prescription: "the ruler should like what the people like, and dislike what the people dislike," he argued that the Confucian political ideal concerns the realization of the preferences of the people. Confucianism also praised the sages Yao and Shun, who yielded their thrones to virtuous persons who had won the heart of the people. From this, we can understand the Confucian belief "Heaven and Earth belong to the public" (*Tianxia weigong*). Finally, Confucianism holds that everybody has the potential to become a sage. This belief in the fundamental equality of moral capacity among people can also be seen as a seed of democracy. Tang held that these beliefs led to the development of institutions and practices in traditional China that aimed at communicating the ideas of the people to the ruler, as seen in the institution of the censorates and in the practice of sending remonstrations to the ruler.

Discussion of Tang's Account of Culture

Tang's claim that Chinese culture contains the seed of democracy and science needs further examination. With regard to democracy, to say that Confucianism recognizes the importance of the people's opinions is very different from the claim that it acknowledges the sovereignty of the people. Central to the ideal of democracy is the belief that the people are the source of political sovereignty. In Confucianism, the idea of the Mandate of Heaven excludes the people from the bestowal of political authority on the ruler by heaven. The source of political authority is very different from the Western contractarian position in which the people delegate their political power to the sovereign and in which the people and the sovereign stand in an equal contractual relationship to each other.

Although Confucianism believes in moral equality among people, this moral equality is distinct from political equality, and it is political equality that is relevant to democracy. Indeed, Confucianism has often been criticized for sanctioning hierarchical and authoritarian rule that is the antithesis of democracy. For example, of the five cardinal human relationships in Confucianism (the ruler–minister, father–son, elder–younger, husband–wife, friend–friend relationships), the first four are hierarchical. To justify the view that Chinese culture contains the seeds of democracy, Tang would have to explain why political hierarchy or even hierarchy in general is not essential to Confucianism or explain how hierarchy is compatible with democracy.

There are also problems with the claim that Chinese culture contains the seeds of science. All of the examples that Tang produced to show a traditional interest in nature reveal an instrumental attitude towards nature. It is the use of nature as exemplified by Xunzi's philosophy, rather than curiosity about the workings of nature, that prompted traditional Confucian scholars to engage in irrigation and farming projects.

Furthermore, we can doubt whether China could introduce the scientific spirit if Tang's cultural theory were true. In Tang's theory, a culture is the particular expression of the mind that follows a particular direction. But the mind that emphasizes integration and the mind that focuses on distinctions are not merely two different minds. Rather, they contradict each other. If science is the result of the mind that focuses on distinctions, and we therefore need to develop this mind, how can this mind coexist with the traditional Chinese mind that seeks integration?

Tang believed that we can temporarily suspend our mind of integration and pursue the mind of distinction when we study science. While this suggestion is worth exploring, a suspension of this sort would risk eroding and weakening the mind of integration, and Chinese culture would have to pay a price for developing science. A sensible approach to the question of modernization requires us to examine the consequences and weigh the costs of the development of science for traditional Chinese values. Tang was perhaps overoptimistic in claiming that science could be built on top of traditional Chinese values.

Conclusion

Tang made important contributions to the modernization of Confucianism. His philosophical ideas are basically a modernized version of many Neo-Confucian ideas. His ethical insights, therefore, may not have broken much new ground, but he placed these ideas in the context of dialogue with Western philosophy. In showing both continuities and contrasts between Neo-Confucianism and Western philosophy, he showed how Confucianism can speak to the modern mind and is not merely an archaic and superseded system of thought.

More significantly, his conception of Confucianism, as evolving around the ideas of *ren* and unity, helped to free Confucianism from any tie to particular institutions and conventions. Tang's Confucianism emphasized the spirit of *ren*, rather than the claims of *li*, which are more closely connected with specific social practices and institutions. In doing so, Tang's thought offers room to define and choose what counts as an appropriate embodiment and expression of Confucian values. New Confucianism, including Tang's philosophy, with its emphasis on metaphysics, has often been criticized as moving in a mistaken direction. The criticism makes sense when we compare New Confucianism with the development of contemporary ethics in the West. Recent Western works on ethics characteristically do not appeal to the notions of metaphysical reality or cosmic truth. Yet, this feature is acceptable on the assumption that ethics can be entirely separate from religion, and this is an assumption that Tang's philosophy challenged. Furthermore, contemporary Western ethicists such as Robert Adams and Philip Quinn also defend a connection between morality and religion. (See Beaty et al., 1988.)

Even if Tang is wrong and ethics can be separated from religion, his philosophy can still help us to understand Confucianism from another perspective, not merely as an ethical theory, but as a religion. A Confucian religion that is free from institutionalization and focuses on a direct connection between the individual and the cosmos perhaps has a special appeal and relevance to our modern society.

Bibliography

Works by Tang Junyi

Tang, Junyi 1974: *Shuo zhonghua minzu zhi huaguo piaoling* 説中國民族之花果飄零 (to speak about the scattering of the Chinese race), Taipei: Sanmin Shuju

Tang, Junyi 1986: *Tang Junyi quanji* 唐君毅全集 (the complete works of Tang Junyi), revised edition, vols. 1–30, Taipei: Taiwan Xuesheng Shuju

Vol. 1 *Rensheng zhi tiyan* 人生之體驗 (the experience of life), 1944; *Daode ziwo zhi jianli* 道德自我之建立 (the establishment of the moral self), 1944

Vol. 2 *Xinwu yu rensheng* 心物與人生 (mind, object, and life), 1954; *Aiqing zhi fuyin* 愛情之福音, (the gospel of love) 1945; *Qingnian yu xuewen* 青年與學問 (youth and learning), 1960

Vol. 3 *Rensheng zhi tiyan xubian* 人生之體驗續篇 (the experience of life II), 1961; *Zhihui yu daode* 智慧與道德 (wisdom and morality), 1963; *Bingli qiankun* 病裡乾坤 (the world of sickness), 1980; *Rensheng suibi* 人生隨筆 (notes on life), 1988

Vol. 4 *Zhongguo wenhua zhi jingshen jiazhi* 中國文化之精神價值 (the development of the spirit of Chinese culture), 1953; *Zhongguo wenhua yu shijie* 中國文化與世界 (Chinese culture and the world), 1958

Vol. 5 *Renwen jingshen zhi chongjian* 人文精神之重建 (the reconstruction of the spirit of humanity), 1955

Vol. 6 *Zhongguo renwen jingshen zhi fazhan* 中國人文精神之發展 (the development of the Chinese humanistic spirit), 1958

Vols 7–8 *Zhonghua renwen yu dangjin shijie* 中華人文與當今世界 (Chinese humanity and the contemporary world), 1975

Vols 9–10 *Zhonghua renwen yu dangjin shijie bupian* 中華人文與當今世界補篇 (Chinese humanity and the contemporary world, supplementary chapter), 1988

Vol. 11 *Zhongxi zhexue sixiang zhi bijiao lunwen ji* 中西哲學思想之比較論文集 (collected essays on the comparisons between Chinese and western philosophical thinking), 1943

Vol. 12 *Zhongguo zhexue yuanlun. Daolun pian* 中國哲學原論導論篇 (original discussions on Chinese philosophy, introductory chapter), 1966

Vol. 13 *Zhongguo zhexue yuanlun. Yuanxing pian: Zhongguo zhexue zhong renxing sixiang zhi fazhan* 中國哲學原論原性篇：中國哲學中人性思想之發展 (original discussions on Chinese philosophy, the original nature chapter: the development of thinking on human nature in Chinese philosophy), 1968

Vols 14–16 *Zhongguo zhexue yuanlun. Yuandao pian: Zhongguo zhexue zhong zhi "dao" zhi jianli ji qi fazhan* 中國哲學原論原道篇：中國哲學中之道之建立及其發 (original discussions on Chinese philosophy, the original dao chapter: the establishment and development of thinking on "dao" in Chinese philosophy), 1973

Vol. 17 *Zhongguo zhexue yuanlun. Yuanjiao pian: Song Ming ruxue sixiang zhi fazhan* 中國哲學原論原教篇：宋明儒學思想之發展 (original discussions on Chinese philosophy, the original teaching chapter: the development of Sung–Ming Confucian thinking), 1975

Vol. 18 *Zhexue lunji* 哲學論集 (collected philosophical essays), 1988

Vol. 19 *Essays on Chinese philosophy and culture*, 1988

Vol. 20 *Wenhua yishi yu daode lixing* 文化意識與道德理性 (cultural ideology and moral rationality), 1958

Vols 21–3 *Zhexue gailun* 哲學概論 (a general discussion on philosophy), 1961

Vol. 24 *Shengming cunzai yu xinling jingjie: shengming cunzai zhi sanxiang yu xinling jiujing* 生命存在與心靈境界：生命存在之三向與心靈九境 (life, existence, and the horizons of the heart–mind), 1977

Vol. 25 *Zhi tingguang shu* 致廷光書 (letters to Tingguang), 1983

Vol. 26 *Shujian* 書簡 (letters), 1988

Vols 27–8 *Riji* 日記 (diary), 1988

Vol. 29 *Nianpu; Zhushu nianbiao; Xianren zhushu* 年譜；著述年表；先人著述 (chronology; chronology of writings; writings), 1988

Vol. 30 *Jinian ji* 紀念集 (collected memorial essays), 1988

Works on Tang Junyi

Li, Du 1982: *Tang Junyi xiansheng de zhexue* 唐君毅先生的哲學 (the philosophy of Mr. Tang Junyi), Taipei: Taiwan Xuesheng Shuju

Zhang, Xiang-hao 1994: *Tang Junyi sixiang yanjiu* 唐君毅思想研究 (research on the thought of Tang Junyi), Tianjin: Tianjin Renmin Chubanshe

Further reading

Beaty, Michael, Fisher, Carlton, and Nelson Mark, eds, *Christian Theism and Moral Philosophy*, Macon: Mercer University Press, 1998

Cheung, Chan-fai 1998: "Tang Chun-i's philosophy of love," *Philosophy East and West* 48–52 April, 1998, 257–71. A critical essay on Tang's idea of love

Feng, Ai-qun, ed. 1979: *Tang Junyi xiansheng jinian ji* 唐君毅先生紀念集 (a collection of essays in memory of Tang Junyi), Taipei: Taiwan Xuesheng Shuju

Huo, Taohui, ed. 1992: *Tang Junyi sixiang guoji huiyi lunwen ji* 唐君毅先生國際會議論文集 (a collection of discussion papers of the international conference on Tang Junyi's thought), vols 1–5, Hong Kong: Fazhu

Metzger, Thomas 1977: *Escape From Predicament*, New York: Columbia University Press. Contains some discussion comparing Tang's ideas and Neo-Confucianism

Ng, William 1988: "T'ang Chun-I On Transcendence: Foundations Of A New-Confucian Religious Humanism," *Monumenta Serica* **46** 1988, 291–322. A detailed and critical discussion of Tang's ideas on transcendence

Taiwan xuesheng shuju bianjubu (Taiwan student publishing house editorial board) ed. 1983: *Tang Junyi xiansheng jinian lunwen ji* 唐君毅先生紀念論文集 (a collection of discussion papers in memory of Mr Tang Junyi), Taipei: Taiwan Xuesheng Shuju

Discussion Questions

1. Can metaphysical reality possess moral qualities?
2. Does moral activity involve transcending the actual self?
3. Does everybody share a universal ethical self or do we all have our own individual ethical selves?
4. If our nature is good, what explains evil and vice?
5. On what basis can we consider one virtue to be more fundamental than others?
6. Can we accept the concept of horizon and the recognition of different horizons?
7. Do Tang Junyi's arguments for the metaphysical reality of the heart–mind succeed?
8. Are all cultural activities manifestations of an ethical self?
9. Should the Western objectifying and differentiating mind be brought into Chinese culture?
10. How can we determine whether Chinese culture contains the seeds of democracy?

16

MOU ZONGSAN ON
INTELLECTUAL INTUITION

Refeng Tang

From its beginning in Ancient Greece, Western philosophy has sought to understand the external world. Because traditional Chinese thought, most notably Confucianism, paid little attention to questions about the world, some commentators have claimed that there is no Chinese philosophy at all. One response to this claim has been to reinterpret traditional Chinese thought within a Western philosophical framework. For example, some commentators sought to identify quasi-Western elements in the thought of Mozi and later Mohists because their work contained rudimentary physics, logic, and epistemology. Others reinterpreted Chinese philosophy in terms of a particular Western doctrine. In *The History of Chinese Philosophy*, Feng Youlan attempted to analyze Chinese philosophy from a Western neorealist perspective and also to define periods of Chinese philosophy in accord with the periods of Western philosophy. At best, such approaches can provide no more than fragile legitimacy to Chinese philosophy and risk massive misinterpretation.

A contrasting response to the rejection of Chinese thought as philosophy has been to revise and develop Confucianism in order to give traditional thought new life in the contemporary world. The most influential contributor to this modern new Confucian project was Mou Zongsan (1909–95). Mou was very critical of the rival approaches mentioned above. He remarked that for a philosopher to look for chance parallels is to "attend to trifles to the neglect of essentials so as to strain his interpretation of Western philosophy of which he only has a shallow knowledge; and as to the mainstream of Chinese learning, he is totally at sea" (Mou, 1963b, p. 2). Mou judged that philosophers who reinterpret Chinese philosophy in terms of a particular Western school have no real understanding of Chinese philosophy at all.

In establishing his own approach to Chinese philosophy, Mou Zongsan epitomized the development of Confucianism in the modern world. Of Xiong Shili's three most gifted pupils, Mou reached the highest level of intellectual achievement. He was widely read and had deep understanding of both Chinese and Western philosophy. This scope of learning provided a unique vantage point from which to compare Chinese and Western thought. His new Confucianism not only established a complete system of Chinese philosophy, but also provided grounds for the critical assessment of Western philosophy.

Mou Zongsan was born in Shandong province in 1909 and studied philosophy in Peking University. He wrote his first book *A Study of Chinese Xuan Xue and Moral Philosophy in Respect of Zhou Yi* when he was still a university student. The work sought to discover a Chinese natural philosophy, philosophy of science, and theory of evolution and used Western categories to provide a framework for his investigation.

After graduation, his study of Russell and Whitehead's *Principia Mathematica* and Wittgenstein's *Tractatus Logico-Philosophicus* led to his second book, *The Model of Logic*. This work established his status as a logician. Indeed, Mou has been the only contemporary Chinese philosopher to move to Confucianism from logic. Mou's fundamental thought was that logic is independent of metaphysics. In retrospect, Mou did not consider *The Model of Logic* to be a good book, but it led to two further works. *On Logic* provided a better treatment of logic itself, and *A Critique of the Cognitive Mind* approached Kant's philosophy from apriorism and subjectivism in logic. He denied that logic is dependent on the actual world and relations in it and sought a different origin of logic. "And this inquiry knocks at the door of 'the subject of knowledge' and establishes a 'transcendental logical I'" (Mou, 1989, p. 72). According to Mou, the cognitive mind is derived from the metaphysical mind and develops from the self-negation of the metaphysical mind. This exploration of Kantian themes about the self is a very important stage in the development of Mou's thought.

In 1949, Mou left Beijing to teach in Taiwan. He had a very strong "cultural consciousness" in this period and published three books of reflections on Chinese culture and politics: *Historical Philosophy*, *Politics and Administration*, and *Moral Idealism*. Mou argued that Chinese culture is positive in terms of morality, but negative in terms of democratic politics and science. In contrast to some other cultural conservatives, he admired Western democracy and science, but in contrast to Westernizers, he insisted that Chinese morality was compatible with democracy and science. He held that Chinese morality must undergo a procedure of self-negation (*zi wo kan xian*) in order to develop democracy and science.

Mou left Taiwan in 1960 to teach at Chinese University of Hong Kong. Until the mid-1970s he devoted himself to close examination of the doctrines of Confucianism, Buddhism, and Daoism. This exploration led to the books *Talent and Mysterious Reasoning* (on Daoism), *Mind and Nature* (on Confucianism), and *Buddha Nature and Prajna* (on Buddhism). *Talent and Mysterious Reasoning* considers the development of Chinese philosophy from the Eastern Han dynasty to the Wei and Jin dynasties and represents Mou's fundamental views on Daoism. *Mind and Nature* and the later work *From Lu Xiang Shan to Liu Ji Shan* concern Confucianism from the North Song dynasty to the end of

Ming dynasty. *Buddha Nature and Prajna* is about Buddhism of the Northern and Southern dynasties and the Sui and Tang dynasties. These works grew from his earlier period of cultural consciousness and were also a necessary preparation for his later philosophical system of moral metaphysics.

Mou retired from Chinese University of Hong Kong in 1974 and began a period of great intellectual achievement that lasted until the end of his life. He traveled back and forth between Hong Kong and Taiwan to give lectures at many institutions and established his philosophical system of moral metaphysics and his moral philosophy. His books *Intellectual Intuition and Chinese Philosophy, Phenomena and Noumena,* and *On the Summum Bonum* constituted his philosophical system. This major revival of Chinese philosophy was based on careful study of Chinese sources and a deeper understanding of Chinese philosophical thought and culture. His response to these traditional sources can be seen in *Nineteen Lectures on Chinese Philosophy* and *Fourteen Lectures on the Route Connecting Chinese and Western Philosophy.*

In what follows, I devote the first section to Mou's understanding of Chinese philosophy; the second section to Mou's moral metaphysics; the third section to his moral philosophy; and the final section to his comparative study of Chinese and Western philosophy.

The Quintessence of Chinese Philosophy

According to Mou, "Chinese philosophy began in the Spring and Autumn and Warring States Periods (770–221 B.C.). It started with the various schools of pre-Qin times" (Mou, 1983b, p. 51). In Mou's view, the four main pre-Qin schools (Confucianism, Daoism, Mohism, and Legalism) were responses to the decline of Zhou Culture. In the Western Zhou dynasty (about 1066 B.C.– 771 B.C.), there was a complete system of social rules or etiquette that lasted for 300 years, but in the Spring and Autumn Period (770–476 B.C.), these rules of Zhou etiquette lost their power. This is what Mou called "the decline of Zhou rites" (1983b, p. 60), and the main pre-Qin schools sought to deal with problems generated by this decline. The Confucian and Daoist schools, in addition to the Buddhism that was later imported from India, provided the major doctrines of Chinese philosophy.

Confucius held a positive attitude toward the Zhou rites. He thought that the Confucian virtue of *ren* (benevolence) gave "life to the Zhou rites" (1983b, p. 61). Confucius saw the decline of Zhou rites as a consequence of the degeneration of the nobility. Although Confucius allowed that the decrees were open to revision, he insisted that the problem was not in the rites themselves, but in the people who no longer followed them. In this way, Confucius turned our attention from objective morality to the moral subject. As Mou put it, "Confucian thought opened up the resources of value and established the moral subject. In this respect, it is unmatched" (1983b, p. 62). In the Song and Ming dynasties, Confucian thought developed into the idealist philosophy of Neo-Confucianism, and Mou's contemporary new Confucianism is a further development of this Neo-Confucian doctrine.

For Confucians, because Zhou rites are based on human nature, they are not purely external. In contrast, Daoism considered Zhou rites to be an external constraint on our lives and thus held a negative attitude toward them. Although Mou thought that Daoism is blind to the connection between Zhou rites and human nature, he recognized that the fundamental spirit of Daoism required a high degree of freedom, which he saw as "unfettered, integrated with the world, and dependent on nothing." Thus "there is a fundamental insight behind Daoism, that is, being free and unrestrained" (1983b, p. 64).

Buddhism, the third major philosophical doctrine in China, was imported and developed in the Sui and Tang dynasties. Mou saw Buddhism as a "very contentful and complicated" doctrine. He held that Buddhist philosophy was "the most illuminating and has opened up the newest states of reason and has involved the most levels" (1983b, p. 253).

Of the three main doctrines, Mou considered Confucianism to be the main trend of Chinese philosophy because the structure of its thought originated in China and because it was centrally concerned with moral consciousness. Mou further explained the concentration on morality in Chinese philosophy in terms of its "concerned consciousness" (*you huan yi shi*), that is, its tendency to bemoan the state of the universe and to pity the fate of mankind. The deeply Confucian commitment to "concerned consciousness" leads naturally to moral consciousness (Mou, 1963b, p. 12). Mou compared Confucian "concerned consciousness" with Buddhist pity and Christian love. He saw all of these as a kind of cosmic feeling, but understood the Confucian spirit to be derived from a consciousness of concern in contrast to a religious spirit that was derived from a Christian consciousness of dread or a Buddhist consciousness of hardship. Thus according to Mou, Confucianism was based on a positive aspect of human life (1963b, pp. 13–14).

Mou considered Daoism to be important as well, because it contained great wisdom. As Mou understood it, Daoist wisdom enabled Chinese scholars to understand Buddhism, and Buddhism provided the greatest philosophical illumination.

Although emphasizing the concentration on morality in Chinese philosophy, Mou did not consider Chinese philosophy to be limited to this one branch of philosophy. According to Mou, Confucian, Daoist, and Buddhist doctrines are all vertical systems that deal in different ways with metaphysics.

Mou thought that Chinese metaphysics displayed its most distinctive features in Confucianism. He explicitly opposed the claim that Confucianism is concerned only with morality and has nothing to do with existence (Mou, 1983b, p. 71). According to Mou, Confucian morality implies a moral metaphysics,

that is, a metaphysics based on morality. Mou held that to have a real understanding of pre-Qin Confucianism, one must take all five Confucian classics
into account: *LunYu* (The Analects), *Mencius, Zhong Yong* (The Doctrine of
the Mean), *Yi Zhuan*, and *Da Xue* (The Great Learning). Only in this way
can we see that Confucianism not only talks about morality in *Lun Yu* and
Mencius, but also discusses existence in *Zhong Yong* and *Yi Zhuan*. According
to Mou, the Confucian conception of existence is derived from the concept
of *tian* (heaven): "[T]he Chinese conception of *tian* is responsible for the
existence of everything" (1983b, p. 75).

Mou held that the characteristic feature of Chinese philosophy is that it starts
with the subject. "The object is taken in through the subject. The subject
projects itself onto the object and takes the object into the subject. Thus it
is based on morality even when it talks about metaphysics." Confucius's concept of *ren* (benevolence) is used to represent the subject. "*Ren* is also mind"
(1983b, p. 79). In this way, Mencius talked about nature through mind. Mou
argued that the nature of *ren* is "real subjectivity." "This real subjectivity is
not the subjective subject in the ordinary sense; it is an objective subject.
Everyone is like this, the sage is like me as well" (1983b, p. 80).

Mou thought that another important concept related to the subject is *shen
du* (behaving oneself even when one is alone) in *Zhong Yong* and *Da Xue*. As
moral consciousness in the strict sense, *shen du* is a *gong fu* (art) presented
through the subject. Later, Wang Yangming derived his notion of "reaching
conscience" from *shen du*.

According to Mou, the concept of *shen* (divine) in *Yi Zhuan* also concerns
the subject. As Mou understands, although *Yi Zhuan* mainly discusses metaphysics, the subject is involved in its metaphysics. One is instructed to "know
changes by exploring *shen*," and *shen* is defined in terms of *cheng* (sincerity).
Cheng, in turn, is a virtue that is based on morality. Thus, for Mou, the metaphysics of *Yi Zhuan* is based on morality.

Mou held that there is also a metaphysics in Daoism. Laozi said, "Everything in the world is produced from being, and being is produced from
nothingness." According to Mou, " 'nothingness' is not an ontological concept, but a practical, life-concerning conception" (1983b, p. 91). What it really
means is letting things be. Mou held that it is indeed great wisdom to let
things take their own course through a mental state of being "empty and with
no attachment." Thus, Daoist metaphysics is based on a practical concept of
"nothingness." In this sense, Daoism has a "practical ontology" or "practical
metaphysics" (1983b, p. 94).

Mou also held that the Daoist concept of being is not an ontological concept, but rather concerns the intentionality of mental states: "Being" is not
taking something to put into empty "nothingness"; it is the directedness of
mental states. And with "nothingness" and "being," we can understand *dao*.
Nothingness and being are double characters of *dao*; the combination of these

two is *xuan* (mystery), and only *xuan* resumes *dao*'s concrete function of creating everything (1983b, p. 103).

Thus Mou claims that Daoist metaphysics is a subjective account of existence. Moreover, Daoism is a pure formation of states. This is to say that "*dao* creates everything" is just an expedient saying. In Daoism, unlike in Confucianism, "the creation is indeed 'creation without creating'" (1983b, p. 104).

Mou held that Buddhist metaphysics is best illustrated in the state of perfect teaching (*yuan jiao*). In the Mahayana teaching, there is a saying that "one mind opens two doors." The "one mind" is the Buddhist empty mind; the two doors are the "suchness door" (*zhen ru men*) and "circulation door" (*sheng mie men*). The Buddhist empty mind is a transcendent mind with no obsession. The suchness door leads to the empty complete law, while the circulation door leads to the circulation law. The Buddhist empty mind can directly "create" the empty complete law, but it can only indirectly "create" the circulation law. The Buddhist empty mind becomes obsessed by the world of circulation through self-negation and in this way can "create" the circulation law.

According to Mou, this account is applicable to Confucianism and Daoism as well as to Buddhism. The Buddhist empty mind is just the Confucian *ben xin* (original mind) or conscience or the Daoist *dao* mind. Mou calls all of these "the infinite mind." To use Kantian terms, the claim that the infinite mind can open two doors to the world just means that the infinite mind can have both intellectual intuition and sensible intuition. The empty complete law and circulation law are the domains of *noumena* and *phenomena* respectively.

In Chinese philosophy, everyone has the capacity to become a sage or Buddha because everyone can have both intellectual intuition and sensible intuition. All of us are born with an infinite mind, although we must preserve it. Many of us do not have intellectual intuition because we have not preserved our infinite mind.

Thus according to Mou, the quintessence of Chinese philosophy is in its metaphysics. This metaphysics sees human beings as moral subjects who have a capacity for intellectual intuition that at the same time creates the world.

Intellectual Intuition and Moral Metaphysics

Mou greatly admired Kant. "[A]ll the ancient philosophies from Greek to Kant converge on Kant, and all kinds of philosophy after Kant develop from Kant" (Mou, 1963b, p. 39). According to Mou, Kantian philosophy is the only philosophy that can engage in dialogue with Chinese philosophy. It is precisely through his dialogue with Kant that Mou established his moral metaphysics.

According to Kant, however, intellectual intuition does not belong to human beings, but belongs solely to God. In his *Critique of Pure Reason*, Kant drew a distinction between *noumena* (things as they are in themselves), and *phenomena* (things as they are experienced as objects in space and time according to the categories of the understanding). There is a corresponding distinction between intellectual intuition, which creates *noumena* as objects of intuition, and sensible intuition, which is aware of independently existing *phenomena* that impinge upon the mind. For Kant, although it is intelligible to attribute intellectual intuition to God, we have no knowledge that God does have this power. We do know, however, that human beings are limited to sensible intuition. Thus, God might have intellectual intuition of things as they are in themselves, but we human beings are limited to sensible intuition of *phenomena*.

Denying intellectual intuition to human beings seemed to Mou to be a crucial flaw in Kant's philosophy. Mou held that human intellectual intuition is crucial for both Kant's philosophy and Chinese philosophy. He argued that for Kant's philosophy to be coherent, human intellectual intuition must be a real possibility. Further, "[I]f it is true that human beings cannot have intellectual intuition, then the whole of Chinese philosophy must collapse completely, and the thousands years of effort must be in vain. It is just an illusion" (Mou, 1975, p. 3). Mou had two lines of reasoning to support his claim that human intellectual intuition is a theoretical necessity for Kant.

Mou's first argument was based on Kant's moral philosophy. He started with the priority of morality. Human beings are first of all moral beings. In Kant's terms, practical reasoning is prior to theoretical reasoning. Following Kant, to act morally is to behave in accord with the categorical imperative. We have a capacity to act according to the categorical imperative through what Kant calls free will or what Mou calls the infinite mind. For Mou, the infinite mind "is the transcendental foundation of moral behavior and is itself absolutely and infinitely universal" (1974, p. 190). Thus, for human beings to be moral beings in the Kantian sense, limited human beings must also be infinite. If human minds are not infinite in this sense, then they cannot issue imperatives with no limitation, and the categorical imperative as the basis of morality is impossible.

Furthermore, human infinite mind must have the features of God's mind. Free will, as the source of the categorical imperative, must be only a cause, and not an effect. It can limit other principles, but cannot be limited by them. This role of "first cause" is filled by God. If the first cause is absolute and infinite, then free will is absolute and infinite as well. Because there cannot be two different absolute and infinite substances in the world, God's mind and human infinite mind must be one and the same. Finally, if God's mind has intellectual intuitions, then human infinite mind must have intellectual intuitions as well.

Mou's second line of reasoning in support of human intellectual intuition is based on Kant's distinction between *phenomena* and *noumena*. Mou argues that to establish this distinction Kant must admit human intellectual intuition. Mou begins by clarifying Kant's concept of *noumena*. He claims that Kant is unclear about the nature of *noumena*. Sometimes it seems that Kant wants *noumena* to be a purely factual concept. We can perfectly well "think the same objects as things in themselves, though we cannot know them." "For otherwise we should arrive at the absurd conclusion that there is phenomenal appearance without something that appears" (Kant, 1881, p. 377). But Mou insists that Kant's *noumena* must be "a concept of value in a very strong sense," since "only in this sense can we understand his transcendental distinction between *phenomena* and *noumena*" (Mou, 1975, p. 8). Thus, the concept of *noumena* is not a concept of the "original appearance"; it is not an objective fact we can always approach but can never reach; it is something we can never approach with our sensibility and understanding. Thus it is a transcendent concept. The inability of our knowledge to reach it is a matter of transcendence, not a matter of extent (Mou, 1975, p. 7). According to Mou, *noumena* are not a purely objective reality, and intellectual intuition is not a kind of absolute representation.

Mou argued that if the concept of *noumena* is a value concept and if only God has intellectual intuition of *noumena*, then there is no way for humans to understand the distinction between *phenomena* and *noumena*. If we cannot understand *noumena* in the sense of value, then Kant's concept of *noumena* is empty, and the distinction between *phenomena* and *noumena* is not secured (Mou, 1975, pp. 13–4). "To secure *noumena* in the sense of value, we must exhibit the subject in ourselves. The subject has intellectual intuition by itself. It can present *noumena* in the sense of value before us. Thus we can represent the concrete and true meaning of *noumena* clearly and distinctly. We should not locate the infinite mind solely in God. It is exhibited on our human being as well" (1975, p. 16).

We can consider why it is so crucial to establish the distinction between *noumena* and *phenomena*. Some critics of Kant argue that the distinction is ultimately unintelligible and that it can be detached from the analytic argument of Kant's positive metaphysics of experience (Strawson, 1966). In contrast, Mou holds that "the transcendental distinction between *phenomena* and *noumena* is crucial for the whole system of Kant's philosophy. It is "the highest and most fundamental insight" (Mou, 1975, p. 4). It is not difficult to see the reason for Mou's view. The distinction between *phenomena* and *noumena* is very congenial to Chinese moral metaphysics.

Intellectual intuition is crucial for Mou's moral metaphysics. For Mou, " 'moral metaphysics' accounts for the existence of things with moral substance which are exhibited by moral consciousness. Thus, moral substance is at the same time metaphysical substance" (Mou, 1975, pp. 92–3). And for Mou, moral substance is infinite mind. The free infinite mind is both a moral substance which opens the way to the domain of morality and a metaphysical substance which opens the way to the domain of existence. The domain of existence is the domain of *noumena*.

Mou explains his position in terms of the creativity of the infinite mind. According to Mou, "there is nothing beyond mind" (Mou, 1975, p. 98).

> In intellectual intuition, things present themselves as they are, that is, things exist as "they are in themselves." Thus things in this case "cannot be treated as objects." . . . Kant talks about "objects" in the case of intellectual intuition for the sake of convenience; in fact this does not really mean "object." . . . Objects are only *phenomena*. We can only talk about objects in the case of *phenomena*. *Phenomena* are placed there in opposition to understanding and sensibility. Thus we can only talk about objects in the case of understanding and sensibility: understanding and sensibility face what is opposed to them and cognize or determine them objectively and cognitively but do not create them. Thus what they face is an external object. In the case of intellectual intuition, things are developed internally in an unrestrained manner. Thus, mind absorbs things into itself. Things are not opposed to mind, but are the exhibition of the infinite mind, that is, the manifestation and openness of the infinite mind: things are where the infinite mind is working, and the infinite mind works where things are. Thus, they are one and the same. For this reason, things are in no sense objects. (Mou, 1975, p. 99)

Sensible intuition is a principle of presentation: it presents a real concrete entity to us, but it cannot create the entity. Thus, it cognitively presents the entity, but does not ontologically create it (Mou, 1975, p. 129). A metaphysics on this basis is derived from the free infinite mind and is therefore a metaphysics with no obsession (*zhi*).

According to Mou, the cognitive mind is derived from the infinite mind. Cognitive character is itself a kind of obsession. It takes *noumena* as its object and thus produces *phenomena*. We thus have "ontology in the domain of *phenomena*" or an "ontology of obsession." With this insight, we can have a clear understanding of the distinction between *phenomena* and *noumena*. *Noumena* can never be the object of cognitive mind. The cognitive mind can never reach *noumena*, which in this sense are transcendent. Thus, Mou understands Kant's domain of *phenomena* in terms of the Buddhist conception of obsession, and completes the conception of obsession with Kant's thought. Since Buddhist obsession emphasizes worry, the obsession of the cognitive mind is not exhibited clearly in Buddhism.

Mou thus suggested that we have two layers of ontology: for the infinite mind, we have "ontology with no obsession"; for the cognitive mind, we have "ontology with obsession." According to this picture, Kant emphasizes the obsessive ontology of the cognitive mind, while Chinese philosophy emphasizes the ontology without obsession of the infinite mind. Mou finds a rich account of "ontology with no obsession" in Buddhism. He thought that the contrast between what is obsessive and what is not obsessive is especially clear in Buddhism and has special ontological significance. But according to Mou, ontology with no obsession in the end belongs to Confucianism because moral consciousness is the best way to exhibit the free infinite mind.

Perfect Teaching and the *Summum Bonum*

Mou greatly admired Kant's moral philosophy and argued that only with Kant did Western philosophy begin to have a real understanding of the nature of morality. Kant was the first in the West to say that "being moral is determined by moral rule, and is not determined by external objects." Furthermore, he agreed with Kant that the highest morality is the *summum bonum*, which brings morality and happiness together. But Mou was dissatisfied with Kant because Kant could not prove that the *summum bonum* is a real possibility in the world. Kant claimed that the existence of God forms the foundation of the possibility of the *summum bonum*. But:

> given that human morality and happiness, which is related to [human] "existence" (that is, physical nature), cannot be harmonious, how can a divine intelligence or divine volition, which is totally different from that of a human being, make them harmonious transcendentally and externally? This is rather difficult to understand. It is the same reality and the same physical nature. How can those which are not coordinate become coordinate simply because there is a God there creating them? (Mou, 1985, pp. 239–40)

Mou thought that it is crucial for a philosophical system to solve the problem of the *summum bonum*. "According to Kant, the accomplishment of a philosophical system depends on two layers of legislation. Of the two layers of legislation, practical reasoning is prior to speculative reasoning. And practical reasoning necessarily points to the *summum bonum*. Thus the *summum bonum* is the mark of the accomplishment of a philosophical system" (Mou, 1985, p. ii). Mou considered this view to be central to the ancient Western understanding of philosophy:

> The term philosophy means "love of wisdom." What is wisdom? To have insight into the *summum bonum* is wisdom. What is it to love wisdom? To yearn for the *summum bonum*, to be sincerely interested in it, to love and desire it ardently is to love wisdom. Thus philosophy or the discipline of wisdom (the practical theory of wisdom) as an area of learning cannot be independent of the *summun bonum*. Thus philosophy, according to its ancient meaning, can be directly called the theory of the *summum bonum*. (Mou, 1985, p. v)

According to Mou, Chinese philosophy has a better understanding of the *summum bonum* than the understanding that we can find in Kant. Mou argued that the *summum bonum* can be explained in terms of the perfect teaching in

Chinese philosophy (Mou, 1985, p. 172). Teaching is a system that "can illuminate human rationality and make a human being purify his life and reach the highest ideal state of rationality through all varieties of practice" (Mou, 1985, p. 269). Mou considered Christianity in the West and Confucianism, Buddhism, and Daoism in the East to be teachings (*jiao*) (Mou, 1985, p. 269). Within any doctrine of this sort, there can be different accounts or teachings, and every account is also a system. Teaching in its perfect form is called perfect teaching.

There is a need to judge which system or account is the perfect teaching. In Buddhism, to judge the teachings (*pan jiao*) is to give the laws of the Buddha and their ways of elaboration a reasonable arrangement (Mou, 1985, p. 266). To judge the teaching is to distinguish merely expedient sayings from the true expressions of the teaching, not to criticize the teaching itself. Great wisdom is needed to make such judgment. One must understand the real intention of the Buddha and judge the teaching objectively, rather than adhering to the teaching subjectively (Mou, 1985, p. 266–7). The perfect teaching, by giving a true expression of the teaching, is the highest grade of judging teaching.

According to Mou, Tian Tai Zong provides the best judgment of the teaching of Chinese Buddhism. In Tian Tai's judgment, "wisdom without getting to the bottom of the matter and kindness without reaching others" characterize the minor teachings of Hinayana (*xiao cheng*). The wisdom of these teachings is limited and their kindness is not enough to ferry others across the sea of bitterness and can only free oneself. In contrast, in the great teachings of Mahayana (*da cheng*), wisdom can reach the domain of the infinite, and extricating all the others is a precondition of extricating oneself.

Nevertheless, not all the teachings of Mahayana count as the perfect teaching. The real perfect teaching is in *Fa Hua*. According to Tian Tai, the fundamental principle of the perfect teaching is exhibited by the word "is" (*ji*). When talking about *bodhi*, the perfect saying is "Vexation is *bodhi*." When talking about *nirvana*, the perfect saying is "Life-and-death (or circulation) is *nirvana*." The "is" in these sayings is a recognition of a real identity. Vexation and *bodhi* and life-and-death and *nirvana* are just *wu ming* and Dharma-nature (*fa xing*), but *wu ming* and Dharma-nature are one and the same. Each is purely dependent on the other, and neither has independent existence.

According to Mou, once the perfect teaching is reached, we can obtain the *summum bonum* in the Buddhist sense. This understanding of the *summum bonum* is based on the saying that "the three principles are three virtues" because the three principles of *banruo*, extrication, and *fa shen* all belong to the moral aspect of human life. The wisdom virtue of *banruo*, the break virtue of extrication, and the *fa shen* virtue of nirvana all concern the law of the three thousand worlds. As a consequence, subjective virtue and objective law have never been separated, and happiness belongs to the domain of law. In this perfect state, happiness is always combined with morality. Existence in this state has no definite features and is not a kind of thing created by God. When virtue is present, the whole world alters and all the laws become Buddhist laws that accord with happiness. Thus, virtue can accord with happiness, and the harmony between virtue and happiness that is established in the perfect teaching is a necessity. This necessity is a matter of real identity rather than a matter of verbal analysis. That is, virtue and happiness are one and the same: virtue is happiness, and happiness is virtue.

Mou held that the perfect teaching can also be found in Daoism, although it has not been expressed clearly. There can also be judgment of teachings in Daoism. In chapter 38 of Daodejing (Lao Tzu, 1970, p. 99), it is said that "one gains virtue when one loses *dao*, gains *ren* when one loses virtue, gains justice when one loses *ren* and gains etiquette when one loses justice. Etiquette is what we have when there is not much honesty and faith, and it is the starting point of disorder." This presentation arranges teachings in order. The highest is *dao*, since it follows nature. By letting things take their own course, one does all. By letting things take their own course, one destroys nothing. Rather, one destroys things when one changes their course. Thus, *dao* is the perfect state. Daoists do not deny virtue, *ren*, justice, and etiquette, but explain how they can really be established only by placing them in relation to the *dao* and by letting things take their own course. Accordingly, "one sustains one's achievement as a sage by discarding the sage and develop one's *ren* by abandoning *ren*" (Wang Bi (226–49) see Lau, D. C., et al, 1996).

Mou argued that the Daoist perfect state is perfect as understood as a state, but is not perfect existentially. Although Laozi said, "Everything in the world is produced from being, and being is produced from nothingness," nothingness, as letting things be, is merely a stance with no ontological significance.

Mou extended his analysis of the perfect teaching to Confucianism, where perfect teaching cannot be exhibited directly by the "is" of identity because Confucianism has a vertical backbone in it, that is, moral creation. According to Mou, the Confucian infinite mind is closely related to *ren*, and the infinite mind's perfect state that "takes everything as a whole" must be established by the fluid creativity of *ren ti*. Thus, it cannot be exhibited by horizontal *banruo* wisdom or *xuan* wisdom and must be exhibited by the vertical structure of *ren ti's* creativity.

Mou admits that the perfect teaching of a vertical theory is difficult to explain. Confucian teaching starts with moral consciousness to "illuminate human rationality and to make people act rationally and reach the highest ideal state" (Mou, 1985, p. 306). Acting upon rational imperatives (the categorical imperative) is moral practice. Through such action, a human's existential state comes into agreement with rationality. Thus moral practice must be related to existence. Because it "either improves existence or creates a new existence," "moral practice improves and creates" (Mou, 1985, p. 306). "Everything in the world is an established existence, but everything is an existence without definite features.

Every existence is moistened by rationality, which, as described in *Zhong Yong* "takes part in the creation of the world and assists in change and cultivation" (Mou, 1985, pp. 306–7).

In this way, the infinite mind moistens and coordinates everything and is exhibited through moral practice. The highest stage of this activity is to take everything in the world as a single whole, with nothing being beyond the fluid creativity of the infinite mind. A life that takes all things in the world as a single whole is a holy life. In Confucianism, this is the life of a sage, the life of a great person, or the life of the benevolent. At this stage of Confucian practice, the perfect teaching can be presented.

The position was already captured in Confucius' injunction to "practice *ren* and know the world." Mencius' view that one should "preserve one's moral mind, develop one's real nature and follow the natural law" was a further development of the same idea. Wang Yangming contributed to the explication of this idea in his discussion of mind, intention, conscience, and world: "There is no benevolence and evil in the mind as an existence. There is benevolence and evil in one's intention. Conscience is consciousness of benevolence and evil. Doing benevolence and removing evil is to correct the world." However, this is still not the perfect teaching. According to Mou, the perfect teaching is contained in Hu Wufeng's claim that "the natural law and human desire are different functions of the same existence" (Mou, 1985, p. 324).

Only through the perfect teaching can the coordination between virtue and happiness be a real possibility. In the state of perfect teaching, mind, intention, conscience, and the world form an integral entity: they are one and the same. To follow the natural law is to do both what one desires and what is morally required. By being moral, we change the world according to the mind. Thus, virtue and happiness coincide: virtue is happiness, and happiness is virtue.

This account of the *summum bonum* is different from Kant's account. According to Kant, the world is created by God, and it cannot change in accord with the cultivation of morality. He, therefore, cannot give a clear explanation of the *summum bonum*. For Mou, an infinite mind is sufficient to account for the possibility of the *summum bonum*, and it is not necessary to personalize the infinite mind as an infinite individual. Confucianism, Daoism, and Buddhism, the three basic doctrines of Chinese culture, all affirm this infinite mind without giving it a personal nature. According to Mou, personalizing the infinite mind is unfounded, and only the three doctrines of Chinese culture can give a rational account of the *summum bonum* (Mou, 1985, p. 244). Thus, the possibility of the *summum bonum* depends on our own wisdom. We can have the *summum bonum* if we are wise enough.

One can object that Mou's account of the *summum bonum* is a gross deception that expresses deep flaws in Chinese philosophical culture. The position diminishes the role of knowledge, and its claim that morality can never be separated from law invites an empty formalism. But it is important to see the significance of bringing wisdom into the domain of morality. And this is indeed the most important difference between Chinese moral philosophy and Western moral philosophy. The orthodoxy of Western moral philosophy is to separate morality from wisdom; thus there is always a difficulty for Western philosophers to coordinate morality and happiness. While Kantian ethics and contemporary deontology give prior status to morality, the social contract tradition, egoism, and consequentialism concentrates on happiness. But they all have their own difficulties. Mou's idea is that the coordination of morality and happiness depends on the highest level of wisdom. Once we are in the highest state of wisdom, morality and happiness are just one and the same. For Mou, the crucial thing for moral philosophy is wisdom, it is neither morality nor happiness.

Admittedly, similar ideas can also be found in Western philosophy. Historically, we find this idea in Hegel; in contemporary thought, Bernard Williams, Charles Taylor, and Hubert and Stuart Dreyfus elaborate the idea in different ways. Nevertheless, this is obviously not the mainstream of Western thought. Moreover, there is still a difference between the kind of moral wisdom we find in Chinese philosophy and in Western philosophy. And to see the real reason for the difference, we need to go deeper to the mentality that underlies Chinese culture and Western culture. This leads us to the difference between Chinese philosophy and Western philosophy.

Chinese Philosophy versus Western Philosophy

To many Western philosophers, Mou's system seems to be a religious faith rather that a philosophy. It is very much like a kind of religion (Berthrong, 1994, p. 107). Although Mou specifically denied that he was a theologian, he was conscious of the religious aspects of Confucianism and argued for accepting them. Nevertheless, Mou considered that Confucian thought qualified as a philosophical doctrine. He had a special understanding of religion and philosophy. "Roughly speaking, whatever a sage or wise person says is a religion. Without mentioning the sage, we may put it in the following way: whatever illuminates human reason and leads a person to purify his life to the highest state by practice can be called a religion. If philosophy is not purely technical and if it is to be distinguished from science, then philosophy is a religion as well" (Mou, 1985, p. ii).

This account is based on Mou's particular understanding of philosophy. "[A]s far as human activity is concerned, whatever reflects and explains with rationality and ideas counts as philosophy" (Mou, 1963b, p. 4). Accordingly, Mou distinguished three kinds of philosophy: Western philosophy, Chinese philosophy, and Indian philosophy. Through their particularity, different kinds of philosophy talk about different things, but through their universality what they talk about is indeed universal. A particular kind of philosophy reflects the universal through a particular aperture. This gives Chinese philosophy and Western philosophy different features. "Chinese culture concerns life while Western culture emphasizes nature or external objects" (Mou, 1963b, p. 11). This "life" is moral, rather than biological. Thus, Chinese culture concentrates on morality while Western culture concentrates on knowledge.

Mou held that Chinese philosophy did not start with figures like the Greek natural philosophers, but began with philosopher-kings like Yao, Shun, Yu, Tang, and Zhong. As a result of this origin, the main concern of Chinese philosophy is life. "Its main aim is to coordinate our lives, to run our lives, to arrange our lives" (Mou, 1963b, p. 15). "This is different from those Greek natural philosophers. Their object is nature. The main theme is nature. And this determines that they later on have cosmology and ontology. The combination of these two is what Aristotle calls metaphysics. . . . The Chinese are different. The Chinese first of all emphasize morality, the concept of virtue comes out first" (Mou, 1983b, p. 15).

According to Mou:

> Western culture looks outwards, either to nature or to God. But Chinese culture is different. Chinese people look up to heaven as well, but "heaven sees what our people see, heaven hears what our people hear." Thus, it is not enough to look up to heaven. One needs to look at the people as well. And what the people see and hear depends on yourself. Thus you must be clear about morality. If you want the support of ordinary people, you must be responsible. Thus, the light gradually turns inwards. (Mou, 1983b, p. 16)

Mou considered moral practice to be the blind spot of Western culture, and this also rendered Western religion empty. "With its blind morality and empty religion, even its science, technology and democratic politics cannot lead society to its perfect state. This is the flaw of Western culture" (Mou, 1985, p. 156). "Where morality is blind, people turn to make a fetish of science as something omnipotent and think that all problems can be solved when we have enough scientific knowledge. At that point, there is nothing that can be called fate. This is the ignorance and conceit of the shallow rationalists" (Mou, 1985, p. 157).

To illustrate the difference between Chinese philosophy and Western philosophy, Mou distinguished two kinds of truth: extensional truth and intensional truth. Roughly speaking, extensional truths are scientific truths. They "do not belong to the subject and can be objectively asserted" (Mou, 1983b, p. 21). Intensional truths have the form of intensional propositions and are propositional attitudes that belong to the subject. Rather than scientific truths, they are truths of humanity or culture. Mou held that we must admit the existence of intensional truth. What is said in Buddhism, Daoism, and Confucianism are intensional truths that have intensional, rather than extensional, universality.

Accordingly, they are not scientific truths, and those who describe Chinese philosophy as science destroy Chinese culture.

Mou further explains that the difference between intensional and extensional truth is that extensional truth has abstract universality while intensional truth has concrete universality. The term "concrete universality" is in fact from Hegel. Mou views Hegel as a philosopher who can get out of the limitation of Western orthodoxy, but he does not appreciate Hegel's way of expressing the idea. He thinks that concrete universality can be better exhibited in Chinese philosophy. According to Mou, concrete universality has a kind of elasticity. It is represented to different extents. It cannot be established forever.

Mou argued that the exploration of extensional truth is well-developed in the West while the exploration of intensional truth is well-developed in China. Because as truth both are universal, China can learn extensional truth from the West while the West can learn intensional truth from China. According to Mou, Chinese people realized their limitations in dealing with extensional truth and became interested in science and democratic politics after the May Fourth Movement. He further argued that to learn extensional truth, it is not enough to gain knowledge. One must acquire the mentality behind this knowledge at a very deep level of culture. In contrast, Western people have not realized their limitations in dealing with intensional truth. Because they do not consider intensional truth to be truth at all, they cannot have a perfect society in spite of their well-developed science and democratic politics. For the West to develop a real understanding of intensional truth, Western people must acquire the kind of mentality behind intensional truth.

It seems that Mou was right to say that Chinese culture emphasizes human life and morality while Western culture emphasizes empirical knowledge, but underlying this difference is a closely related difference in attitude toward nature. In Western culture, nature is a resource with which people can satisfy their desires (including their desire to know). Thus, Western culture stresses the importance of exploring nature and gaining empirical knowledge to make nature work for human ends. In Chinese culture, nature is there for people to respect, integrate, or escape. None of these attitudes motivate people to explore nature and gain empirical knowledge. When there is conflict between human desire and nature, Western culture challenges nature while Chinese culture challenges human desire. Accordingly, Western culture develops empirical science to conquer nature while Chinese culture develops morality to control human desire. For this reason, Chinese culture contains attitudes that are negative towards empirical knowledge and positive towards morality.

In reality, different Chinese doctrines have different attitudes towards morality. Both Daoism and Buddhism propose a morality that denies human desire. For Daoism, there is no point in exploring or attempting to change the world, and the best strategy is "to let things take their own course" (wu wei). This strategy denies human desire and claims that all we can do is to take the processes of the world as they are. Buddhism does not initially deny human desire, but holds that because the world always goes against human desire we see life as a bitter sea. The Buddhist strategy is to escape the bitter sea rather than to change the bitter sea into a happy one by empirical exploration of nature. Buddhist wisdom claims that human life is a bitter sea because one views it as a bitter sea. If one can extricate oneself from the limitations of one's sensibility and escape from human desire, one can take a different view of life and bitter experience can give way to happiness. The great wisdom of Buddhism lies precisely in this change of perspective. This different view that becomes available to us through Buddhism is contained in the perfect teaching of Buddhism. For both Daoism and Buddhism, what has been changed is one's view on the world but not the world itself. Both deny human desire.

A Confucian approach can be more positive. Instead of passively absorbing morality within the natural processes of the world or counseling escape from the world, it actively creates a moral world by seeking to persuade every individual to become a moral person. The Confucian starting point is a pure morality that ignores the desires of the moral subject. But in its highest development, Confucian morality allows moral subjects to do exactly what they desire, although to achieve this Confucianism, like Daoism and Buddhism, requires moral subjects to view the world in a dramatically different way, that is, to view what is morally required as something desirable. And this requires great wisdom.

Now we see that the mentality behind Chinese culture respects nature and controls human desire, while the mentality behind Western culture exploits nature and affirms human desire. While Chinese mentality places great stress on morality, Western mentality provides motives to develop empirical knowledge. The advantage of Western mentality is to satisfy human desire, but this project is flawed. Human desire is infinite, while natural resources are limited. Even if the development of science and technology can keep pace with the development of human desire, limited natural resources will be unable to satisfy infinite human desire. Thus Mou is right in saying that science cannot solve all the problems that we have in this world. And at this point we can see the advantage of Chinese mentality. To establish a harmonious relation with the world, we must control human desire in a certain way. The great wisdom of Chinese philosophy is that it does not deny human desire, but views the world in a way that transcends desire and frees us from obsession with our desires.

There is something very deep here. Human desire is not a scientific fact, it can be altered according to our understanding of the world. We are not justified in being obsessed with our desires, and many of our most difficult problems derive from our inappropriate desires. We can deal with these problems most effectively by extricating ourselves from our obsession with our desires, rather than by seeking to satisfy them. If this is true, then the reality with which human beings must deal is the reality created by our morality, and the only reliable way to achieve the *summum bonum* is to coordinate our desire with the world. Empirical knowledge and social constitution are important only in so far as they are necessary for moral activity. In this sense, Mou's account of the *summum bonum* is the final step in unifying his moral metaphysics and moral philosophy.

Acknowledgment

My thanks to Nick Bunnin, Chung-ying Cheng, and Satoshi Kodama for suggestions and comments.

Bibliography

Works by Mou Zongsan

Mou, Zongsan 1935: *Zhouyi de ziran zhexue yu daode hanyi* 周易的自然哲學與道德涵義 (Zhou Yi's nature philosophy and its moral bearing), Tianjin: Dagong News House

Mou, Zongsan 1941: *Luoji dianfan* 邏輯典範 (the model of logic), Hong Kong: Hong Kong Commercial Publisher

Mou, Zongsan 1955a: *Lishi zhexue* 歷史哲學 (philosophy of history), Taipei: Student Book Company

Mou, Zongsan 1955b: *Lize xue* 理則學 (on logic), Taipei: Zheng Zhong Publisher

Mou, Zongsan 1956: *Renshixin zhi pipan* 認識心之批評 (a critique of the cognitive mind), Taipei: Student Book Company

Mou, Zongsan 1959: *Daode de lixiang zhuyi* 道德的理想主義 (moral idealism), Taipei: Student Book Company

Mou, Zongsan 1961: *Zhengdao yu zhidao* 政道與治道 (politics and administration), Taipei: Student Book Company

Mou, Zongsan 1963a: *Caixin yu xuanli* 才性與玄理 (talent and mysterious reasoning), Taipei: Student Book Company

Mou, Zongsan 1963b: *Zhongguo zhexue de tezhi* 中國哲學的特質 (the uniqueness of Chinese philosophy), Taipei: Student Book Company

Mou, Zongsan 1968–9 *Xinti yu xingti* 心體與性體 (mind and nature), 3 vols, Taipei: Zheng Zhong Book Company

Mou, Zongsan 1970: *Shengming de xuewen* 生命的學問 (learning on life), Taipei: Sanmin Book Company

Mou, Zongsan 1974: *Zhi de zhijue yu zhongguo zhexue* 智的直覺與中國哲學 (intellectual intuition and Chinese philosophy), Taipei: Taiwan Commercial Publisher

Mou, Zongsan 1975: *Xianxiang yu wuzishen* 現象與物自身 (phenomenon and noumena), Taipei: Student Book Company

Mou, Zongsan 1977: *Foxing yu banruo* 佛性與般若 (buddha nature and prajna), 2 vols, Taipei: Student Book Company

Mou, Zongsan 1979a: *Cong Lu Xiangshan dao Liu Jishan* 從陸象山到劉蕺山 (from Lu Xiangshan to Liu Jishan), Taipei: Student Book Company

Mou, Zongsan 1979b: *Mingjia yu Xunzi* 名家與荀子 (Xunzi and the school of logicians), Taipei: Student Book Company

Mou, Zongsan 1982: *Kangde de daode zhexue* 康德的道德哲學 (Kant's moral philosophy), Taipei: Student Book Company

Mou, Zongsan 1983a: *Kangde de chuncui lixing pipan* 康德的純粹理性批判 (Kant's critique of pure reason), 2 vols, Taipei: Student Book Company

Mou, Zongsan 1983b: *Zhongguo zhexue shijiu jiang* 中國哲學十九講 (nineteen lectures on Chinese philosophy), Taipei: Student Book Company

Mou, Zongsan 1984: *Shidai yu ganshou* 時代與感受 (time and experience), Taipei: Goose Lake Publisher

Mou, Zongsan 1985: *Yuanshan lun* 圓善論 (on the *summum bonum*), Taipei: Student Book Company

Mou, Zongsan, 1987: *MingLi Lun* 名理論 (Wittgenstein's tractatus), Taipei: Taiwan Student Book Store

Mou, Zongsan 1989: *Wushi zishu* 五十自述 (autobiography at the age of fifty), Taipei: Goose Lake Publisher

Mou, Zongsan 1990: *Zhongxi zhexue zhi huitong shisi jiang* 中西哲學之會通十四講 (fourteen lectures on the route connecting Chinese and Western philosophy), Taipei: Student Book Company

Mou, Zongsan 1992: *Kangde pangduanli zhi pipan* 康德判斷力之批判 (Kant's critique of judgment), Taipei: Taiwan Student Book Store

Mou, Zongsan 1996: *Renwen jiangxi lu* 人文講習錄 (lectures on humanity), Taipei: Taiwan Xuesheng Shuju

Mou, Zongsan 1997: *Siyin shuo yanjiang lu* 四因説演講錄 (a lecture on the four causes), Taipei: Goose Lake Publisher

Other works

Berthrong, John H. 1994: *All Under Heaven: Transforming Paradigms in Confucian-Christian Dialogue*, New York: SUNY Press

Kant, I. 1881: *Critique of Pure Reason*, vol. 1, trans. F. Max Muller, London: Macmillan (original dates 1781, first edition; 1787, second edition)

Lao, Tzu 1970: *Tao Te Ching*, trans. D. C. Lau, Harmondsworth: Penguin Books

Lau, D. C., Laozi, Heshanggong and Wang, Bi 1996: *A Concordance to the Laozi: Daozang version of the so-called Wangbi text to which Wangbi's commentary is attached, Heshanggong's text, and Heshanggong's commentary*, Xianggang: Shangwu Yinshuguan

Strawson, P. F. 1966: *The Bounds of Sense*, London: Methuen

Discussion Questions

1. What account should we give of the moral subject?
2. What can we learn of philosophical value from the role of Zhou rites in Confucian philosophy?
3. In what sense does Confucian philosophy start with the subject?

4. Is understanding the Daoist account of nothingness important for philosophy?
5. How should we interpret the Buddhist concept of empty mind?
6. Is Mou Zongsan justified in disputing Kant's claim that humans cannot have intellectual intuition?
7. Is *noumena* a purely factual concept or a moral concept as well?
8. Should we accept Mou Zongsan's distinction between cognitive mind and infinite mind?
9. Does Mou Zongsan's philosophical system solve the problem of the *summum bonum*?
10. Does the distinction between extensional truth and intensional truth help us to understand contrasting features of Western and Chinese philosophy?

AFTERWORDS

Recent Trends in Chinese Philosophy in China and the West

Chung-ying Cheng

We will discuss recent trends in Chinese philosophy both in China and the West. This division is important for the immediate future as Chinese philosophy is liberated from an ideological age and enters an age of globalization. In *Modernization and Globalization of Chinese Philosophy* (1973), I argued for the clear and rational articulation of Chinese philosophical concepts, theses, and theories to enable Chinese philosophy, which reflects the deep-seated cultural values and profound experiences of a people, to take part in world-wide philosophical exchanges. History is expressed in the values of the people who created that history, but the values of different people must be understood in a common language of rational description and explanation. The endorsement of this common language is what I call modernization. To communicate and to influence others in an intercultural and global setting is what I call globalization.

To take part in modernization and globalization, Chinese philosophy must begin with a few philosophers whose deep understanding preserves and develops Chinese philosophy. By this standard, Chinese philosophers in China began modernization after the beginning of the policy of openness and reform in 1979. For the globalization of Chinese philosophy, one must look to the efforts of overseas Chinese philosophers. In 1985, at a conference on Xiong Shili in China, modernization and globalization encountered one another. Overseas and mainland Chinese philosophers met for the first time to discuss the significant contributions of Xiong Shili, one of the founding fathers of Contemporary or New Neo-Confucianism.

We shall first note recent philosophical developments in China and then discuss recent contributions by Chinese philosophers in the West who, since 1990, have created a discourse of contemporary Chinese philosophy that has influenced colleagues in China as well. Some of these overseas Chinese philosophers are known as the third generation of New Neo-Confucianism.

Development of Chinese Philosophy in China

In 1985, a group of leading Chinese intellectuals from Peking University under the leadership of Liang Shuming, Ji Xianlin, and Tang Yijie, founded the International Academy of Chinese Culture, which was the first privately formed educational group in China since the founding of the People's Republic. The Academy aimed to promote the study of Chinese philosophy as a cultural philosophy and the study of comparative philosophy to enhance understanding both of the Chinese tradition and of the contemporary West. The Academy continued the unfinished mission of rational enlightenment that was initiated by the May Fourth Movement, a mission that was interrupted by Japanese invasions, the anti-Japanese war, and the subsequent civil war between the Nationalists and Communists. The work of the Academy renewed the interest of Chinese intellectuals and the wider public in assessing the tradition of Chinese philosophy and in reassessing their understanding of the West. I have discussed elsewhere the roles of Marxism and Confucianism in fusing tradition with modernity in the transformation of premodern China into a new modernizing entity. I shall here discuss three currently active Chinese philosophers whose work indicates trends for the future. Many others are worthy of consideration, but these scholars represent the vitality and vision of the most recent Chinese philosophy in China.

Ye Xiushan (1935–)

Born in Jiangsu Province, Ye was educated at Peking University and has been a member of the Institute of Philosophy, Chinese Academy of Social Sciences since 1977. He visited the State University of New York at Albany in 1980–2 and Balliol College, Oxford in 1988.

Ye has contributed primarily in the field of Greek philosophy, which has been studied in China since the 1930s. Ye has contributed to the study of Socratic and pre-Socratic philosophy and has examined how Pythagoreanism transformed the early Ionic School of naïve materialism into the Eleatic School of abstract ontology of oneness followed by Empedocles and Anaxagoras, representing the opposition between objectivity and subjectivity, *logos* and *ousia*. Ye has tried to understand how Socrates and Plato came to formulate philosophical issues centering on knowledge and virtue. In Socrates, knowledge is virtue that commands practice, but in Plato seeking knowledge becomes a speculative enterprise of the soul signifying a transcendence of morality by philosophy. Ye compared the origins of Greek philosophy with studies of Chinese philosophy, especially the origins of Daoism, in order to show the different motivation and patterns of development of the Western and Chinese philosophical traditions. Recognizing this difference is an important step towards mutual understanding and mutual enrichment.

Ye is also interested in modern Western philosophy. He singled out Kant's *Critique of Pure Reason* as the turning point from modern Western philosophy to contemporary Western philosophy, culminating in the analytic reconstruction of a universal logical language in Wittgenstein's *Tractatus*. Ye also recognized the phenomenology of Husserl as a product of the analytical spirit of Kant that led to the existentialism of Heidegger. In Heidegger, Ye sees the transcendence of the Western tradition of philosophy. Heidegger reveals that meaning in our experience of the world is irreducible and has ushered in the development of hermeneutical thinking. For Ye, even more important is Heidegger's achievement of unifying poetry, philosophy, and history and breaking away from the separation of these fields in traditional Western philosophy. However, Ye has not discussed the importance of Heidegger's achievement for Chinese philosophy, which never separated philosophy from history and literature.

Jin Wulun (1937–)

Born in Zejiang Province, Jin studied modern chemistry at the Chinese University of Science and Technology. He then studied dialectics of nature and philosophy of science and joined the Institute of Philosophy, Chinese Academy of Sciences.

In *New Theory on the Divisibility of Matter* Jin argues that the structure of matter is a process of realization of subsistent qualities. He has appropriated two major principles from traditional Chinese philosophy for his interpretation of matter, namely the principle of holism and the principle of natural genesis. Using these two principles, he rejects the traditional Western mechanistic model of matter and argues for a dialectical and organic understanding of matter as a process of genesis, transformation, and extinction. His holism has also been inspired by Thomas Kuhn's work on paradigm shifts and scientific revolutions. Jin hopes to resolve the opposition between humanism and science through a holistic global consciousness incorporating the insights of different traditions. He is presently engaged in integrating social sciences and natural sciences through a multidisciplinary approach.

Chen Lai (1952–)

Chen grew up in Beijing and studied at Peking University. After receiving his Ph.D. in 1985, he remained at Peking University to teach Chinese philosophy. He has taught at Harvard University and in Hong Kong, Korea, and Japan and is now a Professor of Philosophy at Peking University and Secretary of the International Society for Chinese Philosophy.

Chen has studied Song–Ming Neo-Confucianism and the development of New Neo-Confucianism since the May Fourth Movement. In *Zhu Xi zhexue yen jiu* (2000), Chen offers a detailed analysis of the development of Zhu Xi's philosophy of human nature and the human mind, particularly the ways in which Zhu Xi sought to establish the original and ultimate reality of nature–mind. Chen documented the evolution and transformation of Zhu Xi's views in different periods. Chen also published a textual-critical study and chronology of over 3,000 letters of Zhu Xi.

In *You Wu Zhi Jing: Wang Yangming Zhexue De Jing Shen* (1991), Chen expounded Wang's Four Sentence Teaching with many deep insights. He sees Wang Yangming's account of the absence of good and evil of the mind as a reflection of Zhong Yong's notion of spiritual freedom and Cheng Hao's notion of embracing all things without disturbance of feelings. In this interpretation, Wang's attempt to go beyond good and evil is not a return to Daoism but a return to classical Confucianism, in which one is free to care for all people and all things in the world. In Wang Yangming, Chen sees a unity of original reality and its functions and a presentation of the mental understanding of reality.

In analyzing the thought of Zhu Xi and Wang Yangming, Chen has promoted the study of Chinese philosophy as a modern philosophical project. His study also reflects his pro-Confucian orientation. As a scholar belonging to the lost generation of the Cultural Revolution, Chen symbolizes the optimistic revival of Chinese Confucian tradition under the influence of earlier New Neo-Confucianism. In dealing with the conflict between the modern West and Chinese tradition, Chen stresses the importance of learning from tradition and using tradition as a resource for modernization. He does not see any ultimate break between tradition and modernity. As a cultural conservative, he wants to preserve the traditional values of culture as a means of providing social stability in a violently changing society. He sees tradition as the source of national spirit and argues that the *dao* embodies the best spirit and value of humanity.

Development of Chinese Philosophy in the West

We cannot understand recent Chinese philosophy without understanding the history of the study of Chinese philosophy in the West. Chinese philosophy has been known to the West since the seventeenth century when the Jesuit Fathers went to China and communicated with intellectuals and scholars. The Jesuits wished to convert Chinese intellectuals to the Christian faith, but they also gained knowledge of Chinese philosophy, specifically, the philosophy of the Confucianism. They communicated what they learned about the Confucian Classics within their order and to other scholars in Europe. In the middle of the seventeenth century, *Confucius the Philosopher* was published and aroused intense interest in Chinese learning. Notably, Leibniz mentioned this book and also corresponded with the Jesuit Father Buvet in China. Through Buvet, Leibniz learned about the hexagrams and the binary system of numbers in the *Yijing*.

Throughout the next century, Chinese philosophy attracted comments by many philosophers in Germany, France, and England.

Scholarly training in classical Greek and Medieval philosophy had equipped the Jesuits to debate Confucian doctrines and to spread their own teachings, but in the eighteenth century the Rites Controversy led the Catholic Church to restrain its followers in China from maintaining the Confucian rituals of filial piety, and the exchange of ideas between the Chinese scholars and Jesuits came to an abrupt end. Western scholars lost the opportunity to know the Chinese cultural and philosophical tradition and to introduce the Western tradition to China.

For the next two centuries, only a small body of scholars and missionaries in Europe had knowledge of Chinese philosophy, and its true meaning was often misinterpreted. Kant, Rousseau, and Hegel all criticized Chinese philosophy on the basis of gross misunderstanding. There were no new texts to be read in Chinese philosophy, and there were no expounders of Chinese philosophy. No scholars had a real knowledge of Chinese philosophy, and no scholars could discuss issues in both Chinese and Western contexts, let alone evaluate Western philosophy from a Chinese point of view.

The situation did not improve until Bertrand Russell and John Dewey came to lecture in China in 1919–21. No Chinese philosophers sought to discuss philosophical issues with them from a Chinese philosophical point of view. This is no surprise because at the time traditional Chinese philosophy was widely dismissed by Chinese intellectuals, and very few Chinese scholars could argue in the philosophical discourse of the West. Hu Shi, Feng Youlan, and Jin Yuelin wished to promote Western philosophy, not to argue for Chinese philosophy. Xiong Shili and Liang Shuming, who were in the midst of a philosophical transformation from tradition to modernity, were not ready to confront the West.

From the end of the nineteenth century to the middle of the twentieth century, Chinese philosophy was studied in the West in the fossilized form of texts translated from Chinese by nonphilosophical sinologists specializing in ancient Chinese culture. The two most well-known sinologists were James Legge, who translated all the major works of the Classical Confucianism into English, and Richard Wilhelm, who translated the *Yijing* and *Daodejing* into German. They did a great service in introducing Chinese philosophy to the modern West, but their comments revealed their Christian background rather than the living traditions and current issues of Western philosophy. Chinese philosophy was studied as the historical record of a past tradition by a few European and American sinologists. As "Chinese Thought" or "Chinese Intellectual History," it was studied in Departments of Asian Studies or Departments of History rather than in Departments of Philosophy.

Reinforcing this treatment of Chinese philosophy has been the myth that Chinese philosophy is not philosophy at all because it is not expressed in the same form as Western philosophy. Western philosophy is systematic, argumentative, logically presented, and discussed in terms of sharply defined issues and theses. It has diverse and novel positions that are freely investigated from logical and metaphysical perspectives. The close relationships among philosophy, religion, and science are well demarcated. In contrast, the properties that characterize Western philosophy are neither well articulated nor sharply distinguished in Chinese philosophy. But this does not mean that Chinese philosophy lacks logical discourse and clearly stated theses. Arguments may be indicated and understood briefly and allusively, and debates may be conducted over a span of hundred of years. Because of the ways in which the Chinese language differs from Western languages, its persuasive power, meaning, and reference are often hidden. But these variations in the style of expression do not imply that Chinese philosophy lacks positions, novelty, critique, or method. Even today, some Western philosophers argue that there are no concepts of morality and truth in Chinese philosophy. This parochial attitude belittles both humanity and the concepts of truth and morality by seeing them as rooted in the bias and prejudice of one culture or people.

After the May Fourth Movement, Chinese philosophers trained themselves in the universal language of argument and discourse and focused on issues and positions. They learned Western philosophy and the methods of analysis and used these to reconstruct the Chinese philosophical tradition. Since the beginning of twentieth century, Western philosophy was absorbed in China faster than Chinese philosophy was studied in the West. Good examples of the Chinese reception of Western philosophy are found in Kang Youwei, Liang Qichao, and Wang Guowei. These Chinese philosophers tried to catch up with the current trends in Western philosophy. Hence, Bergson and Dewey were translated into Chinese and their thought contributed both to the formation of new Chinese philosophy and to the reconstruction of traditional systems of philosophy. Xiong Shili and Liang Shuming, for example, used Bergson to promote their understanding of Chinese philosophy and Western philosophy. With Fang Dongmei, Mou Zongsan, and Tang Junyi, a critical attitude toward specific Western philosophers was developed.

The Western philosophical works that were studied in modern China transformed the language of Chinese philosophy and helped to reveal the insights of traditional Chinese philosophy. Eventually, contemporary Chinese philosophers were able to hold lively conversations with Western philosophers as colleagues and partners. Such dialogue and conversation took place as early as 1935 at the University of Hawaii at Manoa because Dr. Charles Moore and Dr. Wing-tsit Chan felt the need to bring together philosophers from the East and the West to discuss fundamental issues of philosophy from the perspectives of major cultural traditions. Chinese philosophy, as one of these traditions, was for the first time articulated, discussed, and debated among Chinese and Western philosophers in person. Fang Dongmei, Mou Zongsan, Tang Junyi, Wing-tsit Chan, Shu-hsien Liu, and I participated in subsequent conferences of East–West philosophers in 1965 and 1970.

The recent development of Chinese philosophy in the West can be traced to the International Society for Chinese Philosophy (ISCP), which I founded in 1965 at University of Hawaii at Manoa, and to the *Journal of Chinese Philosophy*, which I founded in 1972. In both cases, these organizations have been motivated by two considerations: first, the great resources of Chinese philosophical wisdom need to be reviewed and systematically presented; secondly, participation in an East–West dialogue will enable Chinese philosophy to become an active force in enriching world civilization and human society. I have sought recognition of Chinese philosophy in the West as a living tradition of philosophical thinking and restoration of Chinese philosophy to a proper place in the world of living philosophy, not simply presenting or repeating the tradition.

We cannot describe the development of Chinese philosophy in the West over the last three decades without mentioning individual Chinese philosophers. We must also mention non-Chinese philosophers who have contributed greatly to the study of Chinese philosophy.

Wing-tsit Chan (1901–94)

Wing-tsit Chan gained his Ph.D. in Chinese Studies in 1929 at Harvard and taught first at University of Hawaii at Manoa and then at Dartmouth College as Professor of Chinese Culture and Philosophy until retirement. He distinguished himself as a great translator of Chinese philosophical works. His classic *Source Book in Chinese Philosophy* (1963a) published selections of major Chinese philosophical texts from ancient times to the works of Xiong Shili. *Instructions for Practical Living* (1963b), his translation the *Chuan Xilu* of Wang Yangming, captures the rational method of understanding and transforming the human self in the Neo-Confucian tradition. *Reflections on Things at Hand* (1967), his annotated translation of Zhu Xi's *Jinsi Lu*, displays his mature style of translation. Both works are important for introducing Neo-Confucian thought to the West. With these two translations, Chan believed that the study of Confucianism in the West would grow into a study of Neo-Confucianism. Unfortunately we do not yet have translations of this standard of other major Chinese philosophical texts, and we must recognize the unique influence of Chan in promoting the study of Chinese philosophy.

Chan held that Chinese philosophy is basically humanistic and criticized Chinese metaphysics as simple and unsystematic. He argued that Western philosophy moves from metaphysics to social and moral philosophy but that the development of Chinese philosophy is the reverse. He held that we must introduce Western logic and science in order to consolidate Chinese metaphysics. What he meant by Chinese metaphysics in asserting its compatibility with Western logic and science remains unclear.

Among his more specialized studies, Chan wrote a useful paper on the meaning of Confucian benevolence (*ren*), tracing the development of *ren* from

Confucius to the present day. He understood *ren* to be the fundamental concept of Confucianism: *ren* as whole virtue in Confucius; *ren* as love; *ren* as universal love, *ren* as nature and principle; *ren* as forming one body with the heaven, earth, and all things; *ren* as creative vitality; *ren* as virtue of heart–mind and the principle of love. Similarly, he provided a historical synopsis of the meanings of principle (*li*) in the Neo-Confucian philosophy.

Chan devoted himself to the study of Song-Ming Neo-Confucianism. He had a special respect for Zhu Xi and considered him to be the most influential Chinese philosopher after Confucius. According to Chan, Zhu Xi founded the tradition of the Confucian *dao* and opened a new direction of learning through the investigation of things. For Chan, Zhu Xi was also important for integrating philosophy, religion, and ethics into one system, although Chan has not demonstrated how this integration took place. Chan was a philosophical scholar rather than a philosopher in his own right. He did not develop new insight into the Confucian *ren* or the Neo-Confucian *li*. Unlike his later colleagues, he did not have a background in Western philosophy and did not provide a systematic comparative study of Chinese and Western philosophy.

Chung-ying Cheng (1935–)

Chung-ying Cheng (*Cheng Zhongying*) was born in Nanjing and went to Taiwan in 1949, where he graduated from National Taiwan University in 1956. He received a Ph.D. in Philosophy from Harvard University in 1964 and wrote his dissertation on *Peirce's and Lewis's Theories of Induction* (published 1966). In this work, he argued for the logical reliability of empirical knowledge. In 1971 he published *T'ai Chen's Inquiry into Goodness*, which was a first study of Dai Zhen with a translation of his work *Yuanshan* in English. Throughout his career, he has taught at University of Hawaii at Manoa, where he has been a Professor of Philosophy since 1972 and has been a visiting professor at many universities in the United States, Asia, and Europe.

Cheng's work has been focused on the nature of Western philosophy; the *Yijing* and the origin of Confucianism and Daoism as complementary aspects of Chinese philosophy; the analytic reconstruction of Chinese philosophy; the ontology and ontologically based cosmology (onto-cosmology) and ethics (onto-ethics) of Confucianism and Neo-Confucianism; the theory of ontologically based hermeneutics (onto-hermeneutics) as a counterpart to Western hermeneutics; and the integration of ethics and theories of management.

In *Choice at the Crossroads of the Century: On Integration and Fusion of Chinese and Western Philosophies* (1991a) he saw the whole history of Western philosophy as a process of differentiation of schools that is occasioned by conscious revision and revolution in methods of approach. Despite questions raised about method in Heidegger and Gadamer, the main trend in Western philosophy remains methodological. In contrast, Chinese philosophy originated in a unifying and holistic vision of reality that includes both constancy and change and has persisted throughout its history. Hence in a broad sense Chinese philosophy is primarily more ontological (or onto-cosmological) than methodological. Because of the persistence of this onto-cosmological commitment, epistemology, ethics, aesthetics, and even politics in Chinese philosophy are not separate from a deeply rooted onto-cosmological understanding.

In *New Dimensions of Confucian/Neo-Confucian Philosophy* (1991b) he distinguished between rationality and "naturality" to explain the difference between Western and Chinese philosophy. The notion of naturality is intended to describe how both Confucianism and Neo-Confucianism have attributed an insight to human beings that reflects the nature of ultimate reality. In more recent work (*Origins of Chinese Philosophy* and *On Guan as Onto-Hermeneutics*), he has focused on the notion of *guan* (comprehensive observation-contemplation) in the *Yijing* as an experience of unity of whole and part in change that leads to the understanding of the *dao* that is eventually recognized in both Confucianism and Daoism. This common grounding in the primordial experience of the *dao* explains the complementarity of Confucianism and Daoism. It is also the basis for a dialectics of harmonization that continues to inspire modern Chinese philosophers in their efforts to integrate ontology with the reason and analysis of Western philosophy.

He has proposed an "analytical reconstruction" of Chinese philosophy based on a conceptual analysis of the original text and one's discovery of a new meaning, a new truth, or a new aspect of reality through reflection and integration of the understanding of the onto-cosmology of the *dao*. Thus, for Cheng an analytical reconstruction must also be ontological because one must begin with some pre-understanding of reality. His main concern has been to reconstruct an onto-cosmology of reality and an onto-ethics of human nature and human will in a Confucian-Neo-Confucian context. He regards Confucianism more as philosophy than religion, even though he recognizes the religious and spiritual import of Confucian philosophy.

He sympathizes with the goals of Xiong Shili and Mou Zongsan, but sees the need to go beyond their present systems. For example, he differs from Mou Zongsan by treating the work of Zhu Xi as a mainstream development of nature and reason as represented by Xunzi and Mencius. He also differs from Mou in speaking of onto-ethics apart from moral metaphysics and in pointing to an onto-moral-hermeneutical circle in the practice and understanding of Confucian and Neo-Confucian philosophy.

Antonio Cua (1932–)

Antonio Cua (*Ke Xiongwen*) was born in the Philippines. He received a Ph.D. at University of California at Berkeley for a dissertation on Richard Price's ethical theory and maintained his interest in ethical analysis and ethical theory throughout his career. His early articles focused on the ethics of the moral agent and led to his book **Dimensions of Moral Creativity** (1978). This book offered a pioneering study of the Confucian notion of the *junzi* as a paradigmatic and exemplary individual and considered how a moral agent can bridge the gap between his moral knowledge of a tradition and his action. Cua discussed three dimensions of ethical practice to which a moral agent can make creative contributions: the exemplary, the reconstitutive, and the ideal.

In the same period, Cua explored Xunzi's philosophy of argumentation and human nature and investigated Daoist ethics. In work published in 1985, he attempted to construct a Confucian theory of ethical argumentation from Xunzi. In 1992, he published *The Unity of Mind and Action*, a study of the development of Confucian moral epistemology that ranges over the desirable qualities of agents, the standards of competence, the nature of moral language and justification, and the diagnosis of erroneous ethical beliefs.

Cua's collection of essays *Moral Vision and Tradition* (1998) provided a conceptual analysis of the development of many aspects of Chinese moral philosophy. In seeking to formulate a Confucian virtue ethics, Cua raised many significant questions rather than providing a system of ethics. He examined the role of tradition in formulating a Confucian ethics and sought to develop a conceptual framework to accommodate basic Confucian concepts, such as *dao* and *ren*. He also considered ways of developing these concepts in order to meet demands of normative regulation in evolving modern life. These questions touch upon the problem of incorporating Confucian insights within a global or intercultural ethics. Cua has proposed ground rules for resolving intercultural conflicts, involving principles of nonprescriptivity, cultural integrity, mutuality, procedural justice, rectification, and reconsideration. These useful rules need further discussion to determine their coherence and applicability.

In relation to his program of formulating a Confucian ethics of virtues, Cua has asked whether an appeal to history or tradition constitutes an essential component of ethical argumentation. It is interesting to note that after the May Fourth Movement, very few contemporary Confucian or Neo-Confucian philosophers have appealed to history or tradition as a ground for the validity of Confucian ethics. Most defenses of Confucian ethics came in the form of an appeal to a descriptive or normative account of human nature. Confucian philosophers such as Mencius, Zhu Xi, and Wang Yangming were often cited to provide grounds for theoretical justifications, not for historical justification.

Fu Weixun (1933–96)

Fu Weixun (*Charles Fu*) graduated from National Taiwan University and obtained his Ph.D. in philosophy from Ohio State University. He taught at National Taiwan University before joining the Department of Religion at

Temple University. Fu devoted himself to the study and teaching of Chinese Buddhism and Chinese religions. He has published edited works on Chinese religion and essays in English and Chinese on various subjects, ranging over Marxist ethics, Zen Buddhism, and what he calls "creative hermeneutics." According to this notion, the meaning of a text is open to various levels of creative interpretation. He was not able to develop his views into a full system before his untimely death in 1996. Shortly before his death, he turned to the study of death as a subject for philosophical and religious thinking. This work has aroused great interest among Chinese Buddhists in Taiwan.

Liu Shuxian (1934–)

Liu Shuxian (*Shu-hsien Liu*) belongs to the same generation as Chung-ying Cheng and Fu Weixun. Liu graduated from National Taiwan University and its Graduate Institute of Philosophy. He gained a Ph.D. from University of Southern Illinois in 1966 and taught in the same Department. In 1981, he moved to Hong Kong and became Professor and Chair of the Department of Philosophy of Chinese University of Hong Kong. After retirement, he moved to the Academia Sinica in Taipei. Liu has served as President of the International Society for Chinese Philosophy.

Liu divides his philosophical development into three periods. From 1955 to 1964, he published books on literary appreciation and on semantics and truth. He explored Western philosophy and culture and compared Chinese and Western views on method. From 1964 to 1978, he completed his dissertation on Paul Tillich and found the future direction of his work. He published essays in *Philosophy East and West* and *Journal of Chinese Philosophy*. His interests centered on the exploration of Confucian and Neo-Confucian philosophy of religion. He also critically commented on Western philosophers and published two collections of essays. From 1978 to 1992, he developed a deeper concern for the future of Chinese culture and reflected on the problems of modernization in China.

The main achievement of his philosophical work was publication of *Development and Completion of Zhu Xi's Philosophical Ideas* (1982). In 1986, he went to the Far East Institute of Philosophy in Singapore for research and published a study of Huang Zongxi. These works show Liu's development as a contemporary Neo-Confucian who shares many insights with Xiong Shili and Mou Zongsan. He is considered to be a representative of the third generation of the Contemporary Neo-Confucians.

Tang Liquan (1935–)

Born in Hong Kong, Tang Liquan (Lik-kuen Tong) studied economics at New York University, but then transferred to philosophy at the New School for

Social Research. He has taught philosophy at Fairfield University, Connecticut and had been once President of the International Society for Chinese Philosophy.

In his work *Between Zhouyi and Whitehead: Introduction to the Philosophy of Field-Being*, Tang used the basic concepts of *Zhouyi* to integrate Whitehead's metaphysics and Heidegger's life philosophy. Tang's central idea is that being depends on and exists in a field. This notion of field-being differs from the notion of substance in traditional Western philosophy. Instead, field-being is inherent in the interrelatedness of things. His account stresses the relativity of things, but field-being also has potency and activity in the power and capacity of things. Tang holds that all things are field-being and that there are no things outside field-being. One cannot see the universe and life from outside the field, but must view the universe from a standpoint within the field.

Tang has a novel interpretation of the statement "The change (*yi*) has its great ultimate (*taiji*)." For him, the *taiji* points to the upright walking body of the human person, whereas the *yi* means our body as capable of reflection and various ways of movement. In this fashion, the two norms and eight triagrams can be described in relation to bodily movement. What Tang called the study of "forms of the root body" seems to reflect someone's experience in performing *taiji quan* exercise.

For Tang, the human being is the locus of two opposing forces: moral nature and natural talent. The manner in which a person combines and develops the two forces determines the way of human behavior. The opposition and combination of the two forces also conditions the differences and development of human cultures. More specifically, they explain the differences between Chinese and Western cultures.

Qin Jiayi (1935–)

Qin Jiayi's (*Julia Ching*) study of Wang Yangming promoted a general wave of interest in Song–Ming Confucianism. Although she was trained in theology and history, her interests include Neo-Confucianism and Chinese culture. She gained a Ph.D. in Australia for her dissertation "To Acquire Wisdom: the Way of Wang Yang-ming." After teaching at Columbia and Yale, Qin became a Professor at Victoria College, University of Toronto in 1979. Her main work has been in the comparative study of Chinese religions and Christianity. *Confucianism and Christianity* (1977) encouraged dialogue among world religions in the hope that each party in the exchange would learn something from the others. Qin also stressed the importance of critique of traditions and held that without critique there would be no progress. As a Catholic she critically examined Catholicism, and as a member of East Asian culture she critically examined East Asian tradition.

Qin has developed the notion of the "critical subject," that is a subject who has moral independence and conscience. On the basis of this notion, Qin promotes a pluralism of religions in which each religion should respect and be open to the others. She treats Confucianism as a religion that should make itself available in dialogues among world religions. In her view, Confucianism as a religion is humanistic, but is open to the transcendent spirit of God. She even holds that Confucianism was originally a religion of prophets with belief in a personal God. She suggests that the unity of heaven and man is derived from an ancient belief in the unity of man and God. She has also interpreted the Neo-Confucian tradition as a tradition full of religious significance.

Du Weiming (1940–)

Du Weiming (*Wei-ming Tu*) was born in China and graduated from Donghai University in Taiwan. He received a Ph.D. in Chinese Intellectual History from Harvard in 1968. After teaching at Princeton and University of California at Berkeley, he returned to Harvard as a Professor of Chinese History and Chinese Philosophy. He is a member of the American Academy of Humanities, Arts, and Sciences and now heads the Harvard-Yenching Institute. He is deeply committed to developing academic exchanges between China and the US.

The central concern of Du's thinking is the modernization of Confucianism. Du approaches Confucianism from a variety of perspectives drawn from modern social science, but he sees his work as interpreting Confucianism as a living religious tradition. He speaks of the need for a living spiritual testimony of Confucianism and opposes the study or reconstruction of Confucianism as an abstract theoretical system of philosophy. He stresses the importance of preserving Confucianism in practice and argues that Confucian thought is never separable from an internal experience of the Confucian spirit. He speaks of the living embodiment of knowing the Confucian spirit. His work on interpreting Zhong Yong in *Centrality and Commonality in Zhong Yong* (1976) attempts to show how a living Confucian spirit can be understood in an important classical Confucian work.

Du criticizes the use of modern philosophical methodology in the study of Confucianism. He wants to defend Confucianism as a religion rather than as a philosophy. We could ask how Du understands Confucianism in light of the work of two generations of contemporary Neo-Confucians and how Du himself testifies to Confucianism in his own words and actions. In his studies of the early life of Wang Yangming, Du was inspired by the use of psychology of religion to understand great religious figures such as Martin Luther. In practical terms, it is interesting to see how much Du's projected future development of Confucianism would constitute a revival of the vitality and creativity of Chinese culture.

As a Confucian activist, Du has been engaged in dialogues with specialists and has edited books on the Confucian subject, but his real important task has been to present Confucianism as a spiritual tradition.

Concluding Remarks

My brief description of some recent contributions to Chinese philosophy overseas is not intended to give a complete picture or systematic assessment. What
is important to recognize is that Chinese philosophy overseas is a developing
field. Its vitality has increased through the accumulated efforts of those working on Chinese philosophy in the last thirty years and through the increasing
frequency of interaction between overseas Chinese philosophers with Chinese
philosophers in China, Hong Kong, and Taiwan. The last three conferences
organized by the International Society for Chinese Philosophy in 1995, 1997,
and 1999 have seen a growing number of dialogues and exchanges among
Chinese philosophers from home and abroad. Contact at international conferences is supplemented by the wide use of modern computer-based communication and the establishment of internet homepages and electronic
publications in philosophy. The impact of easier communications on the
growth of Chinese philosophy overseas has been astonishing.

To understand the richness and dynamism of overseas Chinese philosophy,
one must also recognize the contributions made by non-Chinese scholars and
thinkers who work on Chinese philosophy. Since the late 1970s, there have been
many capable Western scholars who have received training in Chinese philosophy or who have learned Chinese philosophy by reading and discussion. There
have been well-known figures like Benjamin Schwartz at Harvard University, Friedrich Mote at Princeton University, Derk Bodde at University of
Pennsylvania, William Th. de Bary at Columbia University, Donald Monroe
at University of Michigan, and Chad Hansen at Vermont University and
University of Hong Kong, who have worked on the intellectual history of China
in the classical and Neo-Confucian periods. In Europe, A. C. Graham of University of London, François Jullien of University of Paris, and C. Harbsmeier
of University of Oslo have made especially important contributions. We
should also mention Robert Cummings Neville at Boston University as a religious philosopher who has come to appreciate Chinese philosophy and has
long involved himself in the activities of International Society for Chinese
Philosophy. Roger T. Ames and David L. Hall have interpreted Confucius and
Chinese culture from a postmodern point of view. In the last two decades,
many younger Chinese philosophers have emerged from Departments of
Philosophy in the US and from Sinological Seminars in Europe. In the US, there
have been excellent publications, such as Shin Kwong-loi's detailed analytical
study of Mencius. The recently formed Association of Chinese Philosophers
in America contains many promising scholars in Chinese philosophy.

In light of the above, we see a bright future for the development of Chinese
philosophy overseas. This development will quicken with the economic and
cultural processes of globalization and the incorporation of China and the West

in a world system of exchanges As a future trend, one would expect to see growing interaction between Chinese philosophy and Western philosophy overseas, from which more detailed studies of individual Chinese philosophers and more theoretical and comparative works involving Chinese and Western philosophy will emerge.

Bibliography

Chan, Wing-tsit 1963a: *A Source Book in Chinese Philosophy*, Princeton: Princeton University Press

Chan, Wing-tsit 1963b: *Instructions for Practical Living* (translation of Wang, Yangming: *Chuan Xilu*), New York: Columbia University Press

Chan, Wing-tsit 1967: *Reflections on Things at Hand* (annotated translation of Zhu Xi: *Jinsi lu*), New York: Columbia University Press

Chen, Lai 1991: *Youwu zhi jing: Wang Yangming zhexue ti ching shen* 有無之境：王陽明哲學的精神 (the world between being and nonbeing: the spirit of philosophy in Wang Yangming), Beijing: Renmin Chubanshe

Chen, Lai 2000: *Zhuxii zhexue yenjiu* 朱喜哲學研究 (a study of the philosophy of Zhu Xi), Taipei: Wenchiu Chubanshi

Cheng, Chung-ying 1969: *Peirce's and Lewis's Theories of Induction*, The Hague: Nijhoff

Cheng, Chung-ying 1971: *Tai Chan's Inquiry into Goodness*, Honolulu: East-West Center Press

Cheng, Chung-ying: 1973: *Zhongguo zhexue de xiandaihua he shijiehua* 中國哲學的現代化和世界化 (modernization and globalization of Chinese philosophy), Taipei: Linking Publishing

Cheng, Chung-ying 1991a: Shijizhijiao de juece: lun zhongxi zhexue de huitong yu rong he 世紀之交的抉擇：論中西哲學的融合與會通 (choice at the crossroads of the century: on the integration and fusion of Chinese and Western philosophies), Shanghai: Zhishi Chubanshe

Cheng, Chung-ying 1991b: *New Dimensions of Confucian/Neo-Confucian Philosophy*, Albany: SUNY Press

Cheng, Chung-ying 1995a: "Origin of Chinese philosophy," in *Encyclopedia of Asian Philosophy*, London: Routledge, pp. 324–49

Cheng, Chung-ying 1995b: "On guan as onto-hermeneutical understanding", in *The International Journal for Yijing Studies*, issue 1, Beijing 1995, pp. 59–79

Ching, Julia 1977: *Confucianism and Christianity*, Tokyo and New York: Kodansha International

Cua, Antonio 1978: *Dimensions of Moral Creativity*, Pennsylvania: Pennsylvania State University Press

Cua, Antonio 1982: *The Unity of Knowledge and Action: A Study of Wang Yang-Ming's Moral Psychology*, Honolulu: University of Hawaii Press

Cua, Antonio 1998: *Moral Vision and Tradition*, Washington, D.C.: Catholic University of America Press

Jin, Wulun 1988: Wuzhi kefenxing xinlun 物質可分性新論 (new theory of the divisibility of matter), Beijing: Chinese Social Sciences Press

Liu, Shuxian 1982: 朱子哲學思想的發展和完成 (the development and completion of Zhu Xi's philosophical thought), Taipei: Xuesheng Book Company

Tang, Lik-kuen n.d.: Zhouyi yu Whitehead zhi qian – ganyou zhexue xubian 周易與懷特海之間 – 場有哲學續論 (between Zhouyi and Whitehead: introduction to the philosophy of field-being), Taipei: Luming Wenhua Publishing Company

Tu, Wei-ming 1976: *Centrality and Commonality, an Essay on Chung-yung*, Honolulu: University of Hawaii Press

An Onto-Hermeneutic Interpretation of Twentieth-Century Chinese Philosophy: Identity and Vision

Chung-ying Cheng

Contemporary Chinese Philosophy

By inquiring into origins and forces that shaped Chinese philosophical thinking in the twentieth century, we can see that contemporary Chinese philosophy is deeply rooted in the traditions of Chinese philosophy. It has inherited from Confucianism, Daoism, and Chinese Buddhism a structure that is deep, rich, and complex. Its current existence has enabled it to develop its own robust life as a creative response to challenges from Western philosophy. By confronting the reality of its life-world and life-situation, contemporary Chinese philosophy has also confronted these Western challenges. In dealing with issues of knowledge, truth, and reality that largely reflect Western science, culture, and values, it presents a panoramic array of new views and new visions that cope with Western modernity and its own modern world. It also provides a new vitality for transforming human life, human society, and the human world.

The story of twentieth-century Chinese philosophy focuses on the effort of traditional Chinese philosophy to adjust to a new world and to absorb valuable elements from a foreign tradition. It is a positive and creative effort that requires deep understanding. The drive of contemporary Chinese philosophy to break from its past has given it strength to rediscover and revitalize itself. It has transcended itself by creatively seeking to realize a higher goal.

There is no single historical precedent in China for the response of contemporary Chinese philosophy to the demands for change. One might cite the collapse of the Zhou order in the seventh and eighth centuries B.C., when northern barbarians weakened Zhou rule and a new class of people used new inventions to rise to power. But between the Opium War in 1842 and the May Fourth Movement in 1919 continuing crises were driven by foreign invasion and cultural and military domination without a pause for the free development of ideas and talents that took place in the Spring and Autumn Period. Whereas there was an outburst of new energy and new visions in the Spring and Autumn Period, China at the beginning of the twentieth century faced a bleak prospect of drained energy and disintegrating culture. It was not just the decline of Confucianism, but a recession and breakdown of a tradition that sustained culture as a living force. Although the Chinese people did not become enslaved, Chinese tradition lost its confidence and freedom and became a prisoner of Western ideology and values.

Chinese and Western Paradigms: Critical Challenge and Creative Response

Our understanding of the rich content of contemporary Chinese philosophy can serve many purposes. We can learn historical lessons and understand cultural meanings, but above all we must discern philosophical insights. Understanding contemporary Chinese philosophy is a philosophical enterprise that poses a methodological task: we must seek to understand how Chinese philosophers view and appraise Western philosophical thinking and how Chinese philosophy has rediscovered itself and defined its own identity.

It is important to recognize the solid and well-developed philosophical tradition in China that had roots in the classical period and a development that has lasted over 2,000 years. Like Western philosophy, this tradition has its own ontological, cosmological, epistemological, ethical, aesthetical, and religious beliefs and principles. When these two traditions encountered one other, how did each measure, engage, and understand the other? For most of the twentieth century, these questions were difficult to pursue because there was little interaction between the two traditions. Instead, Western tradition was imported by Chinese intellectuals, but, unlike the reciprocal exchanges of the Jesuit missionary period, the Chinese tradition was not exported to the West.

We may note a world of difference between the two traditions. First, there are differences between the Chinese and Western ways of expression: many traditional works in Chinese philosophy have been formulated in conversations, short essays, theses, stories, images, and metaphors, whose logic of presentation is implicit rather than explicit. The logic of discourse in traditional philosophical texts was understood as part of a larger discourse that preserved a coherent vision of reality and suggested practices constituting a form of life. It was a holistic vision whose practical applicability, rather than the abstract logic of argumentation, guaranteed the meaningfulness and validity of Chinese philosophical discourse. Zhang Dongsun saw Western and Chinese languages as two different modes of knowing: one is discursive and the other intuitive. We may add that the Aristotelian subject–predicate construction presupposes an irreducible distinction between subject and object, while the Daoist subjectless presentation of reality in Chinese language and poetry suggests no separation between subject and world. In this light, there is striking contrast between an implicit logic of the concise and often indirect Chinese presentation of reality and its existential and often metaphorical allusion to truth and the explicit logic that since Descartes has made treatises of lengthy reasoning and explicit argumentation the standard mode of Western philosophical discourse.

If we ask why the Chinese philosophical tradition has its characteristic forms of expression, we can see that the tradition originated with broad visions of life and reality that were represented in holistic paradigms of both utter simplicity and rich ambiguity. There are always basic perceptions of unity, identity, nonseparation, and wholeness involved in these experiences, intuitions, and reflections. This is the experience of an original or ultimate reality, *benti* (the root-substance), which is regarded as the source from which everything else arises. All the things that arise from *benti* are the *yong* (function) of *benti* and form a natural part of *benti*. All the basic and persistent theses of Chinese philosophy show a proclivity toward unity versus disunity, oneness versus scatteredness, identity versus difference, and continuity versus discontinuity because the latter term of each polarity is conceived to lack a substance-function relationship of organic unity. In other words, the unity, oneness, identity, and continuity that Chinese philosophy treasures include the variety, diffuseness, difference, and discontinuity as functions of their original reality. Hence there is no real opposition in each kind of contrast. The traditional doctrines of Confucianism, Daoism, and Chinese Buddhism all exhibit these basic tendencies.

Thus in Chinese philosophy we find theses of the unity of heaven and man, the unity of knowledge and action, the nonseparation of substance and function, the nonseparation of subject and object, the nonseparation of principle and vitality, the oneness of principle and nature, and the oneness of principle and mind. All of these preferences for oneness and unity express a perception and insistence on unity as both actuality and ultimate reality (*benti*). There cannot be any unity without an underlying perception of unified reality in a human being's experience of himself, of life, and of the world. Oneness and holism are elaborated as features of the *benti*, whereas distinction and differentiation are taken to be functions (*yong*) of the *benti*.

Traditionally, the distinction between *ti* and *yong*, substance and function, is concretized in many polar distinctions. Hence, the vital force of *qi* is a function derived from the principled order of *li*. The distinction between *ti* and *yong* is also like the distinction between structure and process or between a main source and a derivative development or between the *dao* and the vessels and things (*qi*). In all of these cases, the *yong* must come from the *ti*, but must not be separable from the *ti*. In this sense, there is always a unity between *ti* and *yong* and an organic internal dynamism linking the two. In applying the distinction to human affairs, we may distinguish between means and end. We can use different means to achieve the same end as well as achieving different ends by the same means. There must be a continuum between end and means and thus a continuum between *ti* and *yong* in conduct and goal.

Philosophy is the core of a tradition because it is both a mode of thinking and a normative direction of action towards the ideal values of the tradition. Philosophy is both the consciousness and the conscience of a culture and civilization because philosophical views, formulated by recognized philosophers and accepted by common people over the ages, inspire and guide culture and action. Given the long history of Chinese culture and philosophy, it is no wonder that traditional philosophy has been absorbed in forms of life among the Chinese people and in forms of value and meaningfulness for the Chinese intellectuals. Confucianism is the philosophical mainstay of the culture, but there are other philosophical forces that contribute to the definition of traditional Chinese cultural forms.

With this understanding, we can see how the Chinese philosophical tradition has provided what I have called an *onto-cosmological, onto-epistemological, onto-ethical, and onto-aesthetic understanding of reality as an organic unity of substance and function*. It is a central principle of the Chinese philosophical tradition that the ontological is always basic and, thus, that the cosmological is to be understood against this background vision. Further, epistemological, ethical, and aesthetic experiences are to be understood against this ontological background as well. In understanding each of these fields, there is always an understanding of the substance-function relationship in terms of which a given experience is to be interpreted. This ontological understanding gives rise to and supports the experience and understanding of the oneness and unity, the nonseparation and continuity of all things and sees all principles as functions of an underlying original and ultimate reality. This onto-cosmological presupposition gives rise to additional theses concerning the unity of the internal and external, the unity of mind and nature, the unity of the self and the world, and the unity of being and nonbeing.

Given this holistic view of reality and human life, we can further see that the value of a human person is rooted in one's being endowed with the nature of ultimate reality (*benti*) and in the ability to fulfill one's potentiality of being as functions in one's family, social, and political life. A process of self-cultivation and learning to achieve fulfillment on this basis is both morally necessary and rationally appropriate according to the holistic paradigm of the human person and his humanity. There are two consequences of this understanding of this human–cosmic relationship. First, the human person is the center of human concern, and, secondly, one can strive to achieve the perfection or near perfection of humanity in moral practices and social relations: this is where the ultimate value of human life resides.

We may restate the unitary paradigm of Chinese onto-cosmology and onto-ethics of ultimate reality as an organic unity of substance and function in terms of three basic principles: *the principle of the unity of ultimate reality and the human person (the unity of humanity and heaven); the principle of the unity of nature and mind in the human person; and the principle of the unity of moral understanding and moral action and practice.* These three principles interpenetrate with one other in a common context of culture and understanding. The activity and creativity of the individual are not separated from the whole of reality, but are devoted to the fulfillment of this whole reality. The practice and action of a person are not separable from himself as a whole person: right action is considered to be a trait of the good person and wrong action condemns a human person to shame and social banishment. Society can tolerate a seemingly good person who produces a wrong action more easily than a seemingly bad person who produces a right action.

Given the paradigm of the unity of the human person and the universe as a guiding principle of Chinese philosophy, it is not difficult to understand how Western philosophy was presented as a totally different paradigm. We do not have to go back to the time when the Jesuits in the Ming period tried to establish the theology of a transcendent God in a culture that accepted the Neo-Confucian onto-cosmology of the immanent *dao*. God is a totally transcendent entity that has to be believed in order to be known, whereas the *dao* and heaven are immanent in a world in which we are a part. There is therefore an underlying unity between the human person and the *dao* or heaven. Such a fundamental difference has sources and explanations in the long histories of both traditions. After China closed its doors to the Catholic fathers in 1723, there was a gap of more than one hundred fifty years before Western philosophy was reintroduced. During this period, the influence of Western philosophy in the form of Aristotelian science and Christian theology was unknown. The modern reintroduction of Western philosophy and science began with the translations of Yan Fu (1854–1921).

Yan Fu and the Introduction of Western Philosophical Paradigms

It is important to recognize the role that Yan Fu played in introducing Western philosophy to Chinese intellectuals in the period after China's defeat in the 1842 Opium War. Through Yan Fu's Chinese translations, modern Western philosophy appeared as an agenda and tradition that was largely founded on logical paradigms of analysis, clarity, distinction, difference, separation, individuality, rationality, and nonholistic scientific theory. These paradigms sought to find independent entities or substances in the world, and the properties of these substances were criteria of their independence and autonomy. In the seventeenth century, Euclidean Geometry had been partially translated by Xu Guangqi and a primer of Aristotelian logic was translated by Francisco Furtado and Li Zhizao. These translations introduced the classical methods

of mathematical and logical analysis from the West, but they had no significant influence in China. In a period of over twenty years in the late nineteenth
century, Yan Fu began to reintroduce books of Western logic to China. He
translated the first part of J. S. Mill's *Logic* and William Jevons's *Introduction
to Logic* in an attempt to present explicit definitions of modern logical and
scientific concepts and to employ the notions of inductive and deductive
validity and truth in clear and explicit demonstrations of propositions.

Apart from introducing Western logic as a tool for scientific and logical thinking, Yan Fu, who was deeply concerned with the survival of China as a people
and society, advocated the total reform of Chinese society. He based his proposals for reform on the principles of natural selection and survival of the fittest
that Social-Darwinists drew as the implications of the theory of evolution
for human society. He saw the European nations and Japan after the Meiji
restoration as examples of successful national struggles for survival and pros-
perity. For this reason, he devoted himself to translating many writings that
he considered to embody the keys to successful modernization and development in Europe and Japan. Thus he translated Herbert Spencer's *Sociology*,
Thomas Huxley's *Theory of Evolution and Ethics*, Adam Smith's *Wealth of
Nations*, and Baron de Montesquieu's *The Spirit of the Laws*. He wished to
show how modern Europe, especially England and France, achieved modernity by using reason, science, and a system of modern values to organize their
societies and governments. He particularly appreciated J. S. Mill's essay *On
Liberty*. To be free is to be free from the restraint of tradition, but freedom
must limit itself by respecting the freedom of others. Freedom is the basis for
the moral judgment of human actions, and without such moral judgment there
could be no progress of morality and society. Hence, for Yan Fu, freedom
was both the goal and motive force of human evolution.

Yan's views on philosophy, ethics, and politics reflected his observation that
without freedom one could not do one's best to strive for survival and pros-
perity. His account of freedom also reflected his views on how a modern
society and a modern state should be organized. In a modern state, individual
freedom must be based on a free society, and a free society must be based on
free individuals. Hence, he said: "Consider liberty as substance and consider
democracy as function." He proposed to reform China by reeducating the
Chinese people with the basic ideas of reason, science, and liberty that had
led Western countries to wealth and power and which would also strengthen
and enrich China.

Yan Fu's views differed from the reformist views of Kang Youwei and Liang
Qichao and from the revolutionary views of Sun Zhongshan (Sun Yat-sen). Kang,
Liang, and Sun preserved the value system of Confucian ethics and political
authority, and individuals, who were to define their existence in the context
of family, society, and state, could not be independently conceived as primary
entities. Although Yan Fu upheld Western ideas and visions for reform, his

method for achieving reform retains a Confucian grounding in his desire to accomplish sweeping changes in China through education.

After Yan Fu, Chinese philosophers gradually came to know many other Western philosophers through description or partial translation of their works. Notably, Wang Guowei studied Kant through Japanese sources around 1901, and Zhang Dongsun translated Bergson after May Fourth 1919 and debated with Marxists in the 1920s. Both Bergson and Kant have had a great impact on the development of contemporary Chinese philosophy. Their influence has been a source of development of the paradigmatic claim of Chinese philosophy that ultimate reality is an organic unity of substance and function. This paradigm maintained a powerful presence among Chinese intellectuals after it was deprived of political and social authority in China, and employment and critical reflection on the paradigm will continue to shape the future development of contemporary Chinese philosophy.

Western Philosophy: a Many-Faceted Challenge

Western culture in terms of economic and military strength came to China as an impact, but Western philosophy came to China as a challenge. The challenge has been in the form of the language of modern logic and modern analysis, in the form of an understanding of reason that is embodied in modern science, law, and democracy and in the form of an explicit division, categorization, and systematization of knowledge, truth, reality, morality, and beauty. The demands for organization, explicitness in argument, expression, and definition and precision in meaning and reference are all based on the rational division and logical separation of substance and function and the division and separation of functions into many disciplines.

In these demands we see a logical paradigm that suggests Xunzi rather than Mencius. Xunzi held that heaven and the human person should be separated and that even if man is born of heaven, he has his own substance and function. On this view, human substance and function need not depend on the original substance of heaven for their truth, intelligibility, or value. In this sense, Western philosophy is not simply a challenge of content, but more a challenge of form and method regarding the approach to ontology. In response to this challenge of form and method, Chinese philosophy has had to reformulate its identity and submerge itself in the context of history and ethnology. To gain new life, it first had to take on a new form and new language by reconstructing its vocabulary and discourse in terms of the modern demands for explicitness, precision, independence, and autonomy.

We may formulate the Western logical paradigm as the following dictum: *separate substance from function so that functions become their own substances which need not be understood in relation to an original substance.* This is a demand for autonomy. Physics, for example, was once known as natural philosophy, but once it became a science with its own object and method of investigation, it no longer had to refer to metaphysics for its explanation and prediction of natural events. The modern physics from Newton differed in this way from Aristotelian science, which relied on the categories and principles of metaphysics for its explanations and predictions. If metaphysics and theology (what Heidegger calls *Onto-theo-logik*) concern original reality (*benti*) in a Chinese sense, mathematics was the first branch of science to break off and maintain its distinct autonomous status independent of metaphysics. Next were grammar and logic as the study of abstract forms of thinking and reasoning and then astronomy as the study of nature or the heavens. Through astronomy, the West initiated a modern intellectual revolution that led to the development of Cartesian methods in mathematics. After astronomy came the transformation of physics, chemistry, economics, biology, psychology, and sociology. In the nineteenth century, politics and international law came within the scope of scientific study. In the contemporary period, we have seen the birth of various practical or applied sciences, and even literary studies have acquired an autonomy.

After philosophy gave birth to science, philosophy, as the original substance, could no longer make truth claims about its former function, although one may still ask how a function is related to its original substance and thus begin the philosophical study of an autonomous scientific subject. Interaction between substance and function is both possible and required, but in so far as scientific method and the vision of science prevailed, the substance of philosophy has yielded its many functions to independent sciences. In the end, what remains in philosophy itself is metaphysics. This may be seen to be analogous to the situation of Chinese philosophy, but the analogy is very thin. The Chinese metaphysical tradition continues its consideration of different functions even if the functions gain some relative autonomy from the center.

We have seen how Yan Fu first introduced some modern Western philosophical works into Chinese intellectual life. A later generation further developed a Chinese discourse that would reflect the logical and scientific discourse of the West. Feng Youlan applied the logical and conceptual methods of analysis in his efforts to define the basic terms and categories of traditional Chinese philosophy, more specifically the Neo-Confucian philosophy of principle (*li*) in works of the Cheng brothers and Zhu Xi. Jin Yuelin reconstructed a sophisticated theory of *dao* and *taiji* in terms of the logical methods of analysis, definition, and explication.

There have been two major tasks involved in responding to the challenge posed by Western philosophy. The first task is to understand and interpret the old in the new and to interpret the traditional in the modern. Because the West represents the new and the modern, the second task is to understand and interpret Chinese tradition in light of the West and to understand and interpret Western tradition in light of China. All major Chinese philosophers in the modern period have been engaged in these two tasks. Their work can be further analyzed as transforming the Chinese paradigm of the unity of substance and function into the Western paradigm of the separation of substance and function or in interpreting and integrating Western philosophical positions within the framework of the Chinese paradigm.

In responding to the West and constructing a new identity, it is necessary to distinguish between the modern and the Western. Western modernity overcame the medieval tradition of the West. The Enlightenment philosophers in the eighteenth century, who separated modernity from tradition, considered modernity to be a universal characteristic that could be realized in the name of reason and rationality. But from a postmodern point of view, modernity is a form of cultural identity that need not have universal validity. This is true even though science and technology – and what follows from science and technology – are a culturally neutral practice of seeking scientific truth and technological progress.

We must accept that science and technology can be adopted universally and are neutral regarding cultural values, but everything beyond science and technology is a reflection of traditional values or a reaction against them. There are many systems of traditional values and reactions against them as there are kinds of people. Modernity does not entail the elimination of traditional values unless they come in direct conflict with science and technology. On the contrary, science and technology can revive traditional values by providing better ways of preserving them. Given this understanding, we can see that the task of a contemporary Chinese philosopher has two aspects: the first is to seek forms of rationality that conform to science and democracy; the second is to find a suitable place and voice for traditional values.

The philosophical constructions that we have come to know in this volume focus more on logic and science than on democracy and political philosophy. Despite Yan Fu's introduction of a political philosophy of liberty, the main tendency of contemporary Chinese philosophy has been concerned with ultimate reality, ultimate truth, and ultimate value, concerns that reflect a commitment to the *ti* rather than the *yong* of culture. This mentality has more affinity with the metaphysics of European philosophy than with the practical scientific concerns of the British–American tradition. Certainly, Dewey's pragmatism had an important impact in Chinese educational circles, but his philosophy, like that of Bertrand Russell, had little influence in altering the deepest Chinese concerns with ontologically based ethics and cosmology.

The great tasks of contemporary Chinese philosophy are to accept modernity in a rational form, to transform and express its values and ideas within this new form, and to join genuine dialogues with Western philosophy.

In light of the contrasting paradigms of Chinese and Western philosophy, we may understand the development of contemporary Chinese philosophy as an effort to resolve the differences and contradictions between these two paradigms primarily using the Chinese paradigm of onto-cosmology and onto-ethics. This is understandable because the Chinese paradigm, which is Confucian in character, is deeply entrenched in Chinese life and culture. It acquired a life of its own through embodiment in political and social institutions and practices for over two thousand years. But in the shadow of foreign invasion and the impact of Western culture, Chinese philosophy has come self-consciously to maintain its identity as a system of metaphysical beliefs and human values. This long and tortuous effort has three aspects. First, there is a need to restate in modern terms what can be understood and interpreted in the Chinese philosophical tradition and to jettison or transform what cannot be understood. This work requires the analytic reconstruction of traditional views in a meaningful modern discourse. Secondly, this process of self-understanding requires interpretation of the old in terms of the new Western paradigm and interpretation of the new in terms of the Chinese paradigm, that is interpretation of the familiar in terms of the unfamiliar and the unfamiliar in terms of the familiar. In this way, the intellectual paradigm of the past can become at least partially intelligible according to the new paradigm and the new paradigm can become at least partially intelligible according to the old. Finally, there is a need for intellectual evaluation and appraisal. For critical appraisal, one needs statements of ultimate reality or ultimate value as the highest standard of judgment and justification. But this standard must be justifiable by common reason or by appeal to an ideal value in the traditional paradigm.

Not all Chinese philosophers in the twentieth century have confronted the Western logical and scientific philosophical paradigm with the Chinese paradigm of the organic unity of substance and function. In terms of the urgent need for renewal, distinctions between Confucian and Daoist perceptions of ultimate reality and the human relation to ultimate reality become less significant. Within the paradigm of organic unity, Confucianism, Daoism, and Chinese Buddhism are interrelated as meaningful and useful sources for self-interpretation, self-organization, and self-evaluation in response to the Western tradition. Xiong Shili started with Chinese Buddhism before moving on to Neo-Confucianism. Liang Shuming maintained his appreciation of the value of the Buddhist worldview. Zhang Dongsun, like Xiong, applied Buddhist nonessentialism in constructing his understanding of ultimate reality.

During the May Fourth Period, many Chinese intellectuals completely rejected the Chinese paradigm of philosophy because of its Confucian or Daoist content and enthusiastically embraced the values expressed by the Western paradigm of philosophy. Hu Shi introduced the pragmatic experimentalism of Dewey and advocated a program of piecemeal reform on the basis of a scientific critique of the tradition paradigm. Zhang Dongsun borrowed heavily from Bergson's philosophy of creative evolution and argued for a pluralistic structural epistemology. Li Dazhao and Chen Duxiu accepted Marxist historical and dialectical materialism and criticized and condemned the Chinese tradition.

Although Western liberalism and philosophical scientism have slowly taken root in modern Chinese society, the Confucian and Daoist vision of reality and ethics of virtue have not been absolutely forsaken. Confucianism as a moral-metaphysical paradigm, as a spiritual philosophy, and as a system of moral values and *Yijing*-Daoism as a metaphysics of change and creativity have been deeply consolidated in the minds of modern Chinese intellectuals. For this reason, the drama of contemporary Chinese philosophical development is focused on overcoming the inner weakness of Confucianism as a philosophy and revealing a modern version of the Chinese paradigm of understanding reality and life. This task enables one both to defend Confucian philosophy and to use Western philosophy in exposing and correcting its shortcomings. Hence the central theme of twentieth-century Chinese philosophy is the rediscovery of principles of Confucian-Daoist thought. Through exploring many aspects of the unity of substance and function, modern Chinese philosophy reveals a dialectic of integration, harmonization, inclusion, and comprehension.

Aspects of Transformation

Most modern Chinese intellectuals have been deeply concerned to grasp the difference between Chinese and Western philosophy. They searched for a framework in which to identify the distinctive properties of Chinese and Western minds as a basis for interpreting the difference between Chinese and Western culture. After becoming acquainted with some influential Western philosophical views, they sought to interpret Chinese philosophy and tradition through their understanding of Western philosophy. Dialogue and integration followed this crucial process of self-interpretation.

Thus, Chinese philosophy in the twentieth century started with its discovery of Western philosophy and proceeded to rediscover itself. In the final quarter of the century, there has been a new effort creatively to embrace Chinese and aspects of Western philosophy as contributions toward global understanding of humanity and the world.

In retrospect, twentieth-century Chinese philosophy has been an effort to articulate cultural reform aimed at modernity. It has also sought the rational justification and reconstruction of traditional views of heaven and *dao*, humanity and morality, and the individual and society. It has absorbed selected forms of Western philosophy, but has also sought a standpoint for the critique of Western philosophy. It has searched for new interpretations of Chinese philosophy based on methods linked to modern and Western points of view. New interpretations are needed because a new environment requires Chinese tradition to confront new issues of life and value and to establish new norms. New values are needed to infuse changing forms of life with meaning, and new norms are needed to guide actions and institutions in a modern world.

This account of Chinese philosophical activity will not make sense until we understand that China as a nation had passed through a catastrophic and painful period of frustration and suffering at the dawn of the twentieth century. Despite nineteenth-century efforts to reform, China was unable to regain control of its own destiny. Defeat at the hands of the scientifically and technologically advanced Western Powers and Japan eroded belief in Chinese culture and Chinese tradition, and especially destroyed faith in deeply imbedded Confucian values. In the May Fourth Movement in 1919, university students reacted against the imperialism of foreign powers and the cowardice of the Chinese government. In these conditions, philosophers felt compelled to examine the foundations of traditional culture, to criticize the guiding principles of current thought, to seek standards of justification and criteria of evaluation, to search for human identity, and to pursue human values.

The discovery of Western philosophy was a natural consequence of deepening cultural contact between China and the West. After the Opium War, Chinese intellectuals and administrators had a strong and anxious desire to know Western science and philosophy. We can seek to understand the tradition with which the reformers confronted modernity and to grasp the self-understanding that they brought forward to challenge Western views. These matters did not become intellectually significant until the reformist thinkers relinquished their uncritical visions of the West and gave up their task of emulating the West, that is until the New Confucians worked out their defense of tradition and their understanding of reality and man. Only then did the contest between China and the West in terms of basic values and ways of thinking became a reality.

One way to attempt to catch up with the West was to apply the methods of the West within the existing paradigm of both distinguishing and integrating substance and function. Zhang Shuting's famous dictum: "Use Chinese philosophy as *ti* and Western philosophy as *yong*" applied the model of the unity of substance and function, but he left unclear how Chinese learning could function as a *ti* in relation to the *yong* of Western learning or how both unity and a *ti-yong* internal relationship could be achieved between the two. Each of the *ti-yong* relationships of *li-qi*, *yin-yang*, and end-means requires an underlying principle to unite the two terms. In contemporary discussions, the relationships between knowledge and values, science and religion, and East and West again require a specification of qualities that enable the relationship to be understood and to be functionally operative.

We can regard Western science and technology as tools and Chinese morality and politics as ends-in-view and objectives to be attained. To understand Chinese culture is to understand values while to understand Western culture is to understand knowledge. But it was precisely Chinese ethics and politics that were considered to be responsible for the decline of China as a human society in the modern era. A system of feudalism, autocracy, despotism, and authoritarianism lacked autonomy and responsible individual freedom for human persons, lacked benevolent care from the government, and lacked loyalty and integrity among members of society. All of these shortcomings and weaknesses were protected by the cover of Confucianism, and, hence, Confucianism was held to blame. The social mass was seen to be stagnant and cumbersome due to Confucianism. Confucianism as it existed had to be purged before it could be purified to return to a pristine state of original thinking and being.

At the beginning of the modern era, Chinese science and education were backward and out-of-date. There was simply no systematic research to develop scientific knowledge. Instead, there were otiose organizations, inadequate training, and inefficient management. Within the terms of the traditional paradigm, these weaknesses pointed to a degenerate substance with bad functions. In light of this, one could ask how it was possible to see Chinese tradition and values as substance and Western values as function. Rather, the two seemed to be incompatible: each had its substance and function, and each operated as a whole system on its own.

On a deeper level, however, we can see ideal principles of moral insight and cosmological vision in the Chinese tradition, just as we can see the grim reality of mutual conquest and cruel war in the West. We can also see the beneficial effects of science and democracy in the West and the great disadvantages following from their lack in the East. It is quite reasonable to ask whether a synthesis of the strengths of the East and West could be accomplished while avoiding or limiting the shortcomings on each side. A coherent understanding of the terms of the synthesis would have to be determined over time, and even more time would be needed for any synthesis to become embodied in the practical forms of life and society. From the point of view of the current state of Chinese philosophy, it is not the *ti-yong* model that is in trouble, but the question of what constitutes the *ti* and the *yong* remains unsettled. Further, the distinction between the East and West can be accepted, while our understanding of the possibility of fusing the two according to a *ti-yong* model remains unclear.

Our present understanding of the strengths and weaknesses of the Chinese tradition and the strengths and weaknesses of the West provides a way to test the two to determine their compatibilities and differences. We can also determine the possibilities of dialogue, communication, and interaction and of mutual enrichment, inspiration, and supplementation. In this process, we can discover creative innovative ways to transform and transcend the two. The promise of fusion is not merely a matter of abstract thinking: fusion and interpenetration between Chinese tradition and Western thought can take concrete form in social and ethical practices.

In the context of global economic and political conditions of cultural exchange and philosophical dialogue, mutual accommodation and understanding require a revival of traditional sources and the development of mutual cultural interpenetration. This is needed to understand the human person and the world and as a resource for creating values with a scope, depth, and sophistication to serve humanity. Looking back, we can see how developments in the twentieth century have provided a pathway to this third stage of contemporary Chinese philosophy.

We may also understand the development of contemporary Chinese philosophy in terms of method. The modernization of Chinese philosophy has introduced Western philosophical and scientific method to allow the analysis and reconstruction of Chinese philosophy itself. Chinese philosophers soon discovered, however, that a method can constrain understanding and obstruct discovery. A method can produce a restrictive theory that further conditions the use of the method. In order to go beyond a theory, a new method must be sought that will allow a revolution in both method and theory. Western science has gone through a series of revolutions of theory and method and Western philosophy has experienced revolutions of theory and method as well.

Chinese tradition has not given rise to a similar series of revolutions of theory and method. Instead, it has required an openness of understanding so that we can see what is and what is not presented in experience. Zhu Xi suggested that we shall see *li* by thoroughly investigating all our experiences in time and that we shall recognize our feelings in our self-reflection. These are methods of understanding and discovery rather than methods of critique and justification. The method is incorporated in experience as a creative element in the flow of understanding. It is not formulated as steps like those that are found in Descartes' *Discourse on Method* or Dewey's *How to Think*. Given this difference in method, we can ask whether we are justified in applying Western methods for understanding Chinese philosophy and culture. A method is confined to a theory just as a function is confined to a substance. In this sense, a given scientific method will reduce an experience to a specific form of scientific theoretical knowledge.

Early twentieth-century Chinese philosophy was characterized by methodological reductionism and domination by external Western methods in the works of Liang Qichao, Hu Shi, and the Chinese Marxists, Li Dazhao and Chen Duxiu. Their methods were introduced from the West and used as a tool to evaluate tradition for the purpose of purging and overcoming the tradition and establishing a culture and philosophy to match the West. In the second half of the twentieth century, there were attempts to overcome the domination of external method. It was in accord with the nature of Chinese philosophy to seek a self-critical and self-reflective understanding of its own development. Whether Chinese philosophy leads to a unique methodological consciousness or transcends method by thought that is based on a deeper understanding of the world and humanity has been a central theme of these attempts.

My judgment is that the more a philosopher transcends the domination of an external method, the more he is able to bring forth a new method from his understanding of his own specific situation as a whole. Contemporary Chinese philosophy has depended upon this movement from external thought to internal reflection and on an active creativity that can transcend both the external and the internal. This tendency towards transformation provides a standard vantage point for understanding and evaluating the development of twentieth-century Chinese philosophy and the contributions of individual Chinese philosophers.

The Logic of Four Orientations and the Dialectic of Four Stages

We can now characterize the actual state and process of transformation of contemporary Chinese philosophy. My characterization is not founded solely on the general model of paradigmatic conflict I described above, rather it is a more thorough comparative analysis drawn from my own experience, reflection, and critical understanding of historically informed observations and theory-laden perceptions.

Both historically and theoretically, contemporary Chinese philosophy began with Chinese intellectuals confronting Western culture and Western philosophy at a time when the Chinese system of values and Chinese philosophical paradigm had lost vitality and vision. The intellectuals who were attracted to new values and new ideas from the West had awakened to a crisis for survival. These philosophers, represented by Liang Qichao, Hu Shi, and Wang Guowei, desired to introduce Western values to modernize Chinese philosophy, but they had not consolidated Western philosophy into a system and had not absorbed Western philosophy into either a Western or a Chinese paradigm of thinking. They did not construct any general philosophical theory or positions. We may call these philosophers early modernizers. Their influences were generally felt during the May Fourth Movement.

Philosophers who became interested in specific Western schools or philosophers adopted Western philosophical methods to present, analyze, argue, and develop their philosophical understanding of reality, of the human person, and of other significant matters. Their methods and modes of presentation were Western, but their visions and final concepts were linked to the Chinese philosophical tradition, whether Confucian, Daoist, or Buddhist. Their dominating concern was to apply Western philosophical methods and to develop comparative studies of the East and West. Under this heading, Zhang Dongsun used the philosophy of Kant and Bergson to construct a pluralist epistemology. Jin Yuelin used logical analysis to reconstruct the concept and systematic implications of the *dao*. Feng Youlan formed his new philosophy of *li* by using the method of analysis to reconstruct traditional realism. Fang Dongmei used a phenomenological-existential method to determine what philosophy represents in a culture. Fang attempted to show how a culture formulates and represents philosophical wisdom and how Chinese philosophy embodies a philosophical wisdom that illuminates Chinese culture. We may call these philosophers Western–Chinese synthesizers. They belong to the general category of Chinese philosophers with a Western orientation.

A full-fledged and systematic response to Western philosophy as understood from the standpoint of the Chinese philosophical tradition was found in the Contemporary Neo-Confucians or New Neo-Confucians of the 1930s. They distinguished between Western and Chinese philosophy and recognized the strengths of Western culture and philosophy. But they wished to show how Chinese culture and Confucian philosophy had resources to provide metaphysical insights that were not found in the West. They held that these insights should command our respect and attention because they offered a basis for cultural self-strengthening while adapting and interpreting Western science and democracy.

Within this group, we can distinguish between the moral–metaphysical Confucians and the practical–cultural Confucians. The former concentrated on the primary ontological and cosmological insights of Chinese philosophy and built a metaphysical view of reality that centered on the moral life of the human person. Methodologically, they started from the moral and ethical experiences of humanity and expanded these into a metaphysical understanding of reality based on the paradigm of the unity of substance and function. Thus, they employed the central paradigm of Chinese philosophical thinking that led to the formation of both classical Confucian and Neo-Confucian philosophies in the orthodox tradition. In contrast, the practical–cultural Confucians started by observing the practical and cultural values in the Chinese tradition as forms of life and saw in this practice a wisdom that reached truth and reality. This wisdom was different from that in the West and was possibly a better achievement. The main aim of these philosophers was to show how Chinese culture should be explored and developed to realize the purposes of human life and to establish a culturally richer world.

Xiong Shili represented moral–metaphysical Confucianism, and Liang Shuming represented practical–cultural Confucianism. He Lin, who adopted Hegelian idealism, blended both branches. He was motivated to reconstruct and reconstrue the Chinese tradition, but did not apply the paradigm of the unity of substance and function in his interpretation of the Lu-Wang School of Mind. In another sense, He Lin held a position between the New Neo-Confucians and the Western–Chinese synthesizers such as Jin Yuelin and Feng Youlan.

The New Neo-Confucians continued to develop in the 1960s and afterwards in both Hong Kong and Taiwan, where they became known as Taiwan–Hong Kong New Neo-Confucians or second-generation New Neo-Confucians. Again, we can distinguish between the moral–metaphysical and the practical–cultural branches. Mou Zongsan, following Xiong Shili, developed the moral meta-physics of Confucianism into a post-Kantian system of knowledge and being, whereas Xu Fuguan cultivated the common wisdom of the practical cultural traditions of China into a philosophical understanding of the wisdom of life, morality, and aesthetics. Tang Junyi, with his profound concern with Chinese moral life, developed a comprehensive essentialist, yet dialectical metaphysical view of moral rationality. Tang combined moral metaphysics with practical cultural wisdom in a Confucian system of explanation and understanding.

Due to the efforts of this second generation, New Neo-Confucianism gradually entered the mainstream of Chinese philosophy after the Cultural Revolution in a Chinese world that has encouraged developments over the full range of the Chinese philosophical tradition.

Finally, there were the Chinese philosophers who developed Chinese philosophy under the influence of Marxism or, put another way, formed Chinese Marxist philosophy under Marxist, Confucian, and Daoist influences. These were not the official ideologists or the political leaders, such as Mao Zedong, who developed practical Chinese Marxism for policy and political control. Rather, we are concerned with philosophers who established concepts and principles through close reflective thinking and critique. Their work showed continuity with early Western–Chinese synthetic thinkers like Jin Yuelin and Feng Youlan. They sought to reconstruct Chinese philosophy while maintaining a Marxist perspective and methodology. Through this combination of commitments, they were, perhaps, more culturally representative than many other Chinese philosophical figures from the 1940s through the 1990s. Zhang Dainian, Feng Qi, and Li Zehou are representatives of this group.

Zhang Dainian is a learned Chinese philosopher who has treated the whole history of Chinese philosophy as a theory in his analysis and critique. He gained profound philosophical insights from his brother Zhang Shenfu and metaphysical inspirations from Neo-Confucian *qi* philosophy. In this sense, he is more Confucian than Marxist.

The motivation of Feng Qi's philosophy was derived more from Feng Youlan than from Marxism. He wanted to define a theory of wisdom that embodied the Daoist spirit of openness. He sought freedom as the goal of wisdom and wished to see how freedom and wisdom could be embodied in the concrete individuals of a just and egalitarian society. Feng combined Confucianism and Marxism in the modernizing context of contemporary China.

Li Zehou expressed a romantic reaction against the Cultural Revolution within the framework of Marxism. In holding to the importance of human subjectivity as the motive force for the creation of aesthetic and moral values, Li has offered a new interpretation of Chinese philosophy at the expense of Marxist orthodoxy.

I have characterized the philosophers considered in *Contemporary Chinese Philosophy* according to four main branches:

1. Western orientation:
    *   Enlightenment philosophy: Liang Qichao, Hu Shi, Zhang Dongsun, Wang Guowei
    *   Synthesizing philosophy: Jin Yuelin, Feng Youlan, Fang Dongmei
2. New Neo-Confucian orientation:
    *   Moral–metaphysical philosophy: Xiong Shili
    *   Practical–cultural philosophy: Liang Shuming
    *   In between: He Lin
3. Later New Neo-Confucian orientation:
    *   Moral–metaphysical philosophy: Mou Zongsan
    *   Practical–cultural philosophy: Xu Fuguan
    *   Combining both: Tang Junyi
4. Chinese Marxist Orientation: Zhang Dainian, Feng Qi, and Li Zehou

We can examine the dialectical and logical structure of this scheme: this structure represents the conflict initiated by the introduction and imposition of the Western philosophical paradigm. New Neo-Confucianism can be seen as a natural rebirth and transformation of the Chinese tradition under the challenge of the Western paradigm. Its ability to reflect the deep life of the Chinese philosophical tradition explains how New Neo-Confucianism has gained growing importance in the development of Chinese philosophy in the last half of the twentieth century. There is a dialectical opposition between the West and East involved in the formation of New Neo-Confucianism. Whether this opposition can be resolved and the form that any resolution might take depends on deepening interaction between China and the West. Through this interaction, we can understand more of what lies behind New Neo-Confucianism and more of what lies behind the philosophy of Western figures such as Kant, Hegel, Dewey, and Wittgenstein. Developing this understanding is the challenge of tomorrow.

In this scheme, how do we explain the rise of Chinese Marxist philosophy? At this stage we can say that the sheer force of Marxism as an ideology fostered an interest in Marxist humanist and economic philosophy that shared many common concerns about humanity and human society with Confucianism. The transfer of sentiments from Confucianism to Marxism in China from the 1930s to the 1950s drew on these affinities. Marxism surpassed Confucianism through its claims to economic and scientific knowledge and was perceived to resolve the Chinese demands to embrace science and achieve wealth. Marxist anti-imperialism became a natural weapon against Western domination and in the pursuit of equality and balance between tradition and modernity, between East and West.

Marxism brought a problem of nondemocracy, which negated one of the mainstream values of the May Fourth Movement. Resolving this problem might be one motive for the revival of interest in Confucianism, which can be understood as providing an intellectual basis for the unity of humanity and democracy.

The momentum of development of contemporary Chinese philosophy originated from the matrix of the May Fourth Movement and its articulation of the explicit conflict between the paradigm of Confucianism and the paradigm of modern Western philosophy of science and democratic power. From this source, we can gain a dialectical understanding of the issues of contemporary Chinese philosophy, but can also see contemporary Chinese philosophy as representing a deeply human philosophical need to recognize interparadigmatic conflict and to seek its resolution. For a full understanding of contemporary Chinese philosophy, we must engage in many levels of reflection to examine the sources and natures of related conflicts that are derived from this primary opposition.

We can examine contemporary Chinese philosophy in five stages that reflect its development, progress, return, retrospection, and interaction and recognize both its relation to earlier tradition and its aspiration for the future. The rough dates of each stage are indicated.

1. Pioneering New Thought from the West (1900 to 1930s)
2. Philosophizing in the Neo-Confucian Spirit (1930s to 1950s)
3. Ideological Exposure to Dialectical Materialism (1950s to 1980s)
4. Later Developments of New Neo-Confucianism (1960s to 1990s)
5. Reinterpreting Chinese and Western Philosophies (1960s to present)

The present book concentrated on the first four stages. There is an overlap in the timing of Stage 3, which mainly took place in China, and Stage 4, which mainly took place in Taiwan, Hong Kong, and abroad. To understand the logic of these stages one must understand the dialectical and logical structure of contemporary Chinese philosophy as explained above.

The Roles of Marxism, Confucianism, and Neo-Confucianism

In light of the five-stage development of Chinese philosophy in the contemporary era we can ask: what are the roles of Marxism and Confucianism in this development? Is Neo-Confucianism or Marxism the central force of development? How should their relationship be conceived? What is the present situation of this relationship? Answers to these questions will reveal both the historicity and the logical and metaphysical reasons for the existence of all the varieties of contemporary Chinese philosophy.

Confucianism has unquestionably played the role of substance deprived of its political and social functions in modern Chinese history. After May Fourth

1919, what remained of Confucianism was a spirit of faith and a potential for reconstitution. China was searching for a new substance with a new function. Intellectuals sought a new substance to produce a new faith in life and a new hope for the future. They sought a new function to restore the political sovereignty and social coherence that Confucianism could not then provide. Marxism played the role of the new substance with the potentiality for the new function. In time, Marxism fulfilled this historical mission. It was able to do so because of its holistic philosophy with a clear understanding of reality. It was accepted because of its claims to scientific truth and its pragmatic program that succeeded in founding the Soviet Union.

In many ways, Marxism has satisfied the expectations of a new substance in philosophy to replace Confucianism, while maintaining an equivalence with Confucianism. Not only was Marxism equivalent to Confucianism in its historical role as an organic system of substance and function, it also shared some of the visions and ideal values of Confucianism, for example, its belief in human labor and in social development. Marxism maintained a disciplinary social organization and sought to establish a powerful modern society and economy while advocating principles of equality and social justice. Partly because of their Confucian resonances, these features strongly appealed to Chinese intellectuals, including Mao Zedong and Deng Xiaoping. For these reasons, the rise of Marxism and Maoism in modern China is not an historical accident.

Both Confucianism and Marxism have had crucial importance in contemporary Chinese philosophy. Confucianism was the potential historical force that led to the development of Marxism in China, and Marxism was the actual ideological power that led to the political and social transformation of China. Once the political and social actuality was formed, Confucianism and Neo-Confucianism have returned, not as a political and social force, but as a philosophy of understanding and valuation. This desire to return can be realized on two conditions, namely, Confucianism must have philosophical and ideological importance and it has to be modernized to meet the needs of a modern society.

The Chinese philosophers we have considered have argued that Confucianism is needed as a cosmology and philosophy of human nature and as a philosophy of morality. They have presented arguments transforming Confucianism into a modern materialist or idealist philosophy. These revisions suggest an underlying need and an underlying social transformation that could allow Confucianism to reemerge to provide normative guidance in China. If this occurs, Confucianism will have returned as an intellectual movement and as a social ethic providing a new identity for China as it takes up its role in the world community.

Hence we see a dialectical process of transformation between Marxism and Confucianism. In this dialectical relationship, there is a tension that creates a space for development and a relative positioning of the doctrines for the future. There are two simultaneous forms of transformation: the Marxizing of Confucianism and the Confucianizing of Marxism. Among the philosophers of our volume, Feng Qi, in arguing for a free and egalitarian civil society, is a Confucianized Marxist. Zhang Dainian, who sees Confucian *qi* philosophy in terms of Marxist materialism, is a Marxized Confucian. Li Zehou is a Confucian–Marxist, who could appear as Confucian in one context and as a Marxist in another. From this perspective, we have encountered different blends of Marxism and Confucianism in all the schools that we have considered. Mao himself was identified by Frederick Wakeman as a Nietzschean Wang-Yangming Marxist.

Both Marxism and Confucianism were moving forces throughout a major portion of twentieth-century Chinese history. Their creative tension and transformation generated a momentum that has not yet achieved its culmination. This will be accomplished when an equilibrium is found, with an organic system of substance and function fully established conforming to the needs of the Chinese community and conforming to standards of values that represent the collective history of mankind.

The significance of modern Confucianism is in its revival of the ethical value and cultural form of humanity and in its placement of these concerns within modern scientific and technological culture. In this regard, its significance is global and timely, but it is an open question whether its value as a moral metaphysics or as an onto-cosmology will be fully appreciated.

Criteria of Onto-Hermeneutic Analysis and Evaluation

In order to understand how each strand of contemporary Chinese philosophy has developed a creative response and critical challenge within the framework of conflicting paradigms, we must see them as providing an ontologically based hermeneutical interpretation of what confronts and disturbs them. Their onto-hermeneutic interpretations find answers to questions, an analysis of reality and language, and a method and practical solution. An onto-hermeneutic interpretation is how a philosophy interprets reality and life in light of its understanding of a paradigm based on a tradition of texts or sources from a tradition. Any major tradition of philosophy is a tradition of texts. But an onto-hermeneutic interpretation can also be an effort to reach an interpretation of views of reality and life embodied in another tradition using whatever resources one may command. Since one cannot be separated completely from one's own tradition, onto-hermeneutic interpretation results in an integration and union of one's source tradition and a target tradition of interpretation. We can formulate the following onto-hermeneutic criteria for examining each contemporary Chinese philosopher according to their type and degree of effort and success. We may ask questions related to six areas of onto-hermeneutic understanding and interpretation: tradition, horizon, method, truth, creativity, and application.

1. Tradition: How does a contemporary Chinese philosopher understand the Chinese tradition of philosophy comprising Confucianism, Daoism, and other schools? This is the question of effective history.
2. Horizon: How does a contemporary Chinese philosopher relate himself to classical, Christian, modern, or contemporary Western traditions of philosophy? This is the question of self-transcendence, comparison and contrast, evaluation and integration, and defining or transforming one's identity.
3. Method: What is the method, paradigm, norm, or ideal identified by a contemporary Chinese philosopher and how is it applied and practiced by him? This is the question of justification and discovery and of innovation and knowledge.
4. Truth: What are the ultimate truth and guiding-principle, the vision, and fundamental value to be found in the work of a contemporary Chinese philosopher? How do we describe the reality that emerges from such a system? What is the underlying system, and how far is it systematized? This is the question of the nature and structure of a conceptual system and its ultimate reference to reality.
5. Creativity: How creative, innovative, critical, and systematic is a contemporary Chinese philosopher? This is the question of evaluating the creative and critical contributions of the philosopher.
6. Application: How does a contemporary Chinese philosopher conceive the application and undertake the practice of his philosophy? This is the question of application of a philosophy as a method and as a principle.

Tradition

We may start with the criterion of tradition. With the exception of Hu Shi, all major Chinese philosophers in the contemporary period are in one way or another engaged in preserving the paradigm of organic unity of substance and function from the Chinese philosophical tradition. Specifically, Confucianism and Neo-Confucianism eventually became the ultimate concern for understanding and interpretation. They also became the sources for self-affirmation and self-understanding. As a way of coping with social life and promoting ethical self-cultivation, Confucianism and Neo-Confucianism satisfied the needs for unity, subjective participation, and social practice. On this basis, Liang Shuming defended Confucian rationality. For Xiong Shili, Confucianism provided insight into ultimate reality through the *Yijing* and Neo-Confucianism texts. This provided a strong basis for the Confucian practice of virtue ethics and social life. The tradition developed and strengthened, and Confucianism and Neo-Confucianism were integrated in a larger system of cosmic action and personal understanding. The moral metaphysics and onto-ethics of Contemporary Neo-Confucianism became creatively challenging. This insight was continued and deepened by Mou Zongsan and Tang Junyi. For Tang, Confucianism could absorb Hegelian dialectics and surpass it in its practical and cultural application. Mou used Kant for early guidance but later overcame the Kantian theory of agnosticism concerning reality and the activity of practical morality. Confucian and Neo-Confucian insight into the unity of man and heaven was put to creative and critical use.

From a Western theoretical point of view, it is puzzling how practical reason could reveal an infinite intuition into ultimate reality as *noumenon*. For Kant, the cognitive and practical are separate modes that are unified in their ground, but not in their activity. Yet, our primary intuition shows them to be united in the experience of the human person, the cognitive and the practical merely providing two views of the self. One can seek explanation of this division and their human unity either in the historicity of the tradition or in the different modalities of understanding.

Hu Shi did not work from the basis of tradition, but we may regard his passive and uncritical acceptance of Dewey as both a strength and a weakness. He had given up Chinese philosophy as a tradition and as a base for understanding. Because he insufficiently understood the Western philosophical tradition, Hu could not respond to pragmatism from a Western point of view and had to accept Dewey's position without qualification. He used Dewey's perspective and Dewey's method to interpret Chinese logical thought. Even his research on the history of Chan Buddhism could not penetrate the deep metaphysical meaning of *chan* or *dao*. However, he did reflect, perhaps unselfconsciously, one traditional trait, namely, the preference for simple expression. He simplifies the five steps of Dewey's methodology of problem solving into the two-statement slogan: make bold hypotheses and take care to prove. This is emotionally appealing but epistemologically imprecise.

Horizon

We come to the question of Horizon. Jin Yuelin and Feng Youlan both exemplified a quest for a new horizon by using the methods of logical and conceptual analysis. Unlike Hu Shi, both Jin and Feng were primarily concerned with using Western methodology to build their own philosophy of reality and value. Jin took Russell and Whitehead's *Principia Mathematica* as a model for his analytical-ontological theory in *On Dao*. His method was logical and analytical, but the substance of his philosophy was the holistic notion of the *dao*. His imagination and analysis allowed him to define the *dao* in terms of the concepts of *li* and *qi* from Zhu Xi's Neo-Confucianism because he defined *li* as forms of possibility and *qi* as matter-energy. He described the *dao* as all the combinations of possible forms and matter-energy, although at any time only some forms are realized in matter-energy according to principles of congruence, contingency, and economy of the *dao*. But over time *dao* will produce all forms in matter-energy, and hence there is evolution and movement of the *dao*. With evolution, Jin was further able to explain the emergence of human intelligence, mind, and the formation of society and culture. This richly innovative philosophy was founded on integrating the Chinese metaphysics of *yi* (change) and the modern philosophy of logic and mathematics. Through logical analysis and conceptual definition, he formulated and developed a cogent philosophy of reality and knowledge. Although many things remain unexplained, Jin's philosophy is a good illustration of a fusion of horizons that led to a new horizon for understanding the *dao*.

Similarly, there was an emergence of a new horizon through Feng Youlan's efforts to build his New Principle Learning. Feng was more conservative than Jin in using the methods of logical analysis and critical rationality to reconstruct the Song–Ming philosophy of *li* and *qi*. Following realist models, he distinguished between the realm of truth and the realm of actuality. Whereas the realm of truth contains principles, the realm of actuality contains actual things. Here, Feng diverged from Song–Ming rationalism, according to which *li* as transcendental forms and *qi* as material conditions of actual things are not separable. In addition, Feng's philosophy, unlike Jin's metaphysics of the *dao*, lacked a process of change. Feng's notion of *daquan* (the great whole) represents his highest conceptualization of reality as a universal totality devoid of dynamism. For this reason, Feng's *daquan* cannot to be equated with the traditional concepts of the *taiji* or the *dao* as a creative process of formation and transformation. His awareness of the rich content of the philosophy of the *dao* led Feng to a negative approach to the reality that transcended analysis and logic. Through his combination of the positive method of analysis and the negative approach to the reality of becoming, Feng attempted to integrate Chinese metaphysics with Western methodology. Yet this attempt encountered the limitation of critical reason in describing our profound experience of ultimate reality as explored in Song–Ming Neo-Confucianism.

Zhang Dongsun developed a theory of knowledge that led to a metaphysics based on Chinese Buddhism and Kantian philosophy. He conceived knowledge to be a construction combining subjective concepts as forms, sensations as experiences of unknown entities and postulates determined by a cultural tradition. For Zhang, knowledge is produced by a process of gathering elements under a given condition. This account is derived from the Buddhist notion of relatedness (*yinyuan*), which he later developed into a notion of framework (*jiangou*). He used Bergson's philosophy of creative evolution to introduce an element of openness and creativity into his understanding of unknown reality. Hence, his philosophy clearly offered a new horizon, born from a Chinese sense of reality and a Western epistemology.

Method

We now turn to the problem of method. All major contemporary Chinese philosophers paid attention to the question of philosophical method. In a broad sense, attention to method can be equated with attention to the reason that is required to reach and articulate truth. However, there are two ways in which a narrow sense of method can be conceived: first, method as a skill or *techne* for analysis and construction; second, method as an approach to determining basic issues of reality and value. In the former sense, Jin Yuelin and Feng Youlan applied the method of logic and analysis to reconstruct the notions of *li*, *qi*, and *dao* in a Chinese philosophical system that was separate from the Western tradition that produced the method.

In the latter sense, a method is equivalent to a possible or actually established point of view from which things can be ordered, defined, and explained. A method in this sense can be used for discovery or used for justification, but for this to be possible the method must presuppose a substantive philosophy describing reality and defining issues. Most of the Western philosophy that was introduced to China has been employed as a method to deal with problems defined by Chinese philosophy. Thus, Hu Shi used the methods of science and pragmatism to formulate his views on Chinese culture, literature, and politics. His views on these questions were shaped by methods that integrally contained pragmatic scientific notions of human knowledge and value.

Similarly, Chinese Marxist philosophers used Marxism as a method for explaining, justifying, and evaluating all philosophical positions and social and political issues. The Marxist methodology of dialectical-historical analysis was founded on ontological and axiological premises that, when applied, could yield substantive positions rather than a formal analysis of reality. This was clearly exemplified in the work of Zhang Dainian and Li Zehou. As a dialectical materialist, Zhang interpreted the whole history of Chinese philosophy in terms of materialist categories and paradigms. Li Zehou found a place in materialist methodology for individual and cultural subjectivity in order to construct a philosophy of beauty that aimed to liberate society from its economic and political conditions. In this case, his method of historical materialism led to conclusions that opposed the dialectical materialism of his starting point.

In the corpus of Contemporary Neo-Confucianism, the principle guiding philosophical construction is not a method but an onto-cosmological and axiological vision of the ideal development of the human person. Contemporary Neo-Confucians have methodological concerns, but the method of achieving the ultimate unity of heaven and the human person is internal to their ontological thinking rather than external to it. Their method defines ultimate reality and enables us to discover and justify our understanding of this reality. Their method is one of intellectual intuition and is not prior to or separable from our understanding of reality. This approach to philosophical construction was first developed by He Lin early in the twentieth century. Based on his knowledge of Hegel, He established a philosophical project of interpreting the Lu–Wang school of mind as a system of Absolute Spirit. What had greatest importance for He Lin was not Hegelian dialectics, but the historical and ontological vision that guided his interpretation and justification.

In the second generation of Neo-Confucianism in the middle of the twentieth century, Tang Junyi applied the Hegelian account of Absolute Mind to define his notion of the original substance of the human mind, but he did not adopt Hegelian dialectics. Instead, the method he applied was the dialectical-reflective part of his spiritualistic Confucian philosophy. Similarly, in emulating and criticizing Kant, Mou Zongsan developed a vision of ultimate reality based on his view of critical moral reason. Again, the development of his philosophy depended on the vision that guided his construction rather than on any method independent of the system.

Xu Fuguan's conception of Chinese culture and the moral cultivation of the human person guided his interpretation of the formation of Chinese culture and Confucianism. In Confucianism, it is self-reflection and self-cultivation rather than an external method that discovers and justifies the moral truths realized in the human person. Of course, we can interpret Confucian philosophy as a methodology, but this methodology is one that seeks one's moral nature and its realization in practice. Seeking questions from others, as required by the Great Learning (*Da Xue*), is not solely for conceptual clarification or learning, but rather incorporates clarity and learning in a holistic system of understanding and action. This is a philosophical method of the human person, our moral ability and our moral aspirations. This understanding of method leads us to consider the criterion of ultimate truth.

Feng Qi, in the latter part of the twentieth century, also stressed the importance of method. He advocated the method of intellectual intuition of the *dao* in order to see how distinct things are unified and adopted the notion of sudden enlightenment (*dunwu*). His method does not hamper our perception of things as things nor interfere with the use of logic and observation in science. Rather, as in Zhuangzi's *Qiwulun*, his method aims to equalize all things to produce a wisdom of comprehension and nonselfishness. In this regard he shows the influence of his teacher Feng Youlan. More specifically, Feng Qi enjoined us to transform theory both into method and into virtue. Method for him is the ability to apply wisdom of the *dao* to resolve problems of knowledge and value in order to become a free person. Feng's method is not solely a skill, but results from the use of theory combined with one's understanding of *dao*. By method, we reach knowledge and wisdom, which in turn augments our method for reaching greater knowledge and wisdom. In revealing both this dialectic process and this hermeneutical circle, Feng's transformation of theory into method reflected a deep understanding of ultimate reality in the Chinese metaphysical tradition.

Truth

All philosophers in contemporary China have shown a special concern for the criterion of ultimate truth. Even the pragmatism of the scientifically minded Hu Shi defined ultimate truth, even though Hu did not discuss any metaphysical issues of ultimate reality. From the beginning, Kang Youwei tried to depict a Confucian utopia that realized the ultimate truth for humanity. Further, at the beginning of his career he identified original oneness as the underlying reality of his philosophy. Under the influence of Kant, both Wang Guowei and Zhang Dongsun claimed that ultimate truth cannot be known, but this Kantian constraint was soon rejected in the rise of Contemporary Neo-Confucianism.

For both Xiong Shili and Liang Shuming, ultimate reality was the motivating force for developing their philosophies of morality and culture. Xiong was much more explicit and vocal than Liang in constructing an ontology and cosmology to justify his notions of the human mind and the human cultivation of virtue. Their vision of ultimate reality to inspire human life and inform human nature was derived precisely from their profound concern with human moral development. From this perspective, the second-generation Neo-Confucians determined a challenging task of explanation and construction. Even though Tang and Mou had very different theoretical approaches, the metaphysics of both was based on exploring the ontological implications of moral reason. This was how their vision of ultimate truth was elaborated and expanded.

Xu Fuguan may not have accepted the ontological import of Tang and Mou. His stress on moral practice and his insight into the existential anxiety of self-reflection, self-improvement, and self-realization revealed human nature and the human mind in seeking and practicing virtues. For him, this was the ultimate truth of the human person.

In Fang Dongmei's philosophy of life, creativity, and the realization of value, there is a deep sense of ultimate truth and reality underlying all human cultures and histories. Above all, he saw the comprehensive reality of harmony among all things in the notions of the *dao* and the *yi* as the measure and reality of ultimate truth. In describing major cultures of the world in *Three Wisdoms of Philosophy*, he held that Chinese philosophical wisdom lies precisely in its ability to exhibit the creativity of life in harmony and comprehension. For this reason, he was less appreciative of Indian culture and philosophy than Liang Shuming, but expressed much more appreciation of the systems of Chinese Buddhism than either Liang or Xiong. In Chinese Buddhism, he found a comprehensive harmony that was also realized in Daoism and Confucianism.

Creativity

We can now turn to the criterion of creativity. The very beginning of contemporary Chinese philosophy stressed the importance of evolutionary theory in inspiring the Chinese people to strive to be the fittest in order to survive and in urging intellectuals creatively to evolve a new system of philosophy. We have seen the difficulty of abandoning the very insights from which one's philosophy would have to evolve and of escaping the entrenched values that determined one's ideal standards and goals.

In these circumstances, two forms of creativity were exhibited. The first argued from a Confucian point of view to see how Confucian philosophy could adapt to Western values. The second started from Western philosophical method to reach metaphysical positions that reflected a traditional point of view. Tang Junyi exemplified the first approach, and Jin Yuelin exemplified the second. Jin employed logical method to determine a logical definition of the *dao* and hence a philosophy of the *dao*, whereas Tang used Confucian understanding to comprehend other points of view. In accepting scientific natural reason, he sought not to ignore moral reason.

There is also a variation of the second form of creativity: to regard Western philosophy as substance and to find its function in Chinese philosophy. This happened with Hu Shi and the early Marxists Chen Duxiu and Li Dazhao. Whereas Hu Shi failed to develop any significant metaphysical theory, Chen and Li helped to found the Chinese Marxism that came to dominate China politically. This might have led to Li Zehou's proposal to take Western culture as substance and Chinese culture as function, but this requires thorough scrutiny before we can give it a coherent sense. Theoretically, there is a living organic link between a substance and its function. Without working out a theory of Chinese–Western integration on the basis of Western culture, Li's proposal is as empty as the proposal to take Chinese culture as substance and Western culture as function. Nevertheless, Li's innovative reversal of a standard Chinese view is worth examining.

A deeply inspired creative view is Xiong Shili's claim for the nonduality of substance and function (*tiyong buer*). Although *ti* and *yong* have been held to be related without mediation (*tiyong wujian*) since Song–Ming Neo-Confucianism, no Chinese philosopher before Xiong has focused on the onto-cosmological significance of the inseparability of the two. This reflects Xiong's metaphysical insight and intellectual intuition of the nature of reality. The source of this insight is the account in the *Yijing* of *yi* as creative change, which Xiong attributed to the wisdom of Confucius. This insight serves two main functions: it explicitly identifies the ultimate reality of metaphysics with concrete events of the natural world; and it links metaphysical understanding with the moral wisdom of human life.

Not only did Xiong grasp the Confucian metaphysics of the *yi* as the mainstream tradition of Confucius, Zisi, and Mencius, he also founded the ontological link between reality and morality, which Mou Zongsan called "moral metaphysics." Moral metaphysics is a metaphysics established through the vivid internal experience of the moral development of a human person's mind and nature. It is a theory of the nature of the ultimate reality that is informed and enlightened by human moral self-realization.

There are many implications of this Confucian insight that have not been fully developed but which are implicit in Xiong's insight. One of these is the implication of an ontological ethics that I have discussed in various places. There is also the implication of a moralized epistemology, distinct from an epistemology of morality or a moral psychology, which considers all problems of knowledge as informed with a moral significance reflecting the development of the human person as a moral entity. There are many problems of moral metaphysics that have not yet been articulated and explored, for example, the problem of self-knowledge and self-transcendence as internal, self-determining experiences that do not ground a distinction between right and wrong, the holy and the demonic.

Mou Zongsan, following the insight of his teacher Xiong Shili, developed an account of the basic content of moral metaphysics, but again he did not explore the full significance of this insight. He advanced a controversial theory of "abnegation" or "voluntary suspension" (*kanxian*) that argues that we develop science by suspending moral judgment. At one level the development of science does require us to suspend moral judgment, but at a higher level science requires moral judgment for the integration of knowledge and value. In this sense, there is no real abnegation of the human mind in developing oneself or one's culture toward a higher state. Mou was responsible for valuable innovations, but his claim that Zhu Xi was outside the mainstream of Neo-Confucian philosophy is again questionable. The question raised by this view is whether we should see the development of Confucianism, including Neo-Confucianism, as linear inheritance or as a genuine process of differentiation and integration in which divergent views are also part of the mainstream.

Another important creative insight comes from Fang Dongmei. Again based on the philosophy of the *Yijing*, he considered anything leading to life as creativity and regarded human life and cultures as a rich panorama of the creative impulses of human persons. His insight was to see the highest form of beauty and goodness as an ability to achieve, present, and preserve an all-comprehensive harmony. To offer harmony as an ultimate value or measure of value is important for understanding Chinese philosophy. It is also important for understanding the common nature of reality and human morality as the basis for a moralized ontology and an ontologized morality and for providing the possibility of ranking all human cultures and philosophical thinking. Of course, the nature of harmony and the possibility of regarding harmony as a supreme value require further discussion.

The very principle of creativity is a fundamental focus of contemporary Chinese philosophy. This can be easily understood from the tradition of *Yijing* studies. In *yi*, one finds concepts of change, transformation, ceaseless creativity, and transcendence within change, but the essence of creativity is the production of life. From life comes human nature and the human mind. In the creativity of life, the Neo-Confucian philosopher Cheng Hao found the virtue of benevolence. Giving this new dimension to the meaning of *ren* enabled Confucian ethics to find a further link to metaphysics. This is the true beginning of the concept of moral metaphysics. Zhang Dainian regards the development of Chinese philosophy as comprising the activity of creative synthesis. To be creative is to form new and meaningful views based on a fusion of different positions. For our purposes, these positions can be ancient and modern, Chinese and Western. In this sense of creative synthesis, many major contemporary Chinese philosophers are creative. We can, for example, consider Feng Youlan to be a creative mind. Feng's creative formulation of the negative method led to the formation of the transcendent concept of the great totality (*daquan*) and to the concept of the spirit of heaven and earth, both of which reflect Feng's synthesis of Daoism, Confucianism, Plato, and Aristotle.

Application

Finally, we come to the problem of practice and application. Chinese philosophy has traditionally stressed the importance of the practice concerning what one says and believes. This is also called the problem of *gongfu* (effort-making). It is held that by making enough effort we will get closer to our desired goal. If one has not yet reached a level of perfection, one has made insufficient effort. In contemporary Chinese philosophy, the issue of *gongfu* has been addressed much less than in Song–Ming Neo-Confucianism. The consideration of *gongfu* marks a turn in modern Chinese philosophy from internal to external confirmation and from self-justifying action and practice to the demand for theoretical justification in reason and language. This turn lost sight of the appeal to the internal and action, but at crucial metaphysical points contemporary Chinese philosophers speak of the reality or *jingjie* (realm) of the *dao* by appeal to the internal justification of insight, direct experience, or intellectual intuition.

Contemporary Chinese philosophy is not confined to contemplation and speculation. It also contains an appeal to social action and an effort to realize ideal values. The 1957 Declaration of Chinese Culture is a significant indication of a philosophical willingness to engage in cultural action. It was lack of social action and social concern that led both Xiong Shili and Liang Shuming to turn away from Buddhism to Confucianism. In this sense, all contemporary Chinese philosophers who are Confucians or Neo-Confucians are committed to practice and social action, while only some are committed to a contemplative or speculative self-testifying of ultimate truth.

Liang Shuming's suspension of political activities and his efforts to reconstruct Chinese villages according to his Confucian design expressed a strong commitment to action and practice. Similarly, Tang Junyi and Qian Mu's efforts to found New Asia College in Hong Kong as a Confucian Graduate School that was independent of government and on the model of Song academies showed another commitment to social practice and action. Chinese Marxists have distinguished themselves in their commitment to practice what they believe and say, as exemplified in Mao Zedong's essay "On Practice."

In more recent times, Feng Qi was concerned to transform theory into both method and virtue. For Feng, method is a continuation of knowledge, and virtue is practice according to wisdom. Both are unified in our knowledge and vision of the *dao*. Transforming theory into virtue requires that the theory gives rise to knowledge either mediated by method or directly and that we develop a vision of ideal value as embodied in the *dao*. This transformation can take place because our wisdom inspires us to be more capable and more willing to put what we know into practice. Feng suggests that ideal human persons must believe, achieve, and preserve their vision of the *dao*. To transform the vision of the *dao* into action is to develop a human character that is free from the bondage of desire and seeks self-realization through its own free will. There is no doubt that Feng has been inspired by both Marxism and Neo-Confucianism.

Li Zehou is another philosopher who has used Marxist language to address the Confucian issue of self-cultivation and practice. His account of practice focuses on the subjectivity of the human person. In his Marxist account of subjectivity, Li sees the human subject as composed of structures of culture, psychology, and economic labor. Li argued that the human subject can change his environment and change and even transcend history with his subjectivity. In this regard, he is perhaps more Marxist than Confucian, but in holding beauty to be the supreme realization of the potentiality of subjectivity he is more Confucian than Marxist. He also sees beauty as the form of freedom that represents the spiritual drive for moving history. In this regard, Li is more Hegelian than Marxist or Confucian. Despite his contention that beauty is neither in the nature of things nor in the consciousness of human persons, Li held that beauty is the realization of the subjective and the form of subjective freedom that leads to this realization. But Li's tendency to consider Confucianism as absolutely voluntarist is misleading. In Confucian philosophy, *ming* (destiny) limits what one can will or what willing can accomplish.

Outstanding Characteristics and Issues in Contemporary Chinese Philosophy

Based on our analysis and interpretation, we can identify six significant and historically representative characteristics of contemporary Chinese philosophy. These characteristics are not universal among the philosophers that we have considered and do not define contemporary Chinese philosophy as a genus. Nevertheless, they are not chosen arbitrarily because they arise from a discourse that shares a common origin and a common effective history. They are organically united through their mutual support in a complex and dynamic system. Furthermore, their interrelations can be explained according to an underlying paradigm of the unity of substance and function, being and knowing, knowing and acting, acting and subject, and subject and object. The features can be identified according to important divisions of philosophical thinking, such as metaphysics, epistemology, ethics, value theory, philosophical anthropology, and aesthetics, from the standpoint of the subject who divided philosophy into these subject areas. These features point to issues to consider in comparing Western and contemporary Chinese philosophy, issues that are hidden if we restrict ourselves exclusively to Western philosophy as a base for philosophical critique and interrogation. Ultimately, assessment of the importance of the issues arising from these features depends on deep reflections concerning truth, knowledge, recognition, and judgment.

The *first characteristic* is the dominance of the *Yijing* philosophy of change (*yi*) as a guiding principle that has been deeply embedded in the minds of almost all Chinese philosophers in the twentieth century. The inspiration of the *Yijing* derives from its onto-cosmological unity of substance and function, reality, and process. The *Yijing* provides a picture of experienced reality and a way of thinking that achieves an insight and vision into the basic nature of things. The philosophy of *Yijing* offers understanding of change, innovation, renovation, revolution, transformation, natural and human creative activity, transcendence, and return. In its philosophical role, the *Yijing* has functioned as the source of insight into reality from the time of Confucius continuously through Daoism, Neo-Daoism, Chinese Buddhism, and Neo-Confucianism to the present day. Kang Youwei, the last traditional Confucian and the first twentieth-century Confucian, used the *Yijing* as the foundation of his Confucian philosophy of reform. His disciple Liang Qichao interpreted the *Yijing* claim that "the *yi* has no substance" as showing "the lack of essence of things" to justify the legitimacy of reform.

Although appeal to the *Yijing* has been employed for many philosophical purposes, its main function is still to provide a fundamental ontology and cosmology from which other philosophical theses can take root. Hence, to defend or to revive the Chinese philosophical tradition one cannot forego the metaphysical vision of the *Yijing* that has fundamentally influenced the thought of twentieth-century Chinese philosophers. The most powerful appeal to the *Yijing* came from Xiong Shili, whose philosophy of ultimate reality is an exposition of the creative process philosophy of the *Yizhuan*. Xiong rediscovered the thesis of the nonseparation of substance and function and drew its implications for the creativity of life and reality. He also linked this cosmological insight to his understanding of the human mind and moral virtue.

This led to the founding of moral metaphysics as a unique and influential feature of contemporary Confucianism. Xiong's development of his New Consciousness-Only Theory (*xin weishi lun*) demonstrates the vitality of the *Yijing* onto-cosmological paradigm as a basis for paradigmatic transformation and as a model for onto-hermeneutical interpretation. On this basis, Mou Zongsan's criticism of Kant argued for the recognition of a transcendent, yet immanent reality that is experienced in our moral understanding of the human person and is beyond the reality revealed to us by science. Further, Tang Junyi used his dialectical understanding of the *yi* to transcend Hegel in describing his moral–metaphysical notion of the heart–mind.

Liang Shuming did not make much use of the philosophy of the *Yijing* because he was skeptical of the importance of metaphysical discourse and believed that the fundamental problems of metaphysics had already been solved by Indian and Buddhist philosophy. Liang's position was later held by Xu Fuguan who embraced a practical moral Confucianism that rejected metaphysical Confucianism. Aside from Liang and Xu, all the other Confucian and non-Confucian philosophers explicitly referred to the philosophy of *yi* or used insights based on *yi* to define change and understand the *dao*. Daoism like Confucianism was inspired by the *yi* paradigm of understanding reality. Both Jin Yuelin and Feng Youlan thus relied on the *yi* philosophy of ultimate reality or on a conception of original *yi* as reality (*benti*). Fang Dongmei used the notion of *yi* and method of comprehensive harmony and harmonization to guide the formation of his philosophy of culture and value.

The presence of the *yi* paradigm can be detected in the work of the Chinese Marxists Feng Qi and Zhang Dainian. Even in Li Zehou, it would be difficult to understand the creation of subjective values of the mind and their transformation into the culture of objective values without appeal to the creativity of the *yi* in the philosophy of Zhong Yong and Mencius.

The paradigm of the unity of substance and function poses many problems, including the fundamental problem of understanding their integration. This requires a primordial experience and insight into the reality of organic life and the process of productive and creative change. The very idea of the *dao* of change as ultimate reality may also conflict with the transcendent theology of the Western God. Can God be immanent and naturalistic like the *dao*? Can *dao* be coherently understood and explained in an explicit analytical discourse? These ultimate questions of metaphysics appear to be beyond settlement by common measure and require a deep understanding of our orientation towards reality.

The *second characteristic* is the focus of contemporary Chinese philosophy on the human person. By making the *yi* paradigm the basis of reality, there is no need to worry about a transcendent God. Throughout the whole history of contemporary Chinese philosophy, God has barely been mentioned. Contemporary discussions of the metaphysics of the *Yijing* have not given rise to issues concerning God, because the controversy between the Confucian *dao* and the Christian God had taken place much earlier during the Jesuit mission to China. The Ming Neo-Confucians did not recognize a metaphysical need for the transcendent God of Western theology and practiced religion instead through the performance of rituals toward parents and people with sincerity.

The passionate themes of social reform and societal survival among the philosophers discussed in this volume express their fundamental concern with the human world. This suggests that the development of Chinese Marxism was a reflection of this same person-centered consciousness.

Whether this human-centeredness of contemporary Chinese philosophy poses any questions for Western philosophy of religion depends on how one understands the other in the dialogue between Chinese and Western philosophers. In concerning themselves with self-cultivation and self-transformation, Chinese philosophers are paying attention to nature and ultimate reality and, hence, are nature-centered in ecology and *dao*-centered or universe-centered in cosmology. Their sense of human centrality does not imply an anthropocentrism, but rather a tendency toward a holism and organicism of the human person, nature, and heaven. It is a reflection and articulation of their perception of the cocreativity of nature or heaven and the human.

The *third characteristic* is the articulation and development of moral metaphysics. It is evident that questions of ethics and morality are not separable from considerations of the nature of man and reality. This inseparability is reflected in the traditional priority accorded to ethics in Chinese philosophy. The development of moral metaphysics by Xiong Shili, Tang Junyi, and Mou Zongsan is not at all accidental. It is implicit in both classical Confucianism and is closer to the surface of the Neo-Confucian philosophy of the Song–Ming period. If a Western meta-ethical philosopher asks why ethics must be linked to a cosmology and why morality must be directed toward the *dao*, the Confucian philosopher will answer according to an axiomatic intuition reflecting a fundamental conception of the human person that to become moral is to be and that to be is to become moral. If one does not have a sense of human reality, one cannot see that being and how one ought to be are related.

The claim that being and how one ought to be must be distinguished as independent notions is puzzling and unintelligible to the Confucian way of thinking and the Confucian way of living. In a parallel way, the thesis of moral metaphysics that discloses and discovers being in moral consciousness and moral action can puzzle Western philosophers, even if they endorse virtue ethics. Even in Aristotle, the good life and the rational metaphysical life are distinguished and ranked. The onto-ethical notion of morality and the moral metaphysical notion of reality are incommensurable with the Western tradition of positivism in science, transcendentalism in theology, and dualism in philosophy. None of these link and identify being and morality, but it is precisely in these terms that the *yi* paradigm of the unity of substance and function requires their linkage and identification. This remains an issue between Chinese philosophy and ethics, whether past or contemporary, and the mainstream of Western philosophy and ethics.

The *fourth characteristic* is nonseparation of method and truth. Traditional Chinese philosophy did not develop a strong methodological consciousness in approaching and contemplating the *dao* or ultimate reality, but contemporary Chinese philosophy has conspicuously sought a method to articulate and present the truth of the *dao*. Almost all contemporary Chinese philosophers have searched for a correct method for uncovering and reaching truth.

In Hu Shi, Jin Yuelin, and Feng Youlan, the preoccupation with method was a mark of modernity under the influence of Western philosophy. Every Western philosopher introduced to China in the contemporary period advanced a method. But for Chinese philosophers, a method as a way of thinking is not separable from truth itself. Within the paradigm of the unity of substance and function, a way of thinking reveals itself as an activity aiming towards truth. Hence, in contemporary Chinese philosophy, to speak of method does not raise Heidegger and Gadamer's question of whether seeking truth with a method might block the experience and vision of truth. Even the disclosure of truth without the application of method allows method to vanish to a point. We could justify holding open a place for method, that is to have a method of negating all methods. In this sense, the emphasis on method and the overcoming of method in contemporary Chinese philosophy represents a deep trait of the Chinese philosophical tradition. The phenomenon of transforming method into truth and truth into method marks a creative feature of Chinese philosophy that has been uncovered and realized by contemporary Chinese philosophy as an unintended consequence of the influence of modern Western philosophy and science.

However, one issue has baffled Western philosophers since the first International East–West Philosophers' Conference in the 1930s. In that conference, Chinese philosophers maintained the intuition of the reality of the *dao*, but Western philosophers could not make sense of this understanding and knowledge of reality. The issue remains unresolved. In Xiong Shili's account of the human mind realizing the truth of the ultimate, Mou Zongsan's account of the infinite mind, or Tang Junyi's account of the transcendent dialectics of moral reason or spirit, many modern Western philosophers see a reflection of Hegelian or German idealism, although they could also cite Plato's argument for the intuition of ideal forms and Spinoza's account of a pure intellectual intuition of God. Here we can identify gaps of understanding between the old and the new in Western philosophy as well as between contemporary Chinese and contemporary Western philosophy. Did Western philosophy change too much under the influence of science? Is the Chinese intuition of the reality of the *dao* a genuine insight? An approach to these questions requires an investigation of analysis and analytical understanding within the framework of a naturalized epistemology of the sort elaborated by Quine.

The *fifth characteristic* is the formal accommodation of science and scientific methodology in Chinese philosophy. Since the May Fourth Movement, all contemporary Chinese philosophers have accepted the validity of science and scientific methodology, but the integration of scientific knowledge within Chinese philosophy has not been totally resolved. The holistic paradigm of contemporary Chinese philosophy is dominated by concern with human values. The justification of science and the accommodation of its impact on humanity and the organization of human life remain major issues. Hu Shi's naïve pragmatist scientific methodology offered no solution. Mou Zongsan's theory of abnegation (*kanxian*) accentuated the conflict between morality and science. Feng Qi's transformation of theory to wisdom hid the question of how to transform scientific knowledge into life wisdom. Both Feng Youlan and Jin Yuelin suggested a transcendence beyond science, while Liang Shuming and Xiong Shili did not face the issue. The result of this history has been deep and continuing misunderstanding between philosophers and scientists in China, exemplified in the debate on Science and Metaphysics in the 1920s. Contemporary popular appreciation of science and technology requires reflection on the human ethical values underlying the practice of science and its technological application, but Chinese philosophy has not provided this reflection. These issues could initiate a revolutionary reassessment of Chinese philosophy at the level of cosmology and ontology with application to epistemology and ethics. In any case, analytic philosophy of science and language and the naturalized epistemology of science and philosophy can be a source of new challenges for contemporary Chinese philosophy. This also brings out problems of how to confront recent approaches to these issues in postpositivist Western philosophy of science and of how to introduce them in a globalized philosophical dialogue.

The *sixth and final characteristic* is the relative scarcity of detailed discussion of political philosophy in terms of fundamental concepts of power, common good, freedom, and equality in contrast to the extensive discussion of ethics in contemporary Chinese philosophy. This scarcity may result from features of political reality in China, Taiwan, and Hong Kong and the dominance of political ideology, but the issue of democracy has been recognized since the May Fourth Movement. It would be intriguing to discover how the major orientations of different contemporary Chinese philosophers would issue in ideals for modern society. Given their holistic and organic view of reality, Neo-Confucians must place democracy within the framework of Confucianism. No external value could be transplanted or imposed without being organically integrated within the whole system of values. Hence, Western moral or political values would require transvaluation and integration within Confucian values before they could be appreciated and adopted.

Similarly, questions of authority, rights, and justice must be transformed to fit into the holistic paradigm. This also poses a challenge to the West: whether one can assess another state by one's own political standards without violating one's respect for others. In what respect and to what degree can we justify having different standards for external and domestic affairs? In the global context, questions of political philosophy are thus raised for both contemporary Chinese and contemporary Western philosophy.

The Beginnings of a Great Dialogue and the
Promise of the Future

For most of the twentieth century, Chinese philosophy has encountered Western philosophy through translations and writings, with virtually no direct interaction between philosophers of the two traditions. Although Dewey and Russell lectured in China in the 1920s, their visits did not involve reciprocal understanding between two traditions. In spite of their eminence, the complexity of Western philosophical debate was not fully represented by these philosophers. It would be only a slight exaggeration to say that a great face-to-face dialogue between Chinese and Western philosophers has yet to begin and that a deeper understanding between philosophers from the two traditions has yet to emerge.

There are two important considerations for the dialogue between Chinese and Western philosophy. First, we have to see that each philosophical tradition functions like a scientific theory. A scientific theory is supported by a whole corpus of complex scientific observations that are theoretically structured and theory-laden. As Quine has argued, a scientific theory can maintain its coherence and claims of truth in view of any contravening experiences or new observations. It is the whole system of knowledge that faces external reality, and conceptual adjustments can be made in many ways to protect the essential theory against disconfirmation by an anomalous fact. Even if we wish to make changes to correspond to reality, we cannot alter the whole of the theory at once. There is no theory-free standpoint from which to have knowledge of reality as a whole. Hence, Quine's well-known metaphor of Neurath's ship that is mended bit-by-bit as we voyage over the open sea.

This account of theory and the metaphor of bit-by-bit repair apply to cultural and philosophical systems as well. We must recognize the holistic nature and historicity of our philosophical system with its cultural roots and moral vision practically integrated in a form of life. The whole system is empirically based and entrenched, with our values guiding its internal organization and its responses to reality. The metaphor of piecemeal alteration suggests that Chinese and Western philosophies can use their contact with each other to make adjustments bit-by-bit, but that overall repair once and for all is impossible. Put another way, understanding the position of the other must be from one's own standpoint, although the place that one stands can be altered. Altering one's position in view of the position of the other is not inevitable because one can hold one's theoretical ground.

As a holistic system, each tradition can protect its theoretical presuppositions against the pressure of new observations and experiences. Hence contemporary Chinese philosophy and modern Western philosophy can preserve their cores of belief and value on the basis of internal adjustment, but, like scientific theories, rigid and dogmatic protection can threaten their viability and survival. In choosing adjustments, philosophers should consider both the theoretical and practical consequences of their choices as well as questions of identity, effective history, and communicative rationality and aesthetic prefer- ence. In choosing what to preserve, we want our life to be advanced and uplifted. The greater the communication between traditions and the wider the range of issues that are confronted, the greater the motivation to make significant adjustments. Although not all adjustments will prove to be wise, continuous communication would certainly be of value. In addition to local adjustments, a more radical change of paradigm is theoretically possible without violating Quine's metaphor. Unlike a paradigm-shift in science, however, any major change in philosophical paradigm would need both inner determination and appro- priate circumstances to succeed.

Dialogue is important to articulate peripheral issues in one's system, but dialogue can also create the possibility of fusion of common views. As suggested by Gadamer, two philosophers or two cultures could reach out for each other if they really wished to do so. Holism need not result in a self-centered and enclosed relativism or subjectivism. There need exist no unresolvable incom- mensurability. In this regard, philosophies are more able to take on new ideas than normalized science. Cultures are compelled by the shared circumstances of human life and the world to find a common measure to assess problems and their solution. In light of holistic understanding, however, one would not expect a philosophy or culture suddenly to give up its historically entrenched vision of reality embodied in its ontology and cosmology.

The theology of God and the cosmology of the *dao* could philosophically coexist by covering the same ground and scope of human experiences of reality. Their claims need not become theoretically incompatible because they could avoid entailing contradictory consequences. Mediation of Chinese and Western philosophy through conceptual interpretation and reinterpretation could become a constant requirement of comparative and cross-cultural philosophiz- ing. Within each system, some theses will be strengthened and others will be weakened, with strategic local adjustments responding to these changes. Some of the old theses will receive new life rather than being abandoned. New syntheses drawn from resources of both systems could ground both scientific knowledge and moral tradition.

Two areas of new philosophical thinking will flourish as a consequence of conceiving Chinese philosophy as world philosophy. One is interpretation across ontologies and methodologies and the other is globalization of ethics and epistemology.

Even though entrenched ontologies need not be replaced, we will always be motivated by dialogue to understand another ontology from the standpoint of one's own. How to make sense of another ontology without reducing it to nonsense is an intellectual art of understanding and interpretation. I call under- standing another notion or another system of being or nonbeing through conceptual and textual dialogue *onto-hermeneutics*. The onto-cosmology of the *dao*, heaven, *li*, and *qi* can engage in close and continuous dialogue with the theological and metaphysical traditions of the West. Onto-hermeneutics will remain a vigorous philosophical activity. Given the complexities of both Chinese and Western traditions, it will take many forms and proceed on many levels.

On the practical side, we need ethics and morality to face issues of life and human survival. As the world becomes small and science and technology become more powerful, the need to pursue the right and the good becomes more pressing. We need a practical philosophy to judge persons, motives, actions, consequences, practices, and institutions, just as we need a theoretical philosophy to judge concepts, propositions, theories, and scientific systems. Apart from moral decision making, practical philosophy can guide us to enrich our life and realize our capacity for choice and well-being. We will make our choices on many levels with consequences for the whole world because we are living and interacting globally.

Our philosophy and ethics both need to recognize their global context. We need a global ethics for common measure of rights, obligations, and virtues and utilities. Determining how one's tradition can contribute to forming this common measure becomes a cultural and philosophical duty. The Chinese philosophical tradition has rich resources for a world ethics derived from its roots in the perspectives of Confucianism and Daoism. Contemporary Chinese philosophy has paid attention to the moral wisdom of Confucianism, but it has not dealt with issues arising from the history and variety of Western ethics. A theory of "integrative ethics" could contribute to the internal development of the moral capacity of the individual by encompassing deontology, teleology, utilitarianism, and rights ethics on the basis of Confucian and Neo-Confucian virtue ethics.

We can also follow Hans Küng's external quest to form a global ethical code with justification based on various world religions to build a community of communities that is bound by a moral contract of a common vision for world society. Both internal and external approaches are necessary. They can complement each other and combine to form sustainable moral practices. Contemporary Confucian philosophy has the potential to play an important role in both internal and external approaches to the formation of global ethics. Daoism can also play an active role in the ethical consideration of ecology and the environment. Daoist onto-cosmology is relevant not only for Daoist ethics but also for understanding the world environment as a whole.

Contemporary Chinese philosophy is strong on metaphysics and weak on science and democracy. Nevertheless, through its understanding of the human mind and human nature, it can help face scientific and technological developments, such as genetic biology and its biomedical applications. These fields raise serious problems of value and understanding through their capacity to affect the shape of human life and death and even to change aspects of human

nature. The potential contribution of Chinese philosophy in these areas has
not yet been realized because Chinese philosophers are generally unaware of
the relevance of their studies to coping with these issues. We can look to the
example of rights. It might be conjectured that Confucianism helped to inspire
the enlightenment philosophy of natural rights through John Locke, but it
has lost sight of this dimension of ethical and legal thought in its modern
development. Contemporary Chinese philosophy can be challenged to develop
a holist theory of rights, duties, justice, and benevolence in a modern reconstruction of Confucian theories of government. Chinese philosophy can also
contribute to the theory of organizations mediating between the individual and
the state. In my book *C li lun* (C theory) (1995) I have tried to integrate
concepts from schools of classical Chinese philosophy into contemporary
theories of management, corporate organization, and decision-making.

In dialogue among the metaphysical perspectives and visions that define our
identities, we can at least experiment with an open and pluralistic richness that
would allow us to act in a complex common world of ethical values derived
from many different systems of wisdom and faith.

There is great potential for bringing traditional Chinese culture to bear on
Western philosophy. An old civilization, once revived, can produce new and
vigorous growth. The revival of Europe after the Middle Ages led to a new
civilization through the creative ideas and innovative institutions of the
Renaissance, Reformation, and Enlightenment.

The current situation of contemporary Chinese philosophy bears some likeness to European thought after the Mediaeval period: it has escaped the constraints and stagnation of traditional dogmatism and is prepared to explore
an open arena of free thought. It is possible that we shall see the equivalent of
three hundred years of creative exploration in the Renaissance, Reformation,
and Enlightenment condensed into a brief span. This step can not only
renovate Chinese tradition and revive Chinese civilization, but its momentum
can also fuse with Western growth to create a cosmopolitan world of humane
and progressive thought and practices. Chinese philosophy can contribute to
a global ethics of virtue and right, a global metaphysics of the *dao* and God,
a global epistemology of naturalization and transcendence, a global political
philosophy of justice and harmony, a global aesthetics of genius and refinement, a global logic of communication and understanding, and a global science
of human well–being and liberation. The seeds of these hybrids already exist
in contemporary Chinese and Western philosophy, although the pattern of
their growth must await the stimulating environment of world philosophy.

Bibliography

Cheng, Chung-ying 1995: *C li lun* C理論 (C Theory), Taipei: Dongda Tu Shugangzhi

GLOSSARY

baihua: 白話 spoken language, vernacular

bailü yizhi: 百慮一致 final agreement among a hundred deliberations

bailü: 百慮 many disagreements

banruo: 般若 extrication, prajna

bei tiandi, fu wanwu: 被天地，覆萬物 covering Heaven and Earth, sheathing myriad things

ben: 本 root or substance

benneng: 本能 instinct

benti: 本體 root being, original being, reality, body, substance

ben xin: 本心 original mind

ben-zhi: 本質 essence, root identity

bi mo youxi: 筆墨游戲 play with brush and ink

bianfa: 變法 reform; literally: changing institutions and laws

buge: 不隔 nonseparated, unveiled

cang: 藏 hidden

Chan: 禪 meditation, Zen Buddhism

chao mingyan zhiyu: 超名言之域 the realm of transcending names and speech

chaoyue: 超越 transcendence

chaoyue de baohan: 超越的包含 transcending inclusivity

chaoyue ziwo: 超越自我 transcendental self

chen: 陳 way of addressing

cheng: 誠 sincerity

cheng: 成 to form, become

chuangzao lishi: 創造歷史 making history

Chunqiu: 春秋 the Spring and Autumn Annals

ci: 此 it

ci: 辭 lyric poetry

cunzai: 存在 existence

da cheng: 大乘 Mahayana

da xue: 大學 the Great Learning

dangran zhi li: 當然之理 response to an object or a situation in correct ways

dao: 道 the Way

daode shijian jing: 道德實踐境 horizon of practicing morality

dao-qi: 道器 way and instrument or truth and technology

daoti: 道體 body of the Way or embodiment of the Way

dao tong: 道統 orthodox tradition

daoxue: 道學 learning of the Way or knowledge of the *dao*

daquan: 大全 great whole

de: 德 virtue

dexing: 德性 virtue

di dao: 地道 the *dao* of earth

Dong Zhongshu 董仲舒

dunwu: 頓悟 sudden enlightenment

er chong zhengju fa: 二重證據法 methodology of double proof

fa hua: 法華（經）the Lotus Sutra

fa shen: 法身 Dharma-body or Dharma characters, constantly changing phenomena

fa xiang: 法相 Dharma-nature, absolute unchanging reality

faxian: 發現 discovery

fenshu: 分殊 various manifestations

fenshu biaoxian: 分殊表現 differentiation, particular manifestations

gaizhi: 改制 institutional reform

gan xing zhijue: 感性的直覺 sensible intuition

gang: 綱 standard

ganjue hushe jing: 感覺互攝境 horizon of mutual perception

ganqing: 感情 feelings

gantong: 感通 feeling penetration

ge: 隔 separated, veiled

gongfa: 公法 theorem, public law

gongfu: 功夫 acting with effort and talent or ability gained through training and practice

gongneng xuyun jing: 功能序運境 horizon of functioning in sequence

gu: 古 ancient or age-old

guanzhao lingxu jing: 觀照凌虛境 horizon of observation in suspension

guixiang yishen jing: 歸向一神境 horizon of returning to one God

Guo Xiang (253–312): 郭象 commentator on *Zhuangzi* in the Jin Period

guo: 國 nation or state

guocui pai: 國粹派 national essence

guojia: 國家 nation

guomin: 國民 citizens, people of a nation

guya: 古雅 the refined

han xin ru ku: 含辛茹苦 human existence is saturated with hardship and misery

hanyun: 涵蘊 stored up

hua san jie: 化三界 the universe at three levels, matter, universal law, and the highest standard of value

jiangjie: 疆界 boundary

jiao: 教 teaching

jidian: 積澱 sedimentary accumulation (of rationality)

jie zhuo jing: 接著進 further develop

jietuo shuo: 解脫說 theory of spiritual exoneration

jin: 今 present, modern

jing: 敬 reverence

jing: 景 scene, event

jing: 境 horizon, presented world or realm of objects (Sanskrit: *visaya*)

jingjie: 境界 intellectual–spiritual realm

jingjie shuo: 境界說 theory of the poetic state

jingshen: 精神 spirit

jingshen ziwo: 精神自我 spiritual self

jingwu: 境物 scenes and objects

jingxiang: 鏡像 scene or images in a scene

jingxue shidai: 經學時代 period of scriptural studies

jiran budong: 寂然不動 state of stillness

jiu xue: 舊學 classical learning

jun zi ren ge: 君子人格 the personality of the gentleman

kaichu: 開除 working out

kexue zhexue yu rensheng: 科學哲學與人生 philosophy of science and life

kongjiao: 孔教 the teachings of Confucius

kun: 坤 the soft, the receptive, earth

li: 禮 rituals, rules of propriety

li: 理 principle, law

li xing: 理性 reason

liang: 量 measurement, Sanskrit: *pramana*

liang zhi: 量智 intuitive knowledge, understanding measurement

lijiao: 禮教 the cultivation of character through rituals

lixiang: 理想 imagined principles

lixing: 理性 reason

lixing zhijue: 理性直覺 intellectual intuition

lixue: 理學 School of Principles, primarily referring to the Cheng–Zhu School

liyi fenshu: 理一分殊 the principle is one, its manifestations are many

lizhi: 理智 intellect

lunli ziwo: 倫理自我 ethical self

lun yu: 論語 The Analects

lunli benwei: 倫理本位 ethic-based (society)

meiyu shuo: 美育説 theory of aesthetic education

min: 民 people

ming: 命 fate

ming: 名 name

ming cheng: 名稱 name and way of addressing

ming mingde: 明明德 manifestation of clear character

mingyan zhiyu: 名言之域 the nameable and speakable

nao: 鬧 stir

neisheng waiwang: 內聖外王 sageliness within and kingliness without

neng suo: 能所 subject and object (of knowledge)

ning dao er chengde: 凝道而成德 to focus on the *dao* to form virtue

ningdao er chengde: 凝道而成德 to exemplify *dao* to cultivate virtue

pi: 辟 opening

puti dao: 菩提道 the *dao* of Boddi

qi: 氣 vital energy, material force

qian: 乾 the creative, heaven

qiancun: 潛存 subsistence

qing: 情 feeling, affection

qinggan: 情感 feelings

Qiushui: 秋水 "Autumn Water," a chapter in *Zhuangzi*

Qiwu: 齊物 "Equality of (or Equalizing) Things," a chapter in *Zhuangzi*

qixue: 器學 knowledge of matters, practical know-how

qu: 曲 lyric song as composed in the Yuan Dynasty

quan: 權 rights or powers

qun ji yi ti: 群己一體 individuals are inseparable from their community

ren: 人 human being, person

ren: 仁 humanity, benevolence

ren dao: 人道 the *dao* of man

ren: 認 to recognize

ren-ai: 仁愛 benevolence-love

ren ren you zizhu zhi quan: 人人有自主之權 all human beings have the right to self-mastery or autonomy

ren sheng ku duan: 人生苦短 the life of men is troubled and short

ren ti: 仁體 benevolent nature, entity, substance

ren wei wu yi: 人為物役 "the situation of men enslaved by external things" (*Zhuangzi*)

risun: 日損 daily defection

rixin: 日新 daily renovation

sangang: 三綱 the Three Bonds

sanji: 三祭 the Three Worships (the worship of parents, ancestors and sages)

shang shu: 尚書 the Book of History

shao si gua yu: 少思寡欲 "reducing selfishness and desires" (*Laozi*)

shen: 神 divine

shen du: 慎獨 behaving oneself even when one is alone

sheng mie men: 生滅門 gate of life and death circulation

shengsheng zhi wei yi: 生生之謂易 "Creative creativity is called change" (in *Xici*)

Shengzhi: 聖智 the wisdom of a sage (compare Sanskrit: *prajna*; Greek: *logos*)

shensi: 神似 likeness in spirit

shenyun: 神韻 spirit and tone

shi: 事 events

shi: 是 is

shiji: 實際 dimension of actuality

shijiao: 詩教 the cultivation of character through poetic arts

shijing: 詩境 the poetic realm

shu: 舒 engaging the heart in feeling easiness and uneasiness

shu: 恕 reciprocity

shu er buzuo: 述而不作 commenting without inventing

siduan: 四端 the Four Beginnings (of human goodness)

sifa: 私法 private law

su: 俗 vulgar, popular

tai he: 太和 great harmony

taiji: 太極 the Great Ultimate

ti: 體 body, substance or essential reality

ti-yong: 體用 substance and function or essence and appearance

tian: 天 heaven

tian dao: 天道 the *dao* of Heaven

tian ming: 天命 decree of Heaven

Tiantai Zong 天臺宗

tiancai: 天才 genius

tiande liuxing jing: 天德流行境 horizon of flowing heavenly virtue

tiandi jingjie: 天地境界 the realm of heaven and earth

tianxia: 天下 under heaven, the whole, world, empire

tianxing: 天性 one's nature

tianzi: 天子 emperor

tiren: 體認 bodily or intimate recognition

tiyan: 體驗 bodily or intimate experiencing

tizhi: 體知 bodily knowing

wanguo gongfa: 萬國公法 universal laws of all nations

wanwu sanshu jing: 萬物散殊境 horizon of manifold separate individuals

wei er bu zheng: 為而不爭 "acting instead of competing for gains" (*Laozi*)

weiji zhi xue: 為己之學 learning for the self

wenhua: 文化 culture

wofa erkong jing: 我法二空境 horizon of the dual-emptiness of self and dharma

wu ming: 無明 ignorance

wu nian: 無念 being free of thought

wu wo zhi jing: 無我之境 the state of self-detachment

wu zhi you: 無之有 being of non-being

wulun: 五倫 the five basic Confucian human relationships

xi: 翕 closing

xi xue: 西學 Western culture, Western learning

xianliang jing: 相量境 empirical horizon

xianxing yi hongdao: 顯行以宏道 to practice one's virtue so to expand *dao*

xiao cheng: 小乘 Hinayana

xiao qian: 消遣 unnecessary pastimes

xiao yao you: 逍遙游 "free and easy wandering" (*Zhuangzi*)

xiejing: 寫境 descriptive state

xin er shang xue: 形而上學 metaphysics

xin er xia xue: 形而下學 the learning of what is within *xing*

xin ji li: 心即理 mind is principles

xin lixue: 新理學 New Principle

xin wai wu wu: 心外無物 there is no matter outside of mind

xin xinxue: 新理學 the New School of Mind

xin xue: 新學 modern learning

xin: 心 heart–mind

xing: 性 human nature, essence

xing ji li: 性即理 nature or essence of a thing

xing li: 性理 natural reason

xing zhi: 性智 intuitive understanding by nature

xingqing: 性情 nature and feeling

xingqu: 興趣 inspiration and interest

xingsi: 形似 resemblance in form

xingxiang: 形象 image

Xinxue: 心學 School of Mind, primarily referring to the Lu–Wang School

xuan: 玄 mystery

xue wu zhong xi: 學無中西 learning above any prejudiced preference or distinction between China and the West

xue: 學 learning

xuwu: 虛無 empty being

ya: 雅 elegant, cultivated

yan chu chao ran: 燕處超然 "to live in detachment" (*Laozi*)

yan: 言 words

yang shi: 養士 fostered gentry

yang: 陽 bright, positive principle or force

yi ti chong shi ti: 以體充是體 enriching [Chinese] substance with [Western] substance

yi: 義 meanings

yi: 宜 appropriate, fittingness

yi: 義 righteousness

yi: 易 change

yiban siren: 一般私人 private persons in general

Yijing: 易經 the Book of Changes

yijing: 意境 the mood, state or significance of an artwork

yilei chenghua jing: 依類成化境 horizon of transformation according to classes

yin: 陰 negative principle or force

yinyuan: 姻緣 causal relatedness (Sanskrit: *paccaya*)

yishi: 意識 consciousness

yizhi: 一致 consensus

yong heng liang yi: 永恆兩一 everything is in constant change, and any contradiction has its unification

yong: 用 application, function or appearance

you: 有 to have

you: 游 wandering

youhuan yishi: 憂患意識 concerned consciousness, sense of misgiving or anxiety

you shi: 游士 wandering gentry

you wo zhi jing: 有我之境 the state of self-involvement

you yu yi: 游于藝 take excursions in art; playing with art

youde: 有德 possessing virtues

youmei: 優美 the beautiful

youxi shuo: 游戲說 theory of art as play

yu: 欲 desire

yu jiao yu le: 寓教于樂 hidden education in an appealing form

yu wu wei chun: 與物為春 "be spring with all things" (*Zhuangzi*)

yuan jiao: 圓教 perfect teaching

yuyan: 寓言 metaphorical way to talk about *dao* in *Zhuangzi zaojing*: 造境 creative state

zaoyi: 造詣 academic or artistic attainment

zhao zhe jiang: 照著講 speaking according to

zhe: 這 this

zhen ganqing: 真感情 true emotions and feelings

zhen jingwu: 真境物 true scenes and objects

zhen ru men: 真如門 gate of thusness and suchness

zhen zhi san biao: 真之三表 there are three criteria for true knowledge: consistency, correspondence to sense experience, and the prediction of results

zheng: 政 politics

zheng tong: 正統 orthodox

zheng xue: 政學 political learning, political theory

zhenji: 真際 dimension of truth-and-reality

zhi: 執 obsession

zhi de zhi jue: 智的直覺 intellectual intuition

zhi: 智 intellect, wisdom

zhidao youde: 知道有德 understanding *dao* and possessing virtue

zhijue: 直覺 intuition

zhiyan: 卮言 overflowing words or with unlimited applications (*Zhuangzi*)

zhiye fentu: 職業分途 profession-differentiated (society)

zhong xue: 中學 Chinese learning

Zhong Yong: 中庸 the Doctrine of the Mean

zhong: 中 central-minded, fitting, fair-minded

Zhongguo Dacheng Fojiao: 中國大乘佛教 Chinese Mahayana Buddhism

zhongxue weiti, xixue weiyong: 中學為體，西學為用 Chinese culture as substance, Western culture as function

zhongyan: 重言 quotes from ancient people; one way to talk about the *dao* (*Zhuangzi*)

Zhou li: 周禮 Zhou etiquette

Zhou wen: 周文 Zhou rites

zhu quan: 主權 sovereignty

zhuangmei: 壯美 the sublime

zhuangshi chengzhi: 轉識成智 transforming knowledge into wisdom

Zhuangzi: 莊子

zhui tiyan: 追體驗 tracing-back and bodily experiencing

zhumin: 諸民 all peoples

zhutixing: 主體性 subjectivity

zi wo kan xian: 自我坎陷 self-abnegation, self-negation

zi xing qing jing xin: 自性清淨心 empty mind of self-nature

zifa: 自發 spontaneity

zijue: 自覺 self-consciousness

ziran: 自然 naturalness

ziwo: 自我 individual self

zixue shidai: 子學時代 period of philosophers

ziyou: 自由 freedom

ziyuan: 自願 voluntary

zizhu zhi quan: 自主之權 the right of self-determination or self-mastery, autonomy

INDEX

Note: Pinyin romanization is the main form used for names. Where there are Wade-Giles variants the pinyin form is given in brackets or a cross-reference is given to the main entry.

a priori principles, He Lin   191, 192,
      193, 194–5, 206
abnegation, theory of   393
actuality
   Feng Youlan   166–7, 170, 179, 180
   Jin Yuelin   116, 117
aesthetic criticism   37–40, 43–54
aesthetic education   40, 43, 50
aesthetic spirit   298–301
aesthetics
   Feng Qi   229
   Li Zehou   45, 248, 251, 252, 253–4,
      256, 395
agreement–disagreement dialectic   223–5
alienation   250
ameliorism, antifoundational   231
analogical argument   76, 78
analytic method
   dialectic with synthetic   220–1
   Zhang Dainian   235–6, 243
analytic philosophy   102
analytical logic   166, 169, 170, 174,
      175–6, 177–8, 180
analytical reconstruction, of Chinese
      philosophy   357, 374
anthropocentricity   121–2
anthropological ontology   246–8,
      249–50, 252, 254–6
antifoundational ameliorism   231
anxiety   282–7

application   193, 197–200, 201–2
   onto-hermeneutics   386, 394–5
argumentation   358
Aristotle
   categories   73
   and Feng Youlan   180
   logic   74–5
   practical reason   155
   virtue ethics   142–3, 144
art
   Fang Dongmei   267, 276
   Feng Qi's view   217
   Li Zehou   248, 253, 256
   as play   39–40, 43, 50
   Tang Junyi   320
   Wang Guowei   39–40, 43–54
   Xu Fuguan   299–301
artist as genius   40, 43, 51
atomicity   59, 60, 63

beautiful, the
   and poetic state   47, 50
   and the refined   51–3
beauty
   Fang Dongmei   393
   Feng Qi   229
   Li Zehou   248, 251, 252, 253,
      395
Beijing Massacre   4
benevolence   *see ren*

Bergson, Henri   354
   influence on Fang Dongmei   265–6
   Liang Shuming on intellect   150
   Xiong's theory of change   137–8
   Zhang Dongsun translates   371, 374
biological principles   64
bodily movement   360
bodily recognition   287–94
Book of Change(s)   see Yijing
Buddhism
   empty mind   332
   Fang Dongmei   269–70, 273, 391
   Feng Youlan   174, 175, 183
   Fu Weixun   359
   intellectual intuition   216–17
   knowledge and wisdom   214, 215
   Li Zehou   252, 253–4, 256
   Mou Zongsan   328, 329, 330, 332,
      335–6, 337–8, 342–3
   perfect teaching   337–8, 339
   suffering   284
   Tang Junyi   310–11, 314–15
   Wang Guowei   50
   Xiong Shili   127–8, 130–4, 135, 141–2
   Xu Fuguan   286, 293
   Zhang Dongsun   57, 63, 64–5, 67

Cai, Yuanpei   5, 83
calculative understanding   139–40, 141
categorical imperative, intellectual intuition
      333
categories (postulates)   60–1, 73
Catholic Church   352, 353
Chan, Wing-tsit   354, 355–6
change
   contemporary Chinese philosophy
      396–7
   Fang Dongmei   275, 276
   Jin Yuelin   110, 111–12
   Xiong Shili   135–8
Chen, Duxiu   5, 9, 374, 392
   New Culture Movement   83, 84, 94
Chen, Lai   351–2
Cheng, Chung-ying   356–7
   democracy   297–8
Cheng, Hao   394
Cheng, Yi   272
Cheng-Zhu School of Principles   190,
      193–6

Chiang Kai-shek (Jiang Jieshi)   4
China, development of Chinese
      philosophy in   350–2
Ching, Julia (Qin Jiayi)   360–1
Christianity
   free will   227
   He Lin   202, 203, 205
   Liang Qichao's concept   25
   original sin   284
   Qin Jiayi   360
   Tang Junyi   310–11, 314–15
citizenship   24, 31
civic nationalism   19–24, 29–30
civil associations   31
civil law   29
civil war   3–4
civilization   118
class
   Liang Shuming   160–1
   Tang Junyi   320
classical Chinese philosophy   239–42
closing tendency   135–6, 137
cognition
   Li Zehou   255
   Tang Junyi   308, 309
   Zhang Dongsun   58–62, 64, 67
cognitive mind   328, 335
communication, disagreement–agreement
      dialectic   223–5
communism
   and the individual   230
   Li Zehou   256
Communists, history   3–4, 9, 94
communities
   Feng Qi   230–1
   Liang Qichao   31
   Xu Fuguan   300–1
concepts, hierarchy of   61–2
concrete universality   342
concreteness of reality   109, 110, 111,
      114, 115
Confucianism
   Antonio Cua   358
   Cheng's work on   356, 357
   Du Weiming   361
   and the individual   230
   intuition   152–3, 154, 155
   Li Zehou   252, 253–4, 255–6
   Liu Shuxian   359

metaphysics 330–1
perfect teaching 338–9
Qin Jiayi 360, 361
role in contemporary Chinese
   philosophy 374, 375, 377, 383–5,
   396–7
   onto-hermeneutic analysis 386–8,
     392, 393, 394
   outstanding characteristics 397, 398,
     400
and Western ideas 4–5
  Hu Shi 89–90, 91–3
  Kang Youwei 26
  Liang Qichao 20, 21, 22, 30–1
  Marxism 382–3
  Xiong Shili 127
  Zhang Dongsun 57, 70, 77–8
  Wing-tsit Chan 355
  see also Neo-Confucianism; New
    Neo-Confucianism
congruence principle 109, 111, 115
consistency principle 109–10
constitutionalism 29–30
contemporary Chinese philosophy
   365–6
  dialogue with Western 373–4,
    401–4
  method 378–9, 389–90
  onto-hermeneutics 385–95, 403
  outstanding characteristics 395–400
  roots of 366–9, 379–85
  transformation 375–83
  Western paradigms 366–7, 369
    challenges of 371–5
    logical paradigm 371–2
    Yan Fu's role 369–71
Contemporary Neo-Confucianism *see* New
    Neo-Confucianism
contingency
  Li Zehou 252, 256
  principle of 110–11, 115
continuity 59, 60, 63
correlative logic 74–7, 78
cosmology
  Cheng's work on 356
  Fang Dongmei 274–6
  Feng Youlan 177–8
  fusion of Chinese–Western philosophy
    402

Hu Shi's naturalistic conception 86–7,
  99
  Xiong Shili 138, 143–4
  Zhang Dongsun's panstructuralism 58,
    63–8, 70–1, 77
creative advance 275
creative hermeneutics 359
creative state, poetry 46
creative synthesis 236, 241–3
creativity
  onto-hermeneutics 386, 391–4
  Zhang Dongsun 59, 60, 63
critical attitude 84–5, 86, 90
critical subject 360–1
Cua, Antonio 357–8
cultural epistemology 57, 58, 68–78
cultural monism 19–21
cultural policy, history of 4
Cultural Revolution 4, 26
cultural studies 39
culture(s)
  Chinese–Western synthesis 404
    Zhang Dainian 242–3
  Eastern–Western
    Fang Dongmei 265, 391
    Liang Shuming 149–62
    Lik-kuen Tang 360
    Liu Shuxian 359
    Mou Zongsan 340–2
    Tang Junyi 318, 320–1
    and transformation in China 375–8
    Xu Fuguan 281–7, 297, 300–1
  Fang Dongmei 267, 276
  He Lin 189, 194, 196–202
  New Culture Movement 83
  onto-hermeneutic analysis 391, 392,
    394
  psychological *noumenon* 251
  Tang Junyi 318–23
  universal 162, 199–200, 201–2
  Wang Guowei's intercultural method
    40–4
  Xu Fuguan 281–2
  Zhang Dongsun
    cosmology 66–7, 70–1, 77
    knowledge 68–78
    logic 58, 60–1, 73, 74–7, 78
    scientific knowledge 63
cunning of reason 195–6

daily decrease   130–2, 134
daily renovation   131–2, 134, 143
dao
  Antonio Cua   358
  Chen Lai   352
  Cheng's work on   357
  contemporary Chinese philosophy   397,
    398–9
  Fang Dongmei   268, 269, 270, 275,
    276
  Feng Qi
    dialectical logic   219–25, 231
    human freedom   225–31
    wisdom   213–19, 224–5
  Feng Youlan   176
  fusion of Chinese–Western philosophy
    402
  He Lin   197–9
  Jin Yuelin's theory   102–3, 106–7
    form   104
    man and nature   115–22
    matter   104, 106, 112, 115
    onto-hermeneutic analysis   387–8
    possibility   105, 110–11
    possible worlds   109
    reality and process   109–15, 116,
      117, 118, 119–20
    universal sympathy   108, 121
  Mou Zongsan   331–2, 338, 342–3
  onto-hermeneutic analysis   387–8, 389,
    390, 391, 392, 394, 395
  perfect teaching   338
  root–perfection doctrine   238
  unity between human person and   369
  Wing-tsit Chan   356
  Xiong Shili   127–9, 131, 139
  Xu Fuguan   299, 300
  Zhang Dongsun   72
Daoism
  Antonio Cua   358
  Cheng's work on   356, 357
  in contemporary Chinese philosophy
    374, 375
  Fang Dongmei   269–70, 273, 277
  Feng Youlan   168, 174, 176, 183
  intellectual intuition   216–17
  Li Zehou   252, 253–4, 255–6
  metaphysics   331–2
  Mou Zongsan   328, 330, 331–2, 338

  perfect teaching   338, 339
  substance   72
  Xu Fuguan   293, 300–1
Dasein   249
Decree of Heaven   285, 287, 289, 291, 293
democracy
  contemporary Chinese philosophy   400
  Hu Shi   93, 96–8
  Liang Qichao   22–3, 30
  Mou Zongsan   328
  Tang Junyi   321, 322–3
  Xu Fuguan   294–8
descriptive state, poetry   46
desires
  He Lin   195–6
  Jin Yuelin   119, 120–1
  Mou Zongsan   342–4
  Zhang Dongsun   67, 68, 69
destiny   256, 395
Dewey, John   353, 354
  and Hu Shi   82, 83, 87, 88–9, 374,
    387
dialectical materialism   9–11
  Feng Qi   213–31
  Feng Youlan   181
  He Lin   207, 208
  Li Zehou   246–57
  onto-hermeneutic analysis   389
  Zhang Dainian   235–44
disagreement–agreement dialectic   223–5
Du Weiming (Wei-ming Tu)   361
  family–state relation   31
  on Xu Fuguan   282, 290
duty   204, 205, 206

economic activity   319
economic needs   159, 161–2
economy, principle of   110–11, 115
education, for reform   95–6
egocentricity   121–2
egoism
  Hu Shi   96–7
  Zhang Dongsun   67–8
embodiment   287–94, 299, 300
emotion–reason synthesis
  Fang Dongmei   264, 265–8
  Tang Junyi   308
emotional *noumenon*   255, 256
empty mind   332

end–means
    Chinese philosophical tradition   367–8
    Jin Yuelin   116–18, 120–1
    transformation of Chinese philosophy
        376
enlightenment
    Feng Qi   215–16, 390
    Hu Shi   83, 96, 98–9
    Zhang Dongsun   66, 67–8
enslavement   121–2
epistemology
    Antonio Cua   358
    cultural   57, 58, 68–78
    Jin Yuelin   103, 107
    onto-hermeneutic analysis   388
    pluralist   57–68, 388
    Xu Fuguan   292
    Zhang Dainian   237, 241
    Zhang Dongsun   57–78, 388
equality   27–8
equilibrium   276
essence (*xing*)   *see* human nature (essence,
        xing)
ethic-based society   160, 161
ethical liberty   26–8
ethical relationships   30–1
ethical (genuine) self   306–7, 308,
        319–20
ethical value, art   39, 40
ethics
    Antonio Cua   357–8
    Cheng's work on   356
    contemporary Chinese philosophy   398
    fusion of Chinese–Western philosophy
        403, 404
    He Lin's concept of mind   191–2
    Li Zehou   251, 253
    onto-hermeneutic analysis   386–7, 393
    Tang Junyi   305–18, 320, 323–4
    transformation of Chinese philosophy
        376–7
    Xiong's metaphysics of virtue   131–2,
        138, 142–4
    Yan Fu   370
Euclidean space   113
evolution
    Hu Shi's literary revolution   84
    Yan Fu   370
    Zhang Dongsun's ideas   65

existence   331–2, 334
experimentalism   82, 83, 87–9, 90–1,
        94–5, 98–9, 374
extensional truth   341, 342
extensive connection   276
external world
    Li Zehou   256
    Zhang Dainian   236
    Zhang Dongsun   58–60, 61–3

family
    abolition of, Kang Youwei   25, 26
    Feng Youlan   171
    Liang Qichao   26, 30–1
    Liang Shuming   160
Fang, Dongmei   11–12, 263–4, 354
    Chinese classic philosophy   269–71
    cosmology   274–6
    general philosophy   264–8
    moral philosophy   276–7
    onto-hermeneutic analysis   391, 393
    political philosophy   277–9
    Song–Ming Neo-Confucianism   271–3
Fang, Thomé   *see* Fang, Dongmei
fate, intercultural method   41, 42
feeling-penetration   308, 316
Feng, Qi   10, 213, 381
    antifoundational ameliorism   231
    contemporary Chinese philosophy   390,
        395, 397, 400
    dialectical logic, theory–method
        219–20, 231
        analytic–synthetic   220–1
        disagreement–agreement   223–5
        historical   222–3
        knowledge–practice   221–2
    freedom–virtue transform   225–6, 395
        individual self   229–31
        naturalness   228–9
        self-consciousness   226–7, 228, 229
        voluntariness   227–8, 229
    onto-hermeneutic analysis   390, 395
    wisdom   213–14
        disagreement–agreement dialectic
            223–4
        intellectual intuition   215–18, 390
        language of   218–19
        transforming knowledge into
            214–15

Feng, Youlan 8–9, 165, 353
    contemporary Chinese philosophy 397,
        399, 400
        onto-hermeneutic analysis 387, 388,
            389, 394
    history of Chinese philosophy 165,
        174–9, 184, 239
    New Principle Learning 165, 170–6,
        273, 388
        and history of Chinese philosophy
            174–9, 184
        materialism 178, 179–83
        principles 166–70
    significance of 183–4
    Xu Fuguan's criticism of 291
field-being 360
Five Relations doctrine 202–4, 205
form
    Aristotle 142
    Jin Yuelin 104, 105–6
Foucault, Michel 250, 255
"Fourth Outline of Human Subjectivity"
    254–6
free will
    Feng Qi 227
    He Lin 204, 205
    Li Zehou 251
    Mou Zongsan 333
freedom *see* liberty
Fu, Weixun (Charles Fu) 358–9
function
    Chinese philosophical tradition 367–8
    contemporary Chinese philosophy 397,
        398
    moral-metaphysical Confucians 380
    onto-hermeneutic analysis 392
    principles of unitary paradigm of
        368–9
    reason and intellect 158, 162
    transformation of Chinese philosophy
        376–7
    Xiong Shili 132–4, 135
function philosophy 71
Fung Yu-lan *see* Feng, Youlan

genius
    Liang Shuming 159
    Wang Guowei 40, 43, 51, 52
global philosophy 403, 404

God
    contemporary Chinese philosophy 397
    fusion of Chinese–Western philosophy
        402
    intellectual intuition 332–4
    Tang Junyi 309–12, 315, 320
gonafu (effort-making), onto-hermeneutic
    analysis 394
gradualism 93, 94–8
gratitude 307–8
Guo, Moruo 10
Guomindang, history 3
guya (the refined) 40, 43–4, 51–4

Habermas, Jürgen 224
habituated mind 139, 140
happiness, perfect teaching 337–8, 339
harmony
    Fang Dongmei 265, 266, 276, 391,
        393
    Liang Shuming 152
He, Lin 8, 9, 188–90, 380
    application 193, 197–200, 201–2
    idealism 188, 189–90, 206, 207–8
        Cheng-Zhu and Lu-Wang Schools
            190–6
        philosophy of culture 189, 194,
            196–200
    materialism 190, 207–8
    onto-hermeneutic analysis 390
    reconstruction of Confucianism 200–6
    substance 193, 197–200, 201–2
heart–mind
    Feng Youlan 173, 177, 179
    Tang Junyi 308–9, 311–12, 315–18
    Xu Fuguan 284–7, 289, 295–6,
        299–300, 301
Hegel, G. W. F.
    on Chinese philosophy 353
    Feng Qi's dialectical logic 220
    influence on Fang Dongmei 265–6
    influence on Feng Youlan 180–1
    influence on He Lin 188, 189–90,
        193, 195–6
    Li Zehou's views 251, 252
    Mou Zongsan's concrete universality 342
Heidegger, Martin 249, 254, 255, 256,
    350
heritage, national 85, 89–93, 99

historicism   250, 252, 254
history
    Antonio Cua   358
    of Chinese philosophy
        Fang Dongmei   266–7
        Feng Youlan   165, 174–9, 184, 239
        Hu Shi's method   82, 83, 89–93, 99
        Xu Fuguan   288
        Zhang Dainian   235, 239–42
    cunning of reason   195–6
    historical–logical method dialectic
        222–3
    Liang Qichao's ideas   19–23
    Wang Guowei's method of study   43
holism
    Chinese philosophical tradition   367, 368
    Chinese–Western dialogue   401–2
    Jin Wulun   351
Hong, Qian   6
horizon, onto-hermeneutics   386, 387–8
horizons   308–10
Hu, Shi   6, 7, 82–3, 353, 374
    contemporary Chinese philosophy   399,
        400
        onto-hermeneutic analysis   387, 389,
            391, 392
    as enlightenment philosopher   83, 96,
        98–9
    experimentalism   82, 83, 87–9, 90–1,
        94–5, 98–9, 374
    history of Chinese philosophy   82, 83,
        89–93, 99
    liberalism   93–8
    literary revolution   82, 83, 84–5
    naturalistic conception of universe
        86–7, 99
    political philosophy   93–8
    systematizing the national heritage   85,
        89–93, 99
human being, as *Dasein*   249
human beings
    Aristotle's metaphysics   142–3
    Feng Youlan   172–4
    intellectual intuition   333–4
    Jin Yuelin   108, 118–22
    Li Zehou   254–6
    Liang Shuming   157
    Lik-kuen Tang   360
human development   247–8, 249, 251–2

human freedom   225–31
human life
    Fang Dongmei   264, 269, 270, 274–6,
        277, 278
    Li Zehou   253, 254–6
    Liang Shuming   147–8, 149–50, 151,
        152–3, 156, 160–1
    Xiong Shili   130–1, 134, 138–42,
        143–4
    Zhang Dainian   236–9
    Zhang Dongsun   66–8, 70–1
human mind   138–42
human nature (essence, *xing*)
    Antonio Cua   358
    Che Lin   352
    Fang Dongmei   266, 267, 270
    fusion of Chinese–Western philosophy
        403–4
    He Lin   194–5, 196
    Li Zehou   251, 256
    onto-hermeneutic analysis   391, 393–4
    Tang Junyi   307, 315
    Wang Guowei   41–2
    Xu Fuguan   284–9, 291–2, 295–6
human person   397–8
    paradigm of unity of   368–9
human relationships
    Fang Dongmei   274–5
    He Lin   202–3, 206
    Kang Youwei   26
    Li Zehou   252, 255
    Liang Qichao   26–7, 28–31
    Liang Shuming   149–50, 151, 152–3,
        156, 160–1
    Mencius   288
    Tang Junyi   312–13, 322–3
    Wang Guowei   42
    Xu Fuguan   295–6
    Zhang Dongsun   76
human rights
    Liang Qichao   24, 28
    new Confucianism   28
    Xu Fuguan   297–8
human subjectivity
    Li Zehou   251, 252, 254–6, 395
    Zhang Dongsun   63
humanism
    Jin Wulun   351
    Li Zehou   250

humanity, Xiong Shili 138–42
humanization of nature 255
Hume, David 102
Hundred Day Reform 4, 17–18
Husserl, Edmund 350

Ibsenism 96
idealism
   He Lin 188, 189–200, 206, 207–8
   Hu Shi 93, 94
   Li Zehou 251
   Tang Junyi 313–14, 315
   Wang Guowei 39, 43
   Xiong Shili 136
   Zhang Dainian 235–6, 238–9
identity, Jin Yuelin 111–12
identity logic 74, 75, 77
imagined principles (lixiang) 19–20
implicative relations 60, 61
Indian culture 150, 151, 153, 265,
   391
Indian philosophy
   Mou Zongsan 340–1
   Zhang Dainian 240
individual objects and events 115, 121
individual self, principle of 229–30
individual subjectivity 250, 251, 252,
   254–6
individual–community 300–1
individualism
   Hu Shi 83, 96–7
   Liang Shuming 160
individuality
   Fang Dongmei 269
   Li Zehou 249
indulgence 307, 308
industrialization 171, 178
inference 76, 78
infinite being 312, 315
infinite mind
   Mou Zongsan 332, 333, 334–6,
   339
   Tang Junyi 314, 315
instinct 157
instrumental noumenon 246, 247, 250
intellect 148, 150–2, 153, 157–8, 159
intellectual intuition
   Feng Qi 215–18, 390
   Mou Zongsan 332–6

intellectual policy, history of 4, 17–18
intellectual–spiritual realms 172–4, 181
intellectuality
   Jin Yuelin 103
   Zhang Dongsun 66–8
intellectuals, political influence 296
intelligence
   Fang Dongmei 264
   Liang Qichao 23–4
intensional truth 341–2
intercultural transformation 39, 40–4
internal order 60
International Society for Chinese
   Philosophy 355, 362
intuition
   contemporary Chinese philosophy
   399
   Feng Qi 215–18, 390
   Liang Shuming 150–3, 154, 155
   Mou Zongsan 332–6
   Xiong Shili 141
intuitive cognition 60
intuitive knowledge 154–5
isms 94–5

Jesuits 352, 353, 369
Jiang Jieshi (Chiang Kai-shek) 4
Jin, Wulun 351
Jin, Yuelin 6, 7, 102–3, 353
   contemporary Chinese philosophy 397,
   399, 400
   onto-hermeneutic analysis 387, 389,
   392
   dao 102–3, 106–7
   enslavement 121–2
   and Feng Youlan's philosophy 179
   form 104, 105–6
   man and nature 115–22
   matter 103–4, 105–6, 112, 115
   mind 116, 117–20
   possibility 104, 105–7, 110–11
   possible worlds 109
   purpose 116, 117–18, 119–20
   reality and process 109–15, 116, 117,
   118, 119–20
   time and space 110, 111, 112–16,
   118
   universal sympathy 109, 121
jingjie (poetic state) 40, 44–51, 53–4

Kang, Youwei 4–5, 354
  and Liang Qichao's ideas 17, 21, 22,
    25–6
  onto-hermeneutic analysis 391
Kant, Immanuel
  on Chinese philosophy 353
  Feng Qi's intellectual intuition
    216
  influence on He Lin 191, 192–3, 204,
    206
  Li Zehou's subjectivity 247, 248, 249,
    250, 254, 257
  Mou Zongsan 328, 332–4, 336, 339,
    397
  phenomenon and *noumenon* 241,
    332–5
  practical reason 155
  summum bonum 336, 339
  Tang Junyi's infinite being 312
  Wang Guowei's ideas 37, 41, 42, 50,
    371
  Xiong's original reality 140
  Ye's study of 350
  Zhang Dongsun's epistemology 57–8,
    60, 62
Ke, Xiongwen (Antonio Cua) 357–8
kingliness
  Feng Youlan 169, 182–3
  Li Zehou 256
knowledge
  Fang Dongmei 264
  Feng Qi
    analytic–synthetic dialectic 220–1
    disagreement–agreement dialectic
      224–5
    practice dialectic 221–2
    theory of wisdom 213–15
  Foucault's archaeology of 250
  He Lin 206
  Jin Yuelin 117–18, 119–21
  Li Zehou 250, 255
  Liang Shuming's intuitive 154–5
  Mou Zongsan 341, 342
  Tang Junyi 310
  theory of *see* epistemology
  Wang Guowei's intercultural method
    41–2
  Ye Xiushan 350
  Zhang Dainian 237

labor organization 230
language(s)
  discerning principles in 166, 169
  Foucault's genealogy of 250
  Hu Shi 82, 84, 85
  Li Zehou 249–50, 254, 255
  and philosophy
    Wang Guowei 41
    Zhang Dongsun 41, 72–6, 78
  of wisdom, Feng Qi 218–19
  Ye Xiushan 350
Laozi, Xiong Shili 137
law *see* legal liberty; legal system;
    principle
leadership 182–3
learning
  methodology of, Xu Fuguan
    287–94
  nature of, Wang Guowei 40–2
  political, Liang Qichao on 20–1
  Xiong Shili 130–2, 134, 143
legal liberty 26–8
legal system, and human relationships
    28–30
Legge, James 353
Leibniz, G. W. von 352
li see principle
Li, Dazhao 5, 9, 94, 374, 392
Li, Zehou 10, 11, 246, 381
  aesthetics 45, 248, 251, 252, 253–4,
    256
  anthropological ontology 246–8,
    249–50, 252, 254–6
  contemporary Chinese philosophy 389,
    392, 395, 397
  criticisms of 256–7
  on Foucault 250
  future of philosophy 250–2
  on Heidegger 249
  influence of 257
  Kantian subjectivity 247, 248, 249,
    250, 254
  on Liang Qichao 18–19
  onto-hermeneutic analysis 389, 392,
    395
  the poetic state (*jingjie*) 45
  subjectivity 246–8, 249, 250, 251,
    252, 254–6
  on Wittgenstein 249–50

Liang, Qichao   6, 17–19, 354
   civic nationalism   19–24, 29–30
   cultural monism   19–21
   human relationships   26–7, 28–31
   liberty   22, 23, 24–8
   modernity   28–31
Liang Shuming   8, 147–9, 353, 354, 380
   Chinese society   148, 156, 158–62
   contemporary Chinese philosophy   386,
      391, 394, 397, 400
   Eastern and Western cultures   149–53,
      157–8, 159, 160, 162
   intellect   148, 150–2, 153, 157–8, 159
   intuition   150–3, 154, 155
   intuitive knowledge   154–5
   onto-hermeneutic analysis   386, 391,
      394
   reason   154, 155–60, 161–2
liberalism   375
   Hu Shi   93, 96–8
liberty
   Feng Qi's moral theory   225–31
   Hu Shi   97, 98
   Liang Qichao's concept   22, 23, 24–8
   self-enslavement, Jin Yuelin   121–2
   Yan Fu   370, 373
life
   Fang Dongmei   265–8, 270–1,
      274–6, 277
   Hu Shi's naturalistic conception   86–7
   ideal, Confucian   301
   Mou Zongsan   341
   Zhang Dongsun   63, 64, 66–8, 70–1
   see also   human life
life-ontology   265, 268
literary criticism, Wang Guowei   39, 43–4
   poetic state (jingjie)   44–51, 53–4
literary revolution   82, 83, 84–5
Liu, Shuxian (Shu-hsien Liu)   359
lixiang (imagined principles)   19–20
local self-government   21, 30
logic
   and culture, Zhang Dongsun   58,
      60–1, 73, 74–7, 78
   dialectical, Feng Qi   219–25, 231
   Feng Youlan's New Principle Learning
      166, 169, 170, 174, 175–6,
      177–8, 180
   He Lin's concept of mind   191–2, 198

   introduction of Western   370
   Jin Yuelin   107
   Mou Zongsan   328
logical possibility   104
love, Fang Dongmei   274–5, 278
Lu, Xiangshan   305–6
Lu, Xun   9, 282
Lu-Wang School (School of Mind)
   He Lin   188, 189, 190–6
   Tang Junyi   305

man   see human beings; human life;
      humanity
Mao, Zedong   4, 9–10, 30, 149
Maoism, Feng Youlan   181–3
Marxism   9–10, 381, 382–3
   contemporary Chinese philosophy   383,
      384–5, 389, 395, 398
   Feng Qi   220, 230, 381
   Feng Youlan   178, 179–80, 181–3,
      184
   He Lin   190, 208
   Li Zehou   246–8, 249, 250, 251, 254,
      257, 381
   onto-hermeneutic analysis   392, 395
   and profession-differentiation   160–1
   Tang Junyi   319
   Zhang Dainian   241–2, 381
material force, and principle   134
material needs   159, 161–2
materialism   9–11
   Feng Qi   213–31
   Feng Youlan   178, 179–83
   He Lin   190, 207–8
   Li Zehou   246–57
   onto-hermeneutic analysis   389
   Xiong Shili   136
   Zhang Dainian   235–44
matter
   Aristotle   142
   Jin Wulun   351
   Jin Yuelin   103–4, 105–6, 112, 115
   and mind
      He Lin   193–5, 196, 198, 207
      Xiong Shili   136
      Zhang Dainian   237, 238–9
      Zhang Dongsun   63–4
May Fourth Movement   3, 5, 7, 376,
      382–3

Hu Shi 83, 374
Zhang Dainian 242
Zhang Dongsun 68, 374
means–ends
  Chinese tradition 367–8
  Jin Yuelin 116–18, 120–1
  transformation of Chinese philosophy 376
mediation, Chinese–Western philosophy 404
Mencius
  dao of Confucius 128
  equality 28
  Fang Dongmei on 271, 276–7
  intuitive knowledge 154
  Liang Qichao 28
  mind 139, 192
  new Confucianism 28
  Xu Fuguan on 94–5, 285, 288
mere consciousness Buddhism 127–8, 136
metaphysics
  Chinese–Western fusion 403, 404
  contemporary Chinese 398
  Eastern–Western 151
  Feng Qi's theory of wisdom 213–19
  Hu Shi 98–9
  Jin Yuelin's theory of *dao* 102–3, 106–7
    form 104
    logic 107
    man and nature 115–22
    matter 103–4, 105–6, 112, 115
    possible worlds 109
    reality and process 109–15, 116, 117, 118, 119–20
    universal sympathy 108, 121
  Liang Qichao 28, 151
  Mencius's 28
  Mou Zongsan 330–6, 344, 393
  New Principle Learning 165, 166–84
  onto-hermeneutic analysis 388, 391, 392–4
  Tang Junyi 305–18, 323–4
  of virtue, Xiong Shili 8, 127–44, 392–3
  Wing-tsit Chan 355
  Xu Fuguan 286, 290–1, 293, 299
  Zhang Dainian 237

Zhang Dongsun 63, 69–70, 73–4, 76
method–truth nonseparation 398–9
Mill, J. S. 370
mind
  Chen Lai 352
  Feng Youlan 173, 177, 179
  He Lin 190–6, 197–8, 207
  Jin Yuelin 116, 117–20
  Liang Shuming 156, 157–8
  Mou Zongsan 328, 332, 333, 334–6, 339
  onto-hermeneutic analysis 390, 393–4
  Tang Junyi 305, 306–7, 308–9, 312–14, 315–16, 320, 323
  Xiong Shili 136, 138–42, 143
  Xu Fuguan 284–7, 289, 295–6, 299–300, 301
  Zhang Dainian 237, 238–9
  Zhang Dongsun 63, 64, 66
modernity 4–5, 7
  Chen Lai 352
  contemporary Chinese philosophy 373–4, 375, 376, 378
  Feng Youlan 171–2, 178, 182–3
  He Lin 188, 204, 206
  Hu Shi 83, 85, 90, 98
  Liang Qichao 28–31
  Liang Shuming 153
  Liu Shuxian 359
  New Culture Movement 83, 85, 90
  Tang Junyi 321–3
  Yan Fu 370
Mohism, Fang Dongmei 269, 271, 277
monism, cultural 19–21
Moore, G. E. 236
moral action, principle of unity of 369
moral cultivation 221, 225–31
moral metaphysics
  contemporary Chinese philosophy 398
  Mou Zongsan 332–6, 344, 393
  onto-hermeneutic analysis 392–4
  Xiong Shili 8, 127–44, 392–3
moral-metaphysical Confucians 380–1
  see also Xiong, Shili
moral subject 329–30, 343
moral understanding, principle of unity of 369

morality
  Antonio Cua   358
  Fang Dongmei   268, 276–7
  Feng Youlan   165, 171–2, 173, 177
  fusion of Chinese–Western philosophy
    403
  He Lin   204–5, 206
  Jin Yuelin   118, 119
  Li Zehou   250, 255
  Liang Shuming   155–6, 159, 161
  Mou Zongsan   328, 330–44, 393
  onto-hermeneutic analysis   390, 391,
    392–4
  Tang Junyi   306–13, 315, 318, 319,
    321–2
  Wang Guowei   42
  Xiong Shili   8, 127–44, 392–3
  Xu Fuguan   284–5, 286–7, 288–9,
    290–1, 293–4, 295–8
  Yan Fu   370
  Zhang Dainian   237, 241–2
  Zhang Dongsun   68, 70, 77
Mou, Zongsan   13, 273, 327–9, 354
  anxiety   284
  Cheng's differences with   357
  Chinese philosophy
    quintessence of   329–32
    versus Western   340–4
  contemporary Chinese philosophy   397,
    399, 400
    onto-hermeneutic analysis   387, 390,
      391, 393
  intellectual intuition   332–6
  moral metaphysics   332–6, 344
  moral philosophy   336–40, 344
  perfect teaching   336–40
  summum bonum   336–9, 344
mysticism   165, 168–9, 173, 174, 175,
    180, 181

namable/unnamable   218–19
names, rectification of   75
national heritage   85, 89–93, 99
national rights   22, 23, 24–5
nationalism
  Feng Youlan   165, 182
  Liang Qichao   19–24, 29–30
Nationalists, history   4
nation's essence   195

natural disasters   312–13
natural genesis   351
naturality   357
naturalness, principle of   228–9
nature
  Aristotle   142
  Chen Lai   352
  Fang Dongmei   266, 267, 278
  He Lin   197
  Jin Yuelin   108, 119–22
  Li Zehou   247, 248, 255
  Liang Shuming   150–1
  Mou Zongsan   342
  Xu Fuguan   293
  Zhang Dainian   236–9
  Zhang Dongsun   66
nature understanding   140, 141–2
Neo-Confucianism   129
  contemporary Chinese philosophy   383,
    384, 386–8, 394, 397, 398, 400
  human mind   139
  Liang Qichao   24
  Liu Shuxian   359
  naturality   357
  new   see New Neo-Confucianism
  onto-hermeneutic analysis   386–7
  principle   177
  Qin Jiayi   361
  Song–Ming
    Fang's critique   271–3
    Wing-tsit Chan   356
  Wing-tsit Chan   355
  Zhang Dongsun   70
Neo-Hegelianism   102
New Culture Movement   3, 5
  Hu Shi   83, 84, 85, 90, 94, 98
  and Kang's utopian ideas   26
  Liang Shuming   149
  Zhang Dongsun   68
New Neo-Confucianism   7–9, 380–1, 382
  Chen Lai   351–2
  Feng Youlan   165–84, 273
  He Lin   188–208
  later   11–13
    Fang Dongmei   263–79
    Mou Zongsan   327–44
    Tang Junyi   305–24
    Xu Fuguan   281–301
  Liang Shuming   147–62

Liu Shuxian 359
Mencius's concept of equality 28
role in contemporary philosophy 389, 391
Xiong Shili 127–44
New Principle Learning 165, 166, 183–4, 273
and history of Chinese philosophy 174–9, 184
materialism 178, 179–83
onto-hermeneutic analysis 388
principles 166–70
vital energy 167, 180, 181
New Realism 179, 180
Nietzsche, Friedrich W. 85
nothingness 331
noumenon
Li Zehou 246, 247, 248, 250, 251, 255, 256
Mou Zongsan 332–5
onto-hermeneutic analysis 387
Xiong Shili 134
Zhang Dainian 240, 241
novelty *see* creativity

object nature 108
object–subject relation 60, 73, 221–2, 300–1
objective reality 118, 119–20
objective–subjective unification 308–11
obsession 335–6
One Hundred Day Reform 4, 17–18
oneness, tradition of 367, 368
onto-cosmology 356–7, 368–9, 389–90, 392, 403
Yijing paradigm 396–7
onto-epistemology 368
onto-ethics 368–9, 387, 393, 398
onto-hermeneutics 356, 357, 385–6, 403
application 386, 394–5
creativity 386, 391–4
horizon 386, 387–8
method 386, 389–90
tradition 386–7
truth 386, 391
ontology
anthropological 246–8, 249–50, 252, 254–6

Cheng 356–7
Chinese philosophy's lack of 71–2
Chinese tradition 368
Chinese–Western fusion 402–3
Fang Dongmei 268, 269, 276
Feng Youlan 180
He Lin 192
Mou Zongsan 335–6
Tang Junyi 311–12, 315
Xiong Shili 140–1, 143–4
Zhang Dainian 240–1
opening tendency 135–6, 137
opposites 136–7
orders 58–60, 63–4
original mind 139–40, 141–2, 143
original reality
and function 132–4, 135
and human mind 138–42
and transformation 136, 137, 138

panstructuralism 58, 63–8
pantheism, Fang Dongmei 267
particulars, theory of 114–15
people's power
Liang Qichao 23–4
Tang Junyi 322–3
People's Republic of China 4
people's rights 22, 24, 25, 26, 29
perfect teaching 336–40
perfection 268
and root 237–8, 239
personal cultivation *see* self-cultivation
pervasive unity 269
phenomenalism 74
Tang Junyi 314
phenomenon–noumenon
Mou Zongsan 332–5
Xiong Shili 134
Zhang Dainian 240, 241
physical laws 64
Plato
essence (Ideas) 195
and function philosophy 71
influence on He Lin 195, 204
Ye's study of 350
Platonism, Feng Youlan 165, 180
pluralist epistemology 57–68, 388

poetry
  Li Zehou 45, 252
  Wang Guowei 37
    the poetic state (*jingjie*) 40, 44–51,
      53–4
    the refined (*guya*) 54
political dictatorship 4
political equality 322–3
political ethics 165
political learning 20–1
political liberty 26–7
political philosophy
  contemporary Chinese 400
  Fang Dongmei 277–9
  Feng Qi 230–1
  Feng Youlan 168–9, 171–2, 181–3,
    184
  He Lin 190, 195, 196, 200–8
  Hu Shi 93–8
  Liang Qichao 17–18, 19–31
  Liang Shuming 160–1
  Xu Fuguan 294–8
  Yan Fu 370, 373
  Zhang Dainian 237
political reform
  Hu Shi 94–8, 374
  Li Zehou 251
  Liang Qichao 17–18
  Liang Shuming 148–9
  onto-hermeneutic analysis 394–5
  Yan Fu 370–1
politically-orientated thought 76, 77
politics
  contemporary Chinese philosophy
    376–7
  Yan Fu 370
popular art 53
possibility 104, 105–7, 110–11
possible worlds 109
post-Marxian anthropological ontology
  246–8, 249–50, 252, 254–6
postulates 60–1
potentiality 103–4
power
  He Lin 201–2
  of human species 119, 120–1
  Li Zehou 250
  Liang Qichao's concept 23–4
  Wang Guowei 42

practical–cultural Confucians 380–1
  see also Liang Shuming
practical reason 42, 155, 387
practice
  dialectic with knowledge 221–2
  Li Zehou 247
  onto-hermeneutics 386, 394–5
pragmatism
  He Lin 189
  Hu Shi 82, 83, 87–8, 374
primordial unity 275
principle (*li*)
  Fang Dongmei 273
  He Lin 191–2, 193–6, 197–8, 202,
    206
  imagined (*lixiang*) 19–20
  and material force 134
  New Principle Learning 165, 166–84,
    388
  Wang Guowei 41, 42
  Zhang Dainian 241
process 114–15
profession-differentiation 160–1
psychological *noumenon* 246, 247, 251,
    255, 256
psychology
  Li Zehou 251
  of mind, He Lin 192, 194, 195, 198
  Zhang Dongsun 64
purpose 116, 117–18, 119–20
Pythagoreanism 350

Qi, Liang, democracy 297–8
Qin, Jiayi 360–1
Qing dynasty 3, 4–5
  Hu Shi 94
  Kang Youwei 4, 17, 18
  Liang Qichao 17–18

rationalism 165
rationality
  Cheng's work on 357
  Fang Dongmei 264
  Li Zehou 251, 253
  Xiong's metaphysics of virtue 142–3
reality 368–9, 374
  Cheng 356–7
  Chinese tradition 367, 368
  Fang Dongmei 269

Feng Youlan 165, 170, 171, 179, 180
He Lin 196
Jin Yuelin 109–15, 116, 117, 118, 119–20
onto-hermeneutic analysis 387–8, 389–90, 391, 392–3
original 132–42
Tang Junyi 313–14, 316
Xiong Shili 132–42
Zhang Dainian 240
realizations, change of 111
reason
cunning of 195–6
He Lin 200
Liang Shuming 154, 155–60, 161–2
onto-hermeneutic analysis 387
Tang Junyi 319
Wang Guowei's intercultural method 41, 42
Zhang Dongsun's epistemology 70
see also rationality
reason–emotion synthesis
Fang Dongmei 264, 265–8
Tang Junyi 308
rectification of names 75
refined, the (guya) 40, 43–4, 51–4
regalness 169, 182–3
relatedness 64, 388
relativism 224
religion
Du Weiming 361
Fang Dongmei 265, 267
Feng Qi 217
Feng Youlan 174
Fu Weixun 359
influence on philosophy 76–7
Liang Qichao 21, 22
Liang Shuming 159–60
Liu Shuxian 359
Mou Zongsan 340, 341
Qin Jiayi 360, 361
Tang Junyi 307–8, 310–11, 320, 321
Xu Fuguan 286
religious piety 283
ren (benevolence)
Antonio Cua 358
Mou Zongsan 329, 331, 338, 339

onto-hermeneutic analysis 394
Tang Junyi 307, 316, 320
Wing-tsit Chan 355–6
Xiong Shili 139
Xu Fuguan 284, 285, 287, 289, 290
Republic of China (1912–49) 3–4, 18, 94, 98
reverence 283
revolution
Feng Youlan 183
Hu Shi 95, 98
Li Zehou 251
Liang Shuming 148
rights
fusion of Chinese–Western philosophy 404
Liang Qichao 22, 23, 24–5, 26, 28, 29–30
Wang Guowei 42
Xu Fuguan 297–8
rights-based law 29–30
root 237–8, 239, 240–1
Rosemont Jr., Henry 297, 298
Rousseau, Jean Jacques 353
rulers
Feng Youlan 169, 182–3
He Lin 203, 204
Tang Junyi 322
Xu Fuguan 295–6, 298
Russell, B. 102, 235, 236, 353

sageliness
Feng Youlan 168–9, 181, 182–3
Li Zehou 256
sages
Feng Qi 215, 225, 231
Mou Zongsan 332
Tang Junyi 322
Xu Fuguan 287, 298
Sameness Thesis 134, 135, 139, 141
Schiller, Friedrich 50
scholars 156
scholarship 290
School of Mind (Lu–Wang School)
He Lin 188, 189, 190–6
Tang Junyi 305
School of Principles (Cheng–Zhu School) 190, 193–6
Schopenhauer, Arthur 37, 39, 41, 42

science
  contemporary Chinese philosophy 373,
    375, 376, 377, 399–400
  fusion of Chinese–Western philosophy
    403–4
  Jin Wulun 351
  Li Zehou 248, 252
  Mou Zongsan 328, 341–2, 343
  philosophy gives birth to 372
  Tang Junyi 320, 321–2, 323
  Xiong Shili 140–1
  Xu Fuguan 293–4
scientific knowledge
  contemporary Chinese philosophy
    399–400
  Zhang Dongsun 62–3
scientific practice, Hu Shi 83, 86–9, 90,
    99
scientific theory, Chinese–Western
    dialogue 401
self
  Feng Youlan 173, 174
  Mou Zongsan 328
  Tang Junyi 306–7, 308, 319–20
  Xu Fuguan 284–5, 286, 287
self-consciousness
  principle of 226–7, 228, 229
  Tang Junyi 309
self-cultivation
  Liang Qichao 30–1
  onto-hermeneutic analysis 395
  Wang Guowei 42, 54
self-detachment, poetry 46, 47
self-determination 285
self-development 269
self-enslavement 121–2
self-government
  Kang Youwei 26
  Liang Qichao 21, 23, 24, 30
  Tang Junyi 306
self-involvement, poetry 46–7
self-realization 269
sensation 58–9, 63
sensible intuition 332, 333, 335
Separation Thesis 132, 134
Shu-hsien Liu (Liu Shuxian) 359
social ethics 253
social liberty 26–7
social organizations 319

social philosophy 17–31
social reform
  Hu Shi 84–5, 95–7
  Yan Fu 370–1
  see also society
socially oriented thought 76, 77
society
  contemporary Chinese philosophy
    376–7
  Feng Qi 230–1
  Feng Youlan 171–2
  He Lin 189, 200–6
  Li Zehou 246–8, 249–50, 253–4
  Liang Shuming 148, 156,
    158–62
  Yan Fu 370
Socratic philosophy
  knowledge 68, 264
  Ye's study of 350
space
  Fang Dongmei 270
  Jin Yuelin 112–15
  Zhang Dongsun 60
speakable/unspeakable 218–19
spirit
  Fang Dongmei 267
  He Lin 197, 198–201
spiritual detachment 40, 43, 50
spiritual–intellectual realms 172–4, 181
spontaneity 148
Stalinism 252
state–citizen relationship 28–30
state–family relationship 30–1
structures 59–60, 63–4
stuff see matter
subject 331
subject–object relation
  Feng Qi 221–2
  Xu Fuguan 300–1
  Zhang Dongsun 60, 73
subjective reality 118, 119–20
subjective–objective unification 308–11
subjectivity
  Jin Yuelin 116–17
  Li Zehou 246–8, 249, 250, 251, 252,
    254–6, 395
  onto-hermeneutic analysis 395
  Xu Fuguan 289, 301
  Zhang Dongsun 63, 68

sublime, the   47, 51–3
substance
   Chinese tradition   367–8
   contemporary Chinese philosophy
      376–7, 397, 398
   He Lin   193, 197–200, 201–2
   moral-metaphysical Confucians   380
   onto-hermeneutic analysis   392
   principles of unitary paradigm of   368–9
   reason and intellect   158, 162
   Zhang Dainian   240
   Zhang Dongsun   59, 63, 65, 71–2,
      73–4
sufficient reason   41, 42
summum bonum   336–9, 344
synthesis, creative   236, 241–3
synthetic method   220–1

Tang, Junyi   12, 305, 354
   contemporary Chinese philosophy   397,
      399
      onto-hermeneutic analysis   387, 390,
         391, 392, 394–5
   contribution of   323–4
   culture   318–23
   ethics   305–18, 320, 323–4
   metaphysics   305–18, 320, 323–4
   Xu Fuguan's criticism of   291
Tang, Lik-kuen   359–60
tao   see dao
Taoism   see Daoism
teaching, perfect   336–40
theoretical reason   42
thought, freedom of   22
Three Bonds doctrine   202–6
ti   see substance
Tian Tai Zong, perfect teaching   337
time
   Fang Dongmei   270
   Jin Yuelin   110, 111, 112–16, 118
   Zhang Dongsun   60
tradition, onto-hermeneutics   386–7
transcendent heart–mind   316–18
transcendent mind   312–14
transcendent purpose   116
transcendental intuitive cognition   60
transformation   135–8, 142
trans-subjective–objective horizons
   309–11

truth
   Fang Dongmei   264, 265
   Feng Youlan   170, 179, 180
   He Lin   189, 198
   Hu Shi   88
   Liang Qichao   22
   Mou Zongsan   341–2
   nonseparation from method   398–9
   onto-hermeneutics   386, 390, 391
   Xiong Shili   128, 140–1
Tu, Wei-ming (Du Weiming)   361
   family–state relation   31
   on Xu Fuguan   282, 290

ultimate reality   374
   onto-hermeneutic analysis   388, 390,
      391, 392–3
   principles of   368–9
unity
   Chinese tradition   367, 368
   organic   368–9, 374
universal culture   162, 199–200, 201–2
universal sympathy   108, 121
universality, concrete   342
universe, philosophy of origin of   see
      cosmology
universities   4
utilitarian functions   301
utilitarianism   147–8
utopia
   Kang Youwei   26
   Li Zehou   256

value   267, 271
   ethical, art   39, 40
value-centered-ontology   268
veiled poetry   48
vernacular literary revolution   82, 83,
      84–5
virtue
   Antonio Cua   358
   Fang Dongmei   264
   Feng Qi's moral theory   225–31, 395
   government by, Xu Fuguan   294–8
   perfect teaching   337–8, 339
   Tang Junyi   307–8, 310–11, 316
   Xiong's metaphysics of   8, 127–44,
      392–3
   Ye Xiushan   350

vital energy　166–7, 180, 181
vitality of idealism　194
voluntariness principle　227–8, 229
voluntary association　230, 231
voluntary suspension　393

Wang, Fuzi　216–17
Wang, Guowei　6, 37–8, 354, 371
　intercultural method　39, 40–4
　onto-hermeneutic analysis　391
　the poetic state (*jingjie*)　40, 44–51,
　　53–4
　the refined (*guya*)　40, 43–4, 51–4
　scholarship of　38–40
Wang, Yangming　7
　influence on Tang Junyi　305–6, 308
　intuitive knowledge　154–5
　mind　192
　perfect teaching　339
　study by Chen Lai　352
　study by Qin Jiayi　360
　Xiong's criticism　128–9
　Xu Fuguan's admiration　291
war, Tang Junyi　312–13
West, development of Chinese philosophy
　　in　352–63
Western aesthetics　300
Western cultures
　Fang Dongmei　265
　He Lin　199, 200, 201–2
　Liang Shuming　149–53, 157–8, 159,
　　160, 162
　Liu Shuxian　359
　Mou Zongsan　340–2
　synthesis with Chinese　242–3, 404
　Tang Junyi　318, 320–1
　and transformation in China　375–8
　Xu Fuguan　281–7, 297, 300–1
　Zhang Dainian　242–3
Western ideas
　challenge of　371–5
　Chinese intellectual responses to　4–7,
　　354, 379–83
　　Fang Dongmei　264–6, 273
　　Feng Qi　216, 220
　　Feng Youlan　165, 175, 176, 178,
　　　180–1, 184
　　He Lin　188, 189–90, 192–3,
　　　195–6, 201–6

Hu Shi　82–99
Jin Yuelin　102–22
Li Zehou　246–50, 251, 254–5,
　　256–7
Liang Qichao　17–31, 354
Mou Zongsan　327, 328, 332–4, 336
Tang Junyi　310–12
Wang Guowei　37–54, 354
Xiong Shili　127, 129, 131–2, 134,
　　137–8, 140–1, 142–4
Ye Xiushan　350–1
Zhang Dainian　235, 236, 240–2
Zhang Dongsun　57–78
dialogue with contemporary Chinese
　　401–4
fusion with Chinese　377–9
introduction by Yan Fu　369–71
study by Liu Shuxian　359
and transformation in China　375–9
versus Chinese　353–4, 356–7, 366–7,
　　369
　Mou Zongsan　340–4
　Ye Xiushan　350
Whitehead, A. N.　137, 138, 265–6, 360
Wilhelm, Richard　353
will
　Feng Qi　227
　He Lin　204, 205
　Li Zehou　251
　mind as, Xiong Shili　142
　Mou Zongsan　333
wisdom
　Fang Dongmei　264, 265, 267
　Feng Qi　213–19, 223–4, 225, 390,
　　395
　Mou Zongsan　336, 339–40
　onto-hermeneutic analysis　390
　practical-cultural Confucians　380
　Tang Junyi　310, 320
Wittgenstein, Ludwig J. J.　249–50, 254
world philosophy　403, 404

xing　*see* human nature
xing (human body)　286
Xiong, Shili　353, 354, 380
　contemporary Chinese philosophy　399,
　　400
　onto-hermeneutic analysis　386–7,
　　391, 392–3, 394

metaphysics of virtue 8, 127–30
  change 135–8
  daily decrease 130–2, 134
  daily renovation 131–2, 134, 143
  and ethics 131–2, 138, 142–4
  function 132–4, 135
  human mind 138–42
  original reality 132–42
  transformation 135–8, 142
Xu Fuguan's criticism of 291
Yijing 127–8, 134, 135, 137, 396
Xu, Fuguan 12, 281–2
  anxiety 282–7
  bodily recognition 287–94
  Chinese aesthetic spirit 298–301
  contemporary Chinese philosophy 390, 397
  embodiment 287–94, 299, 300
  heart–mind culture 284–7, 289, 295–6, 299–300, 301
  onto-hermeneutic analysis 390
  political philosophy 294–8

Yan, Fu 4, 5, 369–71
Ye, Xiushan 350–1
yi paradigm 396–7
yijing see *jingjie*
Yijing (*Book of Change(s)*)
  Cheng 357
  contemporary Chinese philosophy 396–7
  Fang Dongmei 265, 267, 269, 270–1, 273, 276, 393
  function philosophy 71

Xiong Shili 127–8, 134, 135, 137, 396
yong see function

Zhang, Dainian 10–11, 235–6, 381
  classical Chinese philosophy 239–42
  contemporary Chinese philosophy 389, 394, 397
  creative synthesis 236, 241–3
  culture 242–3
  importance of 243–4
  man and nature 236–9
  onto-hermeneutic analysis 389, 394
Zhang, Dongsun 6–7, 57–8, 371, 374
  cultural epistemology 57, 58, 68–78
  onto-hermeneutic analysis 388, 391
  pluralist epistemology 57–63, 388
  panstructuralism 58, 63–8
Zhang, Junmai 7
Zhang, Shenfu 9, 235
Zhang, Taiyan 5
Zhang, Zhidong
  learning 162
  rectifying rights 25
Zhou, Dunyi 272
Zhou rites 329–30
Zhu, Guangqian 5–6
Zhu, Xi 7, 256, 272
  Mou Zongsan on 393
  study by Chen Lai 352
  Wing-tsit Chan on 356
  work by Liu Shuxian on 359
Zhuangzi, aesthetic spirit 299, 300, 301
Zong, Baihua 6